The Homeric *Doloneia*

The Homeric *Doloneia*

Evolution and Shaping of Iliad *10*

CHRISTOS C. TSAGALIS

Great Clarendon Street, Oxford, OX2 6DP,
United Kingdom

Oxford University Press is a department of the University of Oxford.
It furthers the University's objective of excellence in research, scholarship,
and education by publishing worldwide. Oxford is a registered trade mark of
Oxford University Press in the UK and in certain other countries

© Christos C. Tsagalis 2024

The moral rights of the author have been asserted

All rights reserved. No part of this publication may be reproduced, stored in
a retrieval system, or transmitted, in any form or by any means, without the
prior permission in writing of Oxford University Press, or as expressly permitted
by law, by licence or under terms agreed with the appropriate reprographics
rights organization. Enquiries concerning reproduction outside the scope of the
above should be sent to the Rights Department, Oxford University Press, at the
address above

You must not circulate this work in any other form
and you must impose this same condition on any acquirer

Published in the United States of America by Oxford University Press
198 Madison Avenue, New York, NY 10016, United States of America

British Library Cataloguing in Publication Data
Data available

Library of Congress Control Number: 2024936502

ISBN 978–0–19–287098–8

DOI: 10.1093/oso/9780192870988.001.0001

Printed and bound in the UK by
Clays Ltd, Elcograf S.p.A.

Links to third party websites are provided by Oxford in good faith and
for information only. Oxford disclaims any responsibility for the materials
contained in any third party website referenced in this work.

For Antonios Rengakos

In the beginning was intertextuality, and a rather complex one, too.

> Edmunds (1995) 22, regarding the inscription
> on the cup of Nestor in Pithecusae
> (an island off the coast of Campania)

Preface

"If we were to assume, as a working hypothesis, that the Pindaric and/or oracle versions are older than the *Doloneia*, we should expect the K poet to have made significant changes in them when composing his own account" (Fenik 1964, 16). "Die stilistische Sonderstellung (des K) legt den Schluß nahe, daß die Dolonie nicht vom Dichter der Ilias stammt, sondern einen fixierten Iliastext voraussetzt, in den sie nachträglich von einem anderen Dichter eingefügt wurde" (Danek 1988, 237). "In an oral tradition it is possible for a poet composing an epic like the *Iliad* to make use of themes and structures of other epic traditional poems in ways that would be meaningful to an audience... We understand *Iliad* 10 to have been composed and performed within a long oral tradition of such poetry, and we argue that it is an example of a very ancient theme, the *lokhos*" (Dué and Ebbott 2010, 28). Arguments such as these have inspired this monograph, in which I aim to explore the coming into being of such a controversial Iliadic book as the *Doloneia*. My own approach shares several assumptions, arguments, and conclusions with the three authoritative studies of *Iliad* 10 quoted above (Fenik 1964, Danek 1988, Dué and Ebbott, 2010), while it also offers several new suggestions and (I hope) insights that may help readers understand and evaluate occasional disagreements.

Except for chapters 2 and 3, earlier versions of which have been published as "The Meta-Narrative Moment: Rhesus' Horses Revisited" (2020a, *TC* 12.1: 92–113) and "The Darkest Hour: Odysseus' Smile and the *Doloneia*" (in A. Rengakos, P. Finglass, and B. Zimmermann [eds.], *"More than Homer Knew"*: *Studies on Homer and his Ancient Commentators*, Berlin 2020b, 53–88), all the other seven chapters, as well as the Introduction and Conclusions, are published here for the first time.

The idea about a monograph on *Iliad* 10 grew slowly and steadily while I was engaged with writing a commentary on *Iliad* 9–12 for the Fondazione Lorenzo Valla. Among the many debts that I have incurred while working on this project, the greatest is to Jonathan Burgess, Bruno Currie, and Jonathan Ready, with whom I was fortunate to discuss the many problems pertaining to this challenging Iliadic book. I have also immensely benefited from the remarks, suggestions, and corrections of the two anonymous readers of OUP, who have helped me improve and organize my work in numerous ways. Their detailed comments, balanced criticism, and thoughtful advice are much appreciated. Equally helpful were the insights and suggestions of Erwin Cook and Lowell Edmunds, who had read my commentary on *Iliad* 10 (as part of the Valla project), thus allowing me to build a more solid basis for undertaking the demanding project of exploring the evolution and shaping of the *Doloneia*. My students who participated in three seminars on the *Doloneia* which I taught at the Aristotle University of Thessaloniki proved to be an invaluable source of assistance by means of their sheer interest in this topic and constant questions about what I (often wrongly) considered obvious. Audiences in Athens, Freiburg, Kalamata, L'Aquila, and Thessaloniki were also obliging. Elton Barker displayed remarkable skill in reading the entire manuscript and making my English more idiomatic. The efficiency of Charlotte Loveridge and Jamie Mortimer of OUP is truly commendable. Their patience, advice, and careful work are greatly appreciated.

Anna, Alexia, and Konstantina were (as usual) always there for me while researching and writing this monograph. The dedication of this book to Antonios Rengakos has a strongly personal tone. It is about a longstanding friendship and scholarly appreciation. It also coincides with his retirement from the Department of Philology of the Aristotle University of Thessaloniki, which he has transformed into a research center of excellence in the study of classical literature.

Christos C. Tsagalis

Thessaloniki
2024

Contents

Bibliographical Conventions and Abbreviations	xiii
Note to the Reader	xv
Introduction	1
1. Theoretical Aspects	28
2. A First Thematic Approach: Intratextual References	67
3. A Second Thematic Approach: The Horses of Rhesus	103
4. The Alleged Un-Iliadic Features of *Iliad* 10: Speeches, Clothing and Arming, and Zielinski's Law	126
5. Putative Clues for the Hector-Version of *Iliad* 10	162
6. Reconstructing the Hector-Version of *Iliad* 10	187
7. The Two Versions of the Rhesus Myth: Reconstruction of Possible Sources	214
8. Comparative Material: The *Mahābhārata* and the *Aeneid*	244
9. The Rhesus Story within the Cyclic and the Iliadic Tradition	278
Conclusions	297
Bibliography	301
General Index	321
Index of Passages	327

Bibliographical Conventions and Abbreviations

ARV	J. D. Beazley, *Attic Red-Figure Vase-Painters* (Oxford, 1963²)
BT	M. L. West (ed.), *Homerus: Ilias*, 2 vols. (Stuttgart, Munich, and Leipzig, 1998–2000)
CGL	J. Diggle (ed. in chief), *The Cambridge Greek Lexicon*, 2 vols. (Cambridge, 2021)
EGEF	C. Tsagalis (ed.), *Early Greek Epic Fragments, Vol. 1: Antiquarian and Genealogical Epic; Vol. 2: Epics on Herakles (Kreophylos and Peisandros)* (Berlin 2017–2022)
EGF	M. Davies (ed.), *Epicorum Graecorum Fragmenta* (Göttingen, 1988)
EGM	R. L. Fowler (ed.), *Early Greek Mythography, Vol. 1: Text and Introduction*; *Vol. 2: Commentary* (Oxford, 2000–2013)
FGrHist	F. Jacoby et al. (eds.), *Die Fragmente der griechischen Historiker* (Leiden, 1961–9)
GEF	M. L. West (ed.), *Greek Epic Fragments from the Seventh to the Fifth Centuries BC* (Cambridge, MA, and London, 2003)
HomEnc	M. Finkelberg (ed.), *The Homer Encyclopedia*, 3 vols. (Chichester, 2011)
IEG	M. L. West (ed.), *Iambi et Elegi Graeci ante Alexandrum cantati*, 2 vols. (Oxford 1989–92²)
KP	K. Ziegler et al. (eds.), *Der Kleine Pauly: Lexikon der Antike*, 25 vols. (Göttingen, 1955–2010)
LIMC	*Lexicon Iconographicum Mythologiae Classicae*, 8 vols. plus indexes (Zurich, Munich, and Düsseldorf, 1981–99)
LSJ	H. G. Liddell, R. Scott, H. S. Jones, and R. McKenzie (eds.), *A Greek-English Lexicon*, with Revised Supplement by P. G. W. Glare (Oxford, 1996⁹)
OCD	*Oxford Classical Dictionary*, 4th edition, digital version. Edited by T. Whitmarsh (Oxford, 2012)
OCT	D. B. Monro, and T. W. Allen (eds.), *Homeri Opera, tomi I–II Iliadis libros I–XXIV continentes* (Oxford, 1920³)
PEG	A. Bernabé (ed.), *Poetae Epici Graeci. Pars I: Testimonia et Fragmenta* (Leipzig, 1996²)
PMG	D. L. Page (ed.), *Poetae Melici Graeci* (Oxford, 1962)
RE	G. Wissowa et al. (eds.), *Paulys Real-Encyclopädie der classischen Altertumswissenschaft* (Stuttgart, 1859–1980)
Roscher	W. H. Roscher (ed.), *Ausführliches Lexikon der griechischen und römischen Mythologie*, 6 vols. (Leipzig and Berlin, 1884–1937)
Severyns	A. Severyns, *Recherches sur la Chrestomathie de Proclos: la Vita Homeri et les sommaires du Cycle* (Paris, 1963)
van der Valk	M. van der Valk (ed.), *Eustathii Archiepiscopi Thessalonicensis Commentarii ad Homeri Iliadem pertinentes*, 5 vols. (Leiden, 1971–87)

Note to the Reader

The text of the *Iliad* is that of M. L. West in the Bibliotheca Teubneriana (1998–2000), with slight modifications. All translations of Iliadic passages (with minor adjustments) are taken from Lattimore (1951), unless stated otherwise. For the *Odyssey* I have used the translation of Rieu (1991 [1946]), and for Proclus' summaries of the Cyclic epics the translation of Burgess (2001). The asterisk (*) indicates unattested poems. The sign > denotes the influence of an earlier poem or epic tradition on a later one. Cyclic with "C" refers to the written poems of the Epic Cycle, whereas cyclic with "c" pertains either to pre-Homeric oral epics with a cyclic tinge or to cyclic myth.

Introduction

1. Main Questions

The title and subtitle of this book make plain the key concerns of this study. The title ("The Homeric *Doloneia*") brings together two important aspects of my interpretive approach. The term "Homeric" does not refer to Homer as the poet of the *Iliad* or of the *Iliad* and the *Odyssey*. It indicates that book 10 belongs both to the same poetic tradition as the rest of the *Iliad*, i.e. the Iliadic epic tradition, and to the larger epic tradition encompassing the *Iliad* and the *Odyssey*. While the terms "Iliadic" and "Odyssean" epic traditions designate oral epics pertaining to the main theme of the *Iliad* (the wrath of Achilles) and the *Odyssey* (the return of Odysseus), respectively, the term "Homeric" encompasses the entire Iliadic and Odyssean epic traditions, which display certain qualitative, stylistic, and narrative features that differentiate them from the rest of early Greek epic.[1] However, if the approach followed is about the Iliadic epic tradition and not about a single poet of the *Iliad*, why should we discuss the question of authenticity of a book of the *Iliad* or of the entire *Iliad*? From this perspective, isn't the question of authenticity pointless?[2]

The notion of authenticity within an oral medium is different from that concerning a text composed by writing. Whereas in the latter case authenticity pertains to the fixed outcome of written composition[3] carried out by a single individual, the author, in the former it is about a fixed story,[4] the essential parts of which remain unchanged.[5] In this framework, variation constitutes an implicit acknowledgment of another notion of fixity, in which different versions of the same story presuppose "a stable skeleton of narrative."[6] The notion of an oral epic

---

[1] On the qualitative, stylistic, and narrative characteristics of Cyclic epic, see Monro (1884) 1–41; Rzach in *RE* s.v. "Kyklos"; Griffin (1977) 39–43; Tsagalis (2011) 214–18 = (2023) 7–11.

[2] See Tsagalis (2011) 218–28 = (2023) 11–22; Currie (2016) 18–21.

[3] However, it is wrong to argue that written composition guarantees text-fixity, just as it is erroneous to claim that all oral traditions are multiform; see Mueller (2009²) 176: "the concept of a fixed text does not depend on writing"; Finkelberg (2000) 9 = (2020) 314; Tsagalis (2011) 235 with n. 86 = (2023) 28 n. 90.

[4] See Kullmann's (1960, 12–13) *Faktenkanon*, which is a standard list of events.

[5] See Dowden (1996) 48: "between the two extremes of total fixity and utter fluidity lie various levels of semi-fixity." On fixity in oral traditions, see, e.g., Finnegan (1988) 95, (1992) 73–8; Nagy (1990) 40–3; Tsagalis (2011) 238–9 = (2023) 31–2.

[6] Lord (2018³) 105; see also Lord (1990) vii–xviii; on simple or essential themes in a given song as opposed to momentary or decorative ones, see also M. Parry (1971) 446.

tradition does not exclude or erase the question of authenticity; rather, it represents a context where authenticity is measured differently from written literature. In this new context, what can be considered genuine or not is not determined by the individual author who uses writing to compose his poem but by the epic tradition to which this poem belongs. In this book, I will explore the relationship between the *Doloneia* and the Iliadic epic tradition, which is one of the two manifestations (the other being the *Odyssey*) of the Homeric epic tradition.

The second term (*Doloneia*) of the first part of the book's title is also worth reflecting on because it refers to the relationship between the ancient title *Doloneia* and the content of *Iliad* 10. *Doloneia* means "the rhapsody of Dolon."[7] The earliest attestation of the name *Doloneia* for *Iliad* 10 is given by Aelian (*V.H.* 13.14),[8] in the context of a long list of Homeric episodes that were sung separately. This is a puzzling designation for a book that also comprises the *Nyktegersia*[9] and the tale of Rhesus. One may counterargue that both these sections are parts of the episode of Dolon, in the sense that the *Nyktegersia* paves the way for the spying mission and the Rhesus story constitutes a side effect of the Dolon episode.[10] Although this could be the case with the *Nyktegersia*,[11] it hardly applies to the Rhesus episode, which is tagged to the Dolon story but involves a major Thracian ally of the Trojans. An impressive night assault, where two chief Achaean leaders, Diomedes and Odysseus, kill a powerful Thracian king and steal his magnificent horses, has not been recorded in the title.[12] However, this is not particular to the *Doloneia*'s title that belongs to a group of ancient designations used for books 8–24 of the *Iliad*, which look more traditional than the designations of books 1–7, since they seem to have been "preserved at the expense of precision."[13] Even so, the silence of the title of book 10 regarding the episode of Rhesus rightly deserves our attention. What does this tell us about the content of

---

[7] The Greeks used the term ῥαψῳδίαι for the books of the *Iliad* and the *Odyssey*. On early book division in Homeric epic, see Mazon (1943) 138–9; Notopoulos (1964) 11–12; S. R. West (1967) 20 and (1988) 39–40 with n. 19; Goold (1977) 26–30; Burgess (2001) 31. Differently, Janko (1992, 31 with n. 47) argues that the division postdates Apollonius of Rhodes; for a thorough discussion of this matter, see the various contributions in a special issue of *Symbolae Osloenses* published by Jensen et al. (1999) 5–91.

[8] Nagy (1996a, 77–9) sees a striking analogy between this passage of Aelian and the Indian evidence of performance segments or episodes in the Palnāḍu, Pābujī, and Ālhā epics.

[9] "The waking up (of the Achaean leaders) in the night." I use the term *Nyktegersia* to designate the first section of book 10 (1–179).

[10] The Achaean spies find out about Rhesus from Dolon and it is then that they decide to ambush the Thracian king.

[11] It is not accidental that *Nyktegersia* and *Doloneia* were the names employed by Alexandrian scholars (Σ *Il.* 10.1a Erbse) and Aelian (*V.H.* 13.14), respectively, to designate *Iliad* 10.

[12] The [Euripidean] *Rhesus*, which does the exact opposite, i.e. highlights Rhesus and downgrades Dolon, is about a first-rank king, not a third-rate spy, who poses a grave threat to the Achaean army. Iliadic book titles regularly mention first-rank heroes: Ἀλεξάνδρου καὶ Μενελάου μονομαχία, Ἀγαμέμνονος ἐπιπώλησις, Διομήδους ἀριστεία, Ἕκτορος καὶ Ἀνδρομάχης ὁμιλία, Ἕκτορος καὶ Αἴαντος μονομαχία, πρεσβεία πρὸς Ἀχιλλέα, Ἀγαμέμνονος ἀριστεία, Μενελάου ἀριστεία, Ἕκτορος ἀναίρεσις, ἆθλα ἐπὶ Πατρόκλῳ, Ἕκτορος λύτρα.

[13] Stanley (1993) 283.

the *Doloneia*? Is there a possibility that the book's title[14] is appropriate to a plot in which the episode of Dolon would have covered book 10 in its entirety and the story of Rhesus would not be part of it?[15] This is a significant question because it gives to the discussion about the book's authenticity a new dimension. Is it conceivable that between wholesale authenticity and inauthenticity of *Iliad* 10 there is room for partial authenticity, which entails that the Dolon episode belongs to an earlier form of the *Iliad*, the Rhesus story being added to it at a later stage?

Another significant question, which is also relevant to the question of the authenticity of the *Doloneia*, refers to its placement between books 9 and 11 of the *Iliad*. It has been argued that Iliadic book divisions occur at junctures preceded by scenes that scarcely affect forthcoming events in the story and are followed by scenes with consequences felt for at least 400 verses.[16] To put it differently, book divisions are preceded and followed by scenes of low and high consequence, respectively. The placement of the *Doloneia* (either with or without the episode of Rhesus) between books 9 and 11 is consistent with this practice, since book 9 does not affect forthcoming events in book 10 and what happens for at least half of book 11 (the wounding of and withdrawal from the battle of the major Achaean heroes) has serious consequences for both the *teichomachia* and the story of Patroclus. On the contrary, if book 10 is omitted, then the last part of *Iliad* 9, in which Diomedes urges Agamemnon to lead the Achaean attack the following day, would become a scene of high consequence, since this is exactly what happens at the beginning of *Iliad* 11. These significant questions, which are related to the authenticity, content, and placement of *Iliad* 10 and are captured in the first part of this book's title ("The Homeric *Doloneia*"), will be systematically examined.

As regards the second part of the title ("Evolution and Shaping of *Iliad* 10"), the terms "evolution" and "shaping" are used here in a complementary manner. Evolution describes a process of (qualitative) change. Shaping refers to the way something is molded into a particular form. Modification pertains to both these

---

[14] See Lohan (1890) 6–7, who has argued that the ancient designations of books of the *Iliad* and the *Odyssey* are not titles but rhapsodic names, i.e. denominations based on content. Some of these denominations are based on comprehensive indications of content, while others pertain to a selective process; see also Castelli (2020) 49–55. A well-known example is offered by Herodotus (2.116), who knew of a Διομήδους ἀριστεία that comprised more than book 5 (he uses this designation for at least *Il.* 6.289–92). It may be the case that the Διομήδους ἀριστεία Herodotus is referring to extended from *Il.* 5.1 to 6.311; see Currie (2021) 5–13. The existence of rhapsodic names for certain Homeric episodes in the classical period suggests that some form of division was already in use; see Thuc. 1.9.4: ἐν τοῦ σκήπτρου...τῇ παραδόσει and 1.10.4: ἐν νεῶν καταλόγῳ; Pl. *Crat.* 428c: ἐν λιταῖς, *Ion* 539b: ἐπὶ τειχομαχίᾳ, *Rep.* 614b: Ἀλκίνου ἀπόλογον; Arist. *Poet.* 1454b30: ἐν τοῖς νίπτροις, 1455a2: ἐν Ἀλκίνου ἀπολόγῳ, *Rhet.* 1417a13: ὁ Ἀλκίνου ἀπόλογος (bibliography in N. J. Richardson 1993, 20–1; Jensen et al. 1999, 10). To this list of names of Homeric episodes used by authors I add ΠΑΤΡΟΚΛΥΣ ΑΤΛΑ (Πατρόκλου ἆθλα), an inscription (*c.* 540 BC) on a *dinos* by Sophilus; see Shapiro (1989) 44.

[15] I agree with Stanley (1993, 285) who sees in the *Doloneia* clear signs of rearrangement and recontextualization, but I disagree with his view that it may be regarded "as an independent narrative" (286).

[16] Heiden (1998) 69.

terms: in the former, it is part of the development towards a certain direction, while in the latter it is about the form of the final product. Taken together, evolution and shaping describe a dynamic, formative process that leads to an outcome, which often bears traces of its earlier stages. The book's subtitle brings to the foreground further significant questions: why did *Iliad* 10 evolve from an earlier version into the current one? How was this evolution carried out?[17] Is it possible to detect the phases through which it has passed until it reached the form with which we are familiar? These questions are important not only with respect to *Iliad* 10 but also because they relate to the genesis and formation of the *Iliad* and Homeric poetry at large.

(a) The first of these questions refers to the evolution of an episode or section that may have been caused by the need or desire to remedy a narrative weakness, to emphasize one or more aspects of the unraveling of the plot, or to improve the presentation of a character or characters. Since evolution is a process that happens over time, it is to be expected that the epic must have undergone various changes. Oral performance is, among other things, an evaluative process, both internally (by the singers themselves) and externally (by the reaction of the audience). Changes, however, tend to group themselves after an epic tradition has acquired a standard form according to a stable narrative skeleton[18] or *Faktenkanon*.[19] They are conditioned by new choices which are made and carried out to a given plan by engaging with specific aspects of the standard event-list.[20] If something is felt to be troublesome or ineffective at the level of the narrative, then a change may be introduced, with the proviso that it does not affect the deep structure of the myth. Sometimes, a change may be due to the need or desire to stress an aspect of the plot. Related to this line of thought is character presentation. In cases like this, the introduction of a new character into the plot is not the reason triggering the change. It is only the by-product of the form of change that is implemented. For example, instead of asking the question why somebody would be interested in introducing Rhesus to the plot of the *Iliad*, it is better to ask how the introduction of the episode of Rhesus improves the characterization of Diomedes.[21]

(b) As regards the question pertaining to the way an episode evolves, a poetic tradition may implement changes by omitting, adding, or reshaping material.[22]

---

[17] The categories of changes in South Slavic song culture, as recorded by Lord (2018³) 131, include: (a) saying the same thing in fewer or more lines; (b) expansion of ornamentation; (c) shifts of order in a sequence; (d) addition of material; (e) omission of material; (f) substitution of one theme for another.
[18] See Lord (1990) vii–xviii, (2018³) 105.
[19] Kullmann (1960) 12–13; (2005) 9–10.   [20] Dowden (1996) 48.
[21] On the contribution of book 10 to characterization, see chapter 2, section 4.
[22] Dowden (1996, 50) argues that Homer emulated earlier masters and advanced on his epic "through incremental variation of an original, much shorter, quarrel poem." He envisages an expansion by means of the composition of new episodes. This approach resembles Hermann's (1832) theory of the *Iliad* growing out of a basic kernel but differs from it as regards authorship, since Dowden does not champion analytical criticism.

On implementing change, it is important to draw a distinction between internal evolution and external adaptation. Internal evolution concerns a given episode or section. It pertains to the omission of material incompatible with the new version, the relocation and adaptation of part of the material of the earlier version, and the addition of new material. External adaptation amounts to the adjustment of the new version to the structure and plot of the entire poem. The *Iliad* and the *Odyssey* acknowledge cyclic traditions and either adapt them to fit their own narrative or tamper with them. This strategy reflects the aim of Homeric epic to claim poetic supremacy since it "deliberately positions itself beyond the tradition to which it ostensibly belongs."[23] The same technique of adaptation and tampering is at work when the *Iliad* and the *Odyssey* are examined as epic traditions evolving throughout the archaic period, until they reach their definitive form. Their evolution and shaping from earlier forms involve changes that aspire to improve previous versions.

(c) With respect to our ability to detect the phases of the evolution of an episode, we need to posit specific criteria which may help us determine the traces left in the text either by an earlier version of the same poem or by a thematically analogous version of a different poem. Such criteria may be narrative inconsistency, weak actorial motivation, and discrepancy between narrator-text and character-text.

Narrative inconsistency refers to discrepancies between "surface" and "deep" layers of narrative. For example, while the "surface" of the text of *Iliad* 16 insists that Sarpedon is not immortalized (16.457 = 675), there are features suggesting at a deeper level his immortalization (the translation of his body by Hypnos and Thanatos, the anointing with ambrosia, and the body's clothing with immortal clothes). Likewise in *Odyssey* 19, where on a "surface" level Penelope does not recognize Odysseus (and does not conspire with him), while on a "deep" level several narrative features hint at recognition and conspiracy. As regards *Iliad* 16, neoanalysts have held that the "deep" level of the text points to another poem (a pre-Homeric *Memnonis featuring the death and immortalization of Memnon) on which the Iliadic version has been modelled, whereas in the case of *Odyssey* 19 they have postulated an earlier version of the *Odyssey* in which Penelope recognized Odysseus and conspired with him with respect to the killing of the suitors.[24]

By weak actorial motivation I am designating an action undertaken by a character or a behavioristic sign that is weakly motivated by the narrative as it stands. Antilochus' tears for the death of Patroclus are weakly motivated both because he is the only one up to this point among the Achaeans to shed tears and because there is not even the slightest hint in the text that he was particularly close to Patroclus. Neoanalysis has suggested that Antilochus' tears for Patroclus aim at

---

[23] Finkelberg (2015) 138 = (2020) 181.
[24] For a recent presentation with updated bibliography, see Currie (2016) 47–72, 89–90.

inviting the audience to perceive the analogy between the fate of Antilochus in the *Memnonis and Patroclus in the *Iliad* (Antilochus is killed by Memnon, whom Achilles kills in revenge; Patroclus is killed by Hector, whom Achilles kills in revenge).[25]

Discrepancies between narrator-text and character-text have also been employed as a criterion for determining earlier and later versions. In *Od.* 24.121–90, Amphimedon's claim (character-text) that Penelope conspired with Odysseus to kill the suitors is inconsistent with the narrator-text in which Penelope plays no such role. Several scholars have argued that in an earlier version Odysseus was assisted by Penelope.

The above criteria had been employed by traditional neoanalysis as indications of the poet's failure to fully assimilate older and recent material. However, certain scholars have argued that instead of poetic weakness we may see here a conscious allusive strategy aiming to alert the audience to the existence of a traditional version from which the new version deviates. Acknowledging an earlier source while refusing to follow it, I may add, is essential to the process of internal evolution and external adaptation of Homeric epic.[26]

2. Wider Implications

The examination of the *Doloneia* on a diachronic axis, i.e. as a part of the Iliadic epic tradition that evolved through time until it was shaped in the form with which we are familiar, has wider implications beyond any narrow interest. These implications concern the composition of the *Iliad*, the notion of authorship, the function of innovation within an oral epic tradition, the issue of stability of oral epic traditions, and the meta-epic nature of Homeric epic.

The discussion of the evolution and shaping of *Iliad* 10 is relevant to the composition of the entire *Iliad* for several reasons. First, it offers an argument from analogy for the evolution and shaping of the Iliadic epic tradition, the kind of changes that were implemented, as well as the reasons that may have caused these changes. Second, the *Doloneia* suggests that the evolution of an epic tradition may not simply be a temporal sequence marked by adaptations, accretions, and omissions of material but a responsive development, during which the tradition matures by creatively reacting both to audience reception and to its own evolving

---

[25] See Currie (2016) 126–8.
[26] Dowden (1996) 51–3; Danek (1998a) 69–72, 235–7, 369–71, 389–91, etc.; Currie (2016) 95. For another representative example, consider the notorious duals in *Iliad* 9. Several scholars have argued that the *Iliad* interacts with and responds to an earlier version of an Embassy to Achilles, in which there were only two ambassadors, Odysseus and Ajax; see, e.g., Hainsworth (1993) 87; Motzkus (1964) 103–4; Goold (1977) 10–11; Cairns (2001a) 36; M. L. West (2011a) 218–19; Currie (2016) 73–4.

sense of poetic effectiveness.[27] Improving the end product is a *conditio sine qua non* for attaining quality in a dynamic environment regulated by continuous epic performances.

The study of the evolution and shaping of *Iliad* 10 is also instructive with respect to the notion of authorship.[28] It is in tune with the view of an oral Iliadic tradition evolving for several generations until it reaches its final form in the archaic period.[29] It therefore aims to provide a working hypothesis that deals in a radically different way with the question of authorship and the related issue of authenticity, which concern the question of whether book 10 is a genuine part of the *Iliad* or not, i.e. whether it is the work of a single author, the same as the poet of the *Iliad*, or of two authors, one of the *Iliad* and another of the *Doloneia*. However, the interpretive approach undertaken in this book does not simply erase the question of the historical author by resorting to the eradication of any interest in the genesis of this part of the *Iliad*. Nor does it view the study of the creation of the *Iliad* as the exclusive field of interest of scholars who adopt a scripsist approach to Homeric poetry. Conversely, by arguing that the making of the *Doloneia* derives from a process of development and adaptation, it claims that the making of the *Iliad* resides in its evolution and shaping.[30] From the making of book 10 and the *Iliad* by one or more poets, we thus move to their evolution and shaping within an oral epic tradition. In this way, the thorny question of authorship, which has dominated the discussion of the *Doloneia*, is viewed in a new light.

In a literate culture, authorship is about the individual writer. In an oral culture, it designates the tradition which has its own distinct identity. As the historical poet

---

[27] See Finkelberg (1990) 301–2 = (2020) 125, who advances the same argument, although she treats creative ability as a personal quality pertaining to a poet operating within an inspiration-oriented tradition.

[28] See Tsagalis (2011) 233–7 = (2023) 26–30.

[29] The making of the *Iliad* during the lifetime of a single author has been advocated by Taplin (1992) and M. L. West (2011a). Taplin argues for a single poet, who has learned his art from other oral singers. Homer performed different parts of the *Iliad* at different venues and continued to shape his poem for an extended period. In this way, he was able to increase the size of his epic, make changes and adaptations, sharpen certain points, and improve the end product. On a similar claim, see R. Thomas (1992) 39–40. M. L. West suggests that the poet of the *Iliad* composed his epic in stages by the use of writing. He first wrote books 1–2, 11, and 16, and then undertook two major expansions (books 3–9 and 12–15), before deciding to continue, at a later stage, his narrative after the death of Patroclus (books 17–24). It is interesting to note that modern unitarians like Taplin and M. L. West believe (a) that an epic of the size and complexity of the *Iliad* can be created either by oral composition or by writing, (b) that fixity can be achieved either by oral or written composition, and (c) that the *Iliad* was made during a prolonged period.

[30] The evolution and shaping of the Iliadic epic tradition, to which I refer here and elsewhere in this book, are not to be confused with Nagy's evolutionary model of Homeric poetry (1996a, 29–63, especially 42). According to my model, Homeric epic has not completed its evolution and shaping until the end of the archaic period. Conversely, Nagy's model involves the following five degrees of increasing crystallization: (a) a fluid period with no written texts from the second millennium to *c.* 750 BC; (b) a more formative or Panhellenic period with no written texts from *c.* 750 BC to 550 BC; (c) an "Athenian period" with potential texts as transcripts from *c.* 550 to 350 BC; (d) a standardizing period from *c.* 317 BC to 250 BC; and a relatively more rigid period from *c.* 250 BC to shortly after 150 BC, which is marked by the philological activity of Aristarchus that leads to a final standardized text.

is recognized as the author of a written poem in a literary milieu, the tradition is recognized as the "author" of an oral poem in a song-culture. This last statement means that in an oral culture individual singers who compose and perform epic songs yield to the tradition. The contribution of each singer to the formation of the epic is gradually absorbed by other singers through a process of continuous performances. The contribution of any given singer is therefore subsumed and incorporated into the collective consciousness of the epic tradition (an oral palimpsest in the case of Homeric epic)[31] within which these singers operate.[32]

The question of authorship in an oral milieu is better captured by the notion of poetic activity. By this term, I designate the driving force behind the evolution and shaping of Homeric epic. Poetic activity operates within a system of commemoration of the past in an oral culture. This system is a traditional structure that cannot be analyzed separately from poetic activity, since structures are created, maintained, and changed through poetic activity, while poetic activity acquires meaning only against the background of, and as the internal development of, the structure. The dilemma between the historical author[33] and the tradition[34] introduces too rigid a dichotomy with respect to the issue of authorship in the oral environment within which Homeric epic operates. The poetic activity of the singers takes place within a traditional structure created by formulaic diction, typical scenes, thematic resonances, rhythm and verse structure, narrative format, and a given set of characters. Along these lines, poetic activity and traditional structure are two sides of the same coin. Singers should not be treated as historical poets[35] with exclusive "proprietorial rights" over their songs.[36] Proprietorial rights are equally asserted by a poetic tradition. The "wide *kleos* of the song, even for those who will be" (*Od.* 3.204; see also 8.580), "the song whose fame had reached wide heaven" (*Od.* 8.74), the "pleasing song" for Penelope (*Od.* 24.197–8), and the "hateful song" for Clytaemestra (*Od.* 24.200): all are manifestations of the "proprietorial rights" of a poetic tradition expressed by recourse to fame and authority. Such predictions, which pertain to self-actualization, may also concern an epic tradition, not only a historical author. The process of self-actualization of an

---

[31] I have explored several aspects of this issue in Tsagalis (2008).
[32] On the corrective influence of the tradition, see Lord (2018³) 126. On the two concepts of song, one pertaining to the "general idea of the story" and the other to the "particular performance or text," see Lord (2018³) 106.
[33] Scodel (2002) 28–9; Pelliccia (2003) 105–9; R. L. Fowler (2004a) 227 with n. 28; A. D. Morrison (2007) 57 with n. 108, 60, 61, 66–7.
[34] Lamberton (1988) 1–37; Foley (1998) 149, 169, (2004) 186.
[35] According to Nagy (1996a, 20–2, 92–3), they are personifications of the tradition.
[36] Currie (2016, 19–20) suggests that the *Homeric Hymn to Apollo* (166–73) allows us to associate "proprietorial rights" with individual poets; behind "the antonomastic *sphragis* of the 'Cean nightingale' type (Bacchylides 3.97–8)" lurks "the constructed persona of 'Homer', self-advertising and celebrity-conscious at that"; on the antiquity of the concern about ownership, see Fowler (2004a) 227: "arguments about authenticity and ownership were rife already in the archaic period, and guilds like the Homeridae and the Creophylii heroized their putative founders."

epic tradition is conditioned by (i) the performative communication with the audience, (ii) the interaction with other epic traditions, (iii) the reaction to larger cultural phenomena, and (iv) the creative combination of a quantitative and qualitative development, the former increasing the epic in size, the latter giving to this expansion a distinct identity.[37]

The main questions with which this book deals are also vital for understanding the meaning and function of innovation within an oral epic tradition. The Homeric epics are marked by restless innovation that does not alter the *Faktenkanon* but entails motif- and episode-transference from one tradition to another or from one setting to another, changes in essential elements, and alterations in the signification of scenes.[38] By studying the evolution and shaping of the *Doloneia*, we may be able to explore, evaluate, and comprehend the way innovation operates in an oral poetic medium.

Another important ramification of the research to be undertaken in this book is the stability of epic traditions.[39] If Homeric epic has been shaped by its creative interaction with earlier oral epics, then the question of fixity of both source- and target-epics comes to the foreground.[40] How did these epics acquire stability? Were they fixed by writing at such an early stage, i.e. before the Homeric epics, or through repeated performance? Regular exposure of singers and audience to such oral epics may have endowed them with the knowledge and familiarity needed for creative interaction and deliberate linking.[41] Concomitant to this issue is the notion of "cyclic tinge."[42] The use of a group of features by certain oral epics that will later influence directly the written Cyclic epics tentatively suggests that a notional Epic Cycle[43] in some form may have existed before the creation of

---

[37] See Tsagalis (2011) 235–7 = (2023) 28–30.   [38] Currie (2016) 73–5.

[39] S. R. West (1988, 67) observes that the proems of the *Iliad* and the *Odyssey* presuppose a general familiarity with the epic tradition. On audience familiarity with fixed epic traditions, see Scodel (1998) 171–94, (2002) 1–41; Burgess (2006) 173; Tsagalis (2011) 229–33 = (2023) 22–6; Kelly (2008) 198–200, (2018) 351–77. If, as Kelly (2012a, 3) has argued, "Homer" manipulates his audience's familiarity with the structural grammar and phraseological idiom of early epic to "create uncertainty, excitement, and meaning, to direct, misdirect, and control their response, and *on the smallest scales of narrative*" (my italics), then *a fortiori* he does the same thing with themes and motifs which are tied to specific epic traditions; see also Porter (2022) 12.

[40] Neoanalysis, which studies the transference of motifs and scenes from pre-Homeric source-texts to the Homeric poems as target-texts, has benefited from interaction with oral theory. For an early attempt to engage in a constructive dialogue, see Kullmann (1984) 307–23 = (1992) 140–55; for recent discussions, see Tsagalis (2011) 209–44 = (2023) 3–33; Barker and Christensen (2020) 15–20.

[41] See Burgess (2019) 13: "For the archaic age, intentional linking between epics would most plausibly be situated in a performance context, with different bards or rhapsodes implementing transitional or recapitulating passages."

[42] Scodel (2012, 515) has used the expression "cyclic impulse" to describe "a basic (though not, of course, universal) characteristic of archaic epic."

[43] On the notional Epic Cycle, see Fantuzzi and Tsagalis (2015a) 9–14; Burgess (2019, 15) envisages a "notional cycle of pre-Homeric myth about the Trojan War and its consequences that existed beyond epic and performance." However, since it is hard to resist the assumption that there existed pre-Homeric oral epics, I see no reason why they have not played their role in the creation of this notional cycle of pre-Homeric myth. In fact, there are reasons to believe that Homeric epic regularly cites pre-Homeric oral poetry on the Theban and Trojan Wars; see pp. 42–3, 278–9.

the written Cyclic epics and long before the establishment of the canon of epics known as the Epic Cycle.[44] Digging into the sources underlying the Homeric *Doloneia* is expected to help us understand more about this notional Epic Cycle, which may have been close to but not identical with the canonical Epic Cycle we are familiar with, mainly through the summaries of Proclus. The conservative[45] and reproductive nature of oral cyclic epic, which was followed by the written Cyclic epics, stands in marked contrast to the especially innovative and interactive nature of Homeric epic,[46] which is distinctly metacyclic.[47] This observation brings us to another crucial ramification of my research on the *Doloneia*.

The aspiration of Homeric epics to be new songs within a pool of traditional oral epics discloses, through the way they exploited earlier traditions, their meta-epic nature, thorough interest in poetry and poetics,[48] systematic engagement with other oral epic poetry, especially of cyclic tinge, and creative interaction with their own earlier versions. All these techniques constitute complementary aspects of the attempt of Homeric epic to excel as inspiring, new song.[49] Exploring these puzzling but fascinating questions is worthwhile not only because it influences our interpretation of the *Doloneia* but also because it affects the way we understand the entire Iliadic and Homeric epic tradition.

All these implications suggest that the problems associated with the *Doloneia* do not belong to an impermeable poetic environment. They have broad consequences for the way we interpret Homeric poetry at large. The evolution and shaping of book 10 concerns how we should think of the making of the Iliadic epic tradition. Evolutionary mutation, to be effective, is a shared and collectively constructed mutation.[50]

---

[44] That the Theban and Trojan stories were paired at least as early as Hesiod is clear from *Op.* 158–73. Since these stories signified the end of the world of heroes, the epic traditions that embodied them may have also been paired; see Scodel (2012) 515; also Most (2024) 131–45.

[45] On the conservatism of the South Slavic tradition, see Lord (2018³) 131.

[46] See Currie (2016) 76, who draws attention to the analogy observed with respect to both lyric poetry and tragedy. Greek lyric strives for innovation (e.g. Pind. *Ol.* 9.48–9), but old songs were also appreciated through reperformance (e.g. Herod. 4.35.3; Timoth. frs. 791.211–12, 791.216–17, 796 *PMG*; Pl. *Leg.* 802a; see Herington 1985, 207–10). Likewise, the annual contests taking place in the City Dionysia speak for the existence of a special venue that attracted innovation like a magnet. On the other hand, reperformances and revivals of old tragedies took place both in the Rural Dionysia (in Attica but outside Athens) and outside Attica (Csapo and Slater 1994, 14–17; Taplin 1999, 37–43; Csapo and Wilson 2015, 316–95; Lamari 2017).

[47] Finkelberg (2015) 126–38 = (2020) 169–81.   [48] See pp. 29–31, 33–5.

[49] Innovation that aims to captivate the audience's interest and thus make the epic song evaluated as inspiring results in epic rivalry. On the competitive impulse in Greek poetry, see Martin (1989), (1992) 11–33; Griffith (1990) 185–207; Nagy (1990) 78–9; Rosen (1990) 99–113; Ford (2002) 272–93; Tsagalis (2006) 79–130, (2009) 131–77 = (2023) 209–55; Barker (2009); Allan and Cairns (2011) 113–46; Bassino, Canevaro, and Graziosi (2017); Gostoli, Fongoni, and Biondi (2017); Damon and Pieper (2019); Nelson (2021) 25–57.

[50] See Havelock (1986) 55: "evolutionary mutation, to be effective, has to be shared mutation," to whose formulation I have added "collectively constructed."

3. Current Status of Research on *Iliad* 10

Previous research on the *Doloneia* can be classified into several categories, according to the arguments and the methodology that have been used by different scholars. The core of the ensuing examination is neither an exhaustive presentation of earlier work on book 10 nor a meticulous investigation of individual arguments. It is the assessment of the theoretical premises on which scholarly debate has been based and the limits to and limitations of certain assumptions that have marked and often disoriented previous research. In this light, the order of presentation and discussion of the relevant material are principally thematical and only partly chronological.

3.1 The *Einzellied* Theory

Building partly on the basis and influential impact of the Townley scholion on *Iliad* 10 (φασὶ τὴν ῥαψῳδίαν ὑφ᾽ [MS: ἐφ᾽] Ὁμήρου ἰδίᾳ τετάχθαι καὶ μὴ εἶναι μέρος τῆς Ἰλιάδος, ὑπὸ δὲ Πεισιστράτου τετάχθαι εἰς τὴν Ἰλιάδα)[51] and on the notion that this Iliadic book is a self-contained episode, various scholars[52] have argued that the *Doloneia* was an *Einzellied*, which enjoyed separate circulation and was incorporated into the *Iliad* at the cost of various contradictions with the rest of the plot, especially with books 8 and 9.

However, the validity of the scholion T on *Il.* 10.1 as evidence of the *Doloneia*'s inauthenticity has been questioned by Gallavotti,[53] who has argued that the term μέρος reflects aesthetic criticism that is based on Aristotelian precepts. Aristotle argues that the unity of Homeric poetry is not undermined by the presence of subordinate episodes (*Po.* 1462b), which give variety to the epic's plot without weakening its coherence.[54] According to this approach, the scholiast's expression μὴ εἶναι μέρος τῆς Ἰλιάδος means that book 10 is not an essential part of the *Iliad*. In fact, this scholion stands in contrast to the relevant expression used by Eustathius (φασὶ δὲ οἱ παλαιοὶ τὴν ῥαψῳδίαν ταύτην ὑφ᾽ Ὁμήρου μὴ ἐγκαταλεγῆναι τοῖς μέρεσι τῆς Ἰλιάδος),[55] which means "the ancients claim that this rhapsody [i.e. book 10] was not included by Homer in the episodes of the *Iliad*," i.e. "does not belong to the *Iliad*." Whereas the scholion T on *Il.* 10.1 expresses an aesthetic judgment, Eustathius' comment states an opinion. A scholion by Dionysius of Thrace stresses the "wholeness" of the *Doloneia* since it is an episode with a

---

[51] "They say that the rhapsody (book 10) has been composed privately by Homer and that it is not part of the *Iliad*, but that it has been placed by Pisistratus in the *Iliad*."
[52] Nitzsch (1862) 408; Ranke (1881) 18–37; Bethe (1914) 123–8; Wilamowitz (1916) 38–9; Theiler (1947) 125–6; M. L. West (2011a) 233–4.
[53] Gallavotti (1969) 203–14.   [54] Gallavotti (1969) 205.
[55] Comm. *Il.* 785.41–2 [III 2.6–7 van der Valk].

beginning and an end.[56] An example from analogy is offered by two scholia on *Od.* 23.296, according to which Aristophanes of Byzantium and Aristarchus regarded this verse as the πέρας/τέλος of the *Odyssey*.[57] Gallavotti[58] and Erbse[59] have argued that Alexandrian criticism about the πέρας/τέλος of the *Odyssey* reflects Aristotelian literary theory, and as such it probably means that the essential part and plan of the epic ("das τέλος des μῦθος")[60] pertaining to the reunion of Odysseus and Penelope have been completed in 23.296. If we endorse this interpretation and apply it to the scholion T *Il.* 10.1, then its validity with respect to the inauthenticity of the *Doloneia* is seriously weakened.

A different approach to this scholion leads also to the conclusion that it is of no importance to the question of the authenticity of the *Doloneia*. Montanari[61] has argued that the scholion of codex Townleianus on *Il.* 10.1 should not be treated as proof for the inauthenticity of book 10, since the manuscript reading ἐφ' Ὁμήρου ("in Homer's time") instead of Eustathius' ὑφ' Ὁμήρου ("by Homer") reflects a viewpoint which was typical of the *Chorizontes*, who may have claimed that, like the *Odyssey*, the *Doloneia* too was by some other poet, different from Homer.[62] Furthermore, the very idea that a self-contained episode is bound to circulate separately does not mean that it has been composed by a different author. The fact that the episode of Penthesileia, which occupies the first part of the Cyclic *Aethiopis*, is a self-contained[63] episode and may have been circulating independently does not mean that it was the work of a different poet (i.e. not Arctinus). According to Aristotle, the *Ilias parva* contains fewer than eight episodes, some of which may have been performed on their own, but this does not mean that they were not composed by Lesches. Demodocus' third song on the Wooden Horse indicates that the last phase of the Trojan War was an episode that would attract the interest of audiences. However, an extended and detailed version of all the events associated with the end of the Trojan War was part of a separate Cyclic epic, the *Iliou persis*, by Arctinus. A version of this same episode was also included in the last part of Lesches' *Ilias parva*. Moreover, even episodes which are not self-contained can be cited on their own without questioning the fact that they belong to a larger poem. Characters in various Platonic dialogues refer to Homeric

---

[56] *Scholia in Dionysii Thracis Artem Grammaticam* 180.1–2 (Hilgard): καὶ τὸ σύνταγμα τὸ ἐν ταὐτῷ ἀρχὴν καὶ τέλος ἔχον, ὁποῖόν ἐστι τὸ Κ τῆς Ἰλιάδος, ἡ νυκτεγερσία καλουμένη.

[57] Ἀριστοφάνης καὶ Ἀρίσταρχος πέρας τῆς Ὀδυσσείας τοῦτο ποιοῦνται (M, V, Vind. 133); τοῦτο τέλος τῆς Ὀδυσσείας φησὶν Ἀρίσταρχος καὶ Ἀριστοφάνης (H, M, Q).

[58] Gallavotti (1969) 208–14. [59] Erbse (1972) 166–77.

[60] Erbse (1972) 176. [61] Montanari (2010) 1–17.

[62] Differently Danek (1988) 236 n. 4, who says that "it is very unlikely that the scholiast or his source did not treat book 10 as the work of Homer" and adds that the ὑφ' Ὁμήρου and ἐφ' Ὁμήρου mean virtually the same thing. However, even if the reading ὑφ' Ὁμήρου (ἰδίᾳ τετάχθαι) is retained, the scholion is at odds with the fact that no other ancient source designates the *Doloneia* as an independent poem by Homer, whereas various ancient sources assign to him several poems, such as the *Thebais*, the *Margites*, the *Homeric Hymns*, certain epigrams, etc.; see Gallavotti (1969) 204.

[63] It has no consequences for the story of Memnon that features in the second part of this epic.

episodes, parts of which they cite, but there is no doubt that the episodes belong to the *Iliad* or the *Odyssey*. The same observation applies to Aristotle and his readers.[64] This treatment of different episodes questions not only the use of separate circulation or quotation as indications of independent authorship but also the very notion of thematic autonomy. An independent citation is a form of autonomy that is not bound to completeness. The idea that the circulation of an episode would be enhanced by its thematic fullness is only partly true, since even parts of an episode could be selected for self-contained presentation. The story of Philoctetes in the *Ilias parva* includes two phases, the episode at Lemnos and the killing of Paris when Philoctetes arrives at Troy. Of these two episodes, the first phase was dramatized by Aeschylus, Euripides, and Sophocles (in this order).[65] Thematic cohesion and autonomy are flexible notions and should be treated with caution when they are used to determine authorship.

Drawing on the scholion T that presents "Homer" as the composer of book 10, Dué[66] argues that this statement is an acknowledgment of the book's traditionality. The scholion does not indicate that the *Doloneia* is by a different poet from the rest of the *Iliad*. On the contrary, it states that it is Homeric and that it was Pisistratus who inserted it in the *Iliad*.[67]

Despite these objections, the *Einzellied* theory has brought to light an important question: was the *Doloneia* composed exactly in the form that is now book 10, or has it been adapted from a more expanded version? Did the poet of the *Iliad* or a different poet find the same episode in another source? Did either of them decide to transfer it to the *Iliad* by making certain changes in order to eliminate features

---

[64] For a list of Homeric passages cited by Plato and Aristotle, see Howes (1895) 153–237. Aristotle quotes three verses of the *Doloneia* in the *Poetics* (1461a10–19).

[65] I am referring to the three plays with the title *Philoctetes* that were written by the three great tragedians. There is also a play by Sophocles referring to Philoctetes' achievements after his arrival at Troy (frs. 697–703 *TrGF*).

[66] Dué (2019) 130; see also Introduction 3.4.

[67] Sbardella (2012, 179–89) argues that the *Doloneia* was inserted into the *Iliad* by Pisistratus because the tyrant aimed at associating this night raid of Diomedes and Odysseus with his own night attack against the Athenians in the Battle of Pallene (see Herod. 1.61.4–62.1 and 1.62.4–63.1). However, there are various counterarguments, of which I cite a few: (a) The information of the scholion T 1 on *Il*. 10.1 that Pisistratus inserted into the *Iliad* the *Doloneia*, which was an independent composition by Homer, belongs to a group of ancient sources (e.g. Ael. *V.H.* 13.14; Plut. *Lyc.* 4.4; Σ Pind. *Nem.* 2.1c [Drachmann]; *Anth. Pal.* 11.442; Eust. 6 [van der Valk]; Tz. *Anecd. Gr.* 1.6 [Cramer]; Cic. *De or.* 3.137) attributing to Pisistratus the joining of various scattered compositions of Homer into a unified whole. If one adopts this line of thought, he would have to make the same assumption for various other parts of the Homeric epics. (b) Herodotus' account of Pisistratus' surprise night attack to the Athenians tallies with Pisistratus' Argive associations (through his Argive wife Timonassa; see Tsagalis 2018b, 47–8 = 2023, 484–5), which would link him to Diomedes, but leaves no room for someone who would have played the role of Odysseus. (c) Pisistratus was exiled in Thrace and exploited the silver and golden mines on Mt Pangaeum. He had in his army auxiliary forces from the area of Strymon (Herod. 1.64.1). In this light, he would have seemed more of a "Rhesus" who comes from Thrace (and whose father was thought by later sources to be the river Strymon) than his adversary. (d) the nocturnal episode of book 10 in the *Iliad* does not determine the course of the Trojan War, whereas Pisistratus' victory at Pallene plays a major role in ensuing political developments.

that would be incompatible with the plot and the viewpoint of this epic,[68] or was the poet of the *Iliad* or a different poet the first who composed this episode? Irrespective of the stance one takes concerning the authenticity of the *Doloneia*, it is crucial to examine the theoretical basis of this issue. At its heart lies not the authenticity of *Iliad* 10 but the existence of another, earlier form of this episode either as an *Einzellied* or as part of another epic poem. Reflexes of this question can be seen as early as Nitzsch,[69] who thought that the *Einzellied* included *Il.* 10.203–579 (the *Nyktegersia*, i.e. 1–202, being composed to allow for the insertion of the *Einzellied* in the *Iliad*), and Witte,[70] who made the same claim for *Il.* 10.299–511. The issue of transfer and adaptation is also crucial because it is related to the way one defines and treats inconcinnities. For if disturbing contradictions and incongruities are found in the *Doloneia*, then the scenario of a single author who has composed and inserted the *Doloneia* into *his* completed *Iliad*[71] at a later stage of his lifetime becomes unlikely. The reason is that it is improbable that the same poet, who decided to add one more episode to his completed oeuvre, would utterly fail to keep up with his compositional technique.[72] Seen from this vantage point, there are three alternatives: (a) the *Doloneia* as we have it is the result of the shaping of an earlier version of book 10 after the addition of new material that was taken from another poetic source and was adapted to the plot of the *Iliad*; (b) book 10 in its entirety has been adapted from some earlier poetic source by another poet who inserted it into the *Iliad*; (c) it has been composed by another poet who did not find it in any other poetic source. This problem may be better stated in the following manner: were the episode of the night raid and the story of Rhesus and his horses composed only within the framework of the Iliadic epic tradition, or had they been part of another epic tradition where they were thematically more at home? The choice between these alternatives rests (a) on one's definition of incongruities of style, language, and composition between the *Doloneia* and the rest of the *Iliad* and (b) on the question of the antiquity of the Rhesus story.

---

[68] The transfer of episodes or scenes rather than entire episodes has been thoroughly studied by neoanalysis. I offer two examples, one pertaining to the *Iliad*, and the other to the *Odyssey*. With respect to the story of Memnon, Schadewaldt (1965⁴, 155–202) undertook a "horizontal" analysis of seven themes that a pre-Homeric *Memnonis* shared with the *Iliad*: Nestor's salvation (scene 3 – *Il.* 8.79–91), *Psychostasia* (scene 7 – *Il.* 22.208–13), the transfer of the bodies of Memnon and Sarpedon after their deaths (scenes 9–10 – *Il.* 16.450, 666–83), the lament for Achilles (scene 18 – *Il.* 18.35–71), Thetis' warning to Achilles about his future death (scene 2 – *Il.* 18.96; also 11.794–5; 16.34–7; 16.51), Achilles lying on the ground (scene 13 – *Il.* 18.26–7), and the assault against Troy (scene 11 – *Il.* 22.378–84). On the basis of two scholia by Servius on Virg. *Aen.* 2.81 and 3.16, P. Kakridis (2001, 481–7) traced the origins of the Odyssean Cicones episode in a pre-Homeric epic (an oral forerunner of the *Cypria*?), in which Odysseus had undertaken the initiative of bringing supplies from Thrace in order to feed the Achaean army that was suffering from hunger.

[69] Nitzsch (1862) 408.

[70] Witte (1908), *non vidi*. I owe this reference to Lucarini (2019) 92 n. 224.

[71] Assuming that he had already composed and finished the rest of it.

[72] See M. L. West (2011a) 233.

3.2 *Quellenforschung*

A first attempt to find the sources of *Iliad* 10 was undertaken by Fenik,[73] who argued that traces in the *Doloneia* point to an earlier Iliadic version in which the target of the spying mission was Hector. Fenik also examined the Rhesus story, distinguishing between two earlier versions, which he called for convenience the "Pindaric" and the "oracle version."[74] According to the former,[75] Rhesus was killed after an *aristeia*. In the latter,[76] an oracle had predicted that if he and his horses drank water from the river Scamander and his horses grazed at its banks, he would be invincible; unfortunately for the enemies of the Achaeans, he is ambushed at night and killed by Diomedes, either alone or accompanied (as in the *Iliad*) by Odysseus, as soon as he arrives at Troy.

Fenik's examination of the sources of *Iliad* 10 is not neoanalytical.[77] Although, like classical neoanalysis,[78] Fenik starts from the observation of irregularities in the *Doloneia*, he does not explain them by means of the neoanalytical method of motif-transference from earlier poems. Moreover, he rejects the association of the Pindaric and oracle versions with single source-texts[79] which the poet of the *Doloneia* used and adapted. He considers these versions of the Rhesus story as reflecting a common tradition, though he acknowledges the cyclic resonances of the story of Rhesus.

3.3 The "Post-Post-Traditional Singer"

The most comprehensive and influential modern study of the *Doloneia* is a monograph by Danek,[80] in which it is argued that the accumulation in a single Iliadic episode of (i) linguistic innovations, (ii) novel combinations and use of formulas,[81] (iii) a taste for the exotic, and (iv) the lack of ring composition and

---

[73] Fenik (1964).   [74] See chapter 7.   [75] Σ [bT, D] on *Il*. 10.435.
[76] Σ [A, D] on *Il*. 10.435.   [77] Fenik (1964) 30–5.
[78] On a brief, yet concise, presentation of neoanalysis, see *HomEnc* s.v. "Neoanalysis" (M. Edwards); *OCD* s.v. "Neoanalysis" (C. Tsagalis).
[79] For the terms source-text and target-text, see Edmunds (2001) 137–9. In this book, these terms designate not only extant texts but also oral epic traditions, mythological traditions, and stories in general.
[80] Danek (1988). Danek is followed by many modern scholars, e.g. Willcock (1989) 178–80; Hainsworth (1993) 154–5; M. L. West (2011a) 233–5, (2014) 40. Danek (2012, 120) refers to the poet of the *Doloneia* as the "post-post-traditional singer". This term designates a singer who "no longer tried to recompose the plot of the *Iliad* in a creative way. He was a rhapsode who learned the *Iliad* by heart, using a written text, and decided to add a new part of his own (even if he used an old story)."
[81] See Ranke (1881); Heusinger (1939); Klingner (1940) 337–68 = (1964) 7–39; also Laser (1949), (1958) 385–425, whose comparison of parallel passages between the *Doloneia* and the *Odyssey* suggests that the former had as its model the latter. The use of diction as a yardstick for determining the authenticity of a book of the *Iliad* has been decisively challenged by Danek (1988, 13–18), who has criticized the fallacy of a "Homeric dictional norm" that runs through the *Iliad* and the *Odyssey* or even an "Iliadic dictional norm" and an "Odyssean dictional norm" against which the diction of any given

parallelism in the speeches makes a deciding case against the book's authenticity. However, as Danek himself acknowledges, only (iii) and (iv) of these four categories of material display a considerable difference from the rest of the epic.[82] The extent of linguistic innovation is not unlike other parts of the *Iliad*, and Odyssean phraseological resonances may be due to older formulas whose existence we simply do not know from other sources.[83]

As regards categories (iii) and (iv), there are important counterarguments that need to be evaluated. The taste for the exotic involves special military gear and clothing. The former is probably determined by the unusual (by Iliadic standards) content of *Iliad* 10, since a night raid and ambush require special equipment which suits their conditions and a different kind of fighting. The latter (dressing in animal skins) is a device employed to evoke other Iliadic passages with which it shares phraseology and content. In this vein, it may be the case that the *Doloneia* uses intratextuality, which is the same associative technique by which Homeric epic creates sense.[84] As regards the striking absence of ring composition and parallelism, which represent two of the standard devices used in the internal structure of Iliadic speeches, it needs to be examined in relation to other considerations pertaining to both the internal and external organization of speeches in book 10.[85]

Danek's central thesis is that *Iliad* 10 was created by a poet trained in epic song-making.[86] He knew the *Iliad* by heart by means of a written text and added a new episode to it not long after the *Iliad* was set down in writing. He neither integrated the *Iliad* into his personal style nor adapted his personal style to the *Iliad*. Being aware of the differences between them, he aimed at highlighting them, often assuming an ironic stance. In the sixth century BC Pisistratus or his son Hipparchus knew of a text or texts of the *Iliad* without the *Doloneia*, but since this episode was not felt to be alien to Homer, no effort was made to exclude it from being recited as part of the *Iliad* by rhapsodes at Athens.[87]

The assumption that the *Doloneia* was an independent episode and its poet an individual who inserted it into the *Iliad* but aimed at stressing the differences between the two texts raises various questions: (a) it postulates a poet with a contradictory mentality. He wants to promote his work by making it part of a

---

book of the Homeric epics should be evaluated. Moreover, the examination of dictional material within the frame of Iliadic and Odyssean books as recognizable narrative entities runs the risk of simplification. The reason is that even within individual books there are significant statistical differences. If, then, statistical variance is observable even within shorter sections of a given book as regards set expressions (and by extension different sorts of similarities and divergencies can be detected in different parts of other books), then book-based statistical data should be also examined with caution.

[82] Likewise, Hainsworth (1993) 154–5.
[83] This is a possibility that previous scholars who dealt with this issue (Laser 1958, 385–425; Ramersdorfer 1981) failed to consider.
[84] For a thorough analysis of arming and clothing in the *Doloneia*, see chapter 4.
[85] See pp. 126–33.   [86] Danek (1988) 234–7, (2012) 121.   [87] Danek (1988) 234.

famous epic,[88] but decides to rival it from within, hence his ironic stance towards it. (b) The end result paints for the poet of the *Doloneia* a rather incongruous picture. While he was successful in promoting his "new" *Iliad*, he failed to make *his own* contribution noticed, since Pisistratus and/or Hipparchus (as well as rhapsodes) did not consider the *Doloneia*'s stylistic oddities to be un-Homeric. (c) It is not clear why this poet[89] learned the *Iliad* by heart. If he aimed to recite it, together with the *Doloneia*, we would be faced with the rather unlikely scenario of a performance of the entire "new" *Iliad* by a single individual who wanted to gain fame and authority by reciting 15,114 verses by another poet and 579 verses of his own, "hidden" in a monumental epic composition. (d) If the poet of the *Doloneia* had a written copy of the *Iliad*, which he used to learn the *Iliad* by heart, it is likely that he would have created a new copy of his *Iliad* (i.e. with the addition of the *Doloneia*), which he would like to proliferate so that his version becomes widely known. Danek[90] dates the addition of the *Doloneia* to the *Iliad*,[91] which means the creation of a new, written copy including book 10, to the early sixth century BC at the latest. How this single written copy rivaled so effectively the earlier written copies of the *Iliad* without the *Doloneia* and became so authoritative that it made the *Doloneia* the dominant version is unclear.[92]

These considerations do not undervalue the main thrust of Danek's argument, which is the special status of the *Doloneia*. However, instead of assuming that the book is the wholesale creation of an individual who inserted it into the made *Iliad*, I will explore an alternative possibility, i.e. that the *Doloneia*'s constant tension between integration and aberrance from the *Iliad* can only partially be explained

---

[88] Although it is argued that it was Pisistratus or Hipparchus who inserted this episode into the *Iliad*, it is clear that the *Doloneia* has been composed to be placed between books 9 and 11, which means that this was the intention of its poet.

[89] Danek's twofold identification of this individual as poet (1988, *passim*) and rhapsode (2012, 120) puts a strain on the way he operated.

[90] Danek (2012) 121.

[91] According to Giuliani (2010, 239–44; also Liapis 2009, 286), the best iconographic representation for the dating of the Homeric *Doloneia* is the depiction of Rhesus, Diomedes, and Odysseus on a Chalcidian neck-amphora by the Inscription Painter (Malibu, Getty Museum 96.AE.1; see also True (1995) 415–29; *LIMC* VIII, s.v. "Rhesos," no. 2 [True]). On side A of this neck-amphora, Diomedes grabs by the throat Rhesus, who is lying to the right and is ready to thrust his sword into his naked chest. The Thracian king has just woken up. On side B, Odysseus grasps a reclining Thracian by the head and cuts his throat. All around the entire vase are depicted twelve Thracians, some of whom are lying on their backs on cushions placed on the ground under trees, and others face down (without cushions). In this long row, all bodies are covered with blankets, heads are turned to the right, while weapons and armor are hanging in the background, either from trees or bushes. The space below both handles is filled with horses, two on one and four on the other. The agitation of the horses is clearly marked, as well as the white stallion among the group of four horses. According to Snodgrass (1998, 73), the fact that Diomedes kills Rhesus first (instead of last in the *Doloneia*) and that the killing is not carried out exclusively by Diomedes do not constitute substantial departures from *Iliad* 10. Furthermore, as Giuliani has argued, the fact that the number of Thracian guards is exactly the same (twelve) as that in *Iliad* 10 leaves little doubt that the painter was reproducing the Homeric version of this episode.

[92] It is equally obscure why Pisistratus or Hipparchus decided to replace with this written copy the earlier ones (without the *Doloneia*) that were circulating in Athens.

by the use of the theme of ambush,[93] and that it results from the evolution and shaping of this book from an earlier form into the current version by means of the addition of the Rhesus episode.

3.4 The Poetics of Ambush

Radically different is the theory of Dué and Ebbott,[94] who argue that *Iliad* 10 belongs, like the rest of the *Iliad*, to a long oral tradition of composition and performance of epic. The *Doloneia* is a fully fledged manifestation of the theme of "ambush" (λόχος). What modern scholars treat as idiosyncratic or aberrant is based on their erroneous identification of the traditionally presented warfare (πόλεμος) with the norm for all military activity. For Dué and Ebbott, the *Doloneia* represents an example of ambush warfare, a theme with its own traditional phraseology and features that differ from those of πόλεμος, which is regularly represented in the *Iliad*. Along analogous lines, Bierl[95] has maintained that the *Doloneia* is an integral part of the Iliadic tradition and that its distinctive features reflect its special narrative function and subgenre. For Bierl, *Iliad* 10 is not only a genuine but also a crucial part of the poem. The fact that it does not fit the geometric form of symmetrical composition of the *Iliad* propagated by unitarians and neo-unitarians is not an indication of its inauthenticity but a deliberate choice made to stress that it stands in the middle of the epic. By endorsing a partly symbolical interpretation, in which Diomedes and Odysseus enter and exit successfully an otherness embodied by ambush, death, night, and the horses of Rhesus, Bierl claims that the *Doloneia* highlights the crisis facing the Achaean army and its overcoming.

3.5 Oral, Intertextual Neoanalysis

In various previous studies,[96] I have argued that one of the most rewarding interpretive methods of Homeric poetry is the application of neoanalysis, as part of a general theory of allusion, to the study of the evolution and shaping of the *Iliad* and the *Odyssey* within an oral culture. Homeric epic resembles an oral palimpsest in the sense that it bears traces of its earlier form through awareness and citation of previous and/or alternative versions. In this vein, some of its source-texts may be pre-Homeric oral epic traditions that have reached a level

---

[93] This is the thesis of Dué and Ebbott (2010); see the next section.
[94] Dué and Ebbott (2010); see also Dué (2012) 175–83, (2019) 128–35.
[95] Bierl (2012) 133–74.
[96] E.g. Tsagalis (2008); (2011) 209–44; *HomEnc* s.v. "Intertextuality"; (2012a) 309–45; (2014b) 357–98; (2016).

of fixity due to the use of the same *Faktenkanon* as Homeric epic.[97] The *Iliad* and the *Odyssey* come into being by creatively responding to these traditions. They are not the first oral epic manifestations of the Trojan War myth but the most developed and successful epic compositions that resonate with mythical material treated in several earlier oral epics dealing with the same subject matter, some of which are marked by the same features that we are used to associating with the post-Homeric Cyclic epics. The making of the *Iliad* and the *Odyssey* amounts to the evolution and shaping of the Iliadic and Odyssean epic traditions throughout a considerable part of the archaic period. In this book these views are applied to the *Doloneia*. In my previous publications, I have concentrated my attention on two issues lying at the heart of the criticism against the authenticity of book 10, i.e. the absence of any reference in the rest of the *Iliad* to the events that happen in the *Doloneia*,[98] and the fact that Diomedes does not use Rhesus' horses to win the chariot race in the funeral games for Patroclus (*Iliad* 23).[99] I have also engaged with various problems of *Iliad* 10 in a forthcoming commentary on *Iliad* 9–12, which is part of the new Italian edition and commentary of the *Iliad* to be published by the Fondazione Lorenzo Valla. It is against the background of my previous work on oral, intertextual neoanalysis in Homeric epic, as well as on intratextual allusions to themes instead of events concerning the relation of book 10 with the rest of the *Iliad*, that I have embarked on the project of offering a systematic study to the making of the *Doloneia*.

4. Method

Iliad 10 is the only part of the *Iliad* where analytical criticism seems to have triumphed. Although the analytical school has practically fallen into oblivion,[100] several of its methods and assumptions concerning authenticity and spuriousness are still used for this book of the epic. The inauthenticity of the *Doloneia* is accepted by the majority of modern scholars, who have enriched the scientific arsenal already provided by the analysts with new arguments, in an attempt to give to the theory of interpolation a contemporary twist.[101] This is perhaps the one field where both adherents to the theory of a historical poet of the *Iliad* who has produced a written fixed text and supporters of oral theory converge. Even some

---

[97] See Dowden (1996) 52: "The *Faktenkanon* is the bottom line of Homeric intertextuality. It is because of its existence that Homer is able to allude—in a way, notably, that Bosnian bards do not—to other epic subjects."
[98] Tsagalis (2020b) 53–88.   [99] Tsagalis (2020a) 92–113.
[100] Lucarini (2019) is an exception. For his analytical approach to *Iliad* 10, see pp. 88–95 of his book.
[101] Ranke (1881); Heusinger (1939); Klingner (1940); Laser (1949) and (1958); Jens (1955) 616–25; Reinhardt (1961) 248–50; Heubeck (1974) 77–9; Danek (1988) and (2012) 106–21.

eminent oralists who are alert to the caveats of adopting the inauthenticity approach have ended up accepting it:[102]

> Any intelligent assessment of the *Iliad*, for example, will have to keep open the possibility that some parts of it, perhaps portions as substantial as the Tenth Book, have been added from an alien source.[103]
>
> The tradition that the *Doloneia* was added at this stage may well be true; it was a separate and post-Homeric composition, perhaps of similar date to the central poems of the Cycle, but too short to survive for long on its own.[104]
>
> It is the one part of the *Iliad* which can be omitted with no damage to the poem at all; the rest is from every point of view profoundly organic... on the other hand, the *Doloneia's* lack of any place in the Geometric pattern, though it creates a strong supposition, hardly seems sufficient proof for unauthenticity. Inconcinnities exist in the design in any case, even though none are so glaring as this would be... Book X bears some significant resemblances to the rest of the *Iliad*, notably in its conception of the relationship between characters, such as Agamemnon and Menelaus, and in the continuation of the fire image.[105]

But what gives us greater pause is that the surprising agreement as to the inauthenticity of the *Doloneia* by a group of scholars endorsing either literary or oralist approaches to Homer is matched by the equally astonishing concurrence as to the book's authenticity by another group of both literary and orally oriented scholars:[106]

> Some Greek exploit is urgently needed if the army is to take the field for tomorrow's battle in fine spirit. To start the battle with the Greeks dispirited would be artistically fatal. The distress which led to Agamemnon's offer to Achilles was crushing in its effect. The rejection of the appeal is a serious matter. Something must clearly happen before the army can be ready for a confident attack. So Diomedes and Odysseus, the two soldiers of Athene, so prominent in the first series, are united in a brilliant nocturnal raid.[107]

---

[102] Hainsworth (1993, 151–3) joins the inauthenticity camp, though he admits that inserting "a substantial episode into a poem such as the *Iliad* is more difficult than some critics of the analytical school have assumed" (152).

[103] This is the formulation by Adam Parry in his Introduction (p. l) to the collected papers of his father, Milman Parry (1971).

[104] Kirk (1962) 311.   [105] Whitman (1958) 283–4.

[106] Apart from the extracts cited below, see also Shewan (1911); Eichhorn (1973); Thornton (1984) 164–9.

[107] Sheppard (1922) 84 (with spelling modifications). Sheppard's observations have been anticipated by the scholia: πολλῶν δὲ κατὰ τὴν ποίησιν διηνυσμένων μετὰ μάχας ἱππικὰς καὶ πεζάς, θεῶν τρώσεις, μονομαχίας, δημηγορίας, ἐκκλησίας ἀνδρῶν τε καὶ θεῶν, πρεσβείας, καὶ μέχρι Ἴδης καταγαγὼν τὸν Δία,

Nestor need only snatch a shield and spear to be fully armed as when he quit the field (11.517ff.); but he has to borrow the shield of his son Thrasumedes, who is using his father's. The motif anticipates how Patroklos borrows Akhilleus' panoply. Thrasumedes lent his own shield to Diomedes the night before, since the latter had left his shield behind (10.255f.). Such lifelike details need no deeper explanation, *pace* the scholia; this curious parallel also helps to prove the *Doloneia* genuine.[108]

...we understand *Iliad* 10 to have been composed and performed within a long oral tradition of such poetry, and we argue that it is an example of a very ancient theme, the *lokhos*... For us, the theme of *lokhos*, with its traditional structure and diction, long predates our received text of the *Iliad*. So too do the narrative traditions about Rhesos predate our *Iliad*.[109]

We are thus faced with a situation in which the authenticity or inauthenticity of an entire Iliadic book is not conditioned by the idea of a written or an oral Homer but by the way scholars—whether they favor a written fixed text of the *Iliad* or an oral epic tradition—define unity of composition or, more generally, literary merit in early Greek epic.

Unity of composition lies, then, at the heart of the discussion with respect to the authenticity of the *Doloneia*. This issue is pertinent even for oralists who see the *Iliad* as an epic tradition evolving throughout the archaic period. This is because the putative difference of book 10 from the rest of the epic would be noticed only when a series of episodes of the *Iliad* was sequentially performed, and *a fortiori* when the entire epic was recited. From an oralist perspective, the question of the authenticity of the *Doloneia* in the sense of being part of multiple Iliadic performances is pertinent. Unity of composition with respect to a long and complex poem such as the *Iliad* must be defined by the study of narrative techniques: intratextual allusion (both backward and forward, sometimes involving shared phraseology), intertextual references, sharing of identical or equivalent metapoetic concerns, repetition of scene and situation, and progressive iteration (something happening on a smaller scale is expanded later in the poem, the second occurrence being narratively more crucial).[110] A special position among narrative techniques is

---

καὶ ἀστραπαῖς καὶ κεραυνοῖς ποιήσας λειπόμενον τὸ Ἑλληνικόν, ἐπ' ἄλλο εἶδος τρέπεται ὁ ποιητής, διὰ δόλου καὶ νυκτὸς ἀναπληρῶν τὴν μεθ' ἡμέραν ἀτυχίαν τῶν Ἑλλήνων ("many things having been poetically presented, after battles of the cavalry and the infantry, woundings of the gods, duels, speeches, councils of men and gods, embassies, and after having Zeus descend to Ida, and making the Greeks fall short by lightnings and thunderbolts, the poet turns to another type [of episode], compensating for the diurnal failure of the Greeks by means of a ruse and the night") [bT on *Il.* 10.3-4, III 2 Erbse]; ἔστι δὲ οἰκονομικὸν τὸ περὶ Δόλωνος, καὶ πίστιν ποιοῦν τοῖς νυκτερινοῖς τῶν Ἑλλήνων κατορθώμασιν ("the story of Dolon is in a well-ordered manner and creates confidence by means of the nocturnal achievements of the Greeks") [T on *Il.* 10.299b, III 64 Erbse].

[108] Janko (1992) 152 on *Il.* 14.9-12. [109] Dué and Ebbott (2010) 28.
[110] Also known as "Fenik's Law"; see Fenik (1974) 180-8.

occupied by intratextual allusion. In this light, I will offer several clarifications with respect to its importance for the question of authenticity versus inauthenticity of *Iliad* 10.[111]

Scholars have claimed that there is nothing in books 1–8 that foreshadows book 10 and equally nothing in books 11–24 that looks back to it.[112] At the core of this matter is the function of foreshadowing and flashback, which are usually limited to their narrative aspect, being employed solely with respect to actual events. This approach seems unjustifiably restrictive. First, an argument *ex contrario*: "not mentioned" is not necessarily equivalent to "unknown."[113] To claim that the *Doloneia* is not an organic part of the *Iliad* because no other book refers to an event taking place in book 10 is so erroneous as to say that the *Odyssey* does not know the *Iliad* because it virtually never refers to an event occurring in the latter poem.[114] Second, "silence" of this sort can be explained otherwise. One putative line of defense would be the lack of a relevant narrative context.[115] What occasion did the poem have to refer to the events of the *Doloneia* by a flashback? The clustering of events around the theme of ambush is difficult to attract references since it is not employed again in the *Iliad*. The horses of Rhesus in the funeral games for Patroclus are not a good example, since Diomedes races with the superior, semi-divine horses he has stolen from Aeneas in *Iliad* 5.[116] Another possible explanation would be to argue that this "silence" is deliberate. The Rhesus story may have been known in two versions, one involving an *aristeia* by the mighty Thracian king as soon as he arrives in Troy, the other an oracle referring to the potential invincibility that Rhesus and his horses would acquire if they drank from Scamander (and the horses grazed at its banks). In both versions, Rhesus was killed in a night ambush by Diomedes and Odysseus. By blacking out these two versions of the Rhesus story and isolating this tale from the rest of the plot, it is possible that the *Iliad* silently expresses its rejection of both the ambush as a form of warfare (by limiting it exclusively to the *Doloneia*) and of the fantastic and miraculous features inherent in the oracle version.[117] It is not unthinkable that the epic may be toying with the audience's knowledge of either or both of these versions which may have been at home in oral epics that focused on the events after the death of Achilles.[118] That Homeric epic engages with this kind of "silence," i.e. blanking out part of a tradition, may be seen, for example, in the story of Bellerophon, who kills the monster Chimaera, though no mention is

---

[111] For a detailed discussion, see chapter 2.
[112] Schadewaldt (1938 = 1966³) 142–3 n. 4; Reinhardt (1961) 248–9; M. L. West (2011a) 233.
[113] Cairns (2001a) 47.
[114] Minchin (2018, 15 with n. 29) rightly states that this claim is not fully accurate, since the *Odyssey* refers to the death of Patroclus and his shared burial with Achilles (in 3.110 and 24.71–9); see p. 123, n. 86.
[115] See Thornton (1984) 168.   [116] On this issue, see pp. 112–15.
[117] See pp. 65, 125, 239, 243, 299.   [118] See chapters 7 and 9.

made of his winged horse, Pegasus, who is essential to this story,[119] or in the depriving of seers like Calchas and Helenus of the ability to foresee future events, restricting them to mere advising.[120] For these reasons, the argument "'not mentioned' means 'unknown'" holds little water. Even if there is no mention in the rest of the poem of the events taking place in a book of the epic, we are not entitled to use this "silence" as an argument supporting the inauthenticity of this book. As for the mechanics of a potential interpolation of this size, let us consider Hainsworth's formulation:[121]

> The interpolated episode must begin from the situation reached at some point and must necessarily then diverge from the main storyline. The trouble comes at the end; if a new situation has been created, there will be a hiatus; the original story, when resumed, will not presuppose the interpolation but what preceded it. That difficulty can be surmounted by making the expansion return to the same situation as obtained at its beginning, but that may not be easy either and, if achieved, may undercut whatever point the expansion ever had.

Although the above formulation has been written for *Iliad* 10, it may equally apply to *Iliad* 9,[122] since circumstances at the end of these two books mirror those at their beginnings. In this respect, it is suggested that this form of reasoning might not be suitable for application to the *Doloneia*.

Allusion to actual events concerns what I would like to call the "range" of the event alluded to and the "weight" of the allusive link. For example, a reference in *Il.* 18.74–7 and 79 to Thetis' meeting with Achilles in book 1 amounts to an allusion of great range and weight. The event alluded to is an entire scene, and the allusive link is an important narrative event for the continuation of the plot. The one end of the allusion pertains to the beginning of Zeus' promise to Thetis to give victory to the Trojans as long as Achilles is not fighting; the other end concerns the change of the course of events after the death of Patroclus. Moreover, the allusion is direct and explicit. The intratextual connection is thus both crucial and easily observable. By contrast, there are cases of small range and weight which can at times be covert (but need not be). As we will see, the evocation of certain details tagged to specific events of the *Doloneia* facilitates the comprehension of an event occurring in another book preceding or following *Iliad* 10.[123]

---

[119] See Gaisser (1969, 170), who rightly argues that this omission creates a gap in the story, since Bellerophon's punishment remains unexplained; see also Dowden (1996) 53.
[120] Kullmann (1960) 221–4; Griffin (1977) 48; Dowden (1996) 53.
[121] Hainsworth (1993) 152.
[122] If books 9 and 10 are omitted, as some analysts suggested, then the Achaean attack in book 11 would proceed smoothly from the end of book 8. We do not need a speech by Diomedes at the end of *Iliad* 9 to suggest it. Eris infuses courage for battle in the hearts of the Achaeans (11.10–14) and Agamemnon hears her and orders the army to prepare for war (11.15–16). The first words of book 11 (1: Ἠὼς δ' ἐκ λεχέων παρ' ἀγαυοῦ Τιθωνοῖο) are a smooth transition from the last words of book 8 (565: εὔθρονον Ἠῶ μίμνον).
[123] See chapter 2.

Since foreshadowing and flashback are important factors with respect to the unity of composition, the focus should be on how they are applied to narrative themes and the forms they may take.[124] The *Doloneia* offers examples of backward and forward references to themes that have been already employed in the poem. The pairing of episodes pertaining to Achilles' withdrawal from fighting (book 1) and Agamemnon's testing of the Achaeans to reinvigorate them (book 2) are doubled by the renewal of Achilles' withdrawal through the failure of the embassy (book 9) and Agamemnon's instigation of the spying mission that will instill courage in the Achaean army (book 10). The theme of "victorious solidarity" that is stressed by the joint mission of Diomedes and Odysseus operates as foil for exposing Dolon's vulnerability in the short run and Patroclus' weakness and failure in the long run. Likewise, verbal associations with a surplus of meaning[125] between *Iliad* 10 and other Iliadic passages add interpretive value to a passage and improve its understanding.[126] Zeus' words ἀλλ' οὐ μὰν ὑμῖν γε καὶ ἅρμασι δαιδαλέοισιν | Ἕκτωρ Πριαμίδης ἐποχήσεται in 17.448–9 acquire a strong ironic connotation only against the backdrop of Hector's arrogant boast, μὴ μὲν τοῖς ἵπποισιν ἀνὴρ ἐποχήσεται ἄλλος, in 10.330.[127]

Intratextual allusion to themes and phraseology is the pillar on which the methodology of my investigation is based. It lies at the heart of unity of composition, which determines the stance one takes concerning the question of authenticity of the *Doloneia*.

5. Organization of the Book

This book, organized in nine chapters, aims to offer a systematic study of the Homeric *Doloneia*. To address issues of authenticity, I have combined intratextual allusion with oral neoanalysis and comparative philology. No approach, however sophisticated and diverse, can hope to address the full host of complicated issues pertaining to *Iliad* 10. Therefore, I make every effort to keep the larger picture in view concerning the evolution and shaping of the *Doloneia*, especially since the

---

[124] The following cases are a few examples; for a detailed analysis, see chapter 2.

[125] With respect to verbal association, the rarity of the phraseological repetition and the specificity of context are crucial; see Pucci (1987) 238; Usener (1990); Bakker (2013) 157–69, especially 159: "the more restricted an expression, the more specific the context in which it is uttered."

[126] Currie (2016) 176, 207, 259. With respect to the *Doloneia*, see Fenik's remarks (1964, 42–3) regarding the adjustment and modification of the story of Rhesus in *Iliad* 10: "the assumption of a 'source'... is no cure-all or automatic solution. It must either remain pure hypothesis or justify itself by its capacity to solve specific problems in the text."

[127] Markedness, which consists in a distinctive manner of association, is key to both foreshadowing/flashback of themes and to verbal associations; see R. F. Thomas (1986) 174; Pucci (1987) 238; D. P. Fowler (1997) 15, 20 = (2000) 118, 122–3; Korenjak (1998) 143; Currie (2016) 11, 33–35, 42, 46, 174, 199, 221, 227, 261.

assessment of these aspects in relation to book 10 will have important implications for understanding the evolution and shaping of the *Iliad*.

Chapter 1 ("Theoretical Aspects") surveys the various theoretical and methodological aspects of using the method of oral, intertextual neoanalysis to study the evolution and shaping of an oral epic tradition. As regards the theoretical part of this chapter, four different aspects are examined: internal criteria, external criteria, entextualization, and the issue of mythological reference and epic allusion.

Chapter 2 ("A First Thematic Approach: Intratextual References") considers the relation between book 10 and the rest of the epic. Several questionable (and rather misconceived) assumptions concerning the absence of foreshadowing and flashbacks to the *Doloneia* in the rest of the *Iliad* are thoroughly examined and evaluated. The core of this chapter rests on drawing the line between references to events and allusions to themes. By means of a detailed analysis it is argued that (a) the *Doloneia* contains various implicit intratextual links to the *Iliad*; (b) it operates on the basis of backward and forward allusions to themes found in other Iliadic books; (c) it works as a bridge contributing to the development of a certain theme linking one part of the epic with another; (d) it shares a significant number of verbal associations with the rest of the epic that make it interpretively richer when examined in combination; and (e) it contributes to the character-drawing of Agamemnon, Diomedes, the pair Diomedes and Odysseus, and Hector.

Chapter 3 ("A Second Thematic Approach: The Horses of Rhesus") revisits one of the main arguments of many modern commentators of book 10 who treat the fact that Rhesus' horses are not used by Diomedes in the chariot race in the funeral games for Patroclus (*Iliad* 23) as a strong indication that the *Doloneia* is a major interpolation. By widening the interpretive lens, I reconsider the function of horses in the *Iliad*, I discuss certain fallacies of modern scholarship with respect to the horses of Rhesus, and I explore why Diomedes, who has already (in book 5) acquired Aeneas' semi-divine horses, will use them to win the chariot race in *Iliad* 23. It is suggested that with respect to the absence of Rhesus' horses from the chariot race in book 23 the Iliadic epic tradition manipulates audience expectations and employs a policy of exclusion that amounts to making a reference by refusing reference. The suppression of a feature such as Rhesus' splendid horses from a context in which their use would be expected constitutes a type of statement towards both the kind of warfare promoted by the *Iliad* and the epic tradition in which this type of warfare would have been at home.

Chapter 4 ("The Alleged Un-Iliadic Features of *Iliad* 10: Speeches, Clothing and Arming, and Zielinski's Law") discusses three of the main arguments that scholars have employed against the authenticity of *Iliad* 10: speeches, the exotic aspect as indicated by the themes of arming and clothing, and the alleged non-observation of Zielinski's Law. With respect to the speeches, it is argued that they are marked by a lack of or weak representation of the internal structuring of other Iliadic speeches, whereas their outer organization and clustering are not different from the rest of the epic. This blurred picture, which is partly un-Iliadic and partly Iliadic, may be reflecting the larger context of the situation at hand. Time pressure and emergency because of the imminent Trojan attack and the putative Achaean departure for Greece leave no room to speakers for elaboration and symmetry that mark speech structuring in the *Iliad*. Instead of detecting poetic deficiency as the explanation of the distinct quality of speeches in book 10, we may arguably see their compressed, often rushed, and even elliptical shape as a deliberate effort of the Iliadic tradition to tamper with the audience's expectations about how characters speak and thus mark the *Doloneia* as a distinct episode. As regards clothing and arming, it will be argued that the special clothing of certain heroes is narratively significant, whereas the unusual picture given in book 10 regarding arming is due to the theme of ambush. With respect to Zielinski's Law, it will be claimed on the basis of several examples that book 10 does not differ from other books of the *Iliad*.

Chapter 5 ("Putative Clues for the Hector-Version of *Iliad* 10") surveys the text of the *Iliad*, the ancient scholia, and the *Mythographus Homericus* for traces of the earlier form of such a plotline. As far as Iliadic evidence is concerned, several passages are examined that allude to a version in which Hector was the target of the spying mission. The fact that these references cover a wide range of text, from book 8 to book 24, tentatively suggests that the earlier version had been part of the Iliadic epic tradition for a considerable amount of time and that it had established itself as a significant part of the plot. Traces of a Hector-version can also be found in the ancient scholia and the *Mythographus Homericus*. A case is made for ancient references to such a putative version that is adduced after careful examination of the Homeric text.

Chapter 6 ("Reconstructing the Hector-Version of *Iliad* 10") argues that in the earlier version the target of Diomedes and Odysseus was Hector, who posed the greatest threat to the Achaeans. However, because of the requirements set by the Trojan War myth, according to which Hector would remain alive for now, until he is killed by Achilles, Diomedes and Odysseus failed in their mission. Therefore, a great deed that would give courage to the Achaeans at this difficult time could only be achieved by means of the murder of another first-rank hero, whose loss would not harm the rest of the epic's plot. It is suggested that this is why Rhesus was brought into the picture.

Chapter 7 ("The Two Versions of the Rhesus Myth: Reconstruction of Possible Sources") examines the Pindaric and oracle versions of the myth of Rhesus by a detailed analysis of the relevant sources that transmit it. The next step is the reconstruction of these sources through a reconsideration of various features that may have been included in them. The main argument is that the *Iliad* employed only those features of the Rhesus myth that were compatible with its storyline, downplaying or erasing all miraculous elements that were nested in the oracle version. The introduction of a first-rank hero such as Rhesus seems to operate as a backdrop against which the epic elaborated the character-drawing of major Iliadic heroes such as Hector, Diomedes, and Odysseus.

Chapter 8 ("Comparative Material: the *Mahābhārata* and the *Aeneid*") embarks on a comparative examination of the *Doloneia*, the massacre at night in book 10 of the *Mahābhārata*, *Aeneid* 1 (Aeneas observing the depiction of the capture of Troy on the walls of the temple of Juno in Carthage), and *Aeneid* 9 (the Nisus and Euryalus episode). The comparison between book 10 of the *Mahābhārata* and book 10 of the *Iliad* discloses their sharing a stable set of features. It also allows us to see that the conditions which should be met in this type of story for the execution of a night attack are similar to those that exist after *Iliad* 9. They pertain to the lack of a major hero who can defeat the enemy in combat and the realization that this goal can only be achieved through treachery. As regards Virgil, who seems to be operating as a neoanalyst *avant la lettre*, it is claimed that he is doing the same thing that has happened in the process of the evolution and shaping of the *Doloneia*. Virgil offers a working analogy for the argument of the shaping of the *Doloneia* by the gradual influence of episodes such as the theft of the Palladium, Coroebus, and the sack of Troy, which belong to the last phase of the Trojan War and may have featured in pre-Homeric oral epic.

Chapter 9 ("The Rhesus Story within the Cyclic and the Iliadic Tradition") investigates the form and function of the cyclic features of the story of Rhesus and argues that it was part of a pre-Homeric oral epic tradition. The similarities shared between the episode of Rhesus and those of late-arriving Achaean and pro-Trojan heroes such as Philoctetes, Eurypylus, Neoptolemus, and Coroebus make a case for its inclusion in an oral epic featuring both the events after the death of Achilles and the sack of Troy. This chapter also traces the process by which the Iliadic epic tradition replaced Hector with Rhesus in the plot of book 10, the changes that needed to be made because of this substitution, and the impact this shaping had on the *Doloneia* and the *Iliad*.

1
Theoretical Aspects

Introduction

The research that will be presented in this book touches on several theoretical aspects which are key to evaluating claims of authenticity and inauthenticity. It is also based on various assumptions that are equally important for studying the evolution and shaping of the *Doloneia*. The present chapter aims at clarifying these issues. The fundamental premise of my approach is the application of oral intertextual neoanalysis to the study of book 10 and the *Iliad* at large. Oral intertextual neoanalysis argues that the Homeric epics have been composed orally, during an extended stretch of time by means of a creative synthesis of material stemming from various oral epic traditions. Homeric poetry systematically alludes to these earlier epic traditions by the transfer of motifs, themes, and phraseology. Since I have already offered a detailed presentation of this theory in a previous publication,[1] I will now focus only on those aspects that relate directly to the applicability of oral intertextual neoanalysis regarding the study of Homeric epic: internal criteria; external criteria; transference of motifs, themes, and phraseology; entextualization; mythological reference and epic allusion.

1.1 Internal Criteria

Internal criteria supporting this theory refer exclusively to Homeric poetry, which is marked by diction pertaining to poetry and poetics.[2] They include (a) the use of metapoetic diction;[3] (b) fate or divine will standing for compliance with or divergence from the epic tradition; (c) *nekyiai*, creating a thematic framework for the interaction of figures of the present with figures of the past; (d) embedded songs; (e) the reference to other genres; (f) the emphasis on the creation and diffusion of epic songs; (g) the indexical potential of time; (h) poetic memory.

---

[1] Tsagalis (2011) 209–44 = (2023) 3–33.
[2] See Thalmann (1984) 116–17, who argues that the interest displayed by Homeric poetry "in speaking about poets and poetry suggests a way to speak about the composer's art by virtually refusing or avoiding speaking directly about oneself."
[3] Metapoetic diction is only one of the manifestations of the pervasive self-consciousness of Homeric epic. Two other aspects include metalepsis (S. Richardson 1990, 170–4; De Jong 2009, 87–116 and 2011, 1–14; Alvensleben 2022) and narrator–narratee communication (S. Richardson 1990, 175–8).

(a) Singer/s (ἀοιδός/-οί), song (ἀοιδή),[4] and stories (φασί) are often mentioned in Homeric epic. Thamyris (2.594-600) and Achilles (9.189-91) in the *Iliad* are presented as singers, the former being punished for boasting that he betters the Muses,[5] the latter singing epic poetry (κλέα ἀνδρῶν), while Patroclus is waiting for him to finish his recital so that he can cap his song with his own.[6] Two named (Phemius and Demodocus) and two anonymous[7] singers in the *Odyssey* are located in Ithaca, Scheria, Argos, and Sparta. The repertory of the two eponymous singers is rich. Phemius sings cyclic epic (1.325-7)[8] and promises to sing before Odysseus as before a god (22.348-9),[9] while Demodocus sings three different songs, a quarrel between Odysseus and Achilles (first song),[10] the adultery of Ares and Aphrodite (second song),[11] and the sack of Troy (third song).[12] Both singers enjoy wide recognition,[13] which is reflected in their rewards[14] as well as in their names: Φήμιος Τερπιάδης ("the famous one, son of him who brings enjoyment"), Δημόδοκος ("the one who is honored by the people"). Homeric epic constantly designates epic poetry either directly by the terms ἀοιδή and κλέος or κλέα ἀνδρῶν or indirectly by combining words like οἶτος or οἴμη or ἔργα with κλέος, κόσμος, or some form of the verb ἀείδω.[15] In *Od.* 1.340-1, Telemachus asks Phemius to cease the sad song[16] pertaining to the return of the Achaeans. This request offers an attractive way of indicating the existence of an epic tradition,[17] a type of oral *Nosti known to the *Odyssey*, which is designated as κακὸς οἶτος. The same is the case with *Od.* 24.197 and 200, where Agamemnon designates the epic tradition of the *Odyssey* as χαρίεσσα ἀοιδή ("graceful song")[18] and the epic tradition of the *Nosti

---

[4] Nagy (1979 = 1999²) 37-8; Ford (1992) 108; Tsagalis (2004) 3; Currie (2016) 19; Ready (2019) 32.
[5] See S. Richardson (1990) 178-82.   [6] See Nagy (1996b) 71-3.
[7] *Od.* 3.267-71 and 4.17-18.
[8] τοῖσι δ' ἀοιδὸς ἄειδε περικλυτός, οἱ δὲ σιωπῇ | εἴατ' ἀκούοντες· ὁ δ' Ἀχαιῶν νόστον ἄειδε | λυγρόν, ὃν ἐκ Τροίης ἐπετείλατο Παλλὰς Ἀθήνη, "he found them listening in silence to a song which their famous bard was singing to them about the Achaeans' return from Troy and the disasters that Pallas Athena made them suffer."
[9] ἔοικα δέ τοι παραείδειν | ὥς τε θεῷ; several scholars (Monro 1901 *ad loc.*; Stanford 1959² *ad loc.*; Fernández-Galiano 1992 *ad loc.*; Pucci 1987, 230; Currie [2016, 143 n. 203] is not absolutely sure) interpret Phemius' words as indicating a promise to become Odysseus' poet, i.e. to sing Odysseus' deeds by applying his "traditional repertory of inherited poetic craft to the particular case relevant to the audience of the moment" (Fernández-Galiano).
[10] *Od.* 8.73-82.   [11] *Od.* 8.266-366.   [12] *Od.* 8.500-20.
[13] *Od.* 1.325, 336, 346; 3.267-71; 4.17; 8.43, 62, 83, 367, 471, 479-81, 483, 487, 521, 539; 9.3-4; 17.385.
[14] On the singer's reward, see Schadewaldt (1965⁴, 70), who refers to treats (*Od.* 8.475) and other gifts, like tripods (*Il.* 22.164, 23.264, 702).
[15] The following cases are representative examples of the use of the relevant terms in Homeric epic. They do not exhaust the use of metapoetic vocabulary in the *Iliad* and the *Odyssey*.
[16] *Od.* 1.326-7. On the metapoetic potential of this and other homecoming narratives in the *Odyssey*, see Barker and Christensen (2016) 85-110.
[17] *Od.* 1.338: "the deeds of men and gods that singers celebrate" (ἔργ' ἀνδρῶν τε θεῶν τε, τά τε κλείουσιν ἀοιδοί).
[18] On the narrator's delight in narrative and his statements concerning the excellence of his product, see S. Richardson (1990) 182-7.

as στυγερὴ ἀοιδή ("loathsome song").[19] In *Od.* 8.73–4, Demodocus sings "famous deeds of men, from a song whose fame had then reached wide heaven" (κλέα ἀνδρῶν, | οἴμης τῆς τότ' ἄρα κλέος οὐρανὸν εὐρὺν ἵκανε). Likewise, Odysseus tells Demodocus that he is inspired and taught either by the Muse or Apollo and sings "in due order the fate of the Achaeans" (κατὰ κόσμον Ἀχαιῶν ἀείδεις). In this context, the term κόσμος has a metapoetic meaning, denoting the archaic practice of performing epic songs. The same observation applies to the term μοῖρα, which has a metapoetic tinge in *Od.* 8.496, where the "ruse" (δόλος, 8.494) of Odysseus to enter Troy in secret and sack it would be an "inspired song" (θέσπις ἀοιδή, 8.498),[20] if recounted "in the proper way" (κατὰ μοῖραν καταλέξῃς, 8.496). Another form of metapoetic diction that marks oral epic intertextuality is the "Alexandrian footnote," which constitutes a dictional mechanism assimilating literary allusion to the communication of talk or rumor.[21] This form of reflexive annotation not only indicates allusion to other epic traditions but also "underlines or intensifies their [sc. of the Alexandrian footnotes] demand to be interpreted *as* allusions."[22] In Homer, the word φασί is sometimes used in this manner.[23] In *Il.* 2.783, the narrator does not simply report the story of Typhon's defeat by Zeus and his final "resting place" in the land of the Arimoi. He also reports a report of this story (ὅθι φασὶ Τυφωέος ἔμμεναι εὐνάς), which implies that "the localization of Typhon 'among the Arimoi' goes back to theogonic poetry predating Homer or Hesiod."[24] In *Il.* 4.375, Diomedes does not simply state that his father, Tydeus, surpassed all other men in bravery and martial skill. He also reveals the source of his knowledge (φασί), since he has not met or seen his father (4.374–5).[25] Likewise, in *Il.* 5.638, where Tlepolemus does not simply tell Sarpedon about Heracles, a true son of Zeus and sacker of Troy, but signals an allusion to a tradition (φασί) relating these events. The same is the case with *Od.* 23.124–5, in which Telemachus alludes to tales praising the outstanding mental skills of his father, Odysseus. The use of this terminology seems to indicate that the narrator employs abbreviated narratives with gaps and holes which the audience can fill through prior knowledge.[26] Furthermore, Homeric epic regularly employs poetic imagery from a variety of semantical fields:[27] animals: *Od.* 19.518–22; craft: *Il.* 13.125–8; healing: *Od.* 17.518–21; agriculture: *Il.* 20.248–9; hunt and sport: *Od.* 21.406–9; light: *Od.*

---

[19] Ready (2018) 329–30.
[20] On κατὰ μοῖραν | ὑπὲρ μοῖραν, see Pestalozzi (1945) 40; Fränkel (1951 = 1976³) 63–4; Kullmann (1956); Schadewaldt (1965⁴) 71; Matthews (1976); Nagy (1979 = 1999²) 40 n. 2; S. Richardson (1990) 194; Janko (1992) 5–6; Currie (2006) 7; Tsagalis (2011) 226 = (2023) 19; González (2013) 194–6.
[21] The expression "Alexandrian footnote" had been first used by Ross (1975, 68), but it has acquired its intertextual aspect after it was employed by Hinds (1987, 58 with n. 22, and 1998, 1–3); see also the extended discussion on the "pre-Alexandrian footnote" in Nelson (2023, 73–175).
[22] Hinds (1998) 1; Nelson (2023) 10.   [23] See Ready (2019) 29.
[24] Currie (forthcoming).   [25] See Barker and Christensen (2011) 9–44.
[26] Scodel (2002) 125. On the form of this knowledge, see pp. 57–8.
[27] The following list is not exhaustive. I offer only one example from some of the relevant categories. This material is based on Nünlist (1998a).

8.63–4; flow (of honey): *Il.* 1.249; walking: *Od.* 8.492–3. It also uses metapoetic metaphors[28] concerning "borrowing" (Patroclus borrows Achilles' arms in *Iliad* 16; Hera borrows Aphrodite's girdle in *Iliad* 14) and "filiation" (the stress on the two successive expeditions of fathers [Tydeus and Capaneus] and sons [Diomedes and Sthenelus] against Thebes "tropes the filiation of *Epigoni* from *Thebaid*").[29] In light of the above, it may be argued that Homeric epic employs allusion in a systematic way. This is an implicit acknowledgment of its preoccupation with stories and storytelling.

(b) Fate or divine will may have narrative significance.[30] They are often used to express agreement or disagreement between the version followed by the *Iliad* or the *Odyssey* and earlier poetic traditions. When Menelaus tells the two Ajaxes that he has sent Antilochus to inform Achilles about the death of Patroclus because he thinks that Achilles will not return to the battlefield immediately since he is deprived of his armor, Telamonian Ajax replies to Menelaus (*Il.* 17.716) that he has spoken κατ' αἶσαν ("according to fate"). In this way, fate stands for the unraveling of the plot, given that what Menelaus says will happen in book 18. In *Il.* 6.487, Hector tells Andromache that he is not going to die against what fate dictates (ὑπὲρ αἶσαν), i.e. unless this is what the tradition determines. In *Od.* 8.496, Odysseus asks Demodocus to recount to him in the proper way (κατὰ μοῖραν) the story of the Wooden Horse, since Demodocus as singer "sings in due order the fate of the Achaeans, all they did and experienced, all they suffered, as if he had experienced these things himself or heard them from someone else"[31] (8.489–91: λίην γὰρ κατὰ κόσμον Ἀχαιῶν οἶτον ἀείδεις, | ὅσσ' ἔρξαν τ' ἔπαθόν τε καὶ ὅσσ' ἐμόγησαν Ἀχαιοί, | ὥς τέ που ἢ αὐτὸς παρεὼν ἢ ἄλλου ἀκούσας). In *Il.* 20.336, Poseidon advises Aeneas to retreat lest he is killed by Achilles, a development that would be ὑπὲρ μοῖραν ("beyond fate"), given that Aeneas is not destined to be killed by Achilles. There are also cases where a putative course of action is rejected because of constraints imposed by fate. In *Il.* 5.671–3, Odysseus hesitates between two courses of action: either to pursue Sarpedon, who had just killed Tlepolemus, or to kill as many Lycians as possible. Athena directs Odysseus to attacking the Lycians because "it was not the destiny of great-hearted Odysseus to kill with sharp bronze the strong son of Zeus" (i.e. Sarpedon).[32] Since several decisions are

---

[28] I restrict the following references to what pertains to Homeric epic; on other relevant cases regarding early Greek poetry, see Currie (2016) 27 with nn. 168 and 179.
[29] Currie (2016) 27.
[30] Hedén (1912) 177; Fränkel (1951 = 1976³) 63–4; Redfield (1975) 133; Nagy (1979 = 1999²) 40 with n. 2; de Jong (1987 = 2004²) 263 n. 76; S. Richardson (1990) 194; Janko (1992) 6 and 371; J. V. Morrison (1997) 284; Scodel (1999) 140–53, (2002) 68; Currie (2006) 7, (2016) 26; Marks (2008) 6; Tsagalis (2011) 226 = (2023) 19.
[31] In the translation I have changed the second person of the Greek text into third for reasons of conformity with the syntax of this period.
[32] *Il.* 5.674–5: οὐδ' ἄρ' Ὀδυσσῆϊ μεγαλήτορι μόρσιμον ἦεν | ἴφθιμον Διὸς υἱὸν ἀποκτάμεν ὀξέϊ χαλκῷ.

determined by tradition, whereas others by the innovative design of the poet, it has been suggested that "fate is plot"[33] and that "fate is Homer."[34]

(c) The Odyssean *nekyiai* (book 11 and the first part of book 24) offer a thematic framework in which figures of the present interact with figures of the past. Since several of these figures refer to past events featured in other epic traditions, there is nothing to rule out the possibility that these scenes in the Underworld allow for an evaluation of the *Odyssey* by comparison to other epic traditions.[35] It has been suggested that the two *nekyiai* enable the *Odyssey* to engage with the *Iliad*, the *Memnonis*, the *Ilias parva*, the *Nosti*, catalogue poetry, as well as poetry on Heracles and Theseus.[36]

(d) Embedded songs suggest continuity of the tradition. They may constitute an acknowledgment of the existence of other poetic traditions with which the Homeric epics are familiar. It may be the case that Homeric epic offers examples of both direct (Demodocus' songs in *Odyssey* 8)[37] and indirect reference (certain para-narratives[38] like the Meleager story in *Iliad* 9 [alluding to a pre-Homeric *Meleagris*][39] and Nestor's youthful adventures in *Iliad* 11 [alluding to a pre-Homeric Pylian epic])[40] to earlier poetry.

(e) The *Iliad* and the *Odyssey* refer to other genres:[41] *linos* (λίνος, *Il.* 18.569–72);[42] *paean* (παιάν, *Il.* 1.472–4, 22.391–4); lament (θρῆνος, *Il.* 24.720–2; *Od.* 24.60–1); wedding song (ὑμέναιος, *Il.* 18.493; *Od.* 4.17, 23.133–6, 23.143–52);[43] women's work songs (*Od.* 5.61, 10.221);[44] shepherds' song (*Il.* 18.526); maiden's song (*Od.* 6.101); maidens' choral song (*Il.* 1.604); "applied song" (ἐπαοιδή, *Od.* 19.547).[45] Homeric epic looks at other genres through a poetic lens. The Iliadic narrator refers to the professional singers of laments but does not cite their words, whereas immediately afterwards he "allows" three characters of his own epic (Andromache, Hecuba, and Helen) to utter their personal laments (γόοι) for Hector;[46] the genre of the antiphonal song and dance performed by Nausicaa and her maids in Scheria is not explicitly designated, but both the

---

[33] Redfield (1975) 194. [34] S. Richardson (1990) 195.
[35] The dead whom Odysseus meets in the Underworld may be seen as emblematizing several earlier poetic traditions; see Most (1992) 1014–26; Kullmann (1995) 50-1 = (2002) 154; Danek (1998a) 230–1; Martin (2001) 23–33 = (2020a) 205–16; Tsagalis (2003a) 43–56 = (2008) 30–43; Currie (2006) 21–2 with n. 102, (2016) 26–7. For a similar argument regarding Virgil's use of the Underworld episode in *Aeneid* 6, see Hardie (1998) 53 n. 1.
[36] *Iliad*: *Od.* 11.482–91; *Memnonis*: *Od.* 24.37–92 (also: 11.522); *Ilias parva*: *Od.* 11.508–37; *Nosti*: *Od.* 24.196–202; catalogue poetry: *Od.* 11.225–32; poetry on Heracles and Theseus: *Od.* 11.601–26, 630–1.
[37] Rinon (2006) 208–25; Currie (2016) 27.   [38] Alden (2000), (2017).
[39] See pp. 39 with n. 92 and 61–2.   [40] See pp. 40, 62 with n. 237.
[41] *HomEnc* s.v. "Songs" (A. L. Ford); Martin (2020b) 36–48. In the following list I cite the Greek terms only when they are used in the Homeric epics.
[42] See Martin (2020b) 41, who draws attention to the word ἀταλά (φρονέοντες) in *Il.* 18.567 and ἀταλότατα (παίζει) that is inscribed on the Dipylon vase (National Archaeological Museum, Athens inv. 192) in the context of a dancing contest.
[43] The term ὑμέναιος is employed solely in *Il.* 18.493.   [44] See Karanika (2014) 52–77.
[45] Martin (2020b) 44.   [46] *Il.* 24.723–76; Tsagalis (2004) 2–8; see also Ford (1997) 412–13.

narrator and Odysseus perceive it by drawing on experiences of maidens' songs, which functioned "as a kind of 'coming out' ball in which well-born women might attract the amorous glance of a spectator (cf. *Il.* 16.179–83)";[47] Odysseus misappropriates the conventions of wedding song, when he asks Phemius to sing such a song after the bloodbath of the *mnesterophonia* (*Od.* 23.133–6).[48] The sophisticated interplay with other poetic genres works better if both the singers and the audience had a notion of the *Iliad* and the *Odyssey* as epic, against the backdrop of which they could place songs belonging to other genres that they had heard performed.

(f) With respect to the creation of epic song, individual creativity on the part of the singer is explained and justified by recourse to his dependence on the Muse that "both allows for greater freedom on his part and gives legitimation to this creative freedom."[49] Phemius asserts (*Od.* 22.347) that he is αὐτοδίδακτος ("self-taught") and that the god has implanted into his heart all manner of songs, which contrasts him "with other singers who learn from others."[50] In this way, the tension between creative freedom on the part of the singer and preservation of the tradition is reflected in the bard's ability to expand his song and in the fixity of the story he is treating in his performance.[51] This is a marked difference between Homeric and South Slavic epic. In the former, the truthfulness of the story is guaranteed by means of divine inspiration, which allows the singer to use motifs and expand his presentation of the story without changing the basic, fixed facts. In Homeric epic, therefore, themes "are more, so to say, 'plot-making' than those encountered in South Slavic epic poetry."[52] Homeric epic refers to the creation of song by various metaphors pertaining to the manufacturing of a product.[53] Characters weave speech and counsels together (*Il.* 3.212: μύθους καὶ μήδεα... ὕφαινον) or only plans (*Il.* 7.324: ὑφαίνειν...μῆτιν; *Od.* 4.678: μῆτιν ὕφαινον), just as they weave a web (*Il.* 6.456: ἱστὸν ὑφαίνοις); they fashion a plan (*Il.* 10.19: μῆτιν...τεκτήναιτο) or a tale (*Od.* 14.131: ἔπος παρατεκτήναιο) in the same manner that they build a ship (*Il.* 5.62: τεκτήνατο νῆας); they bound or fit together a plan (*Od.* 4.777: μῦθον...ἤραρεν) like close-joined timbers (*Il.* 18.275: σανίδες τ' ἐπὶ τῆς ἀραρυῖαι); words (*Il.* 7.375: ἔπος) and plans (*Il.* 3.208: μήδεα) can be designated as "solid" (πυκινόν/-ά), like a house (*Il.* 10.267: δόμον) or bed (*Il.* 9.659: λέχος), i.e. they are well-constructed, dense-packed objects that endure through time. The use of metaphors drawn from weaving, tying, building, bounding, or fitting together reflects the objectification of song, which is treated as a crafted artifact that can be transported. A tale has a shape (*Od.* 11.367: μορφή ἐπέων) and

---

[47] Ford (1997) 412. [48] Ford (1997) 411. [49] Finkelberg (1990) 296 = (2020) 120.
[50] Ready (2019) 31; see also Ford (1992) 90–2 and 95; Ready and Tsagalis (2018) 9. Cf. Scodel (2002) 78.
[51] See Edmunds (1995) 4–6. [52] Finkelberg (1990) 301 = (2020) 125.
[53] The following examples are representative, not exhaustive; see Ready (2019) 28–34 with bibliography. On the Indo-European background of these metaphors, see M. L. West (2007) 26–45.

a speech can be "led" (*Il.* 14.91: μῦθον... ἄγοιτο) like a portable physical object (*Od.* 1.184: ἄγω... σίδηρον). The designation of song as material object speaks for its existence as an independent entity. Just how powerful and important the objectification of song is for Homeric poetry can be seen by means of the impressive step it makes towards self-objectification. In *Il.* 3.125-8, Helen weaves a great web, into which she works the numerous struggles the Trojans and the Achaeans have suffered because of her. This is the crowning moment in the process of song objectification, since the *Iliad* comes very close to objectifying itself.[54] Likewise, in *Od.* 12.189-91 the Sirens pretend to operate as Muse-inspired female bards. By usurping the language of the *Iliad* they promise to sing to Odysseus the epic tradition of the Trojan War,[55] if he abandons his ship and joins them on their island. The meta-epic effect of this passage is based on the objectification of the Iliadic epic tradition, which is known to the deceptive Sirens, Odysseus, as well as the external audience of the *Odyssey*. As the *Iliad* objectifies itself in the tapestry Helen weaves, so the *Odyssey* objectifies the *Iliad* in the song of Sirens. Passing from the creation to the diffusion of epic song, we should turn our attention to the expression κλέα ἀνδρῶν.[56] The etymology of κλέος (< κλύω "to listen and be receptive") and its occasional use with verbs like πεύθομαι ("know or learn by hearing") speak volumes for the existence of other epic traditions, for their oral performance, and for the fact that they are known to the audience.[57] In *Il.* 9.189-91 Achilles sings heroic deeds (κλέα ἀνδρῶν) that the audience is familiar with.[58] He is playing the *phorminx* (9.186), which he keeps holding when he stands up and greets the envoys (9.193-4).[59] In *Il.* 9.524-5 Phoenix begins to recount the story of Meleager by marking it as epic poetry[60] known to him and to the audience who have heard it (οὕτω καὶ τῶν πρόσθεν ἐπευθόμεθα κλέα ἀνδρῶν | ἡρώων, "we

---

[54] Σ *Il.* 3.126-7: ἀξιόχρεων ἀρχέτυπον ἀνέπλασεν ὁ ποιητὴς τῆς ἰδίας ποιήσεως ("the poet made a worthy model of his own poetry"); see, e.g., González (2013) 362 n. 110, 363; Bassino, Canevaro, Graziosi (2017) 3; Ready (2019) 33.

[55] See Pucci (1998) 1-9.

[56] The phrase κλέα ἀνδρῶν, literally "the fames of men," is in epic idiolect the subject matter of bards' songs. For a parallel use in Vedic, where the form śrávāṃsi is used with respect to the "glorious deeds" of Indra, and in Old Irish *clothaib* (dat. pl. of *cloth* < *k̂lutóm*), see M. L. West (2007) 398. On the antiquity of the construction κλέα ἀνδρῶν, see Schmitt (1967) 94-5.

[57] See also *Il.* 1.396-407, where Achilles reminds Thetis of a story she has often (πολλάκι) told him about the way she saved Zeus from an insurrection against him by some other gods and asks her to tell this tale again to Zeus.

[58] On suggestions about the content of Achilles' song, see Tsagalis (forthcoming) on *Il.* 9.189-91 with bibliography.

[59] For a discussion of the antithesis between Achilles' rejection of Agamemnon's authority by throwing the scepter on the ground in *Iliad* 1 and his rejection of Agamemnon's offer while holding his *phorminx* in *Iliad* 9, see Bouvier (2002) 313-14.

[60] Apart from πεύθομαι, *Il.* 9.527-8 (μέμνημαι τόδε ἔργον ἐγὼ πάλαι οὔ τι νέον γε | ὡς ἦν) indicates that the allusion is to poetic rather than mythological material; see Kakridis (1944) 1-53 = (1949) 11-42; Moran (1975) 204; Dickson (1995) 67, 71-2; Mackie (1997) 79 n. 6; Dowden (2004) 197; Currie (2016) 141-3 with more examples.

have heard of such conduct on the part of the deeds of the heroes of the past").[61] The transmission of song is also testified by means of a widespread practice of performances (*Od.* 1.351-2),[62] by the association between "fame" and "song that will report to future generations this fame" (*Od.* 3.203-4),[63] and by the fame a song has acquired (*Il.* 20.204; *Od.* 8.73-4).[64] These passages, which indicate the diffusion of song through singing performances, refer to a process that should be distinguished from the transmission of tales in non-poetic form. In *Od.* 3.94-5 (= 4.324-5) Telemachus thinks that Nestor or Menelaus may have heard about his father from another traveler. In *Od.* 3.186-7, Nestor informs Telemachus that he is ready to tell him whatever stories he learns by inquiry.[65] Likewise, in *Od.* 8.489-91, where Odysseus says that "non-bardic tellers transmit stories to other tellers."[66]

(g) Regarding the indexical potential of time, Homeric epic employs references to the past and future in order to place itself within the larger epic tradition.[67] These references take the form of chronological perspective, marked iteration, and epigonal self-consciousness.[68] The term "chronological perspective" designates a self-conscious acknowledgment of the broader epic tradition: when Antenor recalls a visit by Odysseus and Menelaus to Troy before the beginning of the war, he uses a temporal reference (*Il.* 3.205—6: ἤδη γὰρ καὶ δεῦρό **ποτ'** ἤλυθε δῖος Ὀδυσσεὺς | σεῦ ἕνεκ' ἀγγελίης σὺν ἀρηϊφίλῳ Μενελάῳ, "**Once before now** too godlike Odysseus came here with Menelaus, dear to Ares on an embassy concerning you"), which points to an episode known from the *Cypria* (arg. ll. 152-3 Severyns).[69] Likewise, when in *Od.* 6.162 (Δήλῳ δή **ποτε** τοῖον Ἀπόλλωνος παρὰ βωμῷ | φοίνικος νέον ἔρνος ἀνερχόμενον ἐνόησα), Odysseus compares Nausicaa to "a young sapling of a palm tree" that he "**once** saw on Delos beside the altar of Apollo," the audience may recall Odysseus' visit to this island to fetch the nourishing daughters of Anius to Troy, in order to save the army from famine,

---

[61] See Leaf (1900-2) 409 on *Il.* 9.524. Following Nagy (1990, 196 n. 215), who cites Fraenkel (1950, II, 339), Rawles (2018, 37 and 43 with n. 59) argues that the phrase οὕτω καὶ τῶν πρόσθεν ἐπευθόμεθα κλέα ἀνδρῶν is a way Homer marks the presence of earlier texts or traditions. Rawles also draws attention to οὕτω (*Il.* 9.524), which "is a conventional usage to introduce a paradigmatic tale"; see also Nelson (2023) 1-4 with bibliography.

[62] τὴν γὰρ ἀοιδὴν μᾶλλον ἐπικλείουσ' ἄνθρωποι | ἥ τις ἀκουόντεσσι νεωτάτη ἀμφιπέληται ("for it is always the latest song that an audience applauds the most").

[63] οἱ Ἀχαιοὶ | οἴσουσι κλέος εὐρὺ καὶ ἐσσομένοισιν ἀοιδήν ("the Achaeans will carry his fame widely, even as a song for future generations") [the translation is my own].

[64] πρόκλυτ' ἀκούοντες ἔπεα θνητῶν ἀνθρώπων ("since we have heard the lines of their fame from mortal men"); κλέα ἀνδρῶν, | οἴμης τῆς τότ' ἄρα κλέος οὐρανὸν εὐρὺν ἵκανε ("famous deeds of men, from a song whose fame had then reached wide heaven").

[65] Ford (1992) 105-6; Olson (1995) 13-14; Ready (2019) 31.   [66] Ready (2019) 31.

[67] The use of the same indexical markers intratextually suggests that when employed to point to events beyond the scope of the poem, it is possible that they refer to other poems and not to myth in general: chronological perspective (e.g. *Il.* 1.453 > 1.35-52; *Od.* 22.290-1 > 20.287-302); marked iteration (e.g. *Il.* 5.279 > 5.95-105; *Od.* 16.456 > 13.429-38); see Nelson (2023) 249-52, 262-5. Epigonal self-consciousness can only operate intertextually.

[68] I adopt the terminology of Nelson (2023) 244-91. This section (g) draws on his recent work.

[69] M. L. West (2013a, 42) argues for the antiquity of this episode, which is depicted on a bronze tripod leg at Olympia dating to the period 625-600 BC; see also Nelson (2023) 254.

which is another episode that featured in the *Cypria* (fr. 26 *GEF*).⁷⁰ Marked iteration "involves poets self-reflexively replaying or foreshadowing another event from the poetic tradition in the present."⁷¹ When in *Il.* 23.78–81 the shade of Patroclus tells Achilles that they are destined "to be killed under the wall of the prospering Trojans" (*Il.* 23.80–81: καὶ δέ σοι αὐτῷ **μοῖρα**, θεοῖς ἐπιείκελ' Ἀχιλλεῦ, | τείχει ὕπο Τρώων εὐηφενέων ἀπολέσθαι), the *Iliad* virtually admits that Achilles will die in the same place as Patroclus, an event narrated in the pre-Homeric *Memnonis. However, it reverses the direction of allusion, presenting Achilles' death as doubling or repeating Patroclus' death instead of the other way round.⁷² In this vein, I see no reason to rule out a putative eristic drive between the *Iliad* and the *Memnonis. In the *Odyssey*, the adverbial καί is regularly employed to allude to the story of Agamemnon's death (11.441: **καὶ σύ**) and the revenge of Orestes (**καὶ σύ**/κεῖνος: *Od.* 1.301, 3.197, 3.313).⁷³ That the *Odyssey* adopts for the pairs of fathers (Agamemnon–Odysseus) and sons (Orestes–Telemachus) a policy of rejection and avoidance of the former (Agamemnon) and a policy of imitation of the latter (Orestes),⁷⁴ and that the tale of Agamemnon's murder and Orestes' revenge features at the end of the Cyclic *Nosti* (arg. ll. 301–2 Severyns), allow for the possibility of an intertextual reference to a pre-Homeric epic forerunner of this epic poem. Although extant archaic epic does not directly refer to its predecessors, perhaps because the epic poets present themselves by invoking the Muses instead of their forerunners, epigonal self-consciousness seems to be implicitly discernible.⁷⁵ One major instance of this effect may be seen in the fact that Diomedes' pleas for help to Athena are built on the analogy of Athena's previous assistance to his father Tydeus in the Theban tradition (*Il.* 5.116–17: εἴ **ποτέ** μοι καὶ πατρὶ φίλα φρονέουσα παρέστης | δηΐῳ ἐν πολέμῳ, **νῦν αὖτ'** ἐμὲ φῖλαι, Ἀθήνη; 10.284–5: κέκλυθι **νῦν καὶ** ἐμεῖο, Διὸς τέκος, Ἀτρυτώνη· | σπεῖό μοι ὡς **ὅτε** πατρὶ ἅμ' ἕσπεο Τυδέϊ δίῳ).⁷⁶ In *Odyssey* 11, Odysseus lingers on in the Underworld in the hope that he may see "other men of note who had perished long ago" (11.628–9: ἀνδρῶν ἡρώων, οἳ δὴ **τὸ πρόσθεν** ὄλοντο). He adds that he would have seen "men of earlier times" (11.630: καί νύ κ' **ἔτι προτέρους** ἴδον ἀνέρας), like Theseus and Peirithoos, were it not for the tribes of the dead that surrounded him making their eerie clamor (11.632–3). Preceded by a meeting with Heracles citing his own previous *katabasis* in search of Cerberus (11.617–26),⁷⁷ which suggests an implicit

---

⁷⁰ See Tsagalis (2008) 44–62; Nelson (2023) 253.   ⁷¹ Nelson (2023) 245.
⁷² See Burgess (2001) 74, (2009) 79; Nelson (2023) 266.   ⁷³ Nelson (2023) 265.
⁷⁴ On the *Odyssey* and the Oresteia myth, see *Od.* 1.29, 299, 3.197, 307; also [Hes.] *Cat.* fr. 23a.27–30. On the Oresteia myth as a foil in the *Odyssey*, see D'Arms and Hulley (1946) 207–13; Hölscher (1967) 1–16; Olson (1990) 57–71, (1995) 24–42; Katz (1991) 29–53; Kullmann (1991) 446–9 = (1992) 122–5; Felson (1997²) 93–107; Marks (2008) 17–35; Alden (2017) 77–100.
⁷⁵ Nelson (2023) 273.   ⁷⁶ See pp. 206–7, 250–1.
⁷⁷ Against the authenticity of this scene: Petzl (1969) 28–43; Gee (2020) 15–38; Nesselrath (2020) 32–6; in favor: Hooker (1980) 139–46; Heubeck and Hoekstra (1989) on *Od.* 11.601–27; Karanika (2011) 1–27. M. L. West has not athetized the passage in his Teubner edition (2015).

signaling of the *Odyssey*'s use of Heracles' Underworld adventure as a model for Odysseus' Underworld episode, the reference to Theseus and Peirithoos may be putatively taken as another case of intertextual association, especially since their episode in Hades was associated with Heracles' *katabasis*.[78] If so, it seems that there is a case to be made for the *Odyssey*'s self-conscious presentation of Odysseus' Underworld experience from the perspective of an epigone's engagement with Heracles' *katabasis* and, by extension, with earlier epic poetry featuring this episode.[79]

(h) The indexical potential of poetic memory[80] refers to cases in which a narrator or character of the plot recalls or proleptically knows something that is also recalled by or known to the external audience.[81] The richness of this potential is related to the central role played by memory in early Greek epic, epitomized in the role of the Muses, daughters of *Mnemosyne* ("Memory"), who constitute a source of inspiration for the bards. It is also obvious in the insistence of epic poetry on forgetfulness, which is expressed by the characters' efforts against oblivion. Last, it is manifested in the constant effort of epic poetry to preserve κλέα ἀνδρῶν.[82] I begin by offering two examples of knowledge of past events. When in *Il.* 8.362–9 Athena refers to Zeus' previous support of Heracles, a mythical event falling outside of the Iliadic plot, she uses the language of recollection (362: οὐδέ τι τῶν μέμνηται, ὅ οἱ μάλα πολλάκις υἱόν). Athena's reminiscence coincides with the recall of this event by the external audience that is expected to be familiar with it, putatively, from an early epic on Heracles.[83] Likewise, when in *Od.* 4.187–9 (**μνήσατο** γὰρ κατὰ θυμὸν ἀμύμονος Ἀντιλόχοιο, | τόν ῥ' Ἠοῦς ἔκτεινε φαεινῆς ἀγλαὸς υἱός. | τοῦ ὅ γ' **ἐπιμνησθεὶς** ἔπεα πτερόεντ' ἀγόρευεν) Pisistratus remembers the death of Antilochus at the hands of Memnon, his recollection coincides with the external audience's reminiscence of the same mythical event. The use of the periphrastic matronymic Ἠοῦς ... υἱός that signals the key role of Dawn in an epic tradition which the *Odyssey* seems to cite on

---

[78] See, e.g., [Hes.] *Cat.* fr. 280 M-W = fr. 7* *Min. GEF*; Pan. *Her.* fr. 17 *GEF*; also Gantz (1993) 291–5.

[79] Heubeck and Hoekstra (1989, on *Od.* 11.601-27) suggest that if an epic featuring a *katabasis* of Heracles operated as the model for Odysseus' Underworld episode, one would expect to find in this episode a citation of its source; Nelson (2023) 279–85.

[80] On poetic memory in Homeric epic, see Currie (2016) 140–6.

[81] See Nelson (2023) 181–91. The use of the same indexical markers intratextually suggests that when employed to point to events beyond the scope of the poem, it is possible that they refer to other poems and not to myth in general: e.g. *Il.* 21.394–9 > 5.855–9; *Od.* 12.226–7 > 12.119–20 (forgetfulness: λανθανόμην).

[82] Nelson (2023) 178–81.

[83] Moran (1975) 203; Currie (2016) 141; Nelson (2023) 188. Currie (2016, 141 with n. 188) draws attention, with respect to another similar recollection referring to the story of Laomedon's horses and Heracles' first sack of Troy, to the use of the article (τὸ κῆτος: *Il.* 20.147), which "implies a familiar episode"; see also Moran (1975) 202; M. W. Edwards (1991) on *Il.* 20.145-8; Gantz (1993) 400; N. J. Richardson (1993) on *Il.* 21.441-57; Anderson (1997) 93; M. L. West (2011a) 32; Nelson (2023) 189 n. 47; Bär (2024) 152–3.

other occasions[84] leaves room for the possibility that this is an intertextual allusion to the *Memnonis*. I continue with one example of proleptic knowledge of events that will happen in the mythical future, i.e. after the range of events covered by the *Iliad*. In *Il.* 10.250 Odysseus tells Diomedes not to go on speaking about himself, since "these are the Argives, who know well all these matters you speak of" (εἰδόσι γάρ τοι ταῦτα μετ' Ἀργείοις ἀγορεύεις).[85] Odysseus exhibits knowledge that pertains to events that will happen after the *Iliad*. He thus shares with the poem's audience knowledge that they may have acquired from other epic tellings referring to the events after the death of Hector. Diomedes and Odysseus display a remarkable activity regarding joint missions and nocturnal deeds in various Cyclic epics.[86]

The eight internal criteria presented above suggest that utterances have an object-like status. They are treated as "independently pre-existing entities that performers and audience members know or know of and that can be re-presented as needed: tales and songs exist even when no one is telling or singing them."[87] The use of metapoetic diction and imagery, the reference to other genres, the stress on the creation, repetition, and diffusion of epic songs, the mention of narratives, and their presentation in abbreviated form: all these features seem to indicate that various stories and songs exist before the performance of the poem-in-composition and out of which it is composed. They are "objectified," in the sense that they are recognizable by both singer and audience as autonomous creations with their own identity and status, "which can be lifted from one context and replicated in another."[88] That Homeric epic methodically presents various object-like tales and songs and acknowledges this engagement is a strong indication regarding its nature and formation. It allows us to treat it as the mature product of a synthetic and evolving process based on the creative interaction with song traditions to which it alludes through an entire system of poetic references. To explore the nature, range, and function of these song traditions and, by extension, the applicability of the theory of oral intertextual neoanalysis in the study of Homeric epic, we need to turn our attention to external criteria.

1.2 External Criteria

External criteria for determining allusion to other, identifiable epic traditions are furnished by the *Iliad*'s and the *Odyssey*'s interaction with pre-Homeric poetry. Intertextual allusion in Homeric scholarship is conducted through neoanalysis, an

---

[84] See e.g. *Od.* 5.309–12, 11.543–60, 24.36–92; see M. L. West (2014) 28.
[85] Notice *Il.* 10.243 (πῶς ἂν ἔπειτ' Ὀδυσῆος ἐγὼ θείοιο λαθοίμην) and see Kullmann (1960) 86–7; Fenik (1964) 12–13; Nagy (1979 = 1999²) 34–5; Alden (2017) 10 with n. 38; Nelson (2023) 205.
[86] See, e.g., *Il. parv.* arg. ll. 228–9 Severyns: theft of the Palladium.   [87] Ready (2019) 28.
[88] Siikala (2003) 32.

interpretive method aimed at uncovering the sources of Homeric epic. The term "neoanalysis"[89] was invented as a response to and refutation of the analytical school which dissected Homeric epic into smaller epics. Whereas analysts, who aim to find the "proto-*Iliad*" (*Urilias*) and "proto-*Odyssey*" (*Urodyssee*) that were considered to be the genuine works of Homer, explain logical gaps and thematic oddities as resulting from interpolations, neoanalysts interpret poetic inconcinnities and narrative ruptures by the transfer of motifs (and, to a lesser extent, of phraseology) from pre-Homeric poetry. In contrast to the analytical school, which treats poetic quality as emanating from Homeric inventiveness, neoanalysis claims that it stems from the highly creative interaction between Homeric and earlier epic poetry. Since pre-Homeric poetry does not survive, neoanalysis employs various tools and texts to reconstruct the earlier epics on which the *Iliad* draws:[90] the *Iliad* itself, with both its dense system of forward and backward references to events falling outside the time frame of the epic, and its use of various derivative motifs; the *Odyssey*, with its abundant mention of events pertaining to the Trojan War myth; epic resonances found in Stesichorus, Pindar, Bacchylides, and other poets; vase representations; and the fragments of the Epic Cycle, the summaries of Proclus, and Apollodorus' *Epitome*. In this way, neoanalysis reconstructs various epic traditions as sources of the *Iliad*: the precursors of the Cyclic epics;[91] the *Meleagris,[92] an epic on the story of Meleager; pre-Homeric poetry on Heracles featuring the first sack of Troy[93] and his postwar journey to Cos,[94] as well as poetry referring to other exploits[95] like his *katabasis* to the Underworld;[96] an epic poem

---

[89] Coined by I.-Th. Kakridis (1944; slightly modified version in English 1949); on neoanalysis, see Heubeck (1974) 40–8; Kullmann (1981) 5–41 = (1992) 67–99, (1991) 425–55 = (1992) 100–34, (2002) 162–76; Willcock (1997) 174–89; M. Edwards s.v. "Neoanalysis" (in *HomEnc*); Tsagalis s.v. "Neoanalysis" in *OCD* (4th edition). On neoanalysis and intertextuality, see Dowden (2004) 188–205; Burgess (2006) 148–89; Currie (2006) 1–45, (2012) 543–80; Tsagalis (2011) 209–44 = (2023) 3–33. On oral poetry and neoanalysis, see Kullmann (1984) 307–23.

[90] I restrict my presentation to the *Iliad* because of the topic of my book.

[91] E.g. Kullmann (1960).

[92] I.-Th. Kakridis (1944) 1–53 = (1949) 11–42; see also Howald (1924) 402–25; Bethe (1925) 1–12; Schadewaldt (1938 = 1966³) 139–42; Kraus (1948) 8–21; Willcock (1964) 147–54; March (1987) 22–46; Edmunds (1997) 425–32; Alden (2000) 179–290; Grossardt (2001) 9–50; M. L. West (2011a) 226–30; cf. Bremmer (1988) 37–56; Burgess (2017) 51–76.

[93] Porter (2014) 507–26.

[94] See also [Hes.] *Cat.* fr. 43a.61–4 M–W (the sequence "Heracles sacks Troy > is blown off course to Cos where he fights the Meropes > kills the Giant Alcyoneus in Phlegra while assisting the Olympians who are having a difficult time in defeating the Giants" is also attested in Pind. *Nem.* 4.26–30, *Isthm.* 6.31–3); see Erbse (1970) 94; Moran (1975) 199–200; Janko (1992) 191, 199; Sbardella (1994) 154; Anderson (1997) 93; Danek (1998a) 247; Scodel (2002) 147–50; Hirschberger (2004) 280–1; D'Alessio (2005) 235 n. 72; M. L. West (2011a) 31, 36, 293; Currie (2016) 141; Scodel (2024) 63–86.

[95] In favor of a Heracles cycle or an extended epic: Kullmann (1956) 25–35; Willcock (1964) 145–6; Danek (1998a) 245–50; M. L. West (2003a) 19–24, (2011a) 30–1, (2014) 30–1. Against: Barker and Christensen (2014) 250; Bär (2024) 146–63. On the *Odyssey*'s acknowledgment of earlier Heracles poetry, see Danek (1998a) 23–4; Dowden (2004) 197; Burgess (2012b) 272–3; Andersen (2012, 138–51) remains skeptical.

[96] Currie (2016) 53 n. 94.

or poems on the wars of the Pylians;[97] and pre-Homeric poetry on Aphrodite.[98] The only case in which neoanalysis does not need to resort to reconstruction is furnished by surviving Near Eastern poetry (the Dumuzi-Inanna Sumerian songs, the royal hymns of the Sumerians, the epic of *Gilgamesh*).[99] This "expanded neoanalysis," to use Currie's apt term,[100] has significantly strengthened neoanalytical research because it is based on existing texts and methods that, "if subjective, are clear and open to scrutiny (the criteria of markedness and meaningfulness)",[101] in sharp contrast to all reconstructed pre-Homeric poems of the Greek epic tradition.

Detected allusion between different epics or epic traditions can take various forms. It can be (a) a direct quotation of the source: the "hateful song" (στυγερή ἀοιδή) in *Od.* 24.200 that refers to the song of Agamemnon's return to Greece and murder by Clytaemestra belongs to the epic tradition of the **Nosti*, which involves close and substantial correspondence between two versions[102] and is often marked by metapoetic diction;[103] the reference to the voyage of the Argo, "which is known to all" (*Od.* 12.70: Ἀργὼ πᾶσι μέλουσα), has been interpreted by several scholars as an acknowledgment of an earlier Argonautic epic tradition that may have served as the model for the *Odyssey*'s mythical and poetical *aemulatio*.[104]

(b) Inversion or reversal of the source: Paris' abduction of Helen is mirrored by Agamemnon's abduction of Briseis, but the *Iliad* partly reverses the consequences of the abduction, i.e. from full-scale war between two peoples (Achaeans and Trojans) in the case of Helen to internal strife and withdrawal of Achilles and his troops in the case of Briseis (**Cypria* > *Iliad*: opposition in imitation).[105] The poetic advantages of this innovation are significant. One is to create the conditions for a doubling of the losses for the Achaeans, who perish not only because they fight in Troy for the sake of Helen but also because their best warrior, Achilles,

---

[97] See Bölte (1934) 319–47; also: Cantieni (1942).

[98] In favor: Reinhardt (1956) 7; Penglase (1994) 239; Currie (2016) 156-7. Against: Olson (2012) 1, cf. 165; Baumbach (2012) 139. Not taking sides: Faulkner (2008) 135–6.

[99] This last category of material is not immune to uncertainty, viz. whether there was in fact any influence of Near Eastern poetry on the early Greek epic tradition or we are simply dealing with several types of coincidences. However, the use by early Greek epic "in conjunction, [of] both the same complex motifs and the same complex techniques of allusion as Near Eastern poetry, in not just one, but two sequences of reception ([e.g.] on the one hand, Inanna > Ishtar > Aphrodite > Hera; on the other, Bilgames–Enkidu > Achilleus–Patroklos)" makes it "hard to view these coincidences as just 'coincidental'" (Currie 2016, 217).

[100] Currie (2016) 22; see also Clarke (2019) 31-4.   [101] Currie (2016) 221.

[102] Currie (2006) 6; (2016) 47–55.

[103] In this case, the *Odyssey* acknowledges its existence as a distinct and identifiable poetic tradition that is superior to the epic tradition of the **Nosti*; see Tsagalis (2003a) 53–56 = (2008) 30–43, (2014a) 243.

[104] Kullmann (1991) 449–52 = (1992) 125–9, (2012a, 216–18, 222–3), (2012b, 20–4); M. L. West (2005) 39 = (2011b) 278, (2012) 231–2, (2014) 30; Tsagalis (2011) 221 = (2023) 14, (2014a) 243. Currie (2016, 47 with n. 56) argues that since the language Odysseus employs to introduce himself to the Phaeacians (*Od.* 9.19-20: πᾶσι... | ἀνθρώποισι μέλω) suggests that he knows that he has become the subject of song, this knowledge "tropes the audience's knowledge of other poetry" (see *Od.* 12.70).

[105] Currie (2016) 34; Porter (2022) 11.

abstains from the war. Another one is to bring to the limelight the theme of strife, which is now operating in the world of mortals, whereas in the story of Helen it functions in the world of immortals (Eris > Apple of Discord > *theon krisis* on Mt Ida). It is possible that the inversion of the source constitutes a technique by means of which the *Iliad* "quotes" an earlier poetic tradition that we see later appropriated by the *Cypria*.[106]

(c) Parody of the source: when Odysseus tries to hide his nakedness with a branch and is compared to a lion ready to attack sheep or cattle because it is forced by hunger, the diction employed by the *Odyssey* (κέλεται δέ ἑ γαστήρ) alludes to the formula κέλεται δέ ἑ θυμὸς ἀγήνωρ that has been employed in a lion simile in the *Iliad* (*Il*. 12.299–306 vs. *Od*. 6.130–6: *Iliad* > *Odyssey*). By appropriating the Iliadic dictional and thematical features of this type of expression, the *Odyssey* parodies its source, thus hiding "the embarrassingly elegiac situation of the hero who must *present himself naked*[107] to the young and noble girls."[108]

(d) Splitting of the source: the rejection of Isthtar's proposition by Gilgamesh, who recalls (while washing) a list of Ishtar's former lovers whose negative fate he does not want to share, is split between two different target-texts, the *Homeric Hymn to Aphrodite* and *Iliad* 14. In the former, Aphrodite (performing her toilette and dressing) accepts Anchises' proposition, while a catalogue of love affairs between goddesses and mortals is also presented; in the latter, Hera (performing her toilette and dressing) accepts Zeus' proposition, which is accompanied by a catalogue of his previous love affairs. The rejection of sexual intercourse in the *Gilgamesh* episode is reversed and split in the two Greek texts, where sexual intercourse takes place (*Gilgamesh* SBV VI > *Homeric Hymn to Aphrodite* 202–40 and *Il*. 14.315–27).[109] This kind of literary argument treads on historical unknowns, such as knowledge of the source-text by the target-texts, as well as knowledge of the interaction between *Gilgamesh* SBV VI and the earlier Dumuzi-Inanna songs, in which Dumuzi propositions Inanna[110] while she is performing her toilette, and his proposition leads to sexual intercourse.[111] It also involves twofold interaction of *Homeric Hymn to Aphrodite* 202–40 with *Il*. 14.315–27 and each of these two texts independently with *Gilgamesh* SBV VI.[112]

(e) Explicit or implicit references directing the audience towards familiar epic traditions: Diomedes' plea to Athena to assist him after being wounded by

---

[106] For an analogous argument made with respect to the divine armor of Memnon and Achilles in the **Memnonis* and the *Iliad,* respectively, see Currie (2016) 28–9.
[107] Italics in the original.
[108] Pucci (1987) 159. The idea of making allusion to an earlier epic tradition by denying an alternative version fostered by that tradition finds a revealing parallel in the renewal of phraseology between the *Iliad* and the *Odyssey*: "the *Odyssey*'s simultaneous dependence on and disengagement from the Iliadic tradition are highlighted in those passages of the poems that clearly seem to respond to each other and therefore play with allusion" (Pucci 1987, 18).
[109] See Currie (2016) 178–83.   [110] This scene contains no mythological catalogue.
[111] Currie (2016) 183.   [112] Currie (2016) 217.

Pandarus as she had done with his father, Tydeus, in the past,[113] so that he kills his arrogant adversary, who boasts that he will slay Diomedes, may be considered as an allusion to the *Thebais in which Tydeus' cannibalism may have been caused by similar reasons[114] (*Il*. 5.115–120: *Thebais > Iliad*). In this case the use of the motif of "wrath because of being wounded" seems to have been transferred from the Theban epic tradition (an oral, pre-Homeric *Thebais) to the *Iliad*. The argument that the material used in the post-Homeric written *Thebais* is the source of the *Iliad* is supported by a series of shared features: Athena's intervention, Tydeus (protagonist in the Theban context, recalled in the Iliadic context), the angry reaction by Tydeus and Diomedes in the *Thebais and the *Iliad*, respectively, Diomedes' desire to kill Pandarus because he (Pandarus) had expressed the will to kill him in the first place is not well motivated but seems to have been triggered by Tydeus' eating of Melanippus' brains, the fact that the protagonist asks for the help of a comrade-in-arms, Tydeus of Amphiaraus and Diomedes of Sthenelus.[115] The accumulation of these shared features is at loggerheads with a typological explanation. It is a reasonable assumption that in this episode the *Iliad* is drawing on a pre-Homeric Theban epic tradition, which it signals to its audience. Another case in which the Theban epic tradition may have operated as the source for the *Iliad* is the Achaean Wall,[116] which is protected by seven leaders, each in charge of 100 warriors. This seemingly insignificant detail becomes meaningful when viewed in relation to Theban epic, a key element of which is the siege of seven-gated Thebes.[117] That the *Iliad* refers to Thebes as having seven gates (*Il*. 4.406) enhances the view that the aforementioned association is deliberate. The connection is made even more probable if one considers the semantic surplus created by relating the target-text (*Iliad*) to its possible source-text (*Epigoni*), especially through the polarity between the presence and absence of Diomedes, a key figure in the epic

---

[113] See also *Il*. 4.390.
[114] Fr. 9 *GEF*; see Torres-Guerra (1995) 59; Kullmann (2002) 168; Ebbott (2010) 239–58, (2014) 319–35; Differently Vergados (2014) 438, who admits that φασί (*Il*. 4.375) suggests "the existence of storytelling regarding the expedition of the Seven, an offshoot of which is the cyclic *Thebaid*," but takes it as indicating stories reported to Agamemnon by means of an earlier generation of men who were eyewitnesses of Tydeus fighting at Thebes; Barker and Christensen (2020, 48) argue that the Theban material in the Homeric epics "is put to the service of the narratives of the *Iliad* and *Odyssey*," and that it does not preserve "a remnant of the original focus of a Theban poem"; see also Sammons (2014) 300. However, indexical markers like φασί may suggest a bifurcated mode of reading in which a message is conveyed to both internal and external audiences. The fact that such references operate intratextually does not exclude the possibility that they also function intertextually, more or less as similar indexical markers abundantly used in Hellenistic and Roman poetry (Nelson 2023, 1–5); see also Currie (2016) 26 with n. 163; Ready (2019) 29; Currie (forthcoming).
[115] Torres-Guerra (1995) 60–1 with n. 113.
[116] See Singor 1992, 404; Slatkin (2011, 101, 107–9), who is also in favor of the existence of a constellation of myths referring to the Theban Wars "in narrative form from a period as early as that of the Trojan myths" (109), highlights the fact that Diomedes is more often designated by his patronymic than by his own name.
[117] Reinhardt (1961) 190–206; Kullmann (1981) 12–13 = (1992) 73 with n. 25, (1991) 426–7 = (1992) 101–2; Burkert (1976) 5–21 = (2001) 59–71, (1981) 29–48 = (2001) 198–217; Torres-Guerra (1995) 56.

traditions of the *Epigoni and the Iliad. The audience is thus invited to realize that in contrast to the second Theban War, in which Diomedes overruns the Theban walls and sacks Thebes, the Achaean Wall will be overrun by the Trojans now that Diomedes has been wounded and is unable to protect it.

(f) Self-reflexive tropes of allusion.[118] Helen, a character emblematizing the Trojan War epic tradition, is engaged twice in voicing self-referential comments on the Iliadic epic tradition: in *Il.* 3.125–8 she weaves a great web, into which she works the numerous struggles of the Trojans and the Achaeans,[119] and in *Il.* 6.357–8 she refers to herself as the subject of a future song.[120] In *Od.* 24.196–8, Agamemnon's designation of Odysseus' return tale as "a pleasing song" (ἀοιδήν... χαρίεσσαν, 24.197–8) "comes very close to self-reference."[121] There is also a possibility that in *Od.* 22.345–9 Phemius promises to sing to Odysseus a song about his return in which he himself would feature.[122] These three last cases amount to a form of metalepsis, "where characters 'announce' the text in which they themselves figure."[123]

(g) Compressed indexing of a source-text by means of phraseology. Certain epithets are sometimes particularly associated with an epic tradition which is different from the one in which the epithet is being used. A case in point is the πολυ- compound epithets used for Odysseus, as well as his designation as "city-sacker": πολύαιν'(ε) Ὀδυσεῦ (3x *Il.*, 1x *Od.*); πολύμητις Ὀδυσσεύς (18x *Il.*, 69x *Od.*); πολύτλας Ὀδυσσεύς (5x *Il.*, 37x *Od.*); πτολίπορθος Ὀδυσσεύς (2x *Il.*; 3x *Od.*). These four epithets offer a good case study with respect to the controversy concerning mythological versus poetical allusion. Since they all describe Odysseus and attribute to him features that are foreign to his role in the *Iliad* and pertain either to the continuation of the Trojan saga (πολύμητις, πτολίπορθος) or to his wanderings (πολύτλας), their attestation in the *Iliad* must be explained as a hint to the epic's knowledge of the entirety of Odysseus' myth or to oral epic songs in which Odysseus would have had this role.[124] But in the case of πολύαιν'(ε) sense seems to turn the scales in favor of poetical allusion. An epithet meaning "much-praised"[125] presupposes an utterance or utterances which are repeatedly performed and known to the epic tradition of the *Iliad*. The expression πολύαιν' Ὀδυσεῦ, μέγα κῦδος Ἀχαιῶν is employed twice in the *Iliad*, by Agamemnon in book 9 and Nestor in book 10. Agamemnon and Nestor address Odysseus, who is the leader of the three envoys and one of the two spies, respectively.[126] This expression includes two formulas, πολύαιν' Ὀδυσεῦ and μέγα κῦδος Ἀχαιῶν. The fact that Odysseus is "much-praised" makes him a "great glory of the Achaeans." His fame, which is already established, reflects on the Achaean army. Odysseus'

---

[118] Currie (2016) 26–7.   [119] See p. 34.   [120] De Jong (2009) 98.
[121] R. B. Rutherford (2013²) 79.   [122] See p. 29 with n. 9.   [123] De Jong (2009) 98.
[124] See Haft (1990) 45–55.   [125] See LSJ and *CGL* s.v.
[126] *Il.* 9.673 = 10.544: εἴπ' ἄγε μ', ὦ πολύαιν' Ὀδυσεῦ, μέγα κῦδος Ἀχαιῶν.

reputation and distinction cannot be based on his role in events preceding the *Iliad* or taking place in the *Iliad*. It mirrors his role in what he will do in the rest of the saga, especially in the events covered by the last phase of the war (the *Ptocheia*, the theft of the Palladium, and the sack of Troy). It is exactly these Trojan glories of Odysseus that the Sirens evoke when they use the same expression and address him as πολύαιν' Ὀδυσεῦ, μέγα κῦδος Ἀχαιῶν.[127] They entice him to leave his ship and stay on their island so that he can listen to the sufferings of the Argives and Trojans in the war, as well as to "whatever happens on this fertile earth."[128] In this passage, which is rich in metapoetic overtones,[129] the Sirens use a song of the Trojan War to lure Odysseus and pull him away from the song of the *Odyssey*. They make this attempt by calling him "much-praised," thus acknowledging that he is already the subject of much praise through song. The epithet πολύαινος is also employed by Socus addressing Odysseus in *Il*. 11.430.[130] This time it is followed by the expression δόλων ἆτ' ἠδὲ πόνοιο ("insatiable in cunning and perseverance"), which functions as a poetic exegesis of the epithet πολύαινε. It explains that the reason for Odysseus' wide praise is his unquenchable skill in cunning and perseverance. One important aspect of the use of the designation "much-praised" for Odysseus is that it is always employed in the vocative. The necessary concomitant of this observation is that this word exists only in speeches.[131] To address Odysseus as "much-praised" means that the characters of the plot (Nestor, Agamemnon, Socus, the Sirens) operate *with respect to the use of this epithet* metapoetically, since they endorse the viewpoint of the Homeric epic tradition about a much-praised Odysseus because of his achievements in the last phase of the Trojan War. The above-mentioned speakers become the mouthpiece of the Iliadic and Odyssean traditions which respond to other epic songs that have praised Odysseus. Seen from this vantage point, the use of this epithet only for Odysseus may constitute an allusive reference to the epic traditions which bestowed on him abundant praise. There are good reasons, then, to argue that the reference is not simply mythological but poetical.

The same argument has been made for the epithets ὀϊζυρός[132] and χαλκοκορυστής.[133] In *Od*. 5.105 ὀϊζυρός is used by Hermes in the superlative when conveying Zeus' message to Calypso with respect to the "liberation" of Odysseus from her island. Thematically this epithet is inscribed in the tradition of the *Nosti*, in the sense that the Odyssean Odysseus is designated as representing the most extreme form of return, which lasts more than any other return of an Achaean hero known to the epic tradition. However, the thematical rivalry with the tradition of the *Nosti* may be only one side of the story. The exclusive use of

---

[127] *Od*. 12.184.   [128] *Od*. 12.184-91.   [129] Pucci (1998) 1-9.
[130] ὦ Ὀδυσεῦ πολύαινε, δόλων ἆτ' ἠδὲ πόνοιο.
[131] Technically speaking, it could have been used in a second-person address to Odysseus by the narrator.
[132] Pucci (1987) 38-9.   [133] Mühlestein (1986) 217 = (1987) 182.

the same epithet for Achilles in the *Iliad* (1.417), especially in conjunction with another epithet operating as a trademark of Achilles' fate (νῦν δ' ἅμα τ' ὠκύμορος καὶ ὀϊζυρὸς περὶ πάντων), suggests a comparison between the *Iliad*'s and the *Odyssey*'s "most lamentable of the Achaeans." In this vein, it is possible to argue that phraseology is employed as a vehicle of allusion, allowing the tradition of the *Odyssey* to confront the traditions of the **Nosti* and the *Iliad*. Turning to χαλκοκορυστής, its exclusive use for Memnon (Hes. *Th.* 984), Hector (e.g. *Il.* 5.699; 15.221), and Sarpedon (*Il.* 6.199) in early hexameter verse[134] makes it possible that it has been transferred from the son of Eos, who had an armor made by Hephaestus to his two Iliadic surrogates.[135]

1.3 Transference of Motifs, Themes, and Phraseology

Neoanalysts argue for the transference of motifs, themes, and phraseology from putative source-texts or epic traditions to fully fledged target-texts. Such a kind of relationship between epic poems involves several difficulties, the most important of which is the following: are intertextual references possible in such an early form of poetry? In order to explore this issue, we first need to perform a "control-test" between epics preserved in complete form, and then to carefully determine the criteria by means of which it would be possible to detect allusion.

Regarding the first issue, we may turn our attention to the two Homeric epics. This is not, of course, the place to offer an exhaustive presentation of several test cases that suggest an interaction between the *Iliad* and the *Odyssey*; this is a work that has been largely done by various scholars with very compelling arguments and results.[136] I will, therefore, restrict myself to a single case of allusion on the level of narrative structure, and one example of allusion on the level of wording.

In *Il.* 24.281–508, Priam and Idaeus drive a chariot and a cart, respectively, to the Achaean camp, the latter's cart following the former's chariot and bearing Hector's ransom (265–8, 322–7); they stop at the tomb of Ilus, which is a suitable location for a divine epiphany (349–51); Hermes appears in the disguise of a youth (347–8), becomes Priam's escort (437, 461), and advises him on how to get to Achilles' hut (465–7); Hermes leaves Priam and returns to Olympus (468–9); when Priam arrives at Achilles' hut, a meal is concluded (475–6); Priam gets inside

---

[134] Its use for Ares in *Homeric Hymn to Ares* 2 is not against this argument despite the lateness of the hymn.
[135] Currie (2016, 72) maintains that the same argument can be made for the expression περίφρων Εὐρύκλεια (*Od.* 19.357, 491; 20.134; 21.381) next to περίφρων Πηνελόπεια (*Od.* 22.41); cf. Whallon (2000) 334–5.
[136] On intertextual associations between the *Iliad* and the *Odyssey*, see Maronitis (1983) 279–91 = (2004) 133–46; Pucci (1987); Usener (1990); Di Benedetto (2001) 7–14; R. B. Rutherford (2001) 117–46; Saïd (2011) 373–9; Bakker (2013) 157–69; Currie (2016) 39–47; Schein (2016) 81–91; Minchin (2018) 9–30.

the hut and supplicates Achilles, who is surprised (477–9); Priam delivers a speech of supplication to Achilles (486–506); Achilles hesitates to reply (507–12); the supplication is successful. In *Od.* 6.255–7.154, Odysseus goes on foot to the city of the Phaeacians, while Nausicaa in front drives a chariot with her laundry (6.252–3, 260–1, 317–20); they stop at Athena's grove, which is a suitable location for a divine epiphany (6.291–6, 321–2); Athena appears to Odysseus in the disguise of a young woman (7.20) as Odysseus' guide (7.30) and advises him on how to supplicate the Phaeacian queen, Arete, when he arrives at the city (7.50–77); Athena leaves Odysseus and goes to her temple in Athens (7.78); when Odysseus arrives at Alcinoos' palace, a meal is concluded (7.49–50, 137–8); Odysseus gets inside the palace and supplicates Arete, who is surprised (7.142–3, 145); Odysseus delivers a speech of supplication to Arete (7.146–52); Arete hesitates to reply (7.154–5); the supplication is successful.[137] This list of similarities and analogies shared by *Il.* 24.281–508 and *Od.* 6.255–7.154 is impressive. However, how should we explain it? Is it the outcome of the combination of a "visit type-scene" with a "supplication-scene," or is there a case to be made for allusion? First, I would like to suggest that the possibility that the two poems, independently one from the other, combined two type-scenes in the same way seems rather stretched. It would entail the acceptance of three coincidences, the first referring to the same type-scenes, the second to their number (two), and the third to the same technique of combination.[138] Second, a strong case for allusion may be made by considering the larger context of the two scenes and the poems in which they feature, the specific allusive technique employed in these two scenes in comparison to the usual form of allusion that the *Odyssey* employs in relation to the *Iliad*, and the function of the characters involved in both scenes. Structurally, both scenes belong to the second movement of a process of resolution pertaining to the release of Hector's body in the *Iliad* and the return of Odysseus from Calypso's island and the Phaeacians to Ithaca. The fact that in both poems the first movement involves four similar scenes and that the second movement, as analyzed above, contains the same structural elements in the same order suggests a level of analogy that can hardly be coincidental. Moreover, both *Il.* 24.281–508 and *Od.* 6.255–7.154 use the allusive technique of inversion: while Achilles, the *Iliad*'s protagonist, is supplicated, Odysseus, the *Odyssey*'s main character, supplicates. Since inversion is regularly used by the *Odyssey* to refer to the *Iliad* (e.g. Achilles causes pains, *Il.* 1.2: ἄλγε' ἔθηκε – Odysseus endures pains, *Od.* 1.4: πάθεν ἄλγεα; Achilles excels in fighting skill, *Il.* 1.165–6: ἀλλὰ τὸ μὲν πλεῖον πολυάϊκος πολέμοιο | χεῖρες ἐμαὶ διέπουσ'· – Odysseus excels in *doloi*, *Od.* 9.19–20: εἴμ' Ὀδυσεὺς Λαερτιάδης, ὅς πᾶσι δόλοισιν | ἀνθρώποισι μέλω), the allusive technique observed in *Il.* 24.281–508 and *Od.* 6.255–7.154 conforms with a phenomenon of wide range and application. Furthermore, the antithesis between

---

[137] See Currie (2016) 42–4.   [138] On the evaluation of coincidences, see Currie (2016) 217.

the male figures dominating *Il.* 24.281–508 (Hermes as escort and adviser, Idaeus as Priam's charioteer, and Achilles as the person supplicated) and the female characters playing an analogous role in *Od.* 6.255–7.154 (Nausicaa as escort, Athena as adviser, and Arete as the person supplicated) suggests that "the distinctiveness of the *Odyssey*'s world is revealed through allusion to the *Iliad*."[139] In light of all the above, we cannot rule out the possibility that *Od.* 6.255–7.154 alludes to *Il.* 24.281–508.

Turning to allusion on the level of wording, I will focus on a case of verbatim quotation with a "high contextual surplus" in which two expressions share features "that are not required by the meaning of the line(s) in question."[140] In a state of distress and anger, Achilles dashes to the ground the scepter (*Il.* 1.245: ὣς φάτο Πηλεΐδης, ποτὶ δὲ σκῆπτρον βάλε γαίῃ). Likewise, in a state of distress and anger, Telemachus dashes down the scepter in tears (*Od.* 2.80: ὣς φάτο χωόμενος, ποτὶ δὲ σκῆπτρον βάλε γαίῃ). The two verses are almost identical. Are we dealing here with a formulaic expression that is a manifestation of dictional typology, or is it possible that one of these verses quotes the other? A careful examination of the context suggests that the situations to which these two verses pertain share several similarities and analogies: (i) the verbal similarity of the two verses is paired with corresponding gestures (both Achilles and Telemachus throw down their scepters); (ii) Achilles in *Iliad* 1 and Telemachus in *Odyssey* 2 isolate themselves by walking along the seashore; (iii) both of them ask for divine assistance, Achilles from Thetis and Telemachus from Athena;[141] (iv) in both cases divine help is granted; (v) in both cases the interaction between god and mortal is crucial for the poem: in the *Iliad* a course of the plot is annulled and the groundwork is laid for the unravelling of the theme of *menis*. Likewise in the *Odyssey*, Telemachus' contact with Athena sets the poem in motion; (vi) Nestor in *Iliad* 1 and Halitherses in *Odyssey* 2 intervene in the verbal duel between Agamemnon and Achilles and Antinoos and Telemachus, respectively. The accumulation of similarities and analogies between the contexts in which the two virtually identical verses are placed (*Il.* 1.245 and *Od.* 2.80), the fact that their range of attestation is limited to these two instances, and the different content of the two scenes increase "their potential for signalling meaningful repetition."[142] The interpretive gain from this association is significant. Telemachus initially mirrors Achilles' symbolic act of dissent in a manner similar to the Iliadic hero. However, the *Odyssey* promptly corrects this association by revealing Telemachus' vulnerability as he breaks into tears upon casting aside the scepter. Through his display of restraint and willingness to compromise, Telemachus ultimately fails to become a true embodiment of Achilles. Furthermore, following the scepter's abandonment and Telemachus'

---

[139] Currie (2016) 44.   [140] Mueller (1984) 151.
[141] In *Il.* 1.348–56, Achilles' isolation and request for divine help double Chryses' isolation (he also walks by the seashore) and request for divine help from Apollo in *Il.* 1.34–42; see Usener (1990) 10; Barker (2009) 101–2.
[142] Bakker (2013) 159.

return to the palace after praying to Athena at the seashore, the assertive suitor Antinoos assumes a dominant role, a stark contrast to the eloquent and sagacious Nestor, who immediately follows Achilles in the corresponding scene in the *Iliad*.[143] In this light, it is possible that in this case we are not dealing with formulaic recurrence but with a verbatim quotation on the level of wording of *Il*. 1.245 by *Od*. 2.80.[144]

These two test cases referring to allusion on the level of narrative structure and phraseology between epics preserved in complete form[145] allow for the possibility that the same type of argument could be made with respect to putative source-texts or epic traditions and fully preserved target-texts.

The principal criteria to be used for sustaining such an argument are narrative inconsistency, quotation, markedness, meaningfulness, and opposition in imitation or contrast imitation. A test case will be the cornerstone[146] of neoanalysis, i.e. that the *Memnonis* is a source for the *Iliad*. Neoanalysts have argued that the death of Hector by Achilles, who thus avenges the killing of Patroclus by Hector in the *Iliad*, has been modeled on the demise of Memnon at the hands of Achilles, who is driven by the desire to avenge Antilochus' loss to Memnon in the *Memnonis*.[147] The similarities between the *Memnonis* and the *Iliad* are multiple,[148] but I will concentrate on the most fundamental ones, which I classify into two groups on the basis of the correspondence of Iliadic Achilles with Achilles in the *Memnonis* and of the modeling of Iliadic Patroclus on Achilles in the *Memnonis*.[149] In the first correspondence, we may observe the following series of events that refer to Achilles: withdrawal (after receiving a prophecy from Thetis about Memnon: *Aeth*. arg. ll. 186-7 Severyns — after a disagreement and bitter verbal exchanges with Agamemnon: *Il*. 1.240-4); substitution (Antilochus fights during Achilles' withdrawal: *Aeth*. arg. ll. 188-9 — Patroclus fights during Achilles' withdrawal: *Il*. 16.36-100); friend's death (Memnon kills Antilochus: *Aeth*. arg. ll. 188-9 — Hector kills Patroclus: *Il*. 16.818-57); revenge (Achilles kills Memnon: *Aeth*. arg. l. 189 Severyns — Achilles kills Hector: *Il*. 22.322-63); and death (Paris and Apollo kill Achilles: *Aeth*. arg. ll. 191-2 Severyns — Paris and Apollo will kill Achilles: *Il*. 22.359-60 [foreshadowing]). In the second correspondence, we may note the ensuing series of events that refer to Achilles (*Memnonis*) and Patroclus (*Iliad*): victory over major adversary (Achilles kills Memnon: *Aeth*. arg. l. 189

---

[143] See Barker (2009) 102. [144] Usener (1990) 12-13.
[145] See Currie (2016) 42-5; Minchin (2018, 22-4) has argued that several "story moments" in the *Iliad* are evoked by the *Odyssey*.
[146] Cairns (2001a, 42) claims that the theory that the *Memnonis* is a source for the *Iliad* is "established beyond any reasonable doubt."
[147] Schadewaldt (1965⁴, 155-202) has reconstructed the plot of the *Memnonis* (which some scholars conceive as a song-tradition: Tsagalis 2008, 67-8; Burgess 2009, 60) by means of Arctinus' post-Homeric *Aethiopis*, iconography, Pindar, and Apollodorus; see also p. 14 n. 68.
[148] For a useful list, see Rengakos (2015) 315.
[149] In this respect, I am following the presentation of the argument by Currie (2016) 57.

Severyns — Patroclus kills Sarpedon: *Il.* 16.480–5); death (Achilles is killed by Paris and Apollo [at the Scaean gates]: *Aeth.* arg. ll. 191–2 Severyns; Apollod. *Epit.* 20.1; see also *Il.* 22.360 — Patroclus is killed by Euphorbus, Hector, and Apollo [at the Scaean gates?]: *Il.* 16.788–857); battle over the hero's corpse (Achilles' body is removed by Ajax and Odysseus: *Aeth.* arg. l. 193 Severyns; *Aeth.* fr. 3 *GEF* — Patroclus' body is removed by the two Ajaxes and Menelaus: *Il.* 17.715–61, 18.151–64); mourning (of Achilles by Thetis, the Nereids, and the Muses: *Aeth.* arg. ll. 198–9 Severyns; see also *Od.* 24.47–62 — of Patroclus by Thetis and the Nereids: *Il.* 18.35–71); and funeral and funeral games (for Achilles: *Aeth.* arg. l. 201 Severyns; see also *Od.* 24.85–92 Severyns — for Patroclus: *Il.* 23.110–897).

The five criteria we have mentioned above for sustaining the neoanalytical argument (narrative inconsistency, quotation, markedness, meaningfulness, and opposition in imitation or contrast imitation) are all applicable to the preceding list of similarities.[150]

Thetis' lament in conjunction with the scene of the Nereids beating their breasts in the depths of the sea is narratively inconsistent with its context: Achilles is alive, the performance of the lament and the gestures of lamentation by the Nereids are awkwardly taking place in their watery abode. The narrative gap continues even when Thetis and the Nereids visit Achilles. The scene with the mother holding her son's head is hard to imagine because Achilles is lying face down. This narrative inconsistency seems to have occurred because of the transfer to the *Iliad* of the scene of lamentation for Achilles in the **Memnonis*, where Thetis, together with the Nereids and the Muses, lamented Achilles in his funeral that took place in the Achaean camp, where the deceased's mother may have held in her arms her son's head and sung a dirge for him.[151]

The scene of Thetis and the Nereids in *Il.* 18.35–71 is immediately preceded by a shorter scene of the slave women gathering around Achilles and beating their breasts for Patroclus' death (18.30–1). In this vein, the *Iliad* is able to present in conjunction, albeit incomplete (since fully fledged, antiphonal lament speeches for Patroclus will be expressed in 19.287–300 and 19.315–37 by Briseis and Achilles, respectively), a scene that is fully compatible with its own plot (the mourning for Patroclus) and a scene that was central to the **Memnonis* and is narratively inconsistent with the plot of the *Iliad*. This juxtaposition may be reasonably, I think, interpreted as a way by which the *Iliad* (mourning for Patroclus) "quotes" its source, the **Memnonis* (mourning for Achilles).[152]

Markedness is an important qualitative criterion for determining allusion. One of its manifestations, which is observable in this case, refers to the position of the

---

[150] Hereafter I will mention a few representative examples, which can easily be multiplied if one is to present the entire range of similarities between the **Memnonis* and the *Iliad*.
[151] See *Aeth.* arg. ll. 198–9 Severyns; also *Od.* 24.47–62; I.-Th. Kakridis (1944) 85–100 = (1949) 65–75; Schadewaldt (1965⁴) 167.
[152] For another putative case of the *Iliad* quoting the **Memnonis*, see Currie (2016) 60–1.

series of similarities (not only with respect to the correspondence between Achilles in the *Memnonis* and Achilles in the *Iliad* but also regarding the modeling of Iliadic Patroclus on Achilles in the *Memnonis*). All the fundamental similarities shared by the two epics are located in the last third of the *Iliad*, i.e. in books 16-19 and 22-23,[153] which are devoted to Patroclus (his borrowing of Achilles' armor, initial victory, his death by Hector, the fight over his body) and Achilles (his suffering for the loss of his friend, his return to the fighting, his revenge on Hector, and the funeral games that he organizes in honor of his friend). The concentration of these features in a single and continuous (books 16-23)[154] part of the *Iliad* marks them as a coherent narrative sequence, thus increasing the possibility that they have been taken wholesale from the *Memnonis*, in which similar features formed the entire epic.

Meaningfulness pertains to a dialogue between two contexts.[155] Sometimes it may involve the reversal of a putative source-text by the target-text.[156] The following case refers to both these criteria. In *Il.* 16.480-5 Patroclus kills Sarpedon, and in *Aeth.* arg. l. 189 (Severyns) Achilles kills Memnon. According to the second series of similarities we have presented above, the analogy between Achilles in the *Memnonis* and Patroclus in the *Iliad* allows for a further analogy between Memnon in the *Memnonis* and Sarpedon in the *Iliad*.[157] Is there a dialogue between these two contexts and, if so, is it meaningful? In *Il.* 16.306-27, Nestor's sons Antilochus and Thrasymedes engage in combat against the brothers Atymnius and Maris, who are Sarpedon's comrades. It has been argued that this scene is a reversal of the description of Antilochus' future death, in which Thrasymedes cannot save him.[158] This may well be a case of opposition in imitation or contrast imitation. But why is Antilochus associated in this scene with Sarpedon's comrades? Is this a random incident? Antilochus kills Atymnius and is attacked by his brother Maris, who is killed by Antilochus' brother Thrasymedes. The scene becomes meaningful if Sarpedon is conceived as a second Memnon. The victory of Antilochus and Thrasymedes over Atymnius and Maris, respectively, "stands for the anticipated retribution for Antilochus' death by Memnon in the *Memnonis*. In the Iliadic plot Antilochus could not be associated with Memnon, but with his counterpart Sarpedon."[159]

---

[153] For books 20-21, see the following footnote.

[154] As regards secondary similarities, I also take into account books 20-21 (the routing of the Trojans by Achilles), which seem to reflect Achilles' similar activity in the *Memnonis* (see *Aeth.* arg. l. 191 Severyns: τρεψάμενος δ' Ἀχιλλεὺς τοὺς Τρῶας), in which the pursuit of the Trojans followed the death of Memnon, whereas it preceded the death of Hector in the *Iliad*.

[155] Currie (2016) 261.   [156] Currie (2016) 34.

[157] Notice that Sarpedon and Memnon are both sons of gods (Sarpedon is son of Zeus, Memnon is son of Eos) and that they are both snatched away from the battlefield by Hypnos and Thanatos after their deaths.

[158] Reinhardt (1961) 357.

[159] Kullmann (2005) 22 (paraphrased from the original in German).

At this point, it is important to address two main concerns regarding the relation between the *Memnonis* and the *Iliad* as presented by neoanalysis. The first concern may be designated as "multiple correspondence," the second as "direction of influence." Multiple correspondence between characters is particularly relevant in this case, since it has been contested whether the Iliadic Patroclus can have at the same time two models in the *Memnonis*, i.e. Achilles and Antilochus.[160] The arguments that have been marshaled against this concern are of two types: they refer to the association of Antilochus and Patroclus, and they pertain to the many-to-one and one-to-many correspondence between the *Memnonis* and the *Iliad*.[161] The mythological armature of Patroclus and Antilochus is similar. Both heroes feature exclusively in the contexts of the *Memnonis* and the *Iliad*. In this vein, they do not fall under a pattern that is widely employed to make a case for typological explanation. The intertextual parallelism between these two heroes in the *Memnonis* and the *Iliad* seems to be reflected in their intratextual parallelism:[162] both approach Achilles in tears (Patroclus: *Il.* 16.1–3; Antilochus: *Il.* 18.1–2)[163] and Antilochus is second only to Achilles with respect to the pain he feels about Patroclus' death (*Il.* 17.695–6).[164] The joint burial of Achilles, Patroclus, and Antilochus (*Od.* 24.76–9) suggests an implicit acknowledgment by the *Odyssey* of the *Iliad*'s transference of the friendship between Achilles and Antilochus in the *Memnonis* to the *Iliad*.[165] As regards the many-to-one and one-to-many correspondence between characters, it has been argued that the relation between the *Memnonis* and the *Iliad* is marked by such a polysemic state of affairs. For example, Iliadic Patroclus may have been modeled on Antilochus and Achilles in the *Memnonis*, Hector and Sarpedon in the *Iliad* on Memnon in the *Memnonis*, Antilochus and Patroclus in the *Iliad* on Antilochus in the *Memnonis*.[166] Similar arguments for multiple correspondence have been made for Odyssean allusion to the *Iliad* (e.g. at the beginning of the *Odyssey* Odysseus evokes simultaneously the Iliadic Priam [as suppliant] and the Iliadic Hector [the "dead" person on whose account the supplication is made]).[167] The crucial point is that multiple correspondence between characters shares with motif transference, which is the core characteristic of neoanalytical

---

[160] This is the view of Burgess (1997, 1–19; 2005, 122; 2009, 73, 79–80, 93), who has questioned the neoanalytical argument that Achilles' killing of Memnon in the *Memnonis* was an act of vengeance; see also Allan (2005) 14 and n. 61; Kelly (2006) 6.
[161] See I.-Th. Kakridis (1944) 79–80 = (1949) 60–1; Schadewaldt (1965⁴) 191–2; Lohmann (1970) 193; Tsagalis (2011) 223 = (2023) 16; Currie (2016) 58, 69–70.
[162] Currie (2016) 58–9.
[163] Reinhardt (1961) 357; Schwabl (1986) 59; M. W. Edwards (1991) 143; Di Benedetto (1994) 112; Currie (2016) 58.
[164] Reinhardt (1961) 357; Currie (2016) 59.
[165] Kullmann (1960) 42, (1991) 445–6 = (1992) 121; Reinhardt (1961) 362; Willcock (1983) 484; A. T. Edwards (1985) 223–7; M. W. Edwards (1990) 312; Ford (1992) 158–60; Heubeck (1992) 368; Janko (1992) 314; Danek (1998a) 475; Currie (2016) 59.
[166] Currie (2016) 69.   [167] Currie (2016) 70 with n. 185 (for more examples).

argumentation, the same principle of prismatic reflection[168] and refraction of the model,[169] whether a motif or a character.

As regards "direction of influence," we need to address the possibility that the story of Achilles "was primary and served as a matrix for the narrative about Patroclus in the *Iliad*."[170] According to M. L. West's theory,[171] the poet of the *Iliad* knew the story of Achilles' death at the Scaean Gates and its aftermath (funeral, funeral games) but was unaware of the Memnon story. He had sung an *Iliad* which included the death of Achilles soon after Hector's death,[172] when Achilles (more or less like Patroclus in the *Iliad*) forgot or ignored his mother's prophecy and continued the pursuit of the Trojans to the Scaean Gates, where he was killed by Paris and Apollo. That was, so the argument goes, the *Urilias*. However, the poet changed his mind[173] and at some point in his life decided to exclude from his poem the story of the death of Achilles. He, then, transferred features and scenes which he had used in the *Urilias* for the story of Achilles (funeral and funeral games for Achilles) to the story of Patroclus (funeral and funeral games for Patroclus). Furthermore, he added a final section, i.e. the ransoming of Hector. Years later, a different poet decided to compose a poem on Achilles' death. Since he did not know the *Urilias* that was not a written epic, according to M. L. West, he had to find a solution to the problem of narrating Achilles' death that was not narrated in the written *Iliad*. So he brought in Memnon, a new Trojan ally who arrived at Troy after Hector's death. He then used the story of Patroclus' death in the *Iliad* and Achilles' revenge on Hector as a model for creating a similar plot within his poem: Memnon killed Antilochus (who was Achilles' friend already in the *Iliad*) and Achilles avenged his death by killing Memnon. Last, the funeral and funeral games for Patroclus were transferred to Achilles. Central to M. L. West's theory is the question of the "direction of influence," especially since his approach is not against neoanalysis but against its core results.[174] In fact, M. L. West's argumentation suggests that it was the poet of the *Aethiopis* who operated in neoanalytical manner, transferring motifs and scenes from the *Iliad*, whereas neoanalysis has claimed the exact opposite. In this light, the issue is not about whether we are dealing with the transference of motifs, scenes, and episodes but about the direction of influence.

Among an entire host of contact points between the *Memnonis* and the *Iliad* I will discuss one of them, which is key for deciding about the direction of influence.[175] The armor made by Hephaestus can hardly be primary for Achilles

---

[168] *Prismatisches Auseinanderspiegeln*: Schadewaldt (1965⁴) 191–3.
[169] *Brechung eines Vorbildmotivs*: Schoeck (1961) 11.   [170] M. L. West (2003b) 6.
[171] M. L. West (2003b) 1–14 = (2011b) 242–64.   [172] See *Il*. 18.95–6.
[173] M. L. West does not explain why this poet changed his mind. For discussion and criticism of this view, see the bibliography in Currie (2016) 59 n. 129.
[174] This is not the place to offer a full-scale discussion of M. L. West's theory. Kulmann (2005, 9–28) addresses most of the relevant issues and offers a rebuttal.
[175] See Currie (2016, 60–72), whose interpretation I follow (with some qualifications of my own).

and derivative for Memnon because, as M. L. West contends, only one hero may possess a divine armor and this can only be Achilles, whose acquisition of this armor is fully presented in the *Iliad*.[176] However, if Memnon's divine armor was described in detail in the *Memnonis*, as may be assumed by the fact that the otherwise sparing-in-details summary of Proclus does not fail to tell us that Memnon's armor was made by Hephaestus,[177] the claim about the priority of Achilles' armor is turned on its head. Moreover, the divine armor Achilles acquires in *Iliad* 18 is his second set, since he had received another Hephaestus-made armor from his father Peleus when departing for Troy.[178] It is only because this first divine armor was lent to Patroclus,[179] from whose dead body it was taken by Hector,[180] that Achilles needed a new divine armor. In this light, the situation we encounter in the *Iliad* can hardly be primary. It is the result of the specific way of presentation of the Patroclus story. We may ask: was it necessary for Patroclus to borrow Achilles' armor in order to route the Trojans? The motivation is, of course, that they thought that Achilles had returned to the fighting,[181] but this does not mean that Hector had to take the armor from Patroclus' dead body. After all, he was unable to get Achilles' horses,[182] the other gift of divine origin that Peleus gave Achilles on his departure for Troy.[183] The loss of the first divine armor creates the conditions for a glaring presentation of the manufacturing of Achilles' second armor in book 18. If Memnon's divine armor was described in detail in the *Memnonis*, it is reasonable to think that the *Iliad* transferred this description to Achilles' divine armor. Moreover, that Achilles' divine armor cannot be primary is suggested by the fact that when Hector and Achilles are facing each other in book 22 they have both divine armors; Hector has Achilles' first armor that he took from Patroclus, Achilles has the second divine armor that Hephaestus made for him in book 18. For the *Iliad* there is considerable poetic gain. First, Achilles sees Hector wearing the armor which Patroclus was wearing when he was sent to battle. That the external appearance of his friend's killer reminds Achilles so starkly of the last memory of his friend departing for the battlefield increases the dramatic output of this scene (*Il.* 22.322–3). This significant innovation is important for the *Iliad* but creates problems for the rest of the Trojan saga, since the contest for Achilles' arms between Ajax and Odysseus (ὅπλων κρίσις) makes sense only if there is a single set of arms.[184] Second, the use of divine armors by both Hector and Achilles replicates the climactic encounter between Memnon and

---

[176] See M. L. West (2003b) 9–10 = (2011b) 255.   [177] *Aeth.* arg. ll. 185–6 Severyns.
[178] *Il.* 17.194–7, 18.84–5.   [179] *Il.* 16.130–44.   [180] *Il.* 17.125.   [181] *Il.* 16.41–2.
[182] Zeus' words (*Il.* 17.448–50) suggest a deliberate distinction between Achilles' arms that will be taken by Hector and Achilles' horses that will safely return to the Achaean camp.
[183] Given by the gods as a whole: *Il.* 16.866–7; 17.443; by Poseidon: 23.277–8.
[184] *Il. parv.* arg. ll. 208–9 Severyns.

Achilles in the *Memnonis*, where both had divine armors. Third, the *Iliad* erases, in contrast to the *Memnonis*, the theme of impenetrability of the divine armor, thus stressing the inevitability of death instead of the prospect of immortality (*Memnonis*).

A neglected aspect of the problem, which does not concern a contact point between the two epics, is the *non sequitur* of the end result. If the poem or song on the death of Achilles had been composed by the poet of the *Iliad* before he composed the *Iliad* and served as his model for the resonances of Achilles' death in the *Iliad*, then Arctinus would only have at his disposal the *Iliad* to draw on with respect to Achilles' death. For if Arctinus knew of the poem on the death of Achilles that the poet of the *Iliad* had composed, then he would have been influenced by this poem, which offered a full version of Achilles' death, and not by the *Iliad*, in which Achilles' death did not feature. After all, M. L. West contends that it is the *Iliad* that influenced the *Aethiopis*. In this vein, we would have to assume that the poet of the *Iliad* and Arctinus had both transferred motifs, the former to the *Iliad* from a Homeric but pre-Iliadic poem on the death of Achilles, the latter from the *Iliad* to the *Aethiopis*. Thus, we would have a neoanalytical process of motif transference in which on the one hand the source-text would be the full version of Achilles' death (a lost Homeric epic) and the target-text the elliptical version of Achilles' death (the *Iliad*), and on the other the source-text would be the elliptical version of Achilles' death (the *Iliad*) and the target-text the full version of Achilles' death (the *Aethiopis*). The use of the same text (the *Iliad*) as target-text and source-text for the same topic (the death of Achilles) is unlikely.

1.4 Entextualization

Entextualization is "the process of rendering a given instance of discourse a text, detachable from its local context."[185] It should be distinguished from textualization,[186] which designates the act or process of recording "the verbal component of an oral text in written form."[187] Entextualization is key to the notion of an enduring oral text, which is objectified, concrete, and identified as such by performers and audiences. It is a dynamic process and not an end point in the developing and shaping of an oral tradition. By operating on various levels (conciseness of plot, narrative cohesion, standardized structure, intratextual and intertextual associations, uniformity of diction), entextualization tends towards homogeneity through a process of reshaping material according to a norm that is gradually created as singers

---

[185] Urban (1996) 21; cf. Baumann and Briggs (1990) 73; Wilce (2009) 32–3.

[186] In this study I have decided to adopt the terminology used by Ready (2019) 18. In previous studies (Tsagalis 2011, 211 = 2023, 4–5) I have employed "textuality" in the sense of "entextualization," and "textification" in the sense of "textuality."

[187] Ready (2019) 18.

progressively build on the material not only of their previous performances but also of the performances of other singers to which they had been exposed time and again in their lives. In the Homeric epics some statements suggest transmission from one singer to another.[188] Phoenix says: "thus it was in the old days also, the deeds that we hear of from the great men" (οὕτω καὶ τῶν πρόσθεν ἐπευθόμεθα κλέα ἀνδρῶν | ἡρώων, Il. 9.524–5).[189] Telemachus guesses that Nestor or Menelaus may have "heard the story [sc. of Odysseus] from some wanderer like him" (ἢ ἄλλου μῦθον ἄκουσας | πλαζομένου, Od. 3.94–5). He also defends Phemius because the newest song [that he sings] is what the audience applauds the most (τὴν γὰρ ἀοιδὴν μᾶλλον ἐπικλείουσ' ἄνθρωποι | ἥ τις ἀκουόντεσσι νεωτάτη ἀμφιπέληται, Od. 1.351–2),[190] and adds that the Achaeans "will carry his [sc. Orestes'] fame widely, even as a song for those to be" (οἴσουσι κλέος εὐρὺ καὶ ἐσσομένοισιν ἀοιδήν, Od. 3.204).

Ready[191] has drawn attention to quotations of passages (messages, speech-acts, catalogues)[192] in the Homeric epics. He claimed that these utterances are distinct and detachable[193] from their context and, as such, they are entextualized. Drawing on the work of Barber, who has suggested that performances in oral traditions are not completely instantaneous but involve a "textual dimension,"[194] Minchin argued that "forward planning and rehearsal were essential to a successful oral performance of the Homeric kind" by discussing passages in the *Iliad* and the *Odyssey* that "were the product of composition and rehearsal in tandem."[195] By studying type-scenes, speech-acts (both familiar such as rebukes, protests, threats, expressions of dread, and unfamiliar like question-strings and their responses), as well as lists and catalogues, Minchin suggested that by means of common cognitive scripts reflecting everyday life (type-scenes) or templates (such as address/reproach, problem, generalization/broader perspective, proposal for rebukes) or spatial memory (Catalogue of Ships) or thematical

---

[188] See Ready (2018) 329, to whom I owe the following examples; differently Scodel (2002) 78.
[189] See pp. 34–5, 61; Rawles (2018, 44) draws attention to οὕτω, arguing that it "might function, in Simonides as well as in Homer, as the *introduction* to a paradigmatic narrative" (emphasis in the original).
[190] I have paraphrased the Greek (hence the omission of inverted commas).
[191] Ready (2018) 320–50.
[192] E.g. *Il.* 2.11–15 repeated in 2.28–32, 8.402–8 repeated in 8.416–22 (message); *Il.* 2.317–30 (Calchas' prophecy, which is recalled by Odysseus, is associated with the stone into which Zeus metamorphosed the serpent that ate eight sparrows and the mother bird); *Il.* 14.313–28 (the framing of the catalogue of Zeus' former concubines suggests that the catalogue is a unified, detachable, and perhaps ready-made piece). We may also add object description: *Od.* 4.614–19 (notice the standard, for objects, structure of the description of the mixing bowl [614: summary; 615–16: material; 615, 617: workmanship; 614: value; 616: notable feature; 617–19: history]); see Minchin (2001) 106–12.
[193] On the "portability" of parts of an oral text, see Porter (2022) 59–60.
[194] Barber (2005) 265.
[195] Minchin (forthcoming).; see also Fowler (2004a) 230, who suggests that, in the case of Homer, Greek epic moved from a phase of oral composition with "many consciously fixed passages" through premeditation to a phase of "mostly fixed, and therefore written" compositions.

groupings (Phaeacian nobles), often facilitated by such linguistic features as rhyme, alliteration, and assonance (list of Nereids), oral poets organized and rehearsed several segments prior to performance.[196]

Tracing entextualization in the case of book 10 is important since it implies that its detachability from the *Iliad* should not be explained by assuming that it has been interpolated to a fixed poem. Entextualization marks the ability of a given utterance to endure as a cohesive and coherent entity, an oral text forming part of a larger oral text, the *Iliad*. In this vein, I will briefly explore the following devices which contribute to the entextualization of the *Doloneia*: cohesion, coherence, and evaluation.

A major manifestation of cohesion is the creation of boundaries. Boundaries pertain to the demarcation of beginnings and endings, which delineate an utterance as something concrete and identifiable.[197] By marking the limits of an utterance for his audience, the performer indicates its discrete identity, completeness, and objectification.[198] The *Doloneia* heralds its opening and closure with thematic parallelism. The book begins with the two Atreidae, Agamemnon and Menelaus, in the Achaean camp and ends with the two spies, Odysseus and Diomedes, who return to the Achaean camp. Thematic parallelism is also used to demarcate internal boundaries between the *Nyktegersia* and the *Doloneia* proper (the nocturnal missions of the Achaean and Trojan spies). Two assemblies are held in the first part, one by the Achaeans and another by the Trojans; two spying missions occur in the second, one by the Achaeans (Diomedes and Odysseus) and another by the Trojans (Dolon). Thematic parallelism is further employed to delineate the two phases of the night events, which involve the deaths of Dolon and Rhesus. Furthermore, the *Doloneia* seems to have been based on a structural pattern that is used several times in the *Iliad*[199] and may well reflect a cognitive script by which the mind of the poet organizes and presents information:[200] two narrative lines including certain similar features are first presented separately and then converge:

---

[196] E.g. *Il.* 2.422-9 (type-scene); *Od.* 17.46-51 (speech-act: rebuke), *Od.* 1.169-77 and 1.179-89, 194-5 (speech-act: question and answer); *Il.* 7.161-9, 8.253-7 and 261-6, 18.39-49, *Od.* 8.110-14 (lists and catalogues).

[197] See Bauman (2004) 4.   [198] See Scheub (2002) 95.

[199] *Iliad* 2-3: (A1) 2.455-83: similes for the march of the Achaean army, (A2) 2.494-760: Achaean catalogue of ships, (B2) 2.816-77: Trojan catalogue of forces and allies, (B1) 3.2-7: simile for the Trojans marching, (A) + (B) 3.15ff.: armies clash/*Iliad* 20: (A) 20.33-40: list of pro-Greek gods, (B) 20.68-74: list of pro-Trojan gods, (A) + (B) 20.75ff.: gods clash/*Iliad* 22: (A) 22.7-24: Achilles arrives at the walls of Troy (brief dialogue with Apollo), (B) 22.25-130: Hector stays outside the walls (parents beg him in vain to enter the city, dilemma), (A) + (B) 22.131ff.: Achilles and Hector come close, Achilles pursues Hector, the two heroes fight.

[200] On cognitive scripts lying behind regularly employed structural patterns, such as type-scenes, see Minchin (2001) 33-44.

Achaeans	Trojans
pressing need	desire to find out the enemy's intentions
council of the leaders	assembly
decision to send spies into the enemy camp	decision to send a spy into the enemy camp
preparation of the spies (clothing and arming)	preparation of the spy (clothing and arming)

> The Achaean spies ambush the Trojan spy
> They find out about the purpose of the Trojan spying mission
> They find out about the arrival of Rhesus
> They kill the Trojan spy
> They infiltrate the enemy camp, kill Rhesus and steal his horses
> They return in haste to their camp

Thematic parallelism and structural patterns help define boundaries, and boundaries make an utterance cohesive. As such the utterance is entextualized and may outlast the moment.

Cohesion is one of the ways coherence is created. Coherence means clarity and makes an utterance understandable.[201] In oral texts, coherence is established by both audience and performer. Listeners fill in the gaps by activating their knowledge of the local cultural universe, in which the performed oral text belongs, and of related oral texts.[202] The performer offers gaps that he assumes his audience will be able to fill in or "will not be bothered by if they remain."[203] Gaps may take the form of thematic lacunae only if seen within the boundaries of the given oral text. However, knowledge of both the larger deposit of themes shared by the tradition and allusion to their specific manifestations in other oral texts may render these gaps intelligible to the audience or non-important.[204] Both Dolon and Rhesus fall in the first category. The highly elliptical information given with respect to these two figures suggests that they may have been known to the audience. Dolon recalls the traditional character[205] of the

---

[201] Ready (2019) 19.
[202] See Seitel (2012) 83. That the audience's prior knowledge of abbreviated stories is taken for granted and that this knowledge has been acquired by listening to epic poetry is hinted at by (a) the request for a song (e.g. *Od.* 8.492; 9.263–6; 12.70; 14.196–201) and (b) the use of diction pertaining to an aural reception of stories (e.g. *Od.* 1.298–300; 3.193, 3.203–4).
[203] Ready (2019) 21.
[204] On the narrator relying on audience inattention with respect to several gaps, see Scodel (1999) 59–62.
[205] The earliest (*pace* Schefold 1993, 228 fig. 240) iconographical depiction of Dolon is seen on a Middle Corinthian cup dated to 590–575 BC (Brussels, Bibl. Royale). Telamonian Ajax is facing Aeneas, and Achilles is fighting against Hector. Locrian Ajax and Phoenix are the two Greek cavalrymen who

"arrogant layman"[206] who desires more than he deserves and is punished by real heroes. It is reasonable, I think, to assume that Rhesus was a familiar character to the audience of the *Iliad*, perhaps known from oral epic traditions that featured other versions (the "Pindaric" and "oracle")[207] regarding his involvement in the Trojan War.[208]

Evaluation of an utterance is based on the utterance's distinct identity and consolidation. A character may evaluate a claim by embedding in the text the thoughts of the audience about a feature that is significant to the poem. The *Doloneia* offers an impressive example of this process. When Dolon reveals to the Achaean spies that Hector has promised to give him the horses and chariot of Achilles (10.391–3), Odysseus reacts with an ironic smile before he tells him that these horses are meant to be driven only by Achilles, the son of a goddess. Odysseus' smile suggests a negative evaluation of Dolon's arrogant claim.[209] The horses of Achilles seem to acquire a durability that is not restricted to this context. Three of the four are immortal, the gift of Poseidon or the gods collectively to Peleus when he married Thetis. Their fate will be played out later in the *Iliad*, when Hector (the man who promised them to Dolon) will fail to take them from Patroclus. Achilles' horses have a distinct identity that bridges the epic tradition, since they are associated with events preceding the moment of Dolon's claim and Odysseus' smile[210] and pertain to future events.[211] By evaluating Dolon's contention, Odysseus seems to consolidate and objectify the utterance about Achilles' horses. The audience may soon re-evaluate them against this rich backdrop as the plot unfolds.

---

are balanced by Hippocles and Sarpedon, respectively. Each cavalryman is unarmed and guards a second horse that belongs to the hoplite next to him. Dolon belongs to a separate, third register, which is neither that of hoplite fighting nor that of cavalry. Snodgrass (1998, 121) claimed that the iconography of this vase offers a mixture of scenes from different sources, which may be literary (e.g. the *Iliad* and the *Cypria*) alone or literary and non-literary. The Corinthian cup suggests both that the story of Dolon was strongly associated with the Trojan War myth, and that Dolon may have been so well known to the viewers of the vase that, even when depicted in such an elliptical manner (i.e. without any attribute and in the absence of Diomedes and Odysseus), he could evoke the episode of the *Doloneia* by means of his position on one knee and with his head looking behind.

[206] Thersites too belongs to this category. Physical ugliness (*Il.* 2.217–19, 10.316), which is typical of these characters, is to be contrasted with the good looks of other Homeric heroes. He is punished by Odysseus in *Iliad* 2 and killed by Achilles in the *Aethiopis*. His insolence is epitomized in his enmity towards the two key figures of the Homeric tradition, Achilles and Odysseus (see *Il.* 2.220–1: ἔχθιστος δ' Ἀχιλῆϊ μάλιστ' ἦν ἠδ' Ὀδυσῆϊ | τὼ γὰρ νεικείεσκε). On Thersites, see Chantraine (1963) 18–27; Ebert (1969) 159–75; Rankin (1972) 36–60; Feldman (1979) 3–16; Nagy (1979 = 1999²) 259–62; Funke (1981) 239–58; Andersen (1982) 7–34; Postlethwaite (1988) 123–36; Thalmann (1988) 1–28; Arnould (1989) 510–14; Vodoklys (1992) 21–2 and 37–47; Barker (2009) 56–60.

[207] On these versions, see chapter 7.

[208] The information given about him in the *Doloneia* is elementary since no explanation is offered about his sudden arrival at Troy in the last year of the war. He does not speak or act at all in *Iliad* 10. He is brought into the plot to be killed by Diomedes.

[209] Contrast Nestor's modest offer of "a black sheep, female, with a lamb beneath" (*Il.* 10.215–16); see Fenik (1986) 180 n. 10.

[210] They were a wedding gift from the gods or Poseidon to Peleus; see pp. 107 n. 19, 114 n. 47, 119–20, 240.

[211] After his death, Hector will be dragged by Achilles' horses to the Achaean camp.

1.5 Mythological Reference and Epic Allusion

A central issue associated with oral intertextuality pertains to our ability to determine whether thematic echoes indicate general knowledge of mythological material or specific allusion to other oral epic traditions. This is a bigger topic concerning Homeric epic at large. In this vein, I will first offer some general remarks, then continue with specific observations pertaining to the *Iliad* and the *Odyssey* and conclude with a particular example from the *Doloneia*.

Mythological reference and epic allusion[212] both presuppose that the audience is familiar with a saga or a specific manifestation of it in an oral epic tradition on which the target-text draws. When we discuss these two ways of indexing within the universe of oral epic traditions, absolute dichotomy and mutual exclusion should be avoided.[213] Instead, it is better to speak about "and" than "versus," in the sense that there are cases in which we are dealing with reference to mythical material in general, while in other cases the allusion seems to point to pre-existing oral epics. In the case of Homeric epic, the use of metapoetic diction[214] and imagery,[215] the reference to performance conditions and manner of performance,[216] and the existence of a thick web of intratextual associations within and intertextual references between the *Iliad* and the *Odyssey*[217] suggest a profound self-awareness of both Homeric epics[218] and allow for the possibility that they are marked by a developed and nuanced form of orality, according to which cross-references between oral epic traditions are possible.[219] In this way, we may envisage a situation in which both mythological[220] and poetic allusion are at work as far as the entire poem or epic tradition is concerned.[221] To put it simply: each case should be judged on its own merit. Sometimes we may be dealing with allusion, whereas in other cases reiteration on the level of themes and phraseology

---

[212] See Burgess (2006) 148–89; Currie (2006) 1–45, (2012) 184–209, (2016) 9–11.
[213] Balanced discussions by Dowden (1996) 60–1; Fowler (2004a) 228–30.
[214] See pp. 29–31.   [215] See p. 30.
[216] See Thalmann (1984) 118–24; González (2013) 194–6, 344–8, 419–21; Tsagalis (2018a) 18–29.
[217] See pp. 28, 30, 38, 40, 45–8, 51.
[218] R. B. Rutherford (2001, 135) acknowledges the self-consciousness of both Homeric epics but argues that the *Odyssey* is a much more self-conscious poem than the *Iliad*, since "it includes more overt reference to powers and practitioners of poetry, and specifically heroic epic"; see also Maronitis (1998) 60–1 = (2004) 102–3.
[219] See Dowden (1996) 47–8; Burgess (2001) 61–4 and 132–5, (2006) 148–89; Tsagalis (2008), (2011) 209–44 = (2023) 3–33; Foley and Arft (2015) 91–5; Nelson (2023) 16–72. Differently, R. L. Fowler (1987) 3–52; Kelly (2012b) 221–65.
[220] Mythological allusion may be equally as demanding an enterprise as poetic allusion. It requires from the audience not only familiarity with too many aspects of Greek myth but also the ability to carry out on their own, on the spot, a selection of those features of a figure's mythical pedigree that are applicable to the context generated by the plot of the epic. However, it is important to avoid endorsing a culturally biased approach to sophistication. Treating oral epic as ignorant of or unripe for mythological reference or poetic allusion may seem like a masked redeployment of the now outmoded argument of its primitivity; see Havelock (1986) 37–8, 119, 122.
[221] See Currie (2016) 10.

may be immanent,[222] reflecting the traditional referentiality of the system of epic song.[223]

Neoanalysis and traditional referentiality are not mutually exclusive for the whole of Homeric epic.[224] Since their difference is a matter of degree and direction, it is better to accept that they are both helpful in exploring the vast and complex universe of Homeric poetry, instead of seeing them as representing an absolute dichotomy between literacy and orality. With respect to this issue, some scholars who see these two interpretive methods as representing an unbending polarity have suggested that Homeric epic alludes, through adaptation, refashioning, and distorting to "a distinctive and recognizable sequence of narrative events,"[225] which exist outside the framework of a written or oral text. This "middle road,"[226] which is different from the one presented above, is based on the assumption that distinctive and identifiable sequences of narrative events contain various "core and stable elements that would have been integral to any telling"[227] and that allusion to them is marked by "a sense of design…, even if it is only constructed at the level of audience reception."[228] The idea of a *Faktenkanon* or stable skeleton of narrative events is, of course, not new. Kullmann and Lord, who were the first to argue in favor of it, represent two eminent figures of the neoanalytical school and the oral theory, respectively. The essential question, though, concerns the creation, nesting, and distinctiveness of such a sequence of narrative events. The standardization of such sequences may have come into being through multiple tellings of these stories. However, the strongest and undoubtedly more influential form of telling of these tales may have been oral epics, whose diffusion and performance would have gradually led to the crystallization of certain mythical events *in a given order* and *around specific mythical figures*. It is possible that epic poetry created a suitable environment for the nesting of these sequences because it offered the opportunity for extended and detailed presentation of the relevant events included in them. It may have also given them a sense of authority and distinctiveness, turning them into a canon of events concerning specific mythical figures, who were progressively anchored to certain sagas. Moreover, standardized sequences of narrative events can coexist in Homeric epic with cases of specific, unidirectional phraseological repetition and recontextualization of type-scenes which are better explained by recourse to allusion to oral texts. Neither deliberate dictional repetition nor recontextualization of type-scenes

---

[222] Turkeltaub (2020, 166) has argued that some instantiations of traditional referentiality may have evolved from allusions: Achilles and Odysseus had perhaps been initially designated as "swift-footed" (πόδας ὠκύς, ποδώκης) and "rich in devices" (πολύμητις), respectively, because of certain events in their mythical biographies that had been recorded in pre-Homeric oral epics. According to this suggestion, the progressive diffusion of these expressions to various poetic environments resulted in the substitution of their early, limited scope by a wide, non-context-bound applicability.
[223] Foley (1991) 8; see also Clarke (2019) 32 diagram 2.
[224] See, e.g., M. W. Edwards (1991) 11–16; Currie (2016) 10–11.   [225] Nelson (2022) 57.
[226] Nelson (2022) 57.   [227] Nelson (2022) 57.   [228] Nelson (2022) 58.

are identifiable *in abstracto*. After all, since there are specific reprises between repeated elements over thousands of verses within a single epic, it is difficult to see why this is not the case between elements of different epics irrespective of the position we take with respect to their authorship.[229]

It is against this backdrop that I will continue with several observations in support of specific reprisal and deliberate allusion pertaining to the *Iliad* and the *Odyssey*.

(a) The *Iliad* refers to minor episodes of the Theban saga in a way that suggests that both the singer and the audience knew a fully fledged epic in which these episodes would have been at home.[230] It is even possible that certain verses may have been adapted from pre-Homeric Theban epics.[231] Likewise, with resonances of episodes or characters featuring in the Trojan section of the Epic Cycle. The large number of these resonances, their regular use in Homeric epic, and their diffusion in the entire *Iliad* and *Odyssey* indicate that this material may have featured in pre-Homeric oral epics.[232]

(b) The mythological paradigm of Meleager (*Il.* 9.524–99) and the large digression of Nestor (*Il.* 11.670–762) can neither be simple mythological references nor ad hoc inventions of the Iliadic epic tradition. In the former case, Phoenix's narrative is indexed as a story "of men of the past" that "has been heard." The use of the plural (ἐπευθόμεθα) is a reflexive annotation[233] which discloses not only that this tale is known by both teller and audience but also that they are both familiar with it by hearsay. This means that the story has been presented before, probably by bards who have sung it to different audiences.[234] That the source of this story is an oral epic on Meleager, a **Meleagris*, and not an Aetolian folk tale, has been argued by I.-Th. Kakridis, who drew the line between the firebrand-version that was suitable to a folk tale and the curse-version that is employed by Phoenix and stems from an epic source.[235] Likewise, Phoenix's narrative cannot be an Iliadic *autoschediasma*.[236] There are both internal and external reasons against such a possibility. If this story was invented by the poet of the *Iliad*, then Althaea would not have featured in the ascending scale of affection that included people

---

[229] A. Parry (1971) liv; Schwabl (1982) 14, 18, 32–3; Jones (1997) 36–7; R. B. Rutherford (2001) 126; Kelly (2007) 12 nn. 41–2; Burgess (2009) 64; Currie (2016) 11 and 262.

[230] See *Il.* 2.505, 563–6, 572; 4.8, 372–99, 389–90, 401, 406, 408; 5.125–7, 800–8; 6.222–3; 14.114–25; 20.224; 23.346, 679; on Homeric resonances of Theban epic poetry, see, e.g., Torres-Guerra (1995); Barker and Christensen (2011) 9–44, (2020) 47–89; Slatkin (2011) 99–119.

[231] M. L. West (2011a) 29.

[232] Key studies by Kullmann (1960) on the *Iliad*; Schischwani (1994) and Danek (1998a) on the *Odyssey*.

[233] See Hinds (1998) 1–5; on the plural indicating collective knowledge, see Nelson (2023) 74, 237, 239, 316.

[234] See the discussion of "metapoetic diction," pp. 28, 30, 38, 40, 45–8, 51.

[235] For other arguments in favor of a lost epic source for Phoenix's narrative, see I.-Th. Kakridis (1944) 13–27 = (1949) 18–27.

[236] *Pace* Willcock (1964) 141–54; see also Willcock (1977) 41–53.

who ask Meleager to return to the war. There is nothing in the plot of the *Iliad* that would explain such a radical change in her behavior, since she is the one who has cursed her son. Her presence in the scale of affection may well reflect an earlier epic source. Moreover, the rich iconographical record of the Meleager myth by far exceeds the limited events mentioned in the Iliadic mythological example. Therefore, it can hardly have resulted from an elliptical narrative squeezed in a single Iliadic speech that is foreign to the Trojan War myth. Turning to Nestor's extended digression,[237] the main argument in favor of allusion to pre-Homeric epic is that this Pylian tale is so meticulously reported that it speaks for a knowledge of the landscape of the western Peloponnese. The same is the case with the mention of Ereuthalion in a passage (*Il.* 7.132–56) where the account of a war between the Arcadians and the Pylians is marked by "too much circumstantial detail to have been concocted *ad hoc.*"[238] The existence of a poem or poems on the Pylian wars is also supported by the fact that the various elements of the story (Heracles' sack of Pylos, the Epeians' exploitation of the Pylians, Nestor's cattle raid, the Epeians' counter-reprisal by means of a full-scale attack, Nestor's triumph) are connected by causal links, which makes them stand together as a unified whole.[239]

(c) The argument in favor of exclusive mythological reference instead of epic allusion unavoidably would lead to the assumption that there was no pre-Homeric oral epic or epics dealing with the Trojan saga, since it would be absurd to claim that there were such pre-Homeric epics, but the *Iliad* and the *Odyssey* ignored them or did not know of their existence. If we accept that there were no such epics, we must adopt the view that the key events to this saga like the death of Achilles and the sack of Troy[240] were first rendered in hexameter by such written epics as the *Aethiopis*, the *Ilias parva* (which included the sack of Troy in its last section), and the *Iliou persis*. This line of thought leaves one to assume that the wrath of Achilles, which is the central topic of the *Iliad*, was the first version rendered in dactylic hexameter about the Trojan saga before Arctinus and that Lesches decided

---

[237] Bölte (1934, 343–7) discerns three lays in Nestor's narrative. The deepest lay goes back to the "border wars" in the Late Helladic period between neighbors. The second lay pertains to the "epicization" of the historically based account of a border war by the introduction of mythical characters who belong to local traditions pertaining to the sack of Pylos by Heracles and the reshaping of the tale into a Nestor-centered narrative. The third lay involves the story's infusion in the *Iliad* as an *exemplum* by means of which Nestor aims to convince Patroclus to carry out the difficult task of making Achilles somehow help the Achaeans. As for its transmission and inclusion in the *Iliad*, M. L. West (1988, 160–1) argues that the tradition about the Pylian wars, already shaped in epic form, migrated to Phthiotis and became part of the Iolcos cycle. It was there that it was connected with "the reservoir of late Mycenaean Thessalian epic, which ... must be postulated as the main source of the later Ionian tradition." An epic or epics dealing with this tale in a more expanded version may have been popular in Ionia, where the old stories from the motherland may have always been welcome after the wandering Pylians moved from south-west Peloponnese to Colophon (see also Bölte 1934, 346).

[238] M. L. West (2001) 29.   [239] Cantieni (1942) 67–8.

[240] On a complete list of events of predating and postdating the Iliadic plot to which the *Iliad* alludes, see Kullmann (1960).

to treat the death of Achilles and the sack of Troy. To rephrase: bards unanimously decided to sing only about the wrath of Achilles and not about any other event or phase of the Trojan War. This seems to be a questionable approach. Conversely, the Iliadic tradition displays such a profound and systematic concern with the death of Achilles, which is an event falling outside the limits of its plot, that it is almost certain that it draws on an epic rendering of this event.

(d) Homeric epic contains many resonances of events and themes of the Trojan War and its aftermath which do not fall within its plot and are in agreement with the content of Cyclic epic. These events and themes amount to Homeric allusions to pre-Homeric oral poetry that directly influenced the post-Homeric Cyclic epics and indirectly the *Iliad* and the *Odyssey*.[241] This seems a much more rewarding and possible line of interpretation than an alternative one, which assumes that at different times and places all the Cyclic poets (Stasinus, Arctinus, Lesches, Agias, Eugammon) drew on elliptical and highly abbreviated Homeric references to events and themes that did not fall within the plot of the *Iliad* and the *Odyssey* and developed them into fully fledged episodes and epic poems. Moreover, the diffusion of these events and themes throughout the plot of the two Homeric epics suggests that they have been intentionally used to create a backdrop against which the *Iliad*'s focus on the theme of *menis* and the *Odyssey*'s interest in the fate of a single hero would be evaluated by the audience. Such a strategy reflects the attempt of Homeric epic to highlight and promote its limited thematic focus (one theme: μῆνιν [*Il*. 1.1] and ἄνδρα [*Od*. 1.1]) and differentiate itself from the extended span of events covered in pre-Homeric oral epics dealing with what precedes and follows the events of the *Iliad* and the *Odyssey*. It can hardly be understood as a reaction to mythical material in general.[242]

(e) Allusive motif transference is signaled in Homeric epic. By creating narrative ruptures through the pointed alienation of a motif from a familiar narrative context, Homeric epic marks this estrangement as an allusion to the original context. This is a sophisticated way of writing into Homeric epic priority and direction of influence.[243] In like manner, the *Odyssey* alludes to the *Iliad* not through reference to events that took place within the plot of the latter epic but by means of phraseological reshaping, misuse, parody, adaptation, and expansion.[244] If this notion of influence is eliminated, then we would have to reject any form of influence of the *Iliad* on the *Odyssey*, of the *Theogony* on the *Works and Days*, of the *Thebais* on the *Epigoni*.[245] We would thus be faced with a picture of archaic

---

[241] On a list of cyclic resonances to the *Iliad* and the Odyssey, see Kullmann (2015) 120–5.
[242] See Tsagalis (2014a) 241–2.
[243] Motif transference cannot be explained as resulting from artistic representations (i.e. that a motif has been transferred from a work of art to Homeric epic) or from a vague notion of myth; see Kullmann (1960) 11; Schischwani (1994) 19–21.
[244] Maronitis (1983) 279–91 = (2004) 133–46; Pucci (1987); R. B. Rutherford (2001) 117–46.
[245] Currie (2012) 572–3.

Greek epic where the notions of poetic influence and dependence are completely absent. This seems to me an untenable position.

(f) The "connection" point is vital for deciding about the nature of a resonance. A detail can be either an ad hoc mythological invention of Homeric epic or a citation of another epic tradition. In *Il.* 23.826-9, the iron-weight that Achilles had taken from Eetion when he sacked his city and sets as prize in the funeral games in honor of Patroclus is a free invention of the *Iliad* without mythical precursors, aimed at linking past and present. By having Achilles set as a prize in the funeral games something belonging to Andromache's father (Eetion), the epic tradition of the *Iliad* reactivates the association between the fates of Hector, Patroclus, and Achilles. The iron-weight is unlikely to have featured in an earlier epic tradition that the *Iliad* is quoting. If that was the case, we would have to postulate the existence of a pre-Homeric epic narrating the sack of Eetion's city by Achilles in such detail that there would have been room for the mention of this insignificant object.[246] This is improbable. Equally unlikely is the possibility that this iron-weight featured in the funeral games for Achilles in the pre-Homeric **Memnonis* (the precursor of the post-Homeric *Aethiopis*) and that it was transferred from there to the *Iliad*. It is hard to see how this iron-weight would have been employed in the assumed source-text (the **Memnonis*), the more so since its use in the assumed target-text (the *Iliad*) leaves no narrative ruptures and is anything but secondary. Conversely, the reference to the exile of Philoctetes in Lemnos (*Il.* 2.721-5) seems to stem from a pre-Homeric oral epic, which the Iliadic tradition cites. It cannot have been created by free invention since it serves no purpose in the plot of the *Iliad*. Artistic influence must also be ruled out, given that the depiction of the wounding of Philoctetes is not attested before the fifth century BC,[247] and even if it was, but is simply not extant, it cannot have influenced the *Iliad* with respect to a brief reference to the hero's past and future role in the Trojan War. The reference to Philoctetes in the Catalogue of Ships amounts to an effective way of indexing a hero who plays no part in the Iliadic plot. Despite its condensed nature, his entry summarizes his function in a large part of the tradition of the Trojan War, stretching from his wounding and exile on Lemnos to his return to Troy. The summarizing aspect of the entry is not conditioned by the immediate context, since it exceeds the needs of the Catalogue of Ships by referring to events that happened before the *Iliad* and events that will happen after the *Iliad*. In addition, the entry uses with respect to the hero's wounding phraseology that is shared by Proclus' summary of the *Cypria*. Both employ the rare word ὕδρος for the snake that bit Philoctetes.[248] The use of this Iliadic (and Homeric)

---

[246] See Kullmann (1960) 14-15; Tsagalis (2014a) 242.
[247] See *LIMC* VII.1 s.v. "Philoktetes," nos. 12-78 (Pipili); for the earliest attestation of his wounding, see nos. 12-13; on the embassy to Lemnos, see no. 55a.
[248] *Il.* 2.723: ἕλκεϊ μοχθίζοντα κακῷ ὀλοόφρονος ὕδρου; arg. *Cypr.* l. 145 Severyns: ὑφ' ὕδρου πληγείς; see also Apollod. *Epit.* 3.26: ὕδρος δάκνει Φιλοκτήτην.

hapax legomenon in a digressive reference tagged to an entry of the Catalogue of Ships and its attestation in the summary of Proclus with respect to the same episode leave room for suggesting that the rare word ὕδρος was employed for the snake that wounded Philoctetes in the source-text on which both the *Iliad* and the *Cypria* draw.

(g) A yardstick that helps decide about epic allusion instead of mythological reference is the erasure of the fantastic and miraculous aspect of a story. Such an eradication may indicate epic allusion since it is not about the change of a mythical structure but a qualitative differentiation from the version of a story attested in the source-text. In the case of Iphigenia, criticism of mythical events is not restricted to her sacrifice but extends to the entire time frame within which the sacrifice was placed, i.e. to the expedition to Teuthrania and the second gathering at Aulis, which constitute the non-Homeric rendering of this story in epic form. The story of Telephus with the magical healing of his wound by Achilles' spear and the miraculous salvation of Iphigenia, who was transported from the altar in Aulis to the land of the Taurians, are thus excluded from the *Iliad*'s subject matter. The suppression of the fantastic aspect of this story indicates a process of poetic selection and criticism, not just of differentiation on the level of myth. This criticism pertains to a poetic version covering this mythical time frame.[249] The same observation is applicable to the story of Rhesus, as presented in the *Doloneia*. Only the part of Rhesus' story which is compatible with the subject matter and chronological blueprint of the *Iliad* is narrated. The fantastic element pertaining to the potential invincibility of Rhesus and his horses if they drank Scamander's water (and the horses grazed at its banks) is eradicated.[250] The *Iliad* eliminates the miraculous aspect of the tale of Rhesus in the same way it eliminates miraculous elements when treating material of cyclic provenance.[251] *Iliad* 10, then, conforms to a deep-seated technique that is systematically employed by the *Iliad* and pertains to poetic allusion to a source-text.

(h) The *Odyssey* seems to have incorporated material from west Greek epichoric versions of Odysseus' pre-Homeric past. The preoccupation with specific places (e.g. Aetolia, Elis, Thesprotia) on the mainland points to a sort of west Greek *koine* with respect to local epic poetry about Odysseus, which was absorbed, reshaped, and even obfuscated (to skim over potential disagreements) when the song of Odysseus' return from Troy started acquiring Panhellenic characteristics.[252] The same may be the case with another strand of epic poetry narrating Odysseus' return from Troy, known by the label *alternative Odyssey(s)*.[253] These versions, which may have been influenced by

---

[249] See Kullmann (2005) 26.   [250] See pp. 22, 125, 243, 299.
[251] See Griffin (1977) 39–43; Tsagalis (2011) 214–15 = (2023) 7–8.
[252] See Marks (2008) 83–111.
[253] See S. R. West (1981) 169–75; Reece (1994) 157–73; Danek (1998a); Tsagalis (2011) 222 = (2023) 15, *HomEnc* s.v. "Intertextuality," (2012a) 309–45 = (2023) 163–206.

proto-Panhellenic epic poetry of a cyclic tinge, aimed at placing Odysseus' adventures in the world of the eastern Mediterranean and are embedded in the false tales narrated by Odysseus.[254] The *Odyssey* strives to determine its poetic identity by means of a systematic comparison and rivalry with both the *Iliad* and other epic traditions, some of which narrated Odysseus' *nostos*. The constant and sophisticated manner by which the *Odyssey* pursues this goal and the means it employs to do so suggest that this epic has turned source-indexing into an effective device of self-evaluation. This is carried out by what has been called *Zitat*, a mechanism pertaining to source citation.[255] Since the *Odyssey* allusively captures other Odyssean epic traditions, we can see that Homeric epic engages in quoting its sources on a large scale.

In this chapter I have argued that oral, intertextual neoanalysis allows us to study the evolution and shaping of an oral epic tradition. It is, therefore, an interpretive method that may be fruitfully applied to the *Doloneia*, to which I will now turn my attention.

---

[254] A legitimate objection to this line of interpretation may be summarized as follows: since we are deprived of any direct access to the content of alternative versions of Odysseus' return in dactylic hexameter, how can we determine whether what is presented as an alternative within the Odyssean plot points to an *Odyssey* or even *Odysseys* before our *Odyssey*? In contrast to the Cyclic poems, which can, arguably, provide a thematic platform for evaluating the possibility of the existence of pre-Homeric oral epics to which the Homeric epics allude and/or draw on, the reconstruction of earlier, alternative versions of the *Odyssey* runs the risk of begging the question and may even seem to be a self-fulfilling prophecy. However, an argument from analogy may be helpful. On this issue, Danek (1998a, 16–23) has made important observations which I reproduce in brief. The parallel offered by a regularly used reference technique observable in the South Slavic tradition suggests that a similar technique may have been also employed by the early Greek epic tradition. The South Slavic analogy, which is particularly relevant to the case of the *Odyssey* because of its thematic association with the Serbo-Croatian Return Song, makes it possible that a similar diversity of alternative epic versions of Odysseus' return is to be expected. The South Slavic tradition is particularly useful for both its similarity and its differentiation from Homeric epic: while in the Bosnian-Muslim strand typology dominates as alternative courses of action are interpreted by the audience in accordance with underlying typical structures, in the Christian strand events are narrated in such a way that it is hardly possible to create alternative courses of action within the tight framework of a sequence of events leading to the same goal. Differently from the Bosnian-Muslim strand, the quasi-historical fixity of the material of the Christian strand allows for cross-associations to material beyond the content of the specific song. Within such a strand of the tradition, there are clear cases in which a given song cites concrete circumstances of the mythical material that fall out of the song's storyline and cannot be seen as manifestations of fundamental story types. Comparison with the *Odyssey* suggests that what is observed in both the Christian strand (historicization of mythical material, creation of links within the known myth) and its Bosnian-Muslim counterpart (thematization of alternatives) makes it possible that the alternatives evoked within the *Odyssey* refer to alternative versions of the *Odyssey*, not to an assumed typology of the homecoming song, which did not exist in this specific form in the Greek tradition.

[255] Danek (1998a) 1–28.

2
A First Thematic Approach
Intratextual References

Introduction

Iliad 10 has attracted more negative scholarly criticism than any other book of the poem. Various arguments have been put forward in an attempt to argue that it has been added to the epic at a not much later stage by a different poet, who took pains to integrate it into the plot. This is the view of many modern scholars,[1] who regard Danek's seminal study *Studien zur Dolonie*[2] as the decisive blow to any unitarian aspirations. At the other side of the spectrum stands the collaborative work by Dué and Ebbott, Iliad *10 and the Poetics of Ambush*,[3] that takes its lead from an oralist approach which characterizes research adopting the viewpoint of the Parry–Lord hypothesis. The two authors argue that the *Doloneia* represents the most extended Homeric example at our disposal of what they call "the poetics of ambush." This is a type of warfare markedly distinct from that of traditional fighting, which in the *Iliad* encompasses a wide range of forms of combat (*androktasiai*, duels, *aristeiai*, etc.). These two important works of scholarship set both the tone and pace for any serious engagement with the many thorny questions associated with *Iliad* 10.[4]

This large and complicated issue, which has implications for our understanding of the composition of the entire *Iliad,* constitutes the necessary backdrop to this chapter.[5] One of the main arguments of those scholars who regard the *Doloneia* as a major interpolation to the fixed *Iliad* is that there is absolutely no mention of any of its events in the following books of the epic and that nothing of what happens in *Iliad* 10 influences in any way the ensuing plot.[6] This argument is sometimes

---

[1] See p. 19 with n. 101.   [2] Danek (1988).   [3] Dué and Ebbott (2010).
[4] These two major monographs on *Iliad* 10 (Danek 1988; Dué and Ebbott 2010) are sophisticated and serious pieces of scholarship. They are both alert to the notion of Homer as oral poetry but understand the process of shaping of the *Doloneia* in different ways. Danek argues for a poet different from that of the rest of the epic who is trained in the techniques of oral verse-making, while Dué and Ebbott maintain that *Iliad* 10, as manifestation of "ambush" warfare, a theme with its own typology, is an integral part of the Iliadic epic tradition.
[5] See also my commentary on *Iliad* 9–12 for the Fondazione Lorenzo Valla (Tsagalis forthcoming).
[6] See, e.g., Reinhardt (1961) 248–9; M. L. West (2011a) 233. According to another line of interpretation, the themes of book 10 are Iliadic but their execution idiosyncratic, a sign of different authorship (Hainsworth 1993, 154). Chantraine's (1937, 59–68) argument concerning the high frequency of "late" features in the diction of *Iliad* 10 (pseudo-archaisms and modifications or adaptations of older forms,

paired with the claim that in books 1–9 there are no forward references to any of the events occurring in the *Doloneia*.[7]

The structure of this chapter involves the evaluation of the claim that the lack of reference to events constitutes a reliable yardstick for arguing in favor of interpolation (section 2.1);[8] the examination of intratextual associations on the level of theme and phraseology (sections 2.2.1–2.2.5); the assessment of the putative transference of a narrative sequence (section 2.3); and the interpretive gain from the authenticity of the *Doloneia* (section 2.4).

2.1 Reference to Events and Allusion to Themes: Drawing the Line

The interpolation of a scene, an episode containing multiple scenes, or an even larger section of a poem (e.g. an entire book) constitutes a major philological intervention in the text. In the case of the *Doloneia*, the argument in favor of interpolation has been partly based on the assumption that the "silence" of the rest of the epic regarding events that occur in book 10 indicates that this is a "foreign body" that was inserted into the *Iliad* at a later stage. I will now present and discuss four complementary reasons suggesting that the absence of reference to events does not constitute a dependable benchmark for supporting the argument of interpolation.

(i) The Iliadic tradition criticizes the validity of cunning intelligence ($\mu\hat{\eta}\tau\iota\varsigma$) as an appropriate means of action. Achilles' withdrawal from the Achaean coalition

---

real archaisms, and neologisms) has been seriously questioned; see Danek (1988) 41; Wathelet (1989) 231. For other debatable assumptions about dictional and structural oddities with respect to book 10, see Dué and Ebbott (2010); Tsagalis (forthcoming).

[7] Further ramifications of this line of thought are based on alleged similarities between *Iliad* 10 and the *Odyssey*, which have led to two, partly different, theories: (a) the poet of the *Doloneia* composed this episode after the composition of the *Odyssey* (Klingner 1940, 337–68 = 1964, 7–39); (b) while for most of the *Doloneia* the *Odyssey* must be considered as a source of influence, there is a tiny number of Odyssean passages that may have been influenced by an already fixed *Doloneia*, which means that a *Redaktor* may have changed these Odyssean passages at a later stage (von der Mühll 1940, 80–103) or that the poet of *Iliad* 10 knew of an *Urodyssee*, in which not only was the theme of revenge treated in a different way but also the "Telemachy" had not achieved its final form and the final reworking of the epic's *nostos* core had not yet taken place (Laser 1958, 385–425). Such approaches are of limited, if any, value with respect to the authenticity of *Iliad* 10, since they start from the a priori belief that the *Doloneia* is a major interpolation and only then and on this basis try to interpret similarities with the *Odyssey*. How moot this interpretation is can be seen from the fact that there are other Iliadic books showing a special affinity with the *Odyssey*. Are we to infer from the material shared between *Iliad* 24 and the *Odyssey* that the former is an interpolation? The several affinities between the *Doloneia* and the *Odyssey* may be due to their sharing the theme of ambush, whereas certain phraseological repetitions that are exclusively attested in these two texts show a putative transfer of diction from an *Iliad* with the *Doloneia* to the *Odyssey*; see the careful remarks by Danek (1988) 170–6.

[8] On the methodological assumptions on which these claims stand, see pp. 68–70.

represents a straightforward and transparent act against Agamemnon. His loss of τιμή "controls the plot of the *Iliad* all the way to the death of Patroclus."[9] Contrast this with the *Doloneia*, which celebrates the importance of μῆτις through the killing of Rhesus by Diomedes and Odysseus and the theft of his magnificent horses. The book seems "un-Iliadic" because of its positive presentation of μῆτις that leads to success, not because of its authorship.[10] Moreover, the theme of μῆτις may have been positively evaluated in another version of the *Iliad*, no matter how unusual this seems to be for us who instinctively treat the Homeric *Iliad* as the one and only version of this story. According to a scholion in the Venetus A on *Il.* 22.188, Homer alone is credited with the version of Achilles killing Hector in a duel, whereas "all the rest" (οἱ δὲ λοιποὶ πάντες) present Hector being killed in an ambush by Achilles.[11] An ambush of Hector by Achilles would require a plan based on μῆτις by the latter hero, who in that version may have been endowed with the polytropic skills of Odysseus. In fact, *Il.* 24.778–81 may represent a pointed correction of that tradition, in which Priam reassures the Trojans that they should not fear lest the Argives set an ambush against them while they collect wood for Hector's pyre, since Achilles had promised Priam that he would abstain from war for twelve days.[12] In this vein, it may be suggested that the triumph of μῆτις in the nocturnal spying mission by Diomedes and Odysseus sets book 10 apart from the *Iliad* that is marked by the guileless attitude of its major hero, Achilles. Turning to Odysseus, one of the protagonists of the ambush episode, it should be underscored that the *Iliad* features Odysseus in a key role in the theme of travel which is manifested in the πλοῦς ("sailing") type-scene that is regularly presented in the *Odyssey*. In *Il.* 1.430–87 Odysseus sails to Chryse to return Chryseis to her father. It would be false to treat this theme as un-Homeric because it is employed only in *Iliad* 1, lying outside the context of traditional warfare that dominates the Iliadic plot. On the contrary, it is much more productive to observe that the *Iliad* associates the themes of travel and cunning intelligence with Odysseus, to whom both themes are regularly tied in the *Odyssey*. Moreover, the πλοῦς-scene and the ambush (with which the themes of travel and cunning intelligence are related, respectively) are presented in the *Iliad* in their fullest forms, though it is in the *Odyssey* that they frequently feature. In light of these remarks, it is likely that the Iliadic epic tradition uses sparingly but in fully fledged form themes in which Odysseus is involved and which are repeatedly employed in the Odyssean epic tradition.

---

[9] Wilson (2002) 61 (with spelling modifications).   [10] Dué (2019) 128–34.
[11] σημειῶδες ὅτι μόνος Ὅμηρός φησι μονομαχῆσαι τὸν Ἕκτορα, οἱ δὲ λοιποὶ πάντες ἐνεδρευθῆναι ὑπὸ Ἀχιλλέως ("it is important that Homer alone says that he [Achilles] fought Hector in a duel. All the rest say that he was ambushed by Achilles"); on this point, see Dué and Ebbott (2010) 45: "it is far from clear what the scholiast means by the "rest" (οἱ δὲ λοιποί)...but the implications of the comment are easily grasped: in some versions, Achilles took Hector down by ambush"; see also Lambrou (2015) 130, (2018) 82–3.
[12] Priam's point to the Trojans would then be that they should not fear lest they are ambushed by Achilles in the manner Hector was ambushed by Achilles.

(ii) Book 10 involves events clustering around the theme of ambush, which is otherwise absent from the narrative of the *Iliad*, in which the emphasis is on fighting in the open.[13] Spying missions, night raids, and ambush episodes do occur in the Trojan War epic tradition (the ambush of Troilus,[14] of Helenus,[15] the *Ptocheia*,[16] the theft of the Palladium,[17] the Wooden Horse,[18] etc.), but they are left out of the picture in the *Iliad*, since they either do not belong to its time frame or conform to the poem's focus on battlefield confrontations. The theme of ambush in book 10 allows only for a glimpse into a poetics that differs radically from the *Iliad*'s depiction of warfare. The epic's indifference about events featuring in *Iliad* 10 may stem from the book's thematic marginalization, not from its absence from the "original" poem.

(iii) Reference to events occurring in book 10 may acquire a covert form. Implicit references do exist and are left to the audience to gauge. That they cluster in books flanking *Iliad* 10 is significant, since they are at relatively close distance from the *Doloneia*, allowing the listeners to connect the dots and make sense.[19]

(iv) Defining intratextual references is a vital and decisive matter. Thematic associations and phraseological repetition with an interpretive surplus are a well-known technique that runs through the entire *Iliad*, and it is all-pervasive for the *Doloneia* as well.[20]

2.2 Intratextual Associations on the Level of Theme and Phraseology

In this section I will examine several forms of intratextual associations referring to theme and phraseology. As regards the former, the focus will be on implicit intratextual references, on backward and forward associations with respect to themes, as well as on the bridging of backward and forward references. With respect to the latter, I will examine cases either of (nearly) exclusive use or of high contextual analogy.

2.2.1 Implicit Intratextual References

Even if we adopt the strictest notion of reference, i.e. reference to events, there are a handful of examples which show that events taking place in *Iliad* 10 are known

---

[13] Book 12, which features the siege of the Achaean walled camp, is another exception.
[14] Apollod. *Epit.* 3.32: Ἀχιλλεὺς ἐνεδρεύσας Τρωΐλον ἐν τῷ τοῦ Θυμβραίου Ἀπόλλωνος ἱερῷ φονεύει ("Achilles ambushed Troilus in the sanctuary of Thybraean Apollo and killed him"); see also Σ (A) on *Il.* 24.257b (= fr. 25* *GEF*).
[15] *Ilias parva* arg. l. 211 Severyns.   [16] *Ilias parva* arg. ll. 224–7 Severyns.
[17] *Ilias parva* arg. ll. 228–9 Severyns.
[18] *Ilias parva* arg. ll. 230–6 Severyns; *Iliou persis* arg. ll. 241–5 Severyns.   [19] See section 2.2.1.
[20] See sections 2.2.2–2.2.5.

to the rest of the epic. At *Il.* 8.489-91, Hector leads the army away from the camp by the banks of a swirling river, on "clean ground, where there showed a space not cumbered with corpses,"[21] but with no obvious reason. At *Il.* 10.194-202, the Achaean leaders hold a meeting outside the trench, since Hector's troops are further off. Their meeting is held on "clean ground, where there showed a space not cumbered with corpses, at the place whence Hector the huge had turned back." What is crucial in this case is that the correspondence is bidirectional, i.e. the meaning is constructed by knowledge of both passages (8.489-91→ 10.194-202 and 8.489-91← 10.194-202). The Trojan assembly in book 8 is held in a place like the one where the Achaean council takes place in book 10. At the Trojan assembly Hector speaks in such a way that he implicitly "announces" book 10: he declares his decision to stop fighting because night has fallen, orders that fires are lit while the army camps on the plain, and stresses the need to keep watch during the night. In a masterful narrative move, the *Iliad* has him even mention two key elements that acquire their full semantic potential in book 10: the danger of an Achaean ambush (8.522: λόχος), and the role of Diomedes (8.532: ὁ Τυδείδης κρατερὸς Διομήδης). But these two features are purposefully misdirected,[22] since Hector fears an assault on Troy while the army sleeps out on the plain and imagines Diomedes as the principal opponent of the Trojans when they attack the Achaean Wall.[23] Neither fear comes to pass but instead will assume a different form: the ambush against the Trojan army stationed on the plain, Diomedes as the spy who will kill both Dolon and Rhesus. Hector's speech, which ends with a

---

[21] Τρώων αὖτ' ἀγορὴν ποιήσατο φαίδιμος Ἕκτωρ, | νόσφι νεῶν ἀγαγὼν ποταμῷ ἔπι δινήεντι, | ἐν καθαρῷ, ὅθι δὴ νεκύων διεφαίνετο χῶρος.

[22] For two instructive analogies, see Andromache's and Achilles' speeches to Hector in *Il.* 6.407-39 and 22.351-2, respectively. Andromache expresses her fear about the potential killing of Hector by the Achaeans. She does not mention explicitly Achilles as the man who will kill Hector but does not fail to relate that it was Achilles who had sacked her native city, killed her father, Eetion, and her seven brothers, and taken her mother captive. This passage may be implicitly alluding to *Iliad* 22, when Achilles will "complete" the demise of Andromache's family by killing the most beloved person left to her, Hector. What will happen in the plot is covertly foreshadowed by means of misdirected intratextual references. In *Il.* 22.351-2, Achilles' warning to Hector that Priam will not be able to get back his son's corpse even if he offers to weigh out his bulk in gold (οὐδ' εἴ κέν σ' αὐτὸν χρυσῷ ἐρύσασθαι ἀνώγοι | Δαρδανίδης Πρίαμος) is an intratextual misdirection vis-à-vis Priam's ensuing successful supplication of Achilles in book 24, much as Hector's speech in book 8 is an intratextual misdirection vis-à-vis Diomedes' (and Odysseus') subsequent successful sally in the night in book 10. Moreover, the double naming of Priam by his patronymic next to his proper name (Δαρδανίδης Πρίαμος) in *Il.* 22.352 works similarly as a misdirection to Diomedes' double naming by his patronymic next to his proper name (Τυδείδης κρατερὸς Διομήδης) in *Il.* 8.532. Misdirection is in both passages further enhanced by the conditional/hypothetical formulations (8.532-3: εἴσομαι εἴ κέ μ' ὁ Τυδείδης κρατερὸς Διομήδης | πὰρ νηῶν πρὸς τεῖχος ἀπώσεται — 22.351: οὐδ' εἴ κέν σ' αὐτὸν χρυσῷ ἐρύσασθαι ἀνώγοι). For misdirection with respect to the treatment of Hector's body after his death, see J. V. Morrison (1992) 83-93; Reichel (1994) 192-7; de Jong (2012) 144 on *Il.* 22.337-54.

[23] *Il.* 8.517-22: κήρυκες δ' ἀνὰ ἄστυ Διὶ φίλοι ἀγγελλόντων | παῖδας πρωθήβας πολιοκροτάφους τε γέροντας | λέξασθαι περὶ ἄστυ θεοδμήτων ἐπὶ πύργων· | θηλύτεραι δὲ γυναῖκες ἐνὶ μεγάροισιν ἑκάστη | πῦρ μέγα καιόντων· φυλακὴ δέ τις ἔμπεδος ἔστω, | μὴ λόχος εἰσέλθῃσι πόλιν λαῶν ἀπεόντων; 8.529-34: ἀλλ' ἤτοι ἐπὶ νυκτὶ φυλάξομεν ἡμέας αὐτούς, | πρωῒ δ' ὑπηοῖοι σὺν τεύχεσι θωρηχθέντες | νηυσὶν ἔπι γλαφυρῇσιν ἐγείρομεν ὀξὺν Ἄρηα. | εἴσομαι εἴ κέ μ' ὁ Τυδείδης κρατερὸς Διομήδης | πὰρ νηῶν πρὸς τεῖχος ἀπώσεται, ἦ κεν ἐγὼ τόν | χαλκῷ δῃώσας ἔναρα βροτόεντα φέρωμαι.

reference to the horses "champing white barley and oats" while waiting for the dawn,[24] is a "seed" or "advance mention,"[25] looking forward to *Iliad* 10, where all the aforementioned features (the ambush, Diomedes, the horses) will become fully fledged narrative units. Therefore, the Trojan assembly which takes place in book 8 flags the advent of book 10.[26] Misdirection, both intertextual and intratextual, is a narrative technique that is systematically employed in both Homeric epics. As regards intertextual misdirection, the poet or epic tradition plays with the expectations of the audience, who are familiar with other versions of a scene, episode, or even larger stretches of narrative.[27] In the case of intratextual misdirection, the audience is prepared for an event that in the end does not occur or is delayed or takes place differently. Here, intratextual misdirection of an Achaean ambush and the role of Diomedes makes sense only in view of the *Doloneia*, which contains an ambush with Diomedes in the role of the protagonist. Furthermore, the fact that it is Hector who refers to an Argive λόχος and to Diomedes may also be part of a misdirection, though intertextual this time. By making Hector the speaker to voice these concerns, the *Iliad* creates the expectation of an ambush by Diomedes against Hector for those members of the audience who are familiar with such an alternative plotline for book 10.[28] The link also works backwards, from book 10 to book 8. When the audience hear that the Achaean leaders hold a council outside the trench, "at the place whence Hector the huge had turned back,"[29] they may recall the relevant scene in book 8 and realize that the narrative is picking up from where it left off at the end of *Iliad* 8. One may even argue that the reason the Achaean leaders convene *in this particular area* is to facilitate the association with the Trojan assembly in book 8. It is likely that there is poetic aim here, to create a balance between the Trojan assembly at *Iliad* 8 and the Achaean council at *Iliad* 10. This means that there is unity of composition, the reference in book 8 "announcing" book 10, the reference in book 10 acquiring its full meaning only in combination with the reference in book 8. If book 10 is omitted, then the fact that Hector leads his army away from the camp to hold an assembly in book 8 remains unexplained. In *Il*. 9.76 and 232 the Trojans have encamped near the ships and the Achaean Wall. Such considerations suggest that *Il*. 8.490-1 anticipates *Il*. 10.199-200. M. L. West's proposal that the poet of *Iliad* 10 inserted 8.490-1, "re-using one of his own verses to prepare for

---

[24] οἱ δ' ἵππους μὲν λῦσαν ὑπὸ ζυγοῦ ἱδρώοντας, | δῆσαν δ' ἱμάντεσσι παρ' ἅρμασιν οἷσιν ἕκαστος (*Il*. 8.543-4); see also the very end of book 8 (564-5): ἵπποι δὲ κρῖ λευκὸν ἐρεπτόμενοι καὶ ὀλύρας | ἑσταότες παρ' ὄχεσφιν ἐΰθρονον Ἠῶ μίμνον.

[25] See de Jong (2001) xvii.

[26] Cf. the generalizing statement in *Il*. 9.76 and 9.232-3 that Hector and the Trojans are close to the ships, which means that the danger for the Achaeans is imminent.

[27] On misdirection, see Prince (1973) 178-96; S. Richardson (1990) 174-8; J. V. Morrison (1992); de Jong (2001) xv; Rengakos (2002) 87-98 = (2006) 74-84.

[28] See chapters 5-6.   [29] *Il*. 10.200: ὅθεν αὖτις ἀπετράπετ' ὄβριμος Ἕκτωρ.

the *Doloneia*,"³⁰ postulates an all-powerful K-*Dichter* who composed book 10, added it to the fixed *Iliad*, which he altered in other places to fit his addition and made it the canonical version. This I find hard to accept.³¹ For if that was his plan, he would first and foremost insert in books 11–24 references to events taking place in book 10. But that he has not done, though he had ample opportunity.³²

At *Il.* 13.159–62 Meriones throws his spear against Deiphobus without result, since the spear is broken. We would expect Meriones to use a second spear, but he does not have one. On the way to his hut to get another spear he meets with Idomeneus and gets one from him. This case is markedly different from other instances (*Il.* 14.402–8, 22.289–95) of the pattern "A hits B but breaks or loses his spear,"³³ since at *Il.* 13.168 it is explicitly said that he had left his spear in his hut (ὅ οἱ κλισίηφι λέλειπτο). Why did Meriones have only one spear while fighting Deiphobus? Probably, because when he was on guard the previous night (in book 10) he had only one spear, since he had with him his bow, which he subsequently lends to Odysseus.³⁴ This is a case where an event taking place in book 10 is implicitly *presupposed* in a later part of the *Iliad* (book 13).³⁵

Another example is offered by *Il.* 14.9–10: Nestor takes the shield of his son Thrasymedes that had been left in the hut, because Thrasymedes carried his father's shield.³⁶ One would be left wondering why Nestor took his son's shield, were it not for *Il.* 10.255–7, where we were told that Thrasymedes had given Diomedes his sword and shield. When Diomedes returned from the spying

---

³⁰ M. L. West (2011a) 212 on *Il.* 10.490–1.
³¹ M. L. West's position resembles that of S. R. West (1989, 113–43), according to whom the supposed interpolator of *Odyssey* 24 inserted references to Laertes in the *Odyssey* to justify the presence of Laertes in book 24.
³² Why (e.g.) didn't he make Diomedes use Rhesus' beautiful horses instead of Aeneas' in the chariot race in *Iliad* 23?
³³ Janko (1992) 66 on *Il.* 13.165–8. In *Il.* 22.289–95, Hector asks "Deiphobus" (Athena) for a second spear.
³⁴ *Il.* 3.16–19, where Paris' first appearance in the epic is paired with an overabundance of equipment (he is wearing the hide of a leopard, has a bow, sword, and two spears), is a different case. Paris is even coming in front of the Trojan ranks (16: προμάχιζεν), which is inappropriate for an archer (M. L. West 2011a, 128 on *Il.* 3.16–20). Alexandrian scholars found fault with this description (Zenodotus: Σ[A] on *Il.* 3.18a, Aristarchus: Σ[A] on *Il.* 3.19–20, commenting on Paris' challenge of the Achaeans [19: προκαλίζετο]). Paris' stark presentation makes sense by assuming that "the bow is slung on his shoulder, not his hand" (M. L. West 2011a, 128 on *Il.* 3.16–20) and that his sword is placed inside its case. Moreover, in Homer only the τόξα (and quiver) are occasionally slung on the shoulders (*Il.* 1.45, 3.17), not the βιός (*Il.* 15.468, 24.605, *Od.* 19.577 = 21.75, 22.2), which is always held in one's hand (this difference is perhaps associated to the fact that the βιός, which is the older term, means "string," "cord," hence "bowstring"). This suggests that in *Il.* 10.260 Meriones had his bow in his hands before giving it to Odysseus. As a result, Paris' case should not be used to support the possibility that Meriones too had two spears (the bow being slung on his shoulders).
³⁵ See Shewan (1911) 144.
³⁶ We must assume that Thrasymedes fetched Nestor's shield while the night mission was taking place; otherwise the uncontested fact that he had kept his father's famous shield in *Il.* 14.11 is left unexplained.

mission, he and Odysseus met with Nestor.[37] It is a fair assumption that Odysseus had returned Thrasymedes' shield to his father, Nestor, and not to Thrasymedes himself, who was not inside the camp but among the guards outside of the Achaean Wall (*Il.* 9.81; 10.196, 229, 255).[38] This exchange of shields is not trivial. It is a compliment to Thrasymedes, who had given his shield to Diomedes for his nocturnal mission, and "perhaps implies his present glory in using his father's famous shield in battle."[39] It also anticipates Patroclus' borrowing of Achilles' armor,[40] the more so since Thrasymedes fights close to Patroclus at *Il.* 16.321-7.[41] It may even be the case that the pairing of Nestor's famous golden shield and Diomedes' corselet as the two pieces of armor that Hector sets on capturing at *Il.* 8.191-5 prefigures the association between Thrasymedes, Nestor, and Diomedes that we see in *Il.* 10 and 14.9-10. M. L. West's two alternatives, i.e. that the poet of the *Iliad* not only admitted the addition of the *Doloneia* by a different poet in his own work but also refashioned *Il.* 14.9-10 to make it compatible with book 10 (!), or that the poet of the *Doloneia* modified these lines "to make a link with his own invention," seem untenable.[42] The former scenario requires that the poet of the *Iliad* knew of the "new" *Iliad* that had been expanded by the *Doloneia*, that he found it better than his own, and that he adopted it.[43]

Another relevant case occurs in book 11: at a rather advanced stage of the fighting (Agamemnon and Hector had already routed the Trojans and the Achaeans, respectively), Odysseus and Diomedes join the battle (*Il.* 11.312-19) *without their troops and without any other Achaean leader around them*. When Diomedes is wounded, he mounts a chariot and retires, but we hear nothing of Sthenelus, who regularly accompanies him. When Odysseus is wounded, Menelaus runs to his help *from some distance*.[44] It seems that Diomedes and

---

[37] The only weapons mentioned explicitly after the return of the two spies in the Achaean camp are those of Dolon (*Il.* 10.570), which Odysseus placed in the stern of his ship as an offering to Athena.

[38] See Thornton (1984) 166. The case of Meriones' bow is different, since Odysseus had no reason to return it to Nestor, who was not related to him (i.e. Meriones). It is assumed that Odysseus returned the bow to Meriones, since the hero uses it in *Il.* 13.650.

[39] Thornton (1984) 166.

[40] Janko (1992) 152 on *Il.* 14.9-12. The two passages (*Il.* 10.255-7 and *Il.* 14.9-11) are strongly associated with one another by making unusually specific references to (a) Thrasymedes' shield (σάκος / ἀσπίς), and (b) the loaning of this shield to someone else (Diomedes, Nestor). There are two options: (i) 10.255-7 is composed later in order to explain 14.9-11; (ii) 14.9-11 presupposes 10.255-7—which proves the authenticity of the *Doloneia* or of a version of the *Doloneia* featuring the loaning of Thrasymedes' spear to Diomedes immediately before the nocturnal mission. Those who advocate option (i) must explain why reference is made so incidentally to Thrasymedes' shield in the context of book 14 (I owe this remark to one of the anonymous readers of my book).

[41] In *Il.* 17.377-83, Thrasymedes and his brother Antilochus have still not realized that Patroclus is dead. They learn the bad news much later. It is then that Menelaus sends Antilochus to Achilles, while Thrasymedes stays on the battlefield (*Il.* 17.685-705).

[42] M. L. West (2011a) 288 on *Il.* 14.9-11; see Shewan (1911) 144.

[43] For a refutation of the latter scenario, see p. 73 with n. 32.

[44] See Petegorsky (1982) 218-19, who observes that the theme of companionship between Diomedes and Odysseus in *Iliad* 11 is "prepared" by their joint mission in *Iliad* 10.

Odysseus joined the fighting after the rest of the Achaeans (their own troops included) because the poet had left them eating at the end of *Iliad* 10.[45]

The last case relates to the presentation of the Thracians in the *Iliad*. They are first mentioned in the Trojan Catalogue (*Il.* 2.844–5), where Acamas and Peiroos are named as their leaders. Both of them die before book 10 (Peiroos is killed by Thoas in *Il.* 4.520–38, Acamas by Telamonian Ajax in *Il.* 6.5–11). So, the word νεήλυδες used for Rhesus' troops complies with the extant version of Rhesus' myth of late arrival[46] and his status with the fact that at this point the Thracians are deprived of a leader. The Thracians play no role in the ensuing battle narrative of the poem, but this observation applies both to the troops of Acamas and Peiroos and to those of Rhesus.

All the aforementioned cases involve narrative elements which presuppose that book 10 is an integral part of the *Iliad*. The attempt by certain scholars to argue that a hypothetical K-*Dichter*, as well as inserting book 10, was able to make changes to the rest of the fixed *Iliad* with respect to a few minor features of a limited number of episodes, but *did not* do the same thing with the major events occurring in *Iliad* 10, seems unlikely.

2.2.2 Allusion to Themes: Backward References

Shared themes represent the most fertile field of intratextual associations between the *Doloneia* and the rest of the *Iliad*. Backward references, which refer to themes occurring in books preceding *Iliad* 10, span a range covering books 1–9.

A startling example is offered by the narrative sequence played out over pairs of episodes or, to put it differently, between the members of each of two pairs of episodes in books 1–2 and 9–10. This sequence is of great importance for the matter at hand, since it covers extended text units and concerns the overall cohesion of the plot; indeed, it lies at the heart of the poem's plan. *Iliad* 1–2 constitute the first pole of this narrative sequence. After Achilles' withdrawal in book 1, Agamemnon resorts in book 2 to the πεῖρα of the troops. The result, which is achieved initially with the help of Athena and Odysseus[47] and then by the calming speeches of Nestor, Odysseus, and Agamemnon,[48] is that the Achaeans will be instilled with courage and will fight in high spirits in book 4. We see here a close thematic link involving the insubordination of Achilles and the renewal of the army's desire to fight. Likewise, *Iliad* 9–10 present us with an analogous pair. Book 9 reshuffles the narrative cards played in book 1, since Achilles' defiance is

---

[45] Notice how Diomedes is portrayed in *Iliad* 9. He is not a member of the Embassy to Achilles, and his two speeches are tellingly placed at the beginning and end of the book. His last speech at the closure of book 9 "announces" book 11, in which his late appearance (together with Odysseus) presupposes book 10.
[46] Fenik (1964) 6–7.   [47] *Il.* 2.173–206.   [48] *Il.* 2.279–393.

renewed by means of his staunch refusal to return to the war; his wrath against Agamemnon and everything that man stands for is, if anything, even more forcefully articulated. Book 10[49] plays a role in relation to book 9 equivalent to the one played by book 2 in relation to book 1, since the highly successful spying mission reignites the fighting spirit of the Achaeans, who will launch in book 11 a large-scale attack headed by Agamemnon himself against the Trojans.[50] In these terms, *Iliad* 10 is to *Iliad* 9 what *Iliad* 2 is to *Iliad* 1. Such a symmetrical pairing on the basis of thematic correspondences is a strong sign of compositional unity.[51] Remove *Iliad* 10, and the renewal of Achilles' negative attitude in the Embassy is left suspended, followed by a wholescale attack of the Achaeans, who are left hopeless at the end of *Iliad* 9.[52] Moreover, books 2, 9, and 10 share a triangular relation with respect to certain thematic patterns.[53] *Iliad* 2 begins with Zeus' sleeplessness (A), the sending of the Dream to Agamemnon, and the summoning of an assembly of the Achaean army (B); *Iliad* 9 starts with a storm simile (C) and continues with an assembly of the Achaeans (B); *Iliad* 10 begins with Agamemnon's sleeplessness (A), a storm simile (C), and continues with a council of the Achaean leaders (B). In this vein, book 10 shares with book 2 the same relation it shares with book 9. The kinship between these three books is reinforced both by the role of Agamemnon, who is the key actor in their shared thematic patterns, and by the critical situation the Achaeans are facing. The presence of book 10 seems, therefore, crucial to this triangular relation. It marks an intensification of the patterns used in books 2 and 9, bringing Agamemnon's concern for the army to a climax.

Another example of allusion is offered by a feature of the *Doloneia* that has been considered a stylistic flaw and concerns the series of awakenings of the various Achaean leaders in the first part of the book. Here is what happens:[54]

---

[49] Agamemnon's plan is met with massive volunteering by the Achaean leaders, even in the face of a dangerous nocturnal mission into enemy ground.

[50] Kullmann (1955, 253–73 = 1992, 38–63) argues that Achilles' withdrawal from the fighting is associated with the potential mutiny of the army. He claims that the *Iliad* has reshaped the episode of the epic tradition reflected in the *Cypria*, according to which there was a mutiny of the army that was cut short by Achilles' intervention after his miraculous "meeting" with Helen by means of the aid of Thetis and Aphrodite. This is why we have the (false) impression that the theme of μῆνις is undermined by the potential mutiny of the army in book 2. But the result is that Agamemnon resorts to testing the army in a difficult situation so that their courage is restored.

[51] See also the two pairs of duels that begin and end the first and fourth day of fighting: on day one, the duel between Paris and Menelaus at the beginning, and between Hector and Ajax at the end; then on day four the fight between Aeneas and Achilles at the beginning and between Hector and Achilles at the end (I am grateful to Erwin Cook for this point).

[52] It should not remain unnoticed that the two last speakers at the end of *Iliad* 9 are Odysseus and Diomedes, i.e. the two spies in *Iliad* 10. Although Diomedes suggests that they attack the Trojans the next morning, we never hear Agamemnon's response to the speeches of Odysseus and Diomedes at the end of book 9. The formulaic οἱ δ' ἄρα πάντες ἐπῄνησαν βασιλῆες | μῦθον ἀγασσάμενοι Διομήδεος ἱπποδάμοιο (*Il.* 9.710–11) has no bearing on this. Agamemnon has not been convinced by Diomedes' suggestion and is still troubled by the enormous support Hector is receiving from Zeus. Another initiative must, therefore, be undertaken.

[53] See Lord (2018³) 205.   [54] Italics indicate narrated events.

Agamemnon *cannot sleep*; he plans to go to Nestor
Menelaus *cannot sleep* and *goes to* Agamemnon
Menelaus goes to Ajax and Idomeneus and wakes them up
Agamemnon *goes to* Nestor and *wakes him up*
Agamemnon and Nestor *go to* Odysseus and *wake him up*
Agamemnon, Nestor, and Odysseus *go to* Diomedes and *wake him up*
Diomedes goes to Ajax Oileus and Meges and wakes them up.

This is a typical example of the "chain" pattern,[55] at the end of which is placed the most important member, in our case Diomedes. A manifestation of the "chain" pattern is the "sequence of being woken for a message," which is attested in the Hurro-Hittite *Song of Release* and the Babylonian poem *Atrahasis*. In the former, the Storm-god is roused from bed by a messenger, talks to his brother Suwaliyat, and sends him to Ebla to discuss something with Ishhara.[56] In the latter, Kalkal wakes Nusku, who then wakes Enlil and informs him that the Igigi-gods have surrounded his house and are about to lay siege to it. Enlil follows Nusku's suggestion to summon an assembly, in which it is decided by the gods to send out Nusku to find out why the Igigi-gods are acting in this way.[57] Comparison with these examples suggests an interesting analogy with the sequence of awakenings in the *Doloneia*, irrespective of how one interprets this analogy.[58] In *Iliad* 10, Diomedes will be the first to volunteer when the council will take place, and he will be instrumental in the implementation of the plan. His killing of both Dolon and Rhesus shows that he is the most important Achaean figure in *Iliad* 10. Odysseus, the other member of the spying mission, is placed in the penultimate position within the chain, and it is he who will lead to the next member of the chain (Diomedes). The "chain" pattern involves items or persons appearing in succession and clustering around a given theme (here participation in the spying mission). It belongs to a group of techniques (like the *priamel*) that aim at highlighting a single element in a list, but unlike the *priamel* its constituent elements are not simply placed one after the other but in such an order that one leads to the next. *Iliad* 10 presents exclusively those members of the list who are important for the ensuing episode. The summoning by Menelaus and Diomedes

---

[55] The "chain" pattern is also known as the "Esdras" chain from the relevant story in the Old Testament; see Hansen (2002) 414–25.
[56] *Song of Release*, KBo 32.37 12'–19'; see López-Ruiz (2014) 292; Bachvarova (2015) 145.
[57] *Atrahasis*, I 72–80; see Bachvarova (2015) 145.
[58] For example, Bachvarova (2015, 145) argues that this is "an elaborate version of a traditional narrative sequence, otherwise unattested in the Greek epic tradition." However, it is questionable whether a single occurrence of someone woken up in a Hurro-Hittite composition of the fifteenth century BC, an Akkadian composition of the eleventh century BC, and a Greek composition of the eighth to seventh century BC constitutes a sound basis for a "traditional narrative sequence," especially since the first two are written compositions, while the third may well be oral (I owe this point to one of the anonymous readers of this book).

of Telamonian Ajax and Idomeneus and of Ajax Oileus and Meges, respectively, is not narrated, only mentioned. In terms of the pattern, they are "mute" elements. Though typical, the shape the "chain" pattern takes in *Iliad* 10 is reminiscent of another series of names in *Iliad* 4 that describe which Achaean leaders are preparing for battle. When Menelaus is wounded by Pandarus, Agamemnon sends for Machaon to cure his brother's wound. He then goes to Idomeneus and Meriones to urge them to fight. He does the same with Telamonian Ajax and Teucer, then with Nestor, Menestheus, Odysseus, and Diomedes. Then (*Il.* 4.422) the battle begins. The list in book 4 and the "chain" in book 10 are not identical, but they do share similarities: they both begin with Agamemnon and Menelaus, end with Diomedes, and involve all other shared members in the same order. In both cases, the hero whose action will prove to be the most important for the ensuing narrative is Diomedes, who is mentioned last. It may be suggested that, as the list in book 4 prepares for Diomedes' *aristeia* in regular combat in *Iliad* 5, so the "chain" in the *Nyktegersia* paves the way for Diomedes' *aristeia* in the irregular form of combat highlighted in *Iliad* 10, the ambush. Differences are important too. Unlike the *Epipolesis* (*Il.* 4.223–421), the chain in book 10 does not offer further vignettes of heroes and their troops. Moreover, Agamemnon rouses to action several Achaean leaders, while in book 10 he does so together with Nestor and (partly) Odysseus.[59] However, these differences are interpretively significant. They underline the disparity between regular warfare and a nocturnal mission into enemy territory, which involves a few, selected heroes, and not entire contingents. As for Agamemnon, the help he receives from Nestor and (partly) Odysseus is consonant with the cooperative spirit that marks book 10. Seen from the vantage point of their differences, the *Epipolesis* in book 4 and the *Nyktegersia* in book 10 are in complementary distribution, since together they cover every potential variation of the chain pattern: the initiative of one man (Agamemnon) leading to various fighting scenes that involve several warriors in book 4 is counterbalanced by the collective action of several heroes (Agamemnon, Nestor, and Odysseus) and a single episode (the spying mission) in book 10. In this light, the chain pattern in book 10 invites the audience to recall the list of leaders in book 4. The chain pattern in *Iliad* 10 could have contained Achaean leaders presented in a different order, without having to change the key position of Diomedes at its end. The same ordering of names in equivalent situations amounts to an association that capitalizes on the theme of Diomedes' preeminence and suggests that the allusion of *Iliad* 10 to *Iliad* 4 (10 → 4) is a meaningful and productive one.[60]

---

[59] I am only referring to the awakenings that are narrated (excluding the heroes whom Menelaus and Diomedes wake up).

[60] Handling effectively the parallel dispatching of Agamemnon and Menelaus is not an easy task. The central role of the Atreidae is reminiscent of the mustering of the army in the *Cypria* (arg. ll. 111–21 Severyns), in which Menelaus goes first to Agamemnon, then to Nestor, and then they (Menelaus, Agamemnon, and Nestor?) gather the entire army by visiting one after the other the principal Greek

A different type of allusion is the reversal in paired episodes,[61] which is the intratextual equivalent of "opposition in imitation" or "contrast-imitation."[62] While the latter pertains to a source- and a target-text and operates on an intertextual level between different works, the former works intratextually[63] and becomes more marked when two episodes or scenes are juxtaposed.[64] *Iliad* 9 is marked by the stubborn refusal of Achilles to return to the fighting. The speeches, gifts, and entreaties of the three envoys are given such an extended space in the text so as to highlight even more Achilles' rejection.[65] At the end of the book, we are left with an uncomfortable feeling, because Achilles will not fight. The situation described in book 10 stands in stark contrast with Achilles' refusal. All leaders volunteer to take part in the dangerous spying mission during the night. The *Iliad* makes this amply clear by a sixfold anaphora of the verb ἐθέλω (10.227-31: ἔθελον... ἠθελέτην... ἤθελε... ἤθελε... ἤθελε... ἤθελε) that puts in sharp relief the use of ἐθέλω to describe Achilles' unwillingness at the end of book 9 (ἤ ῥ' ἐθέλει, 674; οὐκ ἐθέλει, 678). There is no effort on the part of Nestor or Agamemnon to convince anybody. Unlike Achilles, they are all ready to do their best. In this way, the unwillingness of one hero to help the army (Achilles in *Iliad* 9) is contrasted with the willingness of every other leader to take part in the night mission (in *Iliad* 10). The same theme (participation in the war) is handled in *Iliad* 10 in a way that contrasts with its use in *Iliad* 9. It seems as if *Iliad* 10 comments on *Iliad* 9 by contrasting Achilles' negative behavior with the positive attitude of all

leaders, though in *Iliad* 10 (probably because of the pressing need of the current situation) the two brothers act in parallel. Here the stress is on Agamemnon, as the most "royal" of the two brothers (Σ[A] bT *Il.* 10.25a). Nestor is then "attached" to Agamemnon because it would have been inappropriate to have the man who is regarded as responsible for the withdrawal of Achilles wake up the Achaean leaders (Σ[A] bT *Il.* 10.108b). In contrast to the comprehensiveness of the mustering of the army in the *Cypria*, the *Nyktegersia* has to be selective. This is why the rousing of the two spies (Odysseus and Diomedes) by Agamemnon and Nestor is narrated, whereas the rousing of Telamonian Ajax and Idomeneus by Menelaus is reported (the same observation applies to the dispatch of Diomedes to Ajax Oileus and Meges). See also pp. 77-8.

[61] On reversal in paired speeches, see Lohmann (1970) 112-30.
[62] See Currie (2016) 27 n. 173, 224, 225-6 with n. 16.
[63] Opposition in imitation can simultaneously operate on an intertextual and intratextual level. A useful example is provided by the theme "siege of a walled city." The Trojan assault on the Achaean Wall in book 12 is a reversal of the siege of Troy, which may have featured in at least one version of an oral *Cypria*, since it occurs in the written *Cypria* (arg. l. 154 Severyns) and is known to the *Iliad* (5.788-90, 9.352-5, 13.105-6, 15.722-3, 18.287, 20.28; see also Bacch. 13.114-20: οἳ πρὶν μὲν [πολύπυργο]ν | [Ἰ]λίου θαητὸν ἄστυ | οὐ λεῖπον, ἀτυζόμενοι [δέ] | πτᾶσσον ὀξεῖαν μάχα[ν,] | εὖτ' ἐν πεδίωι κλονέω[ν] | μαίνοιτ' Ἀχιλλεύς, | λαοφόνον δόρυ σείων). It may have also interacted (again by contrast-imitation) with Troy's siege by Heracles and/or the siege of Thebes by the Seven and the Epigoni. Apart from its intertextual aspect, the siege of the Achaean Wall works also intratextually, since it will be followed by Patroclus' futile attempt to sack Troy when he functions as Achilles' surrogate. The reversal here ends dramatically: Patroclus will be killed by Hector, the man who "sacked" the Achaean Wall.
[64] Lohmann (1988, 64) has described this phenomenon as "Umkehr in (der) Wiederkehr (des Gleichen)," "reversal in recurrence [of the same motif])."
[65] Achilles is also given a lot of space to restate (and expand greatly) his discontent (I owe this point to E. T. E. Barker [private communication]).

other leaders. Such a positive attitude is already implied at the end of book 9, when Diomedes says that they should not have asked Achilles to change his mind in the first place. The stress put by Diomedes on the futility of the embassy and Achilles' unwillingness to fight acquire deeper significance when contrasted with the usefulness of the spying mission and the willingness of the Achaean leaders to participate. Without this contrast, Diomedes' words lose much of their semantic potential.

2.2.3 Allusion to Themes: Forward References

Forward references pertain to intratextual allusion between *Iliad* 10 and books 11–24. They involve four themes: "isolation before defeat," "Achilles" horses', "solidarity brings victory," and "$\lambda\acute{o}\chi os$ and $\pi\acute{o}\lambda\epsilon\mu os$."

The isolation of Dolon in *Iliad* 10 prefigures the future isolation of Hector.[66] Both of them will end up alone, the former caught by the Greek spies, the latter chased by Achilles around the walls of Troy. Both will lose their lives either being promised in vain the horses of Achilles (Dolon) or being unable to get hold of them (Hector).[67] Before their demise they both realize their $\check{\alpha}\tau\eta$: Dolon presents himself as the victim of Hector's folly (*Il.* 10.391–3), while Hector accuses himself of failing to listen to Polydamas' prudent advice (*Il.* 22.99–104). They offer in vain or consider offering ransom to their enemies to escape death (*Il.* 10.378–81 and 22.111–22). They are subsequently killed by Diomedes and Achilles, respectively. Dolon's failure in the field of $\mu\hat{\eta}\tau\iota s$ and in the night ambush prefigures Hector's lack of $\mu\hat{\eta}\tau\iota s$ when he refuses to listen to Polydamas and thinks he can win the war. It will only be a matter of time before his failure in the field of $\beta\acute{\iota}\eta$ against Achilles. We can see here that Dolon does not simply serve the practical "need" of giving information about Rhesus' whereabouts to the Achaean spies. His role is not limited to the *Doloneia* but stretches well beyond the limits of book 10. His story (in the form of an anticipatory doublet) constitutes an allusion to the fate of Hector: his isolation from the rest of the army, his folly, his death.

Another intratextual allusion is triggered by Achilles' horses. Hector's promise to give to a volunteering spy as prize the horses of Achilles means that he is confident that he will defeat the Achaeans and Achilles himself. He so much believes in this that he rejects Polydamas' warning and attacks the Achaean Wall. His loss of $\varphi\rho\acute{\epsilon}\nu\epsilon s$ leads to his defeat. The consequences of his action become

---

[66] On being alone on the battlefield, see *Il.* 8.80 for Nestor being saved by Diomedes after losing his horses; Petegorsky (1982) 253 n. 63.
[67] The contrast between Hector's success in taking Achilles' armor from Patroclus' body and his failure to capture Achilles' horses in *Iliad* 16 indicates that he cannot become a Trojan Achilles. His demise in *Iliad* 22 will be ironically linked with these horses, which will drag his corpse to the ships of the Achaeans.

obvious only when his world is turned upside down, when he refuses to get inside the Trojan walls, although he is pursued by Achilles in *Iliad* 22. Is it really a coincidence that Hector sets as a reward the best chariot and best horses of the Achaeans (*Il.* 10.305–6), that Dolon makes it clear that these belong to Achilles (*Il.* 10.322–3), and that Hector promises to deliver them to him (*Il.* 10.330–1)? Is it a coincidence that this double repetition of the chariot and horses in three instances pertains to the one thing that Hector will *not* take from Patroclus when he kills him in *Iliad* 16, though he strips him of his armor?[68] This is dramatic irony at its best. We experience here the same exquisite *Fernbeziehung* technique that is regularly employed by the Iliadic epic tradition, in which the second reference gives meaning to the first. Achilles' horses are "pregnant with symbolism." As their tears for the dead Patroclus are "pregnant" tears foreshadowing the death of Achilles,[69] so the horses themselves function as a backdrop against which Hector's arrogance is measured. Zeus' determination not to give them to Hector covertly points to Hector's future death. Hector's certainty that he will capture Achilles' horses (and give them to Dolon) somberly alludes not only to the soon-to-follow capture of Rhesus' horses[70] by Diomedes and Odysseus but also to Hector's failure to capture the horses of Achilles, and by extension to Zeus' determination not to allow Hector to have them.

The theme of victorious solidarity is obvious in the joint mission of Diomedes and Odysseus.[71] The two heroes work together in several epic episodes spanning the entire Trojan War tradition (the killing of Palamedes,[72] arguably the fetching of Philoctetes from Lemnos,[73] and the theft of the

---

[68] On the level of the structure of the verse, ἵππους and ἅρματα ποικίλα χαλκῷ are split in two consecutive verses (10.392–3), although they have previously been joined in a single line (10.322). Notice the stress on the outstanding quality of Achilles (10.323: ἀμύμονα Πηλείωνα; 10.392: Πηλείωνος ἀγαυοῦ).

[69] *Il.* 17.426–40 (also: 23.283–4); on this scene, see Schein (2016) 11–26 (a slightly revised version of 2002, 193–205); on pregnant tears, see Currie (2016) 105–46.

[70] On certain "oddities" with respect to the description of Rhesus' horses in *Iliad* 10, see Morard (1963) 385–403. His observations are in tune with the theory of adaptation of the Rhesus story to the *Iliad*. They contribute nothing to the question of the authenticity or inauthenticity of the *Doloneia*.

[71] When Diomedes is wounded and Odysseus fights on his own in *Iliad* 11, his fate is described in similar manner to that of Patroclus (*Il.* 11.471 = 17.690: μεγάλη δὲ ποθὴ Δαναοῖσι γένηται). It is, therefore, possible that the poem stresses a warrior's peril of being alone under difficult circumstances; see Petegorsky (1982) 219.

[72] *Cypr.* fr. 27 GEF.

[73] On the basis of Apollodorus (*Epit.* 5.8), who says that Odysseus and Diomedes went to Lemnos to bring Philoctetes to Troy, Welcker (1835–49 [1865²], 238) suggested that in Proclus' summary, which refers only to Diomedes being sent to Lemnos, the phrase "with Odysseus" had fallen out. Differently M. L. West (2013a, 182 n. 19), who argues that Apollodorus' narrative is based on Euripides' *Philoctetes* (see test. iv c [c] *TrGF* = Dio Chrys. 52); see also Soph. *Phil.* 592; Hyg. *Fab.* 102. However, Pindar's reference to "heroes" who went to Lemnos to fetch Philoctetes (*P.* 1.53) may reflect the *Ilias parva*. As for Welcker's argument, an emendation of Διομήδης into σὺν Διομήδει (see the transmitted text in ll. 211–13 Severyns: μετὰ ταῦτα Ὀδυσσεὺς λοχήσας Ἕλενον λαμβάνει, καὶ χρήσαντος περὶ τῆς ἁλώσεως τούτου Διομήδης ἐκ Λήμνου Φιλοκτήτην ἀνάγει) in light of Ὀδυσσεύς τε αἰκισσάμενος ἑαυτόν... καὶ μετὰ ταῦτα σὺν Διομήδει τὸ Παλλάδιον ἐκκομίζει ἐκ τῆς Ἰλίου (ll. 224–9 Severyns), where the subject Ὀδυσσεύς is not repeated, seems an easier alternative.

Palladium).[74] Their harmonious cooperation in the *Doloneia* aims at exposing Dolon's vulnerability in the short run and Patroclus' weakness in the long run. Patroclus loses his life at the hands of Hector, when he finds himself isolated from the rest of the Achaean army. We see here that "the vulnerability of the Achaean army without Achilles has become personified in Patroclus."[75] The contrast with the joint mission of Odysseus and Diomedes in the *Doloneia* is stark. The pairing of the two heroes, highlighted at *Il.* 10.242–7 when Diomedes selects Odysseus as his companion, stresses the theme of μῆτις, which "will be far more effective if two go instead of one."[76] The antithesis is dictionally highlighted by the use of the word ἀσκηθής ("unscathed"), which occurs exclusively in these two episodes in the entire *Iliad*.[77] Patroclus' mission, then, stands in stark contrast with that of Odysseus and Diomedes in the *Doloneia*. As long as he was fighting together with Achilles, Patroclus was safe, but, the one time he is separated from his friend, he will meet his death. While separation from Achilles leads to Patroclus' death, the combined effort of Diomedes and Odysseus proves successful.[78] The μῆτις of the two heroes wins their νόστος,[79] whereas the βίη of Patroclus, when separated from the βίη of Achilles, costs him his νόστος[80] and leads to his death.

In order to accommodate the λόχος into its plot, the Iliadic tradition has created an association with πόλεμος by means of the "pairing" of Diomedes' two *aristeiai* in *Iliad* 5 and 10. The first pertains to what is regarded as a conventional type of warfare. In book 5, Diomedes performs superbly. He defeats all opponents and wounds even pro-Trojan gods (Aphrodite and Ares). The title Διομήδους ἀριστεία[81] effectively captures Diomedes' exceptional accomplishments. Diomedes looms large in *Iliad* 10 too. In fact, this is the last time he distinguishes himself so starkly in military activity in the entire epic. This means that with *Iliad* 10 Diomedes' outstanding fighting deeds come to an end. We are, therefore, entitled to draw attention even more to the pairing of his exploits in books 5 and 10, the former "introducing" him as a remarkable hero, the latter "completing" his awesome Iliadic performance. Such a pairing gains further weight by considering that Diomedes' skill in a spying mission during the night and its concomitant ambush warfare tactics are, like his performance in *Iliad* 5, an *aristeia*, albeit of a different form. The theme of ambush (λόχος) in the *Iliad* regularly involves the *aristoi*,[82] and Diomedes is an *aristos* par excellence. In this light, the pairing

---

[74] *Il. parv.* arg. ll. 228–9 Severyns.   [75] Petegorsky (1982) 215.   [76] Petegorsky (1982) 218.
[77] *Il.* 10.212 and 16.247; see A. T. Edwards (1981) 169–70; Petegorsky (1982) 220.
[78] Petegorsky (1982) 218.   [79] I.e. their return to the Achaean camp.
[80] I.e. his return to the Achaean camp.
[81] This title is first attested in Herod. 2.116, though the Herodotean quotation pertains to *Il.* 6.289–92; see Introduction.
[82] See *Il.* 1.227 (λόχονδ'...ἀριστήεσσιν), 4.392–3 (λόχον...ἡγήτορες), 6.188–9 (φῶτας ἀρίστους... λόχον), 13.276–7 (ἄριστοι...λόχον). See especially *Il.* 13.274–310, where the λόχος is presented as an alternative type of warfare with its own features and diction.

of *Iliad* 5 and 10 by means of the exceptional performance of Diomedes in two types of warfare, the πόλεμος and the λόχος, testifies to an essential association, one that belongs to the heart of a "martial" epic like the *Iliad*.[83]

A further association between πόλεμος and λόχος relates to the use of the two key characters involved in these two types of warfare. As the Dolon episode alludes to Hector's future death by Achilles, so the Rhesus episode alludes to Patroclus' death and the subsequent Trojan losses inflicted by Achilles after the death of Patroclus but before Hector's demise.

I begin with Patroclus' death. Diomedes ponders whether to take the chariot (he has no time to tie the horses to it) on which Rhesus' armor is placed or to kill more Thracians. Athena intervenes (*Il.* 10.507–8) to tell him to hasten back to the ships before some god informs the Trojans, which is exactly what Apollo does soon after (*Il.* 10.515–19). Diomedes immediately mounts the horses[84] and hurries back to the ships. In *Iliad* 17, Menelaus stands in front of the corpse of Patroclus and ponders whether to protect the armor and body of Patroclus or retreat. Apollo intervenes and tells Hector to stop pursuing the divine horses of Achilles (*Il.* 17.75–81). Instead, he should be fighting Menelaus, who has killed Euphorbus (one of Patroclus' killers). Hector and the Trojan troops approach, and Menelaus retreats and asks Ajax to join him in protecting Patroclus' corpse. Meanwhile, Hector strips Achilles' divine armor from Patroclus' body and then mounts his own chariot (*Il.* 17.130). The audience member who has heard or read book 10 and then hears or reads book 17 realizes that what happens in the latter book is an inversion[85] of what happened to Rhesus' chariot: the whip on it that is not noticed by Odysseus; Diomedes pondering whether to take it or not; Rhesus' armor placed on it. As usual in such cases, the second reference is dramatically the more important.[86] The ambush gives way to full-scale warfare, the person who ponders what to do is the defender of the dead hero, not his killer, while Apollo's intervention is the common denominator. The whole picture becomes clear when one looks at the end result. On the one hand, the splendid armor of Rhesus will be left behind, while the splendid armor of Patroclus (borrowed from Achilles) will be taken by Hector. On the other hand, the beautiful horses of Rhesus will be taken by the spies, whereas the divine horses of Achilles won't be captured by Hector.

---

[83] Dué and Ebbott (2010, 367–9) stress the close relation between ambush and horse-stealing; see also Brillet-Dubois (2011) 130; Strolonga (2018) 194.

[84] The plural is traditional; see Hainsworth (1993) 202 on *Il.* 10.498ff.: "the plural ἵπποι can denote the vehicle drawn by the horses and regularly does so, e.g. 11.94, 109, 143, 179 in Agamemnon's *aristeia*, and in construction with parts of ἐπι-, ἀπο-, and καταβαίνειν alternates with unambiguous terms for the chariot, δίφρος and ὄχεα."

[85] On this technique, see pp. 40–1, 46.

[86] On doublets and anticipatory doublets in Homer and the Epic Cycle, see Fenik (1968) 55–6, 86, 89, 98–9, 119–20, 134, 141, 143, 148–50, 194, 237–9, 213–14; Fenik (1974) 172–207; Sammons (2017) 102–23; Barker and Christensen (2020) 181. On inclusionary and exclusionary doublets, see Currie (2016) 239–45.

As for the analogy between the losses inflicted on the enemy by Diomedes and Odysseus in the *Doloneia* and the Trojan losses inflicted by Achilles after the death of Patroclus but before Hector's death, see the following examples:

1. **Twelve Thracians** are killed by Diomedes (10.488)	1. **Twelve Trojans** are held captive by Achilles (**to be beheaded** during Patroclus' funeral: 23.22–3)
2. **Diomedes and Odysseus wash themselves** after coming back (10.575–9)	2. **Achilles' postpones his washing off the blood** for Patroclus' funeral (23.40–2)
3. **Odysseus places Dolon's armor at a myrike-tree** (10.466–7)	3. **Achilles places his spear by the myrikai** (21.17–18) before entering the river (where he will capture the twelve Trojans)
4. **Diomedes kills the Thracian king Rhesus who is breathing heavily** (10.495: θυμὸν ἀπηύρα), (10.496: ἀσθμαίνοντα)[87]	4a. **Achilles kills the Thracian Asteropaeus who is breathing heavily** (21.182: ἀσθμαίνοντα)
	4b. **Hector**, compared to a lion, **kills Patroclus** (16.828: θυμὸν ἀπηύρα), who is compared to a boar **who is heavily breathing** (16.826: ἀσθμαίνοντα)
5. Odysseus makes room for the μώνυχες ἵπποι **to pass without stepping over the corpses** (10.490–3)	5. Achilles' μώνυχες ἵπποι **step over the corpses** (20.499–500)

Seen together, the Dolon and Rhesus episodes display remarkable similarities, though in reverse order, with the two phases of Achilles' revenge for the death of Patroclus. As such they offer a telling analogy with the plot of the *Doloneia*. The diptych-based plot of *Iliad* 10 is effectively interwoven with the unfolding of the plot of the rest of the epic. Diomedes and Odysseus will do in the specially coded form of warfare known as "ambush" what Achilles will carry out during his revenge for Patroclus' death, first by resorting to mass killings and then by facing his principal adversary, Hector.

2.2.4 Bridging Backward and Forward References

Besides thematic associations with books either side of it, book 10 bridges one part of the epic with another. This function spans a large amount of text and shows

---

[87] See also *Il.* 16.109 (αἰεὶ δ' ἀργαλέῳ ἔχετ' ἄσθματι) with respect to the exhausted (because of intensive fighting) Telamonian Ajax.

how *Iliad* 10 conforms to the evolution and shaping of a given theme throughout the poem. Such kinds of interaction may be activated by a traditional structure or type of tale, but its contextualization abides by the exigencies of a sustained poetic plan that is gradually disclosed as the plot unfolds. My test case is the theme of *overconfidence* that relates to both Hector and Dolon, since the former promises to give as reward the best Achaean horses to the spy who will volunteer for the night mission (*Il.* 10.305-6), while the latter accepts the offer and asks specifically for Achilles' horses (*Il.* 10.322-3).

The theme of overconfidence belongs to a type of tale called "Pride Brought Low," in which someone aspires to great things which he cannot achieve and is soon made to realize painfully the futility of his aspirations.[88] This is the core of the Aesopic fable "The Wolf and his Shadow" (Chambry fab. 219 = Perry fab. 260):

Λύκος γαυρωθεὶς καὶ λέων

Λύκος πλανώμενος <ποτ'> ἐν ἐρήμοις τόποις, | κλίνοντος ἤδη πρὸς δύσιν Ὑπερίονος, | δολιχὴν ἑαυτοῦ τὴν σκιὰν ἰδὼν ἔφη· | «Λέοντ' ἐγὼ δέδοικα, τηλικοῦτος ὤν; | πλέθρου τ' ἔχων τὸ μῆκος, οὐ θηρῶν ἁπλῶς | πάντων δυνάστης ἀθρόων γενήσομαι;» | Λύκον δὲ γαυρωθέντα καρτερὸς λέων | ἑλὼν κατήσθι'· ὁ δ' ἐβόησε μετανοῶν· | «Οἴησις ἡμῖν πημάτων παραιτία.»

There was once a wolf who went wandering in the desert as the sun was sinking and about to set. Seeing his long shadow, the wolf exclaimed, "Should someone as great as myself be afraid of a lion? I'm a hundred feet tall! Clearly, I should be the king of all the animals in the world!" As the wolf was boasting, a mighty lion seized and devoured him. Realizing his mistake after the fact, the wolf exclaimed, "My self-conceit has been my undoing!"[89]

The underlying meaning of this tale pertains to the overconfidence of a person who overestimates his abilities and asks for more than he/she deserves. What makes this story particularly relevant to the plot of *Iliad* 10 is not only that Dolon is disguised as a wolf and Diomedes as a lion but also that "Dolon the wolf" (*Il.* 10.334)[90] is ultimately forced to confront the futility of his arrogant aspirations by being killed by "Diomedes the lion" (*Il.* 10.177-8). Following the reward set by Hector, Dolon, disguised as a wolf, asks for Achilles' horses. This is a gift for which he is anything but worthy. When arrested by Diomedes and Odysseus, and before being killed, Dolon speaks like the wolf in Aesop's tale: "Alas," he cried, "had I not lost sight of the facts, I shouldn't have been ruined *by*

---

[88] See L400–L499 in Thompson (1955-8).   [89] Translation: Gibbs (2002).
[90] On "Dolon the wolf," see Gernet (1936) 189–208; Lissarague (1980) 3–30; Bierl (2012) 151–5. It should be noted that Odysseus wears the cap of his grandfather Auto-lukos, who is mentioned in *Il.* 10.267. It is as if the reference to his grandfather's wolfish name alludes to Odysseus' imminent role in the spying mission and ensuing ambush. Odysseus "out-wolfs" Dolon.

my fancies...Hector led me astray *with much ate*, since he promised me the single-hooved horses of Achilles." This remarkable analogy between the two stories can help us go further. For the story in the *Iliad* is not limited to the wolf-dressed Dolon and the lion-dressed Diomedes (who kills him) but involves Hector and Achilles (through the latter's horses). In this light, it is significant that Hector himself promises as a prize Achilles' horses *before* Dolon volunteers. Hector is the one who initially displays the wolfish overconfidence in his abilities, since he takes it for granted that he will acquire Achilles' horses. As the overconfident wolf will be devoured by the lion, so the overconfident Hector will be killed by Achilles, who will even express his wish to devour him (*Il.* 22.346–7). The two heroes are portrayed, covertly or overtly, as a wolf and a lion, respectively. Hector has been systematically presented as having λύσσα in his desire to destroy the Achaeans (*Il.* 9.239 and 305), a rage that is etymologically associated with the wolf (λύκος). Achilles is portrayed as a lion in *Il.* 18.318–22, 20.164–75, and 24.39–45. What is more, the way the story of Dolon is presented in book 10 looks forward to ultimate Trojan defeat, as encapsulated by the death of Hector. It is the ἄτη (*Il.* 10.391) and ἀτασθαλίαι (*Il.* 22.104) of Hector that have caused Dolon's and the army's huge losses.

In this way, the theme of overconfidence can be productively explored via comparison with this Aesopic fable. In arguing this, I don't see any strong reason against positing a pre-Iliadic fabular narrative with this content or ruling out a putative influence on the *Iliad*.[91] The antiquity of the animal fable in Greece goes back at least to the archaic period. Fables are easily transferred from one culture to the other since they exist in oral form and pertain to situations and/or circumstances shared by various peoples. Scholars have debated about Near Eastern influence, especially since fables, as other forms of cultural transfers, are quickly amalgamated with Greek culture and become an essential part of it. Animal fables are weakly represented in Homeric epic mainly because of its non-didactic nature, its preference for mythical stories with well-known individuals, and its subordination of the animal world to the human. Animals in Homer are mentioned either within the framework of human activity or in similes. Among the earliest uses of the animal fable in Greek literature are the αἶνος of the hawk and the nightingale (Hes. *Op.* 202–12) and the fable of the fox and the eagle (Archil. frs. 172–81 *IEG*), which may well precede Hesiod and Archilochus, respectively.

In this vein, the overconfidence of Dolon in *Iliad* 10 mirrors the overconfidence of Hector in the entire *Iliad*. This would make the *Doloneia* a *texte spéculaire* for the tragedy of Hector. Once more, we observe that *Iliad* 10 displays the same mature narrative technique that we know from the rest of the poem.

---

[91] On the ancient fable in general, see Meuli (1954); Nøjgaard (1964); Adrados (1979); Jedrkiewicz (1989); Holzberg (1993); van Dijk (1997); Grethlein (2011) 321–5.

2.2.5 Verbal associations

In this section I will offer a list of verbal associations between the *Doloneia* and the rest of the *Iliad*.[92]

1. *Il.* 10.43–5: **χρεὼ βουλῆς**, ἐμὲ καὶ σέ, διοτρεφὲς Μενέλαε, | **κερδαλέης**, ἥ τίς κεν ἐρύσσεται ἠδὲ **σαώσει** | **Ἀργείους καὶ νῆας**
Il. 9.74–6: πολλῶν δ' ἀγρομένων τῷ πείσεαι ὅς κεν ἀρίστην | **βουλὴν βουλεύσῃ· μάλα δὲ χρεὼ** πάντας Ἀχαιοὺς | **ἐσθλῆς καὶ πυκινῆς**, ὅτι δήιοι ἐγγύθι **νηῶν**

In *Il.* 10.43–4, Agamemnon tells Menelaus that they need to come up with a crafty counsel in order to save the Argives and their ships. Agamemnon's words echo what Nestor had expressed in *Il.* 9.74–6. How deep the verbal association between the two passages goes can be seen by the fact that in book 9 Nestor initially addresses Diomedes (*Il.* 9.53), but then, in the middle of his speech, he turns to Agamemnon (*Il.* 9.69). The shift of addressees is remarkably in tune with the function of *Il.* 10.43–4. Agamemnon is addressing his brother Menelaus, stressing the need for a crafty counsel. By repeating the phraseology used by Nestor in *Il.* 9.74–6, Agamemnon conjures up to the minds of the members of the external audience the double addressees of Nestor's speech, Agamemnon and Diomedes, and draws attention to the difference: in book 9 Agamemnon had not shown any signs of crafty counsel (or indeed anything other than the usual arrogant overconfidence, when offering his catalogue of gifts).[93] In this way, the *Iliad* makes the second passage in book 10, where the repetition is felt, semantically richer, since meaning is constructed not only in the passage's own right but also, retroactively, by a dynamic interaction with *Il.* 9.74–6, where the same phraseology had been employed. In this light, Agamemnon's words to Menelaus bring to mind Diomedes, who has not yet featured in book 10 but who will become one of the protagonists in the spying mission that follows. In this vein, Nestor too is evoked: as the speaker at *Il.* 9.74–6, he is the one who will come up with the specifics of the Achaean plan in *Iliad* 10. We can see in this case how a passage in *Iliad* 10 becomes significantly more evocative and interpretively richer when it is examined in association with another passage outside book 10 that shares the same phraseology. We also see that *Iliad* 10 employs the same associative technique with which we are familiar from the rest of the epic.

---

[92] This list does not aspire to be comprehensive. There are also some other cases that may have been included here. I have decided to present only the most straightforward examples.
[93] I owe this last point to E. T. E. Barker (by email).

2. *Il.* 10.330: μὴ μὲν τοῖς ἵπποισιν **ἀνὴρ ἐποχήσεται ἄλλος**

Il. 17.448–9: ἀλλ' οὐ μὰν ὑμῖν γε καὶ ἅρμασι δαιδαλέοισιν | **Ἕκτωρ Πριαμίδης ἐποχήσεται**· οὐ γὰρ ἐάσω.

Hector arrogantly promises to give to Dolon the immortal horses of Achilles, i.e. the one thing that Hector will not take from Patroclus when he kills him in *Iliad* 16. When Zeus speaks to Achilles' horses in *Il.* 17.448–9, he uses phraseology that evokes 10.330. The fact that the verb ἐποχεῖσθαι is employed only in these two passages in archaic epic speaks in favor of a deliberate resonance.[94] When the audience hears Zeus' words in book 17,[95] they realize the tragic irony inherent in Hector's arrogant boast in book 10. Moreover, Zeus' determination not to give the horses to Hector is a covert sign pertaining to Hector's future death, which very tellingly involves these very horses, since Achilles will tie Hector's corpse to his chariot and drag him to the Achaean ships. Zeus' language (*Il.* 17.448–9) functions as a reminder of Hector's arrogant boast in the *Doloneia*.[96]

3. *Il.* 10.331: **διαμπερὲς ἀγλαϊεῖσθαι**

Il. 18.133: **δηρὸν ἐπαγλαϊεῖσθαι**

Hector promises Dolon "to take pride forever" in Achilles' horses, while Thetis assures Achilles that Hector will "not take pride for long" in Achilles' armor[97] (which he had taken from Patroclus), since he will soon die. The use of similar diction is sharp and expressively effective. It is strengthened by the expression's non-formulaic character, which makes it context-specific. The full strength of Thetis' prophetic asseveration in the second passage functions as an "answer" to Hector's arrogant claim in the first.[98] The goddess picks up a unique expression employed by Hector and turns it on its head.[99]

4. *Il.* 10.367–8: ἵνα μή τις Ἀχαιῶν χαλκοχιτώνων | φθαίη ἐπευξάμενος **βαλέειν, ὁ δὲ δεύτερος ἔλθοι**

Il. 22.206–7: οὐδ' ἔα ἱέμεναι ἐπὶ Ἕκτορι πικρὰ βέλεμνα, | μή τις κῦδος ἄροιτο **βαλών, ὁ δὲ δεύτερος ἔλθοι**

---

[94] Limited range of repetition, shared phraseology, and similar context increase the possibility for deliberate allusion.
[95] The audience know that Apollo (*Il.* 17.75–8) has dissuaded Hector from trying to acquire Achilles' immortal horses.
[96] Dué and Ebbott (2010) 325.
[97] *Il.* 17.472–3: τεύχεα δ' Ἕκτωρ | αὐτὸς ἔχων ὤμοισιν ἀγάλλεται Αἰακίδαο.
[98] See Dué and Ebbott (2010) 325–6.
[99] The expressions μεγάλων δώρων (*Il.* 10.401) and ἀγλαϊεῖσθαι (*Il.* 10.331), which refer to Achilles' horses and chariot, point to *Il.* 16.867 (ἄμβροτοι, οὓς Πηλῆϊ θεοὶ δόσαν ἀγλαὰ δῶρα) that paves the way for *Il.* 17.75–8 (with the intervening scene of Menelaus); see Heath (1992) 387–400.

The dictional similarity of the two passages is strong. Athena puts μένος in Diomedes so as not to come second in striking Dolon and lose all glory to some other Achaean. Likewise, in *Iliad* 22 Achilles nods to the Achaeans not to strike Hector, in order not to come second and lose the glory of hitting him first. The two cases involve theme (to be the first to strike), phraseological identity (preceded by a negative statement that needs to be avoided), and analogical pairing of the respective protagonists (Diomedes vs. Dolon, Achilles vs. Hector). The allusion is clearly deliberate.

5. *Il.* 10.455–7: ὁ δ' **αὐχένα** μέσσον ἔλασσεν | φασγάνῳ ἀΐξας, **ἀπὸ δ' ἄμφω κέρσε τένοντε**· | φθεγγομένου δ' ἄρα τοῦ γε **κάρη κονίῃσιν** ἐμίχθη

Il. 22.327: δι' **αὐχένος** ἤλυθ' ἀκωκή

Il. 22.396: ἀμφοτέρων μετόπισθε ποδῶν **τέτρηνε τένοντε**

Il. 22.398: **κάρη** δ' **ἕλκεσθαι** ἔασεν

Il. 22.402–3: **κάρη δ' ἅπαν ἐν κονίῃσιν** | κεῖτο πάρος χαρίεν

The description of Dolon's tendons being cut by Diomedes' sword, the middle of his neck being struck, his head falling into the dust—all these gruesome details are repeated in the description of Hector's death at the hands of Achilles. Indeed, Dolon's decapitation[100] (the first in the *Iliad*) encourages the audience to anticipate a putative decapitation of Hector. The *Iliad* steers clear of that scenario, since the gods care for Hector, as Achilles will acknowledge.[101] Book 10 alludes to future developments in the plot: the fate of a minor character prefigures the fate of a major character.

6. *Il.* 10.478: ὃν ἐπέφνομεν ἡμεῖς

Il. 22.393: ἐπέφνομεν Ἕκτορα δῖον

Odysseus uses the same diction for the killing of Dolon that Achilles will use for Hector in book 22, which occurs nowhere else in the *Iliad*. The allusion is secure, especially if we take into account contextual parameters and the general tendency of the *Doloneia* to create intratextual associations between the deaths of Dolon

---

[100] Apart from the case of Dolon, other decapitations in the *Iliad* occur in 11.146–7 (Agamemnon decapitating one of the sons of Antimachus, also cutting off his arms), 11.225–61 (Agamemnon decapitating Coon), 13.202–3 (Ajax Oileus decapitating Imbrius), 14.465–8 (Telamonian Ajax decapitating Archelochus), 14.493–507 (Peneleos decapitating Ilioneus), 16.339–41 (a virtual decapitation of Lycon by Peneleus), 18.334–5 (Achilles intends to decapitate Hector), and 20.481–2 (Achilles decapitating Deucalion). Decapitations are always carried out by Achaeans against Trojans.

[101] Achilles has "promised" to the dead Patroclus in *Il.* 18.333–5 to strip Hector of his armor and decapitate him, whereas in *Il.* 17.126 Hector had planned to decapitate Patroclus but was not able to carry out his threat. On the case of Imbrius in *Il.* 13.202–3, which also prefigures Hector's death, see McClellan (2017) 159–74.

and Hector. It may be no accident that in both cases the plural (ἐπέφνομεν) is not used literally (Dolon is killed by Diomedes, Hector by Achilles).

7. *Il.* 10.515–17: ἀργυρότοξος Ἀπόλλων |...| τῇ κοτέων

Il. 23.383: Τυδέος υἷι κοτέσσατο Φοῖβος Ἀπόλλων

To ask the question why Apollo is angry at Athena in the *Doloneia* would be to miss the point.[102] Since κότος refers to both a lasting grudge and a rivalry-conditioned wrath,[103] the question may be rephrased thus: "why does Apollo feel this kind of wrath against Athena?" Although the obvious answer is her support of Diomedes, Apollo's wrath is related to what Diomedes is doing at the moment, i.e. while he is being helped by Athena. In the chariot race at the funeral games for Patroclus, Apollo "has κότος" (*Il.* 23.383: κοτέσσατο) against Diomedes because he (*sc.* Apollo) wishes Eumelus (see *Il.* 2.763–6) to win the race. To this end, he knocks the whip from Diomedes' hands. Apollo's action does not escape Athena's notice (*Il.* 23.388: οὐδ' ἄρ' Ἀθηναίην ἐλεφηράμενος λάθ' Ἀπόλλων), just as Athena's support of Diomedes does not escape Apollo's notice in *Il.* 10.515 (οὐδ' ἀλαοσκοπιὴν εἶχ' ἀργυρότοξος Ἀπόλλων). She immediately gives the whip to Diomedes and incites his horses on to catch up with Eumelus, "who has κότος."[104] Moreover, Eumelus is the son of Admetus, whose horses had once been under the care of Apollo.[105] It can hardly be a coincidence that Apollo's κότος against Athena in the *Doloneia* concerns Diomedes and horses, just as in book 23, or that upon his return to the Greek camp Diomedes places Rhesus' horses next to his own horses. The point is effective: when Apollo throws away Diomedes' whip in book 23, the earlier scene is recalled (specifically *Il.* 10.504–6 and 10.512–13), when Diomedes leaves behind the chariot in which Odysseus had left the whip (*Il.* 10.500–1). The whip and horses of Rhesus in book 10 give their place to the whip and horses of Diomedes in book 23, the wrath and support of Apollo and Athena making the association even stronger.[106]

8. *Il.* 10.528, 10.570: ἔναρα βροτόεντα

Il. 6.480, 8.534, 15.347, 17.13, 17.540, 22.245: ἔναρα βροτόεντα

This formula (8x *Il.*) nests in contexts in which Hector is involved either directly or indirectly. In his meeting with Andromache in Troy, Hector imagines Astyanax carrying back from battle the ἔναρα βροτόεντα of some Greek (*Il.* 6.480). At *Il.* 8.534, Hector does the same with respect to the arms of Diomedes. At *Il.* 15.347,

---

[102] Apollo and Athena had also featured in similar roles in the scene of the death of Peiroos (another Thracian leader) in *Il.* 4.507–16; see pp. 100–1.
[103] On κότος in Homer, see Walsh (2005) 63–6, 80–1, 83.   [104] *Il.* 23.391: κοτέουσα.
[105] See *Il.* 2.766–7.   [106] On κότος in this episode, see Walsh (2005) 64–7.

Hector advises the Trojans to stop spoiling the ἔναρα βροτόεντα of dead Greeks. At *Il.* 17.13, Euphorbus tells Menelaus to let go the ἔναρα βροτόεντα of Patroclus (who has been killed by Hector). At *Il.* 17.540, Automedon (Achilles' charioteer) avoids Hector's spear and takes the ἔναρα βροτόεντα of Aretus and places them on Patroclus' chariot. At *Il.* 22.245, Achilles gets the ἔναρα βροτόεντα of Hector. The fact that in *Il.* 10 the expression ἔναρα βροτόεντα is used twice for Dolon's arms provides one more allusive link to Hector and his fate in the epic.

The above-mentioned cases suggest that the *Doloneia* interacts with the ensuing books of the *Iliad* in a particularly strong way that either amounts to *verbatim quotation* or to *evocation* by means of shared phraseology. Both terms describe degrees of allusion of decreasing intensity (*verbatim quotation* > *evocation*) and are key to the realization that, as well as sharing themes with the rest of the epic, *Iliad* 10 engages in systematic intratextual associations that involve phraseological transfer or reuse. Contextual factors and/or increasing specificity observable in a limited range of attestations strongly suggest that the links presented above are meaningful and cannot be simply ruled out as mere reflexes on the level of diction within a traditional oral medium.[107]

2.3 A Putative Transference of a Narrative Sequence: *Iliad* 13 Alludes to *Iliad* 10

The argument that will be presented in this section is that the basic narrative sequence observed in the *Doloneia* is also employed in a significant part of book 13.[108] The resemblance concerns at least nine aspects: (1) the Achaeans are facing a difficult situation; (2) a figure decides to do something; (3) he states that Hector is a major threat to the Achaeans; (4) two heroes (of whom he is one or a pair instigated by him) take the initiative and act; (5) he expresses his fear about the situation; (6) he states that the withdrawal of Achilles is responsible for the difficult position of the Achaean army; (7) another pair of heroes, prompted by

---

[107] On this issue, see Usener (1990); Tsagalis (2008); Bakker (2013) 158.

[108] There are various cases of meaningful thematic correspondences within the *Iliad*, the *Odyssey*, and between the *Iliad* and the *Odyssey*: e.g. (*Iliad*) the duel between Diomedes and Aeneas (book 5)—the duel between Achilles and Aeneas (book 20); Aeneas rescued by a Aphrodite (book 5)—Aeneas rescued by Poseidon (book 20); Athena and Hera against Ares and Aphrodite (books 5 and 21); (*Odyssey*) the simile of Odysseus being compared to a father who is restored to his children (5.394–7)—the simile of Penelope who is compared to sailors who arrive at land after a shipwreck (23.233–8); the Phaeacian episode (books 6–8) looks back to Telemachus' visit to Pylos and Sparta (books 3–4) and forward to Odysseus' arrival on Ithaca (book 13); (*Iliad* and *Odyssey*) Priam's journey and supplication to Achilles in *Il.* 24.281–508—Odysseus' journey and supplication to Arete in *Od.* 6.255–7.154; see, e.g., Lang (1969) 159–68; Rüter (1969) 141–2, 220–4, 239–40; Thornton (1970) 40–2; Hansen (1972) 48–57; Eisenberger (1973) 109; Kilb (1973) 188–90; Fenik (1974) 25; R. B. Rutherford (1985) 140–1, 145–6 with n. 5; Taplin (1990) 2; Garvie (1994) 15; R. B. Rutherford (2001) 127–30; Currie (2016) 39–47, 196–7, 259–62.

the initial action of the figure who set in motion the entire sequence or instigated directly by the figure who set this sequence in motion, undertake joint action; (8) a pair of heroes sets an ambush or one of the two heroes delivers a speech on the importance of ambush as a form of warfare; (9) one of them kills an enemy who features only in this episode of the poem. Table 2.1 offers a detailed list of the relevant similarities.

The similarities between the two narrative sequences are significant.[109] Their number, length, and order suggest a complexity of conception[110] that presents a strong case in favor of allusion. Moreover, these two sequences display a remarkable analogy regarding the overarching situation: an initiative is undertaken with respect to Hector, who is posing a major threat to the Achaeans. This is an issue of paramount importance for the central part of the plot. It pertains to the implementation of Zeus' plan to make Hector triumph until the Achaeans realize their fault in dishonoring Achilles. Differences exist (e.g. the role of Poseidon in book 13 is not matched by the role of any other god in book 10;[111] the person who takes the initiative at the beginning of book 10, Agamemnon, is part of the first pair of heroes [together with Menelaus], while the person who takes the initiative in book 13, Poseidon, is not part of the first pair of heroes [the two Ajaxes]), but they do not undermine the impact of similarities.

The association suggested above is further strengthened by the larger narrative blueprint to which the two sequences belong. The gradual unraveling of Hector's dominance is presented in several phases, which involve three groups of four books each. When seen as a whole, each group displays a larger narrative pattern, involving one book of Achaean success, one book of Trojan success, one book of balanced situation between the two armies, and one book featuring a temporary new beginning.

(a) The first phase, which involves books 5–8, begins with Diomedes' *aristeia*. Book 6, which is mainly set in Troy, focuses on Hector's involvement in the war and marks a tentative turning point. Book 7 begins with the duel between Hector and Telamonian Ajax that ends in a draw. The councils of the Achaeans and the Trojans signal a balanced situation that couples the fact that the preceding duel had no victor. Book 8 is about a clear Trojan victory. At its end, Hector camps on the plain, his advance being temporarily stopped by the night, after pushing back the Achaeans, who retreat behind their Wall.

---

[109] It should be made clear that smaller segments of the narrative sequence of *Il.* 13.1–382 display analogies with other narrative segments of the *Iliad*; see Fenik (1968) 115–31. The narrative sequence to which I have drawn attention and its similarities and analogies with the narrative sequence in book 10 cannot be explained by recourse to a pattern. In this vein, it is unlikely to be typical.
[110] I owe the expression "complexity of conception" to Garvie (1994) 15.
[111] Some of the differences are explained by the fact that Poseidon's role pertains to what is expected from a god featuring in a divine chariot journey; compare *Il.* 5.767–93 and see Fenik (1968) 115–17.

Table 2.1 Similar Narrative Sequences in *Iliad* 10 and 13

Iliad 10	*Iliad* 13
1. The Achaeans are facing a difficult situation because of Trojan victory.	1. The Achaeans are facing a difficult situation because of Trojan victory.
2. Agamemnon takes the initiative to consult with Nestor (17–20).	2. Poseidon takes the initiative to instill courage into the Achaeans (43–4).
3. Agamemnon says to Menelaus that Hector is a major threat because he is supported by Zeus (45–6).	3. Poseidon (in the guise of Calchas) tells the Ajaxes that Hector is a major threat because he is supported by Zeus (52–8).
4. A pair of brothers,* Agamemnon and Menelaus, summon the Achaean leaders to a council (53–9).	4. A pair of heroes, Ajax Oileus and Telamonian Ajax, organize the line of defense (126–35).†
5. Agamemnon expresses his intense fear about the situation (93).	5. Disguised as Calchas, Poseidon expresses his intense fear about the situation (52).
6. The dire situation of the Achaeans is explained by means of Achilles' absence (105–7).	6. The dire situation of the Achaeans is explained by means of Achilles' absence (112–14).
7a. The Achaeans decide to send spies to the Achaean camp. Diomedes volunteers and selects Odysseus as his companion (204–53).	7a. Poseidon, disguised as Thoas, urges Idomeneus to fight. Idomeneus asks Meriones to join him (215–38, 249–73).‡
7b. Diomedes and Odysseus are armed (254–71).	7b. Meriones gets his second spear from his hut and joins Idomeneus (295–7).
7c. The importance of undertaking a *joint* mission is underscored (224–6).	7c. The importance of undertaking a *joint* mission is underscored (235–7).
7d. Nocturnal mission begins, as Diomedes and Odysseus join forces and move to the plain (272–3, 295–8).	7d. Battle begins, Idomeneus and Meriones having joined forces (304–62).§
8. The spies set an ambush against Dolon (339–464).	8. Idomeneus delivers a speech about ambush as a form of warfare (275–94).
9a. Diomedes kills Dolon, a character featuring only in this episode.	9a. Idomeneus kills Othryoneus, a character featuring only in this episode.
9b. Diomedes kills a late-arriving ally, Rhesus, who has come to Troy to assist the Trojans (434–5, 494–7).	9b. Idomeneus kills a late-arriving Trojan ally, Othryoneus, who has come to Troy for the hand of Cassandra (363–82).**

* On brothers fighting together, see Trypanis (1963) 289–97; Fenik (1968) 147; Hellmann (2000) 112–16.

† The fact that these two heroes share the same name and are addressed in the dual in this scene facilitates the analogy with the Atreidae, who are also designated in the dual by their patronymic in the *Iliad* (1.16, 375). Scholars have argued that the dual Αἴαντε originally designated a pair of brothers, i.e. Telamonian Ajax and Teucer; see Wackernagel (1877) 302–10 = (1953) 538–46; Merkelbach (1960) 268–70; M. L. West (1988) 158 = (2011b) 49.

‡ On the antiquity of this pair of heroes, see M. L. West (1988) 159 = (2011b) 49.

§ See Hellmann (2000) 116.

** See Fenik (1968) 130–1.

(b) The second phase pertains to books 9–12. Book 9 marks a major acknowledgment of the difficult situation in which the Achaeans have found themselves. The Achaeans try in vain to convince Achilles to return to the war. As book 6 was about Hector in Troy, book 9 is about Achilles in his headquarters. Book 10 signals an Achaean success by means of a night raid that culminates in Rhesus' death and the theft of his splendid horses. Book 11 offers a balanced situation on the battlefield, in the sense that the initial Achaean success is followed by important losses at the hands of the Trojans. Book 12 presents a major Trojan victory: Hector breaches the Achaean Wall and enters with his troops into the Achaean camp.

(c) Phase three refers to books 13–16. Book 13 is about a balanced situation with respect to fighting. The Achaeans resist the Trojan advance and hold their ground. By means of the deception of Zeus in book 14, the Achaeans are able to push back the Trojans. Book 15 presents a major counterattack and victory of Hector, who pushes back the Achaeans. The fight now takes place by the ships. The Achaeans find themselves on the brink of destruction. Book 16 marks a tentative new beginning: Patroclus pushes back the Trojans and the poem flirts with his elusive hope of sacking Troy. This is a crucial step for the future convergence of the storylines of Hector and Achilles.

These correspondences regarding the narrative developments between these three groups can be schematically presented, as shown in table 2.2.

Seen from the vantage point of the larger narrative structure of which books 10 and 13 partake, the similarities we have observed allow for the possibility of a transference of a narrative sequence from book 10 to book 13. The direction of this transference[112] from book 10 to book 13 is determined by at least three factors: (a) The first pair of heroes (the Atreidae) in book 10 play a key role in the unraveling of the narrative sequence, since it is they who take the initiative of

Table 2.2 Correspondences of Narrative Developments in Books 5–8, 9–12, and 13–16

Book 5: Achaean success	Book 9: tentative turning point	Book 13: balanced situation on the battlefield
Book 6: tentative turning point	Book 10: Achaean success	Book 14: Achaean success
Book 7: balanced situation on the battlefield	Book 11: balanced situation on the battlefield	Book 15: Trojan success
Book 8: Trojan success	Book 12: Trojan success	Book 16: tentative turning point

[112] On the "direction of flow" or "line of development," see Currie (2016) 197.

summoning a council, whereas this role is not played by the first pair of heroes, the Ajaxes, in book 13, but by Poseidon. (b) The fact that the features pertaining to the theme of ambush in book 13 can hardly be considered primary, since no ambush warfare takes place in this book; conversely, they are at home in book 10. (c) The lack of Meriones' second spear, which he has left in his hut, makes sense in the light of the arming scene in book 10, where Meriones is, arguably, holding a spear with his one hand and a bow with his other.[113]

The thematic similarities discussed above are further enhanced by a case of verbatim quotation: Agamemnon expresses his fear regarding the safety of the army (10.93: αἰνῶς γὰρ περιδείδια); likewise, Poseidon, having taken the shape of Calchas, states that he is terrified of what might happen to the army (13.52: αἰνότατον περιδείδια). Although the form περιδείδια is attested twice more in the same metrical position (17.240, 17.242) in the *Iliad*, it is only in 10.93 and 13.52 that it is preceded by an adverbial form of the same root (αἰνῶς: 10.93; αἰνότατον: 13.52) and employed with respect to the entire Achaean army. Conversely, in book 17 περιδείδια is not preceded by a form of the adverb αἰνῶς/αἰνότατον, and it is applied only to the lives of Telamonian Ajax and Menelaus. It is exactly this point, i.e. the fear posed by Hector to the entire Achaean army, that belongs to the kernel of the theme running through these two narrative sequences. In this vein, it is reasonable to assume that this is a case of allusive reference by means of wording. The occurrence of this repetition within a similar narrative sequence, the fact that it is employed by two characters (Agamemnon and Poseidon/Calchas) who play similar roles (they set in motion a plan), as well as the placement of this repetition at analogous positions within the two narrative sequences appear to corroborate the possibility of phraseological citation.

But what may be the function of the translation of the narrative sequence of book 10 to book 13 of the *Iliad*? First, the two sequences address the problem of dealing with the danger posed by Hector. This is true for both our tentative earlier version of book 10, in which the target of the nocturnal mission was Hector, and for the current version of the *Doloneia*. In the former case, book 13 may have used the same narrative sequence to help the audience recall the failed ambush attempt against Hector in book 10 and, thus, enhance the need to face him in open combat in book 13. After all, both ended with the killing of a minor warrior of no importance, Dolon (book 10) and Othryoneus (book 13),[114] who feature exclusively in these two episodes[115] and nowhere else in the *Iliad*. These two minor figures are associated by the combination of the same two motifs: (a) undertaking a task beyond their power (Dolon to infiltrate the Achaean camp and overhear

---

[113] See Tsagalis (2020b) 57 with n. 22.   [114] On Othryoneus, see also pp. 93, 96, 289–90.
[115] In *Il.* 13.772 Hector blames Paris for the sufferings and death of several Trojans, among whom is Othryoneus, who has been killed by Idomeneus.

Agamemnon's plan;[116] Othryoneus to protect Troy from the Achaeans) with the result that they lose their lives; (b) they both ask for too great a price (Dolon the horses of Achilles; Othryoneus the hand of Cassandra).[117] In the latter case, Idomeneus' stress on the positive evaluation of ambush warfare, which works as an acid test for the brave and cowardly warrior, allows for the possibility that the transference of this narrative sequence may have operated as a covert comment or afterthought on the success of the bravery of Diomedes and Odysseus, who set two successful ambushes against Dolon and Rhesus in book 10. Second, the analogy between the contexts in which these two narrative sequences are placed—the Achaeans infiltrating the area occupied by the Trojans (book 10) and the Trojans infiltrating the area of the Achaean camp (book 13)—creates a false expectation for the Achaeans, who may entertain the thought that as they had succeeded in achieving a certain victory *within enemy territory* (by killing Dolon in the earlier version and killing both Dolon and Rhesus in the current version of book 10), so *a fortiori* they may defeat or push back Hector now that the fighting takes place *within their own terrain* (in book 13). Third, the translation of this narrative sequence may function on the level of audience reception that is not necessarily the same as the way in which the characters of the plot interpret certain events. The *Iliad* seems to invite its audience to realize that as the result of book 10 was temporary and superficial since it did not change anything, so the result of book 13 will be equally temporary and superficial, in the sense that the Achaean resistance will also be short-lived.

These observations suggest that book 10 forms part of the plan of the *Iliad* and plays its role within a larger structure referring to the organization of the plot with respect to the theme of Hector's gradual victory. Moreover, the argument presented above regarding the backward allusion from book 13 to book 10 involves narrative (on the level of an entire sequence) and phraseological quotation, which results in the creation of an interpretive surplus.

2.4 An Interpretive Gain from the Authenticity of the *Doloneia*: Character-Drawing

A significant interpretive gain from the book's authenticity concerns the character-drawing of several major Iliadic heroes: Agamemnon, Diomedes, Diomedes and Odysseus as a pair, and Hector.

---

[116] The same observation is valid if Dolon played a different role in the earlier version of the *Doloneia*, in which he may have left the Trojan camp to gather booty from the dead Achaean warriors, whose bodies were left on the battlefield; see pp. 209–11, 242, 295.

[117] Strasburger (1954) 72–4; Fenik (1968) 131.

2.4.1 Agamemnon

Agamemnon features only in the first part of *Iliad* 10, the *Nyktegersia*. He is presented in a positive light, since he is concerned about the difficult situation the Achaeans are facing. In the *Doloneia* Agamemnon functions as the driving force for the unfolding of the plot, the more so since it is he who wakes up Nestor, who will devise the plan for a night mission. In *Iliad* 9 Agamemnon has been completely overshadowed by Diomedes, who like a second Achilles had fiercely rejected his accusations and has declared in front of the army that he is willing to stay and fight in Troy to the bitter end, even if he is left alone with Sthenelus. At the end of book 9 it is Diomedes again who not only tells Agamemnon that they should not have asked for Achilles' help in the first place but also advises him to get some rest during what is left of the night and lead the attack the following day. In this light, Agamemnon emerges as a weak, hopeless hero, who has placed himself in such a position that a mirror image of Achilles, the Argive hero Diomedes, sets the tone for the ensuing attack in *Iliad* 11. Remove book 10 and Agamemnon is left doing at the beginning of book 11 what Diomedes had commanded him to do at the end of book 9. Book 10 aims to change this negative situation for Agamemnon. His desperation at the beginning of the *Doloneia* stirs him to action. By taking the initiative on his own, he reasserts himself as the uncontested leader of the Achaean army. He seizes the opportunity, given by the fact that Hector and the Trojans had encamped on the plain without realizing that they are making themselves vulnerable during the night, and tries to exploit it. He summons the Achaean leaders and allows Nestor to devise a plan for a spying mission aimed at finding out Hector's intentions.[118]

2.4.2 Diomedes

Iliad 10 is equally, if not more, important for Diomedes. His impressive Iliadic career as a second Achilles begins with *Iliad* 5, a book devoted to his *aristeia*. His remarkable performance against human and divine enemies allows him to stand apart from all other Achaean heroes, as long as Achilles abstains from fighting. Although the *Iliad* (2.768-9) recognizes Ajax as the second-best hero after Achilles, Diomedes is clearly the best offensive warrior, whereas Telamonian Ajax is the best defensive warrior, the "bulwark of the Achaeans" (ἕρκος Ἀχαιῶν).[119] After his

---

[118] On the contribution of book 10 to the character-drawing of Agamemnon, see Stanley (1993) 126-7.

[119] This expression is employed only for Achilles (*Il.* 1.284) and Telamonian Ajax (*Il.* 3.329, 6.5, 7.211) in the *Iliad*. The latter hero becomes the "bulwark of the Achaeans" as soon as the former hero withdraws from the fighting. On Diomedes and Ajax as second-best Achaean heroes, see Nagy (1979 = 1999²) 30-2.

outstanding martial deeds in book 5 (where he kills numerous Trojans, wounds pro-Trojan gods, and defeats Aeneas), Diomedes comes face to face with his guest-friend Glaucus at *Il.* 6.119–36. The episode, which Zeus concludes by stealing Glaucus' wits, testifies to Diomedes' supremacy by virtue of receiving golden weapons for bronze ones that he gives to his Lycian adversary. In *Iliad* 7 Diomedes volunteers together with other principal Achaean heroes to fight Hector in a duel (163) and later on (399–402) forcefully rejects the Trojan offer to return the possessions stolen by Paris from Sparta, even were that to include the return of Helen herself; that is a stance that is endorsed by the army, who are pleased by his words (7.403–4). In *Iliad* 8 he displays concern for Odysseus, who is forced to retreat (91–5), plays a crucial role in saving Nestor (99–158), and is recognized as the major threat to the Trojans by Hector himself, who in his speech to the Trojan army mentions Diomedes alone as his prime target the following day, since he envisages that he will be the warrior who will try to push back the Trojans from the Achaean Wall (532–4). In *Iliad* 9, Diomedes confirms his heroic prowess, turns against Agamemnon,[120] who accuses the rest of the Achaeans (including Diomedes himself) of cowardice in their desire to return to Greece immediately (32–44). After news that the embassy to Achilles has failed, Diomedes is the hero who changes the mood, not only by robustly criticizing its purpose (698–700) but also by advising Agamemnon to rest and lead the attack the next day against the Trojans (708–9). All in all, Diomedes emerges as an outstanding warrior whose prime concern is the army and victory against the Trojans. He belongs to a world of sheer force. War becomes him, compromise does not.[121] However, after book 10 his presence in the plot gradually fades. Together with Odysseus he makes a late entrance in *Iliad* 11, where he is able finally to try to do to Hector what he was prevented by Zeus from carrying out in *Il.* 8.170. Immediately afterwards, Diomedes is wounded by Paris and retreats to the ships. Because of his wound he does not take part in the *teichomachia* in book 12; in book 14 he expresses his desire to fight despite his wound, given the army's dire straits (109–32), and also marshalls (together with the wounded Odysseus and Agamemnon) the Achaean troops, making them exchange their armor of battle (379–81). In book 16 there is only a passing reference to him being wounded, while in book 21 Ares complains to Athena about the Argive hero's assault on pro-Trojan gods in book 5. It is only in book 23 that Diomedes returns to the limelight. He takes part in two of the eight contests and performs extremely well. He rises victorious with the stolen, semi-divine horses of Aeneas in the chariot race (287–538) and nearly defeats Telamonian Ajax in the duel-in-armor contest (811–25). Seen from this vantage point, books 5 and 23 mark the beginning and end of Diomedes' Iliadic career. The

---

[120] In doing so, "Diomedes not only flags his disagreement with Agamemnon; he also self-consciously parades his act in the precedent established by Achilles in this poem" (Barker 2009, 62).

[121] See Barker and Christensen (2011) 9–44, (2020) 47–89.

former testifies to his military prowess, the latter amounts to a new ranking of the Achaean heroes, one that replaces Ajax (recognized in *Il.* 2.768–9 as the second-best Achaean) with Diomedes. This substitution is jarring without the *Doloneia*. Ajax fought Hector in a duel in book 7 and was instrumental both in the defense of the Achaean Wall in book 12 and in protecting the ships (especially in book 15). His initial identification as second-best warrior after Achilles is acknowledged in book 9 by his participation in the embassy to Achilles. Ajax is there because he is regarded as the representative of the army, next to the cleverest man (Odysseus) and Achilles' tutor (Phoenix). *Iliad* 10 aims to turn the scales in favor of Diomedes, who is the uncontested protagonist of the spying mission. He is the first to volunteer (220–6); the others do so only after he has spoken up (227–32). It is Diomedes who kills Dolon, Rhesus, and twelve Thracians during the night raid. It is Diomedes who is rewarded with Rhesus' splendid horses. Without book 10, the mighty Argive hero against whom Hector expects to fight in the *teichomachia*[122] makes a poor and extremely brief entrance in book 11, only to be wounded and forced to retreat. On the contrary, Diomedes re-emerges in all his heroic splendor at the end of book 10, the more so since he is the only hero who excels in two different types of warfare, fighting on the open ground (*Iliad* 5) and in the ambush (*Iliad* 10). Exhausted from the night raid, he is naturally introduced late in the battle (like Odysseus) and is wounded by Paris, who pointedly ambushes him[123] leaning against the column on the grave-mound of Ilos (*Il.* 11.369). Ambushed by Paris, Diomedes, the great ambusher of the *Doloneia*, is a critical loss for the Achaeans.[124]

2.4.3 Diomedes and Odysseus as a Pair

Iliad 10 is essential for establishing the pairing of Diomedes and Odysseus. It seems that the epic tradition explores the joint undertakings of the two heroes by oscillating between their negative and positive aspects.[125] In the case of the *Cypria*, the sinister side of the murder of a fellow Greek is evident, while in the *Ilias parva*, Odysseus' failed attempt to kill Diomedes after the theft of the Palladium discloses a covert tension between the two heroes.[126] On the contrary, their joint mission to fetch Philoctetes from Lemnos seems rather positive, even if some cunning and, arguably, disturbing tactics were employed to convince Philoctetes to join the army. This tendency to draw a connection between Diomedes and Odysseus is also observed in *Iliad* 8 and *Odyssey* 3, which complement each other in the sense

---

[122] *Il.* 8.532–4.   [123] *Il.* 11.379: ἐκ λόχου ἀμπήδησε.
[124] See pp. 43, 74, 81 n. 71, 98, 108. If so, Diomedes' wounding by Paris would create one more analogy with Achilles. Both heroes would excel in ambushes against major opponents (Rhesus and Hector [Σ (A) on *Il.* 22.188; see pp. 69, 176)]), both heroes would be ambushed by Paris (Diomedes in the *Iliad*, Achilles in the **Memnonis*).
[125] See p. 165 with n. 21.   [126] See *Il. parv.* fr. 11 GEF.

that the two heroes follow different courses of action in scenes in which Nestor is involved.¹²⁷ In *Iliad* 8, Odysseus fails to listen to Diomedes and assist Nestor, with the result that it is Diomedes who has to save him.¹²⁸ In *Odyssey* 3, Odysseus fails to listen to Nestor while on Tenedos and sails back to Agamemnon at Troy, whereas Diomedes follows Nestor and has a safe and speedy return to Greece.¹²⁹

In the light of these events, the joint attempt of Diomedes and Odysseus in *Iliad* 10 reflects an episode where the two heroes operate in perfect harmony. If the Rhesus episode featured in an oral, pre-Homeric tradition including several of the events we encounter in Lesches' *Ilias parva*, it would be interesting to know whether it would have been marked by the kind of harmonious cooperation between Diomedes and Odysseus that we see in *Iliad* 10. The fact that in both episodes it is Diomedes who keeps the prize, the horses of Rhesus and the Palladium, respectively, may be significant. It may also be relevant that, while Diomedes deserves to keep Rhesus' horses as he is the primary actor in the Rhesus episode, in the story of the Palladium it is Odysseus who plays the key role in the sense that he has already made a reconnaissance mission to Troy.

The overall picture shows that the Rhesus episode represents a positive spin on the pairing of Diomedes and Odysseus within the larger epic tradition. Their impeccable teamwork in this nocturnal mission can also be evaluated indirectly within the *Iliad* by means of a comparison of the fate of their victim (Rhesus) with the fate of Peiroos, one of the two Thracian leaders who is killed in book 4.

Both incidents are preceded by a pair of episodes (the *Epipolesis* in book 4 and the *Nyktegersia* in book 10) that share a certain affinity.¹³⁰ Likewise, the deaths of Peiroos and Rhesus are linked by several shared features which combine to mark the difference between the two episodes. They both belong to associated thematic environments, they occur after a pair of interrelated episodes, and they are placed at the very end of their respective books. The contrasting handling of their shared features significantly impacts on the audience's evaluation of the second episode, i.e. the death of Rhesus.

These episodes share the following elements:
(a) they pertain to the death of a Thracian leader (Peiroos [4.527–31] and Rhesus [10.494–6]);
(b) they feature the same two gods (Athena [4.514–16, 10.507–11] and Apollo [4.507–13, 10.515–19]);
(c) they mention what other Thracians do when their leader dies or what happens to them before the death of their leader (4.532–5, 10.483–4);

---

[127] Frame (2009) 556–7.   [128] *Il.* 8.90–117.
[129] *Od.* 3.162–83; Frame (2009, 557 n. 104) allows for the possibility that *Odyssey* 3 alludes to the epic tradition of the *Nosti.
[130] See p. 78.

(d) they refer to what happened to his weapons/belongings (4.532, 10.498–501, and 513–14).

These shared elements are treated in a contrasting manner:

(a) Peiroos is killed during regular warfare by the Aetolian Thoas, who avenges the immediately preceding death of Diores by Peiroos. Conversely, Rhesus is killed in his sleep by Diomedes.
(b) The order, form, and content of the divine interventions are radically different: in book 4, Apollo acts first, Athena second. In book 10, the order is reversed: Athena first and Apollo second. In book 4, Apollo's intervention is expressed in character-text, Athena's in narrator-text. By contrast, in book 10 Athena's intervention is expressed in character-text, Apollo's in narrator-text. In book 4, both Apollo and Athena instill courage in the Trojans and Achaeans, respectively, prompting further warfare. In book 10, Athena advises the spies to return to the ships, while Apollo wakes up Rhesus' cousin Hippocoon.
(c) In book 4, Peiroos' comrades stand around their dead leader (4.530) and drag his body away from the Achaeans (4.535); in book 10, the twelve Thracians who sleep around Rhesus (10.475) are killed by Diomedes before he slays their king; Odysseus drags the bodies of the twelve Thracians so that Rhesus' horses do not step on them (10.489–93). As for the newly arrived Thracian troops of Rhesus, they remain completely unaware of the Achaean spies and the death of their king, until Hippocoon wakes them up.
(d) Whereas in book 4 Thoas is not able to strip Peiroos of his weapons (4.532), in book 10 Diomedes and Odysseus steal Rhesus' horses (10.498–9, 513–14).

In this way, the analogy of the two episodes creates a semantical surplus that is interpretively significant. *Iliad* 10 invites the audience to positively evaluate the successful pairing of Diomedes and Odysseus against a Thracian king (a night raid in which they kill and steal his horses without being noticed) in view of an analogous episode that features a single Achaean warrior confronting a Thracian leader (who is killed in a typical vignette during daytime).

2.4.4 Hector

Iliad 10 contributes significantly to the character-building of Hector. It is in this book that Hector first expresses absolute confidence that he will defeat Achilles, therefore picking up on Odysseus' characterization of him in the Embassy. At *Il.* 10.305-6 he promises to give the best Achaean horses to the Trojan who will undertake the dangerous task of spying on the Achaean camp. Since these horses can only be Achilles' horses, Hector's arrogant promise clearly presupposes Achilles' defeat (for the narrative line of Patroclus acting as Achilles' surrogate has not yet unfolded). Significantly, *Iliad* 10 marks a step in a process. At *Il.* 8.191-7 Hector urges his horses to speed up so that he can get Nestor's golden shield and Diomedes' elaborate corselet, which has been fashioned by Hephaestus himself. He sees these acquisitions as a prerequisite for "the embarking of the Achaeans on their fast-running ships this very night."[131] In book 10, Hector expresses his certainty that he will capture the horses of Achilles (10.330-1) and offers them to Dolon as the prize for undertaking the spying mission.[132] At the end of book 16 (860-1), flushed with the success of killing the surrogate Patroclus, Hector again imagines defeating Achilles. However, in book 17 Apollo (71-81) and Zeus (449-50) make sure that he does not get Achilles' horses,[133] while later on, in an effective display of tragic irony, it will be Hector's dead body that will be tied to the chariot driven by Achilles' horses.[134] One can, therefore, appreciate the gradual build-up of the theme "Hector tries to acquire the enemy's weapons." If book 10 is omitted, Hector's insistence on acquiring Achilles' horses significantly weakens. On the contrary, what is said and done about Achilles' horses in book 17 acquires depth and meaning because of Hector's haughty assurance of Dolon in book 10 and Odysseus' proleptic comment when he arrests Dolon (402-4): ἵππων Αἰακίδαο δαΐφρονος· οἱ δ' ἀλεγεινοί | ἀνδράσι γε θνητοῖσι δαμήμεναι ἠδ' ὀχέεσθαι | ἄλλῳ γ' ἢ Ἀχιλῆϊ, τὸν ἀθανάτη τέκε μήτηρ.[135] Apollo's reiteration of the same lines to Hector in *Il.* 17.76-8 is a powerful reminder about the limits of mortals. In this respect, Diomedes and Hector are alike: the former will not be a second Achilles as far as defeating Hector, the latter will not be the Trojan Achilles even if he wears that man's armor. The promise given in *Iliad* 10 is cut short in *Iliad* 17. Achilles' horses are the measure for evaluating Hector's fate.

This chapter has explored the *Iliad*'s use of themes and phraseology for creating intratextual associations between book 10 and the rest of the epic. It was suggested that these associations deepen the meaning of relevant passages, highlight Hector's overconfidence that constitutes a key topic of the entire epic, and contribute to the character-drawing of several heroes who play a crucial role in the Iliadic plot.

---

[131] *Il.* 8.197: αὐτονυχεὶ νηῶν ἐπιβησέμεν ὠκειάων.
[132] Stanley (1993, 125) argues that in doing so Dolon "exemplifies the same Trojan susceptibility to the lure of *aglaa dora* with which Athena tempted Pandaros into shooting Menelaos in 4.97."
[133] See also *Il.* 17.503-5.   [134] *Il.* 22.396-404.
[135] "They are difficult horses for mortal men to manage, or even to ride behind them for all except Achilles, who was born of an immortal mother."

3
A Second Thematic Approach
The Horses of Rhesus

Introduction

The fact that Rhesus' splendid horses are never mentioned again outside of the *Doloneia*, even when the context seems suitable for such a reference (in the funeral games for Patroclus in *Iliad* 23, Diomedes takes part in the chariot race without using these fabulous Thracian horses),[1] has been time and again used as an argument in favor of the position that *Iliad* 10 is a major interpolation. In the light of the aforementioned mapping of an entire network of internal thematical associations between the *Doloneia* and the rest of the *Iliad*, the time is ripe for a fresh look at Rhesus' horses.

3.1 Horses in the *Iliad*: Some Basic Points

The horse occupies a central position in Indo-European poetry and myth,[2] especially within a martial context in which men and horses fight next to each other. This concept has been crystallized in standard phraseology that spans several Indo-European languages: Greek (*Il.* 9.708: λαόν τε καὶ ἵππους, 17.400: ἀνδρῶν τε καὶ ἵππων, 21.16: ἵππων τε καὶ ἀνδρῶν); Roman (Cic. *De officiis* 3.116: *viris equisque*; Livy 3.70.6: *equos virosque*); Old Persian (*AmH* 6: *huaspā humartiyā* "of good horses, of good men"); Armenian (*ayrewji, ayrowji* "man and horse"); and Welsh (*Y Gododdin* 745: *lledrudd llewyr a meirch a gŵr* "blood-stained throngs, both horses and men").[3] The existence of poetic

---

[1] For an early champion of this argument, see Christ (1884) 76; for a recent advocate, see M. L. West (2011a) 233: "in particular it is remarkable that the wonderful horses captured from Rhesos in this episode are never mentioned again, not even in the context of the chariot race at Patr.'s funeral games, where Diom. races with the horses he captured from Aeneas in E." Shewan's explanation (1911, 179–80), though entirely unitarian, is simplistic.

[2] The close relationship between horses and heroes may stem from "the common predisposition toward the anthropomorphizing of horses and the concomitant hippomorphizing of humans" (Platte 2017, 35). In the *Iliad*, horses and heroes are regarded as superior because they both participate in warfare (horses by means of chariot-driving; see Walker 2016, 315–16). For a brief history of the horse in Indo-European culture, see Delebecque (1951) 217–30; for a thorough analysis of "swift horses" from Proto-Indo-European (PIE) to Greek, see Platte (2017) 7–33.

[3] The references are *exempli gratia*; for more material, see M. L. West (2007) 465.

vocabulary around the pair "man and horse" must have been a standard feature of the Indo-European poetic language.[4]

The horse is by far the most prominent animal in the *Iliad* (and probably in the entire epic tradition of the Trojan War).[5] Although Homeric heroes do not ride them,[6] horses are extensively used in chariot-driving, which constitutes a focal part of Iliadic fighting. Homeric epic preserves all the features pertaining to the Indo-European conception of the horse as an essential part of warfare, and, to this extent, we may speak of a typology: (1) horses are swift. They are characterized by the epithet ὠκύς[7] (ὠκέες ἵπποι: 11x *Il.*, 1x *Od.*; ὠκέας ἵππους: 20x *Il.*, 2x *Od.*; ἵππων ὠκειάων: 3x *Il.*; ὠκύποδες: 12x *Il.*, 2x *Od.*; ἀερσίποδες: 3x *Il.*), and their speed is at times expressed by means of flying imagery or relevant diction (πετέσθην: 11x *Il.*, 3x *Od.*; ὠκυπέτα: *Il.* 8.42 = 13.24).[8] Menelaus' horse is named Πόδαργος ("Swiftfoot": *Il.* 23.295) and Achilles' horses are born to Ζέφυρος, the West Wind, by the Harpy Ποδάργη (*Il.* 16.149–51 and 19.400), probably after she had acquired equine form.[9] Eumelus' horses are ποδώκεας ὄρνιθας ὥς ("swift-moving like birds…": *Il.* 2.764). (2) Horses are prize-winning (ἀεθλοφόροι: 5x *Il.*)[10] and strong-hooved (κρατερώνυχες: 3x *Il.*, 1x *Od.*). (3) Horses are loyal and gifted with mantic abilities. The Myrmidons "miss their warlike master" (*Il.* 2.778: οἱ δ' ἀρχὸν ἀρηΐφιλον ποθέοντες) when he abstains from battle, and the same feeling applies to chariot-horses missing their charioteers (*Il.* 11.161: ἡνιόχους ποθέοντες ἀμύμονας) who have been killed in combat. Xanthus, Achilles' horse, prophesies his master's future death (*Il.* 19.408–17; see 19.420).[11] (4) Horses and men are at times mentioned as parts of a whole (e.g. 17.400–1: τοῖον Ζεὺς ἐπὶ Πατρόκλῳ ἀνδρῶν τε καὶ ἵππων | ἤματι τῷ ἐτάνυσσε κακὸν πόνον; 23.242: ἐσχατιῇ καίοντ' ἐπιμὶξ ἵπποι τε καὶ ἄνδρες).

---

[4] For the possibility that there was a Graeco-Aryan poetic compound *ekwopoti- (or something like it) indicating a "master of horses" (if Greek ἱππότα < *ἱπποπότης, in the manner of δεσπότης, is correct), see M. L. West (2007) 467; Schmitt (1967, 23, 130–1) is of a different opinion, explaining the -τ- in ἱππότα on the analogy of *eques, equitis* in Latin.

[5] The sack of Troy by the stratagem of the Wooden Horse is the crowning manifestation of the horse's preeminence among other animals in the Trojan myth.

[6] There are very few exceptions to this rule: two similes (*Il.* 15.678–86; *Od.* 5.370–1) and *Il.* 10.513–14 (where Diomedes jumps onto the horses that fly away to the Achaean camp). In the latter case, as well as in the whole night episode of the *Doloneia*, note the "tension between the heroic language of chariot driving and the unheroic activity of horse riding" (Walker 2016, 324); see also Hainsworth (1993) 202–3 on *Il.* 10.498ff.; Dué and Ebbott (2010) 367–9 on *Il.* 10.513–14.

[7] See Platte (2017) 7–10, who argues that the phrase ὠκέες ἵπποι goes back to the PIE formula *h₁ōkéu̯-es *h₁éku̯-ōs; see the formula āsauuō aspāṇhō used in the Avestan Gathas and āśavas aśvās in the Sanskrit Vedas.

[8] The epithet ἀελλόπους is used 3x *Il.* for Iris, while in the *Homeric Hymn to Aphrodite* 217 it is applied to horses (ἵπποισιν ἀελλοπόδεσσιν).

[9] This is implied by the fact that she was grazing (βοσκομένη λειμῶνι παρὰ ῥόον Ὠκεανοῖο); see Probert (2016) 377.

[10] See the Vedic equivalent *vājambharā* ("prize-winning") in Rigveda 1.60.5.

[11] See also the speaking horse Arion in the *Thebais* (fr. 11 *GEF*).

On this evidence, we can expect horses to play an important role in the *Iliad*.[12] Their significance and status in the poem are amply on show in a brief "Catalogue of the Best" (of the Achaeans) in 2.761–79, squeezed between the "Catalogue of Ships" (2.494–760) and the "Catalogue of Trojans and Allies" (2.816–77). Given its relevance for my topic, I quote it in full:

τίς ταρ τῶν ὄχ' ἄριστος ἔην, σύ μοι ἔννεπε, Μοῦσα,   761
αὐτῶν ἠδ' ἵππων, οἳ ἅμ' Ἀτρείδῃσιν ἕποντο·
ἵπποι μὲν μέγ' ἄρισται ἔσαν Φηρητιάδαο,
τὰς Εὔμηλος ἔλαυνε ποδώκεας ὄρνιθας ὥς,
ὄτριχας οἰέτεας, σταφύλῃ ἐπὶ νῶτον ἐΐσας·   765
τὰς ἐν Πηρείῃ θρέψ' ἀργυρότοξος Ἀπόλλων,
ἄμφω θηλείας, φόβον Ἄρηος φορεούσας.
ἀνδρῶν αὖ μέγ' ἄριστος ἔην Τελαμώνιος Αἴας,
ὄφρ' Ἀχιλεὺς μήνιεν· ὁ γὰρ πολὺ φέρτατος ἦεν,
ἵπποι θ', οἳ φορέεσκον ἀμύμονα Πηλεΐωνα.   770
ἀλλ' ὁ μὲν ἐν νήεσσι κορωνίσι ποντοπόροισι
κεῖτ' ἀπομηνίσας Ἀγαμέμνονι ποιμένι λαῶν
Ἀτρεΐδῃ· λαοὶ δὲ παρὰ ῥηγμῖνι θαλάσσης
δίσκοισιν τέρποντο καὶ αἰγανέῃσιν ἱέντες
τόξοισίν θ'· ἵπποι δὲ παρ' ἅρμασιν οἷσιν ἕκαστος   775
λωτὸν ἐρεπτόμενοι ἐλεόθρεπτόν τε σέλινον
ἕστασαν· ἅρματα δ' εὖ πεπυκασμένα κεῖτο ἀνάκτων
ἐν κλισίῃς· οἱ δ' ἀρχὸν ἀρηΐφιλον ποθέοντες
φοίτων ἔνθα καὶ ἔνθα κατὰ στρατόν, οὐδ' ἐμάχοντο.

Tell me then, Muse, who of them all was the best and bravest,
of the men, and the men's horses, who went with the sons of Atreus.
Best by far among the horses were the mares of Eumelus,
Pheres' son, that he drove, swift-moving like birds, alike in
texture of coat, in age, both backs drawn level like a plumb-line.
These Apollo of the silver bow had bred in Pereia,
mares alike, who went with the terror of the god of battle.
Among the men far the best was Telamonian Ajax,
while Achilles stayed angry, since he was far best of all of them,
and the horses also, who carried the blameless son of Peleus.
But Achilles lay apart from among his curved sea-wandering
vessels, raging at Agamemnon, the shepherd of the people,
Atreus' son; and his men beside the break of the sea-beach

---

[12] Even their limited use in similes is significant for the poem's plot.

amused themselves with discs and with light spears for throwing
and bows; and the horses, standing each beside his chariot,
champed their clover and the parsley that grows in wet places,
resting, while the chariots of their lords stood covered
in the shelters, and the men forlorn of their warlike leader
wandered here and there in the camp and did no fighting.

This passage is key to unlocking the function of horses in the *Iliad*. First, it should be noted that, despite the preceding "Catalogue of Ships," a hero's excellence is not indicated by the number of ships in his possession. Ships indicate a hero's wealth and the size of an army, but they do not prove excellence in battle and heroic prestige.[13] The same observation may be applied to horses. Eumelus is no special hero. His horses are extremely swift, which makes them, not him, preeminent (763: ἵπποι μὲν μέγ' ἄρισται ἔσαν). He may be a good horse driver,[14] but his horses are exceptional not because of his skill in driving the chariot but because they have been raised by Apollo. We are not told whether they are divine horses, but their association with a god makes them outstanding. Second, what is crucial for the evaluation of one's heroic prowess is fighting ability. Telamonian Ajax is presented as the best warrior (second only to Achilles), though he has no horses. The fact that Ajax has no horses but is the best warrior is telling: just as having the best horses does not make one the best warrior (Eumelus), so being deprived of horses does not prevent one from excelling in battle (Ajax). These two points featuring in this programmatic passage operate as a backdrop against which the *Iliad* will introduce Diomedes, i.e. the hero who will substitute for Achilles until his wounding and withdrawal from battle in book 11. Eumelus' excellent horses and Ajax's heroic prowess will be combined in Diomedes, a hero who will have a passion for horses[15] and will display exceptional fighting skills.[16] The combination of the abilities of these two

---

[13] See Delebecque (1951) 232, who draws attention to the nobility and pride of horses. Platte discusses the identification of horse and hero (2017, 36–45) but does not take into account cases like that of Eumelus and Ajax, the former having the best horses among the Achaeans (after those of Achilles) but being a second-rate hero, the latter being the best Achaean warrior (after Achilles), though he has no horses at all.

[14] *Il.* 23.289: ὃς ἱπποσύνῃ ἐκέκαστο.

[15] He will acquire no fewer than four sets of horses from his opponents (book 5: Phegeus, Echemmon and Chromius, Aeneas; book 10: Rhesus); see below, p. 112. See also Σ (bT) *Il.* 5.25 (ἱππομανὴς ἀεὶ ὁ Διομήδης, "Diomedes is always mad for horses"), though the explanation given by the scholiast is wrong, since Diomedes' passion for horses is explained as stemming from his Argive origin (see, e.g., *Il.* 2.287: ἀπ' Ἄργεος ἱπποβότοιο). Of all the contestants in the chariot race of the funeral games Antilochus is the one who captures horses in the *Iliad*: at 5.576–89 he drives off the horses of Pylaemenes and Mydon, whom he kills together with Menelaus; at 13.400–1 he drives off the horses of Asius. While Menelaus and Antilochus are partners in book 5, they become competitors in book 23, in which the latter fouls the former; while in book 5 they successfully add up to one Diomedes, in book 23 they part ways and fail; see Quint (2022) 18, 23–5.

[16] See *Iliad* 5, 8, and 10.

Achaeans, Eumelus and Ajax—who excel with respect to horses (the former) and bravery (the latter)—represents the two aspects in which Achilles (the great absent hero whom Diomedes temporarily replaces) is truly outstanding, his divine horses and his unsurpassed fighting skill. This essential issue is built into the poem's narrative structure and is explored in a subplot with Diomedes as the protagonist in books 5–11.[17] But even after this point, when Diomedes features again in the plot, it will be in a context that is also associated with horses (the chariot race in the funeral games organized in honor of Patroclus).[18] Since this is the most important contest and Achilles and his horses[19] abstain from the games, as they did for the largest part of the fighting in the poem, Diomedes' victory in the chariot race allows a final glance of the subplot that had been completed in book 11. Moreover, it constitutes the most pronounced mirror-text of the entire episode of the funeral games through which the *Iliad* looks at itself. These two cardinal issues (Diomedes and horses in books 5–11; Diomedes in the funeral games) will be explored in the two following sections of this chapter.

3.2 The Horses of Rhesus and a Telescopic View of the *Iliad*

The theft of Rhesus' horses and the killing of so highly ranked a hero as the newly arrived Thracian king constitute the pinnacle of Diomedes' career as a substitute for Achilles. The process of Diomedes' stepping up while Achilles has withdrawn from fighting follows a carefully planned and gradually developed process. Being absent from the programmatic "Catalogue of the Best" (of the Achaeans) in 2.761–79, which features Eumelus and Ajax as second best in horsemanship and fighting skill, Diomedes will evolve into a hero who is second best only to Achilles. To this end he will excel in both horsemanship and military prowess.[20]

---

[17] See Quint (2022) 18.
[18] This observation is reinforced by their placement in the first position among the contests, the number of contestants, the size of the prizes, and the detailed narrative that is longer than all the other contests together (chariot race: 23.287–538; other contests: 23.651–897).
[19] Achilles has two divine horses (Xanthus and Balius, born to Zephyrus by the Harpy Podarge) and one mortal horse (Pedasus). The former pair were a gift from Poseidon to Peleus at his wedding with Thetis (*Il.* 16.867); the latter horse belongs to the spoils Achilles took when he sacked Hypoplacian Thebes (Eetion's city) in the Troad (*Il.* 16.152-3). The two immortal horses drive his chariot, while the mortal one is a trace-horse, tied to the chariot by παρηορίαι ("ropes"). A three-horse chariot is rare (only here and in *Od.* 4.590; see Delebecque (1951) 16–17; Janko (1992) 337 on *Il.* 16.152–4. Pedasus belongs to a completely different legend from the one pertaining to Xanthus and Balius. His "addition" to the famous pair is poetically motivated: the storyteller aims at "satisfying" Sarpedon, who will kill Pedasus before he is killed by Patroclus. The mortal nature of Pedasus is thus strongly opposed to the immortality of Xanthus and Balius. Notice how the mortal Pedasus is "forgotten" in *Il.* 16.380–1, when Achilles' chariot leaps over the ditch (only the immortal pair of horses being mentioned); conversely, in *Il.* 16.867 (= 16.381) the reference to the immortal horses alone is correct, since Pedasus has been killed by Sarpedon (*Il.* 16.467–9).
[20] Diomedes will also excel in the political arena of assembly and council.

The subplot in which he is the protagonist on the Achaean side extends from book 5 to book 11.[21] Diomedes fights against several pro-Trojan gods in *Iliad* 5, just as Achilles will fight against Scamander in *Iliad* 21. Like Achilles, he has a Hephaestus-made corselet that Hector wants to take from him in *Il.* 8.194–5, just as Hector takes from the dead Patroclus the Hephaestus-made armor he has borrowed from Achilles in *Iliad* 16.[22] Diomedes steals the horses of Phegeus after killing him (*Il.* 5.8–26), those of the pair Echemmon and Chromius whom he also kills (*Il.* 5.159–65), those of Aeneas who remains alive (*Il.* 5.297–327), and those of Rhesus whom he slays together with his guards (*Il.* 10.487–8, 494–6); the last two thefts elevate Diomedes to the rank of an Achilles, famous for his immortal horses.[23] In this vein, the role Diomedes plays in the Rhesus episode represents the apex of his Iliadic performance as the second-best Achaean hero, in that he both steals horses and kills a major enemy (Rhesus). However, the *Iliad* uses the subplot in which Diomedes is the key figure to invite its audience to evaluate him not only as the second-best Achaean hero but also as a new Achilles, i.e. a hero who can defeat Hector. Diomedes succeeds in the former role but fails in the latter. He is the second-best Achaean hero but not a new Achilles.[24] Hector is not defeated but triumphs after Diomedes' failure to kill him in *Il.* 8.117–21 and 8.167–71.[25] Conversely, it is Diomedes who is wounded and withdraws from fighting in book 11. It is at this point that he gives way to another figure, Patroclus, who will also try, albeit in a different way, to be a new Achilles. Patroclus' failure will lead to his death, which in turn redirects Achilles' wrath and causes him finally to return to the war to kill Hector.

In book 23, after Achilles has avenged the death of Patroclus, the *Iliad* recognizes Diomedes as the second-best Achaean warrior through his actions in the prime contest of the funeral games for Patroclus, the chariot race. Using the semi-divine horses that he has stolen from Aeneas in book 5, Diomedes defeats Eumelus

---

[21] With a brief introduction in *Il.* 4.364–421.   [22] See Cook (2009) 149 n. 52.
[23] Quint (2022) 32.
[24] This narrative strategy is paired with the poem's creation of the need for a new Paris, who will play the key role Paris had in the Trojan saga. This new Paris is Hector. As the former's desires and actions have caused the Trojan War, so the latter's actions and decisions seal the fate of Troy. Bakker (2017, 57–74) has argued that Hector gradually becomes in the *Iliad* the equivalent of Paris in the entire Trojan myth, the *aitios* of the Trojan demise in the plot of the epic. This process is partly carried out by three horse similes (6.506–12, 15.263–9, 22.22–4) that belong to the epic's larger architectural design (Bakker 2017, 66). These horse similes link the two brothers and pave the way for Hector's ultimate failure in defeating Achilles in book 22. As these horse similes "rewrite" the story of the Trojan War by associating Paris, Hector, and Achilles, so Diomedes' theft of horses "rewrites" the theme of Achilles' wrath by associating Diomedes, Achilles, and Hector.
[25] Having stolen Aeneas' swift, semi-immortal Trojan horses, Diomedes (with Nestor as charioteer) approaches Hector's own chariot and unsuccessfully attempts to kill him. The stolen horse thus enables him to come as close as possible to killing Hector. Book 8 is the central part of a triad of episodes dispersed in books 5, 8, and 10, which pertain to Diomedes and horses.

and his own exceptional horses that had been raised by Apollo. In contrast, the failure of Telamonian Ajax to win any contest in the funeral games shows that the *Iliad* aims at a new ranking of certain Achaean heroes.[26] The epic thus corrects the "Catalogue of the Best" in which Eumelus and Ajax were presented as the second-best (after Achilles) heroes in horsemanship and military skill. Diomedes is finally recognized as the undisputed second-best Achaean hero, the warrior who achieved this status through the subplot of books 5–11. The Rhesus episode is the climax of this subplot. Not only does it constitute the crowning achievement of Diomedes' role as a substitute for Achilles, since it allows Diomedes to excel simultaneously in the two aspects of Achilles' excellence (horses and fighting), but it also shows what Diomedes cannot achieve—the death of Hector. This will be the work of Achilles, the best of the Achaeans.

3.3 The Horses of Rhesus: Magnificent but not Divine

The horses of Rhesus are described by Dolon at *Il.* 10.436–7. They are subsequently mentioned by Nestor, who hears the noise made by their hooves (*Il.* 10.535) and asks about them when Diomedes and Odysseus return to the Achaean camp (*Il.* 10.547–50). There is one more brief reference to these magnificent horses (*Il.* 10.567–9), when they are placed in the manger next to Diomedes' other horses. Of all these passages I cite only those verses which contain a description of Rhesus' horses:

τοῦ δὴ καλλίστους ἵππους ἴδον ἠδὲ μεγίστους·
λευκότεροι χιόνος, θείειν δ' ἀνέμοισιν ὁμοῖοι.

And his are the finest horses I ever saw, and the biggest;
they are whiter than snow, and their speed of foot is the winds' speed.[27]
(*Il.* 10.436–7)

αἰνῶς ἀκτίνεσσιν ἐοικότες ἠελίοιο.

They shine, like the rays of the sun. (*Il.* 10.547)

Dolon and Nestor express their amazement at Rhesus' horses and describe them in terms of their beauty and size (καλλίστους ἵππους ἴδον ἠδὲ μεγίστους), speed

---

[26] See Wehr (2015) 60–8; Quint (2022) 40.
[27] When applied to swift horses, this expression has a special connotation, since various swift horses have the wind as their father (Erichthonius' mares have been impregnated by Boreas, Achilles' horses are born to Zephyrus by the Harpy Podarge); on the wind impregnating horses, see Zirkle (1936) 95–130.

(θείειν δ' ἀνέμοισιν ὁμοῖοι), and radiance (λευκότεροι χιόνος, ἀκτίνεσσιν ἐοικότες ἠελίοιο). They say nothing about their divine origin or association with a god. Similarly, Rhesus' armor is said to be all gold and silver and his weapons golden as if appropriate to a god. Both references imply that Rhesus' horses and armor are exceptional, but not divine or associated with a specific god.

This is a crucial observation, especially when set against what we know from one of the other versions concerning the Rhesus story.[28] According to the alleged "oracle version" (Σ [AD] Il. 10.435), there was an oracle determining that if he and his horses drank water from the river Scamander and his horses ate the grass growing on its banks, then he would be invincible. Rhesus was killed either by Diomedes alone[29] or by Diomedes and Odysseus[30] during a nocturnal ambush. In the Iliad, Rhesus is not of divine origin (instead he is the son of the herald Eioneus). His horses may be beautiful, impressive, and fast, but they are not of divine origin.

Since Fenik,[31] an argument has been put forward, according to which the "great deed" Odysseus and Diomedes have in mind in their spying mission (Il. 10.282: ῥέξαντας μέγα ἔργον) echoes a plan to kill Hector that may have featured in other versions of this story. This line of thought would be very much in tune with what was said about Hector at Il. 10.51 (ἔργα δ' ἔρεξ' ὅσα φημὶ μελησέμεν Ἀργείοισιν).[32] What is essential to my analysis is that the storylines of Hector and Rhesus are incompatible and that the introduction of the Rhesus story, with the modifications imposed by the Iliadic tradition, may have resulted in the erasure of a plan to kill Hector by ambush. Still, traces of such a plan are discernible in Iliad 10, especially in verses 406-7 (ποῦ νῦν δεῦρο κιὼν λίπες Ἕκτορα ποιμένα λαῶν; | ποῦ δέ οἱ ἔντεα κεῖται ἀρήϊα, ποῦ δέ οἱ ἵπποι;), which allow us to catch a fleeting glimpse of a different version where the target of the spying mission may have been Hector and his horses.[33] It is a plausible hypothesis that Rhesus replaces Hector as the target of the nocturnal mission, complete with details of his weapons and horses.[34] The reason for this replacement may have been that Rhesus offers something to the plotline of book 10 that Hector could not: his death. By killing Rhesus and stealing his weapons and horses, Diomedes and Odysseus return victorious to the Achaean camp and instill courage in the desperate army. This is suggested at the beginning

---

[28] See Fenik (1964) 5-6; Dué and Ebbott (2010) 91-3; Liapis (2012) xviii-xxi.
[29] Σ (bT) Il. 10.435 (Erbse).   [30] Σ (D) on Il. 10.435Zˢ.
[31] Fenik (1964) 16-20; see also Petegorsky (1982) 222-3; differently, Liapis (2012) 234, who treats it as an innovation of the poet of the Rhesus who over-interpreted Il. 10.282.
[32] "He has done things I think the Argives will remember with sorrow."
[33] The swiftness of Hector's horses is deliberately downplayed in the Iliad but lurks at 8.190 and (ironically) at 16.383, when Hector's horses are described as so swift that Achilles' immortal horses (which are also swift: 16.380) cannot catch them. The reason for the emphasis on the swiftness of Hector's horses has its answer in the similar description of Aeneas' swift horses.
[34] See chapters 5-6.

of *Iliad* 11, when Agamemnon leads the great attack against the Trojans and Zeus holds back Hector until Agamemnon is wounded. An Achaean victory during the night would have been impossible had Hector been the target of the spying mission, since, being indispensable to the plot, the spies could not have killed him;[35] in turn, this would mean that there would be no Achaean victory during the night and, hence, no regain of hope at the end of book 10 so as to stir the army to fight in the open the next day. The argument that the killing of Rhesus in *Iliad* 10 stands as a substitute for the attempted killing of Hector in an earlier version of the *Iliad* is analogous to the famous neoanalytical claim that in the *Iliad* Achilles' killing of Hector (to avenge the killing of his best friend, Patroclus, at the hands of Hector) replaces, in an earlier epic tradition, Achilles' killing of Memnon (to avenge the killing of his best friend, Antilochus, at the hands of Memnon).

Seen in these terms, the horses of Rhesus are mere accoutrements of the hero Rhesus, since, together with his weapons, they may have formed part of a narrative unit that has substituted a "Hector-unit" or may have been used as a "response" by the *Iliad* to a rival version of the story. When Rhesus dies, his horses also "die" together with him. We will not hear of them again in the plot; having fulfilled their mission, they fall into oblivion. This development may be helpfully compared to what will happen with the arms of Achilles. Iliadic innovation (the stealing of Achilles' arms by Hector, who takes them from the dead Patroclus) creates a situation where, after Achilles' death, the Achaeans possess two sets of arms belonging to Achilles (the first set given by Peleus to Achilles when he left Phthia to go to Troy and loaned to Patroclus from Achilles, and the second set which Thetis brought to him in the *Iliad* after the death of Patroclus), both made by Hephaestus.[36] Post-Iliadic tradition downplayed the existence of one of the two sets, in order to give sense to the contest of arms between Telamonian Ajax and Odysseus.[37]

---

[35] Diomedes' suggestion to Agamemnon that he lead the attack the next day (*Il.* 9.708–9) may have been met with the approval of the kings (*Il.* 9.710–11) but would have hardly convinced the king of Mycenae, who had at the beginning of book 9 suggested that they should return to Greece and was anxiously waiting for the news about Achilles from the envoys (*Il.* 9.673–5). The approval by the kings of Diomedes' admonition at the end of book 9 caps the approval by the army of his earlier admonition at the beginning of the same book (9.50–1). Both an *Iliad* without book 10 and an *Iliad* with a version of book 10 in which Hector would have been the target of the spy mission would have failed to change Agamemnon's disappointment and lack of courage. By performing outstandingly in book 10, Diomedes enables this change. His admonition at the end of *Iliad* 9 acquires firm support through his action in *Iliad* 10.

[36] Contrast the situation in the *Iliad*, when the two divine armors of Achilles become the possession of Hector and Achilles. Their "coexistence" after book 16 is systematic: see *Il.* 17.194–7, 213–14, 450, 472–3, 693; 18.21, 82–3, 130–2, 335; 19.10–18, 367–83; 22.258–9, 322–3, 368–9. On the contrary, after Hector's death (i.e. when the two armors become the property of a single person, Achilles) the first armor is forgotten.

[37] I owe the analogy with the arms of Achilles to Bruno Currie (private communication).

3.4 The Trojan Horses of Diomedes and the Chariot Race

Diomedes' association with horses is particularly noteworthy. During the unfolding of the plot he acquires no fewer than four new pairs of horses[38] in addition to the ones he had brought with him from Greece. It is these Greek horses that he yokes in his chariot in *Iliad* 5 when the fighting begins. But when he confronts Aeneas and defeats him, he deprives him of his horses, which go back through Tros to Zeus himself. At once, he tells his comrade Sthenelus to "check here these fast-running horses, ours, tethering them with the reins tied to the chariot's rail"[39] and then to lead Aeneas' horses to the Achaean camp.[40] This means that in the rest of book 5 Diomedes will be using the horses that he had brought with him from Greece. However, the *Iliad* makes sure to highlight (even at their first mention in the poem) the importance of the horses Diomedes takes from Aeneas by an external analepsis. The text runs as follows:

τῆς γάρ τοι γενεῆς, ἧς Τρωΐ περ εὐρύοπα Ζεὺς
δῶχ' υἷος ποινὴν Γανυμήδεος, οὕνεκ' ἄριστοι
ἵππων, ὅσσοι ἔασιν ὑπ' ἠῶ τ' ἠέλιόν τε,
τῆς γενεῆς ἔκλεψεν ἄναξ ἀνδρῶν Ἀγχίσης,
λάθρῃ Λαομέδοντος ὑποσχὼν θήλεας ἵππους·
τῶν οἱ ἓξ ἐγένοντο ἐνὶ μεγάροισι γενέθλη.
τοὺς μὲν τέσσαρας αὐτὸς ἔχων ἀτίταλλ' ἐπὶ φάτνῃ,
τὼ δὲ δύ' Αἰνείᾳ δῶκεν, μήστωρε φόβοιο.[41]

These are of that strain of which Zeus of the wide brows granted
once to Tros, as a recompense for his son Ganymedes, and therefore
are the finest of all horses beneath the sun and the daybreak;
and the lord of men Anchises stole horses from this breed,
without the knowledge of Laomedon putting mares under them.

---

[38] See p. 106 n. 15.
[39] *Il.* 5.261-2: σὺ δὲ τούσδε μὲν ὠκέας ἵππους | αὐτοῦ ἐρυκακέειν, ἐξ ἄντυγος ἡνία τείνας.
[40] *Il.* 5.263-4: Αἰνείαο δ' ἐπαΐξαι μεμνημένος ἵππων, | ἐκ δ' ἐλάσαι Τρώων μετ' ἐϋκνήμιδας Ἀχαιούς.
[41] I follow the main paradosis, which gives μήστωρε φόβοιο in both *Il.* 5.272 and 8.108. The application of the expression to horses instead of heroes in guaranteed by *Il.* 8.106-7 that describe both the horses' knowledge of the Trojan plain and their speed. M. L. West (2001, 201) suggests that nothing of the sort is observable at *Il.* 5.272, where "the verse seems to be naturally filled out with a formulaic phrase appended to the name of Aeneas than to a characterization of the horses." To explain his preference for the reading μήστωρι at *Il.* 5.272, he argues that the dual in book 5 has come to the poet's mind after the passage at *Il.* 8.108. M. L. West's arguments are based on context and formulaic use. However, this context equally pertains to the horses' outstanding quality. The ὠκέας ἵππους (5.261) and ἵπποι ὠκύποδες (5.295-6) are all about the horses' speed. As for formulaic use, the phraseology at *Il.* 5.272 and 8.108 is similar and perfectly compatible with traditional use. Since *here* the duals represent *lectiones difficiliores*, their use is *a fortiori* preferable. After all, expressions that are applied to heroes can be "transferred" to animals or things (e.g. *Il.* 11.159-61: πολλοὶ δ' ἐριαύχενες ἵπποι |...| ἡνιόχους ποθέοντες ἀμύμονας; *Il.* 15.314-17: πολλὰ δὲ δοῦρα... λιλαιόμενα χροὸς ἆσαι).

From these there was bred for him a string of six in his great house.
Four of these, keeping them himself, he raised at his manger,
but these two he gave to Aeneas, two horses urgent of terror. (*Il.* 5.265–72)

The horses bred by Zeus and given to Tros are divine. This is not directly stated, but there is no reason to doubt their divine nature, given the indirect and direct acknowledgment of their immortality in *Homeric Hymn to Aphrodite* 210–12[42] and in Hellanicus (26b *EGM*), respectively.[43] Their descendants, interbred with mortal horses (*Il.* 5.269), are not divine[44] but still of divine origin, hence their exceptionality. The case is the same with Eumelus' mares. Their divine nature is stated nowhere, but their exceptionality is clearly indicated by the fact that they have been bred by Apollo (*Il.* 2.766–7). The special abilities of these two groups of horses are flagged in the text by two parallel and highly marked expressions: φόβον Ἄρηος φορεούσας (2.767) and μήστωρε φόβοιο (5.272).[45] Taking this evidence together, it becomes clear that, apart from Achilles' divine horses, the *Iliad* is aware of two other groups of horses that are exceptional because of their divine association, origin, and/or breeding: the horses of Aeneas and the horses of Eumelus.

The account of divine horses given to Tros by Zeus as recompense for the abduction of Ganymedes goes back to the early history of Troy. Laomedon inherited them from Tros, but Anchises, who did not belong to the royal line and so had no chance of inheriting them, stole them from Laomedon[46] and mated them with mares so as to breed other horses for himself.[47] Aeneas' horses are two

---

[42] καί μιν Ζεὺς ἐλέησε, δίδου δέ οἱ υἷος ἄποινα | ἵππους ἀερσίποδας, τοί τ' ἀθανάτους φορέουσι. | τούς οἱ δῶρον ἔδωκεν ἔχειν. The horses that carry the immortals are expected to be divine.

[43] See p. 114 n. 47.

[44] On this point, see Probert (2016, 377 and n. 30). Strolonga (2018, 193 n. 3) speaks of their "semi-immortality," a term she explains as implied immortality. It is important to note that Hector is unaware of this aspect of theirs (Harrison 1991, 253). Moreover, in the chariot race in *Iliad* 23 nothing is said about their divine nature.

[45] With the exception of this passage, the formula μήστωρε/α φόβοιο is always used for heroes in the *Iliad* (6.97, 8.108, 12.39, 23.16). The phraseology in *Il.* 2.767 for Eumelus' horses is also a *hapax*.

[46] Anderson (1997, 68) argues that "in stealing them from this lineage, from the blood of the royal horses, Anchises steals symbols of kingship, thereby appropriating royal prestige for himself and his son Aineias." This theft is a symbolic advance mention of the future transfer of the kingship from the Priamids to the Aeneadae. The royal line of Priam and Hector is destined to perish, together with the city of Troy. Conversely, the survival of the Trojans through the royal line of Aeneas is anticipated in the *Iliad* by the theft of the horses.

[47] In the story of Heracles' sack of Troy, Laomedon's horses are described as immortal (Hellanicus 26b *EGM*; Apollod. *Bibl.* 2.5.9) because this tale takes place before Anchises stole and mated these horses with mortal mares. Laomedon's horses are the immortal horses given to Tros by Zeus in recompense for the abduction of Ganymedes. This story is known to the *Iliad*, since in 5.640–2 it is explicitly stated that Heracles came to Troy "for the sake of Laomedon's horses" (ἕνεχ' ἵππων Λαομέδοντος; see also *Il.* 5.651: ὧν εἵνεκα τηλόθεν ἦλθεν; [Hes.] *Cat.* 43a.64 M–W: ἔνε[χ' ἵπ]πων Λαομέδοντος and fr. 165.10 M–W: εὖτε μεθ' ἵ]ππους στεῖχεν ἀγαυοῦ Λαομέδοντο[ς] and sacked the city with a force of the few men that his six ships could carry, since Laomedon failed to keep his promise and give the horses to Heracles (*Il.* 5.649–51). Heracles' fight with the sea monster is mentioned in *Il.* 20.145–8 in the context of a wall built for him by the Trojans and Athena as protection against the sea

of the six horses born to them, the other four being kept at Anchises' manger. There can hardly be a more emphatic way to indicate the status and prestige of these horses. They are truly "the best" (ἄριστοι), as appropriate for a gift from Zeus. In this vein, Diomedes has achieved a remarkable deed.[48] He has captured the best horses Troy has, an uncontestable token and living symbol of its glory.[49]

The *Iliad* takes pains to further reinforce the importance of these horses. To this end, it employs a whole set of devices. First, the diction employed for the horses of Laomedon (since he inherited them from Tros) and by extension of Aeneas (5.266-7: ἄριστοι | ἵππων, ὅσσοι ἔασιν ὑπ' ἠῶ τ' ἠέλιόν τε) strongly resonates with the language of the programmatic "Catalogue of the Best," in which it is said that (Achilles' horses excluded) Eumelus' mares are the "best" (2.763: ἵπποι μὲν μέγ' ἄρισται ἔσαν Φηρητιάδαο). Second, by having Diomedes capture two other pairs of horses (of the sons of Dares: *Il.* 5.25-6; of Echemmon and Chromius: *Il.* 5.165),[50] the *Iliad* stresses through opposition the vast distance separating the horses of Aeneas from the two other unimportant pairs, which are soon forgotten. Third, at *Il.* 8.105-8 Diomedes "advertises" Aeneas' horses by telling Nestor that he can safely mount his chariot, "so that you may see what the Trojan horses are like, how they understand their plain, and how to traverse it in rapid pursuit and withdrawal; horses I took away from Aeneas that strike men to terror" (ὄφρα ἴδηαι | οἷοι Τρώιοι ἵπποι, ἐπιστάμενοι πεδίοιο | κραιπνὰ μάλ' ἔνθα καὶ ἔνθα διωκέμεν ἠδὲ φέβεσθαι, | οὕς ποτ' ἀπ' Αἰνείαν ἑλόμην, μήστωρε φόβοιο).[51] The exceptional horses of Aeneas have now replaced Diomedes' Greek horses.[52]

---

monster; on Heracles' sack of Troy and its analogy to the Achaean expedition, see Anderson (1997, 92-7); Barker and Christensen (2014) 249-77. It should be noted that Achilles says that his horses (*Il.* 23.277-8) were a gift (from Poseidon to Peleus at the wedding of Peleus and Thetis? Cf. Pind. *Isthm.* 8.26-48), which seems to stand in contrast to other statements (*Il.* 16.381 = 16.867, 17.443-4), i.e. that the gods collectively had given Peleus this gift. Perhaps there were two alternative traditions available; the one featuring Poseidon would draw an effective contrast between Laomedon's divine horses and Achilles'. Both acquired them from their fathers (Tros and Peleus, respectively), but whereas Poseidon was deceived by Laomedon, he was honored by Achilles. See also Schein (2016, 21 n. 26) with further bibliography.

[48] Dué and Ebbott (2010, 352) call attention to the glory Diomedes and Sthenelus will gain upon the acquisition of these divine horses (*Il.* 5.273: εἰ τούτω κε λάβοιμεν, ἀροίμεθά κε κλέος ἐσθλόν).

[49] See Strolonga (2018) 194. The exceptional speed of these horses is also highlighted by the fact that they are placed at the same level with Arion, Adrastus' divine horse (*Il.* 23.345-8, born from the mating of Poseidon and Demeter, the two gods having assumed the form of horses; see Paus. 8.25.5-6).

[50] See pp. 106 n. 15, 108, 124 n. 89.

[51] I have deliberately refrained from mentioning Pandarus' complaint to Aeneas that he has no horses, since he had left them in Lycia against the advice of his father (*Il.* 5.180-216). Although he will join Aeneas on his chariot in the new attack against Diomedes, Pandarus only highlights the importance of chariot fighting when it comes to killing Diomedes, without stressing the special skill of Aeneas' horses.

[52] οἷοι Τρώιοι ἵπποι, ἐπιστάμενοι πεδίοιο has also been used in *Il.* 5.222, when the semi-divine Trojan horses were introduced in the plot. These horses know the plain very well, whereas Rhesus' Thracian horses that have just arrived in Troy obviously do not know the landscape. This may well be another hint to the use of the former in the chariot race, the more so since such experience is essential for winning this contest.

That here the *Iliad* foreshadows the use of Aeneas' horses by Diomedes in the chariot race is signaled by the diction that is employed: the epithet Τρώϊοι is used in the entire epic only four times, always for Aeneas' Trojan horses;[53] Diomedes designates Nestor's horses as "slow" (βραδέες: 8.104), their lack of speed being emphasized again by Nestor when he advises Antilochus before the chariot race in *Il.* 23.309–10 (ἀλλά τοι ἵπποι | βάρδιστοι θείειν).[54] These are the sole two attestations of the epithet βραδύς in its literal sense in the *Iliad*.[55] The similarity of context (horses), of persons involved (in book 8 Nestor is the listener, in 23 the speaker), and of diction applied to these divine horses (Τρώϊοι, βραδέες-βάρδιστοι) suggests that *Il.* 8.105–8 and 23.309–10 are intratextually associated.[56] One could go further. Aeneas' horses are thematically significant. Their semi-association with the gods, superlative quality, and theft by Diomedes foreshadow their use both in book 8 and in book 23. To make this point even more evident, the *Iliad* flags 8.105–8 so as to signal 23.291–2 and 23.309–10. Since Diomedes has substituted his own Greek horses with Aeneas' Trojan horses in book 8, it is expected that he will also use them in book 23.[57] The contrast between these horses and those Diomedes stole from Rhesus is thus clearly delineated. The Trojan horses are on the battlefield (*Il.* 8.105–8), the Thracian ones stay (like the Greek ones)[58] at Diomedes' manger (*Il.* 10.566–9).

---

[53] 5.222 = 8.106, 23.291, 23.378. On the accentuation of this epithet, see Nagy (1979 = 1999²) 352.
[54] According to Platte (2017) 42, "Nestor's old age is mirrored in the slowness of his horses."
[55] The use of βράσσων, the comparative of βραδύς, in *Il.* 10.226 (where it is applied to νόος) is figurative.
[56] See Reichel (1994) 230 n. 19.
[57] The epic is also aware of another tradition of divine Trojan horses, which are tellingly mentioned in Aeneas' reply to Achilles' taunts in their encounter in *Il.* 20.221–9. Aeneas boasts of his divine origin, which he traces back to Dardanus, son of Zeus. That he deems it worthy to embed an "equine genealogy" into a human one is indicative of the importance assigned to these horses. Dardanus' son Erichthonius is reported to have possessed three thousand mares, with some of whom the wind Boreas consorted (after taking the form of a horse) and produced twelve colts, who would run so fast so as to "pass along the tassels of corn and not break the divine yield, but again, when they played across the sea's wide ridges, they would run the edge of the wave where it breaks on the grey salt water" (*Il.* 20.226–9); see the legendary Iphiclus in [Hes.] *Cat.* fr. 62 M-W. In *Il.* 5.265–9, these twelve female horses of divine origin "become" six and male and are given to Tros, not by Erichthonius as we are led to believe by the genealogy in *Iliad* 20, but by Zeus as compensation for the abduction of his son Ganymedes (see Gantz 1993, 557). What matters, though, remains unchanged: first, the horses are of divine origin and of unbeatable speed; second, they are implicitly compared to Achilles' horses, also born to a wind (Zephyrus).
[58] 10.567–8: ἵππους μὲν κατέδησαν ἐϋτμήτοισιν ἱμᾶσι | φάτνῃ ἐφ' ἱππείῃ, ὅθι περ Διομήδεος ἵπποι. It is only appropriate that Diomedes gets Rhesus' horses, both because he has killed Rhesus and the twelve Thracians (he has also killed Dolon, but since Odysseus had promised Dolon's arms to Athena [*Il.* 10.460–3], it is expected that he will dedicate them to her after returning to the Achaean camp [*Il.* 10.570–1]), and because Odysseus, as an islander (like Telamonian Ajax), has no horses and no φάτνη (Σ on *Il.* 10.568a¹; see *Od.* 4.601–8). Rhesus' horses are placed next to those of Diomedes, probably the ones he had brought with him from Greece. This may well be a covert indication that they will not be used again, exactly as is the case with Diomedes' "Greek" horses.

3.5 The Whip

One notable feature of the theft of Rhesus' horses by Diomedes and Odysseus in *Iliad* 10 is the absence of a whip and its offhand substitution for Odysseus' bow. The poet informs the audience that Odysseus did not notice the whip on the chariot and so used his bow to incite the horses and make them run (*Il.* 10.498–501):[59]

τόφρα δ' ἄρ' ὁ τλήμων Ὀδυσεὺς λύε μώνυχας ἵππους,
σὺν δ' ἤειρεν ἱμᾶσι καὶ ἐξήλαυνεν ὁμίλου
τόξῳ ἐπιπλήσσων, ἐπεὶ οὐ μάστιγα φαεινὴν
ποικίλου ἐκ δίφροιο νοήσατο χερσὶν ἑλέσθαι.

Meanwhile patient Odysseus was untying the single-foot horses,
and pulled them together with the reins, and drove them from the confusion
and whipped them with his bow, since he had not noticed nor taken
in his hands the glittering whip that was in the elaborate chariot.

The fleeting reference to an unusual whip could easily seem incidental, were it not for a later passage, where the loss of a whip becomes critical, i.e. *Il.* 23.382–400:

καί νύ κεν ἢ παρέλασσ' ἢ ἀμφήριστον ἔθηκεν,
εἰ μὴ Τυδέος υἷι κοτέσσατο Φοῖβος Ἀπόλλων,
ὅς ῥά οἱ ἐκ χειρῶν ἔβαλεν μάστιγα φαεινήν.
τοῖο δ' ἀπ' ὀφθαλμῶν χύτο δάκρυα χωομένοιο,
οὕνεκα τὰς μὲν ὅρα ἔτι καὶ πολὺ μᾶλλον ἰούσας,
οἱ δ' ἑοὶ ἐβλάφθησαν ἄνευ κέντροιο θέοντες.
οὐδ' ἄρ' Ἀθηναίην ἐλεφηράμενος λάθ' Ἀπόλλων
Τυδείδην, μάλα δ' ὦκα μετέσσυτο ποιμένα λαῶν,
δῶκε δέ οἱ μάστιγα, μένος δ' ἵπποισιν ἐνῆκεν·
ἡ δὲ μετ' Ἀδμήτου υἱὸν κοτέουσα βεβήκει,
ἵππειον δέ οἱ ἔαξε θεὰ ζυγόν, αἱ δέ οἱ ἵπποι
ἀμφὶς ὁδοῦ δραμέτην, ῥυμὸς δ' ἐπὶ γαῖαν ἐλύσθη.
αὐτὸς δ' ἐκ δίφροιο παρὰ τροχὸν ἐξεκυλίσθη,
ἀγκῶνάς τε περιδρύφθη στόμα τε ῥῖνάς τε,
θρυλίχθη δὲ μέτωπον ἐπ' ὀφρύσι· τὼ δέ οἱ ὄσσε
δακρυόφι πλῆσθεν, θαλερὴ δέ οἱ ἔσχετο φωνή.
Τυδείδης δὲ παρατρέψας ἔχε μώνυχας ἵππους,
πολλὸν τῶν ἄλλων ἐξάλμενος· ἐν γὰρ Ἀθήνη
ἵπποις ἧκε μένος καὶ ἐπ' αὐτῷ κῦδος ἔθηκεν.

---

[59] See Frame (2009) 144–7.

And now he might have passed him or run to a doubtful decision,
had not Phoebus Apollo been angry with Diomedes,
Tydeus' son, and dashed the shining whip from his hands, so
that the tears began to stream from his eyes, for his anger
as he watched how the mares of Eumelus drew far ahead of him
while his own horses ran without the whip and were slowed. Yet
Athene did not fail to see the foul play of Apollo
on Tydeus' son. She swept in speed to the shepherd of the people
and gave him back his whip, and inspired strength into his horses.
Then in her wrath she went on after the son of Admetus
and she, a goddess, smashed his chariot yoke, and his horses
ran on either side of the way, the pole dragged, and Eumelus
himself was sent spinning out beside the wheel of the chariot
so that his elbows were all torn, and his mouth, and his nostrils,
and his forehead was lacerated about the brows, and his eyes
filled with tears, and the springing voice was held fast within him.
Then the son of Tydeus, turning his single-foot horses to pass him,
went far out in front of the others, seeing that Athene
had inspired strength in his horses and to himself gave the glory.

This passage from the first contest in the funeral games in honor of Patroclus opens a window on the non-use of the whip in the Rhesus episode. For the whip becomes the decisive factor in the chariot race in *Iliad* 23 and brings with it a host of other associations with that earlier scene in *Iliad* 10. In the *Doloneia*, Athena assists in the theft of Rhesus' horses, while Apollo indirectly intervenes in the death of Rhesus. These same two gods reappear with starring roles in the chariot race, which features Diomedes' Trojan horses. The fact that Apollo had bred Eumelus' horses[60] accounts for his support of this team; more interesting are his actions against Diomedes. In book 5 Apollo intervenes to protect Aeneas and deny Diomedes this prize, the hero being forced to stand down. By way of contrast, in book 10 Diomedes gets his way, two aspects of which are picked up in the later chariot race: the whip and Apollo's κότος ('anger', 'grudge'). His κότος[61] against Tydeus' son in the chariot race stems from his κότος against Athena supporting Diomedes at *Il.* 10.516–17.[62] In *Iliad* 10 Apollo wakes up Hippocoon, Rhesus' cousin, to inform him of Rhesus' murder and the theft of his horses by Diomedes and Odysseus. In *Iliad* 23 it is Apollo who knocks Diomedes' whip from his hands to try to prevent him from overtaking his favorite Eumelus.[63] Diomedes is overcome by anger[64] and sadness[65] at the realization that without a whip his

---

[60] *Il.* 2.766–7.   [61] *Il.* 23.383: κοτέσσατο.
[62] ὡς ἴδ' Ἀθηναίην μετὰ Τυδέος υἱὸν ἕπουσαν | τῇ κοτέων.
[63] *Il.* 23.382: καί νύ κεν ἢ παρέλασσ' ἢ ἀμφήριστον ἔθηκεν.   [64] *Il.* 23.385: χωομένοιο.
[65] *Il.* 23.385: ἀπ' ὀφθαλμῶν χύτο δάκρυα.

horses won't be able to pass those of Eumelus.⁶⁶ Apollo's treachery against Diomedes⁶⁷ does not remain unnoticed by Athena,⁶⁸ who at once goes after Diomedes, gives him his whip, and inspires strength in the horses.⁶⁹ Paying back Apollo for his δόλος, Athena smashes the yoke of Eumelus' chariot in anger.⁷⁰ Eumelus can no longer compete. Diomedes wins the chariot race.

The whip thus becomes a linking device between *Iliad* 10 and 23 involving a series of shared features: the same gods in the same roles, Diomedes, the horses of Rhesus and the horses of Aeneas (both stolen by Diomedes, the former in an ambush, the latter through formal combat), and last but certainly not least, the whip, the formidable symbol of incitement in the chariot race.⁷¹ Its absence in *Iliad* 10 and its substitution by Odysseus' bow stand in contrast to its overarching importance in *Iliad* 23. In the *Doloneia*, the whip of Rhesus' chariot is replaced by the bow, while in the funeral games it is handed back to Diomedes by Athena. The goddess does in the chariot race what she did not do in the Rhesus episode. There she advised Diomedes to hasten back to the ships and said nothing about the whip.⁷² Here she picks it from the ground and gives it to Diomedes. There the whip is forgotten on the chariot from which the horses are cut loose.⁷³ Here it is an indispensable prerequisite for the hero's victory. Apollo's knocking the whip to the ground denotes his attempt to degrade Diomedes' horses, to make them useless for the episode at hand, just as Rhesus' horses remain useless for the rest of the plot. A whip was forgotten in the *Doloneia*, but another one is "remembered" in the funeral games. Just like the horses it was supposed to lash. Deprived of their whip, they cannot compete in the chariot race. Like their whip, they must fall into oblivion.

3.6 *Spiegelungseffekt*

As early as the "Catalogue of the Best" (Achaeans and horses in *Iliad* 2), Achilles and his horses are presented as the apex of excellence. He is the best warrior, while they are the best horses (*Il.* 2.769–70: ὁ γὰρ πολὺ φέρτατος ἦεν, | ἵπποι θ'). This is not only a necessary explanation of the fact that after Achilles' withdrawal the best horses are those of Eumelus and the best warrior is Telamonian Ajax but also a reminder of the absence of Achilles and a covert allusion to his return (at some

---

⁶⁶ *Il.* 23.387: οἱ δ' ἑοὶ ἐβλάφθησαν ἄνευ κέντροιο θέοντες.   ⁶⁷ *Il.* 23.388: ἐλεφηράμενος.
⁶⁸ *Il.* 23.388-9: οὐδ' ἄρ' Ἀθηναίην ἐλεφηράμενος λάθ' Ἀπόλλων | Τυδεΐδην.
⁶⁹ *Il.* 23.389–90: μάλα δ' ὦκα μετέσσυτο ποιμένα λαῶν, | δῶκε δέ οἱ μάστιγα, μένος δ' ἵπποισιν ἐνῆκεν. I am very skeptical about Delebecque's (1951, 21) explanation of Athena's help as a result of the old age of Eumelus' horses.
⁷⁰ *Il.* 23.391–2: ἡ δὲ μετ' Ἀδμήτου υἱὸν κοτέουσα βεβήκει, | ἵππειον οἱ ἔαξε θεὰ ζυγόν.
⁷¹ See how much stress is put to the lashing of the horses by all contestants at the beginning of the chariot race (*Il.* 23.362–4).
⁷² *Il.* 10.509–11.
⁷³ With respect to μάστιξεν in *Il.* 10.530, I concur with Hainsworth's comment (1993, 207): "μάστιξεν is formular and imprecise; as riders they had left the whip behind (500–501)."

point) to the fighting. Moreover, and this point should be strongly stressed, the absence of Achilles' horses from the battlefield is described in terms that bear a certain similarity to the situation we encounter at the funeral games for Patroclus in *Iliad* 23. In book 2, the Myrmidons amuse themselves by the sea, competing with discs, light spear-throwing, and bows (2.773–5). They, therefore, anticipate the games of book 23, when the Achaean heroes compete in the same three sports (as well as others). The analogy becomes even more pronounced when the narrator turns his lens on the horses. They stand beside Achilles' chariot, champ their clover and parsley, and rest (*Il.* 2.775–7). It seems that one (though not the only) function of the "Catalogue of the Best" is to highlight the absence of Achilles and his horses and thus foreshadow the funeral games. A large arc, then, unites this passage in book 2 with the chariot race in book 23.[74] The *Spiegelungseffekt* between the two passages becomes obvious when we turn our attention to what Achilles says at the very start of the games in *Il.* 23.272–86:

Ἀτρείδη τε καὶ ἄλλοι ἐϋκνήμιδες Ἀχαιοί,
ἱππῆας τάδ' ἄεθλα δεδεγμένα κεῖτ' ἐν ἀγῶνι.
εἰ μὲν νῦν ἐπὶ ἄλλῳ ἀεθλεύοιμεν Ἀχαιοί,
ἦ τ' ἂν ἐγὼ τὰ πρῶτα λαβὼν κλισίηνδε φεροίμην.
ἴστε γὰρ ὅσσον ἐμοὶ ἀρετῇ περιβάλλετον ἵπποι·
ἀθάνατοί τε γάρ εἰσι, Ποσειδάων δὲ πόρ' αὐτοὺς
πατρὶ ἐμῷ Πηλῆϊ, ὁ δ' αὖτ' ἐμοὶ ἐγγυάλιξεν.
ἀλλ' ἤτοι μὲν ἐγὼ μενέω καὶ μώνυχες ἵπποι·
τοίου γὰρ κλέος ἐσθλὸν ἀπώλεσαν ἡνιόχοιο,
ἠπίου, ὅς σφωϊν μάλα πολλάκις ὑγρὸν ἔλαιον
χαιτάων κατέχευε, λοέσσας ὕδατι λευκῷ.
τὸν τώ γ' ἑσταότες πενθείετον, οὔδεϊ δέ σφιν
χαῖται ἐρηρέδαται, τὼ δ' ἔστατον ἀχνυμένω κῆρ.
ἄλλοι δὲ στέλλεσθε κατὰ στρατόν, ὅς τις Ἀχαιῶν
ἵπποισίν τε πέποιθε καὶ ἅρμασι κολλητοῖσιν.

Son of Atreus and all your other strong-greaved Achaeans,
these prizes are in the place of games and wait for their horsemen.
Now if we Achaeans were contending for the sake of some other
hero, I myself should take the first prize away to my shelter.
You know how much my horses surpass in their speed all others;
yes, for they are immortal horses, and Poseidon gave them
to Peleus my father, who in turn gave them into my hands.
But I stay here at the side, and my single-foot horses stay with me;

---

[74] See, e.g., Whitman (1958) 261–4; Stanley (1993) 225.

such is the high glory of the charioteer they have lost,
the gentle one, who as many times anointed their manes with
soft olive oil, after he had washed them in shining water.
Therefore, these two horses stand here and grieve, and their manes
are swept along the ground as they stand with hearts full of sorrow.
But take, the rest of you, places in the field, whichever Achaean
has confidence in his horses and his compacted chariot.

The *Iliad* has Achilles stage the chariot race in a way that looks back both at the "Catalogue of the Best" and the plot of the poem with a clear focus on absence and withdrawal. It is, then, within the framework of a mirror-text that we should place the use of Aeneas' immortal horses by Diomedes.

Like mirrors, mirror-texts distort reflections and confound expectations and assumptions. They can do this effectively just by highlighting analogy, as is the case with Diomedes' participation in the chariot race. On the basis of the preeminence of Eumelus' horses (programmatically advertised in the "Catalogue of the Best" in *Il.* 2.763–7), one would expect that Pheres' son would emerge victorious. Indeed, the text toys with this outcome: he is the first to express his will to compete (*Il.* 23.288: ὦρτο πολὺ πρῶτος); the narrator identifies his excellent knowledge of horses and horse-driving (*Il.* 23.289: ὃς ἱπποσύνῃ ἐκέκαστο). But this will not be the case, in the same way that Telamonian Ajax, who has been also programmatically "advertised" as the best warrior (after Achilles) in the "Catalogue of the Best" in *Il.* 2.768–9, does not defeat Odysseus in the wrestling contest (*Il.* 23.700–39) or Diomedes in the spear-fighting (*Il.* 23.798–825). Why do favorites fall short of their and our expectations? Poetic purpose, not coincidence, is here the guiding principle.

The funeral games for Patroclus are framed by the absence of Achilles and his horses from all contests. This absence is twice brought to the fore by Achilles himself before the beginning of the actual contests. The first occasion is when he advises the Myrmidons to desist from unyoking the horses from their chariots, so that they can keep their place close to Patroclus while they grieve for his death. He specifically determines that the unyoking should take place only after the army has satisfied their hearts with lament, when the time comes for the troops to take their supper (*Il.* 23.6–11). The second occasion spells out his absence more sharply, when he introduces the chariot race. Achilles announces that, if the chariot race was in honor of another man, he himself would have competed and won, since everybody knows that his immortal horses (a gift from Poseidon to Peleus at his wedding with Thetis) are exceptional (*Il.* 23.276–8).[75] As it is, both he and his horses will abstain from the contests in honor of Patroclus. The absence of

---

[75] The immortal horses of Achilles can only be yoked in a chariot and driven by the gods or Achilles himself, as Odysseus and Apollo acknowledge at *Il.* 10.402–4 and 17.76–8, respectively (οἱ δ' ἀλεγεινοὶ |

Achilles and his horses from the funeral games in honor of Patroclus "reprises" a situation that is analogous to the conditions that prevail during his absence from the battlefield for most of the *Iliad*. The audience know all too well the consequences of Achilles' decision in book 1 to abstain from the war: Achaean defeat and Patroclus' death. So, it is only too natural for the audience to wonder about the results in the contests of the funeral games, especially in the chariot race when Achilles has so emphatically stated his decision to abstain.

It is exactly within this framework that the victory of Diomedes' Trojan horses should be placed. The *Iliad* looks at itself *sub specie ludorum* so as to comment on its own subject matter.[76] As for the greatest part of the plot, the Trojans were victorious because of Achilles' absence, so in the chariot race the victory belongs to the Trojan horses of Diomedes because of the absence of Achilles' horses. This is the first step the epic takes towards asserting the validity of its plot through analogy. The second step is bolder. It equally aims to assert the poem's authority but this time through opposition. To do so, the epic opens its horizon so as to extend beyond the limits of its plot and encompass the post-Iliadic death of Achilles. According to a well-known neoanalytical argument, the death of Patroclus and the funeral games of the Iliadic *Patrocleia* (books 16–23) are modeled on and substitute for the death and the funeral games for Achilles in a pre-Iliadic **Memnonis*. Seen through this lens, the absence of Achilles and his horses from the funeral games in book 23 has a symbolic-intertextual aspect, reflecting the situation in the **Memnonis*, where Achilles is dead and the funeral games are held in his honor. This is also suggested by the fact that the recognition assigned to Eumelus' mares and Telamonian Ajax, both ranked the best in the absence of Achilles' horses and Achilles, respectively, in book 2, is in tune not with *Iliad* 23 but with the *Aethiopis* (which reflects the **Memnonis*), where Eumelus' mares win the chariot race and Telamonian Ajax the discus-throwing in the funeral games in honor of Achilles. By having Eumelus and Ajax fail to win any contest in book 23,[77] the *Iliad* undermines the "Catalogue of the Best" in book 2[78]

ἀνδράσι γε θνητοῖσι δαμήμεναι ἠδ' ὀχέεσθαι, | ἄλλῳ γ' ἢ' Ἀχιλῆϊ, τὸν ἀθανάτη τέκε μήτηρ); see Delebecque (1951) 18. Stanley (1993, 125) argues that Dolon's and Hector's fascination with Achilles' horses foreshadows the Trojans' final demise because of their fascination with the Wooden Horse. Subterfuge and deception will again be employed in the ultimate act of the Trojan War myth, the sack of Troy, at a time "when Achilles has not simply withdrawn from the fighting but has met the end of his short but glorious life" (128); see also Haft (1990) 54–5.

[76] Achilles' function as ἀθλοθέτης and κριτής in the games amounts to a profound metapoetic gesture. As his anger has made the *Iliad* possible, so his organization of the funeral games is a metanarrative comment on the entire plotline set in motion by his own behavior.

[77] Telamonian Ajax finishes second in discus-throwing, while the result of the wrestling and spear contests against Odysseus and Diomedes, respectively, is a draw. The draw between Ajax and Odysseus in the wrestling contest in *Iliad* 23 is, arguably, a mirroring of their dispute concerning the arms of Achilles in the funeral games of the *Aethiopis*.

[78] The attention with which this effect has been prepared can be seen by the fact that immediately after stating the precondition (Achilles' absence) under which Eumelus' mares were the best Achaean horses, the poet offered the audience a glimpse at the headquarters of Achilles, where the Myrmidons

and diverges from its model in a marked manner. This happens because we are situated at a point in the story that is still clouded by the results of Achilles' μῆνις, which may be over, but its consequences are still strongly felt: in the death of Patroclus, in the victory of Trojan horses, in the complete failure of Ajax as an athletic contestant.

The *Iliad* uses the funeral games to produce a *Spiegelungseffekt* that is played out in the chariot race, which contains resonances with the two principal motifs permeating the entire epic, those of μῆνις ("wrath") and τιμή ("honor").[79] A case in point is Achilles' smile at Antilochus' angry outburst, when he finds out that Achilles is determined to award the second prize to Eumelus (who finished last) instead of Antilochus, who came second. The metapoetic connotations of this smile have been analyzed by Rengakos, who has argued that this is a metanarrative comment, since it "looks back" at Achilles' own anger in *Iliad* 1.[80] This time, it will be none other than Achilles himself, the center of μῆνις throughout the poem, who will prevent a second μῆνις by Antilochus. Achilles is, therefore, presented as a character who realizes the potential consequences for the Achaean army of a new internal strife. He becomes the vehicle through which the epic reflects on its own plot.[81]

Horses can be evaluated on their own, independently of their owner's fighting ability. The audience know all too well that Diomedes is a better warrior by far than Eumelus, but this is not enough to win the chariot race. He therefore uses the best horses he can get, the best horses available. These are the exceptional horses that he has taken from Aeneas in *Iliad* 5, a special gift from Zeus to Tros in compensation for the abduction of Ganymedes. The other horses he has taken from the Trojans, as well as the ones he has brought from Greece, are not of divine origin. This analysis allows us to go one step further, as we realize that even the right form of the question we have asked (why Diomedes employs Aeneas' Trojan horses) has its limitations, for the real question is why Diomedes wins the chariot race. The answer to this question is unmistakable: because he has acquired the best horses available, Aeneas' Trojan horses, a mixed breed going back (at least partly) to Zeus. This conclusion is fully consonant with the observations made

---

were presented passing their time sporting, which included discus- and spear-throwing, as well as arrow-shooting (*Il.* 2.773–5), *but not chariot-driving*. That the omission of chariot-driving from this brief list of sporting activities (within a truly exquisite pre-mirroring of the funeral games) is not a random choice is suggested by the statement that the horses of the Myrmidons were eating their food, being placed next to the huts of their masters, while the Myrmidons, longing for their leader, were going here and there in the camp (*Il.* 2.775–9).

[79] Rengakos (2006) 21–2.

[80] On this topic, see Rengakos (2006) 17–30; also Barker (2009) 87 n. 183. Achilles' privileged role in book 23 concerns the establishment of a novel political relationship, which is based on "the recognition and successful mediation of difference" (Hammer 1997, 21). The *Iliad* "corrects" the lack of such a system that has resulted in Achilles' wrath against Agamemnon in book 1; see also Aeneas' smile in *Aen.* 5.286–361, with which he resolves a squabble between the participants.

[81] See Hammer (1997) 1–24, (2002) 134–43, 153–60; Barker (2009) 86–8.

above with respect to the role of horses in the *Iliad*. The poetic vehicle for bringing about an insightful metanarrative comment in the chariot race is not Diomedes but the horses. They have to be used to defeat the Achaean mares of Eumelus.[82]

To ask the question why Eumelus' horses must be defeated by Aeneas' would lead us astray, since it repeats the same kind of erroneous assumption that we have traced before. What is it, then, that Eumelus' divine horses do not possess to win the chariot race? The answer is that they are not Trojan horses. In the mirror-text of the funeral games in *Iliad* 23, the chariot race becomes the most noteworthy context for metanarrative play and as such offers the opportunity for a telling subversion of the situation presented in the "Catalogue of the Best" in *Iliad* 2. Unlike Achaean horses, there is no catalogue of best horses for the Trojans, and yet it is exactly Trojan horses that must win in the funeral games for Patroclus. This decision speaks volumes for the *Iliad*'s truly exceptional narrative technique, its poetic sophistication and careful planning. By shifting the focus of the plot from the absent Achilles to his non-competing (i.e. absent) horses in the chariot race, the epic makes its comment sound loud and clear. As Trojan victory was evident during Achilles' abstention from the battle, so it must be when Achilles' divine horses stay at their manger. Before it was because of their master's wrath, now it is because of their own grief.[83]

3.7 Homeric Silence and the Policy of Exclusion

Minchin[84] has argued that several "story-moments" and "story-details" in the *Iliad* are evoked by the *Odyssey* and function as a backdrop against which Odyssean "story-moments" should be evaluated. Their specificity makes their recall deliberate and pointed, resulting in a semantic surplus. Typology can hardly account for this phenomenon. This claim makes a case for a type of thematic allusion that goes beyond the mere reference to events. We have seen that a similar technique is used with respect to the relation between the *Doloneia* and the rest of the *Iliad*.[85] This type of association is doubly instructive considering Monro's Law,[86] according to which the *Odyssey* never mentions the main events of the *Iliad*.[87] First, it shows that thematic association between the two Homeric epics takes more subtle

---

[82] The horses of the other participants (Menelaus, Antilochus, and Meriones) are clearly not so swift. In fact, Nestor advises Antilochus how he can win, though his horses cannot compete with those of other participants.

[83] 2.772: κεῖτ' ἀπομηνίσας, 23.283: τὸν τώ γ' ἑσταότες πενθείετον.   [84] Minchin (2018) 22–4.

[85] See chapter 2.

[86] Monro (1901) 325. This Law is not fully accurate. The death of Patroclus and his shared burial with Achilles are mentioned in the *Odyssey* (3.110 and 24.71–9, respectively); see Minchin (2018) 15 with n. 29.

[87] Page (1955, 159) argued that the poet of the *Odyssey* does not know the *Iliad*. In like manner, M. L. West (2003b, 6–7) claimed that the poet of the *Iliad* did not know the episode of Memnon (on the grounds that he never refers to such a person).

forms than a simple mention of events. Second, it suggests that the lack of reference to specific events between two epics may well be a sophisticated mechanism by which an epic tradition makes reference by refusing reference.[88] If this technique is at work between two different poems (the *Iliad* and the *Odyssey*), it may also be applicable both to two different but related references in the same poem, as well as to the relation between a poem that survives intact and a putative earlier poem. Excluding reference to material that would be expected in a given context can be marked. It may create further interpretive ramifications by highlighting the omission of what was anticipated.

The fact that Diomedes uses the semi-divine Trojan horses of Aeneas in his victorious chariot race in the funeral games for Patroclus (*Iliad* 23) is not only triggered by the exceptional quality of these horses. It may operate as a covert comment on the fact that Diomedes does not use the splendid horses that he has stolen from Rhesus in book 10. By having Diomedes select for the chariot race one set of stolen horses (Aeneas' Trojan horses) instead of another set of stolen horses (Rhesus' Thracian horses), the *Iliad* engages its audience in a process of comparison and evaluation of the two episodes in which Diomedes stole horses of prominent enemies.[89] But why does the poem point its audience to the stolen horses Diomedes did not use? What is the poetic effect of this deliberate strategy?

The *Iliad*'s refusal to mention Rhesus' horses in book 23 amounts to a comment on their characteristics. These horses are—like Rhesus and his troops[90]—"newcomers" (νεήλυδες) at Troy since they have just arrived from Thrace. Their lack of knowledge of the plain, a weakness of prime importance regarding success in a chariot race, is at odds with the experience of Aeneas' Trojan horses that Diomedes has stolen and drives in the funeral games. It is exactly this skill that Aeneas highlights to Lycaon at *Il.* 5.221–3: "Therefore mount rather into my chariot, so that you may see what the Trojan horses are like, how much they understand their plain, and how to traverse in rapid pursuit and withdrawal."[91] By making reference to Diomedes' Trojan horses, the poem calls to mind their expert knowledge of the plain. Conversely, by refusing reference to Rhesus' horses in the chariot race, the *Iliad* evokes their lack of experience and unsuitability for this contest in book 23.

With respect to the relation between a poem that survives intact and a putative earlier poem, Homer's silence constitutes a policy of exclusion. He manipulates previous mythical and epic traditions in negative as part of the self-definition of

---

[88] Dowden (1996) 53; Cairns (2001a) 36–7; Finkelberg (2015) 135 = (2020) 178; Currie (2016) 71.
[89] Diomedes had also stolen the horses of Phegeus and those of Echemmon and Chromius in book 5. However, these are the horses of unimportant warriors.
[90] *Il.* 10.434.
[91] Ἀλλ' ἄγ' ἐμῶν ὀχέων ἐπιβήσεο, ὄφρα ἴδηαι | οἷοι Τρώιοι ἵπποι, ἐπιστάμενοι πεδίοιο | κραιπνὰ μάλ' ἔνθα καὶ ἔνθα διωκέμεν ἠδὲ φέβεσθαι.

his poetry.[92] The horses of Rhesus were closely associated with the miraculous, since in another poetic tradition they were destined to become invincible if they drank from the river Scamander and grazed on its banks. By remaining silent on their potential invincibility and instead talking about their outstanding beauty (καλλίστους, 10.436), size (μεγίστους, 10.436), and speed (θείειν δ' ἀνέμοισιν ὁμοῖοι, 10.437), the *Iliad* defines itself as a poem in which the supernatural and miraculous element is downplayed. An instructive analogy is offered by *Il.* 1.106–8,[93] where Agamemnon blames Calchas because he always foretells impending calamities. However, Agamemnon's accusation hardly makes sense if it is not based on a case in which Calchas prophesied a disaster for the Achaeans in the past. Just as Agamemnon's accusation of Calchas for his habit of evil prophecy makes sense if the poet and his audience know about the sacrifice of Iphigenia from another epic tradition,[94] so the description of Rhesus' horses at *Il.* 10.436–7 as "extremely beautiful and very big, whiter than snow, similar to the winds with respect to their speed" acquires greater significance if the audience are familiar with a version in which Rhesus' horses would have been invincible and would have possessed unsurpassed speed if they drank from the river Scamander and grazed on its banks. The absence of Rhesus' horses from the chariot race in book 23 forms part of the same strategy of inclusion by exclusion. By using two interrelated features (the whip and Apollo's κότος), the *Iliad* associates this passage with the description of Rhesus' horses in book 10 and through it with the tradition of the horses' potential invincibility.

This chapter has argued that the "silence" of the *Iliad* with respect to Rhesus' horses in the funeral games in honor of Patroclus does not suggest different authorship regarding the *Doloneia*. It is maintained that since (a) the Trojan horses that Diomedes steals from Aeneas in book 5 are of divine origin, unlike those Diomedes brought from Greece and the ones he stole from Rhesus, and (b) they "understand the plain, and how to traverse in rapid pursuit and withdrawal" (*Il.* 5.222–3), they are perfectly suited for the chariot race. Furthermore, by limiting the use of Rhesus' horses to book 10, the sole ambush episode in the *Iliad*, the epic may be inviting its audience to make an important association: as Hector's death suggests the ensuing fall of Troy, so the nocturnal raid into the enemy camp and the theft of the splendid horses of Rhesus by Diomedes and Odysseus may be alluding to the Wooden Horse by which Odysseus (and Diomedes, who will be in its belly) will bring about the sack of Troy.

---

[92] I have deliberately employed Dowden's (1996, 52) apt formulation (with slight modifications).
[93] Μάντι κακῶν, οὐ πώ ποτέ μοι τὸ κρήγυον εἶπας· | αἰεί τοι τὰ κάκ' ἐστὶ φίλα φρεσὶ μαντεύεσθαι, | ἐσθλὸν δ' οὔτέ τί πω εἶπας ἔπος οὔτ' ἐτέλεσσας.
[94] See Dowden (1996) 52–3; Barker (2009) 43–4; Nelson (2022) 55–101.

4
The Alleged Un-Iliadic Features of *Iliad* 10

Speeches, Clothing and Arming, and Zielinski's Law

Introduction

Besides the thematical aspect referring to the question of authenticity of book 10 that has been discussed in the two previous chapters, some scholars[1] have drawn attention to three other issues (speeches, clothing and arming, and Zielinski's Law) that have arguably been treated as indicating divergence from the rest of the *Iliad*. This chapter is devoted to the examination of these aspects of putative incompatibility.

4.1 Speeches

The absence of ring composition and parallelism, which represent two of the standard devices used in the internal structure of Iliadic speeches, and the preference for ongoing conversations in the *Doloneia* instead of pairs of speeches that are observable in the rest of the *Iliad* have been used as conclusive arguments with respect to the inauthenticity of book 10.[2] Danek, who builds on the earlier work of Klingner[3] and Jens,[4] works with the assumption that there is a single poet of the *Iliad*. It is from there that he proceeds to argue that the speeches of the *Doloneia* display features that are against the standard practice of speech-composition and clustering that we find in the rest of the poem.

Danek's analysis is subtle. It is also crucial for his argument. There are, though, two issues pertaining to his approach that I consider worth exploring. First, we should be asking ourselves why *Iliad* 10 contains a large number of speeches (forty-one) with an average speech-length that is the lowest (7.12 verses per speech)[5] in the

---

[1] See below, pp. 126–7, 133 n. 19, 150–1 nn. 117–18.   [2] Danek (1988) 177–203.
[3] Klingner (1940) 337–68 = (1964) 7–39.   [4] Jens (1955) 616–25.
[5] The average speech-length in the *Iliad* is 10.4 verses. There are 678 speeches in the entire poem, which are delivered by 88 speakers. They represent 44.96% of the *Iliad*.

The Homeric Doloneia: *Evolution and Shaping of* Iliad *10*. Christos C. Tsagalis, Oxford University Press.
© Christos C. Tsagalis 2024. DOI: 10.1093/oso/9780192870988.003.0005

entire *Iliad*. Second, it is crucial to discuss whether the internal (structure) and external (clustering) organization of speeches has an impact on the tone of a given episode, regarding its putative interpretive consequences, and is associated with specific aesthetic preferences. Using speech for highlighting a particular context and/or emotional condition of a character presupposes a deliberate, mentally controlled process, which is unlikely to be useful for detecting authorial trace.

As to the first and second issues, let us begin by presenting some quantifying data that will be important for the ensuing discussion (see table 4.1).

Iliad 10 occupies the third position *qua* number of speeches in the *Iliad*. Book 24 has 47 speeches and book 23 has 43. However, these data should be evaluated with respect to the length of each Iliadic book. In fact, it is book 9 where direct speech really predominates, with 588 out of 713 verses, i.e. a percentage of 82.46%. *Iliad* 10 (50.43%) is much lower, superseded by other books (19: 64.15%; 6: 61.05%; 1: 61.04%; 24: 56.34%; 22: 53.78%; 3: 52.49%; 7: 50.61%). The difference between the number of speeches and the proportion of direct to indirect speech is explained by the fact that the average speech-length in book 10 is only 7.12 verses.

Table 4.1 Quantifying Data Regarding Iliadic Speeches

Book of *Iliad*	Number of Speeches	Number of Verses in Direct Speech	Total Number of Verses	Average Speech-Length	Percentage (%) of Verses in Direct Speech
1	36	373	611	10.36	61.04
2	18	283	877	15.72	32.26
3	28	242	461	8.64	52.49
4	27	242	544	8.96	44.48
5	39	334	909	8.56	36.74
6	23	323	529	14.47	61.05
7	26	244	482	9.38	50.61
8	25	268	565	10.72	47.43
9	17	588	713	34.58	82.46
10	41	292	579	7.12	50.43
11	27	320	848	11.85	37.73
12	11	122	471	11.09	25.90
13	27	254	837	9.40	30.34
14	28	247	552	8.82	44.74
15	34	292	746	8.58	39.14
16	24	256	867	10.66	29.52
17	34	273	761	8.02	35.87
18	25	266	617	10.64	43.11
19	19	272	424	14.31	64.15
20	21	229	504	10.90	45.43
21	31	270	611	8.70	44.18
22	27	277	515	10.25	53.78
23	43	347	897	8.06	38.68
24	47	453	804	9.63	56.34

The picture painted by these data as regards the *Doloneia* is the following: (a) this is a book where speech and narrative are almost equally represented,[6] and (b) this is a book with an average speech-length that is the lowest in the entire poem. Are these two results against common Iliadic practice? As to the former, let us examine what happens in the rest of the poem by using the relevant data from table 4.1. The balanced proportion between narrative and speech is also observable in book 7 (narrative: 49.39%; direct speech: 50.61%), book 22 (narrative: 46.22; direct speech: 53.78%), and book 3 (narrative: 47.51%; direct speech: 52.49%).[7] As to the latter, the average speech-length of 7.12 verses is not very different from 8.02 and 8.06, which is the average speech-length of books 17 and 23, respectively. In view of these observations, *Iliad* 10 does not give a picture that is radically out of step with other books of the *Iliad*.

As to the second issue, I will begin by discussing whether the internal organization of the speeches in book 10 is related to interpretive and aesthetic considerations and then proceed with their external organization. Although Lohmann does not examine the speeches of book 10, he devoted a lengthy footnote to what he considered to be the peculiarities of speech-organization in the *Doloneia*.[8] He argued that apart from some secondary traces of ring composition, none of the forty-one speeches of book 10 displays the three structural laws governing Homeric speeches, that is to say: (a) the beginning of each speech is thematically tagged to the end of the previous one; (b) the number of themes shared between speeches remains basically the same; and (c) new motifs are not developed from the themes treated in the speeches themselves. Lohmann argues that the structural laws about Homeric speeches are part of the poetic technique of scene development in Homeric poetry. They thus pertain to the principle of a strict thematic economy, which (according to Lohmann) is a reliable criterion for recognizing what is genuine and what is not in Homeric epic.[9]

Behind Lohmann's method lurks the belief that these laws and the overarching principle of thematic economy that binds them together can be employed as criteria for detecting authorship. Here, then, lies my main objection to his method. Since it is an objection that pertains to the foundations of his argumentation, it needs to be explained up front.

Speech-organization and distribution are closely related to the thematic framework of a given scene or episode. Speech clustering, length, and ratio to narrative are determined by thematic factors and larger compositional strategies. Books 9 and 10 are both devoted to the events taking place during the night that begins at the end of *Iliad* 8 and ends with the coming of dawn at the beginning of *Iliad* 11.

---

[6] Speech: 292 verses (50.43%); narrative: 287 verses (49.57%).

[7] I cite only those books in which the speech-percentage is slightly over 50% because this is the case with *Iliad* 10.

[8] Lohmann (1970) 134 n. 67.   [9] Lohmann (1970) 132–4.

Both books focus on the same overarching theme, since, for the first time (we are led to believe), the Trojans are camping out on the plain, posing an imminent threat to the Achaeans (rather than vice versa). Asking a single hero, Achilles, to help them is what they do in book 9. Trying to find out the plan of the Trojans is their plan in book 10. This shift from a formal appeal to a single warrior, who ultimately refuses to help, to an impromptu gathering, where the other Achaean leaders volunteer for the common effort to undertake a highly dangerous incursion into enemy territory, marks a powerful transition from *Iliad* 9 to *Iliad* 10. This thematic change is reflected in the way the Achaeans think and operate. The field of prime importance for observing this profound shift is speech. It is when characters speak that an author reveals vividly their emotional state, ideas, and perplexities. How crucial speech is in books 9 and 10 can be seen by the fact that (a) it either outweighs (book 9: 82.46%) or balances (book 10: 50.43%) narrative, (b) it is marked by length (book 9: average speech-length of 34.58%, the highest in the *Iliad*) or brevity (book 10: average speech-length of 7.12, the lowest in the *Iliad*), and (c) it is used only for the main characters of the poem.[10] The brevity of various speeches in *Iliad* 10 is determined by the pressure of time and the anxiety of the situation. In such a context, there is also little room for developing elaborate arguments. Too much needs to happen quickly: wake up the Achaean leaders, organize a council, devise a plan, find volunteers, pray to Athena and ask for her help, plan a spying mission in another council by the Trojans, find out what Dolon is doing when he is arrested, get information from him, have the Achaean spies change their plan and move to the new target, Rhesus, have Athena warn them to hasten back to the ships after they kill him, emphasize the relief of the army for the safe return of the Achaean spies, express amazement at the sight of Rhesus' magnificent horses which the spies bring to the Achaean camp, inform the army about what happened during the spying mission. This list suggests that no fewer than thirteen different aims are addressed by the speeches in book 10.[11]

Building on Lohmann, Danek's analysis of the internal organization of the speeches of the *Doloneia* suggests that they either lack or rarely display the

---

[10] There is no minor character delivering a speech in *Iliad* 9–10, Dolon being a main figure in the *Doloneia*.

[11] Rabel (1997, 136–8) argues that in a book where contrast looms large, there is evidently little room for the rounding effect of ring composition and parallelism within speeches. Relevant to this observation is that the stress on cooperative endeavor and the sense of interdependence displayed by the Achaean leaders in book 10 are mirrored in the polite forms of address they use. Elaborate formal addresses opening various speeches in the *Doloneia* pave the way for the highlighting of the joint effort that the Achaeans will soon be undertaking. However, there are various other cases where contrast does not operate against ring composition and parallelism with respect to the structural organization of speeches. Likewise, cooperative endeavor is also at work in other parts of the *Iliad,* but this does not run against the above-mentioned types of structural organization of speeches. Even more so with polite forms of address. Heroes employ them even for their enemies (e.g. *Il.* 7.234, 21.153) as well as for their allies in circumstances where cooperation is not at hand; on forms of address in Greek (from Herodotus to Lucian), see Dickey (1996).

substructuring observable in speeches attested in other books of the *Iliad*.[12] My own view would be not to insist so much on the weak use of ring composition and parallel structure because the way they can be defined allows for considerable flexibility when one analyses a speech. Arranging thematic material by means of patterns goes against the additive, run-on style of Homeric epic, in which one idea leads to the next. Too rigid schemas for speech structuring are questionable, the more so since they tend to elide the difference between a single point and a topic.[13] In Hainsworth's apt formulation, "Homeric speeches ramble."[14] Nor would I lay too much stress on the principle of "thematic economy" in speech exchange, since it can be easily manipulated by a poet and as such is not a reliable criterion for authorship detection. Overall, I agree with Danek's claim that the speeches in book 10 display a distinct quality, though they also contain features (though few and weakly represented) that remind one of common Iliadic practice. However, before jumping to conclusions we need to examine the outer organization of speeches.

With respect to the outer organization (clustering) of speeches, statistics are equally important as a starting point. Table 4.2 refers to the number, length, and clustering of speeches in each of the three sections of book 10: the *Nyktegersia* (1–179), the Dolon episode (180–464), and the Rhesus episode (465–579).

The tabulated data (table 4.3) indicate that the fourteen speeches of the *Nyktegersia* are organized into four clusters. The average speech-length in this section is seven verses (98 verses: 14 speeches). As far as clustering is concerned, we observe that only two groups (A and B) extend beyond the Iliadic average length of a conversation, which is three turns.[15]

Turning to the Dolon episode, the twenty-two speeches are clustered in nine groups (see table 4.4). The average speech-length in this section is 7.27 verses (160 verses: 22 speeches). With respect to clustering, only one group (L: 8 speeches) extends beyond the Iliadic length of a conversation (3 speeches). Two groups contain 3 speeches, two groups 2 speeches, and there are 4 single speeches.

As regards the Rhesus episode, the 5 speeches cluster in 4 groups (see table 4.5). The average speech-length in this section is 6.8 verses (34 verses: 5 speeches).

These data reveal that there are only three conversations, two in the *Nyktegersia* and one in the Dolon episode, which extend beyond the average Iliadic length of a conversation (three speeches). All the rest are either three- and two-turn conversations, as well as several single speeches. Not only is this a small portion of the total amount of conversation in book 10 but it is also in tune with conversation patterns we come across in other Iliadic books. To offer just a handful of examples, *Iliad* 1 includes an extended conversation of eight speeches (as long as the one [L]

---

[12] Danek (1988) 186–90.
[13] See Hainsworth's review (1972, 187–8) of Lohmann.
[14] Hainsworth (1972) 187.
[15] D. Beck (2005) 127.

THE ALLEGED UN-ILIADIC FEATURES OF *ILIAD* 10   131

Table 4.2 Number, Length, and Clustering of Speeches in *Iliad* 10

	Number of Speeches	Speech-Length (Verses)	Clustering*
Nyktegersia			
37–41	1	5	A
46–59	2	17	A
61–63	3	3	A
65–71	4	7	A
82–85	5	4	B
87–101	6	15	B
103–119	7	16	B
120–127	8	8	B
129–130	9	2	B
141–142	10	2	C
144–147	11	4	C
159–161	12	3	D
164–167	13	4	D
169–176	14	8	D
Dolon Episode			
192–193	15	2	E
204–217	16	14	F
220–226	17	7	F
234–239	18	6	G
242–247	19	6	G
249–253	20	5	G
278–282	21	5	H
284–294	22	11	H
303–312	23	10	I
319–327	24	9	I
329–331	25	3	I
341–348	26	8	J
370–371	27	2	K
378–381	28	4	L
383–389	29	7	L
391–399	30	9	L
401–411	31	11	L
413–422	32	10	L
424–425	33	2	L
427–445	34	19	L
447–453	35	7	L
462–464	36	3	M
Rhesus Episode			
477–481	37	5	N
509–511	38	3	O
533–539	39	7	P
544–553	40	10	Q
555–563	41	9	Q

* Each letter of the alphabet stands for a cluster of speeches. For example, speeches 1–4 belong to the same cluster (A), since they pertain to a double exchange of utterances between Menelaus and Agamemnon.

132   THE HOMERIC *DOLONEIA*

Table 4.3 Clustering of Speeches in the *Nyktegersia*

A: 4 speeches	Dialogue between Menelaus and Agamemnon
B: 5 speeches	Dialogue between Nestor and Agamemnon
C: 2 speeches	Dialogue between Odysseus and Nestor
D: 3 speeches	Dialogue between Nestor and Diomedes

Table 4.4 Clustering of Speeches in the Dolon Episode

E: 1 speech	Nestor addresses the Achaean leaders before crossing the ditch
F: 2 speeches	Dialogue between Nestor and Diomedes
G: 3 speeches	Speeches by Diomedes and Odysseus, who will be the two Achaean spies
H: 2 speeches	Prayers of the two Achaean spies to Athena before they depart for their mission
I: 3 speeches	Dialogue between Hector and Dolon in the Trojan council
J: 1 speech	Odysseus' speech to Diomedes when he spots the Trojan spy Dolon
K: 1 speech	Diomedes addresses Dolon, aiming at preventing him from being killed by his spear
L: 8 speeches	Dialogue between Dolon, Diomedes, and Odysseus
M: 1 speech	Odysseus' speech to Athena

Table 4.5 Clustering of Speeches in the Rhesus Episode

N: 1 speech	Odysseus to Diomedes
O: 1 speech	Athena to Diomedes
P: 1 speech	Monologue by Nestor
Q: 2 speeches	Dialogue between Nestor and Odysseus

we have observed in book 10), as well as two other conversations of four speeches each. As regards the eight-speech conversation in book 1, it involves, exactly as is the case with book 10, three interlocutors. In fact, these two Iliadic books follow a similar pattern with respect to the structure of such extended conversations, given that two of the characters involved in this context are the principal interlocutors. In book 1, Achilles and Agamemnon utter six out of the eight speeches of the conversation, each being given three speeches. Likewise, in book 10 Dolon and Odysseus utter seven out of the eight speeches of the conversation. In *Iliad* 10 the first six speeches take the form of a verbal exchange starting with Dolon. The Trojan spy's fourth speech is not answered by Odysseus but by Diomedes, the man who will decapitate him.

There are also cases of even more extended conversations. Book 24 contains a conversation involving ten speeches between two interlocutors, Hermes and

Priam. It also offers an example of a five-turn conversation between Priam and Achilles. Clusters of four speeches within the framework of a single conversation are also observed in book 4, which shares certain similarities with book 10.[16] Other clusters of a four-speech conversation are traced in book 6, in the meeting between Hector and Andromache, and in book 22 in the scene of the dying Hector and Achilles.

Equally, the number of single speeches in book 10 is not different from the Iliadic average. In fact, shorter books or books with a smaller portion of direct speech occasionally contain more single speeches. Book 3 (461 verses/52.49% direct speech) has ten single speeches, book 12 (471 verses/25.90% direct speech) has nine, book 13 (837 verses/30.34% direct speech) has nine, whereas book 10 (579 verses/50.43% direct speech) has seven single speeches.[17]

Seen against this backdrop, the speeches of *Iliad* 10 give a rather blurred picture. With respect to their internal organization, they are either characterized by a lack of, or they display in a weak manner, the substructuring characterizing other Iliadic speeches, while as far as their outer organization and distribution (clustering) are concerned, there is nothing that separates them from the rest of the poem. Considering these mixed signals and fuzziness, I suggest that the discussion of speeches in book 10 is divorced from the question of poetic quality, which is after all a highly subjective issue. Nor is it the case that we are dealing with a lesser poet or singer.[18] We may arguably see how speeches in book 10 mirror in stark manner the impact of context on how characters speak. Given that too much must happen in too little time, elaborate arguments cannot be developed, pressure and emergency having more edge than contemplation and negotiation. This putative explanation of why the speeches display conflicting signs that draw them close but also apart from the rest of the epic can hardly be an acid test for evaluating and interpreting their distinct quality. However, it seems to me a legitimate way of broaching a thorny issue.

4.2 Clothing and Arming

The taste for the "exotic" with respect to dress or equipment in *Iliad* 10 has been considered untypical and subsequently interpreted as reflecting an author who is not the same as the poet of the rest of the epic.[19] In this section I will revisit this claim and examine clothing and arming in the *Doloneia*.

---

[16] See pp. 78, 100–1, 195.
[17] I basically follow the statistics of D. Beck (2005) 280–1. I differ with respect to the number of single speeches in book 10 (I have 7, whereas she has 5).
[18] Blößner (2020) 25.
[19] See Danek (1988) 203–29; Hainsworth (1993) 154. Differently, Dué and Ebbott (2010) 250–2.

4.2.1 Clothing

Four figures are dressed in animal skin in *Iliad* 10: Agamemnon (10.21–4), Menelaus (10.29–31), Diomedes (10.177–8), and Dolon (10.333–5). However, the first two do not take part in the spying mission, while the third puts on a lionskin as soon as he leaves his headquarters to join the other members of the Achaean council. This is well before the idea for a spying mission is suggested by Nestor and, of course, before Diomedes volunteers to participate. It is not clear whether he is still wearing the lionskin during the spying mission. This is a point which I will revisit in the course of this study. As regards Dolon, he is the only person in *Iliad* 10 who is clearly dressed in animal skin for his own spying mission.

The case of Dolon needs to be stressed in the starkest manner. The reason is that clothing and arming scenes are not identical, although they share certain common features.[20] Of the four clothing scenes of *Iliad* 10, only the one concerning Dolon is part of an arming scene, which takes place immediately before his departure for the spying mission. The other three scenes (featuring Agamemnon, Menelaus, and Diomedes) are of a different nature. The fact that these three Achaean leaders take with them a spear (Menelaus also a bronze helmet) does not turn these descriptions into arming scenes. The only case of a fully fledged arming scene is the arming of Diomedes and Odysseus before departing for their spying mission.

4.2.1.1 Agamemnon, Menelaus, and Diomedes

The dressing in animal skin of Agamemnon, Menelaus, and Diomedes belongs to a type-scene that is poorly represented in the *Iliad*, since it is restricted in *Iliad* 10, with a single exception.[21] However, this does not mean that they are isolated references which exist only in the *Doloneia*. Each of them resonates with a single Iliadic passage in a meaningful way.[22] That the *comparanda* are in each case limited qualifies them for deliberate, intratextual allusion, since the narrow range of association of two scenes sharing similar contexts and/or protagonists suggests that this may not be a symptomatic occurrence of related material but a conscious and planned reprise.[23] Let us look at *Il.* 2.42–6, in which Agamemnon is visited by the Dream (Ὄνειρος), and 10.21–4, when Agamemnon gets dressed:

---

[20] Arend's analysis (1933, 92–8) shows that Homeric epic, and for the purpose of this study the *Iliad*, treats them differently.

[21] *Il.* 3.17–20 (I am considering here only clothing scenes pertaining to mortals).

[22] "Markedness limits the possibility that the connection between two (or more) contexts is due just to coincidence or to typology. The meaningfulness requirement guarantees that a claimed allusion should increase our understanding of a passage or help it to make sense in a larger interpretive framework" (Currie 2016, 33–4).

[23] On limited, intentional, and meaningful repetition, see Pucci (1987) 38–9; Usener (1990); Tsagalis (2011) 219 = (2023) 12; Bakker (2013) 157–69. The term "reprise" means that the reference in *Iliad* 10 has been conditioned by the reference in *Iliad* 2; see Currie (2016) 35.

ἕζετο δ' ὀρθωθείς, μαλακὸν δ' ἔνδυνε χιτῶνα
καλὸν νηγάτεον, περὶ δὲ μέγα βάλλετο φᾶρος·
ποσσὶ δ' ὑπὸ λιπαροῖσιν ἐδήσατο καλὰ πέδιλα,
ἀμφὶ δ' ἄρ' ὤμοισιν βάλετο ξίφος ἀργυρόηλον·
εἵλετο δὲ σκῆπτρον πατρώϊον, ἄφθιτον αἰεί.

(He) sat upright and put on his tunic,
beautiful, fresh woven, and threw the great mantle over it.
Underneath his shining feet he bound the fair sandals
and across his shoulders slung the sword with nails of silver,
and took up the scepter of his fathers, immortal forever.[24] (*Il.* 2.42–6)

ὀρθωθεὶς δ' ἔνδυνε περὶ στήθεσσι χιτῶνα,
ποσσὶ δ' ὑπὸ λιπαροῖσιν ἐδήσατο καλὰ πέδιλα,
ἀμφὶ δ' ἔπειτα δαφοινὸν ἑέσσατο δέρμα λέοντος
αἴθωνος μεγάλοιο ποδηνεκές, εἵλετο δ' ἔγχος.

He stood upright, and slipped the tunic upon his body,
and underneath his shining feet he bound the fair sandals,
and thereafter slung across him the tawny hide of a lion
glowing and huge, that swung to his feet, and took up a spear. (*Il.* 10.21–4)

Comparison of these two scenes creates the impression that the great mantle (μέγα φᾶρος) Agamemnon puts over his *chiton* in *Il.* 2.43 has been replaced by the lionskin in *Il.* 10.23–4. The fact that in both cases Agamemnon takes with him a single weapon, a sword in *Iliad* 2 and a spear in *Iliad* 10, seems to reinforce this analogy. However, close examination suggests otherwise. In contrast to *Iliad* 2, where the great mantle donned by Agamemnon is mentioned immediately after the *chiton* he puts on upon waking up, the mention of the lionskin in *Iliad* 10 occurs not immediately after the *chiton* but, rather, at the conclusion of the clothing description. This is not a trivial rearrangement of the typical elements of a dressing scene but possibly a way to mark a feature as standing out. As the scepter is crucial for Agamemnon's authority, so is his lionskin. On the level of symbolism, it seems to mark Agamemnon's special status as *primus inter pares*.[25] If so, one would expect to find, exactly as is the case with the biography of the scepter in *Il.* 2.101–8, a passage in *Iliad* 10 elaborating on Agamemnon's lionskin. But such a passage is not to be found. The reason for this "absence" may be the deliberate isolation of the reference to the lionskin within the plot of *Iliad* 10.

---

[24] All translations of Homeric passages are by Lattimore (1951) with spelling modifications.
[25] Garments may stand for emotional disposition. Homer employs the same verb for clothing oneself and "clothing in a given emotion" (e.g. *Il.* 1.149: ἀναιδείην ἐπιειμένε; 7.164: θοῦριν ἐπιειμένοι ἀλκήν; 9.372: ἀναιδείην ἐπιειμένος); on garment metaphors and emotions, see Cairns (2016) 25–41.

It is possible that the *Iliad* alludes to the context of *Iliad* 2, when Agamemnon, being unable to sleep, dresses himself and decides to act after Achilles had restated his withdrawal. The similarity of circumstances with the *Doloneia* is only partial. Agamemnon's authority is emphatically undermined in *Iliad* 2 because the army fails his test, since they desire to return to Greece, and this at a point when the disastrous consequences of Achilles' withdrawal have yet to be felt. Conversely, when in *Iliad* 10 Agamemnon cannot sleep, dresses himself, and decides to act, the leaders of the Achaeans display a remarkable willingness not only to continue fighting but also to volunteer for a very dangerous mission into the enemy camp during the night. In this light, the "replacement" of the scepter by the lionskin may be aiming at bringing to the audience's attention an important change by means of a recall of the situation at the beginning of *Iliad* 2. There the scepter's biography and authority of its owner Agamemnon were undermined by the army's failing the test to commit themselves to the war; here a "blank" reference to his lionskin is followed by the mobilization of the leading warriors of the Achaeans.

Similar observations can be made with respect to Menelaus. The *pardalis*[26] he wears recalls his duel with Paris in *Il.* 3.17–20, which is the only other time Paris is described wearing an animal hide.[27]

παρδαλέην ὤμοισιν ἔχων καὶ καμπύλα τόξα
καὶ ξίφος· αὐτὰρ δοῦρε δύω κεκορυθμένα χαλκῷ
πάλλων Ἀργείων προκαλίζετο πάντας ἀρίστους
ἀντίβιον μαχέσασθαι ἐν αἰνῇ δηϊοτῆτι·

Wearing across his shoulders the hide of a leopard,
curved bow and sword; while in his hands shaking the two javelins
pointed with bronze, he challenged all the best of the Argives
to fight man to man against him in bitter combat. (*Il.* 3.17–20)

παρδαλέῃ μὲν πρῶτα μετάφρενον εὐρὺ κάλυψε
ποικίλῃ, αὐτὰρ ἐπὶ στεφάνην κεφαλῆφιν ἀείρας
θήκατο χαλκείην, δόρυ δ' εἵλετο χειρὶ παχείῃ.

First of all he mantled his broad back in a leopard's
spotted hide, then lifting the circle of a brazen helmet
placed it upon his head, and took up a spear in his big hand. (*Il.* 10.29–31)

---

[26] The leopard was an Asiatic animal, according to Aristotle (*HA* 606b). It therefore "belongs" to Paris, not to Menelaus.

[27] The technique of intratextual reprise used by the *Doloneia* is not different from that employed in the rest of the *Iliad*. The prime example is, of course, Achilles' (first) armor. Its use by Patroclus and then by Hector is marked. Achilles is evoked in the audience's minds by his armor, even when he is physically absent from the relevant scenes. *A fortiori*, Paris is not simply evoked but directly alluded to when Menelaus puts on a *pardalis*, especially since this clothing is worn by Paris in a scene in which he fights against Menelaus.

Since the range of the references to the *pardalis* as animal dress is very narrow, including only these two cases in the entire *Iliad*, the association seems to be deliberate, the more so since it involves the same two heroes (Paris and Menelaus). The fact that immediately before his dressing scene in the *Doloneia* Menelaus cannot sleep because of his fear lest the Argives are destroyed, since he holds himself responsible for bringing them to Troy for the sake of Helen, seems also to suggest that the link is intentional.[28] Menelaus' fear reflects the context of his duel with Paris in *Iliad* 3,[29] which is virtually the first appearance of these two heroes in the *Iliad*.[30] It is in this framework that the narrator had explained Menelaus' joy (3.27: ἐχάρη)[31] as soon as he saw Paris leading the Trojan army by means of his hope that he would be able to "punish the robber" (3.28).[32] Moreover, Hector had accused Paris of all the sufferings of the Trojans and tried to find a way out of the impasse of a never-ending war by means of a duel between Paris and Menelaus. This analogy suggests a consistent way of interpreting Menelaus' attire in the *Doloneia*. It is possible that he wears in *Iliad* 10 the same kind of animal hide that Paris wore in *Iliad* 3 because he is to be regarded in a way that it is meant to recall his confrontation with Paris in *Iliad* 3. The aim of this association seems to highlight the difference between these two heroes: while it was Hector who instigated Paris to a duel, thinking about the deaths and pain his brother had caused to his own people by abducting Helen, Menelaus bears the responsibility for the sufferings of his army and acts on his own. The fact that he arrives first at Agamemnon's hut may also point in the same direction. It is along these lines that Nestor's blaming of Menelaus and Agamemnon's response in defense of his brother (*Il.* 10.114–18) may be understood.[33] Although Paris and Menelaus occupy complementary positions next to their older and superior brothers, Hector and Agamemnon, respectively, they are very different as regards their responsibility towards their armies.

The clothing scenes of Agamemnon and Menelaus at the beginning of *Iliad* 10 tag these passages to relevant scenes in books 2 and 3 of the *Iliad*, in order to

---

[28] *Il.* 10.25–8: ὣς δ' αὔτως Μενέλαον ἔχε τρόμος· οὐδὲ γὰρ αὐτῷ | ὕπνος ἐπὶ βλεφάροισιν ἐφίζανε· μή τι πάθοιεν | Ἀργεῖοι, τοὶ δὴ ἔθεν εἵνεκα πουλὺν ἐφ' ὑγρὴν | ἤλυθον ἐς Τροίην πόλεμον θρασὺν ὁρμαίνοντες.

[29] See Reinhardt (1961) 247; Sammons (2009) 30; cf. Shewan (1911) 173; Clay (1983) 76–7; Danek (1988) 220.

[30] This first mention of Paris in the *Iliad* puts stress on his external appearance (3.39–57). Menelaus has been mentioned only *en passant* by Achilles (*Il.* 1.159) and the narrator (*Il.* 2.408, 586).

[31] The reference to Menelaus' joy is preceded by a simile, in which he is compared to a hungry lion that is pleased when he finds the carcass of a horned stag or a wild goat, since he will eagerly eat its prey, although dogs and strong young men hasten against him (*Il.* 3.23–6).

[32] φάτο γὰρ τείσασθαι ἀλείτην. Likewise, Odysseus rejoices at an omen and Zeus' thunder, "for he thought that he'd make the sinners pay" (*Od.* 20.120–1: χαῖρεν δὲ κληηδόνι δῖος Ὀδυσσεύς | Ζηνός τε βροντῇ· φάτο γὰρ τείσασθαι ἀλείτας).

[33] ἀλλὰ φίλον περ ἐόντα καὶ αἰδοῖον Μενέλαον | νεικέσω, εἴ πέρ μοι νεμεσήσεαι, οὐδ' ἐπικεύσω | ὡς εὕδει, σοὶ δ' οἴῳ ἐπέτρεψεν πονέεσθαι. | νῦν ὄφελεν κατὰ πάντας ἀριστῆας πονέεσθαι | λισσόμενος· χρειὼ γὰρ ἱκάνεται οὐκέτ' ἀνεκτός ("But, beloved as he is and respected, I will still blame Menelaus, even though you be angry, and I will not hide it, for the way he sleeps and has given to you alone all the hard work. For now he ought to be hard at work going to all the great men in supplication. This need that has come is no more endurable").

suggest to the audience a putative way of interpreting the actions of the Atreidae in the present context. Observations, already made in the ancient scholia, about the practical aspect of protecting oneself from the cold or rain[34] by wearing animal skin are not off the mark. They are important for decoding the complex case of Odysseus' lack of animal hide. However, they seem to be of limited value with respect to explaining why Agamemnon and Menelaus wore skins of *different* animals[35] and how the comparative and associative aspect of creating sense works in a medium like Homeric poetry.

The other hero who puts on a lionskin when he goes to the meeting of the Achaean council is Diomedes:

ὣς φάθ', ὁ δ' ἀμφ' ὤμοισιν ἐέσσατο δέρμα λέοντος
αἴθωνος μεγάλοιο ποδηνεκές, εἵλετο δ' ἔγχος.

He spoke, and the other wrapped his shoulders in the hide of a lion
glowing and huge, that swung to his feet, and took up the spear. (*Il.* 10.177–8)

Unlike the previous cases, the reference to the lionskin does not seem to allude to a preceding scene but arguably paves the way for the role that Diomedes is going to play in the ensuing spying mission. Before I turn my attention to the way Diomedes functions in the spying mission, there are two heroes in *Iliad* 10 whose dressing must be taken into consideration. Nestor and Odysseus, who also wake up during the night and participate in the council of the leaders, are *not* dressed in animal skin. Nestor wears "a tunic upon his body... and [has] pinned about him a great vermilion mantle sweeping in double fold, with a thick fleece of wool upon it" (*Il.* 10.131–4)[36] to protect an old man like himself from the cold of the night.[37] As regards Odysseus, nothing is said about the way he is dressed. The hero only takes with him his shield (*Il.* 10.149). Since the case of Odysseus is complex, I will treat it later in detail. For the time being, I stress that he will be anchored to Diomedes' feral aspect,[38] when the two heroes become a pair at the very beginning of their mission:

βάν ῥ' ἴμεν ὥς τε λέοντε δύω διὰ νύκτα μέλαιναν,
ἂμ φόνον, ἂν νέκυας, διά τ' ἔντεα καὶ μέλαν αἷμα.

---

[34] Σ *Il.* 10.23d. For animal hide causing fear, see Σ *Il.* 10.23b.
[35] The scholia (on *Il.* 10.23d) explain Agamemnon's wearing a lionskin in terms of his higher status than Menelaus, who is wearing a leopard skin. However, this explanation does not mean that wearing a lionskin makes someone kingly or kinglier. Diomedes is also wearing a lionskin, which would mean (if the scholia's approach is adopted) that he is of equal status to Agamemnon.
[36] ...ἔνδυνε περὶ στήθεσσι χιτῶνα, | ποσσὶ δ' ὑπὸ λιπαροῖσιν ἐδήσατο καλὰ πέδιλα, | ἀμφὶ δ' ἄρα χλαῖναν περονήσατο φοινικόεσσαν | διπλῆν ἐκταδίην, οὔλη δ' ἐπενήνοθε λάχνη.
[37] Σ *Il.* 10.134a (Erbse).
[38] Stanley (1993, 125) suggests that Diomedes' lionskin points to the identity of man and beast, for which he finds confirmation in the repetition of the lion simile while Diomedes slays the Thracians (*Il.* 10.485–7).

They went on their way like two lions into black night
through the carnage and through the corpses, war gear and dark blood.
(*Il.* 10.297–8)

The assimilation of the two spies with lions allows for the possibility that what was symbolically expressed about Diomedes, who was wearing a lionskin on his way to the council, has now been extended to Odysseus, who was not wearing an animal hide.[39]

Returning to Diomedes, his lionskin (as well as his assimilation to a lion at the very beginning of the spying mission)[40] seems to allude to his function in the ensuing spying mission,[41] in which he will act as a predator who ambushes and kills his victims. Attacks by lions on other animals are often mentioned in Iliadic similes,[42] which means that the audience is attuned to the traditional role assigned to lions in Homeric poetry. In this light, it may be expected that Diomedes will display certain characteristics associated with the way lions are presented in the *Iliad*. He becomes a killing machine in the *Doloneia*, since he slays no fewer than fourteen enemies (Dolon, Rhesus, and twelve Thracians). His "lion" aspect covers not only his predatory and killing proclivities but also his belonging to a world that knows of no agreements, arrangements, and compromise.[43] The well-known words of Achilles to Hector in *Il.* 22.262 that "there are no trustworthy oaths between men and lions,"[44] which follow his refusal to reach an agreement with Hector ("Hector, argue me no agreements. I cannot forgive you"),[45] seem to be analogous to Diomedes' rejection of the offer made by Dolon, who tells the two

---

[39] Dinter, Finkmann, and Khoo (2019, 248) draw attention to the fact that Agamemnon, Menelaus, Diomedes, and Dolon wear hides of predatory, aggressive animals. In the case of Diomedes, the symbolism is fully felt when he slaughters the sleeping Thracians, who are described as "helpless herds of unshepherded sheep or goats" (*Il.* 10.485–6).

[40] *Il.* 10.297–8.

[41] There may have been other factors conditioning the use of a lionskin by Diomedes. Lion and boar both belong to the core of animal diction used in epic poetry and at times appear in the same context. It is not a coincidence that the role Diomedes and Odysseus (the latter wearing a helmet made of boar-tusks) play in the spying mission is analogous to the way Homeric poetry describes lions and boars: lions kill other animals, whereas boars do not. So, with the two spies, Diomedes (the lion) kills Dolon, Rhesus, and twelve Thracians. Odysseus (the boar) does not. In the *Thebais*, when Tydeus and Polynices, the two newcomers to Argos, "clash outside the palace of Adrastus wearing skins of, or shields or clothing decorated with, a boar and a lion," King Adrastus recalls an oracle specifying that he should marry his two daughters to a boar and a lion. Reinhardt (1961, 249–50) argues that the *Thebais* had influenced *Iliad* 10 with respect to this issue; see also Davies (2014) 63. Boars fighting lions appear in Homeric similes (*Il.* 16.823–8), and there are cases (both in extended similes and simple comparisons) in which it is said that the animal is either a lion or a boar (e.g. *Il.* 11.292–5, 12.41–9, 17.21–2). In similes sharing the same or analogous *similemes*, the two animals are interchangeable (e.g. *Il.* 15.271–80, 17.281–3), which shows that they can be treated as a pair. When one component is chosen for whatever reason, then the other one is more easily evoked.

[42] Scott (1974) 58–62.   [43] Moulton (1977) 85, 113; Ready (2011) 61–9, 92.

[44] ὡς οὐκ ἔστι λέουσι καὶ ἀνδράσιν ὅρκια πιστά.

[45] *Il.* 22.261: Ἕκτορ μή μοι ἄλαστε συνημοσύνας ἀγόρευε.

Achaean spies that his father will give an enormous ransom to save his life.[46] Although the diction of this passage is similar to the phraseology used by Hector to Achilles in *Il.* 22.339-42,[47] there is a telling difference. Whereas the dying Hector begs Achilles for his body, Dolon implores the spies for his life. Both Diomedes and Achilles will not listen to the entreaty of their victims. Diomedes will not spare Dolon,[48] and Achilles will kill Hector and drag his body (tied to his chariot) to the Achaean camp. The association between the two scenes results in increased meaningfulness. Just as Dolon's decapitated head falls in the dust,[49] so too will Hector's head (although he is not decapitated).[50] The extremely narrow range of repetition suggests that 22.402-3 and 405 may operate as a deliberate allusion to 10.457. The arrogant Hector who promised to deliver Achilles' horses to Dolon and the equally arrogant Dolon who asked for them as his reward for the spying mission will meet the same doom at the hands of lion-like warriors (Achilles and Diomedes, respectively), who will not listen to their entreaties but will kill them, and their heads will mix with the dust. Seen from this vantage point, the lionskin which Diomedes puts on when he leaves his headquarters to join the council of the Achaean leaders may have a twofold function, both on the micro- and the macro-level: it paves the way for his role in the ensuing spying mission, and it will powerfully reverberate when Hector, Dolon's instigator to the spying mission, will meet his fate.

4.2.1.2 Odysseus

The case of Odysseus is more complex. The fact that he is not dressed in animal hide is interpretively meaningful. Odysseus is the only one of the Achaean leaders awakened in *Iliad* 10 who takes with him *his own* shield.[51] Evidence based on the *Odyssey*, as well as on other ancient sources, makes it clear that warriors used their shield to protect themselves from the cold during the night. Of special interest is *Od.* 14.468-503, in which the disguised Odysseus narrates to Eumaeus an episode pertaining to a spying mission (together with Menelaus, the real Odysseus, and other comrades) at Troy during a nocturnal ambush. In this false tale, the disguised Odysseus says that he did not take his cloak with him because he "did

---

[46] *Il.* 10.378-81: ζωγρεῖτ', αὐτὰρ ἐγὼν ἐμὲ λύσομαι· ἔστι γὰρ ἔνδον | χαλκός τε χρυσός τε πολύκμητός τε σίδηρος, | τῶν κ' ὕμμιν χαρίσαιτο πατὴρ ἀπερείσι' ἄποινα | εἴ κεν ἐμὲ ζωὸν πεπύθοιτ' ἐπὶ νηυσὶν Ἀχαιῶν ("take me alive, and I will pay you my ransom; in my house there is bronze, and gold, and difficultly wrought iron, and my father would make you glad with abundant ransom were he to hear that I am alive by the ships of the Achaeans").

[47] μή με ἔα παρὰ νηυσὶ κύνας καταδάψαι Ἀχαιῶν, | ἀλλὰ σὺ μὲν χαλκόν τε ἅλις χρυσόν τε δέδεξο | δῶρα τά τοι δώσουσι πατὴρ καὶ πότνια μήτηρ, | σῶμα δὲ οἴκαδ' ἐμὸν δόμεναι πάλιν ("do not let the dogs feed on me by the ships of the Achaeans, but take yourself the bronze and gold that are there in abundance, those gifts that my father and the lady my mother will give you, and give my body to be taken home again").

[48] *Il.* 10.447-57.   [49] *Il.* 10.457: τοῦ γε κάρη κονίῃσιν ἐμίχθη.

[50] *Il.* 22.402-3: κάρη δ' ἅπαν ἐν κονίῃσι | κεῖτο, 22.405: ὣς τοῦ μὲν κεκόνιτο κάρη ἅπαν.

[51] Diomedes has a shield in the spying mission, but this is given to him by Thrasymedes, son of Nestor (*Il.* 10.255-7).

not think that he would be cold in any case,"[52] although he took his shield (and belt) with him. Conversely, his comrades use their cloaks, *chitons*, and shields to keep themselves as warm as possible during the freezing night.[53] This account suggests that the shields were intended for protection in the fighting which would take place in the ambush, but they could be also employed as protection from the cold. The disguised Odysseus wants to make the point to Eumaeus that since the night has fallen and the West Wind blows, bringing rain,[54] he needs a cloak, just as he needed a cloak in the tale he narrates to him.[55] His shield and *chiton*[56] were not enough protection from the extreme cold of the night.[57] To this end, the disguised Odysseus relates the trick by which the real Odysseus made Thoas (who volunteers to go back to the ships and ask Agamemnon for reinforcements) take off his cloak and give it to him so that he might keep himself warm.[58] Comparison with this false tale[59] that shares various features with the *Doloneia*[60] suggests that, by presenting Odysseus taking his shield with him when he goes to the council, the *Iliad* may be covertly pointing to his participation in the spying mission. Furthermore, the shield is used as a mechanism that alerts the audience to his role in the spying mission. Unlike Diomedes' lionskin, which indicates that he will act as a killer in the night raid, Odysseus will not kill a single enemy.[61]

Odysseus' lack of an animal hide that would be employed as a cloak and its replacement by a shield create a triangular relationship of intratextual and

---

[52] *Od.* 14.481: οὐκ ἐφάμην ῥιγωσέμεν ἔμπης.

[53] As Newton (1997, 149) has nicely put it, "if a shield can double as a cloak,...a cloak may also double as a shield." Immediately after the completion of the disguised Odysseus' narration to Eumaeus follows an "arming" scene, in which the swineherd is presented wearing a cloak (*Od.* 14.529: ἀμφὶ δὲ χλαῖναν ἐέσσατ' ἀλεξάνεμον, μάλα πυκνήν) that takes the place of the shield. The same observation can be applied to the fleece of a goat (*Od.* 14.530: νάκην ἕλετ' αἰγός), which substitutes for the helmet in a typical arming scene.

[54] *Od.* 14.457-8.

[55] The systematic use of the "clothing" motif with respect to Odysseus shows that it is *particular* to him. See Grossardt (1998) 74-82; Tsagalis (2012a) 339 n. 91 = (2023) 201 n. 111.

[56] *Od.* 14.489: οἰοχίτων' ἔμεναι ("dressed only in a tunic").

[57] Notice the emphasis on the cold (*Od.* 14.475-7): νὺξ δ' ἄρ' ἐπῆλθε κακὴ Βορέαο πεσόντος, | πηγυλίς· αὐτὰρ ὕπερθε χιὼν γένετ' ἠΰτε πάχνη, | ψυχρή, καὶ σακέεσσι περιτρέφετο κρύσταλλος ("night came on, a foul one, after North Wind fell, a freezing one. The snow came from above, like frost, cold snow, and ice crystals formed around our shields").

[58] *Od.* 14.484-503.

[59] R. B. Rutherford speaks about "the elusive and kaleidoscopic relationship" between the false tales and Odysseus' "true experiences" (1985, 138). It may be the case that this type of association pertains to the entire spectrum of Odysseus' experiences, covering a span of events beyond the scope of the *Odyssey*.

[60] See *Il.* 10.251-3 (ἀλλ' ἴομεν· μάλα γὰρ νὺξ ἄνεται, ἐγγύθι δ' ἠώς, | ἄστρα δὲ δὴ προβέβηκε, παροίχωκεν δὲ πλέων νὺξ | τῶν δύο μοιράων, τριτάτη δ' ἔτι μοῖρα λέλειπται)—*Od.* 14.483 (ἀλλ' ὅτε δὴ τρίχα νυκτὸς ἔην, μετὰ δ' ἄστρα βεβήκει); *Il.* 10.467 (δόνακας)—*Od.* 14.474 (δόνακας); *Il.* 10.80-1 (ἐπ' ἀγκῶνος, κεφαλὴν ἐπαείρας | Ἀτρεΐδην προσέειπε)—*Od.* 14.485 (ἀγκῶνι νύξας), 14.494 (ἐπ' ἀγκῶνος κεφαλὴν σχέθεν εἶπέ τε μῦθον).

[61] His comparison to a lion is only due to the fact that he is presented as a pair with Diomedes (*Il.* 10.297-8).

intertextual associations.[62] Like Agamemnon's lionskin in *Iliad* 10 that points back to the use of his scepter in *Iliad* 2, Odysseus' shield alludes also to *Iliad* 2, in which he had taken off his cloak and employed Agamemnon's scepter on the backs of the rank and file to get them back to the assembly.[63] By doing so, Odysseus assumes briefly the function of Agamemnon. As the scepter is the trademark of the status of the king of Mycenae, so the cloak is the poetic symbol of Odysseus. It is after all the same cloak that the real Odysseus mentions in *Od.* 14.468–503 and describes in detail in *Od.* 19.221–48. The presence of the Ithacan herald Eurybates only in the relevant scenes in *Iliad* 2 and *Odyssey* 19, both times in the context of Odysseus' cloak, suggests a latent reference of the *Odyssey* to the *Iliad*. As the Iliadic reference to Eurybates became a brief Odyssean description of a man with black skin, curly hair, and round shoulders who follows Odysseus,[64] so the bare Iliadic reference to Odysseus' cloak becomes, arguably, an elaborate description of the cloak with its purple color, its golden brooch with double clasps, its decorated front with a brief snapshot "of a dog holding a fawn with his forepaws, gripping it in its jaws as it gasped and struggled."[65] In this way, "the mantle in the *Odyssey*...finds its origin in the *Iliad* while the mantle in the *Iliad* gains in prehistory from the *Odyssey*."[66] When seen against the background of the false tale to Eumaeus in *Od.* 14.468–503, Odysseus' shield (paired by the lack of gear that would protect him from the cold in *Iliad* 10) invites the audience to assume that he operates in similar manner. As in the false tale to Eumaeus, he deceives Thoas and acquires his cloak, which he gives to the fictive Odysseus, so in the *Doloneia* he will deceive Dolon and acquire from him information about the Trojan army and Rhesus.[67] In this respect, there may be a case that the *Iliad* and the *Odyssey* use Odysseus' cloak (in *Iliad* 2 and *Odyssey* 14 and 19), his shield

---

[62] See Muellner (1976) 96 n. 43: "in the *Doloneia*, a genre piece with many themes and even many details (weather, time, etc.) in common with this story, it is *Odysseus* (not some ragged companion) alone of the five Greek heroes who fails to wear a cloak (χλαῖνα), but carries only his shield (σάκος, K 149, vs. cloaks of other heroes elaborately described: K 23–4, 29–30, 133–4, 177–8). Compare ξ 482: ἀλλ' ἑπόμην σάκος οἷον ἔχων καὶ ζῶμα φαεινόν. The coincidence is all the more striking, since there is no point made of his lack of a cloak in the *Iliad*. Is epic too unsophisticated for a cross-reference here in the *Odyssey* to another version of this tale in which Odysseus himself needed a χλαῖνα – a cross-reference which, like the use of εὐξάμενος, hints broadly that the cloak-less narrator is Odysseus himself?" Danek (1988, 222 n. 106) objects to this interpretation and counterargues that in the *Doloneia* the audience does not know that Odysseus does not wear a cloak.

[63] But contrary to *Iliad* 2, no effort to convince the army to fight needs to be made in the *Doloneia*. Cooperative volunteering is the crowning feature of Achaean attitude in *Iliad* 10.

[64] *Od.* 19.246–7.   [65] *Od.* 19.225–8.   [66] So Maronitis (2004) 140.

[67] Although acknowledging that Odysseus' cloak operates as an associative link between the epic traditions of the *Iliad* and the *Odyssey*, Pucci (1998, 95–6) speaks of a reciprocal relationship between *Il.* 2.182–7 and *Od.* 14.468–503. He therefore favors a bidirectional allusion. On the one hand, the *Iliad* being conscious of the passage from the *Odyssey* employs the cloak to show "how futile is the *metis* of Odysseus, when he uses it to tell parables in order to cadge a cloak from a poor swineherd"; on the other, the *Odyssey* being equally conscious of the passage from the *Iliad* makes its own Odysseus "merge into the Iliadic hero, while...he must perpetually distance himself from him."

(in *Iliad* 10 and *Odyssey* 14), and his lack of animal hide (in *Iliad* 10) to signal his function in the relevant scenes.[68]

4.2.1.3 Dolon

The only case in which dressing in animal hide is part and parcel of a warrior's arming scene is that of the Trojan spy Dolon. Disguise is also used in Odysseus' spying missions in the *Ilias parva*,[69] in which Odysseus wears rags. In various Indo-European traditions, the men's rejection of human clothes goes hand in hand with their assimilation into animals, especially in the framework of their transition into the warrior band or society. In Norse tradition the *berserkir* were sometimes called "wolfskin" (*úlfheðnar*). The same phenomenon is observed in Old Irish (*luchthonn*) and Sanskrit (*Vṛkājina*) traditions.[70] In the case of Dolon, clothing in wolfskin is paired in iconography with wolf-like behavior, like walking on all fours.[71] It is not clear whether Dolon had always been connected to a tradition of ambush and deviousness, which is associated with wolves, hence the wolf-clothing. Wolf names are attested in Homer, but their relation to wolf behavior is indirect at best. Odysseus' grandfather, a famous trickster, was tellingly named Αὐτόλυκος, and it may not be a coincidence that his name comes up in *Il.* 10.266-7 in the context of theft.[72] Although it is not easy to see if the use of "wolf" names (Lycaon: *Il.* 5.229, 20.81; Lycurgus: *Il.* 7.142) is significant, wolfskin seems a suitable choice for Dolon's disguise. The reason may be that his role in the *Doloneia* is closely associated with that of Hector, who sends him as spy to the Achaean camp and whose λύσσα ("mad rage" < λύκος) is a key feature of *Iliad* 9.[73] Dolon's wolfish associations in *Iliad* 10 may well be the result of the "transfer" of Hector's wolfish λύσσα to his spy.[74] The mad rage of Hector, who had inflicted so many losses to the Achaeans within a single day (*Il.* 10.48-9), is ironically

---

[68] Further similarities between *Iliad* 2 and *Odyssey* 14 (*Il.* 2.56 = *Od.* 14.495: κλῦτε, φίλοι· θεῖός μοι ἐνύπνιος ἦλθεν Ὄνειρος; *Il.* 2.183: βῆ δὲ θέειν, ἀπὸ δὲ χλαῖναν βάλε = *Od.* 14.500-1: ἀπὸ δὲ χλαῖναν βάλε φοινικόεσσαν, | βῆ δὲ θέειν ἐπὶ νῆας) suggest the triangular reading I am endorsing; see Alden (2017) 279.

[69] Fr. 9 *GEF*; Odysseus was wounded by Thoas (fr. 8 *GEF*; also arg. ll. 224-5 Severyns) when he entered Troy in disguise; on this episode, see also *Od.* 4.244-6 (αὐτόν μιν πληγῇσιν ἀεικελίῃσι δαμάσσας | σπεῖρα κάκ' ἀμφ' ὤμοισι βαλών, οἰκῆϊ ἐοικώς, | ἀνδρῶν δυσμενέων κατέδυ πόλιν εὐρυάγυιαν, "he disfigured himself with appalling lacerations and then, with dirty rags on his back, looking like a slave, he slunk into the broad streets of the enemy city"); see also M. L. West (2013a) 195-7.

[70] M. L. West (2007) 448-51. "Wolf" is an encomiastic metaphor for the fighting hero in British, Irish, and Norse poetry.

[71] Lissarague (1980) 3-30.

[72] Dolon wears the hide of an animal associated with treachery; see Dinter, Finkmann, and Khoo (2019) 248. The same observation applies to his leather cap that is made of ferret skin.

[73] *Il.* 9.239: κρατερὴ δέ ἑ λύσσα δέδυκεν; 305: λύσσαν ἔχων ὀλοήν.

[74] That Dolon's presentation in the *Doloneia* goes back to a trickster in the manner of another wolf-figure (Odysseus' grandfather Αὐτόλυκος) is a tempting hypothesis (Davidson 1979, 61-6) that cannot be proved. In the case of Dolon, the wolfskin seems to point to the "lone wolf" theme, although the warriors advancing in battle-lines (e.g. *Il.* 4.471-2, 11.72-3) are compared to packs of wolves.

mirrored in the spy he sends to the Achaean camp. Just as Dolon's name is an ironical reminder of his failure to live up to it,[75] since he is arrested by the δόλων ἆτος Odysseus,[76] so his dressing in wolfskin suggests an ironical innuendo to his failure to cause even minimal damage to the Achaeans, very much unlike Hector who dispatched him.

As in the case of Agamemnon, Menelaus, and Diomedes, Dolon's animal hide may be used as an allusive device that recalls another passage which allows the audience to evaluate the situation in *Iliad* 10 by means of comparison. Clothing is, arguably, a mechanism that creates meaning according to the usual epic practice, in which a passage acquires its full semantic potential when associated with other relevant passages or scenes with which it shares phraseology and content. The important lesson to be drawn from this analysis is that the *Doloneia* employs the same techniques of intratextual and intertextual associations as the rest of the *Iliad*, and that in this way our understanding of its poetics is considerably enriched. Compelling commonalities are strongly probative, since they result in an interpretive surplus that is highly suggestive and powerfully allusive.

4.2.2 Arming

Arming scenes in *Iliad* 10 include the arming of the two Achaean spies and Dolon.[77] The arming of Diomedes and Odysseus is the only fully fledged scene of its type in the *Doloneia*. However, it is a unique type-scene for two reasons: first, because of the kind of gear employed by the two spies; second, because this gear is lent to them by others, (the guards Thrasymedes and Meriones). I will explore these two aspects of this type-scene in detail.

In the *Iliad* heroes put on their own armor. Patroclus is a notable exception since he is given the armor of Achilles, which he wears to give the impression to the enemy that Achilles himself has returned to the fighting. Achilles' armor, like all Iliadic armors, is made for protection in regular fighting on open ground between fully equipped armies. This type of gear is unsuitable for ambush warfare, especially of the kind that takes place at night. In this form of warfare, a new type of gear is needed, one that would help those who wear it achieve their goal. The atypicality of the gear worn by the two spies is a result of the fact that the *Iliad* systematically refers to gear that is suitable for regular fighting. Therefore, it may be suggested that subject matter conditions the equipment used in standard

---

[75] "Dolon the 'trickster' will become Dolon the tricked": Stanley (1993) 125.
[76] *Il.* 11.430; see also *Od.* 13.293, where the expression δόλων ἆτ' ("insatiable in your wiles") is employed by Athena when she addresses Odysseus, who has just told her a false tale about himself.
[77] The fact that Agamemnon and Menelaus take with them their spears when they go around in the camp in order to wake up several Achaean leaders does not mean that we are dealing with arming scenes (*pace* Stanley 1993, 123).

arming scenes. In this sense, there is no oddity here. The equipment of the two Achaean spies should be appropriate for their night mission. But is it all suitable for a night mission? The leather skullcaps worn by both Diomedes and Odysseus certainly are. They replace the helmet, which would have been apt for regular fighting. Diomedes' cap is deprived of horn or crest (ἄφαλόν τε καὶ ἄλλοφον) so as not to be spotted by the enemy. The story of Nisus and Euryalus in *Aeneid* 9 and the fact that they are spotted by the enemy because of the shining effect caused by the moonlight reflecting on Euryalus' helmet indicate how crucial are the leather skullcaps worn by the two Achaean spies in the *Doloneia*.[78]

As regards the rest of their equipment, Diomedes is given a double-edged sword and a shield, Odysseus a bow, arrows, and a sword. We are also to understand that both spies take with them the weapons they had when they went to the council— Diomedes a spear (*Il.* 10.178), Odysseus a shield (*Il.* 10.149). They thus have gear that is suitable for both close (sword) and distant (bow and spear) fighting and killing, while their shields would protect them in both types of combat. Their military equipment is complementary. The spies will operate as a single unit (*Il.* 10.222–4), which should be able to meet the needs of different and unexpected forms of fighting. To this end, Diomedes' spear proves useful when he throws it to stop Dolon from running away (*Il.* 10.371–4), while his sword becomes the weapon by which he decapitates Dolon (*Il.* 10.455–6) and stabs twelve Thracians (*Il.* 10.484) and Rhesus (*Il.* 10.495).[79] Since it turns out that all the killings are carried out by Diomedes, Odysseus' bow and sword are not employed as murder weapons. Odysseus uses his bow as a whip for the horses of Rhesus instead of noticing the apparent whip (μάστιγα φαεινήν).[80] For a hero renowned for his mental skill,[81] this inability to notice the whip may raise eyebrows, but it is also a reminder of the fact that as an islander Odysseus does not really know much about horses and chariots.[82] Having said this, it should be made clear that the arming of Odysseus by a bow is contextually appropriate since it would allow him to shoot from a distance at the Trojans, who would be by their campfires (Σ [T] *Il.* 10.260 [Erbse]).[83] That the bow is not used for fighting does not constitute a narrative failure, exactly as is the case with Dolon's weapons, which are also not used despite the fact that they are apt for this kind of mission. The reason is in both cases the same. The spying missions have been planned by the Achaeans and Trojans without knowledge or consideration of the possibility of a counterspying mission. It is the merging of two separate spying missions into a

---

[78] Faint traces of the feature of moonlight in night raids can be found in describing the part of the night during which the episode takes place (*Il.* 10.251–3); for a similar effect, see *Il. parv.* fr. 11 GEF.
[79] Although the sword is not explicitly mentioned in the case of Rhesus, it can be easily assumed that Diomedes used it to kill him, exactly as he did with the other Thracians.
[80] *Il.* 10.500–1.   [81] See *Il.* 10.224–6 and 247.
[82] He does not have a chariot with him at Troy. Σ [bT] 10.499c (Erbse); for other explanations, see Tsagalis (forthcoming) on *Il.* 10.499–506.
[83] See McLeod (1988) 121–5.

single plot (for it was not necessary that the Achaean spies would have come across the Trojan spy) that makes the bow unneeded. Although thematically appropriate, this weapon has become redundant because of the plot of the *Doloneia*. Furthermore, the bow bears a special association with Odysseus. It is an emblematic weapon in the *Odyssey*, since it is closely connected with the climactic episode of Penelope's test to the suitors and the ensuing μνηστηροφονία. Seen against this backdrop, the arming of Odysseus in the *Doloneia* with the type of weapon with which he excels in the major "quasi-ambush" episode of the *Odyssey* suggests that the Iliadic tradition is alert to mythical material pertaining to Odysseus' life after the end of the Trojan War. That Odysseus had left his own bow at home is evident from the fact that he does not have a bow, and so must be given one by another archer.[84]

The arming scene expands only one element, Odysseus' leather cap that is placed last in the list of his equipment (*Il.* 10.266–71) after the description of his cap (*Il.* 10.261–5).[85] The bard's aim is to increase the limited descriptive material with a brief narrative section, and "translate objects in space into actions in time."[86] The appended story fragment invites the audience to conceptualize the described object by understanding how it was acquired.[87] The structure of this "object-biography" is typical: six "owners" of the helmet mentioned in six verses, while the verb δῶκε is used three times, stressing the passing of the helmet from one owner to the next. The less-known figures are accompanied by specific references to their location or family (Amyntor, the son of Ormenus, from Eleon; Amphidamas, who lives in Scandeia on the island of Cythera), whereas the well-known characters are presented only by their bare names (Molus, Meriones, Odysseus).

Aristarchus, who was very attentive in focusing on cases of homonymy in Homer,[88] argued that there were two persons with the name Amyntor and father's name Ormenos: Phoenix's father, who moved from Hellas (southern Thessaly) to

---

[84] This observation is useful for the way Homeric tradition toys with Odysseus' cloak. Bow and cloak are not simply weaponry and clothing but have acquired a special association with Odysseus.

[85] While for Diomedes the leather cap serves only the practical purpose of evading the enemy's notice, Odysseus has a complex relationship with "invisibility." (a) The participle ἀντιτορήσας (*Il.* 10.267) used for Odysseus' maternal grandfather, Autolycus, is also employed for his divine patron, Hermes, who threatens to go to Delphi and "burgle the sizable temple" (*Homeric Hymn to Hermes* 178: μέγαν δόμον ἀντιτορήσων). Apollo says that Hermes "will be frequently entering, nocturnally, prosperous houses and leaving more than one man sitting on the floor while robbing his household without making a sound" (*Homeric Hymn to Hermes* 283–5: πολλάκις ἀντιτοροῦντα δόμους εὖ ναιετάοντας | ἔννυχον οὔ χ' ἕνα μοῦνον ἐπ' οὔδει φῶτα καθέσσαι | σκευάζοντα κατ' οἶκον ἄτερ ψόφου); on these two passages, see the commentaries by Vergados (2013) and O. Thomas (2020) on verse 178. It should be noted that this rare verb is used, apart from book 10, only in *Il.* 5.337 for none other than Diomedes, whose spear pierced the skin of Aphrodite. (b) Hermes, whose cunning association with Odysseus is evident through the intermediary of Autolycus, has also a cap (κυνέη) making the one who wears it invisible (e.g. Athena in *Il.* 5.844–5; Perseus when killing the Gorgon); see Roscher I.1, 735–6; Clay (1983) 83–4.

[86] Becker (1995) 54; see also Minchin (2001) 116. [87] Tsagalis (2012b) 404–6.

[88] van der Valk (1963–4) II, 255–7; Nünlist (2009) 240–2; Schironi (2018) 267–72.

Phthia (northern Thessaly), and another Amyntor living in Eleon (in Boeotia). Demetrius of Scepsis[89] must have had the same view. This is what can be assumed from the fact that he read οἷον ὅτε πρῶτον λίπον Ὀρμένιον πολύμηλον instead of οἷον ὅτε πρῶτον λίπον Ἑλλάδα καλλιγύναικα and argued that Amyntor ruled in Ormenion, a town in the foothills of Mount Pelion by the gulf of Pagasae in southern Thessaly. Wilamowitz-Moellendorff[90] believed that the name and patronymic had been transferred here from *Il.* 9.448 (Ἀμύντορος Ὀρμενίδαο), whereas Leaf[91] suggested that it was the legend that had been transferred from Thessaly to Boeotia (a similar trend having been observed in populations and genealogies).[92] On the basis of three important features of the cap's biography,[93] Danek[94] argued that it is possible that Phoenix's father in *Il.* 9.448 is the same person as the Amyntor mentioned here. It would have been very unlikely for the tradition on the one hand to invent an object's biography by transferring names from another Iliadic book (Ἀμύντορος Ὀρμενίδαο), inventing new ones or transferring them from Hesiodic epic (*Op.* 654: Ἀμφιδάμαντος),[95] and at the same time to create from scratch connections between well-known Iliadic heroes if they did not share any affinities (Meriones and Odysseus). There may be here a deliberate allusion,[96] which must simply remain a riddle for us due to lack of information. This is not contrary to the fact that Odysseus' affinity with the wild boar is traditional: during the flight of the Achaeans, he stands ground like a boar coming out of a thicket (*Il.* 11.411–20); he wounds a Trojan in the shoulder (11.420–1), i.e. at the same spot where he wounds a boar in the *Odyssey* (19.452); the boar's lair on Mount Parnassos is described in similar diction with Odysseus' hiding place in Scheria (*Od.* 5.483, 487; 19.443); Eumaeus first treats Odysseus to the meat of piglets (*Od.* 14.72-7) and then slaughters a boar for him (*Od.* 14.414–39); on his way to the town of Ithaca Odysseus is called a "wild boar piglet" (μολοβρός) by Melanthius (*Od.* 12.219) and later by Irus (*Od.* 17.26-9).[97]

A key person in the helmet's biography is Autolycus, Odysseus' maternal grandfather, who is known from the *Odyssey* (19.394–466), where it is said that

---

[89] Fr. 68 (Gaede).   [90] Wilamowitz-Moellendorff (1916) 62.
[91] Leaf (1900–2) on *Il.* 9.447 and *Il.* 10.266.
[92] Willcock (1978–84, *ad loc.*) has pleaded his ignorance.
[93] Unlike the "biography" of Agamemnon's sceptre (*Il.* 2.101–8), this cap does not pertain to a single lineage; knowledge of the names of Autolycus (*Od.* 19.394–466) and Meriones' father Molus (*Il.* 13.249) by the audience must be taken for granted; the place names Eleon in Boeotia and Scandeia on the island of Cythera, and the mention of a certain Amphidamas, point to some tradition unknown to us.
[94] Danek (1988) 121–2.
[95] So M. L. West (1978) 320–1 on Hes. *Op.* 654. On the contrary, it has been argued that the direction of influence is from Homer to Hesiod; see Most (2024) 131–2: "his [*sc.* Hesiod's] account in the *Theogony* of the wars in heaven is clearly modeled in its general structure and in crucial details upon the Trojan War... Hence we may interpret in general those points in which Hesiod differs from Homer, whether by explicit statement or by tacit omission, as being matters not of chance but of Hesiod's intention"; see also Most (2018) I, xxxi.
[96] Danek (1988) 122.   [97] See Alden (2017) 192–3.

he surpasses all men in thieving and perjury (19.395–6).[98] The hero's Autolycan heritage has been thoroughly discussed, often on the basis of the shaping of Odysseus' persona in the *Odyssey* through a gradual erasing of all the negative qualities he had inherited from his grandfather.[99] If Danek is on the right track to suggest a deliberate allusion to an unknown tale interweaving in a single narrative Phoenix's father, Odysseus' grandfather, and Meriones' father, then perhaps there is more to the fact that Phoenix and Autolycus feature in the *Iliad* and the *Odyssey*, respectively, in the context of a boar-hunt: Phoenix narrates the Calydonian boar-hunt (*Iliad* 9); Autolycus features in an embedded story relating how Odysseus visited him on Mount Parnassos and participated in a boar-hunt in which he was wounded.[100]

The stress put on Odysseus' cap through both its description and the ensuing catalogic expansion, which takes the form of an object biography, reinforces the programmatic aspect of the arming scene. In tune with the general Iliadic practice of placing arming scenes at climactic moments of the plot,[101] the arming of the two Achaean spies has multiple effects: first, it marks the transition to the *Doloneia* proper, which pertains to the spying mission to the Trojan camp; second, by emphasizing the specialist gear of Diomedes and Odysseus, it alerts the audience to the fact that the episode which is about to begin is of a special kind (a spying mission at night); and third, it signals by its sheer length (seventeen verses)[102] and its opposition to the brevity of the ensuing arming scene of Dolon (three verses)[103] that the Achaean spies will succeed, whereas Dolon will fail.[104]

The second special aspect of this arming scene concerns the fact that the spies are given their equipment by two of the guards who are placed outside the Achaean wall—Nestor's son Thrasymedes and Meriones.[105] These two men also put the leather caps on Diomedes' and Odysseus' heads, respectively, in marked contrast to the typical arming scene, in which this is done by the arming warrior himself.[106] These two interrelated issues are less odd than is generally assumed. They suggest a departure, though weakly represented, from the regular process according to which a warrior does *not* usually borrow gear from another person.

---

[98] On the poet's use of narrative to develop or supplement the restricted descriptive material that he offers to his audience, see Minchin (2001) 114–17.
[99] See, e.g., Maronitis (1971) 150–96; Clay (1983) 68–89; M. L. West (2014) 5–23.
[100] *Od.* 19.393–466.   [101] Armstrong (1958); Dué and Ebbott (2010) 290.
[102] *Il.* 10.255–71.   [103] *Il.* 10.333–5.
[104] Similar effect: the description of Hector's putting on Achilles' first armor, which he had taken from Patroclus, is carried out in one verse (*Il.* 17.210), while Achilles' wearing his new, second armor (*Il.* 19.369–91) extends to twenty-two verses. The marked difference in the length of these two descriptions suggests Hector's future demise at the hands of Achilles.
[105] See Stanley (1993) 124–5, who argues that Thrasymedes' name ("Bold-plan") and Odysseus' maternal grandfather Autolycus ("Lone-wolf"), who stole from Ormenos the boar-tusk helmet that Meriones will give to Odysseus, foreshadow the encounter of the two spies with Dolon: "Odysseus as the deceiver, Diomedes the slayer" (125).
[106] Danek (1988) 120.

A notable exception is Patroclus, who wears Achilles' armor. The difference, though, is that he wears Achilles' armor on his own without Achilles' assistance. This case stands out significantly, since Patroclus will serve as Achilles' surrogate in the ensuing battle. The function of Thrasymedes and Meriones in this scene conforms to a pattern used in Greek epic. This is nothing less than a development of a theme that is also observed in the prelude to the seduction type-scene, which is the women's equivalent of an *aristeia*.[107] In the default mode of the seduction scene, adornment includes bathing, anointing, and clothing, which are carried out either by a woman herself or by means of the assistance of other women. In the *Dios apate* in *Iliad* 14, Hera carries out these tasks on her own (165–86), while in the *Homeric Hymn to Aphrodite* (58–65) the bathing and anointing are done by the Charites, whereas the clothing by Hera herself. As for Pandora, she is adorned either by Athena (*Th.* 573–84) or by Athena, the Charites, Peitho, and the Horai (*Op.* 72–6). As regards the placing of the leather caps by Thrasymedes and Meriones on the heads of Diomedes and Odysseus, the seduction type-scene offers a telling analogy: in the adornment of Pandora, Athena (*Th.* 576–7) and the Horai (*Op.* 75) put on her head a wreath made of spring flowers.

These examples suggest that female adornment can be carried out by (a) the woman who is adorned, (b) one or more assistants, or (c) a combination of (a) and (b). Against this background, the function of Thrasymedes and Meriones in the arming scene of Diomedes and Odysseus before the spying mission seems to be equivalent to the role played by different female assistants when adorning a woman before a seduction scene. The assistance given by lesser warriors (Thrasymedes and Meriones) to major ones (Diomedes and Odysseus) stresses the role that the latter will play in the actual mission. They also enhance the cooperative spirit of the whole undertaking. In contrast to the secrecy of Hera's plan to seduce Zeus,[108] in book 10 there is a broad consensus for, as well as widespread knowledge of, the dangerous endeavor.

Dolon's arming scene is the only one that involves special clothing.[109] In this way, arming and clothing that were treated separately in the case of the Achaeans are narratively merged.[110] The entire episode in the Trojan camp is a mirror-scene of the more extended Greek episode of military preparation that precedes it. Like Odysseus, Dolon will be armed with a bow (καμπύλα τόξα),[111] and a sharp-edged spear (ὀξὺν ἄκοντα),[112] which he will not use in the following scene, since he will be

---

[107] See, e.g., Forsyth (1979) 101–20; M. W. Edwards (1987) 248; Alden (2000) 299; on further bibliography on this issue, see Currie (2016) 148 n. 3.
[108] Janko (1992) 173–4.
[109] Diomedes is probably wearing his lionskin when armed for the spying mission, but his animal hide is not part of his arming, since he had put it on much earlier, when he went to the council.
[110] The brevity of this scene is due to the fact that in a sequence of typical scenes epic usually offers a more detailed version of the first and a shorter version of the second (e.g. *Il.* 11.15–46 and 11.56–60).
[111] *Il.* 10.333. [112] *Il.* 10.335.

ambushed.[113] A special case is presented with respect to his cap of marten hide (ἰκτίδεος, < ἴκτις, -ιδος "marten," a kind of weasel).[114] The function of this type of cap is related to the fact that the marten kills birds during their sleep,[115] that it spies during the night, and that it is thought to be a wicked creature (weasels are vicious creatures that eat half their body weight a day and kill animals many times their size).[116] In this vein, Dolon's arming scene is mainly made up of elements that will not be used in the ensuing narrative (the bow and spear), as well as of a kind of cap that signals his role as a spy. We can detect here a covert pairing with Odysseus, enhanced by the fact that neither of them will inflict any deaths during the night mission. Both spies will not use their weapons to kill, neither those they have in common (bow) nor the ones they do not share (Odysseus: sword; Dolon: spear). The wearing of leather caps by both spies is highlighted. In the case of Odysseus this is carried out by its description and prehistory, while in the case of Dolon by its use as an ironic symbol of the failure of the Trojan spy.

4.3 Zielinski's Law

The law of temporal succession, or Zielinski's Law, states that Homer is unable to present events that happen simultaneously[117] and so resorts to presenting them successively, without moving backward in time to recount actions that have been already introduced in the narrative. Zielinski's Law and the representation of simultaneity in Homer has been the subject of debate.[118] It has also been treated

---

[113] On the bow as a standard weapon for night raids, see McLeod (1988) 121–5.

[114] With the exception of *Il.* 10.335 and 10.458, the epithet κτίδεος (that has suffered a loss of initial iota) is not attested in extant Greek literature (I do not count cases in which lexicographers and scholiasts refer to a noun κτίς, which is an artificial back-formation to explain the epithet). This explanation fits the present context and is further suggested by the fact both that the association of κτιδέη with ἴκτις is ancient (e.g. Σ [ATb] on *Il.* 10.335a-c²) and that some MSS give ἐπ' ἰκτιδέην. Leumann (1950, 53–4), who agrees with Maas (1933, 285–6), thought that the false analysis was created by the poet of the *Doloneia*. Differently, Reece (2009, 89–90) takes this as a form of metanalysis and not a scribal error (in *Il.* 10.458 where κτιδέην is guaranteed), "partly motivated by the slight preference in dactylic hexameter for a second-foot masculine caesura over a first-foot diaeresis" (90). The verse is made of formulaic units (κρατὶ δ' ἐπ' -υυ- or --- κυνέην: 5x; ὀξὺν ἄκοντα: 3x [replacing εὔτυκτον ἔθηκεν: 3x*Il.*, 1x*Od.* or θέτο τετραφάληρον: 2x*Il.*]); see Danek (1988) 134–5.

[115] Nic. *Th.* 196–7.

[116] Arist. *H.A.* 612b10; see Wathelet (1989) 220; Dué and Ebbott (2010) 330. This is also the case with the wolfskin worn by Dolon, on which see pp. 143–4; see also Dinter, Finkmann, and Khoo (2019) 248.

[117] Zielinski's Law is against Aristotle's view (*Po.* 1459b26-8) that the narrative mode of Homeric epic allows for the representation of many simultaneous sections (ἐν δὲ τῇ ἐποποιίᾳ διὰ τὸ διήγησιν εἶναι ἔστι πολλὰ μέρη ἅμα ποιεῖν περαινόμενα, ὑφ' ὧν οἰκείων ὄντων αὔξεται ὁ τοῦ ποιήματος ὄγκος, "whereas in epic, given the narrative mode, it is possible for the poem to include simultaneous sections, which, if integral, enhance the poem's dignity"). The result thus is that epic has "an asset for the development of grandeur, variety of the hearer, and diversity of episodes" (ὥστε τοῦτ' ἔχει τὸ ἀγαθὸν εἰς μεγαλοπρέπειαν καὶ τὸ μεταβάλλειν τὸν ἀκούοντα καὶ ἐπεισοδιοῦν ἀνομοίοις ἐπεισοδίοις). Translation: Halliwell et al. (1995). Aristotle's view is shared by Aristarchus: see Rengakos (1995) 5–8 = (2006) 92–4.

[118] Zielinski (1899–1901) 407–49; on time and simultaneity in Homer, see Belzner (1912) 24; Cauer (1921–3) 447; Bowra (1952) 313–14; Heubeck (1954) 44–5; Page (1955) 65 with n. 11; Krischer (1971)

as an indication of written composition of the *Iliad*[119] and its (assumed) violation in the *Doloneia* as the result of different authorship from the rest of the epic.[120] I will revisit this last claim by examining three scenes: the meeting between Agamemnon and Menelaus, the *Nyktegersia* with the branching out of two action sequences, and the two assemblies. I will then turn my attention to what Danek considers a peculiar use of the imperfect instead of the aorist in the arming scene of Odysseus in *Iliad* 10 and his treatment of this change of tense as one more instance of violation of Zielinski's Law.

4.3.1 Agamemnon and Menelaus

With respect to the meeting between Agamemnon and Menelaus, Danek argues that, contrary to Zielinski's Law, which in this aspect is regularly observed in the rest of the *Iliad*,[121] the "poet of the *Doloneia*" steps back in time. His claim is based on the fact that Menelaus' rising and dressing are presented after that of Agamemnon, though he is able to go first to his brother's hut, who is still putting on his clothes.[122] Danek sees a corroboration of his claim that the narrator steps back in time in the use of πρότερος ("but this time he woke far before me, and came to rouse me," *Il.* 10.124) by Agamemnon when he tells Nestor that Menelaus woke him up first.[123] However, when Nestor complains to Agamemnon about Menelaus' hesitancy and procrastination, Agamemnon replies by highlighting Menelaus' recently expressed concern for the army, since he arrived at Agamemnon's headquarters while his brother was still getting prepared and spoke to him first about the difficult situation that the Achaeans were facing. The fact that Menelaus speaks first to Agamemnon remains in the latter's mind as an indication of his brother's willingness to act, and he translates this eagerness into the assumption that Menelaus woke up earlier than him, which explains why he is still in his hut when Menelaus arrives. If ἐμέο πρότερος μάλ' ἐπέγρετο καί μοι ἐπέστη (*Il.* 10.124) is taken at face value,[124] then we would have seen Menelaus

---

71–129; Hainsworth (1974) 285 and (1988) 252; Ruijgh (1974) 419; Hooker (1975) 192; de Jong (1987 = 2004²) xix–xx, (2007) 17–37; M. W. Edwards (1987) 34–5; S. Richardson (1990) 90–1; Lämmert (1991⁸) 85 with n. 36; Janko (1992) 150; Stanley (1993) 6 and n. 18; Rengakos (1995) 1–33 = (2006) 85–134; Danek (1998b) 67–88, (1999) 76–88; Nünlist (1998b) 2–8; Reichel (1998a) 45–61, (1998b) 4–6; Seeck (1998) 131–44; Tsagarakis (2001) 355–66; Belfiore (2002) 25–49; Lundon (2002) 581–91; *HomEnc* s.v. "Time" 878–9 (E. J. Bakker); Danek (2012) 110–16.

[119] See, e.g., Reichel (1998b) 5–6.   [120] Danek (2012) 110–16.
[121] On a comparison between Homer and South Slavic singers with respect to time management, see Danek (2007) 599–618.
[122] *Il.* 10.34: τὸν δ' εὗρε ἀμφ' ὤμοισι τιθήμενον ἔντεα καλά ("he found him putting the splendid armor about his shoulders").
[123] Danek (2012) 112: "the narrator does not only step back in time, contrary to 'Zielinski's Law,' but almost comments on his violation of the rule, signalling that he enjoys the transgression."
[124] So Danek (2012) 111–12.

waking up Agamemnon. But this is not the case. Agamemnon *assumes* that Menelaus had risen earlier because he arrived at his headquarters while he was finishing up his dressing preparations to go to Nestor. In fact, Agamemnon spends some time looking at the campfires of the Trojan army on the plain. It is only after he ponders what to do that he starts getting dressed. This may have given Menelaus enough time to reach Agamemnon while the latter was still getting prepared.

Moreover, the narrator does not pause the first action while turning his attention to the second. In *Il.* 9.712–13, we have been told that each of the leaders of the Achaeans went to his hut and slept. At the beginning of book 10, however, Agamemnon cannot sleep; he observes the Trojans rejoicing in their camp, while his own army is in despair. This means that Agamemnon is in his hut, which must be located at some high point that allows him to see both armies or that the Trojans have camped "on the rise in the plain."[125] We left Agamemnon getting dressed (*chiton*, sandals, lionskin), only grabbing his spear in *Il.* 10.24. Conversely, Menelaus finds him "putting the splendid armor about his shoulders | *beside the stern of his ship*" (*Il.* 10.34–5).[126] This means that Agamemnon is no longer in his hut but outside by the stern of one of his ships and is putting on his armor. Therefore, we are not back to the temporal point the narrator left him in *Il.* 10.24. We are neither told when Agamemnon got out of his hut and stood by his ship nor if he was thinking about his own plan. All this potential information is omitted because, as in several other instances in the *Iliad*, the narrator does not go back in time, i.e. to the exact point he had left Agamemnon. Rather, as for all mortals, time flows forward for Agamemnon, whom Menelaus finds at a later moment in time.[127] A similar example is *Il.* 6.279–80. Hector initiates two actions: he tells Hecuba to go to the temple of Athena and ask for the goddess's help against Diomedes, while he goes to summon Paris to battle. The narrator then presents the first action in detail[128] and then turns his attention to the second action (Hector going to Paris' house). Although one would expect to find Hector beginning his advance to his brother's residence, the narrator presents him as having already arrived there. This is indicated by the pluperfect βεβήκει.[129] Instead of stepping back in time by employing an expression such as βῆ δ' ἰέναι or ἀπέβη, the narrator indicates through the pluperfect that Hector "had been going while the women were praying."[130] As Tsagarakis put it, "the action concerning Hector's

---

[125] See Σ *Il.* 10.11: ἢ ὅτι ἐφ' ὕψους ἡ βασιλικὴ σκηνή, ἢ ὅτι οἱ Τρῶες ἐπὶ θρωσμῷ πεδίοιο, "or because the king's hut is [placed] on an elevated spot, or because the Trojans are on *the rise of the plain*" (10.160). Agamemnon is probably seated when watching what happens (hence ὀρθωθείς: *Il.* 10.21).

[126] τὸν δ' εὗρ' ἀμφ' ὤμοισι τιθήμενον ἔντεα καλὰ | νηΐ πάρα πρύμνῃ ("he found him putting the splendid armor about his shoulders beside the stern of his ship"). Menelaus begins his speech to Agamemnon by asking him "why this arming, my brother" (*Il.* 10.37: τίφθ' οὕτως, ἠθεῖε, κορύσσεαι).

[127] See my examination of the two councils (pp. 156–8). Sometimes the *Iliad* presents background actions and steps back in time, whereas on other occasions it refrains from doing so.

[128] *Il.* 6.286–312.   [129] Tsagarakis (2001) 359–60.   [130] Leaf and Bayfield (1962) 395.

mission to Troy is then not suspended when the poet is not dealing with it directly; it is simply going on off stage, as it were, and at some point the poet catches up on it."[131] Another example is furnished by *Il.* 7.193-4 and 7.206-7, in which the poet refrains from describing the arming scene because it took place during the prayer of the Achaeans to Zeus.[132] Seen from this vantage point, the narrator does not step back in time in the meeting between Agamemnon and Menelaus in the *Doloneia*, which means that he follows what Zielinski has called the *simultaneous analytical-transitional method* ("die gleichzeitige analysierend-desultorische Methode").[133] The aim of this technique is to immerse the audience in the action and help them perceive the unraveling of events not through reflection but by means of observation.[134] This creates the impression that they are not part of a predetermined poetic setting but are actively experiencing reality. Characters continue to act even when their actions are not described or narrated.

4.3.2 The *Nyktegersia*

Turning to the *Nyktegersia*, which is announced by Agamemnon in *Il.* 10.53-6, we see that it involves two simultaneous actions: Agamemnon wakes up Nestor, who goes with him outside of the camp where the guards are stationed, while Menelaus wakes up Telamonian Ajax and Idomeneus. According to Zielinski's Law, "we are forced to expect these two actions to be described one after the other,"[135] which is not the case since the narrator presents only Agamemnon's course of action, leaving Menelaus' mission in the background. Menelaus then asks Agamemnon whether he should stay "in place" (until Agamemnon comes) after waking up Telamonian Ajax and Idomeneus or return to Agamemnon after having carried out his task,[136] which means that Agamemnon would then start his mission to Nestor, possibly with Menelaus.[137] However, since Agamemnon has already told Menelaus that he will go to Nestor, wake him up, and see if he is willing to go to the guards,[138] he clearly draws a line between (a) waking up Nestor and, possibly, various other heroes and (b) going together with him/them or on his own to the guards. This means that it is unclear whether Agamemnon intends to go to the guards together with Nestor. Therefore, Menelaus does not understand whether

---

[131] Tsagarakis (2001) 360.   [132] For more examples, see Tsagarakis (2001) 360-6.
[133] Zielinski (1899-1901) 411.
[134] Zielinski (1899-1901) 413; see also Rengakos (1995) 8-9 = (2006) 95.
[135] Danek (2012) 112.
[136] *Il.* 10.62-3: αὖθι μένω μετὰ τοῖσι, δεδεγμένος εἰς ὅ κεν ἔλθῃς, | ἦε θέω μετὰ σ' αὖτις, ἐπὴν εὖ τοῖς ἐπιτείλω ("shall I wait where I am, with them, and watch for your coming, or run after you, when I have properly given the order?").
[137] Danek (2012) 112-13.
[138] *Il.* 10.55-6: εἶμι, καὶ ὀτρυνέω ἀνστήμεναι, αἴ κ' ἐθέλῃσιν | ἐλθεῖν ἐς φυλάκων ἱερὸν τέλος ἠδ' ἐπιτεῖλαι ("I shall go and waken him (*sc.* Nestor) to rise, if he might be willing to approach the sacred duty of the guards, or give orders to them").

Agamemnon wants him to go together with Telamonian Ajax and Idomeneus to the guards, or return on his own, join Agamemnon (in case he does not accompany Nestor to the guards), and go with him to the meeting place. Such an interpretation gains weight from the fact that Menelaus cannot and does not take it for granted that Agamemnon will convince Nestor to go to the guards.[139] He wants to avoid a situation in which he would have accomplished his mission and show up at the meeting place together with Telamonian Ajax and Idomeneus, whereas Agamemnon would have failed to summon Nestor and would have arrived there on his own. By asking his brother what he should do, he wants to make sure that their actions are coordinated, and that there will be no indication to the other Achaean leaders, no matter what, that his brother will have failed. In this vein, Agamemnon's reply that Menelaus should go directly with Telamonian Ajax and Idomeneus to the guards (or even without them if they are unwilling to wake up) and not return in case they may miss each other makes it clear that we are dealing with simultaneous actions, of which only that of Agamemnon is foregrounded.

However, the assumption that this is an *unparalleled* breach of Zielinski's Law, and therefore an indication that the *Doloneia* has been composed by a poet different from that of the *Iliad*, is questionable. Instead, I suggest that the right question that we should be asking is whether the determination of the converging point of two branching-out actions of which only one is presented amounts to a technique that is observed elsewhere in the epic or not.

In *Il.* 12.366–9, Telamonian Ajax tells Locrian Ajax and Lycomedes to hold their position and continue fighting on the Achaean Wall, while he and Teucer go to a different spot and assist Menestheus, who is pressed by the assault of the Lycian leaders Sarpedon and Glaucus. Telamonian Ajax explicitly tells Locrian Ajax and Lycomedes that he will return to this spot as soon as he saves Menestheus. The narrative then presents the action of Telamonian Ajax and Teucer. However, the parallel, simultaneous fighting of Locrian Ajax and Lycomedes is not presented but remains in the background. The same observation applies to the predetermination of the future convergence of these two coincident actions. The return of Telamonian Ajax and Teucer is not presented or mentioned, but the two Ajaxes are found fighting together immediately before *Il.* 13.46.[140]

At *Il.* 13.751–3 Hector commands Polydamas to summon the leaders of the Trojans, while he continues to fight; he promises to return and meet him again. Hector rejoins the battle, finds Paris and other Trojan heroes, chastises Paris, and returns with all of them, as he had told Polydamas. However, the simultaneous

---

[139] Likewise, Hector in *Il.* 6.279–81 (ἀλλὰ σὺ μὲν πρὸς νηὸν Ἀθηναίης ἀγελείης | ἔρχευ, ἐγὼ δὲ Πάριν μετελεύσομαι ὄφρα καλέσσω, | αἴ κ' ἐθέλῃσ' εἰπόντος ἀκουέμεν, "so go yourself to the temple of the spoiler Athene, while I go in search of Paris, to call him, if he will listen to anything I tell him") is not sure that he will convince Paris to join the battle. Note the stress on the verb ἐθέλῃσιν.

[140] See Rengakos (1995) 18–19 n. 56 = (2006) 110 n. 198.

action of Polydamas is not narrated and lurks in the background. As argued by Rengakos,[141] the difference from the scene between Hector and Hecuba in *Il.* 6.279–81, in which both simultaneous actions are narrated, is that in both *Iliad* 12 and 13 it is only the action undertaken by the main hero/protagonist of the scene (who is also the one who has foretold the branching out of the action) that is presented, whereas the simultaneous actions of the secondary figures (Locrian Ajax and Lycomedes in 12, Polydamas in 13) are not narrated.

These examples suggest that the *Iliad* offers a mixed picture with respect to those simultaneous actions which are announced by characters.[142] Sometimes both contemporaneous actions are presented successively, whereas in other cases only one of these actions is performed and the other one remains in the background. The latter alternative is the case with Agamemnon and Menelaus in *Iliad* 10. Agamemnon, who designates the simultaneous actions to be undertaken by himself and Menelaus, is the one whose action will be foregrounded. In this respect, *Iliad* 10 does not differ from *Iliad* 12 and 13 as regards the presentation of simultaneous actions. Equally, the waking up of Agamemnon and Menelaus in book 10 does not diverge from the scene in *Iliad* 6, in which two simultaneous actions are narrated one after the other. In fact, the *Doloneia* offers two different ways of presenting simultaneous actions, which is exactly the case with the rest of the *Iliad*.

The same branching out of simultaneous actions is observed when Agamemnon, Nestor, and Odysseus wake up Diomedes. The last Achaean leader is subsequently sent to wake up Locrian Ajax and Meges, while Agamemnon, Nestor, and Odysseus go to the guards. Diomedes' action is not presented. The fact that they all arrive at the same time at the meeting place where the guards have been stationed (*Il.* 10.180) does not mean that it is unclear which action the poet understands as foreground and which as background.[143] The narrator treats only one action as foreground after the initial meeting of the Atreidae. This is the action of Agamemnon, to which are progressively added other leaders (Nestor and Odysseus). The aim of this technique foregrounds the waking up of the protagonists of the night mission, and with it Nestor, who devises the plan, and the pair Odysseus and Diomedes, who execute it. Diomedes' action of waking up two other Achaean leaders remains in the background because it is secondary and not instrumental to the plot of *Iliad* 10.

---

[141] Rengakos (1995) 19 n. 56 = (2006) 110 n. 198.

[142] For several examples of Iliadic simultaneous actions which are announced by the narrator, though he presents only one of them, see Tsagarakis (2001) 361–3.

[143] Danek (2012, 114) treats this case as an imprecise use of Iliadic formulation. I do not see anything against *Il.* 3.209–10, where it is said that Odysseus and Menelaus appear before the already assembled Trojans. Here all the leaders appear at the same time before the assembled guards. That only one of these strands is foregrounded, while the other two pertain to background actions, is not a narrative oddity of *Iliad* 10; for a relevant example, see point (c) below (p. 157).

4.3.3 The Two Councils

Another group of scenes pertaining to the debate about the application of Zielinski's Law are the councils of the Achaeans and Trojans. After Diomedes and Odysseus depart for the night mission, the narrator's focus is centered on the Trojans and Hector, who has also summoned a council. He puts forward a plan similar to that of the Achaeans.[144] By employing a double οὐδέ (*Il.* 10.299: οὐδὲ μὲν οὐδὲ Τρῶας ἀγήνορας εἴασεν Ἕκτωρ, "nor did Hector either permit the high-hearted Trojans"), the narrator indicates that the Trojan council takes place simultaneously with the Achaean one. This assumption is indirectly confirmed by Dolon's approach to the Achaean ships, when he is arrested by Diomedes and Odysseus.[145] Danek's claim that the poet has stepped back in time is correct. However, the argument that this is particular to the *Doloneia* and against the handling of time in the rest of the *Iliad* is debatable. Stepping back in time happens in various occasions in the *Iliad*. Let us survey some examples:[146]

(a) The narration in the Iliadic proem looks back to Zeus' plan and the conflict between Agamemnon and Achilles from a temporal point that is later, since it refers to the deaths of heroes and the devouring of their bodies by dogs and birds.[147]
(b) Achilles tells Thetis in *Il.* 1.366-92 about the plague sent by Apollo, his conflict with Agamemnon, the removal of Briseis from his war spoils, etc. These events, which have taken place, have already been narrated in *Iliad* 1. By offering a summary of these events by means of Achilles' speech to Thetis, the poet steps back in time and refers to the same events for a second time.
(c) In *Il.* 2.50-2 Agamemnon commands the heralds to summon the army to the assembly. The heralds do so, and the men are assembled swiftly.[148]

---

[144] *Il.* 10.299-312.
[145] This is the interpretation offered by the scholia (*Il.* 10.299a: οὕτω γὰρ καὶ ἑαυτοῖς συμπεσοῦνται οἱ ἀπεσταλμένοι, "or in this way the envoys will come across each other"; *Il.* 10.299b: ὑπὸ τὸν αὐτὸν χρόνον ἀμφότεροι τοὺς κατασκόπους πέμπουσιν· συντυγχάνουσιν γὰρ ἀλλήλοις ἰόντες, "both send the spies at the same time; for they come across each other as they go"). The *Doloneia* plays with the analogy between the importance given by Agamemnon not to miss Menelaus in the many paths within the Achaean camp and the effort of the Achaean spies not to miss the Trojan spy (after noticing him). Simultaneous actions are orchestrated so that a certain goal is achieved. Agamemnon and Menelaus arrive at the same time at the place where the guards are stationed, Diomedes and Odysseus capture Dolon together. The two pairs, the Atreidae as instigators of the council and the spies as agents executing the council's decision, are thus paralleled. The situation is markedly different from what happens with Hector and Dolon.
[146] See Rengakos (1995) 32-3 = (2006) 131-3.
[147] Krischer (1971) 136-7; Tsagarakis (1992) 781-9.
[148] αὐτὰρ ὁ κηρύκεσσι λιγυφθόγγοισι κέλευσε | κηρύσσειν ἀγορήνδε κάρη κομόωντας Ἀχαιούς· | οἱ μὲν ἐκήρυσσον, τοὶ δ' ἠγείροντο μάλ' ὦκα ("but he [*sc.* Agamemnon] commanded his clear-voiced heralds to summon by proclamation to assembly the flowing-haired Achaeans, and the heralds made their cry and the men were assembled swiftly").

At that point, the narrator tells us that "first Agamemnon held a council of the high-hearted princes beside the ship of Nestor, the king of the race of Pylos" (2.53-4).[149] In this meeting Agamemnon reveals his plan to make trial of the Achaeans and find out whether they are willing to fight (2.72-4),[150] and Nestor agrees, leading the way to the assembly of the army (2.84-6).[151] However, instead of finding the army already assembled as we had been explicitly told in 2.50-2, the narrator steps back in time and describes by means of an extended simile the army going to the assembly (2.87-93).[152] This case in which the "poet" steps back in time results in turning a background action (2.50-2) into a foreground one (2.87-93). Moreover, the two separate strands of action are treated differently as the narrative unfolds: the first time, the heralds summoning the army is the background action, while the council of the leaders is the foreground action, but the second time, the leaders joining the assembly is the background action, whereas the heralds summoning the army is the foreground action. What we see here at work is the subsequent and symmetrical inversion of background and foreground actions, so that the two strands are virtually presented as overlapping, since leaders and army come to the place of the assembly at the same time.

(d) In *Il.* 8.1-56 the epic foregrounds only what happens in the divine council and leaves in the background the feasting and military preparations of both Achaeans and Trojans. What happens on the human level is not foregrounded,[153] and when the narrator turns his attention to men, he refers to the Achaeans as feasting all night long, which he has already mentioned in *Il.* 7.476-7. He therefore steps back in time.

---

[149] βουλὴν δὲ πρῶτον μεγαθύμων ἷζε γερόντων | Νεστορέῃ παρὰ νηῒ Πυλοιγενέος βασιλῆος ("first he held a council session of the high-hearted princes beside the ship of Nestor, the king of the race of Pylos").

[150] ἀλλ' ἄγετ', αἴ κέν πως θωρήξομεν υἷας Ἀχαιῶν· | πρῶτα δ' ἐγὼν ἔπεσιν πειρήσομαι, ἧ θέμις ἐστί, | καὶ φεύγειν σὺν νηυσὶ πολυκλήϊσι κελεύσω ("come then, let us see if we can arm the sons of the Achaeans. Yet first, since it is the right way, I will make trial of them by words, and tell them even to flee in their benched vessels").

[151] ὣς ἄρα φωνήσας βουλῆς ἐξῆρχε νέεσθαι, | οἱ δ' ἐπανέστησαν πείθοντό τε ποιμένι λαῶν | σκηπτοῦχοι βασιλῆες· ἐπεσσεύοντο δὲ λαοί ("so he spoke and led the way departing from the council, and the rest rose to their feet, the sceptred kings, obeying the shepherd of the people, and the army thronged behind them").

[152] ἠΰτε ἔθνεα εἶσι μελισσάων ἀδινάων | πέτρης ἐκ γλαφυρῆς αἰεὶ νέον ἐρχομενάων, | βοτρυδὸν δὲ πέτονται ἐπ' ἄνθεσιν εἰαρινοῖσιν· | αἱ μέν τ' ἔνθα ἅλις πεποτήαται, αἱ δέ τε ἔνθα· | ὣς τῶν ἔθνεα πολλὰ νεῶν ἄπο καὶ κλισιάων | ἠϊόνος προπάροιθε βαθείης ἐστιχόωντο | ἰλαδὸν εἰς ἀγορήν ("like the swarms of clustering bees that issue forever in fresh bursts from the hollow in the stone, and hang like bunched grapes as they hover beneath the flowers in springtime fluttering in swarms together this way and that way, so the many nations of men from the ships and the shelters along the front of the deep sea beach marched in order by companies to the assembly").

[153] Σ *Il.* 8.53a; Rengakos (1995) 32 = (2006) 132.

(e) The reference in *Il.* 15.390-4 to Patroclus' stay at Eurypylus' hut, which has happened at the end of book 11, is a step back in time.

(f) In *Il.* 18.442-56 Thetis steps back in time and narrates to Hephaestus in summary form what has happened with respect to her son since the beginning of the *Iliad*.

(g) The *Iliad* employs the technique of "preliminary overview" when it describes battle scenes. The panoramically massive fighting which comes first is presented as a synopsis in which time flows rapidly. What is foregrounded are the duels and various individual fights which are simultaneous with the general fighting of the armies. A typical example is offered by *Il.* 4.446-5.37. The current stage of the battle is first summarized and then presented in small sections through anachronies pertaining to separate actions.[154]

(h) At the beginning of several Iliadic books[155] and in transitions between episodes the previous action is reviewed by a standard expression consisting in the particle μέν + the imperfect of a verb designating the background action. It is against this backdrop that the new action, which is introduced by δέ/αὐτάρ + imperfect/aorist,[156] is presented.

These representative examples allow for the possibility that occasionally the narrator or a character steps back in time and that the argument that in Homer time flows *only* forward is questionable. Therefore, the situation encountered in the *Doloneia* does not seem to be different from the rest of the *Iliad*.

4.3.4 An Imperfect among Aorists

The arming scene of Diomedes and Odysseus has attracted scholarly interest also with respect to the use of the imperfect δίδου (*Il.* 10.260), which is employed amongst multiple aorists in *Il.* 10.255-61:

Τυδείδῃ μὲν δῶκε μενεπτόλεμος Θρασυμήδης
φάσγανον ἄμφηκες—τὸ δ' ἐὸν παρὰ νηῒ λέλειπτο—
καὶ σάκος· ἀμφὶ δέ οἱ κυνέην κεφαλῆφιν ἔθηκεν
ταυρείην, ἄφαλόν τε καὶ ἄλλοφον, ἥ τε καταῖτυξ

---

[154] Latacz (1977) 78-9; see also Rengakos (1995) 33 = (2006) 133.
[155] E.g. 16.1-2: ὣς οἱ μὲν περὶ νηὸς ἐϋσσέλμοιο μάχοντο· | Πάτροκλος δ' Ἀχιλῆϊ παρίστατο ποιμένι λαῶν ("so they fought on both sides for the sake of the strong-benched vessel. Meanwhile Patroclus came to the shepherd of the people, Achilles"); 18.1-2: ὣς οἱ μὲν μάρναντο δέμας πυρὸς αἰθομένοιο· | Ἀντίλοχος δ' Ἀχιλῆϊ πόδας ταχὺς ἄγγελος ἦλθεν ("so these fought on in the likeness of blazing fire. Meanwhile, Antilochus came, a swift-footed messenger, to Achilles").
[156] See Apthorp (1980) 2; S. Richardson (1990) 94-5, 226 with n. 14, 227 n. 16; Rengakos (1995) 8 and 30 = (2006) 94 and 128; *Hom. Enc.*, s.v. "Time," vol. III, 878 (E. J. Bakker).

κέκληται, ῥύεται δὲ κάρη θαλερῶν αἰζηῶν.
Μηριόνης δ' Ὀδυσῆϊ δίδου βιὸν ἠδὲ φαρέτρην
καὶ ξίφος, ἀμφὶ δέ οἱ κυνέην κεφαλῆφιν ἔθηκεν.

And Thrasymedes the stubborn in battle gave the son of Tydeus
a two-edged sword (his own had been left behind by his vessel)
and a shield; and he put over his head a helmet
of bull's hide with neither horn nor crest, which is known
as the skull cap, and guards the heads of strong men in battle;
while Meriones gave Odysseus a bow and a quiver
and a sword; and he too put over his head a helmet.

It has been maintained that, since the imperfect δίδου ("he was giving," *Il.* 10.260) indicates that the arming of Odysseus was happening simultaneously with that of Diomedes, but the narrator switches to the aorist ἔθηκεν ("he put"), these two simultaneous actions are presented one after the other. This is, the argument goes, against Homeric practice, since in the only other example of a double arming scene, it is solely the arming of the first hero (Paris) that is presented (by aorists),[157] while the arming of the second hero (Menelaus) is expressed by means of a summary reference (*Il.* 3.339) with the imperfect ἔδυνεν. This difference between *Iliad* 10, where the second simultaneous action is foregrounded, and the rest of the poem, in which the second simultaneous action remains in the background, has been interpreted as the result of the *Doloneia*'s different authorship.[158]

However, there are three counterarguments to this line of thought. First, the use of the imperfect δίδου instead of the aorist δῶκε has been conditioned on metrical grounds. The need to place Meriones and Odysseus in the same verse together with the formula βιὸν ἠδὲ φαρέτρην (which is placed after the hephthemimeral caesura)[159] results in the change of δῶκε to δίδου. The same phenomenon is observed in *Od.* 16.118–19, where the imperfect ἔτικτεν is used instead of the aorist τέκε[160]

---

[157] *Il.* 3.330–8: κνημῖδας μὲν πρῶτα περὶ κνήμῃσιν ἔθηκεν | καλάς, ἀργυρέοισιν ἐπισφυρίοις ἀραρυίας· | δεύτερον αὖ θώρηκα περὶ στήθεσσιν ἔδυνεν | οἷο κασιγνήτοιο Λυκάονος· ἥρμοσε δ' αὐτῷ· | ἀμφὶ δ' ἄρ' ὤμοισιν βάλετο ξίφος ἀργυρόηλον | χάλκεον, αὐτὰρ ἔπειτα σάκος μέγα τε στιβαρόν τε· | κρατὶ δ' ἐπ' ἰφθίμῳ κυνέην εὔτυκτον ἔθηκεν | ἵππουριν· δεινὸν δὲ λόφος καθύπερθεν ἔνευεν· | εἵλετο δ' ἄλκιμον ἔγχος, ὅ οἱ παλάμηφιν ἀρήρει ("first he placed along his legs the fair greaves linked with silver fastenings to hold the greaves at the ankles. Afterwards he girt on about his chest the corselet of Lycaon his brother since this fitted him also. Across his shoulders he slung the sword with the nails of silver, a bronze sword, and above it the great shield, huge and heavy. Over his powerful head he set the well-fashioned helmet with the horse-hair crest, and the plumes nodded terribly above it. He took up a strong-shafted spear that fitted his hand's grip").

[158] Danek (2012) 114–15.   [159] *Od.* 21.233, 22.2.

[160] This is the case in the next verse; note that otherwise aorists are employed throughout the passage.

for metrical reasons (under the pressure of the need to have two proper names, Λαέρτης and Ἀρκείσιος, in the same verse).

Second, the successive presentation of simultaneous arming scenes is unique because this is the only example of a double arming scene with four characters involved. In contrast to the double arming scene of Paris and Menelaus (Il. 3.330–9), which also contains both imperfect and aorist tenses (ἔθηκε, ἔδυνεν, ἤρμοσε, ἀμφὶ...βάλετο, ἔθηκεν, ἔνευεν, εἵλετο, ἔδυνεν), the focus of the presentation is not on those who give (Thrasymedes and Meriones) but on those who receive (Diomedes and Odysseus) the weapons. Thrasymedes is the son of Nestor, who had previously woken up Diomedes; Meriones is the *therapon* of Idomeneus, whom Menelaus had woken up. The guards are thus associated with the heroes involved in the *Nyktegersia*. Their pairing with Diomedes and Odysseus is instrumental for the role that the two spies will play. This is because some of the weapons given to them will be employed in the night mission. The "two-edged sword" (φάσγανον ἄμφηκες) given to Diomedes by Thrasymedes will be used in all fourteen killings that will be committed in the *Doloneia*.[161] Likewise, the "bow" (βιός) given to Odysseus by Meriones will be employed as a whip during the spies' theft of Rhesus' horses. Therefore, the stress on the simultaneity of these actions and the fact that they are both narratively presented aims to double and thus intensify the importance of the weapons given to the spies for the ensuing night mission. In contrast to Menelaus' arming in *Iliad* 3, about which "nothing remarkable needs to be said because it is identical with Paris" arming (ὣς δ' αὕτως),[162] there is a lot to be said about Odysseus' weapons, both about the bow he receives from Meriones and the leather cap he puts on his head. A comparison of the gear and weapons given to Diomedes and Odysseus by Thrasymedes and Meriones, respectively, reveals the narrator's attempt to mark their gear and weapons as different.

Thrasymedes > Diomedes Meriones > Odysseus
double-edged sword   bow and quiver
shield   sword
leather cap   leather cap

Both Diomedes and Odysseus received swords, but the former's is double-edged, while the latter's is not. In like manner, the fact that the narrator reports the history of the leather cap given to Odysseus (in which even Odysseus' grandfather Autolycus features) suggests that he wants to indicate to his audience that it is not identical to that of Diomedes. This is part of the reason why the narrator

---

[161] Diomedes will kill Dolon, Rhesus, and twelve Thracians.   [162] Danek (2012) 115.

strives to mark it as "different." The extended history of the leather cap serves this purpose.[163]

Third, the foregrounding of both Diomedes' and Odysseus' arming is partly conditioned by the fact that they borrow their gear and weapons. In Patroclus' arming scene, which consists in the borrowing of Achilles' armor,[164] the ironic reference to the former's inability to use the latter's heavy spear not only makes clear that Patroclus is not Achilles but also hints at his impending doom. Likewise, the successive foregrounding of the arming of Diomedes and Odysseus with the borrowed gear and weapons seems to indicate that this is a temporary condition and that when it is over the two heroes will return to the way they armed themselves and fought in the past. Moreover, the audience is invited to use the success of the night mission in *Iliad* 10, where first-rank heroes (Diomedes and Odysseus) borrowed the gear and weapons of second-rank heroes (Thrasymedes and Meriones), and interpret the borrowing of armor of a first-rank hero (Achilles) by a second-rank warrior (Patroclus) as a foreshadowing of the latter's failure.

In the light of these arguments, I suggest that the successive foregrounding of the arming scenes of Diomedes and Odysseus is a special case with no parallel examples of double arming and double borrowing of gear and weapons in the *Iliad*. Therefore, it does not seem appropriate to use this case to determine whether it adheres to the Homeric norm or not. Furthermore, the double arming scene has a preparatory function since it paves the way for the role of Diomedes and Odysseus in the following narrative.

Having examined the thematic interaction of book 10 with the rest of the *Iliad* (chapters 2 and 3) and its use of three putative divergences (speeches, clothing and arming, and Zielinski's Law) from Iliadic norm (chapter 4), I will next explore the first stage of its evolution and shaping that concerns Hector and his function in an earlier form of the *Doloneia*.

---

[163] See Minchin (2001) 116, who argues that even in descriptive passages the poet finds it difficult "to resist the pull of narrative."
[164] *Il.* 16.131–44.

5
Putative Clues for the Hector-Version of *Iliad* 10

Introduction

Little attention has been paid to the shaping of *Iliad* 10.[1] The dictional oddities of this book, as well as an ancient scholion reported by the *Codex Townleianus*, have cast their shadow on modern notions regarding the way the *Doloneia* has been formed. In this and the following chapters I will trace the process of the shaping of *Iliad* 10 and interpret its function within the poem. First, the structural aspects of book 10 will be explored, before considering whether they can be interpreted in terms of the compositional history of the book.

The shaping of *Iliad* 10 involves at least two phases or stages. The first corresponds to the making of the earliest form that this book had, which for reasons of clarity I will call the "Hector-version." The second phase is called the "Rhesus phase" and involves not only the introduction of the Rhesus story but also a profound reshaping of various elements pertaining to the first phase. For the sake of conciseness, I will begin with a step-by-step presentation of this evolutionary process: chapters 5–6 are therefore dedicated to the Hector-version and chapters 7–9 to the Rhesus phase.

5.1 General Considerations

Let me make it clear up front that I am not the first to argue that the *Doloneia* rests on a version in which the spying mission by Diomedes and Odysseus aimed at killing Hector. When this argument was made by Fenik,[2] it was based explicitly on hints offered by the *Doloneia* as we have it. I will now try to strengthen this approach by adducing further evidence, both from the entire *Iliad* and from ancient criticism on book 10.

Hector is the natural target of the Achaeans after the failed embassy to Achilles in book 9. He is the uncontested leader of the Trojans, the main source of danger for the Achaeans, the one who has camped with the Trojan troops and their allies

---

[1] Fenik (1964) is a notable exception.   [2] Fenik (1964) 58–9.

on the plain³ now that the Achaeans have retreated to the (illusive) safety of their walled camp. This is made evident by the Achaeans themselves in *Iliad* 9. Odysseus as the first speaker (*Il.* 9.237 and 304) stresses the fact that Hector is the main threat against the Achaean army, especially now that his confidence is based on his belief that Zeus stands on his side (*Il.* 9.237–8).⁴ Odysseus' concluding remark to Achilles epitomizes the kernel of his request: "For now you might kill Hector, since he would come very close to you with the wicked fury upon him, since he thinks there is not his equal among the rest of the Danaans the ships carried hither."⁵ Odysseus highlights Hector as the driving force of the Trojan attack and states that only Achilles can kill him in battle. The use of the expression σχεδὸν ἔλθοι covertly alludes to the Achaeans' fear of fighting Hector,⁶ at close quarters, now that he is driven by destructive rage.⁷ In his reply, Achilles takes up the gauntlet and devotes no fewer than six lines to Hector (*Il.* 9.351–6). He agrees that he can defeat him and reminds Odysseus that, as long as he was fighting, Hector had not dared to drive the attack beyond the Trojan walls. When he tried to face Achilles on his own, he barely escaped death.⁸ At *Il.* 9.651 and 655, when Achilles states the conditions under which he is determined to return to the fighting, he only mentions Hector's threat to his own hut and ship.

Since Hector is the real danger for the Achaeans and given that Achilles' current promise to fight him presupposes a catastrophic scenario, according to which Hector breaks the wall of the Achaeans and invades their camp (and perhaps even burns their ships before he reaches the far end of the camp where Achilles' headquarters are placed), there is only one alternative left: a secret mission to the Trojan camp with the sole purpose of killing Hector during the night. This opportunity has been presented to the Achaeans because two different prerequisites are met: Achilles has refused to offer his assistance and Hector has camped on the plain during the night. Such a scenario perfectly conforms to epic practice. Let us recall that the Achaeans will resort to spying missions at a later stage of the

---

³ At the end of *Iliad* 8.
⁴ Ἕκτωρ δὲ μέγα σθένεϊ βλεμεαίνων | μαίνεται ἐκπάγλως, πίσυνος Διί, οὐδέ τι τίει | ἀνέρας οὐδὲ θεούς.
⁵ *Il.* 9.304–6: νῦν γάρ χ'Ἕκτορ' ἕλοις, ἐπεὶ ἂν μάλα τοι σχεδὸν ἔλθοι | λύσσαν ἔχων ὀλοήν, ἐπεὶ οὔ τινά φησιν ὁμοῖον | οἳ ἔμεναι Δαναῶν οὓς ἐνθάδε νῆες ἔνεικαν.
⁶ This fear has been expressed as early as *Il.* 7.93, when the Achaean leaders are afraid to fight Hector in a duel (δεῖσαν δ' ὑποδέχθαι). It is only after Nestor's intervention and the reminding of his past exploits (*Il.* 7.124–60) that the Achaean leaders volunteer. Even so, this is the situation before book 8, when Zeus' support to Hector shows that none of the Achaeans currently on the battlefield can defeat him. In *Il.* 10.104–7 Nestor makes the same point: only Achilles will be able to defeat Hector.
⁷ *Il.* 9.305: λύσσαν ἔχων ὀλοήν.
⁸ With respect to the fighting by the walls of Troy, see, e.g., *Il.* 5.788–90, 13.101–16, 15.722–3, 18.287. On a reflex of a pre-Homeric scene building on this feature, see *Cypr.* arg. l. 154 Severyns (ἐνταῦθα δὴ τειχομαχοῦσιν); also Bacchylides 13.114–20. In an attempt to keep Menelaus away from Hector, Agamemnon distorts the truth and tells him that even Achilles, as long as he was fighting, was afraid to face Hector in battle (*Il.* 7.113–14); see Reichel (1994) 186; Tsagalis (forthcoming) on *Il.* 9.352–5 and 355. On Agamemnon's fear about Menelaus' life, see also *Il.* 10.234–40, where Agamemnon tries to make Diomedes select any other leader but Menelaus as his companion in the spying mission which is about to begin.

war after the death of Achilles. True, they will bring new allies to Troy (Philoctetes[9] and Neoptolemus[10]), but when they realize that these great heroes cannot win the war, spying, night missions, and deceit are what they turn to (*ptocheia*,[11] Palladium,[12] Trojan Horse[13]). This is an important point. It suggests by means of analogy that the motif of the "late-arriving ally"[14] was well established in the Trojan War epic tradition but never acquired a decisive force for the conclusion of the war.[15] The same observation applies to the Trojan side: Penthesileia and Memnon in the *Aethiopis*, Eurypylus in the *Ilias parva*, Coroebus in the *Iliou persis* (and probably in another version of the *Ilias parva*, as we shall see) are epic manifestations of the motif of the "late-arriving ally," who excels on the battlefield for some time but cannot bring the war to an end. All these cases are instructive for another reason too, since they operate principally after the deaths of Achilles and Hector.[16] Achilles and Hector constitute two emblematic heroes who function as *termini post quos* for the motif of the "late-arriving ally," whether pro-Greek or pro-Trojan. Seen against this backdrop, the situation the Achaeans are facing after *Iliad* 9 is similar, for *Achilles is figuratively dead*, since he abstains from fighting. After the failure of the embassy, all hope of bringing him back has been lost.[17] The plot has reached a point when we might expect a pro-Greek hero to come and help the desperate Achaean army.[18] But such an arrival would be unthinkable both for the time frame of the *Iliad*, in which there is no room for such a turn of events, and for the presentation of Achilles. A late-arriving pro-Achaean hero would undermine the status and importance of Achilles, whose exceptionality must be underscored not only by recourse to his outstanding fighting ability but also by means of the fact that he cannot be replaced by anyone else. That Patroclus is killed by

---

[9] *Il. parv.* arg. ll. 212–14 Severyns.
[10] *Il. parv.* arg. ll. 217–18 Severyns.
[11] *Il. parv.* arg. ll. 224–7 Severyns.
[12] *Il. parv.* arg. ll. 228–9 Severyns.
[13] *Il. parv.* arg. ll. 230–2 Severyns.
[14] On this motif, see Fenik (1964) 8–10.
[15] Although the motif of the "late-arriving ally" has been shown to permeate the Epic Cycle, it should be stressed that it does not bring the war to an end. It mainly results in an *aristeia* and/or the death of a major hero: Penthesileia has an *aristeia* (*Aethiopis*), Memnon kills Antilochus (*Aethiopis*), Philoctetes kills Paris (*Ilias parva*), Eurypylus has an *aristeia* (*Ilias parva*), Neoptolemus kills Eurypylus (*Ilias parva*).
[16] The cases of Hippotion's sons Palmys and Ascanius, who have arrived at Troy the previous day (*Il.* 13.792–4), are a minor Iliadic manifestation of this motif. On the contrary, the case of Asteropaeus, who confronts Achilles and is killed by him on the eleventh day after his arrival at Troy (*Il.* 21.139–83), entails multiple associations with Rhesus (late-arriving ally; western ally; troops from his own country have already been at Troy; of non-Asiatic origin; Thracian spear; exceptional fighting skills; breaths heavily before his death [*Il.* 21.182: ἀσθμαίνοντ']); see Tsagalis (2020b 70), which has been now incorporated in this book as chapter 2 (with several modifications). Schoeck (1961, 55–6) saw in Asteropaeus a weak double of Memnon and argued that the Paeonians and Lycians function as "iliadische Nachfahren der Aithiopen" (56). This is a good point, but I would postulate a double shaping of Asteropaeus on the basis of both early versions of the Rhesus myth and the Memnon story. He is after all a late-arriving ally who shares with Rhesus a series of features and with Memnon that he has a duel with Achilles.
[17] See the speeches by Telamonian Ajax (*Il.* 9.624–42) and Diomedes (*Il.* 9.697–709).
[18] Most forms of nocturnal fighting, which amounts to an unusual military operation, are conducted as a last resort by the side facing unsurpassable difficulties; see Dinter, Finkmann, and Khoo (2019) 246.

Hector wearing Achilles' armor reminds one of this reality. Achilles has no equal, only a weak surrogate. Arrivals of pro-Achaean heroes will take place, but only *after the death of Achilles*.

That Diomedes and Odysseus could play this role (and that this role was traditional for them) can be seen by considering the story of Palamedes.[19] In the *Cypria*,[20] Diomedes and Odysseus drowned Palamedes, who had gone on a fishing mission. The context of this episode is probably related to a famine that the Achaean army was facing. Palamedes, who had earlier exposed Odysseus' madness as a ruse to avoid taking part in the Trojan War,[21] attempted to find a solution by undertaking a fishing expedition.[22] Diomedes and Odysseus drowned Palamedes so that they could take the credit for saving the army. To deal with the famine, Odysseus and Menelaus go to Delos,[23] bring the Oenotropi (Οἰνώ, Σπερμώ, and Ἐλαΐς) to Rhoiteion, and feed the troops.[24] Death by drowning is twice called λευγαλέος θάνατος (*Il.* 21.281; *Od.* 5.312) and is clearly un-Homeric.[25] It is also not a heroic way to kill an enemy, the more so if he is a member of the same army. This episode shares with the episode of the attempt on Hector's life the following features: (a) an ambush, (b) deceit and secrecy (Diomedes and Odysseus should not be seen by any other Achaean while drowning Palamedes), (c) the joint effort of Diomedes and Odysseus, and (d) the context of an extreme situation facing the Achaean army (Hector's threat—famine). While it is true that the killing of Palamedes does not in itself deal with the famine, the whole episode shows how the early epic tradition uses Diomedes and Odysseus to rid themselves of a hero rivalling their traditional role of assisting the army in peril.

---

[19] On the complex stratification and relative chronology of the various episodes associated with Palamedes, see Phillips (1957) 267–78.

[20] Fr. 27 GEF.

[21] Diomedes' participation in the drowning of Palamedes may cause frustration, since (a) he rarely features in "cyclic" episodes predating what happens in the Iliadic plot (Andersen 1978, 26), and (b) his enmity against Palamedes seems unmotivated. One is tempted to see in Diomedes' role in this episode a foreshadowing of the cooperation of the two heroes in the *Iliad*. That the version offered by the *Cypria* is earlier can be seen from the Nekyia *krater* (New York 08.258.21: *ARV²* 1086.1: *LIMC* VII.1 s.v. "Palamedes," no. 7 [Woodford and Krauskopf]; see Jacobsthal 1934, 117–45; Davies 2019, 179–80) on which a suffering Palamedes is depicted leaning upon his oar in the Underworld. The vase representation, the *Cypria* version, and the joint action undertaken by Diomedes and Odysseus in the *Iliad*, indicate a typical Diomedes–Odysseus undertaking, not the result of a domino-effect series of causal associations.

[22] This is what Homer's people do when they are short of food; see *Od.* 4.368–9 and 12.330–2.

[23] The choice of Odysseus and Menelaus "echoes their pairing in the embassy to Troy at the start of the war" (M. L. West 2013a, 125).

[24] *Cypria* fr. 26 GEF; for the reconstruction of this episode, see M. L. West (2013a) 123–5, who argues that it was Calchas who told the Achaeans to go to Anius; Davies (2019, 176), who rejects the claim of Immisch (1889, 304; followed by Kullmann 1955, 261 = Kullmann 1992, 47) that the Achaeans had visited Delos before arriving at Troy (probably after the Teuthranian expedition) and so knew of Anius' prophecy about the capture of Troy on the tenth year, does not mention M. L. West's suggestion or any other suggestion about how the Achaeans knew of Anius and the Oenotropi if they had not been to Delos before.

[25] Griffin (1977) 46; Davies (2019) 178–9.

5.2 Putative Clues from the *Iliad*

The internal evidence for a "Hector-phase" of *Iliad* 10 is strong. Already at *Il.* 8.354–6, out of pity for the Achaeans who have found themselves in dire straits, Hera asks Athena to join her in undertaking an initiative, since "these must then fill out an evil destiny, and perish in the wind of one man's fury where none can stand now against him, Hector, Priam's son, who has wrought so much evil already."[26] Agamemnon also emphasizes the grave threat Hector poses to the Achaeans, when he reminds Menelaus that he has "never seen for himself or heard from somebody else of a man who has contrived so much evil (τοσσάδε μέρμερ') in a single day,[27] as Hector, beloved of Zeus, has wrought on the Achaeans" (*Il.* 10.47–9).[28] Moreover, Hector is the only Trojan leader who speaks in *Iliad* 10: he is the one who calls for a night meeting, and the one who promises the horses of Achilles to the spy who will volunteer to penetrate the Achaean camp. The contrast with what happens on the Greek side is marked. Many heroes gather and discuss the best course of action. Nothing of the sort happens in the Trojan camp. This antithesis cannot be put down to the differences of political organization between the centrifugal dynamics of the Achaean council and the centripetal administration of the Trojan army.[29] Hector's domination of Trojan deliberations in books 8 and 10 reinforces his figurative "isolation." The course of the plot is remarkably consonant with this line of thought. Hector is responsible for the initial victory (and final demise) of the Trojan army. It is only too natural that he is the target of a spying mission.

Second, Nestor's desire to find out whether the Trojans intend to spend the night on the plain or withdraw into their city (*Il.* 10.207–10) resonates with Polydamas' advice to Hector that they should retreat into the city and not spend the night on the plain (*Il.* 18.254–66). Polydamas' suggestion is rejected by Hector, who will tragically recall this missed opportunity to save his army when he faces

---

[26] The italics are mine (οἵ κεν δὴ κακὸν οἶτον ἀναπλήσαντες ὄλωνται | ἀνδρὸς ἑνὸς ῥιπῇ; ὁ δὲ μαίνεται οὐκέτ' ἀνεκτῶς | Ἕκτωρ Πριαμίδης, καὶ δὴ κακὰ πολλὰ ἔοργεν).

[27] The italics are mine (οὐ γάρ πω ἰδόμην, οὐδ' ἔκλυον αὐδήσαντος, | ἄνδρ' ἕνα τοσσάδε μέρμερ' ἐπ' ἤματι μητίσασθαι, | ὅσσ' Ἕκτωρ ἔρρεξε διίφιλος υἷας Ἀχαιῶν); see *Il.* 10.289, where Diomedes prays to Athena to stand by him, as she did with his father, Tydeus, when he was sent as an envoy to Thebes. The situations are analogous: father (Tydeus) and son (Diomedes) depart on a mission involving either the delivery of a message (Tydeus) or the gathering of information (Diomedes). The ensuing ambuscades (against Tydeus and the Thebans, against Dolon, Rhesus, and the Thracians by Diomedes) are not planned but occur unexpectedly, which means that Diomedes is not praying to Athena to help him with respect to an unplanned ambush. Moreover, the word μέρμερα used by Diomedes in his prayer resonates with τοσσάδε μέρμερ', which has been used earlier in *Il.* 10.48 for Hector, who has inflicted numerous losses to the Achaeans in a single day (see also *Il.* 10.52: τόσα γὰρ κακὰ μήσατ' Ἀχαιούς).

[28] On the expansion of this thought in *Il.* 10.50–2, see p. 169; see also *Il.* 22.380, where Achilles uses partly similar language to refer to the harm Hector has caused to the Achaean army (ὃς κακὰ πόλλ' ἔρρεξεν, ὅσ' οὐ σύμπαντες οἱ ἄλλοι).

[29] See Elmer (2013) 137–40.

Achilles on his own outside the city walls, just before he meets his doom (*Il.* 22.99–108). The *Iliad* has probably created a link between Polydamas' advice and Nestor's plan in the current version of the poem. "The question raised by Nestor (*Il.* 10.207–10) may be associated in the poet's mind with a threat to Hector's life, and the attempt on Hector's life which motivated the night patrol" in the Hector-version of the *Doloneia* "might explain the appearance of the question in book 10."[30] Working backwards, it is possible to recover the process by which a plan against Hector's life in an earlier version of book 10 was reshaped into a plan to find out whether Hector intended to withdraw into the city or stay on the plain.[31]

Third, *Il.* 10.406–7 invites such an interpretation. Odysseus asks Dolon where Hector is and where he and Diomedes can find his war gear and horses. It is only then that Odysseus asks a clearly "secondary" question concerning the current whereabouts of the Trojan army and where they are camped (*Il.* 10.408). As if this is not enough, the narrator adds, in a syntactically abrupt manner, an indirect question, which repeats verbatim what Nestor has designated as the aim of the spying mission, i.e. to find out what the Trojan plans are and whether the Trojans intend to stay "close to the ships" or return to their city, "now that they have defeated the Achaeans."[32] The loose syntax of this passage, in particular the harsh transition from direct to indirect question, has been met with criticism. Aristarchus (Σ [A] *Il.* 10.409a [Erbse]) athetized 10.409–11.

> ἄσσα τε μητιόωσιν: ἀπὸ τούτου ἕως τοῦ ἂψ ἀναχωρήσουσιν (Κ 411) ἀθετοῦνται στίχοι τρεῖς, καὶ ἀστερίσκοι παράκεινται, ὅτι ἐκ τῶν τοῦ Νέστορος λόγων (sc. e K 208–10) μετενηνεγμένοι εἰσὶν οὐ δεόντως· γελοῖος γὰρ ἔσται ὁ Ὀδυσσεύς, ἤδη τῆς ὥρας προκεκοφυίας ἐρωτῶν, εἰ μένουσιν ἢ ἀπέρχονται ἐπὶ τὴν πόλιν. καὶ ὡς ἂν τούτων μὴ εἰρημένων ὁ Δόλων πρὸς μὲν τὰ ἄλλα ἀποκρίνεται, πρὸς δὲ ταῦτα οὔ.

> ἄσσα τε μητιόωσιν: from this point to ἂψ ἀναχωρήσουσιν (Κ 411) three verses are athetized and asterisks are placed next to them, since they (*sc.* these verses) have been transferred inappropriately from Nestor's speech (*sc.* from K 208–10). For Odysseus will be a laughing stock asking at such a late point of time, whether they (*sc.* the Trojans) will stay or return to their city. Moreover, as if these things were not said, Dolon replies to the other questions, but not to these ones.

Aristarchus' athetesis is based on two grounds: (a) he finds fault with what is said by Odysseus, and (b) he complains that Dolon replies *only* to the question about

---

[30] See Alden (2000) 146, whose interpretation I follow (with minor adaptations).

[31] The Trojan plan of finding out whether the Achaeans will stay and protect their ships or are deliberating with respect to a putative return to Greece (*Il.* 10.309–12) has been modeled on Nestor's plan, in order to create a balanced picture between Achaeans and Trojans (two nocturnal assemblies, analogous plans). It is possible that the Trojan plan has replaced a situation in which Dolon acted on his own initiative; see pp. 96 n. 116, 209–11.

[32] *Il.* 10.208–10 = 10.409–11.

Hector's whereabouts and not to the content of *Il.* 10.409-11.[33] As far as (a) is concerned, Aristarchus regularly targets what he considers as inappropriate or ridiculous in the words of a given character. At *Il.* 8.189 he considers the verse about the horses drinking wine as γελοιότατος ("most ridiculous"), and at *Il.* 24.614-17 he calls the Niobe mythical example a "ridiculous consolation" (παραμυθία γελοία).[34] Likewise, he argues that Odysseus will be ridiculous (γελοῖος γὰρ ἔσται ὁ Ὀδυσσεύς) if he asks at this point whether the Trojans intend to stay on the plain and fight or return to the city (ἤδη τῆς ὥρας προκεκοφυίας ἐρωτῶν, εἰ μένουσιν ἢ ἀπέρχονται ἐπὶ τὴν πόλιν). With respect to (b), Aristarchus observes that Dolon completely ignores Odysseus' indirect question, "as if it was never asked" (ὡς ἂν τούτων μὴ εἰρημένων), and replies only to the direct questions (πρὸς μὲν τὰ ἄλλα ἀποκρίνεται, πρὸς δὲ ταῦτα οὔ). Direct questions pertain to the interest of the spies for Hector, whereas the single indirect question that follows concerns the purpose of the spying mission as set by Nestor at *Il.* 10.207-10. Direct questions show a concern about Hector, which is at odds with the plot of the *Doloneia*, as we have it. Conversely, the ensuing indirect question is perfectly in tune with what has happened before in book 10. The content of the direct questions is unexpected in the context at hand, whereas the content of the indirect question is anticipated and predictable. The direct questions do not match the context of *Iliad* 10. They pertain to circumstances designating an attempt to locate the exact spot where Hector lies. Why, then, should the two Achaean spies be interested in the area where Hector lies together with his arms and horses? It is possible that we may be dealing with a plotline in which Hector was the target of the night mission.[35] If so, that would be a case of the *Iliad* citing an earlier version from which it departs.[36]

Fourth, the language employed in Diomedes' promise (*Il.* 10.292-4) for a sacrifice not only aims at matching the offer made by Nestor to the man who would volunteer for the spying mission (*Il.* 10.214-17) but also bears (together with *Il.* 10.282) a striking similarity to what Agamemnon had said to Menelaus about Hector at *Il.* 10.46-52:

---

[33] Fenik (1964) 58-9. On cross-purpose questions in *Iliad* 10, see p. 193 n. 17.

[34] For more examples and analysis, see Schironi (2018) 435-6, 460; see also Nünlist (2009) 90, who discusses the inversion of the narrative order in Σ *Il.* 24.605b (stressing that the scholia do not take into consideration whether it is a character of the plot or the principal narrator who focalizes): ῥητορικῶς ἀνέστρεψε τὴν διήγησιν· φάγε· καὶ γὰρ Νιόβη. τίς αὕτη; ἀπολέσασα δώδεκα παῖδας. ὑπὸ τίνος; ὑπὸ Ἀπόλλωνος καὶ Ἀρτέμιδος. διὰ τί; δι' ὑπερηφανίαν ("In a rhetorical way he inverted the order of the narrative. 'Eat! For Niobe too ate'. 'Who is she?' 'The one who lost her twelve children'. 'To whom?' 'To Apollo and Artemis'. 'For what reason?' 'Because of her arrogance'").

[35] The possibility that they ask about Hector because they want to avoid him is unlikely. How are they supposed to find out about Hector's intentions if they avoid him? The spies avoid Hector when they find out that he is awake (*Il.* 10.414-15), whereas they are directed to Rhesus because the allies of the Trojans are asleep (*Il.* 10.420-1).

[36] Early Greek epic displays a wide array of self-reflexive manifestations of allusion; see Currie (2016) 26-7; Tsagalis (2011) 221-3 = (2023) 14-16; Nelson (2023) 181-91; see also pp. 36 and 43.

(46) Ἑκτορέοις ἄρα μᾶλλον ἐπὶ φρένα θῆχ᾽ **ἱεροῖσιν**.
(47) οὐ γάρ πω ἰδόμην, οὐδ᾽ ἔκλυον αὐδήσαντος,
(48) ἄνδρ᾽ ἕνα τοσσάδε **μέρμερ᾽**   (289) ἀτὰρ ἂψ ἀπιὼν
ἐπ᾽ ἤματι μητίσασθαι   **μάλα μέρμερα μήσατο ἔργα**
(49) ὅσσ᾽ Ἕκτωρ **ἔρρεξε** διίφιλος υἷας Ἀχαιῶν   (292) σοὶ δ᾽ αὖ ἐγὼ **ῥέξω** βοῦν
                                              ἦνιν εὐρυμέτωπον
                                              (294) τήν τοι ἐγὼ **ῥέξω**, χρυσὸν
                                              κέρασιν περιχεύας
(51) **ἔργα** δ᾽ **ἔρεξ᾽** ὅσα φημὶ μελησέμεν Ἀργείοισιν   (282) **ῥέξαντας μέγα ἔργον**, ὅ κε
                                              Τρώεσσι μελήσει
(52) δηθά τε καὶ δολιχόν· τόσα γὰρ **κακὰ**
μήσατ᾽ Ἀχαιούς.

This internal correspondence (within *Iliad* 10) is intentional. Just as the ἔργα that have saddened the Achaeans have been committed by Hector within a single day of fighting (*Il.* 10.48–9), so the μέγα ἔργον[37] that will sadden the Trojans (*Il.* 10.282) can only be their deprivation of their leader Hector, who has caused so much distress to the Achaeans.[38] The traditional referentiality[39] of this expression within Iliadic diction reveals that it is employed with respect to "fighting" in its various aspects: (a) defensive (building the Achaean Wall: *Il.* 7.444); (b) offensive ([i] lifting a stone to fight: *Il.* 5.303, 20.286; [ii] engaging in typical battle activity: *Il.* 11.734, 12.416, 13.366, 16.208, 19.150; [iii] engaging in unorthodox ambush warfare: *Il.* 10.282). How deeply embedded the expression μέγα ἔργον is within the system of epic diction may be seen from the fact that it is specifically used by Achilles when contemplating revenge for the death of Patroclus. At *Il.* 19.146–53 he replies to Agamemnon in the following manner:

Ἀτρεΐδη κύδιστε, ἄναξ ἀνδρῶν Ἀγάμεμνον,
δῶρα μὲν αἴ κ᾽ ἐθέλησθα παρασχέμεν, ὡς ἐπιεικές,
ἤ τ᾽ ἐχέμεν παρὰ σοί. νῦν δὲ μνησώμεθα χάρμης
αἶψα μάλ᾽—οὐ γὰρ χρὴ κλοτοπεύειν ἐνθάδ᾽ ἐόντας
οὐδὲ διατρίβειν, ἔτι γὰρ **μέγα ἔργον** ἄρεκτον—   150
ὥς κέ τις αὖτ᾽ Ἀχιλῆα μετὰ πρώτοισιν ἴδηται
ἔγχεϊ χαλκείῳ Τρώων ὀλέκοντα φάλαγγας·
ὡς δέ τις ὑμείων μεμνημένος ἀνδρὶ μαχέσθω.

---

[37] On the meaning and function of this expression in Odysseus' Oedipus tale (*Od.* 11.271–4), see Barker and Christensen (2008) 19–22, (2020) 157–63.
[38] See Eust. 788.49–50 (van der Valk).
[39] On this term, see Foley (1991) 24; Danek (2002) 3–19; Tsagalis (2003b) 7 n. 7 = (2008) 154 n. 2; also (2008) 188, 205. On μέγα ἔργον involving violence often escalating to murder, see, e.g., *Od.* 3.261 (Aegisthus kills Agamemnon); Hes. *Th.* 209–10 (castration of Ouranus by Cronus [?]) and 954 (Heracles kills the Giants); Pind. *Nem.* 10.64 (fight between the Dioscuri and the Aphareridae).

Son of Atreus, most lordly and king of men, Agamemnon,
the gifts are yours to give as you wish, and as it is proper,
or to keep with yourself. But now let us remember our joy in warcraft,
immediately, for it is not fitting to stay here and waste time
nor delay, since there is still **a big deed** to be done.
So can a man see once more Achilles among the front fighters
with the bronze spear wrecking the Trojan battalions. Therefore,
let each of you remember this and fight his antagonist.

Achilles designates as μέγα ἔργον his return to the battlefield "among the front fighters | with the bronze spear wrecking the Trojan battalions" and, by extension, the fighting between each Achaean and his antagonist. Achilles' antagonist is none other than the man who has killed Patroclus—Hector. It is to avenge the former that Achilles will rejoin the fight, while it's from Hector that he will gain "great glory" (μέγα κῦδος)[40] when he defeats the man whom the Trojans held as a god in their city.[41] By finding and confronting Hector, Achilles will do what the Achaean spies were prevented from doing by the plot of the *Iliad*. His "big deed" will be to kill Hector. Likewise, the target of the spying mission in *Iliad* 10, the μέγα ἔργον that would sadden the Trojans beyond anything else, may well be the killing of Hector.[42] This is one more trace of an earlier version from which the *Iliad* diverges.

Fifth, the importance of Hector for the Trojans is a topic that permeates the *Iliad*. One manifestation of Hector's importance is the number of losses that he has inflicted on the Achaeans. The theme is prepared at *Il*. 9.236–9, when Odysseus threatens Achilles with the vision of Zeus giving to the Trojans "portents of good, while Hector in the huge pride of his strength rages irresistibly, reliant on Zeus, and gives way to no one, neither god nor man, but the strong fury has descended upon him." At *Il*. 10.45–52, Agamemnon states that the Achaeans are in

---

[40] Thus, the accomplishment of μέγα ἔργον confers μέγα κῦδος.
[41] *Il*. 22.393–4: ἠράμεθα μέγα κῦδος· ἐπέφνομεν Ἕκτορα δῖον, | ᾧ Τρῶες κατὰ ἄστυ θεῷ ὣς εὐχετόωντο.
[42] Although acknowledging that Odysseus does not know at this stage that he and Diomedes will have the opportunity to kill Rhesus, M. L. West (2011a, 241 on *Il*. 10.282) claims that μέγα ἔργον anticipates "the killing of Rhesus and his followers." The implausibility of a lurking anticipation of the killing of Rhesus is suggested by the following considerations: (a) It is not only that Odysseus does not know that he will be directed by Dolon to Rhesus but that he does not know of the existence of Rhesus and his arrival at Troy. (b) The killing of Rhesus is not disastrous to the Trojans as a whole, given that they prevail in the episodes following *Iliad* 10. In this vein, the relative clause ὅ κε Τρώεσσι μελήσει modifying μέγα ἔργον becomes pointless. On the contrary, a potential death of Hector would have serious consequences for the Trojans. This is a pervasive Iliadic theme, which is emphasized when Hector is killed by Achilles (see, e.g., 22.56–77, 22.433–5, 24.728–31). Fries (2016, 320) maintains that "it would be rash to deduce...that there had once been a Greek version of the night raid in which the Trojan chief was the victim," since "the damage to his heroic reputation and to the Trojan story as a whole would have been intolerable." However, Hector would have been the *target* of the spying mission, not the *victim*, since the spies would have failed to kill him and would have returned to the Greek camp with no big trophy. There are other failed attempts to kill Hector in the *Iliad* (e.g. Telamonian Ajax in book 7, Teucer in book 8, Diomedes in book 11).

need of a plan that will save them and their ships, since "the heart of Zeus is turned from them" (45). Agamemnon stresses that Hector's sacrifices have gained Zeus' support and that "he has never seen or heard from the lips of another of a single man" (47-8) who has inflicted so many casualties on the Achaeans, "being called true son neither of a god nor a goddess" (50). Agamemnon's words are especially important to our inquiry because they resonate with the presentation of Rhesus in the overall Trojan saga and in *Iliad* 10. According to the "Pindaric version" of the Rhesus tale, the Thracian king performed an *aristeia* on the battlefield before he was killed at night by Diomedes and Odysseus. The *aristeia* is an exceptional form of warfare in which a single warrior defeats a series of opponents and carries out admirable military deeds. The emphasis Agamemnon puts on Hector's outstanding military accomplishments seems to recall both Hector's previous victory and what Rhesus did in a different, non-Homeric version of his story. Significantly, Agamemnon's phraseology also alludes to the way Nestor will express his awe at the sight of Rhesus' magnificent horses, which Diomedes and Odysseus bring to the Achaean camp upon their return from the spying mission (*Il.* 10.550: ἀλλ' οὔ πω τοίους ἵππους ἴδον οὐδ' ἐνόησα). Nestor's words, which are in tune with Agamemnon's at *Il.* 10.47 (οὐ γάρ πω ἰδόμην οὐδ' ἔκλυον αὐδήσαντος),[43] suggest that the *Iliad* is well aware, by means of its allusive reiterated phraseology,[44] of the fact that Rhesus takes the place that Hector was expected to occupy: that of an outstanding enemy, who must be killed because he has caused much harm to the Achaeans. It is no coincidence that the main threat Hector poses to the Achaeans is particularly linked to the joint role of Diomedes and Odysseus in the war (*Il.* 11.314–15): δὴ γὰρ ἔλεγχος | ἔσσεται, εἴ κεν νῆας ἕλῃ κορυθαίολος Ἕκτωρ ("we will be blamed, if Hector of the shining helmet takes our ships"). Why does Odysseus feel that he and Diomedes together will be the ones blamed if Hector reaches the ships? No other Achaean in book 11 expresses such a concern, not even Agamemnon, whose disagreement with Achilles has led the Achaeans to facing annihilation. A putative explanation is that these words fit perfectly an earlier version of the *Iliad*, in which the target of the *Doloneia* was Hector. Having failed to kill him in book 10, Odysseus and Diomedes would have been the first to get blamed should Hector breach the Achaean camp and set fire to their ships. Odysseus' anxiety in *Iliad* 11 may reflect their joint role in the Hector-version of the *Doloneia*.

---

[43] It should be noticed that in both cases the awe inspired by Hector's accomplishment and Rhesus' horses is explained by means of a reference to the gods. Although this is a typical strategy in Homer, what makes these two references asymptomatic is that in both the "divine" explanation is negated: Hector is not the son of a god or goddess (*Il.* 10.50), and the same applies to Rhesus, who is the son of the herald Eumedes.

[44] On ἔκλυον αὐδήσαντος and its variants, see *Il.* 16.76, *Od.* 3.337, and 4.505, where the subject of the participle is expressed. Thus, *Il.* 10.47 is the only case in which the identity of the subject is not stated; see Danek (1988) 73-4. Agamemnon may well be echoing (10.44: τίς κεν ἐρύσσεται, 10.47: ἔκλυον αὐδήσαντος) the indefiniteness of Menelaus' speech (10.37: τιν' ἑταίρων, 10.39: τίς τοι ὑπόσχηται, 10.41: μάλα τις θρασυκάρδιος ἔσται); see Tsagalis (forthcoming) on *Il.* 10.47–50.

Sixth, the use of αὖτε ("again")[45] in *Il.* 11.362 for Apollo's protection of Hector from Diomedes suggests an earlier incident in which Apollo had saved Hector from Diomedes.[46] Passages like *Il.* 5.601-4, 7.270-2, and 8.309-11 cannot have functioned as the earlier references to which Diomedes alludes because *Il.* 5.601-4 includes a general reference to divine assistance that is then particularized to Ares,[47] while at *Il.* 7.270-2 and 8.309-11 Diomedes is not involved.[48] The suggestion that Diomedes' αὖ designates various earlier instances in which Hector was saved by Apollo, while αὖτε (11.363) refers to an earlier instance in which Apollo saved Hector *from Diomedes*, is strengthened by means of the analogy with *Il.* 20.449-54, in which Achilles speaks the exact same words to Hector. While Achilles' αὖ pertains to various earlier instances in which Hector was protected by Apollo, αὖτε looks back at 20.376-8, where Apollo saves Hector by instructing him to withdraw into the ranks of his fellow Trojans and not stand alone and fight Achilles. Here, then, is a case where a speaker (Achilles) addresses Hector and tells him that Apollo has saved him *again from Achilles* because there is a preceding scene in which the god had done so. Likewise, the use of the same phraseology at *Il.* 11.363, when Diomedes tells Hector that Apollo has saved him again, may presuppose a preceding scene in which the god had done so. This scene may have featured in an earlier version of book 10 in which Hector had been the target of the spying mission and was saved at the last moment by the intervention of Apollo. This interpretation accords well with the theme of Diomedes' limitations as a second Achilles. These limitations reach their peak in Diomedes' failure to kill Hector, who must be killed by Achilles in accordance with the mythological *Faktenkanon*. Diomedes' mention of a future opportunity in which he may defeat Hector if some god helps him[49] suggests a passage in an earlier version of the *Doloneia* where he had failed to kill Hector in his sleep because of the lack of divine support; either Athena advised him and Odysseus to return to the ships since it was not fated that they would slay Hector or (and) Apollo had intervened to wake Hector up. *Il.* 20.438-54 and 22.226-305 form a thematic pair which (contrary to the case of Diomedes) allow for the possibility that Achilles' initial failure to kill Hector will ultimately be corrected when he achieves his goal. The presence of Athena and Apollo in such scenes effectively epitomizes their role in shaping, or even confirming, Hector's destiny:

---

[45] *Il.* 11.363.
[46] *Contra* Schadewaldt (1938 = 1966³) 6, who argues that *Il.* 20.449-54 has been transferred to 11.362-7, where it is not fully at home.
[47] "Yet there goes ever some god beside him, who beats off destruction, | and now, in the likeness of a man mortal, Ares goes with him."
[48] In *Il.* 7.270-1 Apollo helps Hector stand on his feet after being hit by a stone thrown at him by Telamonian Ajax; in *Il.* 8.309-11 Apollo makes Teucer miss when he shoots an arrow at Hector.
[49] *Il.* 11.365-6: ἦ θήν σ' ἐξανύω γε καὶ ὕστερον ἀντιβολήσας, | εἴ πού τις καὶ ἐμοί γε θεῶν ἐπιτάρροθός ἐστιν.

at *Il.* 22.213–14 Apollo leaves him, while Athena approaches Achilles and soon after deceives Hector in the shape of Deiphobus.

A further example is found at *Il.* 22.379–84. After killing Hector, Achilles addresses the Achaeans in the following manner:

ἐπεὶ δὴ τόνδ' ἄνδρα θεοὶ δαμάσασθαι ἔδωκαν,
ὃς κακὰ πόλλ' ἔρρεξεν, ὅσ' οὐ σύμπαντες οἱ ἄλλοι,
εἰ δ' ἄγετ' ἀμφὶ πόλιν σὺν τεύχεσι πειρηθέωμεν,
ὄφρα κ' ἔτι γνῶμεν Τρώων νόον, ὅν τιν' ἔχουσιν,
ἢ καταλείψουσιν πόλιν ἄκρην τοῦδε πεσόντος,
ἦε μένειν μεμάασι καὶ Ἕκτορος οὐκέτ' ἐόντος.

Since the gods have granted me the killing of this man
who has done us much damage, such as not all the others together
have done, come, let us go in armor about the city
to see if we can find out what purpose is in the Trojans,
whether they will abandon their high city, now that this man
has fallen, or are minded to stay, though Hector lives no longer.

This time Achilles' stress on Hector's outstanding military skills, again measured in terms of the losses he has inflicted on the Achaeans, constitutes the pretext for his (sc. Achilles') potential assault on the city, so that it may become clear whether the Trojans are willing to abandon Troy, now that Hector is dead, or will stay inside their walls and fight. This plan is not realized because Achilles will immediately recall that he must first organize Patroclus' funeral. The eagerness of Achilles to find out what the Trojans will do now that Hector is no more recalls the eagerness of Nestor to find out what the Trojans will do while Achilles is abstaining from fighting (*Il.* 10.204-10):

ὦ φίλοι, οὐκ ἂν δή τις ἀνὴρ πεπίθοιθ' ἑῷ αὐτοῦ
θυμῷ τολμήεντι, μετὰ Τρῶας μεγαθύμους   205
ἐλθεῖν, εἴ τινά που δηΐων ἕλοι ἐσχατόωντα,
ἤ τινά που καὶ φῆμιν ἐνὶ Τρώεσσι πύθοιτο,
ἅσσά τε μητιόωσι μετὰ σφίσιν, ἢ μεμάασιν
αὖθι μένειν παρὰ νηυσὶν ἀπόπροθεν, ἦε πόλινδε
ἂψ ἀναχωρήσουσιν, ἐπεὶ δαμάσαντό γ' Ἀχαιούς.

O my friends, is there no man who, trusting in the daring
of his own heart, would go among the high-hearted Trojans?
So he might catch some enemy, who straggled behind them,
or he might overhear something that the Trojans are saying,
what they deliberate among themselves, and whether they purpose
to stay where they are, close to the ships, or else to withdraw back
into their city, now that they have beaten the Achaeans.

In *Il.* 22.379–84 Achilles' words disclose the threat Hector posed to the entire Achaean army. Achilles thus acknowledges, albeit indirectly, that it was during his absence that Hector had inflicted numerous casualties to the Achaeans, since at *Il.* 9.352–5 he had stated to the envoys (Odysseus, Phoenix, and Ajax) that, as long as he was fighting together with the Achaeans, Hector had not dared to attack beyond the Trojan walls but went only as far as the Scaean Gates and the fig tree. It was at that place that he once found the courage to face Achilles alone and barely escaped his onslaught. Seen from this vantage point, Achilles' words at *Il.* 22.379–84 continue a line of thought that was expressed at *Il.* 9.352–5 and *Il.* 10.47–52 but involve a plan based on two possibilities that are never carried out since they run counter to the unfolding of the plot. Nestor's words at *Il.* 10.204–10 are not some random line of thought but relate to a plan based again on two possibilities that do not materialize. The difference between the two plans lies in the fact that, while Nestor's plan is not hindered by plot requirements, Achilles' is. Why then have a plan that is not carried out?[50] The oddity of this situation is further strengthened by the fact that the plan Nestor devises in *Iliad* 9 fails to convince Achilles to return to the war. Moreover, the aim of Nestor's follow-up plan in book 10 is pointless, since the Trojans are clearly going to launch an all-out assault against the Achaeans the next day. As a result, it is worth speculating that the current plan has replaced one that had played a critical role in an earlier version of *Iliad* 10. We have seen that Achilles' plan for an assault on Troy after the death of Hector failed to materialize because he had to organize Patroclus' funeral. Nestor's plan would have targeted Hector, but such a plan could not have been effective in any version of the *Iliad*, because Hector must be killed by Achilles.[51] Further support for this line of argument can be found if we examine Hector's plan at *Il.* 10.309–12, which also consists of two alternatives. Hector tries to lure some Trojan to a spying mission so that the Trojans can find out about the Achaeans' intentions: will they keep protecting their ships or are they thinking of sailing away? In sharp contrast to Nestor's plan, Hector's is anything but odd. It resembles Achilles' plan at *Il.* 22.379–84 not only with respect to its content but also, tellingly, concerning its logic. Like Achilles, who in book 22 wants to test the Trojans *now that Hector is dead*, so Hector wants to learn the intentions of the Achaeans *now that Achilles is not fighting*. The analogy of the two scenarios is enhanced by the fact that in books

---

[50] The way Nestor's plan is expressed is highly complex; Hainsworth (1993, 173 on *Il.* 10.204–10) observes that it contains no fewer than five levels of subordination, a clear (in my view) reflection of its oddity.

[51] This does not mean that the end result of book 10 is a failure. By substituting Hector with Rhesus, who unlike Hector can be killed by the spies without harming the rest of the plot, the epic turns books 9–10 into an "inverted pair": in *Iliad* 9 Nestor's plan is carried out as far as its prerequisites are concerned (the envoys go to Achilles and ask him to return to the war) but fails due to Achilles' refusal, whereas in *Iliad* 10 Nestor's plan is not carried out as far as its technicalities are concerned (the spies do not get information about the Trojan intentions) but ends in victory, signified by the killing of Rhesus and the stealing of his horses. See chapter 7 on the "Rhesus phase."

10 and 22 the Achaeans and Trojans are on the defensive, confined within the walls of Troy and the wall of their camp, respectively. Like Achilles' plan in book 22 (but contrary to Nestor's in *Iliad* 10), Hector's plan in book 10 will not be carried out successfully. The Trojan spy, Dolon, will be arrested and killed by the Greek spies, Odysseus and Diomedes.

There is one more passage where it is emphasized that Hector was a major source of harm for the Achaeans. In her γόος for Hector at *Il.* 24.736–8, Andromache expresses her fear that some Achaean avenging the death of his brother, father, or son will throw Astyanax from the walls of Troy,[52] since "there were so many Achaeans | whose teeth bit the vast earth, beaten down by the hands of Hector."[53] Andromache does not simply recapitulate Hector's exploits; she translates them into the language of lament,[54] which entails fear about the future. Even after his death, Hector's military achievements will be somehow "present," since they will affect those most dear to him.

These testimonies to Hector's success show a consistent, and constant, concern on the part of the *Iliad* to depict Hector as the main threat for the Achaeans, just as the poem depicts Achilles as the main threat for the Trojans. It is only too natural that after the Achaeans fail to bring back the latter in book 9, they must devise a plan against the former in book 10.

5.3 Putative Clues from the Scholia

Besides several indications provided by the *Iliad* regarding a Hector-version of book 10, the scholia also offer material that may putatively support the claim for an earlier version of the *Doloneia*, in which Hector was the target of the nocturnal mission and Rhesus did not feature in the plot. However, before examining the relevant material, we should ask whether the ancient scholia provide indirect evidence for variant mythological episodes or only offer interpretations by ancient critics.

Ancient scholia are often used as evidence for mythological episodes that relate to specific poems and/or poets. Homeric scholia[55] furnish material for numerous episodes of Cyclic epic, some of these scholia being consonant with the

---

[52] By Neoptolemus in the *Ilias parva* (fr. 29.1–5 *GEF*); by Odysseus in the *Iliou persis* (arg. l. 268 Severyns); the future death of Astyanax may have also featured in the *Cypria* (fr. 31 *GEF*); see Kullmann (1960) 186–7, 353 and (1968) 31 n. 39 (= 1992, 236 n. 39); N. J. Richardson (1993) 354 on *Il.* 24.734–9; Anderson (1997) 53–9; Burgess (2001) 66 and 215 n. 67, (2010) 211–24, (2012a) 168–83; Graziosi and Haubold (2010) 7 and 213–14 on *Il.* 6.466–81; Finglass (2015) 348, 350, 353; Kelly (2015) 323, 326–7; 338; Currie (2016) 112–15. On the passage referring to Astyanax's coming death, see G. Beck (1964) 157–68; on iconographic representations, see *LIMC* II.I s.v. "Astyanax I," nos. 1–36 (Touchefeu).
[53] Macleod (1982) 151 on *Il.* 24.736–8.   [54] Tsagalis (2004) 133–6.
[55] The same is the case with the Pindaric and the Euripidean scholia as regards Cyclic epic. The scholia on Apollonius Rhodius are an important source of information for other genealogical and antiquarian epic.

information given either by the summaries of Proclus[56] or by other ancient authors who ascribe a mythological episode to a specific poem.[57] The scholia also record variant details of mythological episodes mentioned in the Homeric text by recourse to a different reading and the scholarly discussion around it.[58] Less often they offer information about a variant mythological version of an episode narrated in the Homeric text either (a) in the context of a different reading, or (b) by comparison with other poets not mentioned in the scholion, or (c) by reference to an ancient critic. So, for example, Zenodotus[59] reports the variant reading Κρήτην (instead of Σπάρτην that is given by the *paradosis*) at *Od.* 1.93 and 1.285 together with παρ' Ἰδομενῆα ἄνακτα instead of παρὰ ξανθὸν Μενέλαον (at *Od.* 1.285) that probably points to a version in which Telemachus traveled to Crete (after Pylos) in search of his father.[60] Σ *Il.* 22.188 (Erbse)[61] records that it is only Homer who presented the fatal encounter between Hector and Achilles as a duel, while other poets had Hector being ambushed by Achilles.[62] Aristarchus' regular designation of "other epic poets as 'younger' than, and derivative on, Homer presupposes the existence of an opposite, neoanalytically minded party, perhaps including Zenodotus."[63] A case in point is furnished by Σ (HMª) *Od.* 3.307a (Pontani), according to which Aristarchus rejected the Zenodotean reading ἂψ ἀπὸ Φωκήων ("back from Phocis") that introduced into the Homeric text a myth used by the *Neoteroi* and opted for the reading

---

[56] E.g. *Cypr.* fr. 20 *PEG* and *Cypr.* arg. ll. 125–6 Severyns.
[57] E.g. *Il. parv.* fr. 14 *GEF* that is cited by Σ Eur. *Hec.* 910 (Schwartz), Clem. *Str.* 1.104.1, Tz. Lyc. 344 (Scheer), and Tz. *Posthom.* 719–21, 773 (Jacobs). For a full list, see Bernabé's *Index Fontium* in *PEG*; see also *Il. parv.* fr. 11 *EGF*.
[58] See (e.g.) Σ (A) *Il.* 1.400a–b (Erbse) and (D) *Il.* 1.399–400 (van Thiel) regarding Aristarchus' defense of the reading Παλλὰς Ἀθήνη against Zenodotus' reading Φοῖβος Ἀπόλλων.
[59] Σ *Od.* 1.93 (Pontani) and *Od.* 3.313 (Pontani).
[60] See Burkert (1995) 147–58 = (2001) 117–26; for a recent discussion with earlier bibliography, see Tsagalis (2023) 169–82.
[61] σημειῶδες ὅτι μόνος Ὅμηρός φησι μονομαχῆσαι τὸν Ἕκτορα, οἱ δὲ λοιποὶ πάντες ἐνεδρευθῆναι ὑπὸ Ἀχιλλέως.
[62] See pp. 69, 99 n. 124. Erbse does not attribute this scholion to Aristonicus (and therefore to Aristarchus), even though it is introduced by σημειῶδες ὅτι. Puzzled by this unique οἱ δὲ λοιποὶ πάντες, Erbse treats it is an exegetical scholion, designating such late authors as Dictys Cretensis (3.15), Ioannes Malalas (5 [p. 123 Ddf. = *P.G.* 97 p. 217 A Migne]), Georgios Cedrenus (*P.G.* 121 p. 257 D Migne), and the anonymous author of the *Ecl. hist.* in An. Ox. 2.216.26, who all mention a version in which Achilles ambushes Hector, when Penthesileia arrives at Troy and Hector falls in love with her (!). However, a comparison with such late authors is awkward, especially since Homer is usually compared with other early poets (this analysis owes a lot to Filippomaria Pontani, who kindly discussed this issue with me by email). It is quite possible, then, that this scholion is drawing an association to other poems of the epic tradition that represent the confrontation between Achilles and Hector differently, in the form of an ambush. What is said at *Il.* 24.779–80, in which Priam reassures the Trojans that the Argives will not ambush them while collecting wood for Hector's funeral since Achilles has promised him so, would be consonant with a version in which Hector has been killed by Achilles in an ambush. Priam's attempt to remove Trojan fear of an ambush may be based on a disastrous event caused by an ambush that occurred recently. It seems no coincidence that this is said as soon as the lamentations for Hector are over. Alternative explanations (a general comment, a reference to Achilles' ambush of Lycaon) are also possible, though not very convincing.
[63] See Currie (2016) 22; also Severyns (1928) 98–9.

ἂψ ἀπ' Ἀθηναίης ("back from Athens") because Homer employs the singular to designate the city of Athens (*Od.* 7.80: ἵκετο δ' ἐς Μαραθῶνα καὶ εὐρυάγυιαν Ἀθήνην). By endorsing the reading ἂψ ἀπὸ Φωκήων ("back from Phocis"), which reflects post-Homeric poets who present Orestes as staying in Strophius' house in Phocis, Zenodotus may have thought that this piece of mythology reflects pre-Homeric use. Moreover, the D-scholia provide information of certain *historiae* which are ascribed to a grammarian (Σ *Il.* 1.399 [Erbse] < Didymus; Σ *Il.* 8.284 [Erbse] < Apollonius [the grammarian]; Σ *Il.* 11.741 [Erbse] < Crates; Σ *Il.* 19.119 [Erbse] < Rhianus)[64] and contain mythological episodes that offer background information to elliptical references in the Homeric text.

In view of the material presented above, it is fair to say that the scholia cite mythological narratives that either (a) reflect a known poetic source (the *Neoteroi*) or (b) derive from unknown poetic sources or are invented by mythographers or even the grammarians themselves. As regards (b), the two alternatives mentioned are not mutually exclusive, and it is advisable to treat each case separately. It seems that material relating to variant versions of mythological episodes is preserved in the scholia in discussions of different readings and/or different versions of an episode.

a1. Σ *Il.* 10.282a [A^ti] (Erbse)
μέγα ἔργον: Ἀρίσταρχος τὸ φονεῦσαι τὸν Ἕκτορα.

a2. Σ [D] *Il.* 10.282a (van Thiel)[65]
μέγα ἔργον: μεγάλην πρᾶξιν· Ἀρίσταρχος δὲ φησὶν τὸ φονεῦσαι Ἕκτορα.

a1. **A great thing**: Aristarchus (says it means) the killing of Hector.

a2. **A great thing**: A great deed. Aristarchus says it means the killing of Hector.

The reference to Aristarchus is consistent with his athetesis of *Il.* 10.409–11, which would leave Hector as the main target of Odysseus' and Diomedes' mission. Aristarchus may have based his approach on his usual practice of Ὅμηρον ἐξ Ὁμήρου χρὴ σαφηνίζειν. Since he had argued that verses 409–11 "have been transferred inappropriately from Nestor's speech"[66] (*Il.* 10.208–10), he may have observed that the first two lines of Nestor's plan that refer to the capture of enemy stragglers or to listening in on discussions had been "reinterpreted" by Odysseus and Diomedes, who opted for Hector's hut. The word ἐσχατόωντα (206) used by Nestor is, tellingly enough, consonant with Dolon's Ἕκτωρ... | ...παρὰ σήματι Ἴλου, | νόσφιν ἀπὸ φλοίσβου ("Hector... by the tomb of Ilus, away from the confusion

---

[64] For a typological analysis of the arrangements of *historiae* within the D-scholia, see Montana and Montanari (2022) 31–56.
[65] On the D-scholia and the *Mythographus Homericus*, see p. 217 n. 8.
[66] μετενηνεγμένοι εἰσὶν οὐ δεόντως ἐκ τῶν τοῦ Νέστορος λόγων.

and noise").⁶⁷ In making this connection, Aristarchus aimed to show that the spies had decided to target not some anonymous enemy lying at the end of the camp but Hector himself, who was also stationed "away from the confusion." This would all be fine, had the scholion not assigned to Aristarchus the interpretation of μέγα ἔργον as *killing* Hector rather than as *gathering information* about his plan. Why did Aristarchus make this claim? This question can be further pressed, if we keep in mind that the vagueness of Nestor's plan concerns the identity of the person whom the spies may capture at the end of the Trojan camp. Aristarchus thought that the change from Nestor's plan is twofold: the spies are no longer interested in arresting some Trojan; they intend to kill Hector. When they learn from Dolon that Hector is well guarded by the Trojans, they turn their attention to their allies. The fact that the spies finally kill Rhesus, who together with his Thracian troops is stationed "separately from the other allies" (*Il.* 10.434: ἔσχατοι ἄλλων), facilitates the transfer of interest from Hector to Rhesus. Although Nestor's initial plan is changed twice, both through the initiative of the Greek spies and then by Dolon's testimony, the goal of killing an enemy at the outer limits of the Trojan camp will be fulfilled.⁶⁸ Thus, getting "intelligence" from an anonymous opponent gives way to finding where Hector lies and in turn to killing Rhesus. Nestor's ἕλοι ἐσχατόωντα⁶⁹ ("might catch some enemy, who straggled behind them") is taken at face value when the spies arrest Dolon⁷⁰ but is then reinterpreted as "kill someone who lies on the outer perimeter of the camp."⁷¹ There is an important lesson to be learned here. Aristarchus "sensed" the oddity of Nestor's plan about a night mission that was not aimed at Hector, the obvious target of the Greeks. He also noticed the oddity of the spies' persistent direct questions to Dolon about Hector followed by a syntactically clumsy reiteration of Nestor's plan in indirect discourse, as well as the further oddity of Dolon's informing them *only* about Hector and ignoring their inquiries about Nestor's plan.

The importance of Aristarchus' approach can be further illuminated by means of a comparison with Σ *Il.* 9.182 Erbse (τὼ δὲ βάτην).⁷² His explanation that the dual is used for Odysseus and Telamonian Ajax, Phoenix being treated separately

---

⁶⁷ *Il.* 10.414–16.

⁶⁸ Danek (1988, 99–100) defends *Il.* 10.147 and argues that it reflects the poet's intention to be vague about the actual spy mission in the first part of the *Doloneia*. Therefore, he concentrates on the various scenes between the Greek leaders. Even when Menelaus asks his brother whether he intends to send a spy to the Trojan camp (*Il.* 10.37–8), Agamemnon does not reply to his questions but speaks about the need for a βουλή (*Il.* 10.43–4).

⁶⁹ *Il.* 10.206. ἐσχατόωντα, just as ἔσχατοι ἄλλων (*Il.* 10.434), designates the lower risk of approaching an enemy who is isolated from the rest of the army; the Σ *Il.* 10.206 (bT) talks about "lack of risk" (τὸ ἀκίνδυνον...τῆς πράξεως).

⁷⁰ *Il.* 10.345: ἔπειτα δέ κ' αὐτὸν ἐπαΐξαντες ἕλωμεν. Notice how the two meanings of αἱρέω converge (despite Σ *Il.* 10.561), when Odysseus reports to Nestor the arrest and death of Dolon (*Il.* 10.561–3: τὸν τρεισκαιδέκατον σκοπὸν εἵλομεν ἐγγύθι νηῶν, | τόν ῥα διοπτῆρα στρατοῦ ἔμμεναι ἡμετέροιο | Ἕκτωρ τε προέηκε καὶ ἄλλοι Τρῶες ἀγαυοί).

⁷¹ On αἱρέω in the sense of "slay" in Homer, see, e.g., *Il.* 4.457, 16.306.

⁷² I restrict myself to this case because I focus on Aristarchus.

from them after Nestor has laid out his plan, is based on a meticulous consideration of the Homeric text. Sensing the oddity of the dual, although the envoys are three, he tried to solve the problem internally, by recourse to the function of Phoenix in this episode. Aristarchus did not go further and argue that it is possible that the duals are vestiges of an earlier version where there were only two envoys, as some modern scholars have maintained.[73] However, this kind of explanation reflects Aristarchus' attempt to explain the text by drawing a line between the factual (three people participating in the Embassy)[74] and the notional (two real envoys). Several modern scholars make a similar argument but claim that what is notional in the *Iliad* was factual in an earlier form of the poem, in which Phoenix did not participate at all in the Embassy.[75]

This example regarding Aristarchus' scholiastic practice is analogous to what is reported with respect to his view that μέγα ἔργον in *Il*. 10.282 points to an attempt to kill Hector.[76] As in Σ *Il*. 9.182 (Erbse),[77] Aristarchus does not suggest that the plan to kill Hector belongs to an earlier version of *Iliad* 10 but explains this rather indeterminate expression by referring to the notional goal Diomedes and Odysseus seem to pursue.[78] His approach, as represented at both Σ *Il*. 9.182 (Erbse) and Σ *Il*. 10.282a (Erbse), accords with his exegetical principle to explain Homer by Homer and avoid digressions "beyond the scope of the poetic account,"[79] while being based on the distinction between the factual and the notional. As such, it indirectly supports the stance of several modern scholars who explain this distinction in terms of the poet's failure "to assimilate fully a new version with an old one"[80] or of an allusive strategy consisting in a "nod" to an earlier or traditional version.[81]

---

[73] Motzkus (1964) 103–4; Goold (1977) 10–11; Hainsworth (1993) 87 on *Il*. 9.182; Griffin (1995) 102; Cairns (2001a) 36; M. L. West (2011a) 218–19; Currie (2016) 74. Cf. Scodel (2002) 162–3.

[74] Apart from the two heralds.

[75] There are various other explanations that have been put forward with respect to the notorious duals of book 9. My aim is not to discuss this problem here but to suggest that the way Aristarchus treated the problem of the duals may be analogous to his comment on μέγα ἔργον in *Il*. 10.282.

[76] On the implausibility of an allusion to the murder of Rhesus, see p. 170 n. 42. Equally unlikely is the possibility that Odysseus speaks more diffusely about some great military dead, in tune with the frequent aim of ambuscades across cultures "to reduce the effectiveness of an enemy force, demoralize a fixed population...demonstrate vulnerability" (Steinen 1992, 135). When Odysseus utters these words (in his prayer to Athena), there is no ambuscade involving murder. The aim of the Greek spying mission is to gather information, not to kill anyone, even less to "demoralize a fixed population" by mass killings. At this stage, the spying mission is a reconnaissance, not an ambuscade. It will become an ambuscade unexpectedly when Diomedes and Odysseus ambush Dolon and subsequently Rhesus and his guards.

[77] See also Σ (A) *Il*. 9.192a and Σ (A^int) *Il*. 9.197a (Erbse).

[78] On the indeterminacy of μέγα ἔργον, see Codino (1951) 138 on *Il*. 10.282.

[79] Montana and Montanari (2022) 39.

[80] E.g. I.-Th. Kakridis (1949) 10 (this point is absent from the Greek version of I.-Th. Kakridis' book [1944]).

[81] Danek (1998a) under "Index," s.v. "konkurrierende Alternativversionen"; Currie (2016) 95. This is the approach I am following, especially since this type of explanation would offer a plausible account of why such features are notional in the text of the *Iliad*.

b. Σ [bT] *Il.* 10.406 (Erbse)
ποῦ <...> λίπες Ἕκτορα: καλῶς τοῦτο πυνθάνεται, ἵνα ἐγρηγορότος μὲν καὶ διέποντος τὰς φυλακὰς ἀπόσχοιντο, εἰ δὲ καθεύδοι, ἐπιχειρήσειαν καὶ αὐτὸν ἀνελεῖν [bT] καὶ τὰ ὅπλα ἀφελέσθαι. [D][82]

Where <...> did you leave Hector: He reasonably tries to find out about this, so that they may keep away from him (Hector), if he is awake and busy with the garrisons, whereas if he is asleep, they may attempt to kill him [bT] and deprive him of his weapons [D].

The scholiast's attempt to explain the spies' interest in Hector's whereabouts ends in the presentation of two alternatives, i.e. whether Hector is asleep or not. The first alternative (ἵνα ἐγρηγορότος μὲν καὶ διέποντος τὰς φυλακὰς ἀπόσχοιντο) seems odd. The spies ask Dolon about Hector, so as to avoid him because they are afraid that he may spot them if he is awake. The *non sequitur* of this line of thought is obvious:[83] why would Hector in particular be able to spot them? The second alternative (εἰ δὲ καθεύδοι, ἐπιχειρήσειαν καὶ αὐτὸν ἀνελεῖν καὶ τὰ ὅπλα ἀφελέσθαι) is more promising. If Hector is sleeping, then he would become the target of the spying mission, since Odysseus and Diomedes should try to kill him and take his weapons.[84] But why are the other Trojans unable to guard Hector and spot the spies? The idea that the guards would not perform their duties and arrest the spies if Hector is not checking them (διέποντος τὰς φυλακάς) is a groundless assumption (provided that this is what the scholiast implies). Both alternatives given by the scholiast are built around the notion of an all-powerful Hector who is a source of danger for the spies if awake but may become their target if asleep. The difficulty that the scholiast has to come up with a plausible explanation of the questions asked by Odysseus to Dolon is evident. The scholion belongs to the same class of scholia that strive to reconcile Nestor's plan to gather information with a plan to kill Hector.

c. Σ [bT] *Il.* 10.407b (Erbse)
ποῦ δέ οἱ ἔντεα κεῖται: εἰκὸς γὰρ ὡς βασιλέα σκηνοποιεῖσθαι στρατηγικώτερον. ἵνα οὖν κἂν ἀφέλωνται τὰ ὅπλα αὐτοῦ [bT] περιϊόντες τὰς φυλακάς. [T]

Where is his gear of war lying: For it is reasonable that he (Hector) as a king fit for command has a hut. (Odysseus asks the question) so that they (Odysseus and Diomedes) may take his (Hector's) weapons [bT] by going the rounds of the guards. [T]

---

[82] The exact form of the D-scholion (van Thiel) is the following: καλῶς περὶ τοῦ Ἕκτορος πυνθάνεται, ἵνα ἐγρηγορότος μὲν ἐκ τούτου ἀπόσχοιντο, εἰ δὲ καθεύδοι, ἐπιχειρήσειε καὶ αὐτὸν ἀνελεῖν καὶ τὰ ὅπλα ἀφελέσθαι.
[83] See p. 168 n. 35.
[84] On stealing Hector's weapons, see my analysis of the following scholion.

Eustathius, *Commentarii ad Homeri Iliadem pertinentes* 813.54-6 (van der Valk)

περὶ Ἕκτορος πρῶτον ἐρωτᾷ ὁ ἥρως. ἴσως γὰρ ὥσπερ ὁ Δόλων τῆς βασιλικῆς σκηνῆς, οὕτως αὐτοὶ τῆς τοῦ Ἕκτορος ἐφίενται. ἐρωτᾷ δὲ καὶ περὶ τῶν ἐκείνου ὅπλων, μέγα ἡγούμενος εἰ καὶ τοιοῦτόν τι ἀνύσουσι καὶ λαθόντες ὑφέλωνται, εἰ καὶ ἡ εὔπλαστος ἄκρα δειλία τοῦ Δόλωνος ἕτερόν τι μεῖζον ποιεῖ ἀνῦσαι αὐτούς.

The hero (Odysseus) asks Dolon first about Hector. Perhaps because just as Dolon aims at the king's hut (Agamemnon's), so they aim at Hector's hut. He also asks him about Hector's arms, considering it a great deed if they accomplish something like this and take the arms without being noticed, although the impressionable extreme cowardice of Dolon makes them accomplish another greater deed.

The ancient scholion on *Il.* 10.407b is elliptical to the point of incomprehensibility. A comparison with the more elaborate comment by Eustathius makes things clear: Hector must have a hut because it is suitable for a king, who is the commander-in-chief. Odysseus asks Dolon so as to take Hector's weapons by avoiding the garrisons of the other Trojans.

When this ancient scholion is taken together with Eustathius' comment, it becomes evident that a new course of action arises for the spies. Their aim is to find Hector's hut (he must have one, since he is a king) and steal his weapons without being noticed. In Σ [bT] on *Il.* 10.406[85] the stealing of the weapons was mentioned in the context of a plan to kill Hector. If so, we may ask: why do the scholia refer to the theft of Hector's weapons irrespective of whether he is killed or not? This question becomes all the more important in light of the absence on the part of the scholia of any association with the fact that Odysseus asks Dolon about Hector's arms and horses immediately after telling him that the promise of Achilles' horses is mere arrogance. By not making this connection, the scholiasts did not reckon on the spies being interested in stealing Hector's arms after killing him (Σ [bT] on *Il.* 10.406). They would thus have returned to the Achaean camp after depriving the Trojans of their best hero. Why, then, should the spies resort only to stealing Hector's weapons without killing him? By doing so they could boast to the Trojans that they had come so close to Hector without being noticed and would have proof of his arms to show for it.[86] This, according to Eustathius, would indeed be a great achievement (ἐρωτᾷ δὲ καὶ περὶ τῶν ἐκείνου ὅπλων, μέγα ἡγούμενος εἰ καὶ τοιοῦτόν τι ἀνύσουσι καὶ λαθόντες ὑφέλωνται). With this example,

---

[85] See p. 180.
[86] In the story of David and Saul in the Hebrew Bible (1 Sam. 26), David and Abishai steal Saul's water jug, which they use as proof that they had infiltrated the enemy camp without being noticed, as well as to boast that they could have killed him if they wanted to.

the two ancient scholia and Eustathius go out of their way to explain something *not stated in the text*, i.e. that the spies aim to steal Hector's weapons.

d. Σ [T] *Il.* 10.414-15 (Erbse)

"Ἕκτωρ μὲν μετὰ τοῖσι<ν.... | βουλὰς βουλεύει>: φυλάσσει μὲν αὐτὸν Ἀχιλλεῖ, ἀπίθανον δὲ ἀδεῶς αὐτὸν κοιμᾶσθαι.

Hector is among those... | they hold their deliberations: He (the poet) reserves him (Hector) for Achilles. It is not convincing that he (Hector) was sleeping without fear.

The scholion testifies to the need to reserve Hector for the encounter with Achilles in *Iliad* 22. We see here once more that there is a tension between the almost instinctive desire to plan a night mission with the aim of killing Hector and the realization that such a mission, should it be successful, would deprive the poem of Achilles' main adversary.

The scholiast's explanation consists in joining two unconnected lines of thought. The fact that the poet "reserves" Hector for the duel with Achilles has nothing whatsoever to do with his being asleep. What are we to gather from this? The stress on the plot's need for Hector, who later must face Achilles, since this encounter belongs to the "deep structure" of the Iliadic plot, would have made sense only if Hector's life was in danger. But who is threatening Hector's life given the plot of *Iliad* 10? The scholion would fit very well a plotline in which Diomedes and Odysseus had as their target Hector. The outcome of that spying mission could never be successful, since the poet "reserves him (sc. Hector) for Achilles" (φυλάσσει μὲν αὐτὸν Ἀχιλλεῖ). That this line of thought is on the right track is suggested by the following two scholia:

(a) Σ *Il.* 3.374b *εἰ μὴ ἄρ' ὀξὺ νόησε*: οὐ βοηθεῖ Ἀθηνᾶ Μενελάῳ, ὅπως ἡ Ἴλιος πορθηθῇ σῳζομένου Ἀλεξάνδρου. [bT][87]

(b) Σ *Il.* 5.662 *πατὴρ δ' ἔτι λοιγὸν ἄμυνεν*: προαναφωνεῖ μὲν τὸν θάνατον τοῦ Σαρπηδόνος διὰ τοῦ ἔτι, παραμυθεῖται δὲ τὴν ἧτταν τοῦ πολεμίου ἀργὸν ποιήσας Σαρπηδόνα. [bT][88]

The first scholion (a) presents a situation which is analogous to Σ *Il.* 10.414-15 [T]. Both of them try to explain why a potential course of the plot—Paris' and Hector's deaths in *Iliad* 3 and 10, respectively—does not take place. Though

---

[87] **If she (sc. Aphrodite) had not watched sharply:** Athena does not help Menelaus, so that Ilium may be sacked while Alexander is safe.
[88] **But his father still fended destruction away from him:** He both foreshadows Sarpedon's death by "still" (ἔτι) and consoles the reader for the enemy's defeat (sc. Tlepolemus) by making Sarpedon lie idle (because he is wounded).

neither course of action is mentioned in the plot,[89] the scholiast thinks that the first instance (Σ *Il.* 3.374b) will occur outside the plot of the *Iliad*, in the continuation of the Trojan saga (the sack of Troy while Alexander is alive), whereas the latter case (Σ *Il.* 10.414–15) takes place within the *Iliad* (the death of Hector by Achilles in book 22). As far as the scholion on *Il.* 3.374b is concerned, the scholiast's point is that if Alexander dies, the war will be over immediately and so Troy will not be sacked, since the war will end at once. The scholion creates the impression that the presence of Alexander among the ranks of the Trojan army is a prerequisite for the continuation of the war and, ultimately, for the sack of Troy, and as such would feature in all versions of the Trojan War. This explanation is false, since Troy falls after Alexander is killed by Philoctetes, which means that the Trojans did not give back Helen when her first Trojan husband perished but married her to Deiphobus and continued to fight the Achaeans.[90] Still, the scholiast's point is valid to the extent that Alexander is needed for the continuation of the plot of the *Iliad* (in which he does not die) and for the Trojan myth, since he will die much later. The analogy between the two scholia is instructive because the stress of Σ *Il.* 3.374b on the plot's need for Alexander, who is required for the continuation of the saga, makes sense *exactly because his life is in danger*. The second scholion (on *Il.* 5.662) explains why another, almost imminent, course of action will not take place. Sarpedon cannot die at the hands of Odysseus because he is needed for the rest of the plot, since he will be killed by Patroclus in book 16.[91] Again, the situation pertains to the *danger Sarpedon faces in Iliad 5*.

Both Σ *Il.* 3.374b and Σ *Il.* 5.662 illustrate that the scholiastic formula "this hero cannot perish now because he is needed for the continuation of the plot/saga" pertains to a *real danger* that a hero is facing (Alexander in book 3, Sarpedon in book 5). This danger is clearly spelled out in the text of the *Iliad*. Conversely, in book 10 the threat to Hector's life is assumed by the scholia.

e. Σ [bT] *Il.* 10.433–4 (Erbse)

εἰ γὰρ δὴ μέματον Τρώων καταδῦναι ὅμιλον, < | Θρήϊκες... νεήλυδες>: οἱ μὲν περὶ τὸν Ὀδυσσέα οὐ τρανότερον ἐξέφηναν τὴν βούλησιν, ὁ δὲ συμβάλλεται αὐτῶν τῇ σκέψει καὶ μιᾶς ψυχῆς ἀτυχίᾳ προδίδωσιν ὅλον τὸ συμμαχικόν. [bT] οἱ δὲ καὶ ἐπαινοῦσιν αὐτὸν ὡς ἀποτρεψάμενον αὐτοὺς Ἕκτορος διὰ τοῦ ἐπαίνου τῶν Θρᾳκῶν [T]

For if you are minded to get among the mass of the Trojans, < | the Thracians... newly come>: Those in the company of Odysseus did not reveal their will in a clearer way, while he (Dolon) converges with their thought and by the loss of a

---

[89] The scholiast may have felt the need to explain why Athena does not assist Menelaus because she will do so when she saves him from Pandarus' arrow in *Il.* 4.127–40.
[90] *Il. parva* arg. ll. 213–16 Severyns.   [91] See pp. 31 with n. 32, 212.

single life betrays the entire allied force. [bT] Others even praise him (Dolon) because he diverted them from Hector by means of praising the Thracians. [T]

The scholiast here comments on Odysseus' questioning of Dolon to find out the whereabouts of the Trojan allies (*Il.* 10.424–5). He claims that Dolon understood the intentions of the two spies but failed to realize that, by providing them with the desired information, he was betraying the entire allied force. The repetition of Odysseus' ἀπάνευθε[92] by Dolon[93] seems to support the accuracy of the scholion's explanation. At this point, the scholiast offers a different line of interpretation which others also put forward, i.e. that Dolon should be praised for having focused attention on the Thracians, since this diverts the Achaean spies away from Hector. This explanation raises the question why Dolon should want to divert the spies away from Hector, if the aim of the spying mission in the *Doloneia* as we have it was simply to gather information and not to kill Hector.[94] One answer might be that we are to assume that the spies would gather information by overhearing Hector's council, hence Odysseus' interest in Hector's whereabouts, much as Dolon tells Hector that he will find out about the Greek plan by approaching Agamemnon's ship, where, so Dolon claims, the Greeks are holding their council (*Il.* 10.325–7).[95] This line of thought would be consonant with the use of parallel, often mirroring, episodes.[96] However, this scenario is unlikely in the current case for the following reasons: (a) when the Achaean spies ask about Hector's whereabouts (*Il.* 10.406–7), they do not know that Hector had held a council;[97] (b) the spies' interest in Hector's weapons and horses rather than in overhearing deliberations in the assembly[98] strongly points to a plan to kill Hector; (c) it would be absurd if the spies reached the place where Hector is deliberating so as to overhear him presenting his plan to the other Trojans and allies instead of trying to kill him

---

[92] *Il.* 10.424–5: "How, then, are these sleeping? And they are mixed with the Trojans, breakers of horses, or apart?"
[93] *Il.* 10.434–5: "Here are the Thracians, newly come, separate, beyond all others in place, and among them lies Rhesus their king, the son of Eioneus."
[94] Dolon could not assume that the spies aimed at killing Hector because they have qualified their questions about Hector's whereabouts with their explicitly stated interest in finding out Hector's plan.
[95] ... ὄφρ' ἂν ἵκωμαι | νῆ' Ἀγαμεμνονέην, ὅθι που μέλλουσιν ἄριστοι | βουλὰς βουλεύειν, ἢ φευγέμεν ἠὲ μάχεσθαι ("...until I come to the ship of Agamemnon, where their greatest men must be gathered to deliberate the question of running away or of fighting"). Dolon, like all Trojans, knows that Agamemnon is the supreme leader of the Achaean army, hence his assumption that assemblies are held in his hut (though this is not always the case, as illustrated in book 10); see pp. 71–2.
[96] See Hainsworth (1993) 155: "Balance rules book 10"; also, Fenik (1986) 34 on the importance of form for the shaping of the content. However, the reciprocity between the two assemblies (the Achaean and Trojan) stems from the two spying missions and the novel role of Dolon in our *Iliad*; on his earlier function in the Hector-version of book 10, see pp. 96 n. 116, 209–11, 242, 295.
[97] At this point, the Achaean spies only know that Hector sent Dolon as a spy to the Achaean camp (they have guessed: *Il.* 10.388–9; Dolon's confirmation: *Il.* 10.391–9). It is only after they have asked about Hector's whereabouts that Dolon tells them about the Trojan council (*Il.* 10.414–16).
[98] *Il.* 10.406–7: ποῦ νῦν δεῦρο κιὼν λίπες Ἕκτορα, ποιμένα λαῶν; | ποῦ δέ οἱ ἔντεα κεῖται ἀρήϊα, ποῦ δέ οἱ ἵπποι;

and solve their problem once and for all;[99] (d) spies engage in eavesdropping,[100] but such tactics are now pointless since Diomedes and Odysseus have captured Dolon. Why are they still interested in Hector's whereabouts, since Dolon can tell them about the Trojan plan? After all, this is exactly what they ask the Trojan spy (*Il.* 10.409–11).

The scholion seems to be perfectly consistent with the explicit references to a plan to kill Hector and steal his weapons which we find in the scholia. It is also important because it informs us about the existence of other scholiasts who argued that the spies' true target was Hector. It is Dolon's eulogy of the Thracians that makes the spies divert from their primary goal.[101]

f. Σ [bT] *Il.* 10.519 (Erbse)

'Ρήσου ἀνεψιόν: οἰκτρὸν τὸ τὸν ἴδιον ἀνεψιὸν ἐπισκέψασθαι τὸ δεινόν. οὐ μὴν θρήνους περιτίθησι καίτοι εὐπορῶν, ἀλλ' ἑτέρῳ μέρει τῆς ποιήσεως (sc. *Il.* 24.720–81) τηρεῖ τοὺς θρήνους ἐπὶ Ἕκτορι τεθνηῶτι.

The cousin of Rhesus: it is lamentable that the disaster befell his (sc. Rhesus') own cousin. He (sc. the poet) does not attach lamentations (sc. for Rhesus to Hippocoon) although he could compose them with ease but reserves the lamentations for Hector after his death in another part of his poem.

The scholion explains the absence of a lament for Rhesus by his cousin Hippocoon by pointing to the formal lamentations for Hector (by Andromache, Hecuba, and Helen) in *Iliad* 24.[102] This association is not immediately clear. Take, for example, Σ *Il.* 16.140c (Erbse), in which the scholiast explains why the poet does not "allow" Patroclus to brandish Achilles' famous ash-spear (although he puts on his armor): τοῦτο Ἀχιλλεῖ τετήρηκε ("he has reserved it [sc. the ash-spear] for Achilles"). In this case, the link is straightforward. Patroclus cannot brandish Achilles' spear because he will not be a second Achilles, since he will soon be killed on the battlefield. Achilles alone is able to use his Pelian ash-spear. This weapon stands (like his horses) for his special, unmatched military skill. The association between Patroclus and Achilles by means of the ash-spear is transparent because it capitalizes on the former's borrowing of the latter's arms. Conversely, why is there

---

[99] The same type of argument is simply not applicable to Dolon because Agamemnon, very much unlike Hector, is *not* a special source of danger for the Trojans by means of his military skills. Book 9 has made it amply clear that he cannot fill the void left by Achilles.

[100] In the *Ilias parva* (fr. 2 GEF) Nestor sent a group of men to the Trojan walls to eavesdrop so that they may find out whom the Trojans consider braver for the arms of Achilles, Telamonian Ajax or Odysseus.

[101] Σ (T) *Il.* 10.433–4 (Erbse): οἱ δὲ καὶ ἐπαινοῦσιν αὐτὸν ὡς ἀποτρεψάμενον αὐτοὺς Ἕκτορος διὰ τοῦ ἐπαίνου τῶν Θρᾳκῶν.

[102] In this climactic scene, the personal laments (γόοι) for Hector by the next of kin, which are paired by antiphonal sobbing and crying by groups of people, are preceded by the dirges (θρῆνοι) sung by professionals; see Alexiou (2002²) 102–3; Tsagalis (2004) 2–8.

an association between Rhesus and Hector? The former has recently arrived at Troy from Thrace together with his fresh troops. Why does the scholiast feel the need to explain the lack of lamentations for Rhesus by Hippocoon? In what way would these dirges "harm" the plot? Judging from the explanation offered, the scholiast clearly felt that, were Hippocoon to lament Rhesus here, this would weaken the effect of the future lamentations for Hector. The poet reserves multiple lamentations (both in *Iliad* 22 and 24) only for Hector. As the uncontested leader of the Trojans, the symbol of the protection and safety of Troy, as well as an ideal father, husband, and patriot, he has to be granted exclusive and extended γόοι to match his status.[103] By lamenting for him, the Trojans proleptically grieve for Troy itself. This line of thought suggests that the scholiast not only regarded Hector as indispensable for the rest of the plot but also treated lamentations on the anti-Achaean side as exclusively his property. In this vein, it may be claimed that Rhesus is handled in such a way so as not to detract from Hector's uncontested preeminence as a fighter and a dramatic figure of the plot. In the *Iliad* Rhesus must be killed before committing himself to the fighting so as not to overshadow Hector by performing a potential *aristeia*.[104] Likewise, his death must be passed over without lamentations so as not to deprive Hector of the privilege of exclusive commemoration as the best of the Trojans. In this way, the scholion seems to confirm the narrative tension and challenge created by the participation of both Hector and Rhesus in the plot, albeit in a single book.[105]

This chapter has been devoted to the examination of putative clues in the text of the *Iliad* and the scholia for the existence of an earlier version of the *Doloneia*, in which Hector may have been the target of a nocturnal mission by Diomedes and Odysseus. The material surveyed and analyzed suggests that a Hector-version of *Iliad* 10 lies behind the current version of this book. In the next chapter I will try to reconstruct the presumptive form of this earlier version.

---

[103] See *Il*. 22.416–28, 431–6, 477–514; 24.725–45, 748–59, 762–75.
[104] On this point, see Fenik (1964) 5–8; Dué and Ebbott (2010) 89–106; Bierl (2012) 139.
[105] καίτοι εὐπορῶν does not mean that the poet had lamentations available to him, i.e. that he knew of lamentations for Rhesus by some other source, but that he could compose them with ease. At Σ *Il*. 2.455–6 (Erbse) the verb εὐπορῶ is used for the poet's ability to create different images for the same thing; in Σ *Il*. 21.76b (Erbse) εὐπορῶ is employed for the poet's inventiveness, who "puts a speech in the mouth of an enemy and still finds a plausible argument for his salvation"; at Σ 13.408b[1–2] (Erbse) εὐπορῶ describes the poet's skill in creating different expressions. All other attestations of εὐπορῶ refer to the characters of the plot.

6
Reconstructing the Hector-Version of *Iliad* 10

Introduction

I will now attempt to reconstruct the putative earlier form of *Iliad* 10, which I have coined the "Hector-version," before the introduction of Rhesus into the plot. I will proceed motif by motif, indicating what would have been the content of an earlier version of the *Doloneia* by discussing, when appropriate, specific scenes and comparing them to other analogous scenes in Homeric and Cyclic epic. In what follows I argue that, while the *Nyktegersia* is largely unchanged, the Dolon episode has been modified substantially to fit the new requirements of the Iliadic plot. But before embarking on this densely argued endeavor, for reasons of clarity I will offer a schematic summary of the proposed hypothetical earlier version of *Iliad* 10.

A. The *Nyktegersia*

I. Summoning the Achaean Leaders
  (1) Tormented by the realization of the extremely difficult situation of the Achaean army, Agamemnon cannot sleep.
    (a) He thinks of undertaking an ambuscade against Hector and decides to hold a meeting of the Achaean leaders to find out whether they agree with him.
    (b) He intends to visit Nestor, who can tell him how to carry out his plan.
    (c) He begins to get prepared.
  (2) Tormented by the realization of the extremely difficult situation of the Achaean army and his personal responsibility regarding the entire war, Menelaus cannot sleep.
    (a) He decides to visit his brother Agamemnon and consult with him.
    (b) He goes to Agamemnon, who is ready to depart for Nestor.
  (3) Agamemnon tells Menelaus that Zeus is supporting Hector, who has inflicted numerous casualties on the Achaean army and can hardly be stopped.

(a) He sends Menelaus to wake up Telamonian Ajax and Idomeneus, while he goes to Nestor, according to his initial plan.

(b) The two brothers agree to meet in the place where the guards have been posted, outside of the Achaean Wall.

(4) Agamemnon wakes up Nestor and suggests that they go to the place where the guards have been posted, so that they may check that all is fine, since it is not unthinkable that the Trojans may attempt a night attack.

(a) Nestor tells Agamemnon about the danger posed by Hector and stresses that only Achilles would be able to stop him. He suggests that they wake up other key heroes, such as Diomedes and Odysseus. He also advises that someone is sent to wake up Telamonian Ajax and Idomeneus, whose headquarters are at the other side of the camp.

(b) Agamemnon agrees and informs Nestor that Menelaus has been already dispatched by him to Telamonian Ajax and Idomeneus.

(5) Nestor and Agamemnon visit Odysseus and wake him up. Odysseus agrees to help.

(6) Agamemnon, Nestor, and Odysseus go to Diomedes' headquarters.

(a) They find Diomedes sleeping outside his hut but with his arms and comrades next to him.

(b) Diomedes agrees to assist them and is dispatched to Locrian Ajax and Meges.

(7) Agamemnon, Nestor, and Odysseus go to the place where the guards have been posted.

(a) There they meet with Menelaus, who has already arrived there together with Telamonian Ajax and Idomeneus.

(b) Diomedes, who has fetched Locrian Ajax and Meges, is also present at the council.

II. The Achaean Council

(1) After checking that the guards hold their posts, Agamemnon allows Nestor to speak first because of his eloquence and wisdom. Nestor says that Hector is the main danger for the Achaean army. Since Achilles abstains from the war and no other hero is able to defeat Hector by means of regular warfare, he suggests that the Achaeans should attempt to kill Hector during the night by infiltrating the Trojan camp. The fact that the enemy has encamped on the plain offers a unique opportunity that should not be missed.

(a) Diomedes takes the floor and declares that he is willing to do so, but it would be better if he is accompanied by another hero.

(b) Several leaders and warriors volunteer, among whom are Menelaus and Odysseus.

(c) Fearing lest Diomedes selects Menelaus and realizing that if he (*sc.* Agamemnon) volunteers, he can hardly exclude his brother from joining him, Agamemnon tells Diomedes to choose whomever hero he desires as his companion for the ambuscade, hoping that Diomedes will not consider Menelaus.
(d) Diomedes selects Odysseus for this nocturnal mission.
(e) They are armed with weapons suitable for an ambush and dress themselves accordingly. They depart for their mission.
(f) Odysseus prays to Athena.

B. The *Doloneia* Proper

I. Dolon and the Failed Attempt at Hector
  (1) Meanwhile, Dolon, a third-rank Trojan warrior, leaves the Trojan camp and enters the area where the bodies of dead Achaeans are lying on the ground with the intention of acquiring spoils for himself.
  (2) Diomedes and Odysseus arrest Dolon and ask him about Hector's whereabouts. After acquiring the desired information, they kill him and rob him of his arms, which they place upon a tamarisk bush that they mark by pulling reeds and placing branches upon it so that they do not miss it on their way back to the ships.
    (a) Diomedes and Odysseus approach the area where Hector is sleeping. They would have killed him if it was not for Athena, who appeared and instructed them that it was not fated for Hector to die at this point, since he will be killed by someone else in the future. She also urged Diomedes and Odysseus to return to the Achaean camp before some pro-Trojan god wakes up Hector, which is what happens soon after with Apollo.
    (b) Mission aborted, Diomedes and Odysseus leave the Trojan camp, pick up Dolon's arms from the tamarisk bush, and return to the Achaean ships.
II. The Return to the Achaean Camp
  (1) Their comrades are happy to see them alive and well, but they are let down by the fact that the mission has failed and Hector is alive.
  (2) Diomedes and Odysseus dedicate Dolon's arms to Athena and prepare themselves for the coming of the next day.
  (3) Having failed to kill Hector, the Achaeans stick to the original plan, suggested by Diomedes to Agamemnon at the end of *Iliad* 9, i.e. to launch a full-scale attack on the Trojans on the plain at dawn.

6.1 The *Nyktegersia*

6.1.1 Sleeplessness Caused by a Pressing Need

After the failure of the embassy to Achilles, the Achaean leaders withdraw, each to his headquarters, to pass the night before launching an attack the following day. Diomedes' scornful tone against the idea that they should have gone to Achilles[1] is a covert prelude to his (*sc.* Diomedes') involvement in the events of book 10. He, a noteworthy absentee from the embassy, will dominate *Iliad* 10.

It is with Agamemnon that book 10 begins. Achilles' refusal to accept his catalogue of gifts and return to battle, the catastrophic turn that the war has taken (as the Achaeans have turned from besiegers to besieged), perhaps even Diomedes' stern rebuke at the beginning of *Iliad* 9, which may have reminded Agamemnon of the fragility of his authority: all these developments are more than enough to make him unable to sleep. Similarly, in *Iliad* 2 Zeus is unable to sleep as he turns his mind to honoring Achilles by assisting the Trojans. On both occasions sleeplessness[2] is precipitated by the problem of Achilles' non-participation—his withdrawal in book 1, his renewed refusal to fight in book 9. Furthermore, the response of both is similar in that their agonized ponderings lead to the wider group being called to deliberate. On the other hand, there are differences: first, in book 2 Zeus' plan unfolds through Agamemnon, whose response to the (lying) dream that Zeus sends him is to call an assembly, while in book 10 Agamemnon acts on his own accord, with no intervention by a god; second, in book 2 the summoning of an assembly happens during the next morning,[3] while in book 10 the Achaean leaders are gathered at night. However, these differences are explained by the practical need to summon the entire army. This event requires in book 2 the involvement of Agamemnon and the coming of dawn, since it is difficult, if not impossible, to summon the entire army during the night. The motif of "sleeplessness caused by a pressing need" is used in book 10 with greater intensity and dramatic force. Agamemnon doesn't wait for day—which signals his desperation. It fits the *Doloneia* much better than the situation in book 2, where both the use of the deceptive dream and the *peira*[4] of the Achaean troops testify to its looser form, perhaps under the influence of an oral, pre-Homeric **Cypria*, in which Achilles stopped the mutiny of the Achaean army that suffered from famine and desired to return to Greece.[5] In book 10 Agamemnon is faced

---

[1] See his speech to Agamemnon at *Il.* 9.697–709.
[2] On troubling sleep or temporal sleeplessness, see *Il.* 23.58–61 and *Od.* 1.421–7 see also Arend (1933) 101.
[3] *Il.* 2.48–52.
[4] Note that in book 2 Agamemnon convokes a council even as the army are gathering to the assembly. A council makes more sense in the context of book 10 (I owe this point to E. T. E. Barker [by email]).
[5] See Kullmann (1955) 253–73 = (1992) 38–63; also pp. 35, 165, 190, 207 (this volume).

with such a pressing need that he must act quickly, during the night, by devising a plan that may save the Achaeans. In this light, this motif may well have featured in an early form of book 10, since it is an integral component of the *Nyktegersia*.

6.1.2 Brothers Deliberating

What happens to Agamemnon happens to his brother Menelaus. He also cannot sleep, as he thinks about his responsibility to the whole army. It is he who has made the Achaeans cross the sea and come to Troy for the sake of Helen. Now that things are on the razor's edge and action is badly needed, Menelaus decides to go to his brother. The presentation of Menelaus going to Agamemnon for help is paralleled by what he has done in another moment of desperation and sadness, when he returned to Sparta from Crete and realized that Helen had been abducted by Paris. According to the *Cypria*, when Menelaus learned from Iris what had happened in his absence, he went immediately to Mycenae to deliberate with his brother Agamemnon,[6] whose status and power was widely recognized among the other Achaean kings.[7] The deliberation between the two brothers in both the *Cypria* and the *Doloneia* concerns the same basic scenario and people, as well as the threat of loss: Menelaus has lost his wife, the Achaeans are about to lose the war.[8] Are these stories parallel, which means that correspondences should be ascribed to a shared typology, or do they speak in favor of unidirectional influence from an oral *Cypria* to an earlier form of the *Doloneia* (within the *Iliad*)? Two factors suggest unidirectional influence: first, the theme of the joint deliberation is primary in the *Cypria* passage (since Menelaus goes to Agamemnon because the abduction of his wife, Helen, concerns him personally), while in the *Doloneia* it is secondary (since the difficult situation of the Achaeans is no more related to him than it is related to Agamemnon, who is already awake when Menelaus visits him); second, the phrasing "they who for his sake over much water | had come to Troy, bearing their bold attack to the Trojans"[9] strongly suggests a source citation (the *Iliad* acknowledges an oral *Cypria* as its source by activating the epic plupast[10]

---

[6] *Cypr.* arg. ll. 110–12 Severyns: καὶ μετὰ ταῦτα Ἴρις ἀγγέλλει τῷ Μενελάῳ τὰ γεγονότα κατὰ τὸν οἶκον. ὁ δὲ παραγενόμενος περὶ τῆς ἐπ' Ἴλιον στρατείας βουλεύεται μετὰ τοῦ ἀδελφοῦ ("and after these events Iris reports to Menelaus what has happened at home. He returns and plans an expedition against Ilion with his brother").

[7] This belief is reflected in *Il.* 10.32–3: ὃς μέγα πάντων | Ἀργείων ἤνασσε, θεὸς δ' ὣς τίετο δήμῳ ("who was the great king of all Argives, one honored in his own land as a god is").

[8] For a negative development of a deliberation between Agamemnon and Menelaus, see *Nost.* arg. ll. 279–80 Severyns (Ἀθηνᾶ Ἀγαμέμνονα καὶ Μενέλαον εἰς ἔριν καθίστησι περὶ τοῦ ἔκπλου), where Athena instigates a quarrel between the two brothers about the sail home.

[9] *Il.* 10.27–8: τοὶ δὴ ἕθεν εἵνεκα πουλὺν ὑφ' ὑγρήν | ἤλυθον ἐς Τροίην πόλεμον θρασὺν ὁρμαίνοντες.

[10] On the term "epic plupast," see Grethlein (2012) 15: "Both the narrator and the characters frequently refer to what we could call the 'epic plupast', the past that preceded the main action of the song. The 'epic plupast' may be read as a *mise en abyme*, that is to say the embedded past of the heroes figures as a mirror to the heroic past presented in epic poetry"; see also Bär (2024) 150 n. 8, 152–3, 159.

of mustering an army that would sail to Troy). If the joint role of the Atreidae in the *Doloneia* was also attested in an oral precursor of the *Cypria*, it may conceivably have featured in an earlier form of book 10 that would have been influenced by this oral **Cypria*.

6.1.3 Brothers Devising a Plan

The making of a plan is a regular feature of deliberation scenes. However, the manner of the devising and the substance of the plan appear confusing, even incoherent in the current version of book 10. When Menelaus arrives at Agamemnon's headquarters, he immediately asks his brother whether he is pondering choosing one of the Achaeans to spy on the Trojans; it would be hard for Agamemnon to find a volunteer for such a dangerous mission. Menelaus' words are odd. How could he know that Agamemnon is thinking of sending a spy? Is Agamemnon really thinking of a spying mission?[11] The only thing we have been told is that Agamemnon will go to Nestor to ask for a plan to save the Achaeans.[12] In his reply to Menelaus Agamemnon stresses the need for crafty counsel. He explains that devising a plan is the utmost priority because of a single man, Hector, who has caused countless losses to the Achaean army.[13] Surprisingly, instead of stating the logical consequence stemming from his previous statement, which can be nothing else than to devise a plan on how to kill Hector, Agamemnon sends Menelaus to Telamonian Ajax and Idomeneus, while he will go to Nestor and ask for his help.

This is a typical case of narrative inconsistency to which various schools of Homeric criticism would provide different answers, although a fair number share the view of lack of poetic skill that seems to be manifested in this passage. Analysts would explain it as the result of the work of various authors, some oralists as the by-product of the imperfect combination by the singer of two traditional themes, the ambush and the spying mission that both suit, but are not limited to, nocturnal adventures, while traditional neoanalysts would opt for the equally imperfect modification of a previous version. My approach is a combination of the oralist and neoanalytical positions, with a certain refinement. The narrative inconsistency observed in this passage is not the result of poetic clumsiness but a planned strategy of allusion. The *Iliad* deliberately manipulates the tension between the traditional themes of ambush and spying mission to meaningfully interact with an earlier version which represented an ambush against Hector, the source of present

---

[11] This cannot be a case of "transference" (μετακένωσις), in which something that the external audience knows is transferred to a character of the plot. On transference, see Bassett (1938) 130–40; I.-Th. Kakridis (1982) 5–12; de Jong (2001) xviii.
[12] *Il.* 10.17–20.   [13] *Il.* 10.47–52.

suffering for the Achaean army. This approach is advanced on the strength of the following considerations: Menelaus' use of the language of arming at the beginning of his speech to his brother[14] and Agamemnon's stress on Hector as a major threat for the Achaeans[15] both square neatly with an earlier version in which Menelaus would have found Agamemnon arming for a night ambuscade against Hector.[16] The poem intentionally uses these two references to alert its audience to the existence of such a version.[17]

6.1.4 Fear in Front of Grave Danger

Agamemnon's concern about the current state of the war and the sufferings of the Achaeans (*Il.* 10.92)[18] is particularized by his focus on Hector (*Il.* 10.46–52). Likewise, Nestor associates the end of Hector's triumph to Achilles' return to the war (*Il.* 10.104–7).[19] Similar observations may be made regarding Menelaus' fear that nobody will volunteer for such a difficult mission (*Il.* 10.39–41). Here intratextuality goes hand in hand with intertextuality. Volunteering for a difficult task, especially when one's life is at risk, has already been highlighted in *Iliad* 7, before Telamonian Ajax ultimately goes head-to-head with Hector. In that case too, Menelaus initially expressed doubt that anybody would be so daring as to confront Hector;[20] hence his intention to volunteer (an intention that is cut short by Agamemnon's intervention).[21] The intratextual association is clear. Fighting Hector is such a dangerous task that it is hard to find anyone willing to take this chance. Likewise in book 10, we might expect Menelaus to express a similar view about attempting a nocturnal ambuscade against Hector. Instead, Menelaus' anxiety is transferred on to a nocturnal spying mission. By transferring the motif of fear of a powerful enemy (Hector) to the undertaking of a spying mission, *Iliad* 10 may be alerting its audience to the existence of a previous version in which Menelaus' fear concerned an ambuscade against Hector. If so, *Il.* 10.37–41 would play off not only *Il.* 7.96–102 but also a scene from an earlier version of book 10.

---

[14] *Il.* 10.37: κορύσσεαι.   [15] *Il.* 10.46–52.
[16] There is nothing to rule out the possibility that Agamemnon, although he was instigated by Diomedes at the end of book 9 to lead a full-scale attack on the plain the next day, had intended to undertake an ambuscade against Hector in the night. This is not against the assumption that this ambuscade was carried out by Diomedes and Odysseus and not by Agamemnon. This decision may have been taken in the council of the Achaean leaders.
[17] Agamemnon never replies to Menelaus' question; on these cross-purpose questions in *Iliad* 10, see Klingner (1940) 341–2 = (1964) 12; Danek (1988) 178; also Sammons (2009, 31), who entertains the possibility that this scene postulates that the Atreidae regularly consult each other over the conduct of war.
[18] μέλει πόλεμος καὶ κήδε' Ἀχαιῶν ("fighting and the cares of the Achaeans perplex me").
[19] Zeus will not make Hector carry out all his designs. Hector will suffer himself, when Achilles puts an end to his wrath and changes his mind with respect to fighting.
[20] *Il.* 7.96–102.   [21] *Il.* 7.109–19.

This line of thought trades on unknowns and as such is tentative. Nevertheless, it is meaningful and significantly rewarding. By alluding both to the preliminaries of the duel with Hector in book 7 and to an earlier version of book 10, this passage suggests that the combination of features of an ambuscade against a specific individual with those belonging to a spying mission may create an interpretive surplus.

6.1.5 Summoning the Leaders

I have argued that in an earlier version Menelaus may have found Agamemnon arming for a night ambuscade against Hector. If so, it is possible that Agamemnon had been deliberating it himself but wanted to consult with other Achaean leaders on the feasibility and implementation of such a plan. The prime source of advice would be, as usual, wise Nestor. In the current version, Nestor specifies the aim of the mission (Il. 10.206-10),[22] asks for a volunteer to undertake this mission (Il. 10.204-6), and sets the award for its successful completion (Il. 10.214-17). Likewise, in an earlier version Nestor may have specified how the plan to kill Hector would be carried out. This line of thought is analogous to the situation we encounter in the *Cypria*, where Agamemnon and Menelaus had decided to muster a huge expeditionary force to send against Troy. In order to put their plan into action, they turned to Nestor, whom Menelaus visited to seek his advice about how this plan could be implemented.[23] Although Proclus does not explicitly tell us what Menelaus discussed with Nestor,[24] we can assume that it concerned *how* Menelaus as the betrayed husband would be able to muster an army of enormous proportions, since after Nestor's episode the summary continues with the phrase ἔπειτα τοὺς ἡγεμόνας ἀθροίζουσιν ἐπελθόντες τὴν Ἑλλάδα (*Cypr.* arg. ll. 118–19 Severyns).[25] Nestor may have initially underlined the need to have Agamemnon

---

[22] Menelaus had assumed that Agamemnon was thinking about sending a spying mission (Il. 10.37-8), but says nothing about the aim of this mission.
[23] It is possible that Menelaus visited Nestor alone (without Agamemnon: *Cypr.* arg. ll. 110-17 Severyns), and that Agamemnon joined Nestor and Menelaus *after* Pylos. Il. 11.767-70 is not against this (*pace* M. L. West 2013a, 102), because the summoning of Achilles happened at a later stage, after the summoning of the suitors of Helen, who were bound by oath to help Menelaus; Odysseus' summoning (who, like Achilles, was not a suitor of Helen) also takes place (Procl. *Cypr.* arg. ll. 119-21 Severyns) *after* the completion of the summoning of all the kings, who were bound by oath (Procl. *Cypr.* arg. ll. 118–19 Severyns). According to Apollodorus (*Epit.* 3.6), a herald was dispatched.
[24] Proclus refers only to the digression of Nestor's lengthy narrative that involved the abduction of Lycurgus' daughter by Epopeus, the story of Oedipus, Heracles' madness, as well as the tale of Theseus and Ariadne.
[25] "Then they gather the leaders, traveling through Greece." This sentence could refer either to Menelaus and Nestor or to Menelaus, Agamemnon, and Nestor. I take *Od.* 24.115-20, where Agamemnon's soul says that he and Menelaus summoned Odysseus to Troy, as reflecting an oral epic precursor of the *Cypria* and as indicating that in some versions Agamemnon traveled together with his brother (and perhaps Nestor) all around Greece to convince various kings to join the expedition.

involved, since he possessed unrivalled authority among the Achaean leaders because of his power and wealth (a status that Menelaus could not possibly match). He may also have reminded Menelaus about the oath that Helen's suitors swore to Tyndareos which would oblige them commit to the common cause. When set against the background of this pre-Homeric tradition and of the association of the *Nyktegersia* with Agamemnon's review of the troops in book 4, the beginning of *Iliad* 10 suggests a pointed twofold interaction not only with a stage in the whole saga, in which the basis for the Trojan War proper is established,[26] but also with a phase within the Iliadic plotline, in which the first day of battle in the epic will take place (in book 4). This doubly allusive reference allows for the possibility that the *Nyktegersia* is solidly built in the Iliadic tradition and may have formed part of the Hector-version.

6.1.6 Seeking Advice about the Implementation of the Plan

Unlike book 2, Agamemnon does not need a Zeus-sent dream to wake up and test his army. Fear has taken him in its grip. As he observes the numerous watch-fires of the Trojans and their allies illuminating the night sky above the plain,[27] he drags the hair by its roots from his head in utter desperation,[28] as if grieving for the Achaean failure. In this hour of need he turns to Nestor, the unquenchable fountain of wise advice. Agamemnon listens unerringly to his admonitions:[29] in book 7 about the building of the wall; in book 9 about the embassy to Achilles. Here he seeks him out for a faultless plan, which may ward off disaster for the Achaeans.[30] He puts on his *chiton* and his sandals, throws about his shoulders a lionskin in haste, grabs his spear, and sets out. The situation we encounter,

---

[26] The *Nyktegersia* is about mustering the leaders for the undertaking of a special and dangerous mission. As such, it may have been shaped upon the narrative skeleton of the mustering of the army in the *Cypria, the more so since the protagonists (Agamemnon, Menelaus, and Nestor) are the same. That the Iliadic tradition is here operating within the framework of a symmetrical plan is suggested by the analogy between books 1 and 9 on the one hand, and books 2 and 10 on the other. Book 1 is about the conflict between Agamemnon and Achilles, while book 9 is a failed attempt to end it. Each of these two books is followed by a book that is partly shaped by two different episodes of the *Cypria*: the presentation of the Achaean forces (reflected in the Catalogue of Ships in *Iliad* 2) and the mustering of the army that included both the meeting with Nestor at Pylos and the traveling all around Greece to summon various Achaean leaders (reflected in Agamemnon's visit of Nestor and their joined waking up of some of the Achaean leaders in *Iliad* 10).

[27] On Agamemnon's gaze, see Hesk (2013) 37–43.

[28] This is a typical gesture of lamentation, which in the *Iliad* is "reserved" for the expression of grief for the deaths of Patroclus (by Achilles at 18.27) and Hector (by Priam at 22.77–8). On other gestures of lamentation (beating the breast, scratching the cheeks), see Tsagalis (2004) 59–60.

[29] At *Il.* 2.79–83 it is Nestor who supports Agamemnon's suggestion in the council that they gather the troops for battle (Nestor does not refer to Agamemnon's decision to test the troops prior to committing them to fight; see *Il.* 2.73–5).

[30] *Il.* 10.19–20: εἴ τινά οἱ σὺν μῆτιν ἀμύμονα τεκτήναιτο, | ἥ τις ἀλεξίκακος πᾶσιν Δαναοῖσι γένοιτο. μῆτις ἀμύμων is an "impeccable plan." Building on Amory-Parry's research on ἀμύμων (1973, 99–103), Danek (1988, 66–7) takes μῆτιν ἀμύμονα as a reinterpretation of μῆτιν ἀμείνω, which was employed by

in which Agamemnon seeks out Nestor, is, therefore, consonant with the importance to the Achaeans and Agamemnon that Nestor has demonstrated.

Furthermore, it resonates with the situation we encounter in the *Cypria*, in which Nestor's advice is sought after an initial meeting between Agamemnon and Menelaus. In particular, we may note the verb πλάζομαι that is employed by Agamemnon while going to Nestor's hut in the middle of the night (*Il.* 10.91). In the middle voice, this verb means "I wander," "I rove," "I roam," which evokes the context of a journey, not of a simple movement from Agamemnon's to Nestor's hut. In Homeric epic, all the examples mentioned by LSJ (s.v. πλάζω (A) I.4) come from the *Odyssey* and pertain to wandering and traveling a great distance.[31] The verb πλάζομαι is also attested in the *Cypria* (fr. 1.1-2 GEF: ἦν ὅτε μυρία φῦλα κατὰ χθόνα πλαζόμενα <αἰεί | ἀνθρώπων ἐ>βάρυ<νε βαθυ>στέρνου πλάτος αἴης), in the context of Zeus' decision to relieve the earth from the weight of the countless peoples roaming over it. Is it possible that the same verb was used for the journey of Menelaus to Nestor's palace at Pylos in the *Cypria* and/or for the journey (all around Greece)[32] involved in the recruitment of the Greek leaders?[33] Intertextuality allows us to widen the horizon of texts involved and the function of meaningful allusion. It may be the case that in an oral *Cypria, during the deliberation with his brother Agamemnon, Menelaus expressed his fear that it would be hard to muster a Panhellenic army (given the power and distance of Troy). Agamemnon may have then suggested a visit to Nestor, whose advice he honored.[34] This intertextual link allows us to gain a better understanding of Agamemnon's suggestion to gather the leaders for consultation. In the *Cypria he dispatched Menelaus to Nestor, while in book 10 he goes to Nestor himself[35] and dispatches Menelaus to Ajax and Idomeneus.

The motif of "seeking advice for the implementation of a plan" is perfectly in tune with an earlier version of book 10, in which the target of the spying mission would be Hector. *Iliad* 10 seems to engage both intratextually (see Agamemnon's consultation of Nestor in the preceding Iliadic books) and intertextually

---

Achilles at *Il.* 9.423 when he urged the Achaeans to come up with a better plan in the future. The semantic difference between the two epithets is not against the resonance created by the recall of Achilles' words, given the aural similarity between the two expressions, as well as the fact that ἀμύμονα is used at *Il.* 10.19 as an "epicized" positive grade of the comparative ἀμείνω; see Tsagalis (forthcoming) on *Il.* 10.17-20. On the "better *menis*" topic, see Dué and Ebbott (2010) 249-50 on *Il.* 10.19; Dué (2019) 128-35.

[31] *Od.* 1.2, 3.95, 3.106, 3.252, 4.325, 13.204, 15.312, 16.64, 16.151. This is one of the cases that have given rise to the theory of the use of "Odyssean" diction in the *Doloneia*; on a cautious evaluation of this theory and of its potential consequences, see Hainsworth (1993) 154; Tsagalis (forthcoming).

[32] *Cypr.* arg. ll. 118-19 Severyns: ἔπειτα τοὺς ἡγεμόνας ἀθροίζουσιν ἐπελθόντες τὴν Ἑλλάδα ("then they gather the leaders, traveling through Greece").

[33] On the transfer of features regarding a meeting between Nestor and Menelaus at Pylos to the discussion between Nestor and Agamemnon in *Iliad* 10, see pp. 194-5, 198-9.

[34] Procl. *Cypr.* arg. ll. 111-13 Severyns.

[35] He already had in mind to do so, as confirmed by *Il.* 10.18-19.

(see Nestor's consultation by the Atreidae in the *Cypria*) with such a version that is deeply rooted in both the Iliadic and Cyclic epic traditions.

6.1.7 Doubting a Hero

The discussion between Nestor and Agamemnon ends with an exchange of speeches concerning Menelaus. Since he does not see Menelaus together with Agamemnon, Nestor assumes he must be sleeping, adding the key sentence "for now he ought to be hard at work going to all the great men in supplication. This need that has come is no more endurable."[36] Agamemnon replies that Menelaus is awake, that he visited him earlier in the night, and that he has been sent by him to summon other Achaean leaders. Reassured, Nestor comments that in this way nobody will accuse or disobey Menelaus' orders.[37] Which of these features may have been found in the Hector-version?

Nestor's concerns about Menelaus belong to the motif of "doubting a hero," in which an important figure questions the heroic prowess of another first-rank warrior regarding his willingness to fight.[38] As in so many other cases, the function of this motif is better understood when examined within the broader Iliadic context. In the assembly of the Achaean army in *Iliad* 9, Diomedes forcefully rejects Agamemnon's latest proposal to give up on Troy and return to Greece. He recalls that earlier he had been unjustly doubted by Agamemnon, who had questioned his heroic prowess.[39] Having proven his fighting qualities in book 5, he now confidently declares that he and Sthenelus will stay and fight until the city of Troy is sacked (*Il.* 9.32–49), even if Agamemnon leaves for Greece and takes the rest of the army with him. This brief scene proves Agamemnon wrong. Diomedes is anything but a coward. A similar situation relates to Menelaus here. Nestor's remarks do not reflect what has happened in the previous Iliadic books but expose Menelaus' poor reputation.[40] Agamemnon's response

---

[36] νῦν ὄφελεν κατὰ πάντας ἀριστῆας πονέεσθαι | λισσόμενος· χρειὼ γὰρ ἱκάνεται οὐκέτ' ἀνεκτός (*Il.* 10.117–18).

[37] See Klingner (1940) 343 = (1964) 13, who has argued that the exchange between Nestor and Agamemnon about Menelaus has been carefully planned since the beginning of book 10, given that Agamemnon has anticipated Nestor's calling a council and asking for the summoning of Telamonian Ajax and Idomeneus (to whom Agamemnon has already dispatched Menelaus); see *Il.* 10.53 and 10.112. Sammons (2009, 37) rightly notes that since Nestor's views have public impact and ramifications, it is important for Agamemnon to clear his brother's name to his authoritative interlocutor.

[38] See, e.g., Sarpedon's rebuke of Hector in *Il.* 5.472–92; Hector's criticism of Paris at *Il.* 6.523 (ἀλλὰ ἑκὼν μεθιεῖς τε καὶ οὐκ ἐθέλεις) that is echoed in Agamemnon's words about Menelaus at *Il.* 10.121 (πολλάκι γὰρ μεθιεῖ τε καὶ οὐκ ἐθέλει πονέεσθαι); see Robert (1950) 248; Sammons (2009) 36 n. 37.

[39] *Il.* 4.368–400. Menelaus' heroic prowess will be amply manifested in book 17, which was called "Menelaus' *aristeia*" (Μενελάου ἀριστεία); see Stelow (2009) 193–205 and (2020) 88–105, 237–8, 248–50, and 256–7 with further bibliography.

[40] Sammons (2009) 34–7; Stelow (2020) 77. Menelaus has performed superbly against Paris in *Iliad* 3, where he has expressed his desire to put an end (by means of a duel) to the sufferings caused to both

corrects Nestor's assumptions by showing that Menelaus is actively engaged in summoning the Achaean leaders, as he is doing.[41] References by both Nestor and Agamemnon to the summoning of the Achaean leaders reflect the plot of the current version of book 10, which is about a spying mission.[42] However, the same kind of discussion may well have featured in the Hector-version, in which Menelaus may have also undertaken to wake up and summon Telamonian Ajax and Idomeneus.[43] The verb πονέεσθαι that is employed by both Nestor (Il. 10.116, 117) and Agamemnon (Il. 10.70) to describe the brothers' actions means "to busy oneself with."[44] Conversely, when employed by Agamemnon at Il. 10.121 it may mean "to fight,"[45] since all the past scenes to which Agamemnon refers concern active warfare.[46] These intratextual considerations suggest that Nestor's doubting of Menelaus may have been used in an earlier version of book 10, when a council of leaders was summoned to plan a covert form of fighting, an ambush against Hector.

Yet intratextual factors are only part of the picture. Returning to the *Cypria* episode of Menelaus' visit to Nestor at Pylos, it should be stressed that

---

Achaeans and Trojans (see also Il. 10.26-8 for his responsibility towards the Achaeans); in *Iliad* 4, Menelaus' critical wounding by the unheroic act of Pandarus, who shoots an arrow at him, is anything but a sign of cowardice (see Agamemnon's lament in Il. 4.155-82; also Sammons 2009, 38-9); at Il. 5.49-58, he joins the battle from the very beginning and slays a Trojan before being so bold as to challenge Aeneas (Il. 5.561-75), the second-best Trojan warrior; at Il. 6.37-65, Menelaus defeats Adrestus, whom he would have pitied and spared had it not been for Agamemnon's rebuke; Menelaus blames the Achaeans for their cowardice at Il. 7.96-102 and volunteers to fight Hector in a duel (though he is restrained by Agamemnon, who fears for his life, as in *Iliad* 4); on the relation of this passage to the *Doloneia*, see Sammons (2009) 34 and 40-1.

[41] On Agamemnon's support of Menelaus in this scene, see Willcock (2002) 223-4.

[42] The poem aims at highlighting Menelaus' concern for the safety of the Achaeans and the success of the expedition. His responsibility is gradually built up from the beginning of book 10, as indicated by the fact that he wakes up on his own and hastens to Agamemnon's hut. By having Menelaus act in parallel with Agamemnon, the *Iliad* raises him, not in terms of status but with respect to his concern for the army, to a level comparable to that of his brother. Agamemnon is the leader of the Achaean army, while Menelaus is the reason for its formation.

[43] Sammons (2009, 28) argues that the *Iliad's* tendency to keep the activity of Agamemnon and Menelaus "as separate as possible," although they "are often spoken as a unit," is also observed by the *Doloneia*. On the division of labor between the Atreidae in the *Doloneia*, see Sammons (2009) 30.

[44] On the constant use of this verb in *Iliad* 10, see Collins (1988) 79-80; Danek (1988) 124; Rousseau (1990) 330.

[45] Cf. Sammons (2009) 32-3, but the reference to Menelaus' past military engagements makes this interpretation very likely, if not unmistakable. This verb is attested eighteen times in the *Iliad*. It means "to fight" in the following seven instances: 4.374, 5.84 = 5.267 = 7.442, 10.121, 13.288, 20.359. Also compare Il. 10.89 with 245 and 279: in the former case, the word πόνος in the plural refers to "the burden of responsibility that comes with Zeus' allotment of authority and its cares to 'scepter-bearing kings'" (Sammons 2009, 33 with n. 26); in the latter cases (Il. 10.245 and 10.279), Diomedes and Odysseus are not referring to the burden of responsibility but to military or quasi-military undertakings.

[46] One of the previous uses of πονέομαι in the sense of "fight" is Il. 4.374, which is directly relevant to the situation we encounter in the *Doloneia*. Alden (2000, 143-9) has argued that the poet has manipulated a story pattern to draw a parallel between Diomedes' and Odysseus' night raid and Tydeus' infiltration into enemy territory (mentioned in books 4 and 5). I concur with this suggestion.

Agamemnon was not present. This scenario postulates a situation that is analogous to the one we encounter in the discussion between Nestor and Agamemnon in *Iliad* 10. Since Menelaus was dispatched alone to Nestor, but then all three (Agamemnon, Menelaus, and Nestor) summoned the rest of the Achaean leaders in the *Cypria*,[47] the discussion between Nestor and Agamemnon on Menelaus' absence in book 10 would be comparable to a discussion between Nestor and Menelaus on Agamemnon's absence at Pylos in the *Cypria*. Both Agamemnon's explanation (*Il.* 10.123) that Menelaus' poor reputation results from his deference to his brother, the commander-in-chief,[48] and Nestor's statement at *Il.* 10.129–30 that "no man of the Argives can disobey him nor find fault with him, whenever he stirs up any of them and gives orders,"[49] would have been remarkably apt to the situation in the *Cypria*, where Menelaus would have assured Nestor that his brother's absence at Pylos is not due to his idleness but to the fact that *in this particular case* he himself must take the initiative. It is he, the husband of Helen, who has been insulted by Paris. It is against this broader Trojan War horizon that the discussion between Nestor and Agamemnon should be placed. We may be dealing here with motif transference from an oral, pre-Homeric *Cypria to the *Iliad* involving its relocation from one character to another, facilitated by contextual similarity and the complementary presence of the same figures in both traditions.[50]

Such transference of motifs may well have been already operating in the Hector-version of *Iliad* 10. Intratextual factors draw attention to relics of a version in which Agamemnon explains to Nestor that Menelaus is willing to fight (by means of an ambuscade), just as he was always eager to fight in the regular warfare in the past. Intertextual considerations suggest that the larger context of the relevant episode in the source-text is about a military operation, not the gathering of information.

---

[47] See Stelow (2020) 77: "Menelaus seeks out Nestor, apparently by himself, although Agamemnon takes credit for the expedition in the *Odyssey* (*Cypr.* frs. 16–17; cf. *Od.* 24.115–17)."
[48] See Barck (1971) 9–14; Parry (1972) 14–19; Rousseau (1990) 325–30; Stelow (2009) 202–4; Sammons (2009) 28.
[49] οὕτως οὔ τίς οἱ νεμεσήσεται οὐδ' ἀπιθήσει | Ἀργείων, ὅτε κέν τιν' ἐποτρύνῃ καὶ ἀνώγῃ.
[50] Such an episode may have featured in an oral, pre-Homeric *Cypria; see Stelow (2020) 77. The shaping of this scene against the backdrop of Menelaus' visit to Nestor at Pylos in the *Cypria* is also suggested by the possibility that in an episode sharing several analogies with the *Nyktegersia* (i.e. Agamemnon's *Epipolesis* of the Achaean army; see chapter 2) we come across a trace of the Palamedes–Odysseus encounter in Ithaca that also featured in the *Cypria*. Scodel (2002, 15–16, 108–9) has made the intriguing suggestion that the fact that Odysseus is the only hero in the poem who names himself by reference to his son ("the dear father of Telemachus": see *Il.* 4.354; also 2.260) alludes by negation to the prewar episode of the joint mission of Palamedes, Nestor, Menelaus, and Agamemnon to Ithaca, where the shrewd Palamedes disclosed Odysseus' fake insanity by taking baby Telemachus from his mother's lap and threatening to kill him (Apollod. *Epit.* 3.7).

6.1.8 Plan Finalized

The expression μῆτιν ἀμύμονα (*Il.* 10.19) that describes the plan determined and finalized by Nestor in book 10 displays a remarkable analogy with the expressions νόον...ἀμείνονα (*Il.* 9.104) and μῆτιν ἀμείνω (*Il.* 9.423), which are employed by Nestor and Achilles, respectively. The former is used with respect to the plan to persuade Achilles to return to the fighting, the latter to the plan that the Achaeans need to devise to save themselves and their ships from Hector. But to understand the meaning of μῆτιν ἀμύμονα at *Il.* 10.19, it will be helpful to compare the two books, which are in many respects symmetrically structured:

Iliad 9	*Iliad* 10
νόον...ἀμείνονα (9.104), μῆτιν ἀμείνω (9.423)	μῆτιν ἀμύμονα (10.19)
three envoys (Odysseus, Phoenix, Ajax)	two spies (Diomedes, Odysseus)
duals (9.182–3, 192–98)	duals (10.254, 272–3, 349–50, 364, 468–9, 577–8)
failure (to persuade Achilles)	accidental success (death of Rhesus)

Putting the comparison this way reveals that in each case there is a major narrative inconsistency. In book 9, duals are used for three envoys; in book 10, the aim of the spying mission is left to one side, as the spies take on, and are successful with, a new goal—the killing of Rhesus. Given the symmetry, it is tempting to look for a connection between the two episodes. Achilles' reference at *Il.* 9.421–6 to a "better metis" (μῆτιν ἀμείνω)[51]—namely a plan that the Achaean leaders will have to come up with if they wish to save themselves and the ships—serves almost as an introduction to book 10 or a version of it in which the Achaeans would attempt do what they had expected from Achilles, i.e. to kill Hector. Along these lines, the narrative inconsistencies of the two symmetrical books 9 and 10 may reflect analogies pertaining to their earlier versions:

*Iliad 9	**Iliad* 10
νόον...ἀμείνονα (9.104), μῆτιν ἀμείνω (9.423)	μῆτιν ἀμύμονα (10.19)
two envoys (Odysseus, Ajax)	two spies (Diomedes and Odysseus)
duals (9.182–3, 192–8)	duals (10.254, 272–3, 349–50, 364, 468–9, 577–8)
failure (to persuade Achilles)	failure (to kill Hector)

---

[51] See Dué (2019) 133.

The duals of *Il.* 9.182-3, 192-8 may be regarded as an example of narrative inconsistency by which the *Iliad* alludes to an earlier version from which it is departing, reminding the audience that in that version there were two, not three, envoys, who were sent to Achilles by Agamemnon.[52] Likewise, the narrative inconsistency related to the spying mission, which takes an unexpected turn for the better as the two spies kill a major new enemy, may function as a reminder to the audience of an earlier version of *Iliad* 10 in which the Achaean spies failed to kill the target of their night ambuscade, Hector.

More broadly, and again bearing in mind the symmetry between books 9 and 10, it is possible to argue that the putative change both books have undergone relates to the introduction of a new character. In the current version of *Iliad* 9, Phoenix assumes the role played by Patroclus in an earlier version, in which Phoenix was in Achilles' hut and played no role. In the current version, Phoenix tells an embedded story in which the name of the wife of the hero who resembles Achilles[53] (he has also withdrawn from the fighting due to his anger) evokes the name of Achilles' best friend (Cleopatra—Patroclus). Likewise Rhesus in *Iliad* 10. That is to say, just as the introduction of Phoenix changed the role of Patroclus in book 9, so the introduction of Rhesus changed the role of Hector in book 10. In cases like this, differences also matter, especially when they are symmetrical.[54] In both books the new role of the two pairs of characters displays a remarkable analogy. The characters who were instrumental in the earlier versions of books 9 and 10 (Patroclus and Hector, respectively) and the characters who were either secondary or absent (Phoenix and Rhesus, respectively) form a tetrad in which speech and silence are (almost fully) complementarily distributed: Patroclus, who may have delivered a speech to Achilles in the earlier version of *Iliad* 9, became completely silent in the current version of this book,[55] while Hector, who was silent in the earlier version of *Iliad* 10,[56] was endowed with the privilege of speech in the current version of this book. Phoenix, who was silent in the earlier version of *Iliad* 9, delivers a lengthy speech to Achilles in the current version of this book, while Rhesus, who was absent from the earlier version of *Iliad* 10, remains silent throughout the current version of this book.

The "better plan" mentioned by Achilles at *Il.* 9.423 and the "blameless plan" mentioned by the narrator at *Il.* 10.19, and finalized by Nestor later in the council, are likely to have been in an earlier version a game changer, just like Nestor's previous plan (*Il.* 9.104: νόον... ἀμείνονα), provided that it had been carried out

---

[52] See Currie (2016) 74 with n. 214; also pp. 179 with n. 73, 200 (this volume).
[53] I.e. Meleager.
[54] On similarities and differences in the context of the discussion about allusion, see Currie (2016) 42, 174, 196.
[55] Notice that Patroclus does not speak in book 9, even when Achilles speaks to him (202-4) or when he orders the maids and his followers to make up the bed for Phoenix (658-9).
[56] Because he was asleep; see below, pp. 208-9.

successfully. As the return of Achilles to the battle would have been a game changer for the Achaeans, so the killing of Hector would also have saved their army and ships. The μῆτιν ἀμύμονα at Il. 10.19 may allude to μῆτιν ἀμείνω at Il. 9.423. Together they speak in favor of a plan that aims to achieve what Nestor's previous plan (Il. 9.104: νόον... ἀμείνονα) had failed to do. Since Achilles does not return to kill Hector, someone else must try to carry out this task: Diomedes, the poem's second Achilles.

6.1.9 Selecting the Protagonists

The motif of selection of those who will undertake a difficult mission can take different forms. The selected person or persons may be (a) appointed by an external key figure[57] (Il. 9.168–70: Nestor appoints Odysseus, Telamonian Ajax, and Phoenix as envoys who will be accompanied by the heralds Hodius and Eurybates); (b) volunteers who are chosen either by (b1) the drawing of lots (Il. 7.171: Telamonian Ajax is selected among nine volunteers) or by (b2) the first volunteer, as an internal key figure,[58] selecting his assistant (Il. 10.242–7: Diomedes is the first to volunteer and then selects Odysseus); (c) bound by a previously given promise to embark on the mission (Cypria [see Apollod. Epit. 3.6: τῶν ὅρκων ὑπεμίμνησκεν ὧν ὤμοσαν]: oath given by Helen's suitors to Tyndareos); (d) figures of exceptional ability who are considered instrumental in the accomplishment of the undertaking (Cypria: Odysseus and Achilles, who are essential for the success of the expedition).

In book 10, the selection process, which pertains to category (b2),[59] is conditioned by the need for two spies (Il. 10.222–6). Its rationale is explicitly stated by Diomedes, who explains it in terms of the mental surplus created by the coordinated action of two men.[60] The presentation of the waking up of Odysseus and

---

[57] By "external key figure" I am referring to a person of high status who will not participate in the mission.
[58] By "internal key figure" I am referring to a person of high status who will participate in the mission.
[59] See this page (above).
[60] Selecting the best comrade is key to the success of the mission. In a night-time mission what matters is not rank and kingly status but ability, i.e. who is truly "best." Agamemnon urges Diomedes to select his assistant on the grounds of skill, not of status and kingship (Il. 10.235–9). In this way, he hopes to exclude Menelaus from the mission, even if he is "more kingly" (10.239: μηδ' εἰ βασιλεύτερός ἐστιν). βασιλεύτερος (and βασιλεύτατος) are only used in Iliad 9 and 10. On Nestor's designation of Agamemnon as βασιλεύτατος, and on Agamemnon's self-designation as βασιλεύτερος with respect to Achilles, see Il. 9.69 and 9.160, respectively, with Tsagalis (forthcoming) on Il. 9.158–61 and 388–92; also Codino (1951) 119–20 on Il. 10.239; on Menelaus, see Rousseau (1992) 69–75, who argues in favor of degrees of royalty, in the manner of degrees of age. He maintains that forms like βασιλεύτερος and βασιλεύτατος were forged by the bards as a means of evoking a social function which both language and institutions did not allow them to represent in a straightforward manner. Heroes are concerned about such values as αἰδώς (237–8) and in this respect Agamemnon's point of view is consonant with the basic

Diomedes foreshadows their participation in the ensuing night mission. The fact that these two heroes engage in dialogue when Nestor wakes them up is balanced by their subsequent engagement in a domino-speech sequence initiated by Agamemnon when they are selected for the night mission.[61] In this way, one member of the pair — the one who wakes them up (Nestor) — speaks to them on the spot,[62] while the other (Agamemnon) speaks to them when they are chosen for the mission.

There is nothing in this process that could not have featured in the Hector-version, in which Diomedes and Odysseus were chosen for the night ambuscade. In fact, the selection of a pair of men for the night mission against Hector would have been symmetrical to the appointment of another pair of men for the embassy to Achilles in an earlier form of book 9. This balanced picture would be consonant with the equally balanced and complementary function of earlier versions of books 9 and 10.[63]

6.1.10 Placing the Council

The place where the Achaean council is held is unusual. The Trojans think that the Achaean leaders hold their meetings near the ships, as Hector says in the council (*Il.* 10.308), or by Agamemnon's ship, as Dolon specifies when he volunteers for the spying mission (*Il.* 10.325–6). However, the placement of the Achaean council has been well prepared in the *Iliad*. The groundwork has been laid in *Il.* 9.66–7 and 80–8. The positioning of seven guards[64] between the ditch and the Achaean

---

tenets of the heroic code. But given the underlying reason for his quarrel with Achilles and the fact that his authority is based on social status, Agamemnon's stance here seems unexpected (Dué and Ebbott 2010, 283–4 on *Il.* 10.237–40). Even so, it may be explained both through his concern for the safety of Menelaus (*Il.* 10.240; see also *Il.* 4.148, 153, 178–81; 7.109–19) and as a marked contrast to the defeatism he had shown in book 9, where he had used the exact opposite line of thought (*Il.* 9.160–1; see also *Il.* 9.392); see also Sammons (2009) 40–2 with n. 53.

[61] See *Il.* 10.234–53: Agamemnon > Diomedes > Odysseus.

[62] On Nestor's adding value, see Diomedes' words at *Il.* 10.164–7 that reflect this assumption: σχέτλιός ἐσσι, γεραιέ· σὺ μὲν πόνου οὔ ποτε λήγεις. | οὔ νυ καὶ ἄλλοι ἔασι νεώτεροι υἷες Ἀχαιῶν, | οἵ κεν ἔπειτα ἕκαστον ἐγείρειαν βασιλήων | πάντῃ ἐποιχόμενοι· σὺ δ' ἀμήχανός ἐσσι, γεραιέ ("Aged sir, you are a hard man. You are never finished with working. Now are there not other sons of the Achaeans younger than you are who could be going about everywhere to each of the princes and waking them up? But you, aged sir, are too much for us"). Nestor's presence guarantees that a wise plan will be devised. His age functions as a further motivation for the Achaean leaders. If an old man undertakes this initiative, the younger ones are expected to follow his lead.

[63] See section 6.1.8, above.

[64] Reichel (1994, 296) has argued that, of the seven principal guards, the four who survive the war (Thrasymedes, Ialmenus, Meriones, and Lycomedes) must have been taken up by the *Iliad* from the larger Trojan War tradition or other earlier oral epics. Conversely, the other three leaders (Ascalaphus, Aphareus, and Deipyrus), who are all killed in the *Iliad*, seem to have been invented by this epic, as they have no other function in the entire epic tradition. They serve to give the sum of the number "seven," by which means Homer draws a connection to the seven gates of the Achaean Wall, i.e. to a motif probably taken from Theban epic; see Reinhardt (1961) 191–206; Torres-Guerra (1995) 55–7; M. L. West (2011a) on *Il.* 9.81–6. Reichel (1994, 296) also draws attention to the fact that the three leaders who die

Wall to protect the camp is due to the fear of an imminent attack by Hector and the Trojans who have been stationed on the battlefield for the night (*Il*. 9.75–9).[65] In book 9 this undertaking was paired with the pressing need for a plan that would save the Achaeans.[66] This plan was the embassy to Achilles. Both initiatives suggested by Nestor in *Iliad* 9 are carried out. However, none of them produces results, unless we take into account book 10, where the former initiative of book 9 (garrison) is activated in order to support the implementation of a plan (the night mission) that presupposes the failure of the latter initiative (embassy to Achilles). The narrative activation of the garrison and of its placement is a well-planned strategy on the part of the *Iliad* so that two of the guards (Thrasymedes and Meriones) join the Achaean leaders, who hold a council beyond the ditch. These two guards are equipped with the special gear that is given to Diomedes and Odysseus for the night mission. The narrative use in book 10 of the garrison and its placement allows us to entertain the thought that the *Doloneia* has turned these two "morbid" elements of book 9 on their head. While in *Iliad* 9 their aim was to protect the Achaeans from Hector, in an earlier version of *Iliad* 10 they may have been part of a plan to kill him.

6.1.11 The Arming Scene

The arming of Diomedes and Odysseus is well suited to a putative version in which the failed attempt to kill a major enemy lies at the heart of the conceived plan. One may counterargue that spies must be armed even if their aim is to retrieve information, since they may have to face enemies. However, the gear with which they are presented is hardly suitable to a spying mission (as shown in table 6.1).

Table 6.1 Gear Used by Diomedes and Odysseus in *Iliad* 10

Spies	Gear when they go the council	Gear they receive from Thrasymedes and Meriones
Diomedes	spear	double-edged sword, shield, and helmet of bull's hide
Odysseus	shield	bow and quiver, sword, and leather helmet

---

in the *Iliad* do so within a range of sixty verses (*Il*. 13.518 [Ascalaphus], 541 [Aphareus], 576 [Deipyrus]) and in the same order. They are also mentioned in the same order (together with Meriones and Antilochus) a few lines before they are killed (*Il*. 13.477–9).

[65] Achaean anxiety about a large-scale attack during the night is consonant with the large number of warriors (100) that each of the seven guards has in his command (*Il*. 9.85–7).

[66] Nestor's diction in *Il*. 9.75–6 (μάλα δὲ χρεὼ πάντας Ἀχαιούς | ἐσθλῆς καὶ πυκινῆς) and 9.78 (διαρραίσει στρατὸν ἠὲ σαώσει) is reiterated by Agamemnon in *Il*. 10.43–5 (χρεὼ βουλῆς ἐμὲ καὶ σέ, διοτρεφὲς ὦ Μενέλαε, | κερδαλέης, ἥ τίς κεν ἐρύσσεται ἠδὲ σαώσει | Ἀργείους καὶ νῆας).

What a spy needs when he is sent on a reconnaissance mission during the night is camouflage and a sword. The latter is the only weapon that can be readily used in close combat, if the spy is discovered by the enemy or if he needs to kill guards in order to get as close as possible to the area where he will find the information he is seeking. In this respect, the leather helmets and swords with which Diomedes and Odysseus are equipped by Thrasymedes and Meriones after the council of the Achaean leaders and the wolfskin, cap of marten's hide, and sword of Dolon are the only type of gear that seem perfectly suited to spying missions.[67]

Conversely, the spear and bow, with which Diomedes and Odysseus are equipped, do not fit a spying mission but, rather, an ambuscade.[68] They are weapons suitable for distant fighting that allow for a surprise attack. The shield is protective gear that may be used to protect an archer.[69] As for the sword, it may occasionally be employed in ambuscades, if the ambushers face the enemy in close combat.

What happens in *Iliad* 10? Diomedes' spear is used for the capture of Dolon.[70] The other weapon that plays a significant role is Diomedes' sword, with which he decapitates Dolon[71] and kills Rhesus and his twelve Thracian guards.[72] As for Odysseus, he does not employ his sword, whereas his bow is put to a totally different use,[73] as a whip to stir Rhesus' horses.[74] As for Dolon, his weapons are completely useless.

In this way, the gear of all three spies in *Iliad* 10 includes weapons that are suitable for both a spying mission and an ambuscade, although the two ambuscades that take place (of Dolon and Rhesus) are completely unplanned when the Achaean spies depart for their night mission.[75] This wide range of weapons belonging to two different types of missions, of which only one is planned, alerts the audience to an earlier version of *Iliad* 10 from which the epic is departing. In that version, there was no spying mission, and Diomedes and Odysseus were armed with weapons fitting for an ambuscade against Hector. However, these

---

[67] Diomedes: *Il.* 10.178 and 256–8; Odysseus: *Il.* 10.149 and 259–61; Dolon: *Il.* 10.333–5 and 458–9.
[68] For the pertinence of the bow in ambush missions during the night, see Farron (2003) 169–84; Dué and Ebbott (2010) 58–62.
[69] In *Il.* 8.266–72, Teucer is protected by the shield of his brother Ajax while he is shooting arrows; see Dué and Ebbott (2010) 60.
[70] *Il.* 10.365–77.
[71] *Il.* 10.455–6: ἁψάμενος λίσσεσθαι, ὁ δ' αὐχένα μέσσον ἔλασσεν | φασγάνῳ ἀΐξας, ἀπὸ δ' ἄμφω κέρσε τένοντε.
[72] *Il.* 10.483–4, 487–8, 494–6.
[73] Dué and Ebbott (2010, 57–62) argue that the bow is a typical ambush weapon and explain the fact that it is misused by Odysseus and not used at all by Dolon as stemming either from a tendency to confound expectations in spying missions and ambush episodes or from the pressure exercised by the thematic typology of these episodes, which virtually dictated the use of regular features, even of those remaining inactive or narratively unexplored.
[74] *Il.* 10.500, 516.
[75] Diomedes' spear (which he already has with him when he goes to the council) is rather oddly used to panic Dolon into being captured.

weapons would not be used against him, who must remain alive, but only in the capture and killing of Dolon, who is essential for the plot, since he would have specified to Diomedes and Odysseus the very spot where Hector was sleeping.

6.1.12 Praying before Undertaking a Difficult Task

The departure of the two Achaean spies is marked by their successive prayers to Athena. Odysseus asks her to help them accomplish a μέγα ἔργον that will cause trouble to the Trojans, reminding her that she had always stood beside him in all hard tasks and never forgotten him as he went his way.[76] "In all hard tasks" (ἐν πάντεσσι πόνοισι, Il. 10.279) is conspicuously vague, though there are some hints that allow us to be more specific.

First, Diomedes explained his choice of Odysseus for the night mission on the basis of (a) Athena's constant support of him (sc. Odysseus) in "all hard tasks"[77] and (b) Odysseus' mental skills that will make their successful return possible.[78] While Diomedes may be basing his judgment on what he has heard about Odysseus, it is more likely that he is referring to a previous collaboration of theirs, under Athena's tutelage. It is also important to note that Diomedes does not mention Athena's support and Odysseus' shrewdness in relation to the success of the mission but, rather, to their safe return. This situation can hardly pertain to the plot of book 10, since Diomedes and Odysseus return safely to the ships after having accomplished an even more important task than the one which they initially planned. Conversely, it is relevant to a situation in which they would not have achieved anything but were able to return safely to the ships.[79]

Second, there is the telling detail about the crying heron, which they interpret as a good sign sent by Athena. The heron is a rapacious bird showing ambush-like behavior when hunting at night.[80] However, Diomedes and Odysseus are at this point departing for a spying mission, not an ambush. The heron would suit a context in which the two heroes were setting out for an ambuscade.

Diomedes too prays to Athena (Il. 10.284–94), citing the help the goddess had previously given to his father, Tydeus. Diomedes could have referred to Athena's help to him during his aristeia in Iliad 5, but chooses not to do so. Instead, his

---

[76] Il. 10.278–82: ...ἥ τέ μοι αἰεί | ἐν πάντεσσι πόνοισι παρίστασαι, οὐδέ σε λήθω | κινύμενος...|...| ῥέξαντας μέγα ἔργον, ὅ κε Τρώεσσι μελήσῃ.
[77] Il. 10.244–5: οὗ πέρι μὲν πρόφρων κραδίη καὶ θυμὸς ἀγήνωρ | ἐν πάντεσσι πόνοισι, φιλεῖ δέ ἑ Παλλὰς Ἀθήνη.
[78] Il. 20.246–7: τούτου γ' ἑσπομένοιο καὶ ἐκ πυρὸς αἰθομένοιο | ἄμφω νοστήσαιμεν, ἐπεὶ περίοιδε νοῆσαι. Odysseus' success in achieving nostos is significantly resonant of his heroic career.
[79] Although in an earlier version Diomedes could not have known that their plan to kill Hector would fail, the way he justifies the selection of Odysseus would have functioned as an ironic hint to such a development.
[80] Dué and Ebbott (2010) 297.

aristeia is framed by two references to Tydeus by Agamemnon (*Il.* 4.384-400) and Athena (*Il.* 5.800-24), respectively, set in the context of the events immediately preceding the expedition of the seven against Thebes, which could have featured in Theban epic.[81] By referencing Athena's assistance to his father, who successfully ambushes the Cadmeans, Diomedes seems to recall Agamemnon's earlier use of the same episode in book 4. But, whereas Agamemnon employed the narrative of Tydeus' victorious ambush to criticize Diomedes, Diomedes uses it to place himself on a par with his father, who had led a successful ambush against his enemies.[82] Thus the *Doloneia* uses this story pattern to create an analogy between Diomedes' and Odysseus' night mission and Tydeus' intrusion into enemy territory in Theban myth.[83] The analogy is further strengthened, if we bear in mind that the initial goal of the mission of both Tydeus and Diomedes was not to inflict injuries on the enemy but to bring a message (Tydeus)[84] and get information (Diomedes). The ambush occurs unexpectedly on both occasions.

The content of the two prayers conforms with two different versions of book 10. Odysseus' prayer depicts a mission that is analogous to a previous task of great importance, a μέγα ἔργον accomplished by him and Diomedes by means of an ambuscade. The only case known to us is the killing of Palamedes in the epic tradition of the *Cypria*, in which the two heroes ambush Palamedes while on a fishing trip, in all likelihood to prevent that hero from stealing the plaudits for saving the Achaeans from famine.[85] Odysseus' prayer alerts the audience to a version of book 10 in which Diomedes and Odysseus would have departed for an ambush in order to accomplish a major deed. As in the *Cypria*, where they ambushed and killed Palamedes, so in an earlier version of *Iliad* 10 they aimed to ambush and kill Hector. Conversely, Diomedes' prayer is more in tune with the current version of book 10. As Tydeus was saved with Athena's help in the unexpected ambush set by the Cadmeans in the Theban tradition, so he will be supported by Athena when he (equally unexpectedly) ambushes Rhesus in *Iliad* 10.[86] In this light, it is possible that only Odysseus would have prayed to Athena in the Hector-version, Diomedes' prayer being devised for the current version of the *Doloneia*.

---

[81] On the Theban resonances of Diomedes' Iliadic career more generally, see pp. 36, 42-3, 166 n. 27.
[82] See Elmer (forthcoming).   [83] See Alden (2000) 143-9; see also p. 198 n. 46 (this volume).
[84] Perhaps aiming at recognizing Polynices' right to kingship in alternative years; for an analogous case, see the embassy of Menelaus and Odysseus to Troy that aimed to convince the Trojans to give Helen back and thus avoid the war. This episode is mentioned at *Il.* 3.204-24 and *Cypr.* arg. ll. 152-3 Severyns.
[85] On Palamedes' murder in the *Cypria*, see arg. l. 166 Severyns and fr. 27 GEF. Notice that νοστήσαιμεν (*Il.* 10.247) is consonant with the fact that Diomedes and Odysseus would have returned to the Greek camp from the place Palamedes had gone (Pausanias' προελθόντα ἐπὶ ἰχθύων θήραν shows that Palamedes had gone on a fishing trip). The episode of Palamedes' murder in the *Cypria* must have preceded that of the daughters of Anius (the Oenotropi); see M. L. West (2013a) 124-5; on the *Iliad*'s knowledge of Palamedes, see Kullmann (1960) 301-2; Wehr (2015) 85-7 with n. 9; Davies (2019) 178-9.
[86] In Theban myth Tydeus is ambushed, in book 10 Diomedes (his son) is the ambusher.

6.2 The Doloneia Proper

6.2.1 The Two-Mission Motif

By turning the focus to Hector, who is not asleep but summons a council of the Trojans, *Iliad* 10 puts in motion the story of Dolon. This figure, who is not the invention of the *Iliad*,[87] is essential for the plot of book 10. Although he never furnishes the spies with the information they are initially seeking, since he does not reveal the Trojan plan for the next day, he does reveal to them Rhesus' whereabouts. This unplanned and accidental shift in the plot of the night mission is probably a development that has originated because of the introduction of the Rhesus episode.

In an earlier version of book 10, Dolon may have been equally, if not more, essential to the plot, since he may have provided Diomedes and Odysseus with the necessary information about Hector's whereabouts. This line of thought capitalizes on the function of the two-mission motif, which is attested in the two missions of Odysseus to Troy in the *Ilias parva*. In that epic the first mission[88] is a reconnaissance that prepares the second,[89] more important mission. Odysseus acquires from Helen the necessary information so that he can subsequently steal the Palladium with the help of Diomedes.[90] In order to accommodate the two-mission motif to its plot, it is suggested that the *Iliad* resorts to the device of *a parallel mission* by Dolon, who would be arrested so that he can provide the necessary information about Hector's whereabouts.[91] In the current version of book 10, the prerequisite for Dolon's parallel mission is the Trojan council that duplicates the preceding Achaean council. The reason that makes the Trojan council necessary is that in the current version Dolon is a spy, so he needs to be appointed by a council. A second prerequisite for Dolon's spying mission is that Hector must be awake, since a Trojan council without him is unthinkable. Moreover, Hector's sleeplessness matches that of Agamemnon and allows the *Iliad* to avoid a situation in which *both* Hector and Rhesus would be asleep, since it would not be possible or effective to justify the interest of the spies in Rhesus instead of Hector.[92]

---

[87] For a thorough analysis, see Dué and Ebbott (2010) 106-19; also pp. 57-8, 228 n. 80 (this volume).

[88] Odysseus and Helen: *Il. parv.* arg. ll. 224-7 Severyns; frs. 8-10 *GEF*.

[89] Odysseus and Diomedes steal the Palladium: *Il. parv.* arg. ll. 228-9 Severyns; fr. 11 *GEF*.

[90] On the use of the same motif in a night mission, see the story of David and Saul in the Hebrew Bible (1 Sam. 26). David and Abishai infiltrate Saul's camp twice—the first time in the context of a reconnaissance mission and the second to ambush and kill Saul.

[91] If so, in typical neoanalytical manner, a motif has been transferred from an earlier to a newer version and has been applied to a new figure.

[92] The two councils of Achaeans and Trojans in *Iliad* 10 are paralleled by the two assemblies of both armies in *Iliad* 2; see Heiden (2008) 73-4.

This interpretation is strongly supported by Dolon's reply to the spies in *Il.* 10.413–22, where he reveals that the Trojans are awake, while their allies are sleeping. It is exactly at this point that Odysseus becomes interested in the allies and asks Dolon if they have camped separately from the Trojans or together with them.[93] Dolon's detailed mapping of the area in which the allies are stationed paves the way for the night raid.[94] Therefore, it may be argued that when the story of Rhesus was introduced into *Iliad* 10, Hector had to acquire an active role, given that he could not be sleeping. As a result, Dolon was, arguably, anchored to Hector by means of the council, in which Hector would ask for a volunteer spy.

There are further traces of the introduction of the Trojan council in book 10. Dolon is the only one to answer Hector's call. This is a marked antithesis to the Achaean council, in which various heroes volunteer.[95] Moreover, Hector's plan is odd. What is the purpose of finding out whether the Achaeans are guarding their ships, since the latter constitute a *conditio sine qua non* for their return to Greece? Whether they intend to sail right away or not, their ships have to be protected.[96] They are their only means of successfully returning home. The only factor of consideration to Hector is whether the Achaeans are about to make a run for it during the night, since he intends to cause them even more losses. This is exactly his plan at *Il.* 8.510–16. It is for this reason that he has ordered the Trojans to illuminate the night sky by burning many fires,[97] since they will thus be able to see whether the Achaeans intend to sail away back to Greece.[98]

The Trojan council in *Iliad* 10 and the selection of Dolon as a spy with a plan that is at least unnecessary after Hector's "first" plan in *Il.* 8.510–11 may be the result of the changes implemented in the *Doloneia* after the introduction of the episode of Rhesus.

6.2.2 Dolon in the Hector-Version

In the Hector-version Dolon may not have been a spy sent by Hector but a Trojan who left his camp to loot the bodies of the dead warriors that filled the plain, until he was caught, interrogated, killed, and finally stripped of his weapons by Diomedes and Odysseus. Hector, like Rhesus in the current version of book 10, was asleep and, therefore, not involved in Dolon's undertaking.

---

[93] *Il.* 10.424–5: πῶς γὰρ νῦν, Τρώεσσι μεμιγμένοι ἱπποδάμοισιν | εὕδουσ', ἦ ἀπάνευθε; δίειπέ μοι, ὄφρα δαείω.
[94] *Il.* 10.427–41.
[95] *Il.* 10.227–31: Diomedes, the two Ajaxes, Meriones, Thrasymedes, Menelaus, and Odysseus.
[96] On the analogous oddity of Nestor's plan in book 10, see pp. 174 with n. 50 and 178.
[97] *Il.* 8.508–9: ὥς κεν παννύχιοι μέσφ' ἠοῦς ἠριγενείης | καίωμεν πυρὰ πολλά, σέλας δ' εἰς οὐρανὸν ἵκῃ; also *Il.* 8.553–63; see especially *Il.* 8.562: 1,000 fires.
[98] *Il.* 8.510–11: μή πως καὶ διὰ νύκτα κάρη κομόωντες Ἀχαιοί | φεύγειν ὁρμήσωνται ἐπ' εὐρέα νῶτα θαλάσσης.

The *Iliad* provides several putative traces for this plotline. First, Odysseus asks Dolon whether he has left the Trojan camp on his own initiative, with the intention of "stripping someone of the perished corpses" (ἤ τινα συλήσων νεκύων κατατεθνηώτων),[99] or is a spy sent by Hector or acting on his own.[100] Respectively, these alternatives stem from the Hector-version, the current plotline, and an attempt to combine the two (where Dolon acts as a spy on his own initiative). A second trace is found at *Il.* 10.354–6, where the narrator reveals the reason why Dolon stops in his tracks when he hears a noise made by the Achaean spies.[101] Dolon thinks that his comrades have come to call him back, arguably because in the Hector-version he knew that he had not obeyed orders and had acted on his own. In the current version, it seems inexplicable why Dolon would have thought so if he was obeying orders. Why would he think that Hector had changed a plan that he had just devised? The phrase Ἕκτορος ὀτρύναντος may well reflect the Hector-version, in which Hector had ordered that no warrior was allowed to exit the Trojan camp and that everybody should wait until dawn, when he would attack the Achaeans. πάλιν ("again") seems to reflect the attempt of the current version of book 10 to explain Dolon's awkward interpretation of the noise made by the Achaean spies that he mistakes for Trojan activity. A third trace is suggested by the name of Dolon itself. Although most obviously associated with δόλος, Dolon is the antithesis of trickery in book 10. In sharp contrast to what the name of his father Eumedes (< εὖ + μήδομαι, "the Goodplotter") signifies, Dolon is "unusually forthcoming with helpful information when being interrogated by Odysseus and Diomedes."[102] The disjunction is all the more jarring because we do not know anything about his father, Eumedes, apart from the fact that he is a herald. The possibility that Dolon had earned his name not because of trickery but through an ironic contrast to his father would presuppose that his father had devised and/or carried out a "good plot," as his name suggests.[103] This is not the case. There is no oddity or inconsistency, if we follow the reconstruction of the Hector-version that I have suggested. In this earlier form of the *Doloneia*, so this account goes, Dolon would have attempted to trick (and thus deceive) Hector by

---

[99] *Il.* 10.387.
[100] *Il.* 10.388–9: ἤ σ' Ἕκτωρ προέηκε διασκοπιᾶσθαι ἕκαστα | νῆας ἔπι γλαφυράς; ἦ σ' αὐτὸν θυμὸς ἀνῆκε.
[101] τὼ μὲν ἐπεδραμέτην, ὁ δ' ἄρ' ἔστη δοῦπον ἀκούσας. | ἔλπετο γὰρ κατὰ θυμὸν ἀποστρέψοντας ἑταίρους | ἐκ Τρώων ἰέναι, πάλιν Ἕκτορος ὀτρύναντος.
[102] See Duffy (2019) 101 with n. 14, who objects to Hesk's suggestion (2013, 51–2) that Dolon tries to distract the Achaean spies from the Trojans by sending them to Rhesus. There is no trick here at all, the more so since Rhesus and twelve of his troops are killed by Diomedes.
[103] On the contrary, since tricksters are tricked too, Dolon must have been presented as attempting to trick someone, even if he failed; see Duffy (2019)101–2: "It is rare for a Homeric hero to have a name that does not connect to his own attributes and actions, particularly those that have a name as unusual as Dolon. Furthermore, while trickster figures can suffer deception, this usually happens to characters who are at least attempting to engage in trickery on their own, with Prometheus providing a particularly good example from Greek myth."

leaving the Trojan camp in secret to loot the bodies of the dead on the battlefield. However, instead of looting the dead warriors he would be killed and subsequently stripped of his weapons by Diomedes and Odysseus. His δόλος, albeit short-lived, would justify his speaking name.[104]

6.2.3 The Disclosure of Information

In the Hector-version the spies would have arrested Dolon and asked him about Hector's whereabouts. Traces of this scene may be found at *Il.* 10.406-8 (ποῦ νῦν δεῦρο κιὼν λίπες Ἕκτορα, ποιμένα λαῶν; | ποῦ δέ οἱ ἔντεα κεῖται ἀρήϊα, ποῦ δέ οἱ ἵπποι; | πῶς δαὶ τῶν ἄλλων Τρώων φυλακαί τε καὶ εὐναί;).[105] Dolon would have revealed to the spies where Hector was sleeping. Diomedes would have subsequently killed Dolon, and the spies would have stored his weapons next to a bush, so that they could take them back to their camp on their return and dedicate them to Athena, i.e. exactly as happens at *Il.* 10.458–68 and 10.526-31.[106]

6.2.4 Mission Aborted

The killing of Hector that was the target of the night mission in the Hector-version was not carried out. The reason is simple: Hector had to be spared for he was instrumental in the unraveling of the plot. His death at the hands of Achilles was a fixed element of the epic *Faktenkanon*.[107] A hint to this fleeting reference to the frustration of this plan seems to be found in [Eur.] *Rhesus*, when Athena realizes that Odysseus and Diomedes are about to return to the Greek camp after having failed to kill Hector (580–1: οὐ γὰρ ηὕρομεν | τὸν ἄνδρ' ἐν εὐναῖς, ἐλπίδων δ' ἡμάρτομεν). Because of this, the goddess directs them to Rhesus, adding...τὰς δ' Ἕκτορος | εὐνὰς ἔασον καὶ καρατόμους σφαγάς (605–6). Odysseus and Diomedes have decided to return to the ships and not try to kill some other major Trojan

---

[104] Aristophanes of Byzantium's ἤπαφεν Ἕκτωρ (Σ [Aim Til] *Il.* 10.391b [Erbse]) instead of ἤγαγεν Ἕκτωρ at *Il.* 10.391 may be an attempt to explain Dolon's speaking name by having him present himself to the Achaean spies as the victim of Hector's deception; on this interpretation, see Duffy (2019) 101–2, who treats ἤπαφεν Ἕκτωρ as a multiform.

[105] On these verses, see pp. 167, 180–1, 184 with n. 98.

[106] Verses 10.391–411, which are the part of the dialogue between Odysseus and Dolon that pertains to Hector's deception of Dolon and the horses of Achilles, would not have featured in the earlier version of book 10. These verses continue a line of thought that has started in the dialogue between Hector and Dolon in the Trojan council, which (as argued above) was not part of the Hector-version of the *Doloneia*. These two dialogue scenes (10.303-31 and 10.391-411) were shaped when the Rhesus episode was added to the earlier version. On the poetic gain of this shaping, see pp. 242–3.

[107] The same is the case in the Saul and David story in the Hebrew Bible (1 Sam. 26). After infiltrating the enemy camp, David and Abishai do not kill Saul because David declares that Saul is the Lord's anointed and, as such, must be spared. The Lord will in his own good time bring his end either in battle or in some other way; on this episode, see briefly M. L. West (1997) 374–5.

(like Aeneas or Paris), though they have been frustrated in their desire to kill Hector. Athena consoles them in their grief that a god has not allowed them to kill Hector or Paris, but proposes a new task, the killing of the Thracian king Rhesus (595-607), adding that "death will come to him from another hand" (607: ἔσται γὰρ αὐτῷ θάνατος ἐξ ἄλλης χερός).[108] I suggest that in the Hector-version of *Iliad* 10 the plot may have continued more or less in the following way: the Achaean spies find Hector sleeping and, when they are ready to strike him a mortal blow, Athena appears to instruct them that it is not destined for Hector to die at this point and that they should return to their camp before the Trojans are woken by some god (see *Il.* 10.509-10).

This line of thought is supported by the fact that such an allusive technique reflects Homeric practice and that Athena features in such a role. At *Il.* 5.662 (ἔτι) and 5.674-5 (οὐδ' ἄρ' Ὀδυσῆϊ...μόρσιμον ἦεν | ...Διὸς υἱὸν ἀποκτάμεν, "yet, as it was not the destiny of Odysseus...to kill the son of Zeus"), the poet hints at his plan to let Sarpedon live for the time being.[109] Athena becomes the means by which the poet carries out this aim: "she steered his (*sc.* Odysseus') anger against the host of the Lycians" (τώ ῥα κατὰ πληθὺν Λυκίων τράπεν θυμὸν Ἀθήνη, *Il.* 5.676). Likewise, in *Od.* 19.478-9, Athena prevents Penelope from recognizing Odysseus "by turning her mind away" (τῇ γὰρ Ἀθηναίη νόον ἔτραπεν). As Currie has put it, "Athene's intervention here, dispensable as it is, arguably serves to draw attention to the fact that the poet is denying the audience a recognition between husband and wife at this point."[110] Furthermore and returning to the *Iliad*, a failed attempt to kill Hector in an earlier version of book 10 would have been in tune with a series of failed attempts to kill him at *Il.* 7.260-2 and 7.268-72 (Ajax), 8.309-11 (Teucer),[111] 11.349-67 (Diomedes).[112]

---

[108] This *hysteron proteron* in literary terms capitalizes on the rich allusive force of the phrase ἐξ ἄλλης χερός. For an audience familiar with archaic Greek epic, the use of this expression flags an interaction with the tradition of the *Iliad*. Fact (Hector's death by Achilles) is here presented as a future possibility (without specific designation of Hector's killer). This is a case of "future reflexive", since what is presented as a potential future outcome has happened in an earlier text (the *Iliad*); on such signaling of the source, see Currie (2016) 66-7; on "future reflexive," see Barchiesi (2001) 105-27.

[109] Likewise, the expression κακοῦ δ' ἄρα οἱ πέλεν ἀρχή ("and this was the beginning of his evil") in *Il.* 11.604 refers to the unfolding of events that will lead to the death of Patroclus. On innovation within tradition as represented by the example of Sarpedon, see Barker (2011) 1-17.

[110] This may well be a hint that a recognition between Penelope and Odysseus happened before the killing of the suitors in an earlier poem about Odysseus' homecoming; see Currie (2016) 47-55 with further bibliography.

[111] I omit *Il.* 8.167-70 because Diomedes is not allowed even to attempt to kill Hector because of the early intervention of Zeus.

[112] These considerations are not weakened by the fact that unlike *Il.* 16.431-61, which not only dramatizes Sarpedon's fate (Schmitz 1994, 11; J. V. Morrison 1997, 283-5; S. Richardson 1990, 193-5) and Zeus' dilemma about whether to save his son (gods can operate as figures of tradition; see Rutherford 2013², 51) but also reflects the *Memnonis* (Currie 2016, 66-7), [Eur.] *Rh.* 607 does not acknowledge the poetic context from which the motif has been transferred, since an earlier version of *Iliad* 10 was probably unknown to the poet of the *Rhesus*. In this vein, the playwright may have used a Homeric technique that he had observed in the case of Sarpedon and applied it to Rhesus; see Fantuzzi (2020) 472 on [Eur.] *Rh.* 605-7.

Athena's intervention would have made the spies return to the Achaean camp. Upon their return, they would have been received with joy by Nestor, as well as perhaps by Agamemnon, Menelaus, and others. The phrase τοὶ δὲ χαρέντες | δεξιῇ ἠσπάζοντο ἔπεσσί τε μειλιχίοισι[113] fits well any dangerous mission, be it the one in the Hector-version or the one in the current version of book 10. But the level of satisfaction that the leaders experience upon seeing the spies return safely to the camp differs enormously between the two storylines. In the Hector-version, initial relief must have soon given way to disappointment, when it became known that the mission had not been successful, since Hector was not killed.

6.2.5 Dedicating the Spolia

In the current version of book 10, the Achaean spies take Dolon's weapons, store them in a safe place next to a tamarisk or marsh-shrub, and ultimately dedicate them to Athena by placing them on the prow of Odysseus' ship upon their return to the camp. This is a surprising development, since the spies do not dedicate to Athena their most important prize, the wonderful horses of Rhesus. After all it was Athena who advised Diomedes when to leave the enemy camp, lest some other god wake up the Trojans.[114] The oddity of having the spies keep the exceptional part of the booty and offer Athena the weapons of a completely unimportant, third-rate warrior may be easily solved, if we consider the possibility that Dolon's weapons would have been the *only* trophy of Diomedes and Odysseus in the Hector-version in which there was no Rhesus and, therefore, no horses of his to steal.

The suggested reconstruction of the Hector-version of *Iliad* 10 is, like all reconstructions, a putative endeavor trading on unknowns. What has been argued is undeniably provisional. However, this was not, I hope, a leap into the dark. After using several arguments based on analogy and comparison to offer a potential restoration of an earlier version of book 10, many features of the current version are, arguably, explained in a more rewarding way than they have been up to now. Coarse-grained answers to such thorny questions as the creation and function of the *Doloneia* can hardly be given. Nor is there an acid test that would decide such an issue once and for all. After all, much in classical scholarship is about weighing probabilities. The proposed reconstruction has no claim on perfection. Nevertheless, it may be suggested that it has more edge than its dismissive alternative, according to which there was an *Iliad* without the *Doloneia* that was composed by a different poet who imposed his will to the entire Iliadic tradition by making his version the canonical one.

---

[113] *Il*. 10.541–2.
[114] *Il*. 10.509–11: νόστου δὴ μνῆσαι, μεγαθύμου Τυδέος υἱέ, | νῆας ἔπι γλαφυράς, μὴ καὶ πεφοβημένος ἔλθῃς, | μή πού τις καὶ Τρῶας ἐγείρῃσιν θεὸς ἄλλος.

7
The Two Versions of the Rhesus Myth
Reconstruction of Possible Sources

Introduction

So far my argument builds on Fenik's approach,[1] though (I hope) in a more robust and detailed manner. But unlike Fenik, I have maintained that the *Doloneia* did not involve the Rhesus episode in the "Hector-phase." It entailed only a failed attempt to kill Hector. In this chapter, I suggest that the "Rhesus-phase" represents the second stage in the shaping of *Iliad* 10. This phase starts when the Iliadic tradition moves away from having Hector as the main target of the spying mission. Key to the interpretation of the story of Rhesus is what has been known (after Fenik) as the Pindaric and oracle versions which are reported by the Homeric scholia.

This chapter contains the following sections: transmission of the Pindaric and oracle versions of Rhesus' story (section 7.1); examination of the scholia transmitting these versions (section 7.2); evaluation of the results of this examination (section 7.3); reconstruction of the possible sources of the Pindaric and oracle versions (section 7.4); putative poetic gains from the addition of the episode of Rhesus to book 10 (section 7.5).

7.1 Transmission

1. Σ Il. 10.435 (bT): Ῥῆσος Στρυμόνος τοῦ ποταμοῦ τῆς Θράκης υἱὸς καὶ Εὐτέρπης Μούσης. ἱστορεῖ δὲ Πίνδαρος (fr. 262 S–M) ὅτι καὶ μίαν ἡμέραν πολεμήσας πρὸς Ἕλληνας μέγιστα αὐτοῖς ἐνεδείξατο κακά, κατὰ δὲ πρόνοιαν Ἥρας καὶ Ἀθηνᾶς ἀναστάντες οἱ περὶ Διομήδεα ἀναιροῦσιν αὐτόν.

3 κατὰ δὲ πρόνοιαν Ἥρας καὶ Ἀθηνᾶς T: κατὰ δὲ θείαν πρόνοιαν b ‖ 4 ἀναστάντες οἱ περὶ Διομήδεα ἀναιροῦσιν αὐτόν T: νυκτὸς αὐτὸν Διομήδης ἀναιρεῖ b

Rhesus, the son of the river Strymon of Thrace and of the Muse Euterpe. Pindar records that though he fought against the Greeks for one day, he caused to them

---

[1] Fenik (1964).

the greatest harm. Owing to the foresight of Hera and Athena, those in the company of Diomedes[2] wake up and kill him.

2. *Σ Il.* 10.435/Z^S (D [ZYQXAIG]): Ῥῆσος γένει μὲν Θρᾷξ ἦν, υἱὸς δὲ Στρυμόνος, τοῦ αὐτόθι ποταμοῦ, καὶ Εὐτέρπης, μιᾶς τῶν Μουσῶν. διάφορος δὲ τῶν καθ' αὑτὸν γενόμενος ἐν πολεμικοῖς ἔργοις ἐπῆλθε τοῖς Ἕλλησιν, ὅπως Τρωσὶ συμμαχήσῃ, καὶ συμβαλὼν πολλοὺς τῶν Ἑλλήνων ἀπέκτεινεν. δείσασα δὲ Ἥρα περὶ τῶν Ἑλλήνων Ἀθηνᾶν ἐπὶ τὴν τούτου διαφθορὰν πέμπει, κατελθοῦσα δὲ ἡ θεὸς Ὀδυσσέα τε καὶ Διομήδην ἐπὶ τὴν κατασκοπὴν ἐποίησεν προελθεῖν. ἐπιστάντες δὲ ἐκεῖνοι κοιμωμένῳ Ῥήσῳ αὐτόν τε καὶ τοὺς ἑταίρους αὐτοῦ κτείνουσιν, ὡς ἱστορεῖ Πίνδαρος (fr. 262 S–M). (D [ZYQ(X)AUIG~T^r]): ἔνιοι δὲ λέγουσιν νυκτὸς παραγεγονέναι τὸν Ῥῆσον εἰς τὴν Τροίαν, καὶ πρὶν γεύσασθαι αὐτὸν τοῦ ὕδατος τῆς χώρας φονευθῆναι. χρησμὸς γὰρ ἐδέδοτο αὐτῷ φασιν, ὅτι εἰ αὐτός τε γεύσεται τοῦ ὕδατος καὶ οἱ ἵπποι αὐτοῦ τοῦ Σκαμάνδρου πίωσι καὶ τῆς αὐτόθι νομῆς, ἀκαταμάχητος ἔσται εἰς τὸ παντελές.

Rhesus was Thracian by descent, the son of Strymon, a river in the same region, and of Euterpe, one of the Muses. Since he excelled among the people of his age in warlike deeds, he came upon the Greeks, in order to be an ally of the Trojans and, after engaging in battle he killed many of the Greeks. Being worried about the Greeks, Hera sends Athena to destroy him. The goddess came down and made Odysseus and Diomedes go forth as spies. After standing next to Rhesus who was sleeping, they kill him and his comrades, as Pindar records.

But some say that Rhesus arrived at Troy in the night and was killed before he could taste the water of the land. For, they say, an oracle had been given about him, that if he tasted the water and his horses drank from the Scamander and the pasture there, he would be entirely invincible.

7.2 Examination

7.2.1 The Pindaric Version

The first scholion that cites the Pindaric version of the Rhesus story belongs to the *scholia vetera*. It is reported by b[3] and T,[4] as well as by A.[5] Since the text given by b and T is basically the same as A, I have decided to quote them together and append a critical apparatus containing variant readings.[6] The second scholion that reports both the Pindaric and the oracle version comes from the D-scholia. It comprises two parts, the Pindaric version and the oracle version, which are

---

[2] See p. 229 n. 81.
[3] *Corpus exegeticum codicum BCE³E⁴ quem Erbse b [codicem archetypum] nominavit.*
[4] Codex Townleianus (Brit. Mus. Burney 86, a.D. 1014 or 1059).
[5] Venetus graec. 882 (*olim* Marcianus graecus 454), tenth century.   [6] See p. 214.

clearly distinguished by the formula ἔνιοι δὲ λέγουσιν that introduces the oracle version.

As for the Pindaric version, the first part of the D-scholion offers an extended and more detailed presentation of the Rhesus story than bT. By comparing the two scholia we can trace the following similarities and differences:

Similarities:
1. Rhesus is Thracian.
2. He causes many losses to the Achaean army upon his arrival at Troy.
3. Hera and Athena, who support the Achaeans, undertake an initiative against him.
4. He is killed by Diomedes.

Differences:
1. In b and T Rhesus inflicts losses to the Achaeans in a single day (μίαν ἡμέραν);[7] this detail is missing from the D-scholion.
2. In the D-scholion Rhesus' military excellence is highlighted *before* coming to Troy (διάφορος δὲ τῶν καθ' αὐτὸν γενόμενος ἐν πολεμικοῖς ἔργοις) and inflicting great losses on the Achaeans.
3. In the D-scholion it is explicitly stated that he came to assist the Trojans (ὅπως Τρωσὶ συμμαχήσῃ), while b and T omit this detail.
4. In T the two divinities are mentioned by name (κατὰ δὲ πρόνοιαν Ἥρας καὶ Ἀθηνᾶς), in b they are grouped under the generalizing statement κατὰ δὲ θείαν πρόνοιαν, whereas in D it is Hera who incites Athena to visit Odysseus and Diomedes and suggests to them the idea of a spying mission (δείσασα δὲ Ἥρα περὶ τῶν Ἑλλήνων Ἀθηνᾶν ἐπὶ τὴν τούτου διαφθορὰν πέμπει).
5. In the D-scholion the reason for Hera's action is stated (δείσασα "because of fear").
6. In T the detail that the killing of Rhesus happened during the night is implied (ἀναστάντες), in b it is stated briefly (νυκτός), while in the D-scholion it is explained that Odysseus and Diomedes went on a spying mission, found Rhesus sleeping (D: ἐπιστάντες δὲ ἐκεῖνοι κοιμωμένῳ Ῥήσῳ), and killed him and his comrades (αὐτόν τε καὶ τοὺς ἑταίρους αὐτοῦ κτείνουσιν).

---

[7] In the *Rhesus* (447–9), Rhesus' boast that one day will be enough for him in order to invade the enemy camp, fall upon their ships, and kill the Achaeans may well reflect the Pindaric version that featured his *aristeia* in a single day. Rhesus' arrogant overconfidence, which is contradicted by his lengthy war against the Scythians (that passes unnoticed: Liapis 2012, 191 on [Eur.] *Rh.* 447–9) and aims to assert his superiority towards Hector, who has been unable to defeat the Achaeans after fighting them day after day for years (444–6), recalls Hector's arrogant overconfidence in the *Doloneia* that he will be able to defeat Achilles and acquire his immortal horses, which he will give to Dolon (*Il.* 10.305–6, 330–1); see also Nestor's assertion that he has never seen or heard of a man who has inflicted so many casualties to the Achaeans as Hector in a single day (*Il.* 10.47–9).

7. In b, only the killing of Rhesus is mentioned (ἀναιροῦσιν αὐτόν); in the D-scholion the two spies kill Rhesus and his comrades (αὐτόν τε καὶ τοὺς ἑταίρους αὐτοῦ κτείνουσιν).

As regards the Pindaric version of the Rhesus episode, b, T, and D share several similarities. Their differences are easily reconciled, if we treat the first section of the D-scholion as an expanded and more detailed version of b and T. This is not to say that the D-scholion has originated from b and T or that b and T are abbreviated or cropped versions of D. The picture is rather different.

A crucial issue in cases like this pertains to the extent and authority of the subscriptions (bT: ἱστορεῖ δὲ Πίνδαρος; D [ZYQXAIG]). The b and T exegetical scholia on *Il.* 10.435 contain parallel versions to the D-scholion on *Il.* 10.435,[8] which is more extended and detailed.[9] Van der Valk[10] treats the mythographical D-scholia as equally consistent with and not later than the material cited in analogous versions found in the Homeric exegetical scholia. This line of thought suggests that the D-scholion on *Il.* 10.435 runs parallel to the exegetical scholia b and T on the same Iliadic verse (all having as their starting point the first mention of the Thracian king Rhesus in the *Iliad*). As regards the subscriptions attributing the first version to Pindar, Lünstedt[11] has argued that the subscriptions incorporated in the *historiae* of the D-scholia are not unfounded.[12] They disclose the existence of a link between the *historia* and the author cited. This broad understanding of the poet's name so as to include both his own work and the scholiastic tradition on it is likely to point to ancient commentaries, in which the various lemmata followed the order of the text and were appended to specific words and phrases mentioned in the text. In this light, the formula ὡς ἱστορεῖ Πίνδαρος placed at the end of the first section of the D-scholion on *Il.* 10.435 may well refer to both Pindar's poetry and the ancient scholia on it.[13] At the same time,

---

[8] What is included in the D-scholion derives from the *Mythographus Homericus*. The term *Mythographus Homericus* refers to a lost *hypomnema* or commentary containing summaries of myths (*historiae fabulares*) that were briefly mentioned or alluded to in the Homeric epics. Each *historia* was tagged to a feature of the text, be it a word or expression which the compiler of the commentary thought needed to be elucidated for readers of Homer. The surviving material is found in several papyrus fragments dated from the first/second to the fifth century AD, as well as in the D-scholia (*Iliad*) and V-scholia (*Odyssey*). The compilation of such a work probably aimed at providing the necessary background information on the level of myth for a better understanding of the Homeric poems. Montanari (1995, 145) stresses the need to abandon the earlier designation of the *Mythographus Homericus* as a handbook. Differently Pagès (2017) 66, who still calls it a "handbook"; see Montanari (1995) 135–72, (2002) 129–44; van Rossum-Steenbeek (1998) 278–309; Montana and Montanari (2022) 31–56.

[9] It contains not only details that are absent from the b and T scholia but also, in its second part, a different version of the Rhesus episode, one in which the Thracian king has no *aristeia*, since he is killed during the first night he arrives at Troy, after Athena reveals to Odysseus and Diomedes that if he drinks from the water of Scamander and his horses graze at its banks he will be invincible.

[10] Van der Valk (1963–4) I 7, 303–14.   [11] Lünstedt (1961).

[12] See pp. 230 n. 83, 235 n. 103.

[13] By "ancient scholia on it" I am referring not only or exclusively to the ancient scholia on Pindar but also to topics mentioned in Pindaric poetry.

no subscription should lay a claim on exclusiveness, since some of the material of these *historiae* is derived from other sources, such as parallel texts by other authors or references to other texts mentioned in ancient *hypomnemata* and *syggrammata* transmitting a different version or part of a version of the same story.[14] For example, the initial designation (in both bT and D) of Rhesus' parents as the river Strymon and the Muse Euterpe should not be attributed to Pindar, who is mentioned in the second sentence for the testimony of Rhesus' *aristeia* in Troy and not in the first, which pertains to his parentage.[15] It is likely that Rhesus' divine parentage is based on [Euripides'] *Rhesus* and its own scholiastic tradition.[16]

The salient suggestion of this examination is that the subscriptions and authority of the Pindaric version recorded in the two scholia are trustworthy, with the exception of Rhesus' divine parentage and, arguably, previous military achievements, which do not come from Pindar.[17] I will now turn my focus to the diction of the D-scholion in an attempt to trace the origin of various features that have been fused into a unified short narrative.[18]

'Ῥῆσος γένει μὲν Θρᾷξ ἦν, υἱὸς δὲ Στρυμόνος, τοῦ αὐτόθι ποταμοῦ:
Although the divine parentage of Rhesus (mentioned in the two Homeric scholia) does not derive from Pindar but reflects the *Rhesus* and its scholiastic tradition, it is worth investigating the designation of Strymon as Rhesus' father, the more so since Rhesus' father in the *Iliad* is called Eioneus, whose name is based on Ἠιών ("riverbank or seashore") and refers to a town situated at the mouth of the river Strymon (Herod. 7.25).[19]

On these grounds Wilamowitz-Moellendorff[20] argued that Eioneus is the eponym of Eion by the river Strymon at the "border" of Macedonia and Thrace.[21] According to this line of reasoning, the water association of the name Eioneus is evident. Additionally, it is recorded that Strymon was king of the

---

[14] See Montanari (1995) 143–4, (2002) 134.
[15] Moreover, ancient sources offer various names for the Muse; see p. 221 with n. 49.
[16] See Rempe (1927) 38–9; Fries (2014) 13–14, (2016) 295 n. 10; Fantuzzi (2020) 334 on [Eur.] *Rh.* 346–8a.
[17] See the discussion on pp. 218–22 and 222–7, respectively. [18] See Pagès (2007) 323–5.
[19] Rhesus' Thracian origin and the fact that his father was the river Strymon is a feature also shared by the bT and D scholia. The beginning of the scholion, though conforming to the layout of a mythographic *historia*, is similar to the introduction of various late-arriving allies of the Trojans in the Proclan summaries of different Cyclic epics (I also append in each case the relevant passages from Apollodorus' *Epitome*): (a) *Aeth.* arg. ll. 175–6 Severyns: Ἀμαζὼν Πενθεσίλεια...Ἄρεως μὲν θυγάτηρ, Θρᾷσσα δὲ τὸ γένος / Apollod. *Epit.* 5.1 (epitoma Vaticana): ὅτι Πενθεσίλεια, Ὀτρηρῆς καὶ Ἄρεος; (b) *Aeth.* arg. ll. 185 Severyns: Μέμνων δὲ ὁ Ἠοῦς υἱός / Apollod. *Epit.* 5.3 (epitoma Vaticana): ὅτι Μέμνονα τὸν Τιθωνοῦ καὶ Ἠοῦς; (fragmenta Sabbaitica): Μέμνων δὲ ὁ Τιθωνοῦ καὶ Ἠοῦς; (c) *Il. parv.* arg. l. 219 Severyns: Εὐρύπυλος δὲ ὁ Τηλέφου / Apollod. *Epit.* 5.11 (epitoma Vaticana et fragmenta Sabbaitica): Εὐρύπυλος ὁ Τηλέφου (see also: P. Ryl. 22: [Εὐρύπυλος ὁ Τηλέφου υἱός]). In all these cases, the name of the late-arriving hero is given together with information concerning the hero's parents (and, in the case of Penthesileia, place of origin).
[20] Wilamowitz-Moellendorff (1884) 27 n. 15.
[21] See von Kamptz (1982) §§13a1, 80a1; also Herod. 7.25.

Thracians, Eioneus was his nickname, and Rhesus one of his three sons (the other two were Braggas and Olynthus).[22] Even if this is an attempt to reconcile the Homeric[23] with the Pindaric version of the story, the water association of Eioneus, his geographical link with Strymon, the fact that they are both presented as fathers of Rhesus in early versions of the story,[24] the use of the name Rhesus not only for a king but also for a river in the Troad,[25] and the fact that both Strymon (who is not attested in Homer) and Rhesus feature together in river catalogues as early as Hesiod[26] suggest the antiquity of their association. In this vein, there is nothing to rule out an early correlation of Strymon and Eioneus.[27] After all, rivers were often considered to have been the earliest kings and progenitors in a given region, like Scamander in the Troad, Inachus in Argos, Asopus in Phlius and Sicyon, Cephisus in Boeotia, Peneius in Thessaly, etc.[28] Linguistic evidence is also helpful in this respect, since Ἠιονεύς is Greek for "the man of the riverbank" or "the man of the seashore," whereas Strymon is Phrygian[29] for "stream" and Rhesus is Thracian[30] for "king." This makes it possible that the naming of Rhesus' father as Eioneus in the *Iliad* reflects an identification of the river Eioneus with the river Strymon, the latter being a nickname of the former.

The argument about Rhesus' father, Eioneus, squares neatly with the function of another Eioneus who fights on the Trojan side against the Greeks during the sack of Troy.[31] The use of the same name for the Trojan ally killed by Neoptolemus during the sack of Troy as for Rhesus' father in the *Iliad* suggests the presence of Thracians at Troy's sack, as there were Phrygian allies under Coroebus, who is

---

[22] Conon 4 (Brown): Ἡ τοίνυν δ᾽ διήγησις τὰ περὶ Ὀλύνθου τῆς πόλεως καὶ Στρυμόνος τοῦ Θρᾳκῶν βασιλεύσαντος ἀπαγγέλλει, οὗ καὶ ὁ πάλαι Ἠιονεὺς ποταμὸς ἐπώνυμος· καὶ ὅτι παῖδες αὐτῷ τρεῖς γεγόνασι, Βράγγας καὶ Ῥῆσσος [sic] καὶ Ὄλυνθος· καὶ Ῥῆσσος μὲν ἐπὶ Τροίαν Πριάμῳ συστρατεύσας ἀναιρεῖται χειρὶ Διομήδους. Pagès (2007, 323) talks about a μετονομασία ("renaming").

[23] Eioneus is also father of Rhesus in Dict. Cret. 2.45.

[24] In the *Iliad* and the *Rhesus*, respectively.   [25] See *Il.* 12.20.   [26] Th. 339–40.

[27] See Wilamowitz-Moellendorff (1884) 413; Hiller von Gaertringen (1886) 81.

[28] See Roscher I, 642–4 (Asopos); I, 1114–15 (Cephisos); II.1, 125–7 (Inachos); III, 1898–1900 (Peneios); IV, 976–983 (Scamander).

[29] Tomaschek (1893–4) I, 32 and 58. The IE root *srev/sru* can be seen in Germanic *Strom* (English "stream"), Latvian *straume*, and Slavic *struna*; see the river nymph Στρυμώ, daughter of Scamander, who is glossed in Greek as Ῥοιώ (< ῥέω), the Thasian city of Στρύμη, the overflowing stream Στρυμών, and the place Στρυμόνιον that is a sobriquet of the Brygian city of Mieza on the eastern slopes of Mt Bermion.

[30] From the IE stem **(H)rēǵ-* (see Vedic *rāj* and Latin *rēx*). This etymology has been put forward for the first time by Tomaschek (1893–4) II.1, 53; see also, e.g., Pedrizet (1910) 17–18; *RE* Suppl. III s.v. "Heros Equitans," col. 1147 (Kazarow); Boisacq (1926) 332–4; Rempe (1927) 26; Wathelet (1989) 213–31; Ustinova (2002) 253 n. 153; M. L. West (2007) 412–13; Liapis (2011) 99 with n. 26; Fries (2014) 15 n. 21.

[31] Robert (1901, 502) has argued that the author of the *Doloneia* had taken the name from the *Ilias parva* (fr. 23 *GEF*), adding that Polygnotus (whose painting, the content of which is described by Pausanias [10.27.1], is the earliest source of the relevant fragment of the *Ilias parva*) named him Eioneus after the same poem. Robert's observation is acute, but his interpretation is less convincing. For why would the *Doloneia* name Rhesus' father Eioneus because of a certain Eioneus killed by Neoptolemus in the *Ilias parva*? What association made the Iliadic tradition choose *this* name? In my view, the association works better the other way round.

also killed during the fall of the city by Neoptolemus[32] or by Diomedes.[33] This may be the relic of a version in which allied troops fought on the side of the Trojans against the Achaeans during the sack of Troy.[34] Eioneus may well have been someone important among Rhesus' troops (perhaps a relative of his) who stayed and fought in Troy even after their king's death. His presence during the sack makes more sense if Rhesus' arrival at Troy and his death at the hands of Diomedes and Odysseus featured in a pre-Homeric oral version of the *Ilias parva* (that differed in some way from Lesches' epic), in which Eioneus would have been already mentioned amongst Rhesus' Thracian troops.[35]

This line of interpretation is also suggested by the names of all minor figures who feature in the episode of the sack of Troy as reported by the extant fragments of Lesches' *Ilias parva*. They can be classified into the following groups with respect to their names:

1. Those known from both the *Iliad* and Cyclic epic (Achaeans: Eurypylus son of Euaemon, Meges, Lycomedes; Trojans: Agenor, Helicaon).
2. Those who have featured in the preceding sections of Lesches' *Ilias parva* (Trojans: Admetus, Agenor; allies of the Trojans: Coroebus).
3. Heroes bearing names of other heroes in the *Iliad*: a Trojan Astynoos is killed by Diomedes at *Il.* 5.144, and another Astynoos (son of Protiaon and charioteer of Polydamas) features at *Il.* 15.455; their namesake is killed by Neoptolemus at *Il. parv.* fr. 21 GEF. The Thracian Eioneus is Rhesus' father at *Il.* 10.435 (cf. an Achaean Eioneus killed by Hector at *Il.* 7.11–12); his namesake is killed by Neoptolemus at *Il. parv.* fr. 23 GEF.
4. Pre-Homeric figures who are cited only here but may have featured in earlier accounts of the sack of Troy known to Homer (Priam's son Axion: *Il.* 6.447–9, 20.306, 22.58–68, 22.408–11, 24.550–1).[36]

The majority (categories 1, 2, and 4) of minor figures featuring in the sack of Troy according to Lesches' *Ilias parva* are known from Cyclic epic (and occasionally the *Iliad*). As for Astynoos and Eioneus (category 3), they bear the names of other heroes in the *Iliad* and probably also in other epic poetry. The name of the former's father Protiaon is based on the Aeolic form $\pi\rho o \tau \iota$-[37] and is therefore

---

[32] Paus. 10.27.1: ὡς ὁ μὲν πλείων λόγος "in the majority version."   [33] *Il. parv.* fr. 24 GEF.

[34] The troops (*Il.* 2.844–5) of Acamas and Peiroos fought on the Trojan side together with Rhesus' troops until the end of the war. All three Thracian leaders are killed in the *Iliad* (Peiroos is killed by Thoas at *Il.* 4.527–31; Acamas is killed by Telamonian Ajax at *Il.* 6.5–11; Rhesus is killed by Diomedes at *Il.* 10.495).

[35] See chapter 9.

[36] Kullmann (1960) 349. I see no reason to include Pelis in Lesches' poem, despite the view of all modern editors. The same reason that excludes Leiocritus (mentioned by Pausanias in exactly the same context) from the *Ilias parva* applies to Pelis.

[37] See *GH* II, 131 (§ 191).

unlikely to have been invented ad hoc. The latter designates both Rhesus' father and an Achaean warrior who is a shadowy figure lacking any information (place of origin, name of father or mother, etc.). In both cases, Lesches' *Ilias parva* uses a name for which only one of its two attestations in the *Iliad* makes sense (since the other Astynoos and Eioneus are killed in Homer). In this light, Astynoos and Eioneus, who are both killed by Neoptolemus during the sack of Troy in the *Ilias parva*, may well be either identified with (Astynoos son of Protiaon and charioteer of Polydamas) or associated with (Eioneus, father of Rhesus)[38] their Iliadic namesakes.

καὶ Εὐτέρπης, μιᾶς τῶν Μουσῶν

Homer omits any mention of Rhesus' mother. The poet of the tragedy *Rhesus* designates her as one of the Muses without naming her,[39] while other sources identify her with Euterpe,[40] Clio,[41] Terpsichore,[42] or Calliope.[43] As to the *Mythographus Homericus*, which follows the more widely reported version that Euterpe was Rhesus' mother,[44] the expression μιᾶς τῶν Μουσῶν juxtaposed with Εὐτέρπης recalls τῆς μελῳδοῦ μητέρος, Μουσῶν μιᾶς that is employed by the poet of the *Rhesus* (393). Is this the only source on which the *Mythographus Homericus* draws this information?[45] Fenik, who claimed that the Homeric scholia are heavily based on Pind. fr. 262 S–M, thinks that the name of Rhesus' mother also comes from that source. However, the anonymity of Rhesus' mother in the *Rhesus* and the disagreement of later sources over her name[46] suggest otherwise,[47] since it seems that there was no fixed tradition. Scholars[48] have maintained that the presentation of the Muse as Rhesus' mother is either the invention of the poet of the *Rhesus*, perhaps under the influence of the tradition of Orpheus, or it reflects local Thracian beliefs.[49] The second alternative is less likely, since the

---

[38] With respect to his origin, see above, pp. 218–21.
[39] See also Σ at Eur. *Rh.* 346 (Schwartz); see also Pagès (2007) 323.
[40] Heracl. Pont. fr. 111 Schütrumpf (*apud* Σ [Eur.] *Rh.* 346 [Schwartz]); Apollod. *FGrHist* 244 F 146 (*apud* Σ [Eur.] *Rh.* 346 [Schwartz]); Apollod. *Bibl.* 1.3.4; Σ (bT) *Il.* 10.435 (Erbse); Σ (D) *Il.* 10.435 [van Thiel]; Σ (V) [Eur.] *Rh.* 393 (Schwartz); Serv. Auct. on Virg. *Aen.* 1.469; Eust. 817.27 (van der Valk).
[41] Marsyas II *FGrHist* 136 F 7 (*apud* Σ [Eur.] *Rh.* 346 and 393 [Schwartz]).
[42] Hyp. *Rh.* (c) (Diggle); Σ (D) *Il.* 10.435 (van Thiel); Σ Tz. Lyc. 831 (Scheer); Σ 190b on Tz. *Carm. Il.* 2.190 (Leone).
[43] Hyp. *Rh.* (a) (Diggle); ὡς δὲ ἔνιοι λέγουσι: *apud* Apollod. *Bibl.* 1.3.4.
[44] This is also the case with Apollod. *Bibl.* 1.3.4.   [45] See Pagès (2007) 323.
[46] There is also the further problem of whether the ascription to Pindar refers to the whole *historia* of the D-scholion or only to part of it; see the analysis of the expression διάφορος δὲ τῶν καθ' αὑτὸν γενόμενος ἐν πολεμικοῖς ἔργοις (pp. 222–5).
[47] See Leaf (1915) 2 n. 5; Rempe (1927) 38–43, 53; Fries (2014) 13; Fantuzzi (2020) 334 on [Eur.] *Rh.* 346–8a.
[48] See the previous footnote.
[49] The Corinthian Eumelus is an early Greek epic poet who speaks of three Muses, daughters of Apollo, who all have river names (Cephiso, Achelois, Borysthenis); see Tsagalis (2017) 166–72. However, this does not mean that the presentation of Rhesus' mother as a Muse goes back to the archaic period. Unlike the water-associated Muses of Eumelus, the designations of all those Muses featuring in the role of Rhesus' mother in later sources (Calliope, Clio, Euterpe, Terpsichore) are not hydronyms.

Muses are a quintessentially Greek phenomenon. Moreover, it is possible that the poet of the Rhesus was aware that the sanctuary dedicated to the Muse Clio was situated near the μνημεῖον of Rhesus in Amphipolis.[50]

διάφορος δὲ τῶν καθ' αὑτὸν γενόμενος ἐν πολεμικοῖς ἔργοις
The scholion clearly states that Rhesus possessed exceptional fighting skills when he arrived at Troy. This feature is also mentioned in the *Rhesus*.[51] While some scholars[52] think that this element relates to Rhesus' mythical armature, Fries argues that "the mythical pre-existence of Rhesus' earlier campaigns...is not guaranteed by the extended narrative of Σ^AD *Il.* 10.435."[53] Fries proposes instead that this element may have been extrapolated from "Homer" and that διάφορος δὲ τῶν καθ' αὑτὸν γενόμενος ἐν πολεμικοῖς ἔργοις has been influenced by the *Rhesus* rather than by Pindar or some anonymous source. In order to settle the debate, we need to revisit Fries's explanation that the scholiastic reference is an extrapolation from "Homer,"[54] and take into account both Σ (bT) on *Il.* 10.435 and Σ (D) on *Il.* 10.435. With respect to Fries's first argument, it is likely that the scholiast may have extrapolated from *Il.* 10.436–41 that Rhesus had accomplished glorious deeds before coming to Troy.[55] Fries's second argument has also much to commend it. Just as Σ (bT) on *Il.* 10.435 and Σ (D) on *Il.* 10.435 agree that Rhesus excelled in Troy[56] before being killed by Diomedes and Odysseus, so Σ (D) on *Il.* 10.435 emphasizes Rhesus' exceptional fighting skills: he has excelled in the past in Thrace; he also excels in Troy. This "doubling" seems like a deliberate effort to create a link between his earlier glorious status as a warrior and its reconfirmation in Troy. Rhesus' excellence in Troy amounts to an *aristeia*, which is a feature frequently anchored to the motif of the "late-arriving ally." Penthesileia (*Aeth.* arg. l. 177 Severyns),[57] Memnon (Apollod. *Epit.* 5.3),[58] and Eurypylus (*Il. parva* arg. l. 220 Severyns)[59] are allies of the Trojans who perform an *aristeia* before being killed by Achilles (Penthesileia, Memnon) and Neoptolemus, (Eurypylus). But what about Rhesus' past exploits? Of these three late-coming allies, we only possess the relevant lemma of the *Mythographus Homericus* with respect to

---

[50] Rempe (1927) 40; Fries (2014) 13. The information comes from Marsyas II *FGrHist* 136 F 7 (*apud* Σ [Eur.] *Rh.* 346 [Schwartz]).
[51] 932–3: καὶ σ' ἀμφὶ γῆν μὲν πατρίαν φιλαιμάτους | ἀλκὰς κορύσσοντ' οὐκ ἐδείμαινον θανεῖν ("I had no fear for your death when you were marshaling bloody battles in defense of your country"). Translation: Kovacs (2002).
[52] Fenik (1964) 30; Ritchie (1964) 63; Jouan (2004) 54 n. 275.   [53] Fries (2014) 12.
[54] The inverted commas in "Homer" are used by Fries (2014, 12).
[55] I would like to make it clear that (as will be shown in the ensuing analysis) I am not excluding extrapolation as an explanation of such references.
[56] On this expression, see Thuc. 2.39: διαφέρομεν δὲ καὶ ταῖς τῶν πολεμικῶν μελέταις τῶν ἐναντίων ("we also surpass our enemies with respect to military security").
[57] ἀριστεύουσαν.
[58] καὶ πολλοὺς τῶν Ἑλλήνων κτείναντα (epitoma Vaticana), καὶ τῶν Ἑλλήνων οὐκ ὀλίγους ἀναιρεῖ (fragmenta Sabbaitica).
[59] ἀριστεύοντα.

Eurypylus.⁶⁰ In this case too, as with Rhesus, his military fame before his arrival at Troy is also highlighted:⁶¹

Εὐρύπυλος ὁ Ἀστυόχης καὶ Τηλέφου τοῦ Ἡρακλέος παῖς λαχὼν τὴν πατρῴαν ἀρχὴν τῆς Μυσίας {ἀρχῆς} προΐσταται. πυθόμενος δὲ Πρίαμος **τῆς περὶ τούτου δυνάμεως** ἔπεμψεν ὡς αὐτόν, ἵνα παραγένηται σύμμαχος.

Eurypylus, the son of Astyoche and Telephus who was Heracles' son, was allotted his father's rule and took the lead of Mysia. After learning about his power, Priam sent a messenger to him in order that he may come (to Troy) as an ally of the Trojans.

The reference to Eurypylus' might before the Trojan War, about which all extant sources are silent, seems similarly to be an extrapolation from *Od*. 11.519-20: ἀλλ' οἷον τὸν Τηλεφίδην κατενήρατο χαλκῷ | **ἥρω' Εὐρύπυλον** ("but [I remember] how he [*sc*. Neoptolemus] killed with his bronze weapon the hero Eurypylus, son of Telephus").

Since, then, it is exclusively in the two extant lemmata of the *Mythographus Homericus* concerning the motif of the "late-arriving ally" that the hero's previous military fame is highlighted as a prelude to his *aristeia* in Troy, it is conceivable that this is a technique used by the compiler of the *Mythographus Homericus* and not a feature imposed by an external source describing these episodes. In fact, this amounts to a standard process that is not limited to the motif of the "late-arriving ally," since the compiler of the *Mythographus Homericus* employed it each and every time he used the pattern "superlative + τῶν καθ' αὑτόν/ἑαυτόν or κατ' αὐτὸν γενόμενος."⁶² As will become clear from the following list, the compiler either extrapolated from Homer or added the relevant feature on his own to create a link with the ensuing narrative of each *historia* where this feature is developed:

---

⁶⁰ Σ (D) *Od*. 11.519-21 (Ernst).

⁶¹ The summoning of Eurypylus to Troy was effected by Priam's bribing of his mother, Astyoche, since Telephus had given his word after being healed by Achilles' spear that neither he nor his descendants would fight the Achaeans in the future; see Σ Iuv. 6.655 (Wessner), which may have come from the *Cypria* (Kullmann 1960, 213): "*atque Eriphyle*": *Eriphyle, uxor Eurypili* [sic], *filii Telephi. qui Telephus cum venisset ad auxilium Priamo, plagatus est ab Achille, et cum non posset curari, sortitus est, ab Achille se solo posse curare. venit supplex, petit se curari, promisso hoc, ut nunquam iam auxilio ferat Troianis, nec ipse, nec de suis aliquis. curatus est; recessit. post mortem huius, filius Eurypilus* [sic] *vir fortis fuit. hunc saepius ad auxilium petit Priamus. ille negavit, monitus scilicet a patre suo. ergo cum non posset aliter Priamus eum sollicitare, fecit vitem ex auro, et misit ad uxorem eius Eriphylem. haec, accepto munere tanto, marito persuasit. venit in Troiam auxilium ferens. hunc occidit Pyrrhus filius Achillis.* This suggestion is partly corroborated by Σ (D) *Il*. 1.59 (van Thiel): Τήλεφος δὲ ἀνίατον ἔχων τὸ τραῦμα, εἰπόντος θεοῦ μηδένα δύνασθαι αὐτὸν θεραπεῦσαι ἢ τὸν τρώσαντα, ἦλθεν εἰς Ἄργος, καὶ πίστιν δοὺς μὴ ἐπικουρήσειν (ἐπικοινωνήσειν UG) Τρωσὶν ἐθεραπεύθη ὑπὸ Ἀχιλλέως καὶ αὑτὸς (αὑτοῖς UG) ἔδειξε τὸν ἐπὶ Τροίαν πλοῦν. ταῦτα <μὲν U> οἱ νεώτεροι· ὁ δὲ ποιητὴς λέγει Κάλχαντα ὑφηγήσασθαι τὸν ἐπὶ Ἴλιον πλοῦν (ἀφηγήσασθαι τοῦ ἐπὶ Ἴλιον πλοῦ U).

⁶² Van Rossum-Steenbeek (1998) 91-2.

(i) Σ (D) *Il.* 1.264: ὁ δὲ Καινεὺς Ἐλάτου μὲν {ἦν} παῖς, Λαπιθῶν δὲ βασιλεύς, ...ἄτρωτος γίνεται, **γενναιότατος τῶν καθ' αὑτὸν** (ἑαυτὸν pap.) **ὑπάρξας** (subscription lacking).
Extrapolation from *Il.* 1.264-7: Καινέα...| **κάρτιστοι** δὴ κεῖνοι ἐπιχθονίων τράφεν ἀνδρῶν· | **κάρτιστοι μὲν ἔσαν** καὶ καρτίστοις ἐμάχοντο.

(ii) Σ (D) *Il.* 7.9: Ἀρηΐθοος ὁ Βοιωτὸς **ἄριστος τῶν κατ' αὐτὸν ἀνθρώπων** (subscription: Pherecydes).
Extrapolation from *Il.* 7.9: ὃν **κορυνήτης** | γείνατ' Ἀρηΐθοος, and 7.138-41: **δίου Ἀρηϊθόου, τὸν ἐπίκλησιν Κορυνήτην** | **ἄνδρες κίκλησκον καλλίζωνοί τε γυναῖκες,** | οὕνεκ' ἄρ' οὐ τόξοισι μαχέσκετο δουρί τε μακρῷ, | ἀλλὰ σιδηρείῃ **κορύνῃ ῥήγνυσκε φάλαγγας·**

(iii) Σ (D) *Il.* 11.1: μυθεύεται, ὅτι Τιθωνὸν τὸν Λαομέδοντος **ἐκπρεπέστατον τῶν καθ' ἑαυτὸν ἐν Ἰλίῳ γενόμενον** ἐρασθεῖσα ἀνήρπασεν ἡ Ἡμέρα καὶ τῆς τούτου μετέβαλεν κοίτης, αἰτησαμένῳ δὲ αὐτῷ παρέσχεν ἀθανασίαν (subscription lacking).
Extrapolation from *Il.* 11.1: Ἠὼς δ' ἐκ λεχέων παρ' **ἀγαυοῦ Τιθωνοῖο** (= *Od.* 5.1).

(iv) Σ (D) *Il.* 11.672: Νηλεὺς ὁ Ποσειδῶνος, **ἱππικώτατος τῶν καθ' αὑτὸν γενόμενος** (subscription: Pherecydes).
Extrapolation from *Il.* 11.717-21: οὐδέ με Νηλεύς | εἴα θωρήσσεσθαι, **ἀπέκρυψεν δέ μοι ἵππους·** | οὐ γάρ πώ τί μ' ἔφη ἴδμεν πολεμήϊα ἔργα. | ἀλλὰ καὶ **ὣς ἱππεῦσι μετέπρεπον ἡμετέροισιν** | καὶ πεζός περ ἐών, ἐπεὶ ὣς ἄγε νεῖκος Ἀθήνη.

(v) Σ (D) *Il.* 14.119: Τυδεὺς ὁ Οἰνέως Αἰτωλὸς μὲν ἦν τὸ γένος, **ἀνδρειότατος δὲ τῶν καθ' ἑαυτὸν γενόμενος** (subscription: Pherecydes).
Extrapolation from *Il.* 14.113-14: **πατρὸς δ' ἐξ ἀγαθοῦ** καὶ ἐγὼ γένος εὔχομαι εἶναι, | **Τυδέος**, and from 14.124-5: **κέκαστο δὲ πάντας Ἀχαιούς** | **ἐγχείῃ**.

(vi) Σ (D) *Il.* 18.486: Ὑριεὺς ὁ Ποσειδῶνος καὶ Ἀλκυόνης, μιᾶς τῶν Ἄτλαντος θυγατρῶν, ᾤκει μὲν ἐν Τανάγρᾳ τῆς Βοιωτίας, **φιλοξενώτατος δὲ γενόμενος** ὑπεδέξατο ποτὲ καὶ θεούς. Ζεὺς δὲ καὶ Ποσειδῶν καὶ Ἑρμῆς ἐπιξενωθέντες αὐτῷ καὶ τὴν φιλοφροσύνην ἀποδεξάμενοι παρῄνεσαν αἰτεῖν ὅ τι ἂν βούλοιτο. ὁ δὲ ἄτεκνος ὢν ᾐτήσατο παῖδα (subscription: Euphorion).
No extrapolation from Homer. The expression φιλοξενώτατος δὲ γενόμενος (without τῶν καθ' αὐτὸν/ἑαυτόν or κατ' αὐτὸν) is probably due to the continuation of the narrative, since Hyrieus offers hospitality to Zeus, Poseidon, and Hermes. The extrapolation from [Hes.] *Cat.* 148(b) M-W[63] (*Aristomachus ait Hyriea quendam Thebis voto petisse, ut filium*

---

[63] *Apud* Σ in Germanici *Aratea* p. 93.13 (Breysig).

haberet. penes quem Iovis et Mercurius et Neptunus in hospitio devenerunt imperaveruntque ei, hostiam deiceret uti filius nasceretur) is less likely.

(vii) Σ (D) *Il.* 23.660: Φόρβας ἀνδρειότατος τῶν καθ' ἑαυτὸν γενόμενος, ὑπερήφανος δὲ πυγμὴν ἤσκησεν καὶ τοὺς μὲν παριόντας ἀναγκάζων ἀγωνίζεσθαι ἀνῄρει. ὑπὸ δὲ τῆς πολλῆς ὑπερηφανείας ἠβούλετο καὶ πρὸς τοὺς θεοὺς τὸ τοιοῦτο φρόνημα ἔχειν. διὸ Ἀπόλλων παραγενόμενος καὶ συστὰς αὐτῷ ἀπέκτεινεν αὐτόν. ὅθεν ἐξ ἐκείνου καὶ τῆς πυκτικῆς ἔφορος ἐνομίσθη ὁ θεός (subscription: Cyclic poets).

No extrapolation from Homer. The expression ἀνδρειότατος τῶν καθ' ἑαυτὸν γενόμενος is due to the continuation of the narrative, since it operates as the backdrop that explains Phorbas' arrogance towards the gods.

(viii) Σ (D) *Od.* 15.16–17: πυθόμενος δὲ Λαέρτης περὶ τῆς Πηνελόπης ὅτι καὶ τῷ κάλλει καὶ ταῖς φρεσὶ **διαφέρει πασῶν τῶν καθ' ἑαυτὴν γυναικῶν** (subscription: Philostephanus and Pherecydes).

Extrapolation from *Od.* 15.15: ἀμύμονα μητέρα.

On the basis of this evidence, Fries seems to be right that the compiler of the *Mythographus Homericus* is responsible for referring to Rhesus' previous military triumphs by the phrase διάφορος δὲ τῶν καθ' αὐτὸν γενόμενος ἐν πολεμικοῖς ἔργοις.[64] However, Fantuzzi argues that the *Rhesus*, Parthenius, and Σ (D) *Il.* 10.435 may have followed an independent, local tradition[65] of Rhesus' wars of conquest, "parallel to the archaic tradition (and poems?) of Achilles' various expeditions and sacking of cities around Troy before or during the first years of the Trojan War."[66] As to the influence of the *Rhesus* on this issue, I remain skeptical, since the picture of Rhesus' previous military excellence is rather obscure. On the one hand, Rhesus needed Hector's assistance to gain the Thracian throne (that is why he owes him);[67] on the other hand, he was able to defeat the Scythians without Hector's help before coming to Troy (hence his delay).[68] Parthenius' description of Rhesus as "winning over allies and imposing tribute,"[69] as well as "the pressure from the 'kings' (Priam and family?) on him to come to Troy,"[70] look like direct points of contact with the *Rhesus*,[71] though the tragedy is not Parthenius' only source.

---

[64] The phrase διάφορος δὲ τῶν καθ' αὐτὸν γενόμενος ἐν πολεμικοῖς ἔργοις refers to Rhesus' martial excellence, not just to his involvement in wars.
[65] I assume that Fantuzzi (rightly; also Fries) does not consider Pindar to be the source of the information concerning Rhesus' past military exploits, since he refers to an independent, local tradition.
[66] Fantuzzi (2020) 379 on *Rh.* 426–8a; see also Lightfoot (1999, 555–6 on Parth. *Narr. am.* 36.1), who draws attention to the generalizing and unspecific tone of Parthenius, and suggests that the author "makes Rhesus sound like a second Achilles, winning over cities to his side before he joins the Greeks at Troy" (556).
[67] *Rh.* 407–11.   [68] *Rh.* 426–33; see also 931–3.
[69] *Narr. am.* 36.1: προσαγόμενόν τε καὶ δασμὸν ἐπιτιθέντα.
[70] Fantuzzi (2020) 366 on *Rh.* 399–403; *Narr. am.* 36.4.
[71] Fantuzzi (2020) 366 on *Rh.* 399–403.

ἐπῆλθε τοῖς Ἕλλησιν, ὅπως Τρωσὶ συμμαχήσῃ

The same stress on the arrival and its purpose is observed in the Proclan summaries of various Cyclic epics which deal with motif of the "late-arriving ally":

Penthesileia:

Aeth. arg. ll. 175–6 Severyns: Ἀμαζὼν Πενθεσίλεια παραγίνεται Τρωσὶ συμμαχήσουσα.

Memnon:

Aeth. arg. ll. 185–6 Severyns: Μέμνων... παραγίνεται τοῖς Τρωσὶ βοηθήσων

Apollod. Epit. 5.3 (fragmenta Vaticana): ὅτι Μέμνονα... μετὰ πολλῆς Αἰθιόπων δυνάμεως παραγενόμενον ἐν Τροίᾳ, (fragmenta Sabbaitica): Μέμνων... πολλὴν Αἰθιόπων δύναμιν ἀθροίσας παραγίνεται.

Eurypylus:

Il. parv. arg. l. 219 Severyns: Εὐρύπυλος... ἐπίκουρος τοῖς Τρωσὶ παραγίνεται.

Apollod. Epit. 5.12 (epitoma Vaticana et fragmenta Sabbaitica): ἀφικνεῖται δὲ ὕστερον Τρωσὶ σύμμαχος Εὐρύπυλος ὁ Τηλέφου πολλὴν Μυσῶν δύναμιν ἄγων·

See also: P. Ryl. 22: [Εὐρύπυλος ὁ Τηλέφου υἱὸς] ἐκ τῆς Μυ[σίας παραγ{ε}ίνεται βοηθῶν] τοῖς Τρωσ[ί·

While Rhesus' arrival is expressed differently from the language employed in Proclus' summaries, his aim is described in remarkably similar terms. The aorist ἐπῆλθε matches the aorist ἀπέκτεινε,[72] though they contrast with the historical presents that dominate the rest of the scholion. The historical present is systematically used in Proclus' summaries.

καὶ συμβαλὼν πολλοὺς τῶν Ἑλλήνων ἀπέκτεινεν
See also Σ (bT) Il. 10.435: καὶ μίαν ἡμέραν πολεμήσας πρὸς Ἕλληνας μέγιστα αὐτοῖς ἐνεδείξατο κακά

Rhesus' aristeia is highlighted, very much like the aristeiai of Penthesileia, Memnon, and Eurypylus. The emphasis on the hero's military skills does not belong to the kernel of the motif of the "late-arriving ally." This feature relates only to first-rank allies, not to unimportant ones, who join the war at a late stage, have no aristeia, and meet their death:[73]

Penthesileia:

Aeth. arg. l. 177 Severyns: ἀριστεύουσαν·

---

[72] See pp. 215, 226–7, 263 n. 64.
[73] See, e.g., the cases of Hippotion's sons Ascanius and Morys (Il. 13.792–4; I follow Janko [1992, 143 on Il. 13.792–4], who argues that υἷ' stands for the dual υἷε, not the accusative singular υἷα, because of the ensuing plurals) and of the Paeonian Asteropaeus (Il. 21.155–6); Fenik (1964) 9.

Apollod. *Epit.* 5.1 (epitoma Vaticana): μάχης γεγομένης πολλοὺς κτείνει, ἐν οἷς καὶ Μαχάονα.

Memnon:

Aeth. arg. l. 188 Severyns: καὶ συμβολῆς γενομένης.

Apollod. *Epit.* 5.3: καὶ πολλοὺς τῶν Ἑλλήνων κτείναντα καὶ Ἀντίλοχον κτείνει (epitoma Vaticana) and καὶ τῶν Ἑλλήνων οὐκ ὀλίγους ἀναιρεῖ, κτείνει καὶ Ἀντίλοχον (fragmenta Sabbaitica).

Eurypylus:

Il. parv. arg. l. 220 Severyns: ἀριστεύοντα.

Apollod. *Epit.* 5.12–13 (epitoma Vaticana et fragmenta Sabbaitica): τοῦτον ἀριστεύσαντα Νεοπτόλεμος ἀπέκτεινεν.

Rhesus' *aristeia* belongs to the so-called Pindaric version.[74] Conversely, the oracle version is devoid of an *aristeia*, just as in *Iliad* 10, where the Thracian king is killed during his first night at Troy, before he has the chance to join the fighting.[75]

Of special importance is the Apollodoran passage (*Epit.* 4.4) that refers to Rhesus and his death at the hands of Diomedes and Odysseus:

Apollodorus (*Epit.* 4.4)	Σ(D) and Σ(bT) *Il.* 10.435
ὃς πρὸ μιᾶς ἡμέρας παραγενόμενος Τρωσὶ σύμμαχος οὐ συμβαλὼν ... ἀπέκτεινεν	μίαν ἡμέραν πολεμήσας πρὸς Ἕλληνας ἐπῆλθε τοῖς Ἕλλησιν, ὅπως Τρωσὶ συμμαχήσῃ καὶ συμβαλὼν πολλοὺς τῶν Ἑλλήνων
τούς τε περὶ αὐτὸν δώδεκα κοιμωμένους ἑταίρους κτείνουσι καὶ τοὺς ἵππους ἐπὶ τὰς ναῦς ἄγουσι	αὐτόν τε καὶ τοὺς ἑταίρους αὐτοῦ κτείνουσιν

The dictional similarities between Apollodorus, who reports the Iliadic version of the Rhesus episode, and Σ (D) and Σ (bT) *Il.* 10.435 suggest that Apollodorus consulted the same source as the compiler of the *Mythographus Homericus*.

δείσασα δὲ Ἥρα περὶ τῶν Ἑλλήνων Ἀθηνᾶν ἐπὶ τὴν τούτου διαφθορὰν πέμπει
See also Σ (bT) *Il.* 10.435: κατὰ δὲ πρόνοιαν Ἥρας καὶ Ἀθηνᾶς

The cooperation of Hera and Athena when the Achaeans are in trouble is attested throughout the *Iliad*. The two goddesses belong to a patterned scheme of intervention in human affairs, with Hera instigating action and Athena implementing it either together with Hera or on her own. At *Il.* 1.194–5 Hera sends

---

[74] Pagès (2007) 324. [75] On the oracle version of the Rhesus story, see pp. 230–4.

Athena to restrain the angered Achilles against Agamemnon. At *Il.* 2.156–81 she advises Athena to restrain the Achaeans, who are thinking of returning to Greece; Athena descends immediately from Olympos and advises Odysseus accordingly.[76] At *Il.* 5.711–845 Hera realizes that the pro-Trojan gods are turning the scales against the Achaeans and calls on Athena to join her in retaking the initiative. The two goddesses prepare themselves, mount Hera's chariot, and go to Zeus to ask for his permission for intervention. When consent is granted, they descend to the Trojan plain at the spot where the rivers Simoeis and Scamander meet. Hera takes the shape of Stentor and speaks loudly to all the Achaeans, urging them to regain their courage by addressing them (*Il.* 5.787) exactly as Agamemnon will address them at *Il.* 8.228.[77] Athena approaches Diomedes and, after mounting his chariot, they engage together in fierce combat against the Trojans. At *Il.* 8.350–96 Hera sees the dire situation of the Achaeans and tells Athena that they should do something because otherwise the Achaeans will perish under the force of a single man, Hector. The two goddesses prepare themselves, mount Hera's chariot, and ride to the gates of the sky. This time Zeus prevents them from helping the Achaeans. Hector will triumph and dominate until Achilles returns to battle. The goddesses' intervention will not take place. Night falls.

The scholion offers a version[78] in which Hera realizes the grave danger facing the Achaeans and incites Athena to action. Since this plotline is taken neither from *Iliad* 10 (where Hera is absent[79] and Athena's intervention at the last moment is extremely limited)[80] nor from the *Rhesus* (where Hera is equally absent), it must

---

[76] Odysseus' compliance with Athena's advice is expressed with a line (*Il.* 2.182: ὣς φάθ', ὁ δὲ ξυνέηκε θεᾶς ὄπα φωνησάσης, "so she spoke, and he knew of the voice of the goddess speaking") that is repeated verbatim at *Il.* 10.512, when Athena advises Diomedes (and by extension Odysseus, who is standing next to him) to "remember his *nostos*" and return immediately to the Achaean camp before some other god wakes up the Trojans. In *Iliad* 2 Athena's advice aims to deter the Achaeans from their *nostos* to Greece, while in *Iliad* 10 she aims at reminding them of their immediate *nostos* to their ships.

[77] αἰδώς, Ἀργεῖοι, κάκ' ἐλέγχεα, εἶδος ἀγητοί ("shame, you Argives, poor nonentities splendid to look on").

[78] Pagès (2007, 324) attributes it to Pindar.

[79] She is only mentioned in the portentous simile at *Il.* 10.5 and in an oath to Zeus at *Il.* 10.329. In both cases, she is cited in a phrase used as a designation of Zeus, which is either a unique expression (*Il.* 10.5: πόσις Ἥρης ἠϋκόμοιο) or a formula (*Il.* 10.329: ἐρίγδουπος πόσις Ἥρης); see Hainsworth (1993) 157 on *Il.* 10.5 and 188 on *Il.* 10.329–31, respectively.

[80] See also Σ [bT] *Il.* 10.496–7 Erbse (τὸ βαθὺ γὰρ τοῦ ὕπνου δι' αὐτῆς ἐγένετο), which represents a free-floating attempt by the scholiast to explain the "unintelligible" phrase διὰ μῆτιν Ἀθήνης, although the narrator has explained the Thracians' sleep as a result of exhaustion (*Il.* 10.471: οἱ δ' εὗδον καμάτῳ ἀδηκότες), obviously because of their long journey. This is also how the poet of the *Rhesus* (763–4: ηὕδομεν πεδοστιβεῖ | κόπῳ δαμέντες, "overcome by fatigue from our long journey") has interpreted *Il.* 10.511 (μή πού τις καὶ Τρῶας ἐγείρῃσιν θεὸς ἄλλος). Although the Trojans are not sleeping in the *Doloneia* (*Il.* 10.419–20: οἱ δ' ἐγρηγόρθασι φυλασσέμεναί τε κέλονται | ἀλλήλοις), whereas their allies (including the Thracians) are (*Il.* 10.420–1: ἀτὰρ αὖτε πολύκλητοι ἐπίκουροι | εὕδουσι), the point should not be pressed. The ethnic term "Trojans" is employed here in the general sense of "enemy." As Fenik (1964, 53 with n. 3) has forcefully argued, the presentation of Athena as unseen by the spies (*Il.* 10.275–6, 512) and unheralded (*Il.* 10.507–8) "looks like an unsuccessful attempt to retain [her] role..., as far as possible, from the Pindaric/oracle version, in which she played a leading role, along with the new figure of Dolon and the relative naturalism which the *Iliad* as a whole demanded." Although I agree about the awkwardness of Athena's role, I disagree with Fenik's claim that Dolon is a "new figure"; on the traditionality of Dolon, see Dué-Ebbott (2010) 106–19.

belong (at least) to the Pindaric version, as the scholion says. A comparison with the Cyclic material pertaining to the motif of the "late-arriving ally" is again revealing. In the cases of Penthesileia, Memnon, and Eurypylus there is no divine intervention (from what we can tell on the basis of Proclus' summaries). The reason is that an Aeacid is involved in the defense of the Achaeans in all three episodes: Achilles kills Penthesileia and Memnon; Neoptolemus slays Eurypylus. The patterned scheme of the intervention of Hera and Athena when they aim at saving the Achaeans from peril takes place only when an Aeacid is not involved. In the *Iliad* the threat is posed by Hector, who threatens to destroy them. In the Rhesus story it is Rhesus who plays a similar role. Once again, an Aeacid is absent.

ἐπιστάντες δὲ ἐκεῖνοι (sc. Διομήδης καὶ Ὀδυσσεύς) κοιμωμένῳ Ῥήσῳ αὐτόν τε καὶ τοὺς ἑταίρους αὐτοῦ κτείνουσιν
See also Σ (bT) *Il.* 10.435: ἀναστάντες οἱ περὶ Διομήδεα ἀναιροῦσιν αὐτόν

The abbreviated style of the scholion is matched by an equally abbreviated style of the Proclan summaries marked by the use of the verb (ἀπο)κτείνειν, which is employed at the completion of a train of thought including what the victim did before his death.

Penthesileia:

Aeth. arg. ll. 176–7 Severyns: κτείνει αὐτήν.

Memnon:

Aeth. arg. l. 189 Severyns: Ἀχιλλεὺς Μέμνονα κτείνει.

Eurypylus:

Il. parv. arg. l. 220 Severyns: αὐτὸν ἀποκτείνει Νεοπτόλεμος.

In all three examples from Proclus, Penthesileia, Memnon, and Eurypylus are killed after having performed an *aristeia*; in Σ (D) on *Il.* 10.435, Rhesus is killed while sleeping (κοιμωμένῳ Ῥήσῳ). In the Cyclic examples no mention is made of the losses inflicted on the late-coming hero's troops, while in the case of Rhesus the slaying of his comrades who are sleeping next to him is narrated. Both Σ (bT) and Σ (D) on *Il.* 10.435 stress, through the use of plural and compound forms of the verb ἱστάναι (ἀναστάντες οἱ περὶ Διομήδεα,[81] ἐπιστάντες δὲ ἐκεῖνοι κοιμωμένῳ Ῥήσῳ), the united action by a pair of heroes, Odysseus and Diomedes, who wake up in the middle of the night, infiltrate the enemy camp, stand over the sleeping Rhesus, and kill him.

---

[81] The expression οἱ περὶ Διομήδεα "those in the company of Diomedes" that is used for "Odysseus and Diomedes" is scholiastic jargon (Liapis 2012, xix n. 9 and 57); see Hypothesis (a) of *Rhesus*: οἱ περὶ τὸν Ὀδυσσέα ("those in the company of Odysseus," i.e. Diomedes and Odysseus) and οἱ περὶ τὸν Διομήδην ("those in the company of Diomedes," i.e. Odysseus and Diomedes).

ὡς ἱστορεῖ Πίνδαρος
This explicit ascription at the very end of the first *historia* of the *Mythographus Homericus* cannot refer to the last phrase that is consonant with what happens in the *Iliad*. It probably refers to the preceding statements which report material that is neither Homeric nor Euripidean.[82] If so, apart from the initial sentence that describes Rhesus' parentage and (perhaps) his earlier (pre-Troy) heroic excellence, this scholion seems to quote a version that was used in a lost poem by Pindar.[83] The cyclic features observable in the diction and themes of the scholion may be explained, if Pindar is following a cyclic source which included the Rhesus story. Since this source cannot be identified with any of the extant summaries and fragments of the Cyclic epics, it may belong to alternative cyclic epic versions which have not survived the test of time, being overshadowed by the canonical Epic Cycle.[84]

7.2.2 The Oracle Version

As for the oracle version of the Rhesus story, the erudite compiler of the *Mythographus Homericus* may have taken it from a source in which there was no subscription. It seems difficult to believe that the same source gave both Pindar's name for the origin of the first section of what now is the D-scholion on *Il.* 10.435 and the names of the authors who present the oracle version. Yet, the compiler of the *Mythographus Homericus* mentions only Pindar, whereas he summed up the other authors under the vague ἔνιοι. Perhaps the cropping of the name of the author or authors who reported the oracle version had happened in an intermediate source from which the compiler of the *Mythographus Homericus* took both *historiae*. There are two possibilities: (a) the compiler of the *Mythographus Homericus* drew both *historiae* (i.e. the first and second sections of the D-scholion) from the same source which mentioned only Pindar as the source of the first *historia* but attributed the second to ἔνιοι without giving any name(s); or (b) he drew the second *historia* from a different source in which he found it introduced by ἔνιοι δὲ λέγουσιν or something like it.

ἔνιοι δὲ λέγουσιν
Since (a) neither Homer nor Pindar nor pseudo-Euripides belong to this group and (b) the oracle version is consonant with what is said in Virgil[85]

---

[82] Pagès (2007) 324.
[83] See Lünstedt (1961), who has argued that subscriptions in the *Mythographus Homericus* are to be trusted; also Montanari (1995) 143–4.
[84] On this line of thought, see chapter 9.
[85] *Aen.* 1.469–73: *nec procul hinc Rhesi niveis tentoria velis | adgnoscit lacrimans, primo quae prodita somno | Tydides multa vastabat caede cruentus, | ardentisque avertit equos in castra, prius quam | pabula gustassent Troiae Xanthumque bibissent* ("not far away he discerns with tears the snowy-canvassed tents

and Eustathius,[86] Pagès has argued that we can postulate the existence of a Hellenistic poet who reports a local version associated with the cult of Rhesus.[87] This line of thought should not be taken as proof of the lateness of this version. The oracle version contains various features which may well be quite old, even if the Homeric scholia, which are followed by both Virgil and Eustathius, had access to it through a Hellenistic source unknown to us.

νυκτὸς παραγεγονέναι τὸν Ῥῆσον εἰς τὴν Τροίαν
The arrival of Rhesus at Troy within the night is consistent with the oracle version, in which there is no time for an *aristeia* for the Thracian king, since he is slain on arrival by Diomedes (and Odysseus). It is also consistent with the Homeric *Doloneia*, even if there is no oracle, since there too Rhesus is granted no time for an *aristeia*. Virgil, who follows the oracle version, emphasizes that Rhesus was killed in his "first sleep" (*Aen.* 1.469: *primo... somno*), i.e. the first time he slept after his arrival at Troy. The same observation applies to Eustathius, who reports that Rhesus died the same night he arrived at Troy (αὐτονυχὶ ἀνηρέθη).[88]

καὶ πρὶν γεύσασθαι αὐτὸν τοῦ ὕδατος τῆς χώρας φονευθῆναι
Both Virgil and Eustathius report the same version.[89] The diction employed by Virgil contains the same type of temporal clause (*prius quam*) as the scholion, though Virgil applies it to Rhesus' horses,[90] whereas the scholion uses it for Rhesus.[91]

χρησμὸς γὰρ ἐδέδοτο αὐτῷ, φασίν, ὅτι εἰ αὐτός τε γεύσεται τοῦ ὕδατος καὶ οἱ ἵπποι αὐτοῦ τοῦ Σκαμάνδρου πίωσι καὶ τῆς αὐτόθι νομῆς <ἔδονται>, ἀκαταμάχητος ἔσται εἰς τὸ παντελές
The ensuing discussion of this part of the scholion involves two issues: the oracle and the role of Scamander.

---

of Rhesus, which, betrayed in their first sleep, the blood-stained son of Tydeus laid waste with many a death, and turned the fiery steeds away to the camp, before they could taste the Trojan fodder or drink of Xanthus"). Translation: Fairclough 1935 (revised by Goold).

[86] Eust. 817.27–8 (van der Valk): λέγουσι (sc. οἱ νεώτεροι) δὲ καὶ χρησμὸν ἀποκεῖσθαι αὐτῷ, εἰ τῆς ἐν Τροίᾳ βοτάνης φάγοιεν οἱ ἵπποι αὐτοῦ καὶ τοῦ ἐκεῖσε πίοιεν ὕδατος, ἀπρόσμαχον αὐτὸν ἔσεσθαι. τὰ δ' οὐκ ἐγένετο. ἅμα γὰρ κατέλαβε, καὶ αὐτονυχὶ ἀνηρέθη ὑπὸ Διομήδους ὑπνώττων ἀφύλακτος ("The *neoteroi* say that an oracle lay in store for him that if his horses eat Trojan fodder and drink the water of that place, he will become invincible. But these things did not happen. For as soon as he arrived, he was slain in his sleep by Diomedes, being unprotected").

[87] Pagès (2007) 324.

[88] According to Fries (2014) 349 and 352 on [Eur.] *Rh.* 595–641 and 600–4, respectively (mainly on the basis of the phrase διοίσει νύκτα τήνδ' ἐς αὔριον, [Eur.] *Rh.* 600), the author of the *Rhesus* has adapted the oracle version "to give Rhesus' death a more elevated note" (349) but suppressed the magic element of invincibility; see also Fenik (1964) 15 n. 4, 16, 26; Griffin (1977) 40. Differently, Fantuzzi (2020, 470 on [Eur.] *Rh.* 600–4) notes that "Athena authoritatively confirms Rhesus' boastful claim at 447–50 that he could prevail over the Greeks in a single day" and takes both statements as reflecting the Pindaric version, providing Rhesus "with a sort of epic greatness" (2020, 470); however, Fantuzzi (2020, 468 on [Eur.] *Rh.* 595–605a) does not exclude a reference to the oracle version in 600–4.

[89] See pp. 230–1 with n. 85, 234, 261–2 (Virgil); pp. 230 n. 86 and 234 (Eustathius).

[90] See pp. 234 and 261–2.

[91] The expression "the water of the country" is then specified as "the water of Scamander."

The Oracle

The meaning of the expression χρησμὸς γὰρ ἐδέδοτο αὐτῷ translates as "an oracle had been given to him."[92] The way that Eustathius refers to the oracle (λέγουσι δὲ καὶ χρησμὸν ἀποκεῖσθαι αὐτῷ, "an oracle lay in store for him") indicates that at some point in the past the oracle had foretold his possibly glorious future (i.e. that Rhesus would become invincible under certain conditions).[93]

The diction εἰ αὐτός τε γεύσεται τοῦ ὕδατος καὶ οἱ ἵπποι αὐτοῦ τοῦ Σκαμάνδρου πίωσι καὶ τῆς αὐτόθι νομῆς <ἔδονται>, ἀκαταμάχητος ἔσται εἰς τὸ παντελές, which is rendered by Eustathius as (λέγουσι)... εἰ τῆς ἐν Τροίᾳ βοτάνης φάγοιεν οἱ ἵπποι αὐτῷ καὶ τοῦ ἐκεῖσε πίοιεν ὕδατος, ἀπρόσμαχον αὐτὸν ἔσεσθαι, suggests that the oracle concerns a threat Rhesus poses for the Achaeans. That is to say, the oracle version concerns the Achaeans as much as it does Rhesus. Its association with Rhesus' murder allows for the possibility that its content was revealed to the Achaeans, who acted immediately, i.e. πρὶν γεύσασθαι αὐτὸν τοῦ ὕδατος τῆς χώρας. If so, the oracle was made known to them as soon as Rhesus arrived at Troy. But how did the Achaeans find out about the oracle? It may be the case that Hera (and Athena), who urged the Achaeans to kill Rhesus during the night after his *aristeia* in the Pindaric version, are the ones who also disclosed the oracle's content to the Achaeans in the oracle version.[94] Alternatively, this role may have been taken by Calchas, who functions in similar manner in the context of the events following the death of Achilles and the suicide of Telamonian Ajax. Calchas both prophesies that Philoctetes, the hero currently in possession of Heracles' bow, needs to be brought from Lemnos to Troy[95] and advises that the Achaeans should capture the Trojan seer Helenus, since he will disclose to them the oracles that need to be fulfilled for Troy to fall.[96] The way Servius[97] refers to Rhesus reveals that his death was a prerequisite for the fall of Troy. This feature points to the viewpoint of a cyclic epic like the *Ilias parva* (not Lesches' poem but an oral predecessor of it), in which Helenus disclosed to the Achaeans the conditions that need to be met for the sack of Troy. Since Virgil knows and cites the oracle version at *Aen*. 1.470–3, it is likely that Servius' comment refers to the oracle version. We are therefore faced with a situation that is reminiscent of the theft of the Palladium in the *Ilias parva*. If the Palladium is not stolen, Troy will remain impregnable. Likewise, if Rhesus is not killed, he will be invincible, and Troy will never fall. On this basis, we can

---

[92] Fantuzzi (2020) 8.
[93] I owe this clarification to one of anonymous readers selected by OUP for evaluating my manuscript.
[94] This seems to be what Fenik (1964, 37) believes.   [95] Apollod. *Epit*. 5.8.
[96] Apollod. *Epit*. 5.9–10.
[97] On Virg. *Aen*. 1.469 (Thilo and Hagen): *abducti sunt equi, quibus pendebant fata Troiana, ut, si pabulo Troiano usi essent vel de Xantho Troiae fluvio bibissent, Troia perire non posset*; 2.13 [Thilo and Hagen] (*fatisque repulsi oraculis*): *secundum Plautum tribus...; secundum alios vero pluribus: ut de Aeaci gente aliquis interesset, unde Pyrrhus admodum puer evocatus ad bellum est; ut Rhesi equi tollerentur a Graecis; ut Herculis interessent sagittae, quas misit Philoctetes, quibus Paris peremptus est, cum ipse non potuisset adferre morte praeventus.*

postulate that someone (Hera and/or Athena, or Calchas on the analogy of Helenus?) revealed to the Achaeans the existence of this oracle about Rhesus, and that subsequently Odysseus and Diomedes take the initiative to kill the Thracian king before he can drink water from Scamander. Either way, the context is unquestionably cyclic.

Scamander
The identification of Scamander as the river whose waters would render Rhesus invincible is of key importance for the oracle version.[98] The *Iliad* contains multiple cases which testify to the importance Scamander, called Xanthus by the gods, had for the Trojans:

(a) Certain Trojans are named after Scamander: the son of Strophius, who is killed by Menelaus (*Il.* 5.49–50); likewise, Hector's son, who is also called Astyanax (*Il.* 6.402–3).
(b) Scamander has its own seer, i.e. Hypsenor, son of Dolopion, who is killed by Eurypylus, son of Euaemon. This seer is honored by the Trojans like a god (*Il.* 5.76–8).
(c) Ambrosia (the immortals' food) is produced by Simoeis at the point it meets with the river Scamander, so that Hera's horses can graze at its banks after being unyoked from her chariot (*Il.* 5.773–7).
(d) Scamander's water helps the wounded Hector temporarily recover, vomit a dark clot of blood, and even lean on his knee before lying again on the ground under persisting pain (*Il.* 14.433–9).
(e) Scamander instills "valor" ($\mu\acute{\epsilon}\nu os$) to the Paeonian Asteropaeus as he comes out of the river to face Achilles because the latter had slaughtered without pity young Trojan warriors beside its waters (*Il.* 21.144–7).
(f) Scamander fights alongside other pro-Trojan gods in the Theomachia. He is the only river presented on a par with several pro-Trojan Olympian deities (*Il.* 20.40), and faces the pro-Achaean god Hephaestus (*Il.* 20.73–4). Scamander turns against Achilles to put a stop to the slaughtering of Trojans in its waters. The speech exchange between Scamander and Achilles does not restrain the latter's fury and the river god asks Apollo to intervene (*Il.* 21.214–32). Scamander's anger against Achilles persists and the

---

[98] Several sources associate Strymon and Scamander: (a) horses are sacrificed to both (Herod. 7.114 – *Il.* 21.131). It is interesting that the ones mentioned by Herodotus are white and that Scamander had a daughter named $\Lambda\epsilon\nu\kappa\acute{\iota}\pi\pi\eta$, who was the wife of Laomedon and the mother of Priam (Hellan. fr. 139 *EGM*; Apollod. *Bibl.* 3.12.8; Σ Lyc. 18 [Scheer]; Eud. *Viol.* 920 [Flach]; Tz. *Prol. Alleg. Il.* 172 [Boissonade]). One is reminded of Rhesus' white horses (*Il.* 10.437). (b) According to another tradition, Scamander had a daughter named Strymo, who was the wife of Laomedon and the mother of Tithonus (Apollod. *Bibl.* 3.12.8; Σ *Il.* 20.237 [Erbse]; Σ Lyc. 18 [Scheer]; Eud. *Viol.* 920 [Flach]; Tz. *Prol. Alleg. Il.* 173 [Boissonade]).

river god asks for the help of his brother Simoeis, who is another river god of the Troad (*Il.* 21.305–23). In turn, Hera asks Hephaestus to assault Scamander, since she is afraid for Achilles' life (*Il.* 21.328–41).

These features attest to the importance of Scamander for the Trojans and for the Trojan War myth. Elements (c), (d), and (e) resonate with the oracle version of Rhesus' story: horses eating immortal food at the meeting point of the brother-rivers Scamander and Simoeis (c), Scamander's water temporarily healing the wounded Hector (d), Scamander giving strength to the Paeonian Asteropaeus[99] *as he comes out of its waters* (e). There is, arguably, a background in all this, which means that the oracle version (in which Scamander is important) cannot have been shaped by the *Iliad* and is unlikely to have been formed at a later date.

The strength Rhesus and his horses will acquire if they drink water from Scamander (and if the horses also eat fodder from its banks) presupposes a special connection between Rhesus and rivers.[100] This line of thought is corroborated by the origin of Rhesus, whose father, Eioneus, has fluvial associations and whose name (*sc.* Rhesus) is also employed for a river in the Troad within a list of other rivers, among whose number is Scamander.[101] Rhesus' affiliation with rivers reflects a belief in the regeneration of one's powers through contact with an element akin to his origins. The diction employed by Virgil and Eustathius is reminiscent of the language of the scholion:

Scholion	Virgil	Eustathius
χρησμὸς γὰρ ἐδέδοτο αὐτῷ		χρησμὸν ἀποκεῖσθαι αὐτῷ
γεύσεται τοῦ ὕδατος		εἰ τῆς ἐν Τροίᾳ βοτάνης φάγοιεν
καὶ οἱ ἵπποι αὐτοῦ	equos	οἱ ἵπποι αὐτῷ
τοῦ Σκαμάνδρου	Troiae Xanthumque	καὶ τοῦ ἐκεῖσε
πίωσι καὶ τῆς αὐτόθι	bibissent	πίοιεν ὕδατος
νομῆς <ἔδονται>	pabula gustassent	
ἀκαταμάχητος ἔσται		ἀπρόσμαχον αὐτὸν ἔσεσθαι

7.3 Evaluation

The stylistic similarities of the scholia reporting the Pindaric version of the Rhesus story and the summaries of Proclus that describe the shared motif of the "late-arriving ally" are clear and self-evident. The crucial question concerns how these points of contact should be explained. Are they due to a common source from which they all derive, perhaps through various intermediaries, or are they incidental in the sense that they reproduce scholiastic language? In my view, the number of similarities, the

---

[99] Like Rhesus, Asteropaeus traces his origin to a river god, since Axius is his grandfather.
[100] See pp. 219 and 239 with n. 114. [101] *Il.* 12.20–22.

analogies in diction and structure of these passages, and the fact that they all cluster around the same motif turn the scales in favor of the first alternative. This line of thought is further reinforced by the fact that (like the Σ (D) *Il.* 10.435 on Rhesus) the Σ (D) *Od.* 11.519–21 on Eurypylus displays the same diction and structure relating to the motif of the "late-arriving ally," which we have examined above:

Εὐρύπυλος ὁ Ἀστυόχης καὶ Τηλέφου τοῦ Ἡρακλέος παῖς... ἵνα παραγένηται σύμμαχος... Νεοπτόλεμος δὲ ὁ Ἀχιλλέως αὐτὸν ἀναιρεῖ.[102]

Since these scholia belong to *historiae* which formed part of the *Mythographus Homericus*, we can hazard an explanation about the derivation of the dictional and structural similarities between the Rhesus and Eurypylus scholia and the relevant passages from Proclus (and Apollodorus). The *Mythographus Homericus* was created by a compiler who drew material from learned sources like *hypomnemata*[103] and shaped it into a commentary that enjoyed an independent life, since it circulated separately from other sorts of exegetical material. The *Mythographus Homericus* included various mythographical *historiae* on Homer, a small part of which we can trace through papyrus fragments and the D-scholia.[104] As can be seen from both Σ (D) *Il.* 10.435 on Rhesus and Σ (D) *Od.* 11.519–21 on Eurypylus, in its original and complete form the *Mythographus Homericus* must have contained references to other figures who, like Rhesus and Eurypylus, were mentioned in Homer *en passant* and for whom readers needed some background information. Such *historiae* may have existed in the original *Mythographus Homericus* for both Penthesileia and Memnon, who are mentioned at *Il.* 24.804–5* and *Od.* 11.522, respectively. The compiler of the *Mythographus Homericus* did not compose these *historiae* on his own. He used material from

---

[102] Σ (D) *Od.* 11.519–21 (Ernst). On the "special" feature of the late-coming ally's previous military excellence and fame, see the discussion of the phrase διάφορος δὲ τῶν καθ' αὐτὸν γενόμενος ἐν πολεμικοῖς ἔργοις (above, pp. 222–5).

[103] Cf. Cameron (2004) 104, who follows Schwartz's theory (accepted by Bethe 1887, 80–90; Maass 1884, 537 n. and 563–4; Panzer 1892, 61–3; Wilamowitz-Moellendorff 1925, 76–7) that the compiler of the *Mythographus Homericus* drew mainly on a mythographical compendium of a later age and of low quality. Cameron disputes Montanari's suggestion that the *Mythographus Homericus* used "high-quality learned commentaries of the Alexandrian age" (1995, 163) by arguing that learned citations do not necessarily imply a learned writer or compiler and that the "great Alexandrian critics did not spend their time on such unscholarly activities as compiling potted mythological biographies, biographies that they were very ill-suited to the Homeric passage they were supposed to be explaining" (Cameron 2004, 104). I side with Montanari (1995), who builds on the results of Lünstedt's analysis (1961), according to which the examination of subscriptions regarding extant authors suggests the validity of the subscriptions, as well as that certain elements are derived not only from the author's text but also from the scholastic tradition on this text, which points to the use of ancient commentaries. I, therefore, see the *Mythographus Homericus* as a lemmata-organized commentary on the Homeric text, with each lemma including a *historia* taking its lead from a specific reference in the *Iliad* and the *Odyssey*. This is not a mythological handbook in the manner of Apollodorus' *Bibliotheca* but a mythographical commentary; see also p. 217 n. 8.

[104] See Montanari (1995) 135–72.

ancient *hypomnemata* on the *Iliad* and the *Odyssey*. After all, this must have been his starting point for the compilation of an independent, self-contained set of mythographical stories built around a single word or expression that was thought to need explanation or commentary. It is possible that, in the case of heroes who did not feature as acting characters in the *Iliad* and the *Odyssey* but were only briefly mentioned, the Homeric *hypomnemata* drew on Cyclic material available at the time either through the archetypal summary of the Epic Cycle,[105] which must have been available from the fourth century BC onwards, or from some other early summaries. This line of argument is based on the fact that the references to the Cyclic poets that we find in D-scholia which reproduce material belonging to the *Mythographus Homericus* derive from the use of early summaries of the Epic Cycle. In this respect, the similarities in diction and structure observed between the *Mythographus Homericus* (not the D-scholia) and the recurrence of the motif of the "late-arriving ally" in the summaries of Proclus (and Apollodorus) may be due to the fact that they may both ultimately derive from early summaries of the Epic Cycle, the former through the intermediary of ancient Homeric *hypomnemata* which drew on early summaries of the Epic Cycle when dealing with heroes who featured in the Cyclic epics (like Penthesileia, Memnon, and Eurypylus), the latter (i.e. Proclus and Apollodorus) from other intermediary summaries of the Epic Cycle.[106] With respect to the *historia* about Rhesus (found in Σ [D] *Il*. 10.435), which was not included in any summary of the Epic Cycle, the similarities in diction and structure observed above may be due to the assimilation and unification of the relevant material which were effected by the compiler when the *Mythographus Homericus* circulated separately from other exegetical material. The reference to Pindar as the source of the *historia* must have existed in the Iliadic *hypomnema* from which this material was excerpted by the compiler of the *Mythographus Homericus*.

As far as the diction of the oracle version is concerned, its departure from the language employed in the Pindaric version is due to its different content (inclusion of magical elements and lack of an *aristeia*). Therefore, it did not undergo the influence of early summaries of the Epic Cycle, although it may have belonged, like the Pindaric version, to ancient *hypomnemata* on the *Iliad* and the *Odyssey*.

---

[105] See Davies (1986) 104–6; M. L. West (2013a) 14–15, 23–26; Fantuzzi and Tsagalis (2015a) 35.

[106] In order to come up with a satisfactory explanation of the fact that sometimes the D-scholia contain details not featuring in Apollodorus' *Bibliotheca*, Pagès (2007, 110–11, and 2017, 72–3) puts forward two hypotheses, which may both be correct if applied to different cases: (a) both Apollodorus and the *Mythographus Homericus* (not the D-scholiast) drew on the same source but omitted certain elements on the basis of what interested them most in a given story; (b) the D-scholiast used the *Bibliotheca* when he had in front of him an abridged version of a story (such as those attested in some of the extant papyri) of the *Mythographus Homericus* and wanted to offer to his readers a fuller version. He therefore copied material from the *Bibliotheca* but kept features (missing from the *Bibliotheca*) of the abridged version of the *Mythographus Homericus* that was available to him. One of the features he preserved from the *Mythographus Homericus* was the *subscriptio* at the end of each *historia*. See also Diller (1935) 298; Cameron (2004) 97–8.

7.4 Reconstruction of Possible Sources

Having discussed the transmission of the Pindaric and oracle version and suggested a tentative explanation of the points of contact between the Pindaric version and the summaries of Proclus, I will now turn my attention to the reconstruction of the possible sources the two versions rely on. I will then proceed with some observations concerning the Homeric version of the Rhesus episode and its usefulness for the *Iliad* at the particular point of the plot, in which it features. I begin by offering a schematic presentation of the Pindaric and oracle versions side by side:

Pindaric version	*Oracle version*
Rhesus arrives late at Troy	Rhesus arrives late at Troy (at night)
He has an *aristeia*, causing the Greeks many casualties	He has no *aristeia*
Hera sends Athena to Diomedes and Odysseus	There is an oracle about the potential invincibility of Rhesus, if he drinks from the Scamander and his horses graze at its banks
Athena advises Diomedes and Odysseus to go on a spying mission during the night	Diomedes and Odysseus go on a spying mission during the night
They find Rhesus sleeping, surrounded by his companions, and kill him	They find Rhesus sleeping and kill him

The first question that needs to be asked concerns the relative chronology of the two versions. It is a question which lies at the heart of this investigation. In my view, we are dealing not with an evolutionary process from an earlier, folktale-oriented oracle version to an epicized account with an *aristeia* but with two different types of story that existed in epic poetry.

With respect to the version of the Rhesus story in which he excels in the battlefield before being killed by Diomedes and Odysseus, it is possible that its introduction into Greek epic did not begin with the *Iliad*. This is suggested by the fact that the Iliadic version of the Rhesus story is deprived of crucial elements like an *aristeia* and the divine intervention of Hera and Athena, which feature in the Pindaric version. These are constitutive elements that may well have an epic origin, since they are attested in Homeric epic in relation to other figures and contexts.[107] They probably come from an epic version which is earlier than not

---

[107] There are various *aristeiai* (e.g. of Diomedes, Agamemnon, Menelaus) in the *Iliad*. As to Hera and Athena, they intervene to assist the Achaeans either together or independently several times (e.g. in *Il.* 5.711–846, 8.350–484, 14.153–362, 20.112–55, 22.214–47).

only Pindar but also the *Iliad*. The need to postulate such a version and reject the possibility that it was Pindar who introduced these elements results not only from the epic tonality of the *aristeia* of Rhesus[108] and the divine intervention features of the Pindaric version but also from the fact that this epic coloring has an even more precise imprint, which I have called cyclic. It consists in the nesting of the aforementioned features in a motif that is cyclic par excellence: the late-coming ally. In this version, in which the magical elements of the reinvigoration of Rhesus and his horses by the water of Scamander were not used, there would have been no reason why the Thracian hero would not fight against the Achaeans before being slain. Since his arrival at Troy conformed with the motif of the late-coming ally, an *aristeia* would have been integral to his story, in the manner of Penthesileia, Memnon, and Eurypylus.[109] A great ally should prove himself on the battlefield before being killed. The *aristeia*, which required the lapse of a day, as our sources stress,[110] would have given time for the epic poet to display to his audience not only Rhesus' military skills but also his *ethopoiia*. The Thracian king may well have engaged in dialogue with his comrades, with his Trojan allies, and perhaps with some of his Achaean victims. His personality would thus be explored—both his willingness to help the Trojans and his cruelty and arrogance. A good analogy is with the way the Iliadic tradition treats the Lycians, who provide important military assistance throughout the war, even accuse the Trojans as cowards,[111] and at times disclose a certain arrogance, as the case of Sarpedon amply testifies. This would have made Rhesus a more human warrior and, in this way, more emotionally identifiable to the audience. Conversely, the Rhesus of the oracle version was a rather arcane character, since he did not engage in any activity in Troy but is killed as soon as he arrives. The poetic gain from removing the magical elements and introducing an *aristeia* would have been significant.

The oracle version recalls the situation of the giant Antaeus, whose power was reinvigorated every time he touched the ground, since he was the son of Gaia.[112] Heracles had to defeat him by lifting him in the air, so that he would not be in contact with an external element that would continuously restore him. The brevity

---

[108] The fact that no Trojan or ally of the Trojans has a typical *aristeia* in the *Iliad*, whereas pro-Trojan allies consistently have *aristeiai* in the Epic Cycle (Penthesileia and Memnon in the *Aethiopis*, Eurypylus in the *Ilias parva*), suggests that Rhesus' *aristeia* is a cyclic feature.

[109] The reason is that Rhesus could not have been killed by an Aeacid, as was the case with Penthesileia and Memnon (who were slain by Achilles) or Eurypylus (who was killed by Neoptolemus). On the reasons that may have suggested that Diomedes and Odysseus killed Rhesus, see pp. 286, 291, 300.

[110] Apollod. *Epit.* 4.4 (ὃς πρὸ μιᾶς ἡμέρας); Σ (D) and Σ (bT) *Il.* 10.435 (μίαν ἡμέραν πολεμήσας πρὸς Ἕλληνας).

[111] See Tsagalis (2012b) 242–4.

[112] Marsyas of Philippi (*FGrHist* 136 F 7) reports that the Muse Clio was abducted by Strymon and gave birth to Rhesus, in front of whose tomb on a hill in Amphipolis she had a sanctuary; see Pagès (2007, 325), who argues that Rhesus was an ancient river god who became the object of a cult and was subsequently introduced in archaic literature referring to the Trojan myth.

of the scholion that reports the oracle version leaves us in the dark about the miraculous association of Rhesus and his horses with the river Scamander. Why would only *he and his horses* gain invincible strength if they drank water from this river? A possible explanation is that, on the analogy of Antaeus whose reinvigorated strength every time he touched the ground stems from the association of his father, Poseidon, with the earth, Rhesus was associated with rivers, as suggested by the river-like name of his father, Eioneus, in the *Iliad*. In accordance with this view, Rhesus would gain insuperable strength if he drank of the element, the water of a river, which was linked to him through his father.[113] The fact that his reinvigoration and invincibility are projected on to his horses may be explained by the typical association of horses with water, be it that of rivers or of the sea.[114] The brevity of the D-scholion, which reports an oracle version that featured in some authors (ἔνιοι δὲ λέγουσιν), leaves us with many questions concerning a fully fledged account of this story. However, it seems fair to assume that in the oracle version, even if the relevant scholion in its extant form does not state it explicitly, Diomedes and Odysseus stole Rhesus' horses after killing him. This observation may indicate that the theft of Rhesus' horses was due to the danger they posed to the Achaeans, which means that they were particular to the oracle version.[115] Being on a par with Rhesus as regards their potential invincibility, his horses could be used by some other Thracian or Trojan or other Trojan ally after Rhesus' death unless they were stolen. The way they are described in the *Iliad*, i.e. as "finest and biggest,"[116] "whiter than snow and their speed of foot being the winds' speed,"[117] and "shining, like the rays of the sun, terribly,"[118] is revealing.

As regards their description as "finest and biggest," it should be stressed that the superlative of these adjectives is never employed for any other horses in Homeric epic.[119] This may reflect their special status in the oracle version, in which they may have been divine, though their highly elliptical Iliadic presentation does not refer at all to their immortality. A relic of their divine nature is that they are not killed

---

[113] As noted above (p. 218), this does not mean that in the Pindaric version Rhesus' father was Strymon and his mother the Muse Euterpe. On criticism of this erroneous assumption by Fenik (1964), see Fries (2014) 13–14, (2016) 295.

[114] See p. 234. An interesting analogy is provided by the fact that one of Achilles' horses (Xanthus) bears the same name as the river Scamander in the Troad (Xanthus being the river's divine name). It can hardly be a coincidence that the name Rhesus is employed for both the Thracian king and a river in the Troad (*Il.* 12.20). It should be noted that the Greeks kill several enemies who are named after rivers in the Troad: Menelaus slays Scamandrius (*Il.* 5.49–50), Diomedes kills Xanthus (*Il.* 5.152–5) and Eurypylus, a priest of Scamander (*Il.* 5.76–8), and Ajax Oileus puts to death Satnius (*Il.* 14.443–4).

[115] If so, the coexistence of the killing of Rhesus' comrades and the theft of his horses in *Iliad* 10 shows that the *Doloneia* has conflated features pertaining to the Pindaric and oracle versions.

[116] *Il.* 10.436: καλλίστους ἵππους ... ἠδὲ μεγίστους.

[117] *Il.* 10.437: λευκότεροι χιόνος, θείειν δ' ἀνέμοισιν ὁμοῖοι.

[118] *Il.* 10.547: αἰνῶς ἀκτίνεσσιν ἐοικότες ἠελίοιο.

[119] The superlative ἄρισται that is used for Eumelus' horses at *Il.* 2.763 refers to their highest evaluation among the horses of the Achaeans, since they are second only to Achilles' horses.

(a reflex of their immortality in the earlier tradition), only stolen.[120] As for the comparison of their speed to the wind, there may be something at work here that goes beyond the common metaphor of "flying" that is employed for horses running swiftly,[121] especially since this is the only case that horses are likened to having the speed of the winds. The analogy with Achilles' divine horses that are born to the wind god Zephyrus and the Harpy Podarge, who bore them "as she grazed in the meadow beside the swirl of the Ocean,"[122] is instructive. As for the comparison of their brightness to the rays of the sun, it may be a reflex of their divine radiance. Likewise, when Achilles speaks to his immortal horses, whose names indicate their distinctiveness,[123] he is compared by virtue of his divine shining weapons to Hyperion.[124] The case of Achilles and his horses is helpful for what may have happened to the earliest version of the Rhesus story. Achilles is the son of a goddess who is associated with water (Thetis is a Nereid). He receives the immortal horses given to his father, Peleus, by Poseidon or the gods collectively as gift when he married Thetis.[125] He also possesses divine armor, which is a gift to Peleus from Hephaestus. How much this armor is interwoven with Achilles can be seen from the fact that he acquires new, Hephaestus-made armor in the *Iliad*, when the old armor is taken by Hector from the corpse of Patroclus (who had borrowed it from Achilles). These divine gifts possess no magical force. Neither the divine armor of Achilles nor his divine horses make him invincible. In similar vein, in the Iliadic rendering of Rhesus' story the supernatural and magical features of his horses are clearly downplayed, if not fully erased.

Turning to the question of the source in which the oracle version of the Rhesus story existed, we are faced with considerable difficulties. The vague ἔνιοι δὲ λέγουσιν of the D-scholion does not help. The central issue here is whether this version also has a cyclic imprint or not. Does the lack of an *aristeia* and the magical element of the empowering waters (of Scamander) and grass (growing at its banks) mean that we are now situated in the realm of folklore and not epic poetry? The following considerations may help us answer this question:

---

[120] The stealing of the horses may also have been linked to the fact that in the oracle version of the Rhesus story their theft was a prerequisite for the sack of Troy; see Servius on Virg. *Aen.* 2.13; also Fenik (1964) 12.

[121] E.g. *Il.* 5.366 = 5.768 = 8.45 = 10.530; see also *Il.* 10.514.

[122] *Il.* 16.149-51 (Ξάνθον καὶ Βαλίον, τὼ ἅμα πνοιῇσι πετέσθην, | τοὺς ἔτεκε Ζεφύρῳ ἀνέμῳ ἅρπυια Ποδάργη, | βοσκομένη λειμῶνι παρὰ ῥόον Ὠκεανοῖο); see also *Il.* 19.400 (Ξάνθέ τε καὶ Βαλίε, τηλεκλυτὰ τέκνα Ποδάργης).

[123] Ξάνθος ("Golden") and Βαλίος ("Dappled").

[124] *Il.* 19.398 (τεύχεσι παμφαίνων ὥς τ' Ἠλέκτωρ Ὑπερίων). Achilles' corselet has been compared with fire (*Il.* 18.610), his shield with the moon (*Il.* 19.374), his helmet with a star (*Il.* 19.381); see Σ (bT) *Il.* 19.398a[1-2].

[125] Poseidon: *Il.* 23.277-8; the gods collectively: *Il.* 16.381 = 16.867, 17.443-4.

a) We know that in the *Ilias parva* the advent of Philoctetes, who has Heracles' bow, is of prime importance for the sack of Troy.[126] The special bow and arrows of Heracles, who has sacked Troy in the past, have a magical dimension, not because of some special feature these weapons possess but because they become a prerequisite for the fall of the besieged city.

b) Helenus' (conditional) oracle, which belongs to Cyclic epic,[127] that Troy's protection depends on the Palladium also has a magical filter. As long as the sacred xoanon of Athena remains in the city, Troy is impregnable.

c) The inclusion of the oracle version of the Rhesus story in the ecphrasis of Juno's temple at Virg. *Aen.* 1.472–3 is implicitly advertised as a Cyclic account. The expressions *ex ordine* and *per orbem* (1.456–7: *videt Iliacas ex ordine pugnas | bellaque iam fama totum vulgata per orbem*) may well be buzzwords of the Epic Cycle.[128]

d) A faint echo of the magical connection between the death of a hero and the fall of a city is still traceable in the case of Hector, whose death signifies the future sack of Troy.[129] Likewise with Rhesus. According to Servius' commentary on Virg. *Aen.* 1.469–73 and 2.13, the Achaeans were given various oracles about the sack of Troy, one of which stipulated that the theft of Rhesus' horses was a prerequisite for the city's fall.[130]

The oracle version,[131] then, belongs to a type of story in which a relic of magic that recalls folk-tale material has found its way into the Trojan saga. The generic acculturation of such features consists in the downplaying or complete erasure of the special abilities of the magical elements and their systematic anchoring to the sack of Troy.

Both the Pindaric and oracle versions are likely to be older than the *Iliad*. They share a simple structure which is at odds with the *Doloneia* that is marked by motif-doubling.[132] It may be argued that the *Iliad* was, because of its plotline, not able to follow either the version with Rhesus' *aristeia* or that of the oracle. It was evident that the Achaean spies should triumph at the end of book 10. Triumph involved the death of a major enemy. But who could be this first-rank hero who

---

[126] *Il. parv.* arg. ll. 211–15 Severyns.
[127] *Il. parv.* arg. ll. 211–12 and 228–9 (Severyns) with Apollod. *Epit.* 5.9–10; see Fries (2016) 294–5.
[128] See Barchiesi (1994) 117–18 = (1999) 333–4; Currie (2016) 68 n. 176.
[129] See Reinhardt (1961) 361.
[130] Fenik (1964, 12) refers only to Servius' comment on *Aen.* 2.13.
[131] See also Parthenius (*Narr. am.* 36), according to whom Rhesus was killed (after traveling widely and falling in love with the huntress Arganthone) by Diomedes in a duel by the banks of a river that was named after him. Parthenius draws on previous sources, like the tragedy *Rhesus* from which he has taken the idea of Rhesus' imposing tribute on foreign people (see [Eur.] *Rh.* 426–42 with Liapis 2012, xxvi). Lightfoot (1999, 554) has argued that the combat by the riverbank may have been triggered by Diomedes' attempt to prevent Rhesus from becoming invincible after drinking from its water. If so, Parthenius (first century BC) knew both the oracle version and the *Rhesus*.
[132] See Fries (2016) 295.

would be killed by Diomedes and Odysseus *without creating new problems for the rest of the poem*? Hector, Sarpedon, Glaucus, Paris, and Aeneas were all needed for the plot and the last two for the next phases of the Trojan War myth. A first prerequisite that this new major hero should meet was that his death had no consequences for the rest of the poem and the Trojan saga. A second prerequisite should be that this hero was of outstanding merit. This meant that he should be not simply a king and leader of a contingent of Trojans or of one of their allies but someone who possessed special abilities and, as a result, posed *a great threat* to the Achaeans. A third prerequisite should be that this hero had no association with Achilles, such as a confrontation on the battlefield. Otherwise, his transfer to the Iliadic plot, at a point when Achilles could not possibly face him (since he was sitting out the war by his ships), would defy the stable skeleton of mythical events that the Trojan War saga had to follow faithfully. Rhesus fulfilled all three prerequisites.

7.5 Putative Poetic Gains

The putative poetic gains from the addition of this episode to an earlier form of book 10 can be classified into two groups: (a) those pertaining to the improvement of the Hector-version, and (b) those referring to the plot of the entire *Iliad*.

As to (a), it may be argued that Hector is not presented as a weak warrior who is saved in the nick of time by means of divine intervention. Moreover, the dramatic irony consisting in the reversal of Dolon's fate in the Hector-version (the would-be looter of the dead is killed and stripped of his weapons) would be deepened in the current version, in which it was extended to the fate of Hector. What he promises (Achilles' horses), he will not get; what his promise presupposes (victory over Achilles), he will suffer himself (death at the hands of Achilles). The poetic gain from this shaping is noteworthy.[133]

As to (b), the first step is made towards building up Hector's arrogant profile, since it is in the Rhesus version that he boasts that he will acquire Achilles' horses (and give them to Dolon). The dialogue between Hector and Dolon about the spying mission in the Trojan council and the dialogue between Odysseus and Dolon about Hector's promise of the horses of Achilles create the necessary

---

[133] Dihle's claim (1970, 35–6) that the abbreviated form of the scholia on *Il.* 10.435 allows for the possibility that Dolon featured in the earliest form of the Rhesus story is methodologically questionable. The lack of comprehensiveness cannot be used as proof that something or someone not mentioned in the relevant scholia was part of the story. Moreover, what role would Dolon play in a story in which Diomedes and Odysseus would have found their way to Rhesus' camp by means of information given to them by Athena? As for the fact that Dolon's role in the *Rhesus* is redundant, Dihle's approach is equally off the mark. This defect of the tragic play is due not to Dolon's inclusion in earlier forms of the Rhesus story but to the influence of *Iliad* 10. On further criticism of Dihle, see Kullmann (1977, 536 = 1992, 206–7).

framework for the formation of a cohesive, deep, and dramatic association with the unraveling of the Iliadic plot. The fact that Rhesus possessed beautiful and fast horses created a link with Achilles' divine and amazingly swift horses, which are the prize Dolon asked from Hector for volunteering to enter the Achaean camp as a spy. By having Hector promise to deliver Achilles' horses to Dolon, which presupposed his victory over Achilles, the *Iliad* establishes the framework for a significant reversal of fortune, rich in dramatic irony. Odysseus' ironic smile and reply to Dolon, after being informed by him about Hector's promise, suggest a carefully designed allusion to the continuation of the plot. Hector will fail not only to defeat Achilles, who will kill him instead (*Iliad* 22), but also to capture Achilles' horses (for himself, since Dolon is dead) in *Iliad* 16, when these horses are driven by Patroclus.[134] Furthermore, the introduction of the Rhesus episode contributes to enhancing the importance of the pair Diomedes–Odysseus. Their triumph in the absence of Achilles establishes them as an important military asset of which the Achaeans will be deprived when the two heroes are successively wounded in book 11.

By conducting a comprehensive analysis of the ancient scholia reporting the Rhesus story, I have suggested that both the Pindaric and oracle versions are marked by a cyclic tinge. The Iliadic epic tradition seems to have employed those features of the Rhesus tale that could be adapted to its plot and were consonant with its tacit downplaying or full erasure of miraculous features, such as the motif of invincibility that referred to both Rhesus and his horses in the oracle version. The addition of the Rhesus story to an earlier form of book 10 had, arguably, important poetic gains: by stressing Hector's arrogant overconfidence through his promise of Achilles' horses to Dolon, it further deepened the process of the dramatic reversal of Hector's fate; by having Diomedes and Odysseus accomplish a dangerous night mission, it allowed the audience to evaluate how much they would be missed (due to their successive wounding in book 11) regarding the protection of the Achaean army in the ensuing episodes of the epic, until the return of Achilles.

---

[134] The fact that Hector will acquire Achilles' divine armor, after stripping it from Patroclus' body, but not Achilles' horses, which will escape back to the ships, shows the effectiveness of the new development where Hector promises Achilles' horses to Dolon. This is undoubtedly a noteworthy narrative improvement.

8
Comparative Material
The *Mahābhārata* and the *Aeneid*

Introduction

Comparative material is useful to our inquiry not only with respect to the similarities and/or analogies it shares with the Rhesus story but also in view of the wider context within which it is placed.[1] By wider context I am referring to the events with which it is related and the order of their presentation. As we will see, an array of internal and external similarities and analogies links the Rhesus story with the night raid in book 10 of the *Mahābhārata*[2] and with the episode of Nisus and Euryalus in *Aeneid* 9.[3]

Before we begin, it is useful to keep in mind two important observations. First, nyctomachies can take various forms: (a) scouting expeditions; (b) ambushes of single individuals or groups of enemies; (c) a raid on the enemy's camp; and (d) the sack of a city by attack or infiltration.[4] As I have argued above, the *Doloneia*, which seems to represent the fusion of two different phases of composition, may (Hector-version) have initially belonged to type (b), whereas its current form begins as (a) and ends as (b) and (c). Second, nyctomachies display a typology based on four tropes: (i) they follow a period of calm or at least non-fighting (*Iliad* 9); (ii) the tranquility is interrupted when a leader who is worried about the situation takes action that leads to a night mission (Agamemnon); (iii) those who volunteer for

---

[1] The detection of features shared by two different texts may in general be explained by their sharing a certain typology which pertains either to their analogous content or to the transfer of motifs and features from one to the other. When these texts belong to different cultures and have been composed or written in different languages, the *onus probandi* falls even more on the following criteria: (a) the quantity of the shared features; (b) the level of their integration in two different episodes; (c) the featuring of some of the principal characters in other episodes of the same text; (d) the level of internal cohesion of each episode; (e) the existence of narrative breaches created by these features in one or both of these texts; (f) the detection of dictional elements that are functional in the language of one of the two texts but extinct in the other; and (g) the question and direction of transferability of material on the basis of analogous transfers from other episodes that have been already identified with respect to these two texts.

[2] The following material is based on Johnson's summary (1998, 98–9) of the initial part of book 10 of the *Mahābhārata*; see also Fries (2016) 289–324.

[3] The episode of Nisus and Euryalus will be the main subject of the relevant section, though I will also draw attention to other material from the *Aeneid* which is associated (directly or indirectly) with the Rhesus episode.

[4] See Dinter, Finkmann, and Khoo (2019) 246.

such a dangerous mission are lured by rewards (Nestor's promises constitute rewards that increase the spies' property and social recognition); and (iv) the spies or ambushers acquire spoils (Dolon's weapons, Rhesus' beautiful white horses).

8.1 The *Mahābhārata* and *Iliad* 10

Book 10 of the *Mahābhārata* is known as the *Sauptikaparvan* ("The [book of the] Massacre at Night"). The relevant events are, in brief, as follows. After the death of the mighty warrior Duryodhana, Aśvatthāman, Kṛpa, and Kṛtavarman take refuge in a forest. When Aśvatthāman sees an owl killing other owls he interprets it as a bird-omen indicating that they should launch a night raid against his sleeping enemies, in order to avenge the death of his father, Droṇa. Despite Kṛpa's different opinion, Aśvatthāman departs for the enemy camp followed by Kṛpa and Kṛtavarman. Leaving his two companions at the camp's gates with the order to kill anyone who attempts to escape, Aśvatthāman enters the camp and slaughters many of his sleeping enemies, including the entire host of Pāñcālas and Pāṇḍavas, with the exception of Dhṛṣṭadyumna's charioteer, who escapes and breaks the news to the Pāṇḍavas.

Even on the basis of this summary it is possible to discern an entire set of external and internal thematic similarities, as well as structural analogies, with the Rhesus story.[5] These similarities and analogies seem to reflect an inherited narrative pattern pertaining to the theme of night attack that is shared by the Rhesus episode and the night raid of Aśvatthāman on the Pāṇḍavas' camp.[6]

8.1.1 External Similarities

Mahābhārata
(a) The enemy is victorious
The Pāṇḍavas defeat the Kauravas
books 6–9

(b) Major warriors of the defeated side have been killed
book 6: Bhīṣma; Book 7: Droṇa;
book 8: Karṇa;
book 9: Śalya (beginning) and Duryodhana (climax and end)

Iliad
The enemy is victorious
The Trojans defeat the Achaeans
book 8

The best warrior of the defeated side abstains from war
books 1–8: Achilles

---

[5] Liapis (2012, xxxii) offers a brief discussion of some analogies between the *Sauptikaparvan*, *Iliad* 10, and the *Rhesus*; a thorough analysis is offered by Fries (2016) 289–324.

[6] See M. L. West (2007) 475; Fries (2016) 296–7, 319. Fries's analysis is based on "ten corresponding elements between *Iliad* 10 and its alternatives and the *Sauptikaparvan*" (297). My own examination is structured in a slightly different way.

(c) The enemy cannot be defeated in regular warfare but through treachery	The enemy's plan may be revealed by deception
book 10	book 10

External similarities concern the context within which these two episodes are placed. In both cases the night raid is undertaken by the side that has been defeated up to this point in the war (a).[7] The inherent danger and high risk of a nocturnal endeavor reflect the desperate condition of the defeated side. In the *Sauptikaparvan*, defeat takes the form of the loss of many major heroes, while in the *Iliad* it is expressed by the absence of Achilles on the Achaean side, the dominance of Hector in the field of battle, and the retreat of the Achaeans into their camp (b). A solution can be found only by recourse to a risky endeavor involving treachery and deceit, a night raid in the *Sauptikaparvan*, a night mission, which unexpectedly becomes a raid, in *Iliad* 10 (c). Fries[8] rightly claims that the implications of this comparison are that the night raid is not an independent type of story that could stand on its own but "part of an extended complex of martial epic,"[9] and that its placement in the *Iliad* at this particular point of the plot is explained by its narrative background as manifested in two different epic traditions.[10]

8.1.2 Internal Similarities

Mahābhārata	*Iliad* 10
(a) Sleeplessness	**Sleeplessness**
10.1.32–3: But Droṇa's son	*Il.* 10.3–4: ἀλλ' οὐκ Ἀτρείδην Ἀγαμέμνονα, ποιμένα λαῶν,
could not sleep...sleep lay beyond	ὕπνος ἔχε γλυκερὸς πολλὰ φρεσὶν
his grasp	ὁρμαίνοντα
(a1) Many/all were asleep, but one person did not sleep	**Many/all were asleep, but one person did not sleep**

---

[7] The defeat of the Kauravas is permanent, whereas that of the Achaeans is temporary (as well as in the Pindaric and oracle versions).
[8] Fries (2016) 297–8.   [9] Fries (2016) 298.
[10] The next night (after the long day starting at *Il.* 11.1) occurs in book 18 (239–42), i.e. after the news of Patroclus' death has reached Achilles. Because of this fact, the night raid could not have been placed anywhere in books 11–18, during which time all action takes place during the day and the Achaeans are pushed to the brink of defeat.

10.1.30: Then limbs dragged down by sleep, they lay on the bare earth...	*Il.* 10.1–4: ἄλλοι μὲν παρὰ νηυσὶν ἀριστῆες Παναχαιῶν εὗδον παννύχιοι...
10.1.33: sleep lay beyond his grasp	ἀλλ' οὐκ Ἀτρείδην Ἀγαμέμνονα, ποιμένα λαῶν | ὕπνος ἔχε γλυκερὸς
(a2) Designation of the sleepless hero by his patronymic	Designation of the sleepless hero by his patronymic
Droṇa's son	*Il.* 10.3: Ἀτρείδην
(a3) Stress on the emotional state of the hero by means of participial clauses	Stress on the emotional state of the hero by means of participial clauses
10.1.32–3: overpowered by shame, and wrath, burnt up by rage	*Il.* 10.4: πολλὰ φρεσὶν ὁρμαίνοντα
(a4) Use of a simile	Use of a simile
10.1.32: hissing like a snake	*Il.* 10.5–10: ὡς δ' ὅτ' ἂν ἀστράπτῃ πόσις Ἥρης ἠϋκόμοιο, | τεύχων ἢ πολὺν ὄμβρον ἀθέσφατον ἠὲ χάλαζαν | ἢ νιφετόν, ὅτε πέρ τε χιὼν ἐπάλυνεν ἀρούρας, | ἠέ ποθι πτολέμοιο μέγα στόμα πευκεδανοῖο, | ὣς πυκίν' ἐν στήθεσσιν ἀνεστενάχιζ' Ἀγαμέμνων | νειόθεν ἐκ κραδίης, τρομέοντο δέ οἱ φρένες ἐντός
(a5) The sleepless hero surveys the scene	The sleepless hero surveys the scene
10.1.34–5: great-armed Aśvatthāman surveyed the terrible forest and its lurid sights	*Il.* 10.11: ἤτοι ὅτ' ἐς πεδίον τὸ Τρωϊκὸν ἀθρήσειε
(a6) While they suffer, the enemy rejoices	While they suffer, the enemy rejoices
10.1.3–4: bruised and tenderized by blades, all seeping wounds, and panting... they thought on... Paṇḍu's sons, whose shouts	*Il.* 10.12–16: θαύμαζεν πυρὰ πολλά, τὰ καίετο Ἰλιόθι πρό, αὐλῶν συρίγγων τ' ἐνοπὴν ὅμαδόν τ' ἀνθρώπων. αὐτὰρ ὅτ' ἐς νῆάς τε ἴδοι καὶ λαὸν Ἀχαιῶν, πολλὰς ἐκ κεφαλῆς προθελύμνους ἕλκετο χαίτας

of dreadful triumph filled the air;   ὑψόθ' ἐόντι Διί, μέγα δ' ἔστενε κυδάλιμον κῆρ

10.1.59: The Pāñcālas are buzzing,
they bellow and laugh;
jubilant, they blow their conches
by the hundred, and batter
their drums

(b) Plan for Night Mission   **Plan for a Night Mission**

10.1.44: my thoughts are locked   *Il.* 10.43–4: χρεὼ βουλῆς... | κερδαλέης, ἥ τις κεν

onto my enemies' death, and   ἐρύσσεται ἠδὲ σαώσει | Ἀργείους καὶ νῆας

now the time has come   *Il.* 10.204–10: ... οὐκ ἂν δή τις ἀνὴρ πεπίθοιθ' ἑῷ αὐτοῦ

10.1.53: resolved to massacre at night   θυμῷ τολμήεντι μετὰ Τρῶας μεγαθύμους

10.3.24–5, 28–9 *passim*: tonight   ἐλθεῖν, εἴ τινά που δηΐων ἕλοι ἐσχατόωντα,

10.3.26: in the dead of night   ἤ τινά που καὶ φῆμιν ἐνὶ Τρώεσσι πύθοιτο,

I shall make an irresistible assault   ἄσσά τε μητιόωσι μετὰ σφίσιν, ἢ μεμάασιν

10.3.29: so shall I roam tonight   αὖθι μένειν παρὰ νηυσὶν ἀπόπροθεν, ἦε πόλινδε

among the Pāñcālas, slaughtering   ἂψ ἀναχωρήσουσιν, ἐπεὶ δαμάσαντό γ' Ἀχαιούς.

them in war   *Il.* 10.251–3: ἀλλ' ἴομεν· μάλα γὰρ νὺξ ἄνεται, ἐγγύθι δ' ἠώς,

10.3.30: I shall then torment in   ἄστρα δὲ δὴ προβέβηκε, παροίχωκεν δὲ πλέων νύξ

combat Pāṇḍu's sons tonight.   τῶν δύο μοιράων, τριτάτη δ' ἔτι μοῖρα λέλειπται

(b1) Consulting with the wise   **Consulting with the wise**

10.2.31: So let's approach   *Il.* 10.54–6: ... ἐγὼ δ' ἐπὶ Νέστορα δῖον

Dhṛtarāṣṭra, Gāndhārī,   εἶμι, καὶ ὀτρυνέω ἀνστήμεναι, αἴ κ' ἐθέλῃσιν

and clever Vidura—   ἐλθεῖν ἐς φυλάκων ἱερὸν τέλος ἠδ' ἐπιτεῖλαι

let's consult with them.

COMPARATIVE MATERIAL 249

(b2) Selecting companions

10.4.8: For who would fight

Droṇa's son in battle,

with Kṛpa and Kṛtavarman

at his side?

Selecting a companion

Il. 10.242–7: εἰ μὲν δὴ ἕταρόν γε κελεύετέ
μ' αὐτὸν ἑλέσθαι,

πῶς ἂν ἔπειτ' Ὀδυσῆος ἐγὼ θείοιο
λαθοίμην,

οὗ πέρι μὲν πρόφρων κραδίη καὶ θυμὸς
ἀγήνωρ

ἐν πάντεσσι πόνοισι, φιλεῖ δέ ἑ Παλλὰς
Ἀθήνη.

τούτου γ' ἑσπομένοιο καὶ ἐκ πυρὸς
αἰθομένοιο

ἄμφω νοστήσαιμεν, ἐπεὶ περίοιδε νοῆσαι

(c) Arming

10.5.35–6: Take up your bows

and swords, buckle your armor

without delay, and wait on me.

Mounting his chariot with these

words, he then set out towards the foe.

And Kṛpa and Kṛtavarman

of the Satvas followed him.

Il. 10.254–71: ὣς εἰπόνθ' ὅπλοισιν ἔνι
δεινοῖσιν ἐδύτην.

Τυδεΐδῃ μὲν δῶκε μενεπτόλεμος
Θρασυμήδης

φάσγανον ἄμφηκες—τὸ δ' ἐὸν παρὰ νηῒ
λέλειπτο—

καὶ σάκος· ἀμφὶ δέ οἱ κυνέην κεφαλῆφιν
ἔθηκεν

ταυρείην, ἄφαλόν τε καὶ ἄλλοφον, ἥ τε
καταῖτυξ

κέκληται, ῥύεται δὲ κάρη θαλερῶν
αἰζηῶν.

Μηριόνης δ' Ὀδυσῆϊ δίδου βιὸν ἠδὲ
φαρέτρην

καὶ ξίφος, ἀμφὶ δέ οἱ κυνέην κεφαλῆφιν
ἔθηκεν

ῥινοῦ ποιητήν· πολέσιν δ' ἔντοσθεν ἱμᾶσιν
ἐντέτατο στερεῶς· ἔκτοσθε δὲ λευκοὶ
ὀδόντες

ἀργιόδοντος ὑὸς θαμέες ἔχον ἔνθα καὶ
ἔνθα

εὖ καὶ ἐπισταμένως· μέσσῃ δ' ἐνὶ πῖλος
ἀρήρει.

τήν ῥά ποτ' ἐξ Ἐλεῶνος Ἀμύντορος
Ὀρμενίδαο

250 THE HOMERIC *DOLONEIA*

	ἐξέλετ᾽ Αὐτόλυκος πυκινὸν δόμον ἀντιτορήσας,
	Σκάνδειαν δ᾽ ἄρα δῶκε Κυθηρίῳ Ἀμφιδάμαντι·
	Ἀμφιδάμας δὲ Μόλῳ δῶκε ξεινήϊον εἶναι,
	αὐτὰρ ὁ Μηριόνῃ δῶκεν ᾧ παιδὶ φορῆναι·
	δὴ τότ᾽ Ὀδυσσῆος πύκασεν κάρη ἀμφιτεθεῖσα
(c1) Departure expressed by a simile	Departure expressed by a simile
10.5.37: shining like three enkindled	*Il.* 10.297–8: βάν ῥ᾽ ἴμεν ὥς τε λέοντε δύω διὰ νύκτα
sacrificial fires, fed with ghee, those	μέλαιναν, | ἂμ φόνον, ἂν νέκυας, διά τ᾽ ἔντεα
three advanced towards the foe	καὶ μέλαν αἷμα.
(d) Divine assistance	Divine assistance
10.1.64: With these words Lord Śiva	*Il.* 10.366–7: τότε δὴ μένος ἔμβαλ᾽ Ἀθήνη | Τυδεΐδῃ
gave the warrior a spotless sword,	*Il.* 10.482: τῷ δ᾽ ἔμπνευσε μένος γλαυκῶπις Ἀθήνη
and entered his body	*Il.* 10.509–11: νόστου δὴ μνῆσαι, μεγαθύμου Τυδέος υἱέ,
	νῆας ἔπι γλαφυράς, μὴ καὶ πεφοβημένος ἔλθῃς,
	μή πού τις καὶ Τρῶας ἐγείρῃσιν θεὸς ἄλλος
(d1) Self-sacrifice	Prayers
10.7.2–66: By an act beyond the	*Il.* 10.278–82: κλῦθί μοι, αἰγιόχοιο Διὸς τέκος, ἥ τέ μοι αἰεί
unintelligent—by an act which,	ἐν πάντεσσι πόνοισι παρίστασαι, οὐδέ σε λήθω
even for those with a mind,	κινύμενος· νῦν αὖτε μάλιστά με φίλαι, Ἀθήνη,
is barely imaginable—I shall offer myself in sacrifice to the destroyer	δὸς δὲ πάλιν ἐπὶ νῆας ἐϋκλεῖας ἀφικέσθαι, ῥέξαντας μέγα ἔργον, ὅ κε Τρώεσσι μελήσῃ.
of the citadel...	*Il.* 10.284–94:
Then, being possessed by God,	κέκλυθι νῦν καὶ ἐμεῖο, Διὸς τέκος, Ἀτρυτώνη·

Aśvatthaāman blazed with divine energy,	σπεῖό μοι ὡς ὅτε πατρὶ ἅμ' ἕσπεο Τυδέϊ δίῳ
and with that fiery,	ἐς Θήβας, ὅτε τε πρὸ Ἀχαιῶν ἄγγελος ᾔει.
God-engendered power,	τοὺς δ' ἄρ' ἐπ' Ἀσωπῷ λίπε χαλκοχίτωνας Ἀχαιούς,
he was transformed into the embodiment of battle	αὐτὰρ ὁ μειλίχιον μῦθον φέρε Καδμείοισι κεῖσ'· ἀτὰρ ἂψ ἀπιὼν μάλα μέρμερα μήσατο ἔργα
	σὺν σοὶ δῖα θεά, ὅτε οἱ πρόφρασσα παρέστης.
	ὣς νῦν μοι ἐθέλουσα παρίσταο καί με φύλασσε.
	σοὶ δ' αὖ ἐγὼ ῥέξω βοῦν ἦνιν εὐρυμέτωπον,
	ἀδμήτην, ἣν οὔ πω ὑπὸ ζυγὸν ἤγαγεν ἀνήρ·
	τήν τοι ἐγὼ ῥέξω χρυσὸν κέρασιν περιχεύας.
	Il. 10.366–8: ...τότε δὴ μένος ἔμβαλ' Ἀθήνη
	Τυδείδῃ, ἵνα μή τις Ἀχαιῶν χαλκοχιτώνων
	φθαίη ἐπευξάμενος βαλέειν, ὁ δὲ δεύτερος ἔλθοι.
	Il. 10.482–3: τῷ δ' ἔμπνευσε μένος γλαυκῶπις Ἀθήνη,
	κτεῖνε δ' ἐπιστροφάδην
(d2) Bird-omen	**Bird-omen**
10.1.34–42: The warrior saw a fig tree	Il. 10.274–6: τοῖσι δὲ δεξιὸν ἧκεν ἐρῳδιὸν ἐγγὺς ὁδοῖο
covered in crows—... beheld an owl	Παλλὰς Ἀθηναίη· τοὶ δ' οὐκ ἴδον ὀφθαλμοῖσι
... uttering soft, deceitful cries,	νύκτα δι' ὀρφναίην, ἀλλὰ κλάγξαντος ἄκουσαν
like any bird come down to roost, it fell upon the tree— stopped on a branch, and slaughtered countless sleeping crows	

(e) Division of duties

10.8.8: I shall penetrate the camp

and career about like Time

[the Destroyer]. The two of you

must ensure that not a man escapes you

alive—I have decided that it must be so.

(f) Unconcerned and tired enemy killed in his sleep

10.8.11: the Pāñcālas, exhausted by great deeds done in the intensity of battle, slept unconcerned, surrounded by their fellows

(f1) Enemy lying among his people

10.3.26: as they are lying prone within their camp, among their own people

(f2) Killing the enemy

10.3.26: I shall make an irresistible assault

10.3.27: I shall attack and slaughter them

10.3.28: I shall...consume all those whose

lord is Dhṛṣṭadyumna

10.1.53: Aśvatthāman massacres the enemy

10.3.33–5: I shall...tear the shoulders of...the Pāñcāla king...his head... I shall strike in battle the sleeping sons of the Pāñcālas and Pāṇḍavas alike

Division of duties

Il. 10.479–81: ...πρόφερε κρατερὸν μένος· οὐδέ τί σε χρὴ ἑστάμεναι μέλεον σὺν τεύχεσιν, ἀλλὰ λύ' ἵππους·

ἠὲ σύ γ' ἄνδρας ἔναιρε, μελήσουσιν δ' ἐμοὶ ἵπποι

Unconcerned and tired enemy killed in his sleep

Il. 10.471: οἱ δ' εὗδον καμάτῳ ἀδηκότες

Enemy lying among his people

Il. 10.474: Ῥῆσος δ' ἐν μέσῳ εὗδε

Killing the enemy

Il. 10.483: κτεῖνε δ' ἐπιστροφάδην

Il. 10.487–8: ὣς μὲν Θρήϊκας ἄνδρας ἐπώχετο Τυδέος υἱός, | ὄφρα δυώδεκ' ἔπεφνεν

Il. 10.494–5: βασιλῆα...τὸν τρισκαιδέκατον μελιηδέα θυμὸν ἀπηύρα

10.8.37: slew the others, man by man, careering through the camp, path after path

(g) "Oracular" dream

10.64–7: Then, chanting, there appeared

before them a black-skinned Woman, the Night of all-destroying Time... on other nights, the greatest of those warriors had seen her in their dreams, leading the sleepers away— and Droṇa's son, forever killing them see also 8.69: and those fate-afflicted heroes, remembering such former sights, understood that what they had dreamt then was now being realized in fact

(h) Charioteer breaks the news

10.1–25: he reports to Yudhiṣṭhira

the slaughter done on the sleeping

warriors by Aśvatthāman

(i) Lament

10.8.26–7: Then, after that great warrior,

Droṇa's son, had gone, the women

and the guards began to cry out loud. 10.10.9–25 and 10.11.4–25: King Yudhiṣṭhira and Draupadī utter laments

(j) Joy after the safe return of the hero

10.8.140–1: Kṛpa and Kṛtavarman

"Oracular" dream

Il. 10.496–7: κακὸν γὰρ ὄναρ κεφαλῆφιν ἐπέστη

τὴν νύκτ᾽, Οἰνείδαο πάϊς

Charioteer breaks the news

Il. 10.522–3: ᾤμωξέν τ᾽ ἄρ᾽ ἔπειτα φίλον τ᾽ ὀνόμηνεν ἑταῖρον.

Τρώων δὲ κλαγγή τε καὶ ἄσπετος ὦρτο κυδοιμός

Lament

Il. 10.522–3: ᾤμωξέν τ᾽ ἄρ᾽ ἔπειτα φίλον τ᾽ ὀνόμηνεν ἑταῖρον

Τρώων δὲ κλαγγή τε καὶ ἄσπετος ὦρτο κυδοιμός

Joy after the safe return of the hero

Il. 10.541–2: τοὶ δὲ χαρέντες | δεξιῇ ἠσπάζοντο

with high-pitched cries of joy exulted and clapped their hands,	ἔπεσσί τε μειλιχίοισι *Il.* 10.565: ἅμα δ' ἄλλοι ἴσαν χαίροντες Ἀχαιοί

when they saw Aśvatthāman return safe

from the enemy camp

10.8.148–9: Warriors greeted one another,
exclaiming, "Well done! Well done, indeed!"
Saluted by the others, Droṇa's great son
embraced them and, with joy, uttered this high speech

Internal similarities between the *Sauptikaparvan* and *Iliad* 10 are numerous. I offer a brief commentary on each of them:

(a) Sleeplessness: Aśvatthāman and Agamemnon are lying awake. This similarity is reinforced by (a1) the use of similar phraseology ('many/all were asleep, but one person was not sleeping);[11] (a2) the designation of the sleepless figure by his patronymic (Droṇa's son/son of Atreus); (a3) the stress on the emotional state of the hero by means of participial clauses (overpowered by shame and wrath, burnt up by rage/pondering in his mind); (a4) the use of a simile (hissing like a snake/as when Hera... such was Agamemnon); (a5) the picture of the sleepless hero surveying the scene (Aśvatthāman surveys the forest and its sights); (a6) the contrast between the rejoicing enemy and the suffering army of the protagonist (the protagonists' army is presented as seeping wounds and panting, while the enemy is jubilant, blowing their conches by the hundred, and battering their drums/the Trojans and their allies are celebrating with flutes and pipes, while Agamemnon is desperate, pulling his hair and stricken in lamentation).

(b) Plan for the night mission: Aśvatthāman wakes up Kṛpa and Kṛtavarman and thinks of launching a night assault. Agamemnon and Menelaus wake up various Achaean leaders. Kṛpa suggests that they approach Dhṛtarāṣṭra, Gāndhārī, and clever Vidura to consult with them, but this plan is not carried out. Agamemnon suggests that they consult Nestor, and this decision is carried out. After some

---

[11] The expression "he pondered in his mind" that follows in *Iliad* 10 is not attested in the *Sauptikaparvan*. Even in Old Norse poetry, where Gunnar is awake, he ponders about something that has happened, not about what he should do (like Agamemnon in the *Doloneia*); see M. L. West (2007) 475; Fries (2016) 300.

deliberating, Aśvatthāman's plan for a night raid and assault on the enemy prevails. Nestor advises that the Achaeans send a spying mission to find out Hector's plan (this plan may have already been in Agamemnon's mind, since Menelaus had asked him about it earlier on). The three men (Aśvatthāman, Kṛpa, and Kṛtavarman, though Kṛpa and Kṛtavarman act as one person)[12] set out for the night raid. Diomedes and Odysseus set out for the nocturnal spying mission.

(c) Arming: Aśvatthāman urges Kṛpa and Kṛtavarman to arm themselves and follow him. Diomedes and Odysseus receive special gear from Thrasymedes and Meriones, respectively, before they depart for the night mission. In the *Sauptikaparvan*, the heroes arm for a raid, while in *Iliad* 10 for a reconnaissance mission.[13] The departure of Aśvatthāman, Kṛpa, and Kṛtavarman is marked by a simile. Likewise, the departure of Diomedes and Odysseus.

(d) Divine assistance: In the *Sauptikaparvan*, when Aśvatthāman arrives at the threshold of the camp, he sees a guardian great-bodied spirit, Lord Śiva, standing in front of the gate. After being unable to kill Śiva, Aśvatthāman offers himself in sacrifice and the god enters his body and arms him with a sword. With his powers renewed and filled with battle frenzy, Aśvatthāman enters the enemy camp ready to slaughter his enemies. In *Iliad* 10, Odysseus and Diomedes pray to Athena and ask for her assistance. The goddess gives might to Diomedes both when he captures Dolon and when he slays Rhesus and his guards. Aśvatthāman's decision for a night raid rests on spotting an owl slaughtering countless sleeping crows. Although this seems analogous to the portent of the sparrows and their mother in Aulis,[14] it is striking that Athena makes her presence felt by means of a night heron,[15] immediately before the two spies pray to her in the *Doloneia*, as if an indication of a divine portent.[16] The Pindaric version and the *Rhesus* both testify to the motif of divine assistance, as Athena orchestrates the night ambush.[17]

(e) Division of duties: Aśvatthāman will penetrate the enemy camp, while Kṛpa and Kṛtavarman will make sure that nobody escapes. (This seems the most likely scenario for the *Sauptikaparvan*, despite the textual problem posed by *vāṃ* ("you," gen. dual), which in other texts that do not have the line "I decided that it must be so" is replaced by *me* ["me," gen. sing.]). Fries rightly argues that the undisputed fact that Kṛpa and Kṛtavarman have a different role in this episode, since they do no follow Aśvatthāman inside the camp, is better explained if we read *vāṃ* ("you"), which shows that there was a division of duties. The division of duties also features in *Iliad* 10,[18]

---

[12] See Garbutt (2006) 187.
[13] On arming in the *Doloneia*, see pp. 144–50, 153, 158–61.
[14] Mentioned at *Il.* 2.308-19.
[15] *Il.* 10.274-6.
[16] Fries (2016, 304) draws attention to Athena's assistance to Diomedes and Achilles by means of a golden halo cast around their heads in *Il.* 5.4-7 and 18.203-31, respectively.
[17] See Fries (2014) 11-12, 369 on *Rhesus* 670-1a, (2016) 304.
[18] However, it seems that in the Pindaric version there is no division of duties, since both Diomedes and Odysseus kill Rhesus and his comrades (Σ (D) *Il.* 10.435: ἐπιστάντες δὲ ἐκεῖνοι κοιμωμένῳ Ῥήσῳ αὐτόν τε καὶ τοὺς ἑταίρους αὐτοῦ κτείνουσιν); the same is the case in a Chalcidian neck-amphora by the Inscription Painter, dating to the middle of the sixth century BC (Malibu, Getty Museum 96.AE.1); see pp. 17 n. 91 and 291.

in which Diomedes tells Odysseus to take care of Rhesus' horses and let him do all the killing.[19] A further argument corroborating Fries's analysis is that even in the Dolon episode there are traces of a division of duties (this time by the narrator) since Diomedes captures the Trojan spy and Odysseus interrogates him.[20]

(f) An unconcerned and tired enemy is killed in his sleep. In the *Sauptikaparvan*, Aśvatthāman slays the Pāñcāla prince Dhṛṣṭadyumna in his tent, while all the Pāñcālas are sleeping, surrounded by their comrades, after being worn out by the intensity of battle. He then kills Sikhaṇḍin, Draupadī's five sons, and the entire army of the Pāñcālas and the Pāṇḍavas (except Dhṛṣṭadyumna's charioteer). The successive killings of Aśvatthāman are emphasized.[21] Aśvatthāman's assault takes the enemy by surprise. Nobody has noticed him entering the camp, not even the guards at the gates. Likewise, in the *Doloneia* the Thracians are sleeping exhausted from fatigue (which must refer to their journey from Thrace to Troy since they have not yet done any fighting).[22] The same is the case in the *Rhesus*.[23] Rhesus is sleeping surrounded by his men; nobody notices the Achaean spies; the successive killings of the guards by Diomedes are stressed.[24] In the Pindaric version, the exhaustion of Rhesus and the Thracians may have been explained because of their fighting the previous day at Troy. In the *Rhesus* the carelessness of the Thracians is highlighted.[25] Fries argues that the carelessness of the enemy who are taken by surprise may belong to the original story pattern on which the *Sauptikaparvan*, *Iliad* 10, and the *Rhesus* draw. This fatal negligence is mentioned in both Yudhiṣṭhira's and the Charioteer's lament in the *Sauptikaparvan*[26] and the *Rhesus*[27], respectively.

(g) "Oracular" dream: This type of dream is characteristic of both the *Sauptikaparvan* and *Iliad* 10. It is deprived of a prophetic aspect and is marked by its tragic overtones, since the victims see a bad dream, in which their killer

---

[19] This motif is also attested at *Il.* 5.221–38, in which Aeneas and Pandarus discuss who will be the charioteer when they attack Diomedes; see Danek (1988) 152–3, who observes that in *Iliad* 10 there is no discussion between the two Achaean spies, Diomedes dictating to Odysseus what he should do; see also Fries (2016) 305–6, whose analysis I follow.

[20] Diomedes addresses Dolon (*Il.* 10.447–53), only to tell him that he will kill him. Diomedes explains his decision to Dolon by saying that, if they let him go, he will either carry out his own spying mission or fight against them later. This speech is reminiscent of the task imposed on Kṛpa and Kṛtavarman that no enemy should escape from the camp. In the *Rhesus* (622–6), there is also a division of duties: Odysseus steals the horses, Diomedes kills Rhesus and the Thracians. However, this division is achieved after a brief dialogue between the two heroes, whereas at *Il.* 10.479–81 it is Odysseus who decides about the division. See Fries (2014) 358 on [Eur.] *Rh.* 622–3, who notes that the alternatives mentioned in the Iliadic text are presented in reverse order in the *Rhesus*.

[21] 10.8.37: slew the others, man by man careering through the camp, path after path.

[22] Exhaustion from fatigue because of a long journey features in the night raid narrated in the *Rāmāyana* (6.22.18).

[23] 763–4: πεδοστιβεῖ | κόπῳ δαμέντες.   [24] *Il.* 10.483: κτεῖνε δ' ἐπιστροφάδην.

[25] 761–9: ἡμεῖς δ' ἀβούλως κἀκλεῶς ὀλώλαμεν. | ἐπεὶ γὰρ ἡμᾶς ηὔνασ' Ἑκτόρεια χείρ, | ξύνθημα λέξας, | ηὕδομεν πεδοστιβεῖ | κόπῳ δαμέντες, οὐδ' ἐφρουρεῖτο στρατός | φυλακαῖσι νυκτέροισιν οὐδ' ἐν τάξεσιν | ἔκειτο τεύχη πλῆκτρά τ' οὐκ ἐπὶ ζυγοῖς | ἵππων καθήρμοσθ', ὡς ἄναξ ἐπεύθετο | κρατοῦντας ὑμᾶς κἀφεδρεύοντας νεῶν | πρύμναισι· φαύλως δ' ηὕδομεν πεπτωκότες.

[26] 10.10.9–25.   [27] 761, 769.

features, at the very moment he is about to slay them. This is the crucial difference separating these two dreams from prophetic dreams in Near Eastern tradition,[28] in which the dreams are interpreted.[29] Two other secondary features strengthen the similarity between the two contexts: the killer is described by paronomasia (periphrastic patronymic [Droṇa's son] for Aśvatthāman, periphrastic designation consisting of patronymic [Οἰνεΐδαο] + "son" [πάϊς] for Diomedes),[30] and a goddess is mentioned either together with the killer as part of the victims' dream (a baleful goddess [Kālī?] and Aśvatthāman) or in association with the killer who is the victim's dream (Athena and Diomedes). Although the correspondence is not perfect and the Greek version is more complicated and interpretively difficult, the similarities are too pointed to be overlooked. Fries[31] argues in favor of common heritage.

(h) Charioteer breaks the news: In the *Mahābhārata*, Yudhiṣṭhira finds out about the carnage by a nameless charioteer, while in *Iliad* 10 the news is broken to the army by Hippocoon, Rhesus' cousin, who is woken up by Apollo. The name Hippocoon (< ἵππος + κοέω, "the one who looks after the horses")[32] allows for the possibility that the charioteer was nameless in the traditional story lying behind the *Sauptikaparvan* and the *Doloneia*.[33] Likewise, the Charioteer is not named in the *Rhesus*, although we cannot tell whether this figure has been modeled on Hippocoon of *Iliad* 10 or the poet of this play drew on another story that we are unaware of.[34] Fries[35] suggests that Rhesus' cousin Hippocoon was originally a charioteer, which is certainly possible. However, the motif of the "only survivor," which she traces in both the *Mahābhārata* and the *Doloneia*, is attested only in the former poem, since at *Il.* 10.506 it is explicitly stated that after killing Rhesus and his twelve guards Diomedes ponders whether to seize the king's chariot or "strip the life from still more Thracians."[36] Although no other Thracian is named, it is clear that Hippocoon is not the only survivor among the army brought by Rhesus to Troy (which after all could not have included only fourteen men).[37]

(i) Lament: In the *Sauptikaparvan*, after Aśvatthāman (who is again designated by his periphrastic patronymic [Droṇa's son]) had finished killing enemies and

---

[28] In Sumerian tradition, Dumuzi dreams of his death; in Babylonian tradition, Gilgamesh has many dreams, among which is the coming of Enkidu; in Hittite tradition, Kessi has seven dreams in a single night; in the Bible, the Pharaoh has various prophetic dreams.; see M. L. West (1997) 188, 375; Garbutt (2006) 193.
[29] Garbutt (2006) 193.
[30] Οἰνεΐδαο πάϊς means "the son (πάϊς) of the son of Oeneus (Οἰνεΐδαο)." The son of Oeneus is Tydeus, Diomedes' father.
[31] Fries (2016) 311.   [32] See also p. 275.
[33] Fries (2016, 312–13) offers a helpful excursus suggesting that the speakers of Graeco-Aryan or Proto-Indo-European knew of two-wheeled chariots pulled by horses.
[34] Fries (2016) 312.
[35] Fries (2016) 314 with n. 30 on how highly charioteers are valued in the *Iliad* and the *Mahābhārata*.
[36] ἢ ἔτι τῶν πλεόνων Θρῃκῶν ἀπὸ θυμὸν ἕλοιτο.
[37] I.e. Rhesus, Hippocoon, and the twelve guards.

departed, the women and the guards cry out loud. A formal lament is expressed by Yudhiṣṭhira and Draupadī after the news of the deaths has been announced. In *Iliad* 10, after Hippocoon sees the carnage, he "groans aloud and calls on his dear companion by name."[38] The Trojans shout and flock to the area where Rhesus and his comrades lie dead. The use of the formula ᾤμωξέν τ' ἄρ' ἔπειτα, φίλον τ' ὀνόμηνεν ἑταῖρον, which is employed in lament contexts immediately before an actual speech (*Il.* 23.178 and 24.591), suggests that this line introduces a lament.[39] It is therefore possible that another version of the Rhesus story which preceded the *Doloneia* included a lament for Rhesus, and that a lament for him could not be included in book 10 since it would have undermined the laments for Hector in *Iliad* 22 and 24.[40] It is Hector who will be the only non-Achaean hero for whom the *Iliad* reserves a formal lament. Furthermore, had Rhesus received a lament, he would have become sympathetic, which would have undermined the pro-Greek tone of *Iliad* 10.[41] In the *Rhesus*,[42] where the story is presented from the Trojan point of view, and in the *Sauptikaparvan*, where the victims are the sympathetic focus of the narrative, the laments of the defeated are well placed.[43]

(j) Joy after the safe return of the hero: When they saw Aśvatthāman return safe from the enemy camp, Kṛpa and Kṛtavarman exulted in joy and clapped their hands. Aśvatthāman embraced them and they congratulated each other. Likewise, when Diomedes and Odysseus return to the Achaean camp, their fellow Achaeans "rejoiced and congratulated them with clasped hands and words of welcome."[44]

8.1.3 Structural Analogies

Mahābhārata	*Iliad* 10
(a) Extended exchange of speeches before the night raid is launched	Extended exchange of speeches before the night raid is launched
book 10.2–5	*Il.* 10.1–253
(b) Discussion of the plan that is contested (by Kṛpa) book 10.2–5	Discussion of the plan that is met with unanimous approval *Il.* 10.227–31

---

[38] *Il.* 10.522–3.   [39] Fenik (1964) 55; Fries (2016) 315–16.
[40] Σ [bT] *Il.* 10.519 (Erbse): οὐ μὴν θρήνους περιτίθησι καίτοι εὐπορῶν, ἀλλ' ἑτέρῳ μέρει τῆς ποιήσεως (sc. *Il.* 24.720–81) τηρεῖ τοὺς θρήνους ἐπὶ Ἕκτορι τεθνηῶτι; see Fenik (1964) 54–5; Danek (1988) 158; also pp. 185–6.
[41] Fries (2016) 316.   [42] Rhesus is lamented by his mother, the unnamed Muse (890–982).
[43] Garbutt (2006) 184; Fries (2016) 316; see also *Rāmāyaṇa* (6.23.7–31) for Sītā's lament for Rāma.
[44] *Il.* 10.541–2; see also *Il.* 10.565.

(c) Greatest warrior of the defeated side has been killed
book 9: Duryodhana

Greatest warrior of the defeated side abstains from fighting
books 1–9: Achilles

With respect to structural analogies, there is an extended exchange of speeches before the night raid is launched, though the two traditions present this in different ways, either as a contested topic (*Sauptikaparvan*) or as a matter of unanimous assent (*Iliad* 10). The key element is that there must be a preparatory discussion and that, no matter what will be said during this discussion, the plan will be finally approved and executed. Moreover, the night raid or mission is undertaken by the defeated side and is thus presented as an extreme measure to turn the tide of war. This analogy is better presented in the Indian epic because the highly abbreviated version of the Rhesus story in the *Iliad* probably goes back to an earlier, fully fledged version that no longer survives.

What are the implications comparing *Iliad* 10 with the *Sauptikaparvan* according to the theme of the night raid? First, the impressive range of external and internal similarities,[45] as well as structural analogies, may be explained by a common Indo-European or Graeco-Aryan origin.[46] Second, the cumulative effect of these similarities strengthens the argument for earlier forms of the Rhesus story that may have employed this fixed pattern, since it is unlikely that the highly condensed form of this episode in *Iliad* 10 constitutes the earliest application of this pattern to the myth of Rhesus. Since the Pindaric and oracle version are independent descendants of this fixed narrative pattern,[47] they may reflect similar instantiations of it that are earlier than *Iliad* 10. Third, the vast array of correspondences renders unlikely the possibility of the episode's independent existence.[48] As suggested by the examination of the *Sauptikaparvan*, night raids of this type require a developed narrative that forms part of a larger work. The need to resort to this kind of dangerous and risky night activity presupposes an extended plot presenting both the desperate situation of the side to which the raiders belong and the aftermath of the successful night raid. Fourth, the thematic ecosystem, in which a pre-Iliadic fully fledged version of the Rhesus story nested, may have been regulated by three essential external factors, which are shared by the *Doloneia* and the *Sauptikaparvan*: that the side launching the night raid faces a critical situation which may involve defeat or the failure to achieve its military goals; that it is deprived of a warrior who could win the war by regular combat; and that the enemy leader who is killed in the night raid could only be eliminated by treachery. Before book 10 of the *Mahābhārata*, Duryodhana, a

---

[45] Differences indicate what I would call "an adjusted flexibility" of the narrative pattern's constituting features that are adapted to different cultural contexts.
[46] Fries (2016) 319.   [47] Fries (2016) 320.   [48] Fries (2016) 320.

major warrior among the army of the Kauravas, has been killed.[49] His death made his comrades realize that the Pāṇḍavas could only be defeated by treachery, which is permissible even within the heroic code of fighting when a Brahmin lives according to the *kṣatriya dharma*.[50] Likewise, the (temporary) withdrawal of Achilles from the war in the *Iliad* and the killing of Rhesus by a night raid may well presuppose an earlier version of the story placed in a context similar to that of the *Mahābhārata*, i.e. a context in which Achilles would be dead and the Achaeans would have realized that Rhesus could only be eliminated by a night raid (either after his initial *aristeia* or because of the revelation of an oracle). Such a context may have featured in an epic poem pertaining to the events after the death of Achilles.

8.2 Virgil and *Iliad* 10

8.2.1 Preliminary Remarks

"[T]he *Aeneid* offers an invaluable extant poetic commentary on the relationship of Homer and the Epic Cycle."[51] Virgil's knowledge of both Homer and the Cycle is profound. With respect to the former, he used not only his detailed knowledge of the Homeric poems but also the profuse philological material offered by the Homeric scholia.[52] Concerning the latter, irrespective of whether he had direct access to the content of the Cyclic epics[53] or indirect knowledge through mythological compendia and summaries,[54] Virgil displays a sophisticated and highly creative reading of Homeric and Cyclic epic that is remarkably similar to the way the Homeric epic tradition engages with other oral epic traditions.[55]

In this context, we are entitled to ponder whether Virgil does something similar with respect to the episodes of Dolon and Rhesus. I will therefore examine all the relevant references to these two figures, Coroebus, and the Nisus and Euryalus

---

[49] In *Śalyaparvan* (book 9 of the *Mahābhārata*). For other important losses of the Kauravas, see pp. 245–6.
[50] True law (*dharma*) and unlawfulness (*adharma*) refer to the maintenance or destruction of universal order; see Johnson (1998) xxiii–xxviii.
[51] Currie (2016) 173.
[52] On Virgil's knowledge of ancient Homeric criticism by means of the scholia vetera, see Schlunk (1974); Schmit-Neuerburg (1999); Hexter (2010) 26–36.
[53] Ehwald (1894) 732–3; Fraenkel (1932) 247–2; Manton (1962) 16; Assereto (1970) 56; Kopff (1981) 920–1; Burgess (2001) 45; M. L. West (2013a) 48.
[54] Heinze (1915³) 198; Norden (1926³) 261; Horsfall (1979) 46–7, (2003) 466, 468, (2008) xx; Scafoglio (2004) 44; Gärtner (2015) 543–64.
[55] See Kopff (1981) 919–47; N. J. Richardson (1993) 43; Hardie (1998) 55; Currie (2016) 64–71, 248–9. A case in point is *Aeneid* 10–11, which shows that Virgil employs Homeric epic in a way that is analogous to the way the Iliadic tradition uses the *Memnonis* (the deaths of Pallas, Lausus, and Camilla evoke the deaths of Sarpedon and Patroclus in the *Iliad*, of Troilus in the *Cypria*, and of Antilochus and Memnon in the *Memnonis*).

episode against the backdrop of the conditions that need to be met for the sack of Troy. It will be argued that Virgil's engagement with Homeric epic goes beyond a mere reuse of material. He delves into the text of the *Iliad* by juxtaposing it with the oracle version of the Rhesus story, which he reconstructs by means of analogous episodes of the Cyclic *Ilias parva* that have Diomedes and Odysseus as their main actors. Virgil operates as a "neoanalyst pioneer," offering insight into the connection between *Iliad* 10 and its epic forerunners. These forerunners collectively belong to a notional Epic Cycle of several pre-Homeric oral epics dealing with the Trojan War. This examination amounts to a litmus test for the validity of my claim that the Rhesus episode thematically nests in a phase of the war after the death of Achilles. This may be so because, as in the case of the *Sauptikaparvan*, the episodes of Coroebus and of Nisus and Euryalus are associated with a context in which the side whose perspective is presented has been deprived, temporarily or permanently, of a hero of preeminent importance (Duryodhana in the *Sauptikaparvan*, Hector in the *Ilias parva* and the *Iliou persis*, Aeneas in the *Aeneid*). The risky and perilous undertakings of these episodes seem to result from a pressing need that is based not only on defeat or a difficult situation but also on the absence or death of a major hero who could have turned around the tide of events.

8.2.2 The Oracle Version and *Aeneid* 1

In *Aeneid* 1 (469–73), while Aeneas observes the Trojan War paintings on the walls of the temple of Juno in Carthage, he sees the white tents of Rhesus and Diomedes, who is red with the blood of the men he had killed while stealing the horses of Rhesus, "*before they could taste the grass of Troy and drink the water of the Xanthus.*"[56] This description suggests that Virgil is aware of the oracle version of the Rhesus story,[57] despite the fact that the oracle is not directly mentioned. In fact, the phraseology employed (*Aen.* 1.472–3: *prius quam | pabula gustassent Troiae Xanthumque bibissent*) reproduces part of the diction of Σ (D) *Il.* 10.435 [van Thiel] (πρὶν γεύσασθαι αὐτὸν τοῦ ὕδατος τῆς χώρας φονευθῆναι. χρησμὸς γὰρ ἐδέδοτο αὐτῷ, φασίν, ὅτι εἰ αὐτὸς γεύσεται τοῦ ὕδατος καὶ οἱ ἵπποι αὐτοῦ τοῦ Σκαμάνδρου πίωσι καὶ τῆς αὐτόθι νομῆς <ἔδονται>, ἀκαταμάχητος ἔσται εἰς τὸ παντελές).[58] Virgil adds to his reference to Rhesus two more features, which are

---

[56] The italics are my own.
[57] Virgil is not following the Pindaric version of the Rhesus story. Allusions to Pindar are minor in the *Aeneid*; see Fraenkel (1932) 247; Willcock (1983) 482–3 and 484–5 n. 7, (1997) 180; Kullmann (2015) 114; Currie (2016) 248–9; cf. Kelly (2006) 13 n. 57; Gärtner (2015) 557–8 with n. 55, 563.
[58] 1.470 (*primo...somno*) may well refer to the fact that this was the first time Rhesus slept in Troy, since he had just arrived; see *Il.* 10.434 (νεήλυδες) and [Eur.] *Rh.* 763–4 (πεδοστιβεῖ | κόπῳ δαμέντες); see also my previous discussion of this passage on pp. 228 n. 80, 256 with nn. 23 and 25.

not recorded in the *Doloneia* and may well belong to the oracle version of the Rhesus story: the location of Rhesus' camp near the walls of Troy and the white canvas of his tents. Commenting on this passage, Servius relates that, when Rhesus arrived at Troy, he set his camp by Scamander's bank (*in litore*)[59] because he found the gates of the city closed. He then refers to the Trojan spy Dolon and to the Achaean spies Diomedes and Odysseus, who had also been sent to spy (*qui et ipsi speculatum venerant*).[60] For Servius the theft of Rhesus' horses was essential, since it was on them that the fate of Troy depended. If they ate the grass of Troy and drank water from the river Xanthus, Troy would never be sacked (*abducti sunt equi, quibus pendebant fata Troiana, ut, si pabulo Troiano usi essent vel de Xantho Troiae fluvio bibissent, Troia perire non posset*).[61] Servius' commentary combines features from both *Iliad* 10 (Dolon the spy, Diomedes and Odysseus infiltrating the enemy camp to spy) with certain features from the oracle version (the setting of Rhesus' tent by the riverbank because he found the city gates closed, the magical association between Rhesus' horses and the fate of Troy). The detail about the location of Rhesus' camp, which is not included in the form of the D-scholion as it has been preserved for us, may be explained if Rhesus had arrived at Troy at night and was afraid for the safety of his Thracian army. Although he was aware of the prophecy about his potential invincibility, he did not go immediately to Scamander to have his horses drink from its water and eat from the grass at its banks, since the prophecy concerned only him and his horses, not his entire army, which would be thus dangerously exposed to the Achaean host during the night.[62] Thus we can surmise that in the oracle version, when Rhesus arrived at Troy, he intended to enter the city and camp there for the night out of concern for his men. The necessary condition under which this scenario could take place is if the Trojans had not camped on the plain, as is the case in *Iliad* 10. In this way, we may envisage a context for Rhesus' arrival which is radically different from that presented in the *Doloneia*. This may well be a context with no room for Hector,[63] i.e. a putative episode taking place *after* Hector's death.[64] The detail that Rhesus found the gates of the city shut when he arrived at night at Troy and camped by

---

[59] On this meaning of *litus*, see Virg. *Aen.* 8.83 (*viridique in litore conspicitur sus*).
[60] Serv. on Virg. *Aen.* 1.469 (Thilo and Hagen).
[61] Serv. on Virg. *Aen.* 1.469 (Thilo and Hagen).
[62] See the relevant discussion about the oracle on pp. 230–4.
[63] Rhesus' arrival at Troy while Hector is alive would have seriously weakened Hector's heroic preeminence since Rhesus' martial skills would have put the spotlight on him. To avoid this undesirable outcome, Hector does not refer to him at all in the *Doloneia*, in which the Achaean spies find about the arrival of Rhesus accidentally (through Dolon). In similar vein, the Rhesus episode could not be placed in a context before Hector decided to have the army camp out on the plain. The problem would again be the weakening of Hector's status, who would have been overshadowed by a hero like Rhesus, about whom an oracle predicted that if certain conditions were met, he and his horses would be invincible.
[64] It is possible that the Trojans went out and fought the Achaeans on the plain only when they had an exceptional hero on their side. After Hector's death they engaged with the Achaeans on the plain when Penthesileia and Memnon came to their assistance. They may have stayed inside their walled city

Scamander, which is close to the Scaean gates, aligns remarkably well with the earliest (post-*Iliad*) reference to Rhesus. According to the lyric poet Hipponax, whose *floruit* is the middle of the sixth century BC,[65]

ἐπ' [ἁρμάτων τε καὶ Θρεϊκίων πώλων
λε[υκῶν †ὀείους κατεγγὺς† Ἰλίου πύργων
ἀπ[ηναρίσθη Ῥῆσος, Αἰνειῶν πάλμυς.

On chariots and Thracian, white horses, † ... † close to the towers of Ilium, Rhesus was despoiled, the king of the Aineians.[66]

Despite the various emendations proposed for †ὀείους κατεγγὺς†,[67] the reading ἐγγύς Ἰλίου πύργων is likely to be correct. Hipponax's placement of Rhesus' camp "close to the walls of Ilium" is fully consonant with Servius' placement of his camp "by the river's bank," which in the context of Servius' scholion can only be Scamander's bank, lying close to the walls of Troy. If Servius is in this respect reproducing material from the oracle version, it is possible that Hipponax is also using a detail drawn from the same version. This is also suggested by Hipponax's stress on the theft of Rhesus' armor and horses (ἀπ[ηναρίσθη Ῥῆσος) that suits a version in which stealing the horses is a prerequisite for the future sack of Troy. In this light, it is conceivable that the oracle version was known to Hipponax and is therefore earlier (at least) than the middle of the sixth century BC.

Let us review this section. Virgil is aware of the oracle version of the Rhesus story, arguably by access to a more detailed form of Σ (D) on *Il.* 10.435 that is, in its cropped form, also our source for this version. Servius not only combines material from *Iliad* 10 and Virgil's text but also adds two features (Rhesus' encampment by Scamander and the closed gates of Troy) that are absent from

---

after the fight about Achilles' body that took place near the city walls where Achilles had pursued them (*Aeth.* arg. ll. 191-5). There is a case that they came out only when a new ally came to their support, Eurypylus son of Telephus, after whose death they returned to Troy (*Il. parv.* l. 221: καὶ οἱ Τρῶες πολιορκοῦνται); cf. Apollod. *Epit.* 5.11-12 (παραγενόμενος δὲ οὗτος [sc. Νεοπτόλεμος] εἰς τὸ στρατόπεδον...πολλοὺς τῶν Τρώων ἀναιρεῖ. ἀφικνεῖται δὲ ὕστερον Τρωσὶ σύμμαχος Εὐρύπυλος... τοῦτον ἀριστεύσαντα Νεοπτόλεμος ἀπέκτεινεν), but see M. L. West (2013a) 18. Furthermore, the three nocturnal missions by Odysseus alone (ambush of Helenus [see p. 281 n. 22]; *Ptocheia*) or together with Diomedes (theft of the Palladium) in the *Ilias parva* suggest that the Trojan army was not camping on the plain (Helenus had gone on his own for some religious business to the shrine of Thymbraean Apollo, which was close to the city; see M. L. West 2013a, 180). As for Proclus' phraseology regarding the death of Paris at the hands of Philoctetes, it clearly refers to a duel (*Il. parv.* ll. 213-14: καὶ μονομαχήσας Ἀλέξανδρον κτείνει), perhaps after a challenge. The situation is unclear in Apollod. *Epit.* 5.9 (ὁ δὲ [sc. Φιλοκτήτης] παραγενόμενος καὶ θεραπευθεὶς ὑπὸ Ποδαλειρίου Ἀλέξανδρον τοξεύει), but since Apollodorus presents Podaleirius as curing Philoctetes, given that Machaon has been killed by Penthesileia (Apollod. *Epit.* 5.1), it is likely that (concerning these details) he is drawing on a source differing from the *Ilias parva*, in which it is Machaon who cures Philoctetes (and is later killed by Eurypylus: fr. 7 GEF).

[65] Fr. 72 IEG.   [66] Translation by Kelly (forthcoming) (with modifications).
[67] See the critical apparatus ad loc. in IEG and Degani's edition (1991²) of Hipponax.

both the *Doloneia* and the *Aeneid*.⁶⁸ How did Servius come up with these features? Is it possible that he found in one or more of his sources the information that upon his arrival at Troy Rhesus camped by Scamander, near the city walls, because he found the gates of the city closed? In my view, this is a reasonable possibility, given that all the other features of his report belong to the oracle version. This line of interpretation is suggested by the fact that Servius' scholion on *Aen.* 1.469 is introduced by the phrase *(ut) quidam tradunt Martis, ut alii Hebri vel Strymonis et Euterpes Musae filius*,⁶⁹ the last part of which corresponds to the information found in the Homeric scholion. Servius appears to have access to several sources (among which was a fuller form of Σ [D] on *Il.* 10.435) that he used together with features belonging to *Iliad* 10 (Dolon, Diomedes, and Odysseus being designated as spies). If so, Virgil and Servius become crucial sources for accessing several features of the oracle version of Rhesus' story. As Virgil was trying to emulate Homer, so Servius (and or his predecessors) seem to have been trying to emulate the Homeric exegetes.⁷⁰

8.2.3 *Iliad* 10 and *Aeneid* 2

Aeneid 2 also includes features which can be traced back to the Homeric *Doloneia*, though Virgil fuses Trojan elements with features referring to the Achaeans in a new, unified narrative. Like Dolon, who is wearing a wolfskin and departs on the spying mission,⁷¹ Aeneas and the Trojans set out ("like ravening wolves in a black mist" [*lupi ceu | raptores atra in nebula*]).⁷² Like Diomedes and Odysseus, who move through the black night, through weapons and dark blood,⁷³ Aeneas and his comrades pass "through spears and enemies" (*per tela, per hostis*).⁷⁴ As Dolon is not destined to return safe from his mission and report back to Hector,⁷⁵ so Aeneas and his companions are going "to certain death" (*haud dubiam in mortem*).⁷⁶

Virgil's narrative of the sack of Troy not only reshuffles features that belong to the Trojan and the Achaean side in *Iliad* 10 but undertakes a bold and profound blending of elements from the *Doloneia* with the episode of Coroebus, which

---

[68] It is unlikely that Servius was influenced by Virgil as regards the location of Rhesus' camp near the Trojan walls because he criticizes the poet's use of the phrase *bellantes Pergama circum* (*Aen.* 1.466), "pointing out that this is a figure of speech, since *Pergama* properly denotes the citadel, whereas the scenes being described are of battles that took place over a wider area" (Farrell 2008, 113–14). I am referring to this point because Virgil (*Aen.* 1.469) says that Rhesus had encamped *nec procul hinc* ("not far from this place").

[69] "(As) some report he (*sc.* Rhesus) was the son of Ares, as others (report) of Hebrus or of Strymon and the Muse Euterpe."

[70] See Farrell (2008) 121, 131.   [71] *Il.* 10.334: ἕσσατο δ' ἔκτοσθεν ῥινὸν πολιοῖο λύκοιο.

[72] *Aen.* 2.355–6; translation: Fairclough 1935 (revised by Goold); see Dinter, Finkmann, and Khoo (2019, 255–6), who stress the antithesis between the use of the wolf (through Dolon's wolfskin) as a symbol of deceit in *Iliad* 10 and Virgil's depiction of the Trojans as wolves so as to highlight "their heroic desperation."

[73] *Il.* 10.468–9: διὰ νύκταν μέλαιναν | ...διά τ' ἔντεα καὶ μέλαν αἷμα.   [74] *Aen.* 2.358.

[75] *Il.* 10.336–7: οὐδ' ἄρ' ἔμελλεν | ἐλθὼν ἐκ νηῶν ἂψ Ἕκτορι μῦθον ἀποίσειν.   [76] *Aen.* 2.359.

belong to different phases of the Trojan War saga but are associated with the themes of nocturnal ambush, disguise,[77] and treachery. Coroebus, who is marked out by his age and patronymic (*iuvenisque Coroebus | Mygdonides*),[78] has recently come to Troy[79] to help in the war against the Achaeans on the back of the promise of Cassandra's hand.[80] He suggests to the Trojans that they disguise themselves as Achaeans by wearing the helmets and insignia of the enemies they had killed.[81] This scene brings to mind the *Doloneia*, in which Dolon, Diomedes, and Odysseus wear animal skins for the night-time spying missions. We may assume that Virgil realized that a dangerous nocturnal mission required disguise, noticed its application to both Trojans and Achaeans, and decided to transfer it to his narrative. However, he changed the balanced distribution of the theme of disguise between Trojan and Achaean spies into a unilateral but subversive application to Coroebus and his men. He thus turned this transference into a highly dramatic scene by presenting Coroebus and his comrades disguising themselves as their enemy, at whose hands they would soon lose their lives. Virgil may have also been influenced by the *Ptocheia* episode of the *Ilias parva*, in which Odysseus enters Troy disguised as a beggar, in order to acquire information about the Palladium.[82] We see here Virgil alluding to his sources by intensification of effect[83] and reverse imitation.[84]

---

[77] The disguise of the Trojans as Achaeans produces a short-lived victory at the beginning but ends in complete disaster as the Trojans are killed by other Trojans, who mistake them for Achaeans (*Aen.* 2.410–12). In Apollonius Rhodius nightfall causes confusion as both the Argonauts and the Doliones fail to recognize each other during the night-time massacre (1.1015–52); see Dinter, Finkmann, and Khoo (2019) 250–4.

[78] *Aen.* 2.341–2; see also Pap. Ryl. 22 (Κόροιβον τὸν Μυγδῶν[ος τὸν ἐκ Φρυγίας] ἐληλυθότα); Quintus Smyrnaeus 13.169 (αἰχμητῆρα Κόροιβον, <ἀγαυοῦ> Μυγδόνος υἷα).

[79] This is another feature in which Virgil (*Aen.* 2.342–3: *ad Troiam forte diebus | venerat*) agrees with Quintus Smyrnaeus (13.174–5: ἵκανε | χθιζός ἐπὶ Πριάμοιο <πόλιν>).

[80] *Il. parv.* fr. 24 GEF (ἀφίκετο μὲν δὴ ἐπὶ τὸν Κασσάνδρας ὁ Κόροιβος γάμον); *Aen.* 2.343–4 (*insano Cassandrae incensus amore, | et gener auxilium Priamo Phrygibusque ferebat*); Quintus Smyrnaeus 13.174 (γάμων, ὧν οὕνεχ' ἵκανε) and 13.176–7 (καὶ ὑπέσχετ' Ἀχαιοὺς | Ἰλίου ἄψ ὤσαι). The similarities between Virgil's and Quintus Smyrnaeus' references to Coroebus can be seen even in the way they mention Coroebus' failure to marry Cassandra (Virg. *Aen.* 2.345–6: *infelix qui non sponsae praecepta furentis | audierit*—Quintus Smyrnaeus 13.174: νήπιος, οὐδ' ἀπόνητο γάμων, ὧν οὕνεχ' ἵκανε); on the Coroebus episode in the *Aeneid*, see Monda (2011) 199–208.

[81] *Aen.* 2.389–90 (*mutemus clipeos, Danaumque insignia nobis | aptemus*).

[82] See Kopff (1981) 937. Commenting on *fatisque repulsi* (*Aen.* 2.13), Servius lists two series of oracles. The source of the first series regarding what the Trojans need to preserve to ensure that their city is not sacked (three conditions: the life of Troilus, the preservation of the Palladium, and the tomb of Laomedon at the Scaean Gates) is Plautus' *Bacchides* (954–5). The source of the second series referring to what the Achaeans must carry out so that Troy can be sacked (three conditions: the arrival of an Aeacid, the theft of Rhesus' horses, and the use of the arrows of Heracles) is assigned to the vague phrase *secundum alios*. It is not clear whether these three prerequisites were all mentioned by each of these unnamed authors or whether Servius presents a compilation of prerequisites that he found in different authors. However, it is possible that the theft of the Palladium was included in all versions of the preconditions. Drawing on the second series of prerequisites mentioned by Servius, we may tentatively suggest that, with respect to the oracle version of the Rhesus episode: (a) the Palladium was a prerequisite for the sack of Troy; (b) it was mentioned together with other preconditions pertaining to the fall of Troy; (c) it belonged to events that take place after the death of Achilles; and (d) it was given to the Achaeans (*Aen.* 2.13–14: *fatisque repulsi | ductores Danaum*).

[83] On several analogous cases in Quintus Smyrnaeus, see Currie (2016) 123.

[84] See pp. 269, 271.

The comparison between *Aeneid* 2 and the *Doloneia* suggests that in his presentation of the sack of Troy Virgil has fused certain features of *Iliad* 10 with episodes and characters (the theft of the Palladium, the story of Coroebus, and the fall of the city) that belong to the last stage of the Trojan War. His reconfiguring of the sack of Troy evokes Trojan War material that clusters in three distinct episodes associated with night raid, theft, and disguise. In this way, he brings together episodes that share certain features, belong to the same time span of the Trojan War, i.e. after the death of Achilles, and are marked by the presence of Diomedes and Odysseus.

8.2.4 *Iliad* 10 and *Aeneid* 9

The importance of the preceding analysis lies not so much and not exclusively in the comparison between the *Doloneia* and *Aeneid* 2 but in the way *Iliad* 10 may be effectively associated with episodes relating to the sack of Troy. For a truly close relationship between the *Doloneia* and a Virgilian episode we will turn our attention to *Aeneid* 9, which is dominated by the episode of Nisus and Euryalus. This episode amounts to an impressive blend of elements of the *Doloneia* with (1) the oracle version of the Rhesus story, (2) the theft of the Palladium in the *Ilias parva*, (3) *Iliad* 9, and (4) *Odyssey* 8. There are also some cases in which Virgil seems to have used the *Doloneia* as his only source (5). I will now examine these features.

(1) Blending Elements of the Doloneia with the Oracle Version of the Rhesus Story
(a) In *Aen.* 9.186 Nisus tells Euryalus that his mind drives him into battle or *some great deed* (*aut pugnam aut aliquid iamdudum invadere magnum*). Virgil's phraseology recalls the μέγα ἔργον which Odysseus and Diomedes plan to carry out at *Il.* 10.282. Since the dictional analogy occurs in a similar context (a nocturnal ambush episode with two protagonists), it is interesting to observe that the great deed Nisus and Euryalus will try to achieve is to bring back Aeneas (*Aen.* 9.192–3: *Aenean acciri omnes, populusque patresque, | exposcunt mittique viros, qui certa reportent*). Virgil "interprets" Homer in a way that is consonant with the interpretation of μέγα ἔργον by Aristarchus, who took it as an indication of the spies' plan to kill Hector.[85] The aim of μέγα ἔργον and *aliquid magnum*, respectively, concerns a key figure of the plot.

---

[85] Σ (D) *Il.* 10.282 (van Thiel): μέγα ἔργον· μεγάλην πρᾶξιν· Ἀρίσταρχος δέ φησιν τὸ φονεῦσαι Ἕκτορα; see the discussion on pp. 177–9.

(b) At *Aen.* 9.189-90, Nisus says to Euryalus that the Rutulians "lie prone relaxed with sleep and wine" (*somno vinoque solute | procubuere*).[86] The phrase *somno vinoque soluti* echoes οἱ δ' εὗδον καμάτῳ ἀδηκότες (*Il.* 10.471), which refers to the sleeping Thracians.[87] But again, it is Σ (T) *Il.* 10.496-7 (ἔλαβε δὲ καὶ τὸ φίλοινον Θρᾳκῶν πρὸς τὸ μὴ αἰσθέσθαι "he takes the Thracians' love for wine as lack of perception"), which explains a feature of *Iliad* 10 in a way that reflects Virgil's transference of it to the Trojans in the episode of Troy's fall.[88] This does not exclude the possibility that Virgil is here echoing Ennius *Annales* 288 (*nunc hostes vino domiti somnoque sepulti*), the more so since "in the historians such nocturnal drunkenness in the field is typically the mark of barbarian enemies (e.g. Tac. *Ann.* 4.48.1)."[89] Still, since the particular situational context relates both to *Iliad* 10 (the spies exit the walled Achaean camp and enter the vast night camp of the Trojans on the plain) and Ennius, Virgil may have used both texts as his source.

(c) At *Aen.* 9.192-3,[90] it is explicitly said that the messengers will inform Aeneas about the critical (even desperate) situation in which the Trojans find themselves, in order to persuade him to return and help them. In *Iliad* 10, Diomedes and Odysseus initially set out to acquire information about Hector's plan but then forget their mission, kill Rhesus, and steal his horses. Seen through this lens, Virgil's narrative amounts to a triple imitation in opposition, since in *Aeneid* 9 (i) information is not sought but disclosed, (ii) the key figure (Aeneas) belongs to the same side as the spies and must be brought back, not killed (Rhesus), and (iii) the disclosure of information and the return of Aeneas are connected, since the former is a precondition of the latter, while in *Iliad* 10 these two features are not associated, given that knowledge of Hector's plan (which is never gained by the spies) is not a prerequisite for the killing of Rhesus. Having said this, we may also entertain the possibility that Virgil, who is after all aware of the oracle version of the Rhesus story,[91] is alert to the *Iliad*'s reception of its models for the *Doloneia*. The information that must be reported to Aeneas by Nisus and Euryalus reflects the information about the content of the oracle that is revealed to the Achaeans

---

[86] See also Virg. *Aen.* 9.236-7 (*Rutuli somno vinoque solute | conticuere*). The drunkenness of the Trojans during the very night that Troy would be sacked is also mentioned by Quintus Smyrnaeus (13.21-2: εὖτε γὰρ ὕπνος ἔρυκεν ἀνὰ πτόλιν ἄλλοθεν ἄλλον | οἴνῳ ἐνιπλήθοντας ἀπειρεσίῳ καὶ ἐδωδῇ) and is implied in his presentation of the episode of Coroebus (13.171: ᾗχι θοαὶ πόσιός τε καὶ εἴδατός εἰσι κέλευθοι).

[87] See also καμάτῳ ἀδηκότες ἠδὲ καὶ ὕπνῳ | κοιμήσωνται (*Il.* 10.98-9), which is used for the Achaean guards outside the camp.

[88] The drunkenness of the Thracians occurs at [Eur.] *Rh.* 418-19 (see also 438), where Hector accuses Rhesus that he and the Thracians "lie in blankets and toast each other in deep drafts of wine," but it is not employed as an explanation of their deep sleep. On the drinking habits associated with the Thracians, see Liapis (2012) on [Eur.] *Rh.* 418-19; Fantuzzi (2020) 376 on [Eur.] *Rh.* 418b-19.

[89] Hardie (1994) 110 on Virg. *Aen.* 9.189.

[90] *Aenean acciri omnes, populusque patresque, | exposcunt, mittique viros qui certa reportent.*

[91] *Aen.* 1.472-3.

either by Calchas or by Hera and Athena in the oracle version of the Rhesus story. Moreover, the association between the disclosure of information to Aeneas and his subsequent return to the Trojan camp may not simply be a Virgilian invention but a sensitive response to the close link between the disclosure of the oracle's content about Rhesus' potential invincibility (and Troy's impregnability) and the Achaeans' successful act of killing him and stealing his horses.[92]

(d) At *Aen.* 9.240-3,[93] Nisus elaborates on the aims of the spying mission by adding that, apart from getting intelligence to Aeneas, the spies will kill the sleeping Rutulians and take spoils. Although the syntax of these verses has attracted different interpretations, it is fair to say that the spies on their way back with Aeneas aim to slaughter defenseless Rutulians and despoil them.[94] But, as the narrative of *Aeneid* 9 unfolds, Nisus and Euryalus have to cut their path through the middle of sleeping enemies in order to get Aeneas to the city of Pallanteum.[95] This change in the order of events becomes even more pronounced when their final goal is not achieved, since Nisus and Euryalus do not find Aeneas but are both killed. In the Homeric *Doloneia* there is also a duality of aims initially presented by Nestor (10.206-7), to capture some enemy or overhear something that the Trojans are saying.[96] Like the duality of the aims of the spying mission in *Aeneid* 9, the two aims in *Iliad* 10 are presented as alternatives, since they refer to two distinct ways of acquiring information. That said, both aims are ignored in the rest of the plot of *Iliad* 10, only to be replaced by the capturing and killing of Dolon (ἕλοι suits both meanings; see 10.345: ἕλωμεν) and the killing of Rhesus, whose Thracian troops are positioned on the edge of the Trojan camp (10.434: ἔσχατοι ἄλλων).[97] Along these lines, it is fair to say that Virgil noticed the divergence between the initial aim of the spying mission and the unraveling of the plot of the *Doloneia* and reconfigured it in *Aeneid* 9 so that Nisus and Euryalus accomplish only one aim—the one that had been initially secondary. Having said this, it is important to bear in mind that in the *Doloneia* the internal divergence between the initial aim (acquiring information) and final outcome (killing Rhesus and stealing his horses) may have resulted from the integration of the Rhesus story into an earlier form of *Iliad* 10 in which the target was Hector. In its desire to keep Hector within the range of events taking place during the nocturnal mission and

---

[92] A similar case may be the fact that in *Aeneid* 9 the Trojans defend their own city wall, whereas the Achaeans in *Iliad* 12 defend the wall around their ships (Hardie 1994, 10-11). Given that the Achaean seven-gate wall may involve the transference of a feature pertaining to the defense of the seven-gate city wall of Thebes in the Theban epic tradition (Singor 1992, 404), it is possible that the Virgilian narrative involves not only opposition in imitation of the *Iliad* but also transference of already contaminated Iliadic material that the *Iliad* had received from an earlier (epic) source; see Currie (2016) 68 n. 174.

[93] *si fortuna permittitis uti* | *quaesitum Aenean et moenia Pallantea,* | *mox hic cum spoliis ingenti caede peracta* | *adfore cernetis.*

[94] See the discussion by Hardie (1994) 118 on Virg. *Aen.* 9.241.   [95] Virg. *Aen.* 9.314-66.

[96] εἴ τινά που δηΐων ἕλοι ἐσχατόωντα, | ἤ τινά που καὶ φῆμιν ἐνὶ Τρώεσσι πύθοιτο.

[97] Tsagalis (forthcoming) *ad loc.*; see Dué and Ebbott (2010, 275-6 on *Il.* 10.206-10), against Fenik (1964) 41-2, who speaks about the poet's failure here.

have the spies kill Rhesus, the *Iliad* depicts a gradual shift in the objectives of the two Achaean spies. In the earlier form of the Rhesus story, either in the version involving an *aristeia* or in the oracle version, such a shift was not needed. The spies would have had as a single aim to kill Rhesus and steal his horses. Since Virgil is aware of the oracle version of the Rhesus story, it is possible that the shift from the initial reference to two independent aims (bring Aeneas back, kill and despoil Rutulians) to two associated ones (kill Rutulians in order to cut a path to Pallanteum for Aeneas) amounts to a sophisticated reaction by the Roman epic poet to the *Doloneia*'s shift from two independent aims (acquisition of information either by arresting an enemy or by overhearing the Trojans) to two associated ones (killing of Dolon and Rhesus, since the former has led them to the latter). In this way, Virgil would be citing not only his immediate (*Iliad* 10) and remote (the oracle version) source but also, in a typically neoanalytical manner, the relation between these two sources and the very form by which the immediate source cites its model.

(2) Blending Elements of the Doloneia with the Theft of the Palladium in the Ilias parva
(a) At *Aen.* 9.195–6,[98] Nisus claims that he is able to find the way around the foot of a hill to the walls of Pallanteum. Likewise at *Aen.* 9.243–5,[99] Nisus and Euryalus state that they know how to get to Pallanteum because they have been hunting in this area and are therefore familiar with it. In the *Doloneia*, it is Dolon who tells the Achaean spies where to find Rhesus. This opposition in imitation goes deeper than these passages allow us to assume. In order to see the wider picture, we turn to Servius, where we find a reference to a tunnel or vault (in different versions) as a way into entering Troy, the existence of which Diomedes and Odysseus know about and use in order to steal the Palladium.[100] Servius' comment probably reflects the *Ilias parva*, as can be surmised by a comparison to the Tabula Capitolina.[101] The convergence between the *Aeneid* and the *Ilias parva* regarding Diomedes' and Odysseus' knowledge in the context of another episode with remarkable similarities to the episode of the night raid against Rhesus suggests that the opposition in imitation observed above concerns only the surface level of *Iliad* 10 and may have been caused by the combination of the Dolon and Rhesus stories in the *Doloneia*. In the oracle version of the Rhesus episode, the Achaean spies may have known the way to the walls of Troy, close to which Rhesus had

---

[98] *tumulo videor reperire sub illo | posse viam ad muros et moenia Pallantea.*
[99] *nec nos via fallit euntis: | vidimus obscuris primam sub vallibus urbem | venatu adsiduo et totum congovimus amnem.*
[100] Serv. on Virg. *Aen.* 2.166: *tunc Diomedes et Ulixes, ut alii dicunt, cuniculis, ut alii, cloacis, ascenderunt arcem, et occisis custodibus sustulere simulacrum.*
[101] In the Tabula Capitolina Diomedes holds the Palladium and is followed by Odysseus, who is stepping from a low vaulted opening in a stone structure; see M. L. West (2013a) 165 and 200.

encamped.[102] Accordingly, Virgil's stress on the knowledge Nisus and Euryalus possess of the way to Pallanteum would be analogous to the familiarity of Diomedes and Odysseus concerning the way to the camp of Rhesus in the oracle version of this episode. What can be learnt from his line of thought is that Lesches' poem may have followed its oral forerunner by identifying the vault by which Diomedes and Odysseus entered and exited Troy. In fact, it is likely that the episode of the Palladium shared certain features with the night raid against Rhesus, both episodes featuring in an oral epic presenting the events after the death of Achilles. The choice of Lesches to include the former but omit the latter from his written, post-Homeric *Ilias parva* sealed the fate of the Rhesus story, creating the false impression that the mythically contaminated version of *Iliad* 10 contains its pristine form. Virgil's text proves, once again, an invaluable poetic commentary on C/cyclic epic (in both its oral, pre-Homeric and written, post-Homeric form) and its relation to Homer. Virgil had no access to the fully fledged narrative of the oracle version of the Rhesus story but he nevertheless was able to break it down to its constituent parts and configure their relation to the *Doloneia*.

(b) The theme of solidarity, which runs through the Nisus and Euryalus episode in *Aeneid* 9, is also strong in *Iliad* 10, where the overwhelmingly positive reaction of the Achaean leaders to a spying mission during the night counterbalances Achilles' stubborn refusal to assist the Achaeans and return to the war in *Iliad* 9. In *Aeneid* 9, the failure of Nisus and Euryalus is caused by the fact that they operate on a more intimate and narrower level of loyalty as lovers. If Nisus had abandoned Euryalus, when the latter was caught, he may have been able to contact Aeneas.[103] In *Iliad* 10, Diomedes and Odysseus act as a cohesive pair, though we can detect a certain tension with regard to who will be the first to capture Dolon.[104] This antagonism has deeper roots. It is manifested in its most extreme form in the episode of the theft of the Palladium in the *Ilias parva*.[105] Diomedes realizes (by the shadow of Odysseus' sword in the moonlight) that Odysseus is ready to strike him dead and take the Palladium back to the Achaean camp on his own, so as to gain all the glory for this remarkable achievement. To avoid this outcome, Diomedes forces Odysseus to go on ahead by beating his back with the sword. In this way, the extreme and potentially deadly antagonism between Odysseus and Diomedes in a pre-Homeric oral epic,[106] which may have been transferred to Lesches' *Ilias parva*,

---

[102] See Hipponax fr. 72 *IEG* and the discussion on p. 263.   [103] Hardie (1994) 13.
[104] *Il.* 10.367-8 (ἵνα μή τις Ἀχαιῶν χαλκοχιτώνων | φθαίη ἐπευξάμενος βαλέειν, ὁ δὲ δεύτερος ἔλθοι).
[105] Fr. 11 *GEF*.
[106] The *Ilias parva* begins with the strife between Telamonian Ajax and Odysseus for the arms of Achilles (*Il. parv.* arg. ll. 208-10 Severyns; fr. 2 *GEF*) and includes the antagonism between Diomedes and Odysseus for the Palladium (fr. 11 *GEF*). In *Il.* 10.367-8 Diomedes "is remembering" the episode of the Διομήδεος ἀνάγκη and tries to get the glory for himself. This means that this episode could not pertain to the killing of a third-rate warrior like Dolon but to an incident that originally happened in the Rhesus story, which (as I have argued) could very well "nest" in the plot of an alternative *Ilias parva*. It may well be the case that the antagonism between Diomedes and Odysseus concerned the killing of Rhesus, not the capture of Dolon. The motif of the "division of duties" that we have observed in the

is downgraded to a low-level competition for glory in the *Doloneia*.[107] We can therefore assume that Virgil's version is based on the transferred reversal (the love of Nisus and Euryalus leads to the failure of the greater plan, whereas the lurking antagonism between Diomedes and Odysseus in the *Doloneia* does not prevent their success) of an already contaminated scene of *Iliad* 10.

(c) At *Aen.* 9.373–4[108], the reflection of the moonlight on Euryalus' helmet, which he has forgotten to take off, betrays him to the enemy.[109] There is nothing similar in the *Doloneia*, where it is not explained how Odysseus spots Dolon in the darkness.[110] The reference to the two parts of the night that have already passed indicates only the limited amount of time available for the two Achaean spies,[111] not their ability to see clearly under these circumstances. On the other hand, in the episode of the theft of the Palladium in the *Iliad parva* (fr. 11 GEF), the moonlight betrays Odysseus, who attempts to kill Diomedes and gain all the glory for himself in bringing the Palladium to the Achaean camp. Odysseus fails, since Diomedes notices the shadow of his sword. This is a case of opposition in imitation. By using the two characters (Diomedes and Odysseus) as vehicles of allusion, Virgil preserves the theme "moonlight betrays a hero during a night mission" but transfers it from the personal antagonism between the two protagonists of the night mission (Diomedes and Odysseus) to the danger presented by an external enemy (Volcens). Moreover, he dramatizes it, as the episode ends peacefully in the *Ilias parva* but fatally in the *Aeneid*, where Euryalus is killed, and Nisus directly after him.[112] The

---

Sauptikaparvan, Iliad 10, and the *Rhesus* may have taken a less agreeable form in a pre-Homeric *Ilias parva, creating a doublet with the antagonism between Diomedes and Odysseus in the theft of the Palladium.

[107] It should be emphasized that since in *Iliad* 10 the competition for glory takes place in the night in the context of a spying mission, its basic prerequisite (the recognition and acknowledgment of the person who is responsible for the capture of Dolon) remains unfulfilled. This stands in contrast to the story of the theft of the Palladium, since the Achaeans would assume (when Diomedes and Odysseus returned to the camp) that the one who bears the Palladium is the person responsible for this remarkable achievement. Likewise, at *Il.* 22.206–7 (οὐδ' ἔα ἱέμεναι ἐπὶ Ἕκτορι πικρὰ βέλεμνα, | μή τις κῦδος ἄροιτο βαλών, ὁ δὲ δεύτερος ἔλθοι), Achilles' concern to acquire the glory for killing Hector is based on the fact that the entire Achaean army is watching him pursue Hector around the walls of the city. Recognition and acknowledgment of his achievement are, therefore, guaranteed; on the association between *Il.* 10.367–8 and 22.206–7, see pp. 88–9.

[108] *et galea Euryalum sublustri noctis in umbra | prodidit immemorem radiisque adversa refulsit.*

[109] It is noteworthy that Servius, in his desire to emulate the Homeric scholia, understands a perfectly ordinary helmet (*galea*) to be of a special type used by scouts, "as shown by Homer" (*sicut etiam Homerus ostendit*: on *Aen.* 9.307). He is thus reproducing a Homeric scholium (on *Il.* 10.258) pertaining to a Homeric *zetema*, which is about the meaning of καταῖτυξ that is worn by each of the two Achaean spies in the *Doloneia*; on this passage, see Farrell (2008) 124–5.

[110] 10.339–40: τὸν δὲ φράσατο προσιόντα | διογενὴς Ὀδυσεύς, Διομήδεα δὲ προσέειπεν. At *Il.* 10.152–4, the flashing armor of Diomedes, who is woken up by Nestor, Agamemnon, and Odysseus, remains narratively inactive; see Dinter, Finkmann, and Khoo (2019) 257–8.

[111] 10.251–3: μάλα γὰρ νὺξ ἄνεται, ἐγγύθι δ' ἠώς, | ἄστρα δὲ δὴ προβέβηκε, παρῴχωκεν δὲ πλέων νύξ | τῶν δύο μοιράων, τριτάτη δ' ἔτι μοῖρα λέλειπται.

[112] Nisus' prayer to the Moon at *Aen.* 9.404–9 is a case of tragic irony. The hero asks the Moon to give him victory (presumably by making his vision clear through its light), but it is the Moon's light that will betray Euryalus and cause his death.

theme of the moonlight gleaming at night is also used in the sack of Troy that featured in the last part of the *Ilias parva*.[113] In this respect, it has been argued that the reference at *Il.* 10.251-3 to the heroes being impatient that the night is coming to an end reflects other versions of the Rhesus story, notably the oracle version, in which the situation was critical, since if Rhesus was not killed during the night, the next day he would be invincible.[114] The similarity in phrasing to the *Ilias parva* (fr. 14 GEF) suggests that the oracle version of the Rhesus story belonged to an oral epic tradition similar to that of Lesches' *Ilias parva*.[115] This line of thought is of special importance to our investigation. Whether Virgil transferred the motif of the moonlight from the episode of the Palladium to the *Doloneia* or found it in an expanded and more detailed Homeric scholion reporting the oracle version or sensed that it connoted a scene pertaining to a nocturnal mission and decided to include it in his poem, he successfully draws on the analogy between the two night missions, that of the Rhesus story and that of the Palladium, which organically belong to the same phase of the Trojan War and as such may well have featured in a pre-Homeric oral epic similar (but not identical) to Lesches' *Ilias parva*.

(3) Blending Elements of the Doloneia with Iliad 9
At *Aen.* 9.263-74,[116] Ascanius promises Nisus two silver embossed cups, a pair of tripods, two talents of gold, an ancient mixing bowl, the horse, helmet, and shield of Turnus, twelve beautiful women, many captive men in full armor, and the entire land now owned by King Latinus as rewards for his undertaking a dangerous night mission. As for Euryalus, Ascanius promises to have him as his beloved comrade-in-arms and share all glory with him (*Aen.* 9.275-80).[117] Likewise, in the *Doloneia* Hector promises Dolon the best Achaean horses, Dolon asks for the horses of Achilles, and Hector confirms that he will deliver them to him (*Il.* 10.305-6, 322-3, and 330-1).[118] Virgil is here expanding the list of offerings by activating

---

[113] Fr. 14 GEF: νὺξ μὲν ἔην μέσση, λαμπρὰ δ' ἐπέτελλε σελήνη. In both literature and art night is connected to murder, violence, and intense cruelty. The Trojan saga is full of such incidents occurring at night (Dolon, Rhesus, Ajax's suicide, abduction of Cassandra, sack of Troy). On night ambushes in Greek and Roman epic, see Casali (2004) 319-54 and (2018) 209-37, respectively.
[114] Hainsworth (1993) 177 on *Il.* 10.252.
[115] For a similar approach, which is based on thematic and phraseological factors, in an oral precursor of the Cyclic *Thebais*, see Wood (2022) 51-68; also Torres-Guerra (2015) 226-43.
[116] *bina dabo argento perfecta atque aspera signis | pocula, devicta genitor quae cepit Arisba, | et tripodas geminos, auri duo magna talenta, | cratera antiquum quem dat Sidonia Dido. | si vero capere Italiam sceptrisque potiri | contigerit victori et praedae dicere sortem, | vidisti, quo Turnus equo, quibus ibat in armis | aureus; ipsum illum, clipeum cristasque rubentis | excipiam sorti, iam nunc tua praemia, Nise. | praeterea bis sex genitor lectissima matrum | corpora captivosque dabit suaque omnibus arma, | insuper his campi quod rex habet ipse Latinus.*
[117] *te vero, mea quem spatiis propioribus aetas | insequitur, venerande puer, iam pectore toto | accipio et comitem casus complector in omnis. | nulla meis sine te quaeretur gloria rebus: | seu pacem seu bella geram, tibi maxima rerum | verborumque fides.*
[118] 10.305-6: δώσω γὰρ δίφρον τε δύω τ' ἐριαύχενας ἵππους, | οἵ κεν ἄριστοι ἔωσι θοῆς ἐπὶ νηυσὶν Ἀχαιῶν; 10.322-3: ἦ μὲν τοὺς ἵππους τε καὶ ἅρματα ποικίλα χαλκῷ | δωσέμεν, οἳ φορέουσιν ἀμύμονα Πηλεΐωνα; 10.330-1: μὴ μὲν τοῖς ἵπποισιν ἀνὴρ ἐποχήσεται ἄλλος | Τρώων, ἀλλά σέ φημι διαμπερὲς ἀγλαϊεῖσθαι.

two more passages of the *Iliad*, the catalogue of gifts offered to Achilles by Agamemnon in his vain attempt to lure him to battle,[119] and the gift of a black sheep to the man who agrees to participate in the perilous night mission to the Trojan camp (*Il.* 10.214–17).[120] The combination of these Iliadic references allows Virgil to turn the list of gifts and rewards to Nisus and Euryalus from mere description to a sophisticated comment on the two heroes' future fate, the more so since intertextual associations play a central role in character-construction.[121] At the same time, the stark imbalance between the multiple and impressive material gifts promised to Nisus and the single, non-material reward promised to Euryalus builds on the equally stark imbalance between the impressive gift promised to Dolon by Hector and the humble offering of a sheep to each Achaean spy promised by Nestor in *Iliad* 10. Virgil's reading of *Iliad* 10 is enriched not by a simple addition of prizes but by means of a close reading of an Iliadic passage (*Iliad* 9) concerning Achilles. In this way, the gifts Ascanius promises to Nisus amount to a combination of the gifts offered to Achilles by Agamemnon and the gift promised to Dolon by Hector. Together with the gifts come the characters to whom the gifts have been promised. As a result of this combination, Nisus takes on features pertaining to both Achilles and Dolon. Like Achilles and Dolon, Nisus is promised great gifts. Unlike Achilles he accepts the offer and undertakes the night mission. Like Dolon he will not get the horse, helmet, and shield of Tyrnus because he (*sc.* Nisus) will die. Whereas Nisus evokes (through the gifts) Achilles and Dolon, Euryalus recalls (again through the single gift) the Achaean spies. Thus, the duality of Virgil's pair of night-time operatives in *Aeneid* 9 works against the backdrop of the two spying missions in *Iliad* 10, as well as of the promised gifts to Achilles in *Iliad* 9.[122] Virgil's refined and complex reading of the *Iliad* does not exhaust the range of texts that he employed for representing the gifts promised but not given to Nisus and Euryalus in *Aeneid* 9. There is an essential element underlying the promise of gifts for such a dangerous undertaking as a night mission to the enemy camp. It is based on the idea that a night mission does not belong to regular warfare and is therefore not expected to be voluntarily undertaken by any hero who is used to engaging in standard fighting during daylight. It is a non-heroic and dangerous form of war to which warriors must be lured by gifts.[123] In *Iliad* 10, the gathering of information is the aim of both spying missions, Trojan and Achaean alike, and as such it requires remuneration. Likewise, in the oracle version, in which the target was Rhesus and his horses

---

[119] See Knauer (1964) 269.
[120] ὅσσοι γὰρ νήεσσιν ἐπικρατέουσιν ἄριστοι, | τῶν πάντων οἱ ἕκαστος ὄϊν δώσουσι μέλαιναν | θῆλυν ὑπόρρηνον· τῇ μὲν κτέρας οὐδὲν ὁμοῖον, | αἰεὶ δ' ἐν δαίτῃσι καὶ εἰλαπίνῃσι παρέσται.
[121] Lyne (1987) 100–44; D. P. Fowler (1997) 17 = (2000) 120.
[122] Achilles is covertly drawn into the picture in *Iliad* 10 through the reference to his immortal horses that Hector promises to Dolon.
[123] Dinter, Finkmann, and Khoo (2019, 245–81) consider this feature typical of the *Bauform* of the nocturnal battle.

and whose purpose was of prime importance for the successful completion of the whole expedition (the sack of Troy), the promise of gifts may have been further stressed, the more so since Rhesus' horses (and perhaps his armor) would be a major reward for the successful spies.[124] In this respect, Virgil is doing something much more profound than engaging with *Iliad* 9 and 10. He is reading the text of the *Iliad* against the backdrop of the oracle version of the Rhesus story as he reconstructs it on the basis of analogous episodes featuring Diomedes and Odysseus in the Cyclic *Ilias parva*.

(4) Blending Elements of the Doloneia with Odyssey 8
At *Aen.* 9.303-7,[125] Iulus gives the sword made by the Cnossian Lycaon to Euryalus, while Mnestheus and Aletes equip Nisus with a lionskin and a helmet, respectively. At *Il.* 10.255-62,[126] Thrasymedes gives his two-edged sword, shield, and a bull's hide as a head cap to Diomedes, while Meriones gives a bow, quiver, sword, and leather-made head cap to Odysseus. Beyond the primary Iliadic model of the *Doloneia* arming scene lurks the secondary model of *Od.* 8.403-5,[127] where Odysseus receives from the Phaeacian Euryalus a bronze sword with a silver hilt upon it, and a sheath of fresh ivory.[128] The association of Virgil's Euryalus with the Phaeacian Euryalus goes beyond the arming scene, as the former has been the model for the latter with respect to his beauty.[129] In this light, Virgil's Euryalus is a figure of heavy allusive weight, given that he has been shaped by features relating to both Diomedes (they are both armed with a sword with which they kill their enemies during the night mission) and the Phaeacian Euryalus.

(5) Virgil Using the Doloneia as his Only Source
(a) At *Aen.* 9.324-8,[130] Euryalus kills the seer Rhamnes, who combines characteristics of Rhesus and his cousin Hippocoon as presented in *Iliad* 10. Rhamnes resembles Rhesus, in that they are both breathing heavily in their sleep,[131] and

---

[124] In the *Doloneia* the horses are given as reward to Diomedes, who kills Rhesus.
[125] *umero simul exuit ensem | auratum, mira quem fecerat arte Lycaon | Cnosius atque habilem vagina aptarat eburna. | dat Niso Mnestheus pellem, horrentisque leonis | exuvias, galeam fidus permutat Aletes.*
[126] Τυδείδῃ μὲν δῶκε μενεπτόλεμος Θρασυμήδης | φάσγανον ἄμφηκες—τὸ δ' ἑὸν παρὰ νηΐ λέλειπτο—| καὶ σάκος· ἀμφὶ δέ οἱ κυνέην κεφαλῆφιν ἔθηκεν | ταυρείην, ἄφαλόν τε καὶ ἄλλοφον, ἥ τε καταῖτυξ | κέκληται, ῥύεται δὲ κάρη θαλερῶν αἰζηῶν. | Μηριόνης δ' Ὀδυσῆϊ δίδου βιὸν ἠδὲ φαρέτρην | καὶ ξίφος· ἀμφὶ δέ οἱ κυνέην κεφαλῆφιν ἔθηκεν | ῥινοῦ ποιητήν.
[127] δώσω οἱ τόδ' ἄορ παγχάλκεον, ᾧ ἔπι κώπη | ἀργυρέη, κολεὸν δὲ νεοπρίστου ἐλέφαντος | ἀμφιδεδίνηται.
[128] Hardie (1994) on Virg. *Aen.* 9.303-7.
[129] At *Od.* 8.115-17, Euryalus is designated as the most beautiful among the Phaeacians after Laodamas; see *Aen.* 9.179-80 (*comes Euryalus, quo pulchrior alter | non fuit Aeneadum Troiana neque induit arma*); on Euryalus' beauty, see also *Aen.* 5.295 (*Euryalus forma insignis viridique iuventa*).
[130] *sic memorat vocemque premit, simul ense superbum | Rhamnetem adgreditur, qui forte tapetibus altis | exstructus toto proflabat pectore somnum, | rex idem et regi Turno gratissimus augur | sed non augurio potuit depellere pestem.*
[131] *Aen.* 9.326; *Il.* 10.496: ἀσθμαίνοντα.

Hippocoon, in that they both fail to prevent or realize what was going on despite the fact that Rhamnes is a seer[132] and Hippocoon's name (< ἵππος + κοέω) should mean "the one who looks after the horses"; ironically, he fails to protect Rhesus' horses. Virgil transfers to Rhamnes a feature that belongs to Diomedes (Rhesus' killer in the *Doloneia* and partly the model for Virgil's Euryalus): Rhamnes is lying on a deep pile of coverings,[133] just as Diomedes lies on the hide of a field-ranging ox laid beneath him with his head on a blanket at *Il*. 10.155–6.[134]

(b) At *Aeneid* 9.420–45 Nisus and Euryalus are killed while engaged in their mission, in contrast to Diomedes and Odysseus, who in *Iliad* 10 return safe and victorious to the Achaean camp. The episode with Volcens is another case of opposition in imitation, though only partial. Volcens is the one who spots Nisus and Euryalus, who are both killed, but only after Nisus kills Volcens.

On the basis of the arguments presented above I argue that in *Aeneid* 2 Virgil transferred features of the *Doloneia* to the episode of Coroebus, which originally belongs to the sack of Troy in the *Ilias parva*. In the episode of Nisus and Euryalus in *Aeneid* 9, which is extremely rich in intertextual resonances, Virgil blends several features pertaining (mainly) to the oracle version and the story of the Palladium in the *Ilias parva* with the *Doloneia*. We therefore see Virgil doing something that, according to my argument, is similar to what happened in the shaping of the *Doloneia*, i.e. its incorporation of elements of a pre-Homeric oral version of the *Ilias parva*, which included the episodes of the Palladium, Coroebus, and the sack of Troy. According to this approach, Virgil shows himself to be operating as a neoanalyst *avant la lettre*, since he allows us, by means of his keen interest in motif transference, to glimpse at the relation between *Iliad* 10 and its epic predecessors that seem to belong to a notional Epic Cycle.[135]

Until now, scholars have been divided over determining the process by which Virgil has conducted a highly elaborate reception of Cyclic epic that bears similarity to the reception of earlier epic poetry by Homeric epic. According to one line of thought, Virgil learned various techniques such as "quotation (non-verbatim) with inversion, explicit acknowledgment of the model, and the gods as representatives of the poet's will"[136] from his study of the Homeric poems. This means that Virgil discovered that Homer was employing these techniques, considered them effective, and decided to apply them to the relation of his poem with his sources. Dekel argues that Virgil was able to make this discovery by comparing the two Homeric epics because he realized that "the *Odyssey* is...an interpretation, or perhaps even a rendition, of the *Iliad*. Characters, themes, and conflicts from the war are evaluated and reconfigured as an authoritative account of central

---

[132] *Aen.* 9.327–8.   [133] *Aen.* 9.325–6: *tapetipus altis | exstructus.*
[134] εὗδ', ὑπὸ δ' ἔστρωτο ῥινὸν βοὸς ἀγραύλοιο, | αὐτὰρ ὑπὸ κράτεσφι τάπης τετάνυστο φαεινός; see Hardie (1994) 132 on Virg. *Aen.* 9.325–6.
[135] See Fantuzzi and Tsagalis (2015a) 9–14.   [136] Currie (2016) 68.

Iliadic concerns."[137] Another factor that may also have contributed to Virgil's discovery of the way Homer deals with earlier oral epics is the Homeric scholia. Virgil had access to and systematically employed the Homeric scholia that were written before his time. He occasionally used them to avoid criticism that had been exercised by scholars on the *Iliad* and the *Odyssey*.[138] Conversely, it has been claimed that Virgil simply interacted with earlier poetry in a way similar to how Homer had interacted with pre-Homeric epic.[139]

Knowledge of the bare bones of the oracle version of the Rhesus story by Virgil suggests that it is much more likely that it is the first line of thought that is closer to the truth. It is improbable that Virgil had access to a fully fledged text of the oracle version of the Rhesus story, which he probably knew from a more extended narrative included in an expanded form of the Homeric scholion on *Il.* 10.435 that may have been available to him. He also had access to at least an epitomized form of Lesches' *Ilias parva*. His knowledge of the Odyssean references to events of the Trojan War that were mentioned in the summary of the *Ilias parva* made him realize that the *Odyssey* knew of these events from earlier poetry which had also influenced Lesches' epic. He must have arrived at this conclusion for two reasons: (a) he was too well versed in the tradition of Homeric criticism to believe that Lesches was earlier than Homer (and consequently Homer had in the *Odyssey* engaged in a reception of Lesches' *Ilias parva*); and (b) he had realized that the analogies and similarities between the oracle version of the Rhesus story and several episodes of the epitomized form of the *Ilias parva* (the theft of the Palladium, the Coroebus story) could not be explained by Lesches' influence on the *Doloneia*. This is because Virgil knew that the Rhesus episode was not included in the epitomized form available to him and that *Iliad* 10 was an abridged and highly elliptical version which involved no oracle.

This chapter has been devoted to a comparison between *Iliad* 10 and (a) book 10 of the *Mahābhārata*, and (b) Virgil's *Aeneid*. The various features pertaining both to the content and structure of the *Sauptikaparvan* and *Iliad* 10 make it possible that they are rooted in a narrative pattern whose origins are traced in the Indo-European or Graeco-Aryan tradition. This pattern involves a stable skeleton of features, as well as occasional differences that refer to secondary elements of presentation and do not affect the kernel of those episodes sharing the theme of night raid.[140] Moreover, the implications of this comparison are that the night raid is not an independent, standalone narrative but relies on being integrated into the

---

[137] Dekel (2012) 1.   [138] Schlunk (1974); Schmit-Neuerburg (1999).

[139] See Currie (2016) 69; on the relativization of the strict dichotomy between the oral and literary poet, see D. P. Fowler (1997) 31 = (2000) 134.

[140] See Allen (2020) 223, who focuses on the analogy between this part of the *Mahābhārata* and the wider context of the μνηστηροφονία in the *Odyssey* (books 19–22) and argues that the various similarities detected can be explained if we postulate a common origin. In fact, the flexibility of such analyses shows that a typical theme or sequence of themes can generate more than one analogous thematic structure.

broader complex of a martial epic. While the comparative examination of the *Sauptikaparvan* and *Iliad* 10 refers to the type and order of episodes in which the theme of the night raid nests, Virgil's *Aeneid*, which is a text that feeds, like the *Doloneia*, on the tradition of the Trojan War, offers ample material allowing us to suggest a tentative process regarding the specific adaptation of the theme of the night raid to the plot of *Iliad* 10. It has been argued that in this process certain episodes of the Trojan saga, such as the Palladium, Coroebus, and the sack of Troy, may have played a key role.

9
The Rhesus Story within the Cyclic and the Iliadic Tradition

Introduction

I have argued that the Rhesus story was not an independent poem[1] but a fully fledged episode within a larger epic, in the same way that *Sauptikaparvan* is book 10 of the *Mahābhārata* and the Nisus and Euryalus episode is part of *Aeneid* 9. The cyclic elements within the Pindaric and oracle versions of the Rhesus story indicate that the poem in which the Rhesus story belonged may have had a cyclic tonality. But what does "cyclic" mean in this context, since the Rhesus episode is not attested in any of the poems of the Epic Cycle?

9.1 Cyclic Epic

It is a reasonable assumption that various oral epics on the Theban and Trojan Wars were performed during the archaic period. The Homeric epics include numerous allusions to events both predating and postdating them. This means that "poems existed containing much the same material, not necessarily in written form and not necessarily corresponding to the later ones [*sc.* the Cyclic epics] in coverage."[2] It is possible that some of these poems that may have drawn on the Theban and Trojan sagas formed a notional group around these two famous mythical traditions. The tendency to group poems or separate mythical episodes featuring a single protagonist is a phenomenon attested in both Near Eastern (a Sumerian Bilgames Cycle or a Hurro-Hittite Kumarbi Cycle)[3] and Greek poetry (a Heracles Cycle).[4] The pairing of the Theban and Trojan Wars as early as Hesiod (*Op.* 161–8) is marked as cyclic in the sense that the poet assumes that his audience know that Thebes and Troy constitute a canon of stories associated

---

[1] See pp. 259, 276–7.   [2] M. L. West (2015) 97.   [3] See I. Rutherford (2009) 9–35.
[4] Note that the canon of Heracles' labors may be as old as the seventh century BC, since we know (via Theocr. *Epigr.* 22 = Pis. test. 2 *EGEF*) that the Rhodian poet Pisander (from Camiros) wrote a *Heracleia* in which he included all the labors of Heracles; see Tsagalis (2022) 121–9. Another putative Cycle may have been a Corinthian one which comprised the epics of Eumelus of Corinth (*Titanomachy*, the *Corinthiaca*, and the *Europeia*; see Tsagalis 2017, 17–174). The *Titanomachy* became later part of the "Canonical Epic Cycle"; see M. L. West (2002) 109–33 = (2011b) 353–91.

The Homeric Doloneia: *Evolution and Shaping of* Iliad 10. Christos C. Tsagalis, Oxford University Press.
© Christos C. Tsagalis 2024. DOI: 10.1093/oso/9780192870988.003.0010

with the end of the age of heroes (Hesiod's fourth race)[5] and that they have a fixed mythical chronology (the Theban Wars preceding the Trojan War).[6] It also points to an early canonization of mythical events, which are treated in several epic poems covering aspects of the Theban and Trojan sagas. Thebes and Troy seem to have been for the early Greeks "notional mega-epics"[7] which constituted a mythical and perhaps epic continuum.[8] Resonances in lyric poetry and in particular Pindar[9] and various Stesichorean poems (*Iliou persis, Oresteia, Nosti, Helen*) on themes that feature in Cyclic epic,[10] as well as Iliadic and Odyssean allusions to the Trojan section of the Epic Cycle,[11] may reflect pre-Homeric epic traditions.[12] A by-product of this poetry, which was thematically related to the Homeric poems, was the composition of written epics on Theban and Trojan storylines (*Oedipodea, Thebais, Epigoni, Alcmeonis* on Thebes; *Cypria, Aethiopis, Ilias parva, Iliou persis, Nosti, Telegonia* on Troy). At a later stage, poems of theogonic scope (*Theogony, Titanomachy*) were incorporated into what became the canonical Epic Cycle.[13]

The Rhesus story (in both the Pindaric and oracle versions) displays cyclic features which bring it within the framework of cyclic epic. It therefore closely relates to episodes like those of Penthesileia, Memnon, and Eurypylus that are Cyclic representatives of the motif of the "late-arriving ally," as well as to those of Hippotion's sons and Asteropaeus that reflect the same motif in the *Iliad*. The repercussions of these observations have not been sufficiently examined before. Even Fenik, who is alert to the neoanalytical argument about the pre-Homeric myth complex in which Memnon, Penthesileia, and Eurypylus are involved, is quick to dismiss the possibility that Rhesus too belonged to a pre-Homeric mythical network.[14] Fenik believes that Rhesus belongs to a group of stories sharing the motif of the "late-arriving ally," but he does not have a place in pre-Homeric myth, "regardless of the age of his story." This formulation discloses a certain limitation in perspective. The phrasing "regardless of the age of his story" both leaves the question of the relative date of the Rhesus episode open and dissociates it completely from "the pre-Homeric myth complex." But, if the Rhesus story was known before the creation of *Iliad* 10, as implied by his presentation in the *Iliad*, which displays clear signs of a reshaping of an older and fuller version

---

[5] *Op.* 161–8; see Barker and Christensen (2020) 3–6, 81–2, 247–8.
[6] See Most (2024) 131–2; also Most (1997) 104–27.   [7] Scodel (2012) 511.
[8] Fantuzzi and Tsagalis (2015a) 9–10; M. L. West (2015) 96.
[9] I. Rutherford (2015) 450–60; Spelman (2018) 182–201.
[10] See Burkert (1987, 43–62 = 2001, 198–217) on the possible influence of Stesichorean choral lyric performance on the performance of epic by the *aoidoi*; Fantuzzi and Tsagalis (2015a) 11; Noussia-Fantuzzi (2015) 430–2.
[11] See Kullmann (1960).
[12] On the early status of Theban epic and its association with Trojan epic, see Fantuzzi and Tsagalis (2015a) 11–14; Tsagalis (2016) 55–66.
[13] On the formation of the Epic Cycle, see M. L. West (2015) 96–107.
[14] Fenik (1964) 9–10: "This does not, of course, prove a similar case for Rhesus, but that he belongs within this group, regardless of the age of his story, there can be no doubt."

(as Fenik himself has argued), how is it possible that it does not belong to a pre-Homeric myth complex? The Pindaric and/or oracle versions reflect earlier, pre-Homeric treatments of the Rhesus story and share with the episodes of Penthesileia, Memnon, and Eurypylus the motif of the "late-arriving ally"[15] and with the episodes of Helenus, Philoctetes, Neoptolemus, the *Ptocheia*, and the Palladium the theme of "special mission" (sometimes involving spying and ambush).[16] Taken together, these stories display features that signal cyclic epic and nest in the post-Hector and post-Achilles stages of the war, respectively. Kullmann seems reluctant to interpret the myth of Rhesus as part and parcel of a pre-Homeric myth complex. His neoanalytical approach treats the Rhesus story as an ἀπόκρυφον, a variant story which did not belong to cyclic epic.[17] The reason for this assumption was that, despite its pronounced cyclic nature, the story of Rhesus was neither mentioned in the summaries of the Trojan War Cyclic epics that have come down to us via Proclus nor included in the extant fragments attributed to the Epic Cycle. In my view, this approach is not without problems. I will now suggest a putative context for the Rhesus episode in pre-Homeric epic and will discuss the absence of any reference to Rhesus in Proclus' summaries.[18]

9.2 Contextualizing the Rhesus Episode

9.2.1 Thematic Kernel, Narrative Pattern, and Autonomy

In assessing an episode, what matter most are its thematic kernel, narrative pattern, and autonomy. The thematic nucleus of the Rhesus episode is a night-time mission that culminates in the ambush and death of the Thracian king and some of his men. The narrative pattern is fixed, the protagonists are the same: Diomedes and Odysseus infiltrate the enemy camp at night, remain unnoticed, approach, and kill Rhesus and his guards, and return safely to their camp. The clustering of these features of the Rhesus story in various versions (*Iliad* 10, the Pindaric version, the oracle version, the *Rhesus*) suggests that, despite the differences in secondary elements, the episode has been organized into a cohesive whole that displays a high level of systematization.[19] Its crystallization makes it likely that it constitutes a distinct mythical unit with its own identity.

---

[15] These episodes feature a triumphant Aeacid (Achilles: Penthesileia, Memnon; Neoptolemus: Eurypylus) operating *after the death of Hector*.

[16] In these episodes Diomedes (Philoctetes) or Odysseus (Helenus, *Ptocheia*) or both (Palladium) operate *after the death of Achilles*.

[17] See Kullmann (1977) 536 = (1992) 207. Kullmann's criticism on Dihle's attempt to refute Fenik's claim about an early cyclic background of *Iliad* 10 is decisive. There is no indication whatsoever in the scholia that the tradition about Rhesus originates with book 10 of the *Iliad*.

[18] On Proclus and the Epic Cycle, see Fantuzzi and Tsagalis (2015a) 1–40; Currie (2016) 229–33.

[19] On the fixed narrative pattern lying behind the Rhesus story, see pp. 244–60.

A corollary to this argument is the story's autonomy. Just as the episodes of Penthesileia, Eurypylus, and Coroebus,[20] which also share the motif of "the late-arriving ally" and occur after the death of either Hector (Penthesileia)[21] or Achilles (Eurypylus and Coroebus),[22] are marked by a noteworthy autonomy, so the Rhesus story, whose thematic "habitat" is also stamped by the motif of "the late-arriving ally," enjoys a high degree of self-sufficiency. This is because none of these episodes entail consequences for the rest of the Trojan War.[23] The autonomy of the stories of Penthesileia, Eurypylus, and Coroebus makes them transferable from one epic to the other. Penthesileia may have featured in an *Amazonis*, from where she was transferred to the *Aethiopis*. The same may have been the case with respect to Eurypylus.[24] The case of Coroebus is more complex, but it is plausible that his episode was transferred[25] from a poem on the sack of Troy to an epic like the *Ilias parva*, in which the sack of the city was only one component of its plot.[26]

---

[20] See pp. 93, 164 with nn. 15–6, 222–3, 226, 229, 234–6, 279–80, 286–90.

[21] In the *Aethiopis* the Penthesileia and Memnon episodes constitute two independent exploits by Achilles against a female enemy from the North and a male enemy from the South. The death of Antilochus by Memnon, which leads to Achilles' confrontation with and death of Memnon, is a prerequisite for the death of Achilles (*Aeth*. arg. ll. 186–7 Severyns) that must happen before the end of the war and the fall of Troy, since it is fated that Achilles will not sack the city.

[22] The advent of Neoptolemus, Philoctetes, and the theft of the Palladium are all prerequisites for the sack of Troy, according to Helenus' prophecy. See *Il. parv.* arg. ll. 211–12 Severyns: μετὰ ταῦτα Ὀδυσσεὺς λοχήσας Ἕλενον λαμβάνει, καὶ χρήσαντος περὶ τῆς ἁλώσεως τούτου Διομήδης ἐκ Λήμνου Φιλοκτήτην ἀνάγει ("after this Odysseus seizes Helenus in ambush, and when that one foretells about the sack of the city, Diomedes brings Philoctetes back from Lemnos"); *Il. parv.* arg. ll. 217–18 Severyns: καὶ Νεοπτόλεμον Ὀδυσσεὺς ἐκ Σκύρου ἀγαγὼν τὰ ὅπλα δίδωσι τὰ τοῦ πατρός ("and Odysseus brings Neoptolemus from Scyros and gives him the arms of his father"); *Il. parv.* arg. ll. 228–9 Severyns: καὶ μετὰ ταῦτα σὺν Διομήδει τὸ παλλάδιον ἐκκομίζει (sc. Ὀδυσσεὺς) ἐκ τῆς Ἰλίου ("and after that he conveys the Palladium out of Ilium with Diomedes"); see also Apollod. *Epit.* 5.9–10.

[23] The death of Penthesileia by Achilles is not a prerequisite for the continuation of the story of the Trojan War. The Memnon story does not presuppose it. Likewise, the death of Eurypylus by Neoptolemus is a self-contained episode, since no prophecy or prerequisite is met because Eurypylus dies. That this is so can be covertly seen by the fact that there was no funeral for him (M. L. West 2013a, 193). The advent of Telephus' son, his *aristeia*, and death at the hands of Neoptolemus (*Il. parv.* arg. ll. 219–20 Severyns) constitute a doublet of Telephus' victory over the Achaeans and wounding by Achilles (*Cypr.* arg. ll. 125–8 Severyns). Along the same lines, Coroebus' death at the hands of Diomedes (*Il. parv.* fr. 24 GEF; see also Pap. Ryl. 22) is not necessary at all for the continuation of the war.

[24] See Kullmann (1960) 189–203, (2012b) 15–20; Tsagalis (2014b) 373 = (2023) 328–9; see also M. L. West (2006) 17 = (2013b) 16, who has argued that Archilochus' version of the Telephus episode and the final victory of Neoptolemus/Pyrrhus over Eurypylus may have been taken from a lost epic or pair of epics relating the entire Telephus myth from the arrival of the Achaeans in Mysia to the death of Eurypylus in Troy; see *EGM* 542: "the Odyssey passage and a depiction of Eurypylos slain by Neoptolemos on a late sixth-century hydria (*LIMC* Eurypylos no. 1) indicate the same conclusion."

[25] For the "special" association between the Coroebus and Rhesus episodes, see pp. 287–93.

[26] Coroebus' absence from the extant summaries of Proclus may be due to cropping in the Proclus or pre-Proclus prose tradition so as to avoid repetition of events which also featured in Proclus' summary of the *Iliou persis*. In fact, we can identify a principle of citation used by Proclus in his summary of the capture of Troy in the *Iliou persis*: "only one violent act per scene or episode, only one violent act per person is mentioned": Neoptolemus kills Priam, Menelaus kills Deiphobus, Ajax Oileus takes from Cassandra by violence the xoanon of Athena, Odysseus kills Astyanax, the Achaeans sacrifice Polyxena on Achilles' grave. It is possible that Coroebus may have featured in the Cassandra episode in the *Iliou persis*, although he is not mentioned in Proclus' summary, which focuses only on Ajax Oileus and Cassandra. This would be in tune with fr. 24 GEF, where it is stated that other authors presented

Viewed against this backdrop, the Rhesus story, which belongs to a category of successive enemies of the Achaeans (Telephus, Cycnus, Penthesileia, Memnon, Eurypylus, Coroebus), shares with the episodes of Penthesileia, Eurypylus, and Coroebus a level of autonomy that makes it transferable from one epic poem to another. However, autonomy should not be confused with independence. None of all the extant examples of this type of story exists as an independent poem. This observation, which is true for the *Sauptikaparvan*, the Nisus and Euryalus episode, and the Cyclic stories of Penthesileia, Eurypylus, and Coroebus, may well be applied to the tale of Rhesus.

If so, where is it likely for the story of Rhesus to be nested? It may have existed as part of an epic tradition of cyclic nature that featured similar episodes. We have seen that such episodes tend to cluster in the time frame after the deaths of Hector and Achilles, in which various new heroes come to Troy, both Achaean (Philoctetes, Neoptolemus) and pro-Trojan (Eurypylus, Coroebus).

9.2.2 Relation to Episodes with the Same Protagonists

Another important factor in the evaluation of an episode is the way it is related to other episodes with the same protagonists. The Rhesus story shows affinities not only with other episodes of the Trojan War that use the motif of the "late-arriving ally" but also with episodes marked by the intense activity of Diomedes and Odysseus. These two heroes are associated with ambushes (Helenus, Trojan Horse), spying (*Ptocheia*, Palladium), nocturnal missions (Odysseus ambushing Helenus;[27] *Ptocheia*; theft of the Palladium), or other special missions (fetching Philoctetes from Lemnos and Neoptolemus from Scyros) which feature in the *Ilias parva*. Diomedes and Odysseus act (a) individually (Odysseus in the *Ptocheia*); (b) separately, but in accordance with a plan (after Odysseus' capture of Helenus and the seer's subsequent prophecy about the requirements that needed to be fulfilled for Troy to fall, Diomedes fetches Philoctetes from Lemnos and Odysseus brings Neoptolemus from Scyros); or (c) together (Palladium).

How intense this activity is can be also seen from certain "side effects," which refer to material that may have been shaped under the influence of this chain of events and in which Diomedes and Odysseus play a prominent role. The Eurytus *krater* from Cerveteri dating to the last quarter of the seventh century BC

Neoptolemus as the killer of Coroebus, while Lesches opted for Diomedes. In this light, Arctinus (the poet of the *Iliou persis*) may be one of the authors obliquely referenced by Pausanias' ὡς μὲν ὁ πλείων λόγος, on the killing of Coroebus by Neoptolemus.

[27] See M. L. West (2013a) 179, who argues that this was also a nocturnal episode since it is possible that Soph. *Phil.* 606–8 (Ἕλενος, ὃν οὗτος νυκτὸς ἐξελθὼν μόνος | ὁ πάντ' ἀκούων αἰσχρὰ καὶ λωβήτ' ἔπη | δόλοις Ὀδυσσεὺς εἷλε) draws on it.

(c. 625–600)[28] presents the suicide of Ajax, who lies prostrate over his sword, his body supported on his knees and arms. The artist has decided to stage a particular phase of the episode, not with Ajax alone (as in so many other early depictions of this episode) but flanked by Diomedes and Odysseus in full armor. The decision to depict a moment after Ajax's suicide may have been related to the artist's desire to invite his viewers to think about the impact of this suicide on the Achaean army. Diomedes' posture is marked by a stroke of artistic brilliance. In a powerful display of utter dismay and worry, Diomedes grasps his neck. On the other side, Odysseus stares at the sight of the great dead warrior over his sword. Diomedes' size (he is much taller than Odysseus) is a graphic reminder of the traditional presentation of the two heroes, the great warrior and the man of *metis*. This is all well and good, but we are left with a disturbing feeling as far as the depiction of Diomedes is concerned. The hero has no connection whatsoever with the episode of Ajax's suicide. Why not Agamemnon, Menelaus, or Athena? Odysseus is, of course, the one who got the arms of Achilles in the *hoplon krisis*, so his presence is justified. But what about Diomedes? In my view this is the wrong question. The right one would be: why Diomedes *together* with Odysseus? As argued above, what matters is the context in which the episode is placed. The artist seems to have in mind the sequence of events that takes place after the suicide of Ajax. Is it possible that he was also thinking of Lesches' *Ilias parva*, in which Diomedes *and* Odysseus dominate? The plot of the *Ilias parva* allows us to realize that the two heroes come to the fore after Ajax's suicide, when Odysseus ambushes Helenus, who reveals that one of the requirements for Troy to fall is the arrival of Philoctetes with Heracles' bow. This task is undertaken by Diomedes, who brings the great archer from Lemnos.[29] However, if a date between 640 and 630 BC for this epic is accepted,[30] there is a very brief time-lapse for a potential influence on the artist, given that the vase is dated to 625–600 BC. If the artist was drawing on myth in general, it seems that he knew of a fixed order of events. In this vein, there is nothing to rule out the possibility that, besides this artist (and arguably others), there may have been one or more versions of these events narrated in oral epic poetry.

This line of thought is supported by the depiction of Diomedes next to the dead Ajax immediately after his suicide and especially the emphatic expression of his consternation that reflects his concern about the future of the war. By losing Ajax, the Achaeans are deprived of a great warrior who was second only to Achilles.[31] In fact, they find themselves in a situation of utter despair. The war goes on but at the highest cost. The fact that Ajax's suicide follows the death of Achilles works cumulatively. The Achaeans are faced with a situation that, *mutatis mutandis*, could be like the one they were facing in the *Iliad*, when Achilles was sitting out the

---

[28] Louvre E 635; see Ahlberg-Cornell (1992) 74 and fig. 113.   [29] Ahlberg-Cornell (1992) 74.
[30] M. L. West (2012) 240, (2013a) 181–2.   [31] See *Il.* 2.768.

war because of his quarrel with Agamemnon. By giving Odysseus Achilles' weapons, which precipitates Ajax's suicide, the Atreidae have harmed the army in a manner that is analogous to the harm Agamemnon had caused when he insulted Achilles. In this respect, Diomedes' gesture of consternation while standing together with Odysseus by Ajax may suggest that the artist is alerting viewers of the vase to the events that are about to unfold.

It is in such a framework and at such a point in the myth that the arrival of a new, pro-Trojan ally like Rhesus may have been at home. The Eurytus *krater* does not and cannot prove that the artist had the Rhesus episode in mind, but it points to its putative context, which is marked by the joint activity of Diomedes and Odysseus after Achilles' death and Ajax's suicide.[32]

9.2.3 Balancing the Antagonism of the Protagonists

The *Ilias parva* begins with the *hoplon krisis*, an episode in which Odysseus' strained relationship with first-rank heroes comes to the fore. Odysseus is awarded Achilles' arms instead of Telamonian Ajax (another Aeacid), who has been recognized as the second-best warrior among the Achaeans,[33] has significantly contributed to the protection of the Achaean ships, and has played an eminent role in the recovery of Achilles' body.[34] Ajax considers Odysseus (and the Atreidae for their unjust verdict) to be responsible.[35] In the wake of this event, he resorts, like his cousin Achilles, who had withdrawn from battle, to an extreme decision: suicide.[36] Odysseus' troubled relationship with another first-rank hero, Diomedes,

---

[32] The importance of the successive deaths of Achilles and Telamonian Ajax is often neglected. This point underlies the emphasis on Rhesus' fighting ability in [Eur.] *Rh.* 461–2, where the Chorus refers to these two Aeacids only to imply that they will not be able to withstand the Thracian king's might (πῶς μοι τὸ σὸν ἔγχος Ἀχιλλεὺς ἂν δύναιτο, | πῶς δ' Αἴας ὑπομεῖναι, "Tell me, how can Achilles withstand your spear, how can Ajax?"). Translation: Kovacs (2002).

[33] See *Il.* 2.768.

[34] The controversy with respect to which of the two, Telamonian Ajax or Odysseus, is worthy of receiving the arms of Achilles is an issue with various ramifications, one of which pertains to determining their specific role in the process of saving Achilles' body. The most common version (starting with the *Aeth.* arg. ll. 193–5 [Severyns] and followed by most literary sources: Pind. *Nem.* 8.26; Soph. *Aj.* 445–9, 1135–6, 1243; Antisth. *Ajax* 1, *Od.* 1; on iconographical sources, see Gantz 1993, 633) has Ajax carry the body, while Odysseus wards off the Trojans. The roles are reversed in P. Oxy. 2510 (third–fourth century AD; see *Il. parv.* fr. dub. 32 PEG). According to *Il. parv.* fr. 2 GEF, Nestor proposed that the dispute between Odysseus and Ajax about the arms of Achilles should be solved by sending some men to the walls of Troy to eavesdrop so that they might find out whom the Trojans consider to be the best among the Achaeans after Achilles. The source for this version are the scholia to Ar. *Eq.* 1056a (Mervyn Jones and Wilson); see M. L. West (2013a) 175–6.

[35] Pindar has interpreted the awarding of the arms of Achilles to Odysseus rather than Ajax through φθόνος in its two aspects, an external one that was felt by others (especially Odysseus) for Ajax's martial superiority and an internal one felt by Ajax for Odysseus, who was awarded the arms of Achilles; see Köhnken (1971) 25–7.

[36] Odysseus' strained relationship with Ajax is so strong that it is reflected even in the Underworld scene in *Od.* 11.543–64, when Ajax's *eidolon* neither comes close nor speaks to Odysseus, since he still holds a grudge against him for the arms of Achilles.

is observable in the episode of the Palladium, which also belongs to the *Ilias parva*.[37] On their way back from Troy after the theft of the Palladium, Odysseus tries to kill Diomedes, who was in front of him, so as to gain all the glory for himself. Due to the moonlight, Diomedes is able to see the shadow of Odysseus' sword.[38] As a result, Diomedes makes Odysseus go first while slapping him on the back with the flat of his sword.[39]

Since both episodes featured in the *Ilias parva*, we can see that Lesches' epic offered the right context for the presentation of Odysseus' tense relationship with two first-rank Achaean heroes. This observation seems disconcerting, especially since Odysseus comes out as a leading hero in this epic.[40] The unsettling aspect of these two relationships, which are both at odds with the otherwise good relationship of Odysseus with Telamonian Ajax[41] and Diomedes, creates a backdrop against which the troubled situation of the Achaeans is presented after such a deeply disturbing event as Achilles' death. These two relationships are about who will "shine" more, now that the incontestably "best" of the Achaeans is no more. In both relationships, there is initial cooperation. In the case of Ajax and Odysseus in the *Iliad*, in both the Embassy and on the battlefield, the two heroes cooperate. In book 9 Odysseus and Ajax try to convince Achilles to return to the war; in book 11 Ajax comes to the rescue of Odysseus in his hour of need;[42] in the *Aethiopis* and (perhaps) in the beginning of the *Ilias parva* they fight jointly to recover Achilles' dead body. As for Diomedes and Odysseus, they join forces in the episode of Palamedes in the *Cypria* and in the *Doloneia* in the *Iliad*. Although they undertake several different missions after Helenus' prophecy in the *Ilias parva*,[43] their actions are clearly parallel and aim at achieving a common goal.

Since the *Ilias parva* tries to strike a balance between the successful collaboration of Odysseus with Diomedes in the events following Ajax's suicide and their tense relationship in the theft of the Palladium, it seems like the ideal environment for a major episode of harmonious and successful collaboration between the two heroes. This episode may have been the Rhesus story. That Lesches had not made this choice should in no way prohibit us from considering

---

[37] Fr. 11 *GEF*.
[38] The fact that Odysseus tries to kill Diomedes and claim the theft of the Palladium as his own achievement suggests that he may have thought that he had done more regarding the accomplishment of this difficult endeavor. Odysseus had gone alone to Troy in the episode of the *Ptocheia*, which paves the way for the theft of the Palladium.
[39] See the proverbial expression Διομήδειος ἀνάγκη in Hesych. δ 1881 (Cunningham); Paus. Att. δ 14 (Phot. *Lex.* δ 637 [Theodoridis] = *Suda* δ 1164 [Adler]); Eust. 822.19 (van der Valk), Ar. *Eccl.* 1029; Pl. *Rep.* 493d. Conon 34 (Brown) reverses the roles of Diomedes and Odysseus.
[40] See Kelly (2015) 324 and 343.
[41] The relationship between Odysseus and Telamonian Ajax is rather harmonious in *Iliad* 9.
[42] *Il.* 11.472–97.   [43] See p. 263 n. 64.

the possibility that the episode featured in some oral epic focusing on the events after Achilles' death that may have existed prior and next to Lesches' written epic.

9.2.4 Relation to Episodes Sharing the Motif of the "Late-Arriving Ally"

The Rhesus story falls within a range of episodes, which are marked by the same motif of the "late-arriving ally." This motif undergoes a progressive development over the course of the Trojan War after the death of Hector and the end of the *Iliad*. The first two late-arriving allies are Penthesileia and Memnon, who support the Trojans. Their arrival at Troy aims to fill the void left after the loss of the major Trojan hero, Hector. Both the Thracian Amazon and the Aethiopian king are killed by Achilles, who in turn is killed after the death of Memnon. Ajax's suicide, which occurs soon after Achilles' loss, marks a turning point for the use of the motif of the "late-arriving ally,"[44] given that both Achilles and Ajax are dead. This is the moment for a new beginning. It is exactly at this point that Diomedes and Odysseus, these two non-Aeacid heroes, come to the fore. When we look at the plot of the *Ilias parva*, we realize not only that this powerful pair dominates the entire action but also that it gives to the motif of the "late-arriving ally" a new twist: first, Diomedes and Odysseus become instrumental in "transferring" this motif from the Trojans to the Achaeans, since it is they who bring Philoctetes and Neoptolemus to Troy; second, they do not engage in the typical battlefield confrontation with the new pro-Trojan allies (Eurypylus and Coroebus), but either leave this role to be played by the new Achaean allies they themselves bring to Troy (Neoptolemus kills Eurypylus) or kill them during a night ambush (Diomedes kills Coroebus after the ambush of the Wooden Horse).[45] This new deployment of the motif of the "late-arriving ally" is instructive, since it suggests both sophisticated elaboration and interdependence between a motif and the characters with whom it is associated. Likewise, the Rhesus episode is a manifestation not simply of the motif of the "late-arriving ally" but especially of one of its two developments which we have traced above. It has the same protagonists (Diomedes and Odysseus) and features a night ambush, not an open martial engagement. This conformity with a development and use that we have observed in the plot of the *Ilias parva*, an epic which encompasses all the events from the death of Achilles to the sack of Troy, may indicate that this is the environment in which this episode belongs.

---

[44] It should be noted that only late-arriving pro-Achaean allies excel in regular combat in the *Ilias parva* (Philoctetes and Neoptolemus).

[45] In another version, it is Neoptolemus who kills Coroebus; see *Il. parv.* fr. 24 *GEF*.

9.2.5 The Special Affinity between the Rhesus and Coroebus Episodes

Coroebus occupies a special position regarding the Rhesus story.[46] This is because the Coroebus episode is the only case featuring a pro-Trojan late-arriving ally who comes to Troy after the death of Achilles and is killed by Diomedes in a night assault. The story of Coroebus is reported by Pausanias[47] (= *Il. parv.* fr. 24 *GEF*) and a summary of events featuring in the *Ilias parva* that is cited in P. Rylands 22 (first century BC, ed. Hunt). Before looking at the stories of Coroebus and Rhesus side by side, I will quote, for reasons of convenience, the text of P. Rylands 22 and offer some brief comments:

Ὀδυσσεὺς καὶ Διομήδη]ς εἰσελθόντες εἰς {ε} Ἴλι[ον, ὅπως ἐκκλέψωσιν] τὸ τῆς
Ἀθηνᾶς οὐράνι[ον ἄγαλμα, τοῦτο Ἑλ]ένου πάλιν αὐτοῖς εἴπαν[τος, ἀποκτείνουσι]ν
Κόροιβον τὸν Μυγδῶ[νος τὸν ἐκ Φρυγίας] ἐληλυθότα ἐπὶ συμμα[χίαν τοῖς Τρωσὶν]
καὶ ἄλλους αὐτοῦ ἑταίρο[υς . . . .] καὶ σώζονται πρὸς τοὺ[ς Ἕλληνας
ἔχοντες] τὸ παλλάδιον. εἶτα γ{ε}[ίνεται τούτοις μὲν] χαρά, τῶν δὲ Τρώων [. . . . . .
. . . .] τροπὴ ἐπὶ τοῖς γεγεν[ημένοις. Ὀδυσσεὺ]ς δὲ καὶ Φοῖνιξ πλε[υσάμενοι
εἰς τὴν] Σκῦρον ἄγουσι τὸν Ν[εοπτόλεμον, καὶ δ]ὴ ἀποδίδωσιν αὐτῶ<ι> τὰ ὅπλα
τοῦ πατρὸ]ς αὐτοῦ. Ἀ[χιλλεὺς δὲ αὐτῶ<ι> φαντάζε]ται παρὰ τῶ<ι> [τύμβω<ι> . . .
καὶ κατὰ τὸν αὐ]τὸν καιρὸν [Εὐρύπυλος ὁ Τηλέφου υἱὸς] ἐκ τῆς Μυ[σίας παραγ{ε}
ίνεται βοηθῶν] τοῖς Τρωσ[ί . . . . Πριά]μω<ι> εἶτα . . [. . . . .
γ{ε}ίνε]ται μάχη[. . . . .

3 Κόροιβον Bernabé: Κόρυβον Π ∥ 4 ἑταίρο[υς Bernabé: ἑτέρο[υς Π ∥ 7 καὶ δ]ὴ Ebert: ἤδη κα]ὶ Hunt ∥ 10 Πριά]μω<ι Bernabé: πολέ]μω<ι> Hunt

P. Rylands 22 agrees with Apollodorus' *Epitome* (5.11–13) and the Proclan summary of the *Ilias parva* (ll. 212, 217–21, 224–9 Severyns) regarding (a) the mission of Odysseus and Diomedes to Ilium in accordance to the prophecy of Helenus, (b) their theft of the Palladium after the killing of the guards, (c) the fetching of Neoptolemus from Scyros and Odysseus' offering to him of Achilles' arms, (d) the apparition of Achilles' ghost to Neoptolemus, (e) the arrival of Eurypylus at Troy, his *aristeia*, and death at the hands of Neoptolemus. However, these three texts differ with respect to (a) the order of events concerning the arrival of Neoptolemus in Troy: in Apollodorus and Proclus, Neoptolemus is brought to Troy from Scyros by Odysseus *before* the theft of the Palladium by Odysseus and Diomedes; in P. Rylands 22, the order is reversed; (b) the association of the death of Coroebus with the protection of the Palladium, not with the

---

[46] Fenik (1964) does not discuss in detail this Cyclic example of a late-arriving ally of the Trojans.
[47] 10.27.1.

sack of Troy as is the case in Lesches' *Ilias parva*. The coexistence of stunning similarities in diction and content in the narrative of P. Rylands 22 and the summaries of Apollodorus (*Epitome*) and Proclus (*Ilias parva*) on the one hand,[48] and of two important divergencies on the other, allows for the possibility that the Proclan version was not the only one with respect to the *Ilias parva*.[49] If the version reported by P. Rylands 22 was non-Aristotelian, it is likely that it never obtained the status of a canon.[50]

Let us now turn our attention to a comparative examination of the stories of Coroebus (as reported by Pausanias 10.27.1 = *Il. parv.* fr. 24 *GEF* and P. Rylands 22)[51] and Rhesus (oracle version reported by Σ [D] Il. 10.435):

Coroebus story (*Il. parv.* and *IlParvPapRyl*)	Rhesus story (oracle version)
Helenus' prophecy	oracle
theft of Palladium by Diomedes and Odysseus[52]	theft of Rhesus' horses
as magic symbol for the safety of Troy	as magic symbol for the safety of Troy by means of Trojan victory
Diomedes and Odysseus kill the late-arriving ally Coroebus and his comrades	Diomedes kills the late-arriving ally Rhesus and his twelve Thracian guards

---

[48] The summaries of Proclus and Apollodorus match the order of episodes given for the *Ilias parva* by Arist. *Po.* 1459b4–7 and Pausanias 10.27.1 (= *Il. parv.* fr. 24 *GEF*).

[49] See Bernabé (1984, 148 and 150), who argues that more than one epic covered the events included in the *Ilias parva*. A similar argument has been put forward by Finkelberg (2002, 156 = 2020, 145) as regards the *Cypria*. Discrepancies in certain features or episodes of Cyclic epics have either been treated as a sign indicating the existence of more than one version or been explained by interpolation or by the "cropping" of individual Cyclic epics around the Homeric epics; see Currie (2016) 229 with nn. 2–3.

[50] Notice that in the version given by P. Rylands 22 Coroebus dies before the fall of Troy, whereas in Lesches' *Ilias parva* and in Arctinus' *Iliou persis* he is killed during the sack of Ilium. The dictional similarities that we have observed are likely to be due to the influence of the canonical summary of the Epic Cycle, which had greater authority and was widely diffused and consulted.

[51] The abbreviation *IlParvPapRyl* refers to P. Rylands 22.

[52] It should be stressed that in the *Rhesus* certain events (the theft of the Palladium [501–7] and the arrival of Coroebus, who is assigned the first night watch [538–9]) that belong to the last phase of the Trojan war, i.e. the sack of Troy, are presented as prior to the advent of Rhesus; see Liapis (2012) 205–7 and 223 on [Eur.] *Rh.* 498–509 and 539, respectively; Fries (2014) 309 and 328–9 on [Eur.] *Rh.* 501–2 and 539, respectively; Fantuzzi (2020) 418–20 and 442–3 on [Eur.] *Rh.* on 501–9 and 539–41, respectively. Drawing on Σ exeg. *Od.* 4.425, Fantuzzi (1996, 175–85) has argued that the author of the *Rhesus* allowed this chronological discrepancy "because he wanted the πτωχεία...to have in his play a prefigurative function similar to that of the πτωχεία narrated by Helen at *Od.* 4.242–58." As Helen's recollection of Odysseus' disguise as a beggar in *Odyssey* 4 prefigured his beggar disguise in the *mnesterophonia*, so the reference to his disguise in the *Ptocheia* (*Rh.* 501–9, 710–19) prefigures his killing of the Thracians in the *Rhesus*. This is an ingenious interpretation with which I agree. In my view, apart from the reasons that have caused the use of the two anachronisms in the *Rhesus* (*Ptocheia*-Palladium and Coroebus), it is important to stress that their similarities with the episode of Rhesus (talismanic aspect of the Palladium—oracle version of Rhesus' story, "late-arriving ally") have suppressed the chronological incompatibility; see Fries (2014) 329 on [Eur.] *Rh.* 539.

Coroebus has come to Troy because of the obligation of his father, Mygdon, to Priam,	Rhesus has come to Troy because of the obligation he had to Hector,
who had helped the Phrygians against the Amazons (*Il.* 3.184–9)	who had helped him against other Thracian princes ([Eur.] *Rh.* 406–11;[53] see also *Il.* 24.234–7)

The essential question to emerge from the impressive number of these close analogies is whether we are dealing with a traditional pattern or a unidirectional influence and shaping of one story by another. The former alternative seems unlikely. The first reason is that the Rhesus and Coroebus stories display a range of accumulated similarities that bring them closer than the other extant examples of the motif of the pro-Trojan "late-arriving ally." They both represent an intensified and focused version of this motif. The second reason is that the extant version of the Rhesus story diverges between his death after an *aristeia* (the Pindaric version) and his immediate death without an *aristeia* (the oracle version). This divergence speaks in favor of the view that Rhesus' *aristeia* does not belong to the nucleus of the Rhesus story, but is a secondary element that could vary.

As regards the second alternative (unidirectional influence), we need to determine the direction of the influence. The motival priority of the Rhesus story over Coroebus must be ruled out for the following reasons:

(a) Coroebus, who is attached to the figure of Cassandra and the sack of Troy, is more monumental than the completely peripheral Rhesus story, which was not included in any of the three post-Iliadic Cyclic epics,[54] though there was a place for pro-Trojan late-arriving allies like him (Penthesileia and Memnon in the *Aethiopis*, Eurypylus in the *Ilias parva*). On the contrary, Cassandra (and Coroebus with her) featured in two different Cyclic epics (in the *Ilias parva* and in the *Iliou persis*).

(b) The Coroebus story must have exercised its influence on the Rhesus story at an early stage, before the former incurred certain secondary elements whose later popularity has wrongly created the impression that they belong to the story's kernel. This is exactly the case with Cassandra as Coroebus' future wife. A further clue is offered by *Il.* 13.365–7 (ᾔτεε δὲ Πριάμοιο θυγατρῶν εἶδος ἀρίστην | Κασσάνδρην, ἀνάεδνον, ὑπέσχετο δὲ **μέγα ἔργον**, | ἐκ Τροίης ἀέκοντας ἀπωσέμεν υἷας Ἀχαιῶν). Othryoneus promises the Trojans in the *Iliad* what Coroebus will promise them in the *Ilias parva*. This may be the result of the transfer in miniature

---

[53] See Fantuzzi (2020) 370 on [Eur.] *Rh.* 408–11a.

[54] Likewise with the Cassandra and Chryseis episodes: Cassandra must have provided the model for Chryseis rather than vice versa, since Cassandra's story is "more familiar and the Ilioupersis the more monumental capture" (Anderson 1997, 52).

of the bare bones of the Coroebus episode from a pre-Homeric oral tradition to Othryoneus in the *Iliad*.[55] What is of special interest to our inquiry is the use of the expression μέγα ἔργον, which is regularly employed in the *Iliad* for a military feat, operating in book 10 as a relic of the failed attempt to eliminate Hector by means of a night ambush in the Hector-version of the *Doloneia*.[56] The use of this expression in *Iliad* 13 for Othryoneus, a character sharing several similarities with Coroebus within the larger epic tradition of the Trojan War, may indicate that it was previously used for Coroebus and Rhesus, who have also promised to defeat the Achaeans.[57]

(c) The joy of the Achaeans in Pap. Ryl. 22 results from the theft of the Palladium, as Helenus has prophesied.[58] Their exultation comes from the fact that they believe that a basic prerequisite for the fall of Troy has been fulfilled (no matter if the actual sack will take more time). In contrast, at *Il.* 10.541 the joy of the Achaeans is due to the safe return of Diomedes and Odysseus, while at 10.565 it may be (additionally) associated with the theft of Rhesus' horses.[59] The joy of the Achaeans in the Coroebus story (Pap. Ryl. 22) cannot have been a reflex of their joy in the Iliadic version of the Rhesus story, since a motival influence of the Rhesus story on the Coroebus story based on widely *disiecta membra* (*Il.* 3.186[60] and the Rhesus episode in the *Iliad*) is unlikely.

---

[55] Fantuzzi (2020, 442 on [Eur.] *Rh.* 539–41) treats the two episodes as doublets. I treat the Othryoneus episode as derivative, since it is elliptical and narratively insignificant.

[56] In Odysseus' prayer to Athena (*Il.* 10.278–82), Odysseus cannot ask for the goddess's help against Rhesus because at this stage he (as well as Diomedes) does not know that Rhesus has come to Troy.

[57] See Quintus Smyrnaeus 13.174–5 (ὑπέσχετ' Ἀχαιούς | Ἰλίου ἄψ ὦσαι), where Coroebus boasts that he would drive the Achaeans away from Troy, and the use of similar diction with respect to Othryoneus at *Il.* 13.366–7 (ὑπέσχετο δὲ μέγα ἔργον, | ἐκ Τροίης ἀέκοντας ἀπωσέμεν υἷας Ἀχαιῶν). This arrogant promise made Coroebus a "by-word for stupidity"; for the relevant ancient sources, see Fantuzzi (2020) 442 n. 76 on [Eur.] *Rh.* 539–41; for Rhesus' arrogance, see [Eur.] *Rhes.* 447–9, where the Thracian king boasts that one day will be enough time for him to invade the enemy camp and fall upon the Achaean ships.

[58] For the discussion of this motif in the *Sauptikaparvan*, see pp. 253–4 and 258.

[59] Having said this, I would like to record the possibility that the joy of the Achaeans regarding the horses, which in the *Iliad* is due to their impressiveness, has been adapted from the oracle version, in which the theft of the horses was a prerequisite for the fall of Troy. If so, then the joy would be similar to and derivative of the joy of the Achaeans over the theft of the Palladium, which was also one of the conditions that had to be met for Troy's sack.

[60] In *Il.* 3.186–90, Priam recalls that he had assisted the Phrygians in a war against the Amazons in the past. Such a detail speaks of an obligation on the part of the Phrygians to the Trojans. Is it a coincidence that the two Phrygian figures mentioned in this passage are Otreus and Mygdon, both being Hecuba's brothers, the latter the father of Coroebus, who is, like Rhesus, another late-arriving ally who comes to Troy to assist the Trojans and is killed by none other than Diomedes inside Troy? Is this a piece of circumstantial detail or a relic of a version in which Coroebus' assistance to the Trojans resulted from a Phrygian obligation to Priam and the Trojans, while in the other version he was lured to Troy with the promise of marrying Cassandra (*Il. parv.* fr. 24 *GEF*)? Rhesus too had an obligation to Hector according to [Eur.] *Rh.* 399–403 (see Liapis 2012, 176; Fries 2014, 269–71; Fantuzzi 2020, 366–8), where it is stated that the Trojans had sent a herald and an embassy of elders together with gifts in order to persuade him to come to Troy. This last reference is not mentioned in the *Iliad* and, therefore, cannot have originated from it. Furthermore, the analogy with the Embassy to Achilles can hardly be used as an explanation since, unlike Achilles who was angry with Agamemnon, Rhesus was not angry with Hector.

(d) The early influence of the Coroebus tale on the story of Rhesus is suggested by the following observation: in the story of Coroebus, when attached to the theft of the Palladium (Pap. Ryl. 22), both Diomedes and Odysseus kill Coroebus and his comrades (arguably in this order).[61] The same seems to be the case in the Pindaric and oracle[62] versions of the Rhesus tale, in which both Diomedes and Odysseus kill Rhesus and his own comrades (again, probably, in this order).[63] A combined (by Diomedes and Odysseus) killing of Rhesus and his twelve Thracian guards/comrades also features in a Chalcidian neck-amphora by the Inscription Painter, dated to the middle of the sixth century BC (again in this order, according to the standard interpretation of the iconography).[64] The correspondence with respect to (a) the joint killings by Diomedes and Odysseus and (b) the order of the killings makes it possible that the story of Coroebus' death in the context of the theft of the Palladium has influenced the Pindaric and oracle versions of the Rhesus story as regards the joint killings and the order of deaths. That Odysseus, like Diomedes, was actively engaged in the elimination of enemies in such stories can be also seen from the *Ptocheia*, which is the prelude to the episode of the Palladium: see *Odyssey* 4.257 (πολλοὺς δὲ Τρώων κτείνας ταναήκεϊ χαλκῷ) and *Ilias parva* (arg. ll. 226–7 Severyns: κτείνας τέ τινας τῶν Τρώων). On the contrary, it is unlikely that the Pindaric and oracle versions had influenced the episode of Coroebus referring to the theft of the Palladium (P. Ryl. 22) with respect to the joint killings and the order of deaths, and simultaneously *Iliad* 10 regarding the joy of the Achaeans (see point c, above). As for the *Doloneia*, in which it is solely Diomedes who kills Rhesus and his comrades and the order of deaths is different (Rhesus is killed last), it is possible that it has not been influenced by the story of Coroebus in the context of the sack of Troy. The killing of Coroebus by Diomedes alone in the *Ilias parva* seems to be Lesches' innovation, other versions featuring Neoptolemus in this role (see fr. 24 *GEF*), and, in addition, Diomedes and Odysseus do not act as a pair in the Coroebus episode when it concerns the sack of Troy.

In fact, it may be suggested that the motif of the "distribution of duties" between Diomedes, who carries out all the killings, and Odysseus, who drags away the

---

[61] ἀποκτείνουσι]ν Κόροιβον τὸν Μυγδῶ[νος τὸν ἐκ Φρυγίας] ἐληλυθότα ἐπὶ συμμα[χίαν τοῖς Τρωσὶν] καὶ ἄλλους αὐτοῦ ἑταίρο[υς ... ...].

[62] It can be assumed that in the oracle version Rhesus and his comrades are killed (in this order) by both Diomedes and Odysseus, since the part of Σ (D) *Il.* 10.435 relating the oracle version is a direct continuation of the scholium referring to the Pindaric version. The scholiast did not repeat the features that both episodes shared; instead, he added only those elements that differ in the two versions.

[63] Σ (D) *Il.* 10.435: ἐπιστάντες δὲ ἐκεῖνοι κοιμωμένῳ Ῥήσῳ αὐτόν τε καὶ τοὺς ἑταίρους αὐτοῦ κτείνουσιν; see pp. 215–16, 229, 255 n. 18.

[64] This is a point on which both True (1995, 416) and Giuliani (2010, 244) agree. However, the two scholars differ regarding the source of influence on the painter: while True (1995, 419) favors a non-Iliadic version, Giuliani (2010, 244 n. 5) suggests *Iliad* 10. This is not the place to deal with this issue in detail. The only thing I would like to highlight here is that the text to which True points as a tentative source is neither hypothetical nor dependent on the iconography of the Chalcidian neck-amphora. This text is known to us by means of the ancient scholia to *Iliad* 10, and we are aware of its content with respect to the point of the Rhesus story described on the vase.

bodies of the dead, in *Iliad* 10 conforms with the situation we have encountered in the *Sauptikaparvan*, in which Aśvatthāman penetrates the enemy camp, while Kṛpa and Kṛtavarman make sure that nobody escapes.[65] The *Doloneia* may simply be reflecting this traditional motif.

Having argued in favor of a unidirectional influence of the Coroebus story on the Rhesus episode, we now need to shift the focus to the way this episode may have influenced the Rhesus story. To pursue this goal, we should consider both the placement of the two episodes within the larger context of the *Iliad* (Rhesus) in comparison to that of the pair *Ilias parva–Iliou persis* (Coroebus) and the technique by means of which the motival influence Coroebus > Rhesus is realized.

In these two Cyclic epics (*Ilias parva–Iliou persis*), Cassandra and Coroebus are linked to events pertaining directly or indirectly to the sack of Troy, which is the climactic event of the entire tradition. It is solely in this context that the Coroebus episode nests. It can hardly be a coincidence that the Rhesus episode is placed in the *Iliad* in proximity to the sack of the Greek camp in book 12, the figurative city of the Achaeans which stands for the inverted miniature of Troy. This allows for the possibility that the *Iliad* is using the Rhesus episode to allude to the manner in which the Coroebus episode was used in earlier oral epics, in which it was placed before the events that led to the sack of Troy. The correlation between the episodes of Rhesus and Coroebus can also be seen in relation to the preconditions that need to be fulfilled for Troy to be sacked. Helenus names various preconditions, which include the arrival of Philoctetes and Neoptolemus, as well as the theft of the Palladium. Likewise, there are certain prerequisites that need to be satisfied for the sack of the Achaean city-camp.[66] They all follow under the general pattern "Achaean leaders are wounded and withdraw from fighting." This is exactly what happens in *Iliad* 11, where Agamemnon, Diomedes, Odysseus, Machaon, and Eurypylus are all injured. None of them can take part in the defense of the Achaean Wall in *Iliad* 12. The *Iliad* may be here employing the technique of opposition in imitation or contrast-imitation by means of which it cites its source. The sack of Troy after the arrival of Coroebus (in the Cyclic tradition)[67] is transferred to the temporary sack of the Achaean camp after the arrival of Rhesus (in the *Iliad*). What was narratively consistent in the Cyclic tradition (Troy is sacked after the new ally Coroebus fails to save it) becomes narratively inconsistent in the *Iliad* (Rhesus is an enemy of the Achaeans whose camp is sacked).

---

[65] See pp. 245, 252, 255–6.

[66] The *Iliad* "sees," through Poseidon's words (7.452–3), the construction of the Achaean Wall as a rival to the glorious, impenetrable walls of Troy that he and Apollo had built as a penalty to Laomedon; see also *Il.* 8.47–52—by presenting Zeus traveling to Mount Ida to watch "the city of the Trojans and the ships of the Achaeans," the *Iliad* reinforces the analogy between the literal city of Troy and the figurative city of the Achaeans.

[67] The sack of Troy forms the last part of the *Ilias parva* and the thematic core of the *Iliou persis*; on the *Ilias parva* and its relation to the Homeric epics and the *Iliou persis*, see Wehr (2015) 325–33.

Following the suggestion of Burgess that there may have existed various epic poems of different length and boundaries that shared certain features and episodes with Lesches' epic,[68] I suggest that the Coroebus episode in one or more of them may have influenced the Rhesus episode. One cannot exclude the possibility that the episodes of Rhesus and Coroebus were at some point in the evolution of the tradition "inclusionary doublets" occurring in the same epic version of post-Iliadic events, from which the Rhesus episode was transferred with multiple adaptations to the *Iliad*. However, it is possible that the "inclusionary doublets" became "exclusionary," since they span different poems, each member of the pair excluding the possibility of coexistence with the other member in the "new text" in which they are now attested, the *Iliad* (Rhesus) and Lesches' *Ilias parva* (Coroebus).[69]

9.3 The Absence of the Rhesus Episode from the Summaries of Proclus

The highly abbreviated summaries of Proclus and the fragmentary nature of our evidence for Cyclic epic can hardly be used as a secure basis for excluding from Cyclic poetry episodes not mentioned by Proclus or not attested among the extant fragments available to us. Because of their abbreviated structure, selectiveness, tendency to avoid repetition, as well as possible cropping[70] and interpolation,[71] Proclus' summaries cannot sustain a claim to exclusiveness, a point that is readily observable from the fragments with secure ascription to the Cyclic epics which are not included in the summaries. Some representative examples include a series of scenes pertaining to the sack of Troy in the *Ilias parva*. The wounding of Meges by Admetus,[72] of Lycomedes by Agenor,[73] of Helicaon who was recognized by Odysseus and dragged out of the battle;[74] the death of Astynoos who fell on his knees by Neoptolemus,[75] of Pelis, of Eioneus by Neoptolemus, and Admetus by Philoctetes,[76] of Coroebus by Diomedes,[77] of Axion by Eurypylus son of Euaemon,[78] of Agenor by Neoptolemus;[79] Menelaus dropping his sword upon seeing Helen's bare breasts;[80] Aethra being recognized by her children and being given to Demophon:[81] all these scenes that featured in Lesches' *Ilias parva* are absent from Proclus' summary. This phenomenon is especially relevant to the

---

[68] "The more one studies the Cycle, the more he or she touches upon a big and perhaps depressing truth: there must have been countless separate epic poems on the material found in the *Ilias parva* of various boundaries" (Jonathan Burgess by email).
[69] On inclusionary and exclusionary doublets, see Currie (2016) 239–45.
[70] Davies (1989) 62; Burgess (2001) 24; M. L. West (2003a) 12–13, (2013a) 15–16; Barker (2008) 5; Currie (2016) 229.
[71] See Currie (2016) 229 n. 3.   [72] Fr. 15 *GEF*.   [73] Fr. 16 *GEF*.   [74] Fr. 22 *GEF*.
[75] Fr. 21 *GEF*.   [76] Fr. 23 *GEF*.   [77] Fr. 24 *GEF*.   [78] Fr. 26 *GEF*.
[79] Fr. 27 *GEF*.   [80] Fr. 28 *GEF*.   [81] Fr. 17 *GEF*.

standard scope of this epic and should always be taken into consideration when discussing Cyclic poetry. Of no less importance is the highly fragmentary nature of our evidence. The limitations stemming from it are further worsened by the problem of ascription. There is material deprived of an ascription but marked by cyclic elements that could well fit the content of Cyclic epic. A fair amount of *dubia* belong to this category. In the end, it is all a matter of balance, though the scales are turned this side or that depending on how strict one is concerning the trustworthiness of the available material.

Another aspect relating to the limitations inherent in Proclus' summaries is that the *Ilias parva* may have existed in more than one form during the archaic period. In the case of the latter epic, there is a very good possibility that there were even more versions available, among which the one by Lesches became the established version at a later point in time, when it was selected for inclusion in the "canonical" Epic Cycle. It is possible that some of these alternative *Iliades parvae* existed from a time anterior to the final shaping of the Iliadic tradition. They obviously go back to mythical material about the latter phase of the Trojan War, covering the events after the death of Achilles. It is likely that they were quite popular, since they presented material pertaining to the end of the war, including the sack of Troy, which constituted the thematic apex of the entire expedition and the topic that every audience would like to hear, just as in *Odyssey* 8 the Phaeacians listen to Demodocus' third song about the Wooden Horse and the capture of Troy. One or more of the pre-Homeric, oral *Iliades parvae* may well have provided the seed out of which the Rhesus story grew.

9.4 The Adaptation of the Rhesus Story and its Use by the Iliadic Tradition

The replacement of Hector by a first-rank enemy of the Achaeans who could be killed as the target of a night raid in the Trojan camp may have resulted from two causes: the realization of the negative impact an attempt to kill Hector had on his heroic persona, and the *non sequitur* of the Achaeans' failure to kill their chief enemy in the older version of *Iliad* 10 and their renewed courage at the beginning of *Iliad* 11. The substitution of Hector by Rhesus would have derived from similarities between the two heroes regarding their personal contribution to the immense damage they had caused to their enemies,[82] the fact that both of them had brought about such destruction in a single day,[83] and their close association

---

[82] *Il.* 8.355–6 and Rhesus' *aristeia* in the Pindaric version (Σ [bT] *Il.* 10.435: μέγιστα αὐτοῖς [sc. τοῖς Ἕλλησι] ἐνεδείξατο κακά).

[83] *Il.* 10.47–9: οὐ γάρ πω ἰδόμην, οὐδ' ἔκλυον αὐδήσαντος, | ἄνδρ' ἕνα τοσσάδε μέρμερ' ἐπ' ἤματι μητίσασθαι, | ὅσσ' Ἕκτωρ ἔρρεξε διίφιλος υἷας Ἀχαιῶν; Σ (bT) *Il.* 10.435: ἱστορεῖ δὲ Πίνδαρος (fr. 262 S–M) ὅτι καὶ μίαν ἡμέραν πολεμήσας πρὸς Ἕλληνας μέγιστα αὐτοῖς ἐνεδείξατο κακά.

with the fall of Troy.[84] This replacement was further enhanced by the participation of the same two heroes, Diomedes and Odysseus, in the night raids against Hector (in the earlier version of *Iliad* 10) and Rhesus (in an oral epic or epics encompassing the events after the death of Achilles and up to the sack of Troy). The fact that some of these similarities pertained to the Pindaric version which had an *aristeia* and others to the oracle version with its magical component suggests that the bards who sang the *Iliad* may have been aware of both.

In the Iliadic epic tradition, the replacement of Hector by Rhesus was not a mechanical process. It probably required a fair number of changes pertaining both to Hector's role in *Iliad* 10 and to the story of Rhesus that had to be shortened and adapted to the Iliadic plotline.[85] Hector's role would have changed from a (failed) target of an Achaean night raid to an agent of the plot of the *Doloneia* who formulates a plan to send a Trojan spy to gather information about the future intentions of the Achaeans. Concomitantly, Dolon the putative looter would be transformed into a spy, and his role would have shifted from revealing to the Achaean spies Hector's whereabouts to telling them about the arrival of Rhesus and informing them about the exact location of his camp. As for Rhesus, the Pindaric version with its *aristeia* would be eliminated, since it would have violated the Iliadic plot. As for the oracle version, the *Iliad* had to dispense with the oracle about Rhesus' potential invincibility, as well as of the importance of Scamander, to the point where it preserves only the faintest echoes of his impressive armor and horses.[86]

Reshaped by the profound adaptation of the Rhesus story in an extremely abridged form, the Iliadic tradition would have been able to "restore" Hector's heroic status and create an effective transition to the beginning of book 11, where the Achaeans find the courage to exit their camp and wage a massive assault on the Trojans.[87] The impact of this change may have been strong. It would have resulted

---

[84] *Il.* 24.728–30; Servius' commentary on Virg. *Aen.* 2.13: *ut Rhesi equi tollerentur a Graecis*; see Reinhardt (1961) 361; Fenik (1964) 12.

[85] The *Iliad* could not present an *aristeia* by Rhesus because it would have weakened Hector's heroic status. Moreover, the poem has no room for major late-arriving pro-Trojan allies.

[86] The embedding of the Rhesus episode in its Iliadic context displays traces of a specific technique of allusion, *narrative inconsistency*. Narrative inconsistency exists between the "surface" insistence of the *Iliad* on the magnificent armor and horses of Rhesus and the "deep"-level suggestion that there is something divine about Rhesus and his horses. At *Il.* 10.440-1, Dolon describes Rhesus' armor as "suitable for the gods to bear," and at *Il.* 10.545–51 Nestor says that these white horses are "similar to the sun's rays...that only some god could have given to Diomedes and Odysseus." The "otherworldly" aspect of Rhesus and his horses is a fundamental feature of the oracle version, according to which, if Rhesus drank from Scamander's water and his horses grazed at its banks, they would all be invincible. The tension between the "surface" and "deep" layers of the narrative amounts to an inconsistency that orients the audience to two different directions: the oracle version and its adaptation by the *Iliad*. This case is analogous to two well-known examples of narrative inconsistency pertaining to Homeric epic, the death of Memnon in the *Aethiopis* and the death of Sarpedon in *Iliad* 16, as well as the Attic version of the rape of Persephone in P. Berol. 13044 and the same episode as narrated in *Homeric Hymn to Demeter*; see Currie (2016) 89–93.

[87] The fact that this attack had been proposed by Diomedes to Agamemnon at the end of book 9 (707–9) may have operated as a further reason for the need to prepare the attack by a feat that would boost the Achaeans' shattered morale.

in nothing less than including Rhesus in the *Iliad*. The Pindaric treatment of the Rhesus myth in the fifth century BC discloses an early but certainly not the earliest (the *Iliad* excluded) interest in this tale. The existence of a tragedy on Rhesus during the fourth century BC, with two surviving prologues, suggests a rekindled interest during a period that is immediately antecedent to the creation of the canonical Epic Cycle that is surely pre-Aristotelian. Both Pindaric poetry and the play *Rhesus* are marked by C/cyclic resonances of which the *Aethiopis* and the *Ilias parva* are the most pronounced. It may be the case that the Rhesus story is one more trace of this C/cyclic predilection observable in Pindar and the *Rhesus*, despite the fact that it is not included in the extant summaries of Proclus or the few surviving fragments of the Epic Cycle.[88]

I have argued that the Rhesus story as reported by the scholia is cyclic in its nature and function; that it formed part of one or more pre-Homeric oral epics on the events that took place after the death of Achilles including the sack of Troy; that it featured as protagonists Diomedes and Odysseus; and that it had been influenced by the Coroebus story. I have also suggested that since the summaries by Proclus cannot and should not be treated as the ultimate measure of exclusivity with respect to the material of the "canonical" Epic Cycle, the absence of the Rhesus episode from them should be treated with caution.

The Rhesus story is unlikely to have existed as an independent poem. It may have formed part of a pre-Homeric oral epic or epics, in which a fixed narrative of Indo-European or Graeco-Aryan origin acquired its specific characteristics through its thematic symbiosis with episodes of Achaean (Philoctetes, Neoptolemus) or pro-Trojan (Eurypylus, Coroebus) heroes, who arrived late at Troy as allies of the Greeks and the Trojans, respectively. Since the fixed narrative pattern of this story pertained to a context marked by (a) the previous defeat of the army undertaking the night raid, (b) the lack or absence of a major hero on the defeated side, and (c) the elimination of a major enemy by treachery, the fully fledged version of the Rhesus story may have featured in a pre-Homeric oral epic like the *Ilias parva*, where all these conditions are met. The transfer of this episode from such an oral epic tradition to the *Iliad* would have been partly facilitated by the existence of an earlier, shorter form of the *Doloneia* in the *Iliad* featuring an unsuccessful night raid on Hector. When the Rhesus story was transferred to *Iliad* 10, the aim of the night mission changed (from attempting to kill Hector to acquiring information about his plan), and the Rhesus episode was presented in a highly elliptical form.

---

[88] See Fantuzzi and Tsagalis (2015a) 34–6; Currie (2016) 229–33.

Conclusions

The aim of this book has been to offer a systematic and comprehensive study of the *Doloneia*, which represents one of the most notorious cruces of the *Iliad* with respect to the book's authenticity. To this day, scholarly opinion is divided between those who argue that the *Doloneia* has been composed by a poet well versed in the epic tradition, but different from the poet of the *Iliad*, and those who adopt the approach of the oral theory and treat book 10 as an integral part of the Iliadic epic tradition and a manifestation of the theme of "ambush," which is poorly represented in the extant remains of early Greek epic.

The main argument of this book is that a more rewarding way to study the *Doloneia* may be to consider the possibility that it was neither composed wholesale by a different poet than the rest of the epic nor that it always formed part, in the shape that we now have it, of the Iliadic epic tradition. Instead, it is suggested that it evolved from an earlier version in which the Achaeans undertook an unsuccessful nocturnal mission against Hector and was profoundly reshaped after the introduction of the Rhesus episode. This process was, arguably, not the work of a single individual. It is more likely that it marked one of the final stages in the shaping of the Iliadic epic tradition before it was fixed by means of dictation.[1]

The complexity of this interpretive endeavor asks for serious theoretical clarifications, especially given the heavy interpretive burden created by the conflicting approaches undertaken by various scholars. In this vein, chapter 1 has been devoted to the examination of the theoretical aspects pertaining to oral intertextual neoanalysis, the principal interpretive tool used in this book. This is a method that provides us with the means to explore the development of and influence between oral epic traditions. The legitimacy of the application of this method of analysis on Homeric epic is based on internal (metapoetic diction, generic reference, stress on the creation and diffusion of epic poetry) and external (interaction with pre-Homeric oral poetry) criteria, on the notion of entextualization (the act or process of rendering an utterance as text), on the transference of motifs, themes, and phraseology, as well as on epic quotation as distinct from mythological reference (the ability of Homeric epic to cite other epic poetry, as well as alternative versions of the same subject matter, or even its own earlier versions). The cumulative force of the criteria and factors discussed in chapter 1 suggests

---

[1] See Lord (1953) 38–48, (2018³) 138–9, 163; Jensen (1980); Powell (1991) 221–37; Janko (1998) 1–13; Foley (2005) 209; *HomEnc* s.v. "Oral Dictated Texts" (J. M. Foley); Ready (2019).

(a) that Homeric epic is a highly developed type of oral poetry, which has been shaped in the form that we are familiar with through creative interaction with other oral epic traditions, and (b) that it has embedded this intertextual epic dialogue in its plot and diction. Seen from this vantage point, oral intertextual neoanalysis is ideally suited to the examination of the evolution and shaping of the *Doloneia*.

In chapter 2, I have argued that book 10 mainly interacts with the rest of the *Iliad* not through references to events but by means of allusion to themes. It creates implicit intratextual associations, facilitates backward and forward allusions to themes featuring in other Iliadic books, and operates as a bridge that contributes to the development of the theme of overconfidence that spans a large part of the epic and concerns one of its main figures, Hector. *Iliad* 10 also shares phraseology with the rest of the poem in a pointed manner that results in an interpretive surplus of the relevant passages when examined together. Furthermore, it makes a significant contribution to the character-drawing of major Iliadic heroes (Agamemnon, Diomedes, the pair Diomedes and Odysseus, and Hector).

Chapter 3 argued that by equating Hector's death with the fall of Troy, the *Iliad* honors its chief hero, Achilles, as well as elevates its own limited plot to put it on a par with the core of the Trojan War story, the sack of Troy. Analogously, the night raid on the enemy camp and the theft of the splendid horses of Rhesus by Diomedes and Odysseus represent a sophisticated take on the tradition. Instead of the ambush of Achilles feared by the Trojans (*Il.* 24.778–81) or the Wooden Horse by which means Odysseus, designated as δόλων ἆτος ("insatiate in cunning") at *Il.* 11.430, will bring about the sack of the city, the *Iliad* narrates the ambush of Odysseus and Diomedes. In a superb move, the epic allows Odysseus, the hero who will bring the war to an end, to use Dolon and the horses of Achilles (10.401–4) as a "window" allowing us a glimpse into both plot and subplot. The Trojan spy has asked for something too great for his stature. Hector has promised him something not in his gift. Likewise, Patroclus will only be Achilles' surrogate, not a second Achilles, because he is unable to brandish his friend's Pelian ashspear. Achilles' armor and immortal horses, a gift of the gods, will not suffice to sack Troy. The former will go to Hector, while the latter will be returned to the real master, Achilles, on whose chariot Hector's dead body will later be tied and driven to the ships. But even Achilles' divine horses are not enough to sack Troy. For that, a different kind of horse is needed, one made of wood, built with the help of Athena, a gift to resourceful Odysseus. It is this horse, with Odysseus and Diomedes in its belly, that will finally sack the holy citadel of Troy.

Chapter 4 was devoted to the examination of three alleged un-Iliadic features of book 10 (speeches, clothing and arming, and Zielinksi's Law). The result is a rather blurred picture with respect to the question of authenticity. The speeches combine an un-Iliadic internal structure with an Iliadic external organization. Clothing and arming not only are in tune with the requirements of an episode involving a night mission and ambush but also have an important narrative function, as they are associated with specific characters who (with the exception of Dolon) play a major role in the *Iliad*. As regards Zielinski's Law, I have argued that book 10 does not differ from other Iliadic books.

In chapter 5, I have suggested that putative clues provided by the *Iliad* and the scholia allow for the possibility that an older form of the *Doloneia* lurks in what is now *Iliad* 10. In that earlier version, the target of the spying mission was Hector, the chief threat to the Achaean army. The *Iliad* has retained several features of this previous version, which should be treated neither as traces of an incomplete transition from the earlier version to the current one nor as indications of the poor poetic quality of book 10 but, rather, as an allusive strategy that alerts the audience to the fact that the current version of book 10 grew out of its predecessor. Several features in our current version of the *Doloneia* make notional what was factual in the earlier version.

Chapter 6 dealt with a putative reconstruction of the Hector-version of the *Doloneia*. It was argued that this earlier version did not end with the triumph we come across in the current version of *Iliad* 10. No major opponent was killed, no impressive horses were stolen. Dolon was a poor catch for heroes of the rank and skill of Diomedes and Odysseus. More importantly, the Achaeans found themselves in the same position they were in before the embassy (*Iliad* 9) and the night mission (*Iliad* 10). They had tried in vain both to persuade Achilles to return to the war and to kill Hector. How, then, would they find the courage to risk a dangerous operation the next day? What would they hope to achieve by leaving the safety of their wall and waging a wholesale attack against the Trojans? This disturbing paradox was at some point in the evolution of the Iliadic tradition felt, and a new narrative path was followed. It was a path that would profoundly change the *Doloneia*, since it required the introduction of a new hero who would play no other role in the epic: Rhesus.

In chapter 7, I embarked on a systematic examination of the ancient scholia referring to the story of Rhesus, suggesting that the Pindaric and oracle versions exhibit a cyclic quality. The Iliadic epic tradition appears to have incorporated elements of the Rhesus tale that could seamlessly align with its narrative and were consistent with its implicit tendency to downplay or entirely omit miraculous elements, such as the motif of invincibility attributed to both Rhesus and his horses in the oracle version. The introduction of a first-rank hero such as Rhesus may have operated as a backdrop against which the epic elaborated the character-drawing of major Iliadic heroes such as Hector, Diomedes, and Odysseus.

In chapter 8, I compared the *Doloneia* with two non-Greek episodes, one from the *Mahābhārata* and the other from the *Aeneid*, that refer to the theme of nocturnal raid. I suggested that the *Sauptikaparvan* and *Iliad* 10 share a stable set of features that go back to a fixed narrative pattern of Indo-European or Graeco-Aryan origin. The night raid is not a self-contained, independent narrative. Instead, it depends on being incorporated into the larger context of a martial epic. In this vein, it can hardly, especially in the mixed form that it has in the *Doloneia*, have been composed as an integral narrative that was added to a martial epic like the *Iliad*. The Pindaric and oracle versions, which are independent descendants of this pattern, may be earlier than *Iliad* 10 and probably belong to developed narratives that formed part of a larger poem or poems. The context in which this fixed narrative pattern nests describes a difficult situation experienced by an army that has been defeated, that is temporarily or permanently deprived of its major hero, and that resorts to a night raid, which ends with the death of a major enemy who is killed by treachery. With respect to Virgil, it has been argued that the Roman epic poet offers an instructive example and working analogy for the claim that the fixed narrative pattern used by *Doloneia* has been gradually shaped under the influence of a series of epic episodes such as the Palladium, Coroebus, and the sack of Troy, which belong to the last phase of the Trojan War.

In chapter 9, I explored a tentative pre-Homeric context for the Rhesus story, i.e. an oral epic including several events taking place after the death of Achilles. I suggested that in that epic the Rhesus episode could have been placed after the suicide of Ajax, when the Achaeans found themselves in a situation bearing a striking analogy to the situation they are facing after *Iliad* 9. The withdrawal of Achilles from the war in the *Iliad* is parallel to his death at the end of the *Aethiopis*, since in both cases he is not fighting. The ensuing suicide of the other great Aeacid, Telamonian Ajax, in the *Ilias parva* deprives the Achaeans of their second-best hero too. The prevalent role of Diomedes and Odysseus in this epic, in which they undertake various missions either separately (Diomedes brings Philoctetes from Lemnos and Odysseus brings Neoptolemus from Scyros to Troy) or jointly (the theft of the Palladium), seems to be the necessary poetic environment for hosting the Rhesus episode. Furthermore, I have offered several suggestions about the process concerning how the Iliadic epic tradition substituted Hector with Rhesus in the storyline of book 10. The examination delved into the alterations necessitated by this replacement and explored the consequential influence on both the *Doloneia* and the broader narrative of the *Iliad*.

Bibliography

Adrados, F. R. (1979), *Historia de la fábula greco-latina: Introducción y de los orígines a la edad helenística*, vol. I (Madrid).
Ahlberg-Cornell, G. (1992), *Myth and Epos in Early Greek Art. Representation and Interpretation* (Jonsered).
Alden, M. (2000), *Homer Beside Himself: Para-Narratives in the* Iliad (Oxford).
Alden, M. (2017), *Para-Narratives in the* Odyssey: *Stories in the Frame* (Oxford).
Alexiou, M. (2002²) [= 1974]. *The Ritual Lament in Greek Tradition* (Lanham, MD, and Oxford, revised by D. Yatromanolakis and P. Roilos).
Allan, W. (2005), "Arms and the Man: Euphorbus, Hector, and the Death of Patroclus," *CQ* 55: 1–16.
Allan, W., and D. L. Cairns (2011), "Conflict and Community in the *Iliad*," in N. Fisher and H. van Wees (eds.), *Competition in the Ancient World* (Swansea): 113–46.
Allen, N. J. (2020), *Arjuna-Odysseus: Shared Heritage in Indian and Greek Epic* (Abingdon).
Alvensleben, L. von (2022), *Erzähler und Figur in Interaktion: Metalepsen in Homers Ilias.* (Berlin).
Amory-Parry, A. (1973), *Blameless Aegisthus: A Study of ἀμύμων and Other Homeric Epithets* (Leiden).
Andersen, Ø. (1978), *Die Diomedesgestalt in der Ilias* (Oslo).
Andersen, Ø. (1982), "Thersites und Thoas vor Troia," *SO* 57: 7–34.
Andersen, Ø. (2012), "Older Heroes and Earlier Poems: The Case of Heracles in the *Odyssey*," in Andersen and Haug: 138–51.
Andersen, Ø., and D. T. T. Haug (eds.) (2012), *Relative Chronology in Early Greek Epic Poetry* (Cambridge).
Anderson, M. J. (1997), *The Fall of Troy in Early Greek Poetry and Art* (Oxford).
Apthorp, M. J. (1980), "The Obstacles to Telemachus' Return," *CQ* 30.1: 1–22.
Arend, W. (1933), *Die Typischen Scenen bei Homer* (Berlin).
Armstrong, J. I. (1958), "The Arming Motif in the *Iliad*," *AJP* 79: 337–54.
Arnould, D. (1989), "Le chauve et le glouton chez Homère: Remarques sur le personnage d'Ulysse," *REG* 102: 510–14.
Assereto, A. M. (1970), "Dall'*Etiopide* all'*Eneide*," in *Mythos: Scripta in honorem Marii Untersteiner* (Genoa): 51–8.
Bachvarova, M. (2015), *From Hittite to Homer: The Anatolian Background of Ancient Greek Epic* (Cambridge).
Bakker, E. J. (2013), *The Meaning of Meat and the Structure of the* Odyssey (Cambridge).
Bakker, E. J. (2017), "Hector (and) the Race Horse: The Telescopic Vision of the *Iliad*," in C. Tsagalis and A. Markantonatos (eds.) (2017), *The Winnowing Oar—New Perspectives in Homeric Studies* (Berlin): 57–74.
Bär, S. (2024), "Heracles and Hesione in the *Iliad*," in Tsagalis: 146–63.
Barber, K. (2005), "Text and Performance in Africa," *OT* 20: 264–77.
Barchiesi, A. (1994), "Rappresentazioni del dolore e interpretazione nell'Eneide," *A&A* 40: 109–24; = "Representations of Suffering and Interpretation in the *Aeneid*," in P. Hardie (ed.), *Virgil: Critical Assessments of Classical Authors* (London and New York, 1999): iii.324–44.
Barchiesi, A. (2001), "Future Reflexive: Two Modes of Allusion and Ovid's *Heroides*," in A. Barchiesi (ed.), *Speaking Volumes. Narrative and Intertext in Ovid and Other Latin Poets* (London): 105–27.
Barck, C. (1971), "Menelaos bei Homer," *WS* 84: 5–28.

Barker, E. T. E. (2008), "Momos Advises Zeus: Changing Representations of 'Cypria' Fragment 1," in E. Cingano and L. Milano (eds.), *Papers on Ancient Literatures: Greece, Rome, and the Near East. Proceedings of the Advanced Seminar in the Humanities, Venice International University 2004–2005* (Padua): 33–73.
Barker, E. T. E. (2009), *Entering the Agon: Dissent and Authority in Homer, Historiography, and Tragedy* (Oxford).
Barker, E. T. E. (2011), "The *Iliad*'s Big Swoon: A Case of Innovation within the Epic Tradition," *TC* 3.1: 1–17.
Barker, E. T. E., and J. P. Christensen (2008), "Oedipus of Many Pains: Strategies of Contest in Homeric Poetry," *Leeds International Classical Studies* 7.2: 1–30.
Barker, E. T. E., and J. P. Christensen (2011), "On Not Remembering Tydeus: Diomedes and the Contest for Thebes," *Materiali e discussioni per l'analisi dei testi classici* 66.1: 9–44.
Barker, E. T. E., and J. P. Christensen (2014), "Even Herakles Had to Die: Homeric 'Heroism', Mortality, and the Epic Tradition," *TC* 6.2: 249–77.
Barker, E. T. E., and J. P. Christensen (2016), "Odysseus's nostos and the *Odyssey*'s nostoi: Rivalry within the Epic Cycle," *Philologia Antiqua* 7: 85–110.
Barker, E. T. E., and J. P. Christensen (2020), *Homer's Thebes: Epic Rivalries and the Appropriation of Mythical Pasts* (Washington, DC).
Bassett, S. E. (1938), *The Poetry of Homer* (Berkeley).
Bassino, P., L. G. Canevaro, and B. Graziosi (eds.) (2017), *Conflict and Consensus in Early Hexameter Poetry* (Cambridge).
Bauman, R. (2004), *A World of Others' Words: Cross-Cultural Perspectives on Intertextuality* (Malden).
Bauman, R., and C. L. Briggs (1990), "Poetics and Performance as Critical Perspectives on Language and Social Life," *Annual Review of Anthropology* 19: 59–88.
Baumbach, M. (2012), "Borderline Experiences with Genre: the Homeric Hymn to Aphrodite between Epic, Hymn and Epyllic Poetry," in M. Baumbach and S. Bär (eds.), *Brill's Companion to Greek and Latin Epyllion and Its Reception* (Leiden and Boston): 135–48.
Beck, D. (2005), *Homeric Conversation* (Washington, DC).
Beck, G. (1964), *Die Stellung des 24. Buches der Ilias in der alten Epentradition* (Diss., University of Tübingen).
Becker, A. S. (1995), *The Shield of Achilles and the Poetics of Ekphrasis* (Lanham, MD).
Belfiore, E. (2002), "Dramatic and Epic Time: 'Magnitude' and 'Length' in Aristotle's *Poetics*," in Ø. Andersen and J. Harberg (eds.), *Making Sense of Aristotle: Essays in Poetics* (London): 25–49.
Belzner, E. (1912), *Homerische Probleme, II: Die Komposition der Odyssee* (Leipzig and Berlin).
Bernabé, A. (1984), "¿Más de una *Ilias parva*?," in L. Gil and Rosa M. Aguilar (eds.), *Apophoreta Philologica Emmanueli Fernández-Galiano a sodalibus oblata*, pars prior (Madrid): 141–50.
Bethe, E. (1887), *Quaestiones Diodoreae mythographae* (Göttingen).
Bethe, E. (1914), *Homer. Dichtung und Sage*, vol. 1 (Leipzig).
Bethe, E. (1925), "Ilias und Meleager," *RhM* 74: 1–12.
Bierl, A. (2012), "Orality, Fluid Textualization and Interweaving Themes. Some Remarks on the *Doloneia*: Magical Horses from Night to Light and Death to Life," in Montanari, Rengakos, and Tsagalis: 133–74.
Blößner, N. (2020), "The State of the Homeric Question," in M. Fritz, T. Kitazumi, and M. Veksina (eds.), *Maiores philologiae pontes. Festschrift für Michael Meier-Brügger zum 70. Geburtstag* (Ann Arbor and New York): 13–49.
Boisacq, É. (1926), "L'étymologie du grec 'Ῥῆσος," *REG* 39: 332–4.
Boissonade J. F. (1851), *Tzetzae Allegoriae Iliadis (accedunt Pselli Allegoriae)* (Paris).
Bölte, F. (1934), "Ein pylisches Epos," *RhM* n.s. 83.4: 319–47.
Bouvier, D. (2002), *Le sceptre et la lyre. L'Iliade ou les héros de la mémoire* (Grenoble).
Bowra, C. M. (1952), *Heroic Poetry* (London).
Bremmer, J. N. (1988), "La plasticité du mythe: Méléagre dans la poésie homérique," in C. Calame (ed.), *Métamorphose du mythe en Grèce antique* (Geneva): 37–56.

Brillet-Dubois, P. (2011), "An Erotic *aristeia*: The *Homeric Hymn to Aphrodite* and its Relation to the Iliadic Tradition," in A. Faulkner (ed.), *The Homeric Hymns: Interpretative Essays* (Oxford): 105–32.
Brown, M. K. (2002), *The Narratives of Konon. Text, Translation, and Commentary of the Diegeseis* (Munich and Leipzig).
Burgess, J. S. (1997), "Beyond Neoanalysis: Problems with the Vengeance Theory," *AJP* 118: 1–19.
Burgess, J. S. (2001), *The Tradition of the Trojan War in Homer and the Epic Cycle* (Baltimore and London).
Burgess, J. S. (2005), "The Death of Achilles by Rhapsodes," in R. Rabel (ed.), *Approaches to Homer, Ancient and Modern* (Swansea): 119–34.
Burgess, J. S. (2006), "Neoanalysis, Orality, and Intertextuality: An Examination of Homeric Motif Transference," *OT* 21: 148–89.
Burgess, J. S. (2009), *The Death and Afterlife of Achilles* (Baltimore).
Burgess, J. S. (2010), "The Hypertext of Astyanax," in C. Tsagalis (ed.), *Homeric Hypertextuality*, *TC* 2.2: 211–24.
Burgess, J. S. (2012a), "Intertextuality without Text in Early Greek Epic," in Andersen and Haug: 168–83.
Burgess, J. S. (2012b), "Belatedness in the Travels of Odysseus," in Montanari, Rengakos, and Tsagalis: 269–90.
Burgess, J. S. (2017), "The Tale of Meleager in the *Iliad*," *OT* 31.1: 51–76.
Burgess, J. S. (2019), "Introduction," *YAGE* 3: 1–47.
Burkert, W. (1976), "Das hunderttorige Theben und die Datierung der Ilias," *WS* 89: 5–21 (= 2001: 59–71).
Burkert, W. (1981), "Seven Against Thebes: An Oral Tradition Between Babylonian Magic and Greek Literature," in C. Brillante, M. Cantilena, and C. O. Pavese (eds.), *I poemi rapsodici non omerici e la tradizione orale* (Padua): 29–48 (= 2001: 150–6).
Burkert, W. (1987), "The Making of Homer in the Sixth Century B.C.: Rhapsodes versus Stesichoros," in *Papers on the Amasis Painter and his World* (Malibu): 43–62 (= 2001: 198–217).
Burkert, W. (1995), "'Irrevocabile verbum'. Spuren mündlichen Erzählens in der Odyssee," in U. Brunold-Bigler and H. Bausinger (eds.), *Hören–Sagen–Lesen–Lernen: Bausteine zu einer Geschichte der kommunikativen Kultur*, Festschrift für Rudolf Schenda zum 65. Geburtstag (Bern): 147–58 (= 2001: 117–26).
Burkert, W. (2001), *Kleine Schriften I, Homerica* (Göttingen).
Cairns, D. L. (2001a), "Introduction," in Cairns (2001b): 1–56.
Cairns, D. L. (ed.) (2001b), *Oxford Readings in Homer's* Iliad (Oxford).
Cairns, D. L. (2016), "Clothed in Shamelessness, Shrouded in Grief: The Role of 'Garment' Metaphors in Ancient Greek Concepts of Emotion," in G. Fanfani, M. Harlow, and M.-L. Nosch (eds.), *Spinning Fates and the Song of the Loom: The Use of Textiles, Clothing and Cloth Production as Metaphor, Symbol, and Narrative* (Oxford): 25–41.
Cameron, A. (2004), *Greek Mythography in the Roman World* (Oxford).
Cantieni, R. (1942), *Die Nestorerzählung im XI. Gesang der Ilias (V. 670–762)* (Diss., University of Zurich).
Casali, S. (2004), "Nisus and Euryalus: Exploiting the Contradictions in Virgil's Doloneia," *HSCP* 102: 319–54.
Casali, S. (2018), "Imboscate notturne nell'epica romana," in A. Chaniotis, *La Nuit: imaginaire et réalités nocturnes dans le monde gréco-romain. Entretiens sur l'antiquité classique* (Geneva): 209–56.
Castelli, E. (2020), *La nascita del titolo nella letteratura greca: dall' epica arcaica alla prosa di età classica* (Berlin).
Cauer, P. (1921–3), *Grundfragen der Homerkritik* (Leipzig).
Chambry, É. (1927), *Ésope: Fables* (Paris).

Chantraine, P. (1937), "Remarques critiques et grammaticales sur le chant K de l'Iliade," in *Mélanges offerts à A. M. Desrousseaux* (Paris): 59–68.
Chantraine, P. (1963), "À propos de Thersite," *AC* 32: 18–27.
Christ, W. von (1884), *Homeri Iliadis carmina seiuncta discreta emendata* (Leipzig).
Clarke, M. (2019), *Achilles beside Gilgamesh: Mortality and Wisdom in Early Epic Poetry* (Cambridge).
Clay, J. S. (1983), *The Wrath of Athena. Gods and Men in the* Odyssey (Lanham, MD).
Codino, F. (1951), *Omero: Dolonia* (Bari).
Collins, L. (1988), *Studies in Characterization in the* Iliad (Frankfurt).
Cook, E. (2009), "On the 'Importance' of *Iliad* Book 8," *CP* 104.2: 133–61.
Cramer, J. A. (1836), *Anecdota Graeca*, vol. III (Oxford).
Csapo, E., and W. J. Slater (1994), *The Context of Ancient Drama* (Ann Arbor).
Csapo, E., and P. Wilson (2015), "Drama Outside Athens in the Fifth and Fourth Centuries BC," in A. A. Lamari (ed.), *Reperformances of Drama in the Fifth and Fourth Centuries BC: Authors and Contexts*, *TC* 7.2: 316–95.
Currie, B. (2006), "Homer and the Early Epic Tradition," in M. J. Clarke, B. G. F. Currie, and R. O. A. M. Lyne (eds.), *Epic Interactions: Perspectives on Homer, Virgil, and the Epic Tradition Presented to Jasper Griffin by Former Pupils* (Oxford): 1–45.
Currie, B. (2012), "The *Iliad*, *Gilgamesh*, and Neoanalysis," in Montanari, Rengakos, and Tsagalis: 543–80.
Currie, B. (2016), *Homer's Allusive Art* (Oxford).
Currie, B. (2021), *Herodotus as Homeric Critic* (Oxford, Edmonton, and Tallahassee).
Currie, B. (forthcoming), "Theogonic Allusions in the *Iliad*."
D'Alessio, G. B. (2005), "Pindar, Bacchylides, and Hesiodic Genealogical Poetry," in R. Hunter (ed.), *The Hesiodic* Catalogue of Women: *Constructions and Reconstructions* (Cambridge): 217–38.
Damon, C., and C. Pieper (eds.) (2019), *Eris vs. Aemulatio: Valuing Competition in Classical Antiquity* (Leiden).
Danek, G. (1988), *Studien zur Dolonie* (Vienna).
Danek, G. (1998a), *Epos und Zitat: Studien zu den Quellen der Odyssee* (Vienna).
Danek G. (1998b), "Darstellung verdeckter Handlung bei Homer und in der südslawischen Heldenlied-Tradition," *WS* 111: 67–88.
Danek, G. (1999), "Synchronisation von Handlungssträngen in Ilias 14, 1-40," in J. N. Kazazis and A. Rengakos (eds.), *Euphrosyne. Studies in Ancient Epic and its Legacy in Honor of Dimitris N. Maronitis* (Stuttgart): 76–88.
Danek, G. (2002), "Traditional Referentiality and Homeric Intertextuality," in F. Montanari and P. Ascheri (eds.), *Omero tremila anni dopo* (Rome): 3–19.
Danek, G. (2007), "Developments of Traditional Narrative Techniques: Flashback Accounts in Homer and Avdo Međedović," in Z. Čolacović (ed.), *The Epics of Avdo Međedovic: A Critical Edition*, with Introduction by R. L. Fowler, 2 vols. (Podgorica): 599–618.
Danek, G. (2012), "The *Doloneia* Revisited," in Andersen and Haug: 106–21.
D'Arms, E. F., and K. K. Hulley (1946), "The Oresteia-Story in the *Odyssey*," *TAPA* 77: 207–13.
Davidson, O. (1979), "Dolon and the Rhesus in the *Iliad*," *QUCC* 30: 61–6.
Davies, M. (1986), "Prolegomena and Paralegomena to a New Edition (with Commentary) of the Fragments of Early Greek Epic," *Nachr. Akad. Wissensch. Göttingen (phil.-hist. Kl.)* 2: 91–111.
Davies, M. (1989), *The Epic Cycle* (Bristol).
Davies, M. (2014), *The Theban Epics* (Washington, DC).
Davies, M. (2019), *The Cypria* (Washington, DC).
Degani, E. (1991²), *Hipponactis Testimonia et Fragmenta* (Stuttgart and Leipzig).
de Jong, I. J. F. (2001), *A Narratological Commentary on the* Odyssey (Cambridge).
de Jong, I. J. F. (2004² [1st ed. 1987]), *Narrators and Focalizers. The Presentation of the Story in the* Iliad (London).
de Jong, I. J. F. (2007), "Homer," in I. J. F. de Jong and R. Nünlist (eds.), *Studies in Ancient Greek Narrative* (Leiden): 17–37.

de Jong, I. J. F. (2009), "Metalepsis in Ancient Greek Literature," in J. Grethlein and A. Rengakos (eds.), *Narratology and Interpretation: The Content of Narrative Form in Ancient Literature* (Berlin): 87-115.
de Jong, I. J. F. (2011), "The Shield of Achilles: From Metalepsis to Mise en Abyme," *Ramus* 40.1: 1-14.
de Jong, I. J. F. (2012), *Homer:* Iliad *XXII* (Cambridge).
Dekel, E. (2012), *Virgil's Homeric Lens* (New York and London).
Delebecque E. (1951), *Le cheval dans l'Iliade* (Paris).
Di Benedetto, V. (1994), *Nel laboratorio di Omero* (Turin).
Di Benedetto, V. (2001), "Reuses of Iliadic Patterns in the *Odyssey*," *RCCM* 43.7-14; reprinted in V. Di Benedetto, *Il Richiamo del Testo: Contributi di filologia e letteratura* (Pisa, 2007): ii. 691-700.
Dickey, E. (1996), *Greek Forms of Address: From Herodotus to Lucian* (Oxford).
Dickson, K. M. (1995), *Nestor: Poetic Memory in Greek Epic* (New York and London).
Diggle, J. (1981-94), *Euripidis Fabulae*, 3 vols. (Oxford).
Dihle, A. (1970), *Homer-Problem* (Opladen).
Diller, A. (1935), "The Text History of the *Bibliotheca* of Pseudo-Apollodorus," *TAPA* 66: 296-313.
Dinter, M., S. Finkmann, and A. Khoo (2019), "Nyktomachies in Graeco-Roman Epic," in C. Reiz and S. Finkmann (eds.), *Structures of Epic Poetry, vol. II.1: Configuration* (Berlin): 245-81.
Dowden, K. (1996), "Homer's Sense of Text," *JHS* 116: 47-61.
Dowden, K. (2004), "The Epic Tradition in Greece," in Fowler (2004b): 188-205.
Dué, C. (2012), "Maneuvers in the Dark of Night: *Iliad* 10 in the Twenty-First Century," in Montanari, Rengakos, and Tsagalis: 175-83.
Dué, C. (2019), *Achilles Unbound: Multiformity and Tradition in the Homeric Epics* (Washington, DC).
Dué, C., and M. Ebbott (2010), Iliad *10 and the Poetics of Ambush. A Multitext Edition with Essays and Commentary* (Washington, DC).
Duffy, W. (2019), "Dolon's δόλος: Aristophanes of Byzantium's Version of *Iliad* 10.391," *CP* 115.1: 99-104.
Ebbott, M. (2010), "Error 404: Theban Epic Not Found," *TC* 2.2: 239-58.
Ebbott, M. (2014), "Allies in Fame: Recruiting Warriors in the Theban and Trojan Epic Tradition," *TC* 6.2: 319-35.
Ebert, J. (1969), "Die Gestalt des Thersites in der Ilias," *Philologus* 113: 159-75.
Edmunds, L. (1995), "Intertextuality Today," *Lexis* 13: 3-22.
Edmunds, L. (1997), "Myth in Homer," in Morris and Powell: 425-41.
Edmunds, L. (2001), *Intertextuality and the Reading of Roman Poetry* (Baltimore and London).
Edwards, A. T. (1981), *Odysseus against Achilles: The Role of Allusion in the Homeric Epic* (Ph.D. diss., Cornell University).
Edwards, A. T. (1985), "Achilles in the Underworld: *Iliad, Odyssey,* and *Aethiopis*," *GRBS* 26: 215-27.
Edwards, M. W. (1987), *Homer: Poet of the* Iliad (Baltimore and London).
Edwards, M. W. (1990), "Neoanalysis and Beyond," *CA* 9: 311-25.
Edwards, M. W. (1991), The Iliad: *A Commentary, Vol. V: Books 17-20* (Cambridge).
Ehwald, R. (1894), "Vergilische Vergleiche," *Philologus* 53: 729-44.
Eichhorn, F. (1973), *Die Dolonie* (Garmisch-Partenkirchen).
Eisenberger, H. (1973), *Studien zur Odyssee* (Wiesbaden).
Elmer, D. (2013), *The Poetics of Consent: Collective Decision-Making & the* Iliad (Baltimore).
Elmer, D. (forthcoming), *Omero: Iliade, vol. II: Libri V-VIII (testo e commento)*, Fondazione Lorenzo Valla-Mondadori (Milan).
Erbse, H. (1969-83), *Scholia Graeca in Homeri Iliadem (scholia vetera)*, 6 vols. (Berlin).
Erbse, H. (1970), "Zeus und Here auf dem Idagebirge," *A&A* 16: 93-112.
Erbse, H. (1972), *Beiträge zum Verständnis der Odyssee* (Berlin).
Ernst, N. (2006), *Die D-Scholien zur Odyssee. Kritische Ausgabe* (Cologne).

Fairclough, H. R. (1935, revised edition by G. P. Goold [1999]), *Virgil:* Eclogues, Georgics, Aeneid I–VI (Cambridge, MA, and London).
Fantuzzi, M. (1996), "Odisseo mendicante a Troia e a Itaca: su [Eur.] *Rh.* 498–507; 710–719 e Hom. *Od.* 4, 244–58," *MD* 36: 175–85.
Fantuzzi, M. (2020), *The* Rhesus *Attributed to Euripides* (Cambridge).
Fantuzzi, M., and C. Tsagalis (2015a), "Introduction: *Kyklos*, the Epic Cycle, and Cyclic Poetry," in Fantuzzi and Tsagalis (2015b): 1–40.
Fantuzzi, M., and C. Tsagalis (eds.) (2015b), *The Greek Epic Cycle and its Ancient Reception: A Companion* (Cambridge).
Farrell, J. (2008), "Servius and the Homeric Scholia," in S. Casali and F. Stok (eds.), *Servio: stratificazioni esegetiche e modelli culturali/Servius: Exegetical Stratifications and Cultural Models* (Brussels): 112–31.
Farron, S. (2003), "Attitudes to Military Archery in the *Iliad*," in A. Basson and W. Dominik (eds.), *Literature, Art, History: Studies on Classical Antiquity and Tradition in Honor of W. J. Henderson* (Frankfurt am Main): 169–84.
Faulkner, A. (2008), *The Homeric Hymn to Aphrodite. Introduction, Text, and Commentary* (Oxford).
Feldman, T. P. (1979), "The Taunter in Ancient Epic: The *Iliad, Odyssey, Aeneid*, and *Beowulf*," *Papers on Language & Literature* 15: 3–16.
Felson, N. (1997²), *Regarding Penelope: from Character to Poetics* (Norman, OK).
Fenik, B. (1964), *«Iliad X» and the «Rhesus»: The Myth* (Brussels).
Fenik, B. (1968), *Typical Battle Scenes in the* Iliad. *Studies in the Narrative Techniques of Homeric Battle Description* (Wiesbaden).
Fenik, B. (1974), *Studies in the* Odyssey (Wiesbaden).
Fenik, B. (1986), *Homer and the Nibelungenlied* (Cambridge, MA, and London).
Fernández-Galiano, M. (1992), "Books xxi–xxii," in Russo, Fernández-Galiano, and Heubeck: 131–310.
Finglass, P. J. (2015), "*Iliou persis*," in Fantuzzi and Tsagalis (2015b): 344–54.
Finkelberg, M. (1990), "A Creative Oral Poet and the Muse," *AJP* 11: 293–303 (= 2020: 118–26).
Finkelberg, M. (2000), "The *Cypria*, the *Iliad*, and the Problem of Multiformity in Oral and Written Tradition," *CP* 95: 1–11 (= 2020: 305–17).
Finkelberg, M. (2002), "The Sources of *Iliad* 7," in H. M. Roisman and J. Roisman (eds.), *Essays on Homeric Epic* (*Colby Quarterly* 38.2): 151–61 (= 2020, 140–9).
Finkelberg, M. (2015), "Meta-Cyclic Epic and Homeric Poetry," in Fantuzzi and Tsagalis (2015b): 126–38 (= 2020: 169–81).
Finkelberg, M. (2020), *Homer and Early Greek Epic: Collected Essays* (Berlin).
Finnegan, R. (1988), *Literacy and Orality: Studies in the Technology of Communication* (Oxford).
Finnegan, R. (1992), *Oral Poetry: Its Nature, Significance and Social Context* (Bloomington, IN).
Flach, I. (1880), *Eudociae Augustae Violarium* (Leipzig).
Foley, J. M. (1991), *Immanent Art: From Structure to Meaning in Traditional Oral Art* (Bloomington, IN).
Foley, J. M. (1998), "Individual Poet and Epic Tradition: Homer as Legendary Singer," *Arethusa* 31: 149–78.
Foley, J. M. (2004), "Epic as Genre," in Fowler (2004b): 171–87.
Foley, J. M. (2005), "Analogues: Modern Oral Epics," in J. M. Foley (ed.), *A Companion to Ancient Epic* (Malden, MA): 196–212.
Foley, J. M., and J. Arft (2015), "The Epic Cycle and Oral Tradition," in Fantuzzi and Tsagalis (2015b): 78–95.
Ford, A. L. (1992), *Homer: The Poetry of the Past* (Ithaca, NY).
Ford, A. L. (1997), "Epic as Genre," in Morris and Powell: 380–414.
Ford, A. L. (2002), *The Origins of Criticism: Literary Culture and Poetic Theory in Classical Greece* (Princeton, NJ).
Forsyth, N. (1979), "The Allurement Scene: A Typical Pattern in Greek Oral Epic," *ClAnt* 12: 101–20.

Fowler, D. P. (1997), "On the Shoulders of Giants: Intertextuality and Classical Studies," *MD* 39: 13–24 (= 2000. *Roman Constructions: Readings in Postmodern Latin* [Oxford]: 115–37).
Fowler, R. L. (1987), *The Nature of Early Greek Lyric: Three Preliminary Studies* (Toronto).
Fowler, R. L. (2004a), "The Homeric Question," in Fowler (2004b): 220–32.
Fowler, R. L. (ed.) (2004b), *The Cambridge Companion to Homer* (Cambridge).
Fraenkel, E. (1932), "Vergil und die Aethiopis," *Philologus* 87: 242–8.
Fraenkel, E. (1950), *Aeschylus*: Agamemnon, 3 vols. (Oxford).
Frame, D. (2009), *Hippota Nestor* (Washington, DC).
Fränkel, H. (1976^3 [1st ed. 1951]), *Dichtung und Philosophie des frühen Griechentums* (Munich).
Fries, A. (2014), *Pseudo-Euripides*, Rhesus (Berlin).
Fries, A. (2016), "Indo-European Night Raid Revisited," *JIES* 44.3–4: 289–324.
Funke, H. (1981), "Zu den Vorläufern der Militärgroteske," in H. J. Horn and H. Laufhütte (eds.), *Ares und Dionysos: Das Furchtbare und das Lächerliche in der europäischen Literatur* (Heidelberg): 239–58.
Gaede, R. (1880), *Demetrii Scepsii quae supersunt* (Greifswald).
Gaisser, J. H. (1969), "Adaptation of Traditional Material in the Glaucus-Diomedes Episode," *TAPA* 100: 165–76.
Gallavotti, C. (1969), "Tracce di Poetica di Aristotele negli scolii Omerici," *Maia* 21: 203–14.
Gantz, T. (1993), *Early Greek Myth: A Guide to Literary and Artistic Sources*, 2 vols. (Baltimore).
Garbutt, K. (2006), "An Indo-European Night Raid?," *JIES* 34.1–2: 183–200.
Gärtner, U. (2015), "Virgil and the Epic Cycle," in Fantuzzi and Tsagalis (2015b): 543–64.
Garvie, A. F. (1994), *Homer. Odyssey: Books VI–VII* (Cambridge).
Gee, E. (2020), *Mapping the Afterlife: From Homer to Dante* (Oxford).
Gernet, L. (1936), "Dolon le loup (à propos d'Homère et du Rhésus d'Euripide)," *Annuaire de l'Institut de Philologie et d'Histoire orientales et slaves, vol. IV (Mélanges Franz Cumont)* (Brussels): 189–208.
Gibbs, L. (2002), *Aesop's Fables. Translated with Introduction and Notes.* Oxford. Online at http://mythfolklore.net/aesopica/oxford/265.htm.
Giuliani, L. (2010), "Rhesos: On the Production of Images and the Reading of Texts," in E. Walter-Karydi (ed.), *Myths, Texts, Images: Homeric Epics and Ancient Greek Art* (Ithaki): 239–56.
González, J. M. (2013), *The Epic Rhapsode and His Craft* (Washington, DC).
Goold, G. P. (1977), "The Nature of Homeric Composition," *ICS* 2: 1–34.
Gostoli, A., A. Fongoni, and F. Biondi (eds.) (2017), *Poeti in agone: competizioni poetiche e musicali nella Grecia antica* (Turnhout).
Graziosi, B., and J. Haubold (2010), *Homer*: Iliad, Book VI (Cambridge).
Grethlein, J. (2011), "Die Fabel," in B. Zimmermann (ed.), *Handbuch der griechischen Literatur der Antike*, vol. I: *Die Literatur der archaischen und klassischen Zeit* (Munich): 321–5.
Grethlein, J. (2012), "Homer and Heroic History," in J. Marincola, L. Llewellyn-Jones, and C. Maciver (eds.), *Greek Notions of the Past in Archaic and Classical Eras: History without Historians* (Edinburgh): 14–36.
Griffin, J. (1977), "The Epic Cycle and the Uniqueness of Homer," *JHS* 97: 39–53.
Griffin, J. (1995), *Homer*: Iliad IX (Oxford).
Griffith, M. (1990), "Contest and Contradiction in Early Greek Poetry," in M. Griffith and D. J. Mastronarde (eds.), *Cabinet of the Muses: Essays on Classical and Comparative Literature in Honor of Thomas G. Rosenmeyer* (Atlanta): 185–207.
Grossardt, P. (1998), *Die Trugreden in der Odyssee und ihre Rezeption in der antiken Literatur* (Frankfurt).
Grossardt, P. (2001), *Die Erzählung von Meleagros: zur literarischen Entwicklung der kalydonischen Kultlegende* (Leiden).
Haft, A. J. (1990), "'The City-Sacker Odysseus' in *Iliad* 2 and 10," *TAPA* 120: 37–56.
Hainsworth, J. B. (1972), "Review of D. Lohmann, *Die Komposition der Reden in der Ilias*. Berlin," *JHS* 92: 187–8.
Hainsworth, J. B. (1974), "Review of T. Krischer, *Formale Konventionen der homerischen Epik* (München) 1971," *CR* 24: 285.

Hainsworth, J. B. (1988), "Books v–viii," in Heubeck, West, and Hainsworth: 249–385.
Hainsworth, J. B. (1993), *The* Iliad: *A Commentary, Volume III: Books 9–12* (Cambridge).
Halliwell, S., et al. (1995), *Aristotle:* Poetics, *Longinus:* On the Sublime, *Demetrius:* On Style (Cambridge, MA, and London).
Hammer, D. (1997), "'Who Shall Readily Obey?' Authority and Politics in the *Iliad*," *Phoenix* 51: 1–24.
Hammer, D. (2002), *The* Iliad *as Politics: The Performance of Political Thought* (Norman, OK).
Hansen, W. (1972), *The Conference Sequence: Patterned Narration and Narrative Inconsistency in the* Odyssey (Berkeley, Los Angeles, and London).
Hansen, W. (2002), *Ariadne's Thread: A Guide to International Tales Found in Classical Literature* (Ithaca and London).
Hardie, P. (1994), *Virgil:* Aeneid *Book IX* (Cambridge).
Hardie, P. (1998), *Virgil* (Oxford).
Harrison, E. L. (1991), "Homeric Wonder-Horses," *Hermes* 119.2: 252–4.
Havelock, E. A. (1986), *The Muse Learns to Write: Reflections on Orality and Literacy from Antiquity to the Present* (New Haven and London).
Heath, J. (1992), "The Legacy of Peleus: Death and Divine Gifts in the *Iliad*," *Hermes* 120.4: 387–400.
Hedén, E. (1912), *Homerische Götterstudien* (Uppsala).
Heiden, B. (1998), "The Placement of 'Book Divisions' in the *Iliad*," *JHS* 118: 68–81.
Heiden, B. (2008), *Homer's Cosmic Fabrication: Choice and Design in the* Iliad (Oxford).
Heinze, R. (1915³; repr. Darmstadt 1976), *Virgils Epische Technik* (Leipzig and Berlin).
Hellmann, O. (2000), *Die Schlachtszenen der Ilias* (Stuttgart).
Herington, J. (1985), *Poetry into Drama: Early Tragedy and the Greek Poetic Tradition* (Berkeley, Los Angeles, and London).
Hermann, G. (1832), *De interpolationibus Homeri* (Leipzig).
Hesk, J. (2013), "Seeing in the Dark: Kleos, Tragedy, and Perception in *Iliad* 10," in H. Lovatt and C. Vout (eds.), *Epic Visions: Visuality in the Greek and Latin Epic and Its Reception* (Cambridge): 32–59.
Heubeck, A. (1954), *Die Odyssee-Dichter und die Ilias* (Erlangen).
Heubeck, A. (1974), *Die homerische Frage: ein Bericht über die Forschung der letzten Jahrzehnte* (Darmstadt).
Heubeck, A. (1992), "Books xxii–xxiv," in Russo, Fernández-Galiano, and Heubeck: 313–418.
Heubeck, A., and A. Hoekstra (1989), *A Commentary on Homer's* Odyssey, *vol. II: Books ix–xvi* (Oxford).
Heubeck, A., S. R. West, and J. B. Hainsworth (1988), *A Commentary on Homer's* Odyssey, *vol. I: Introduction and Books i–viii* (Oxford).
Heusinger, H. (1939), *Stilistische Untersuchungen zur Dolonie. Ein Beitrag zur Echtheitsfrage des K der Ilias* (Leipzig).
Hexter, R. (2010), "On First Looking into Vergil's Homer," in J. Farrell and M. C. J. Putnam (eds.), *A Companion to Vergil's* Aeneid *and Its Tradition. Blackwell Companions to the Ancient World. Literature and Culture* (Chichester and Malden, MA): 26–36.
Hilgard, A. (1901), *Scholia in Dionysii Thracis Artem Grammaticam* (Leipzig).
Hiller von Gaertringen, F. (1886), *De Graecorum fabulis ad Thraces pertinentibus* (Berlin).
Hinds, S. (1987), *The Metamorphoses of Persephone: Ovid and the Self-Conscious Muse* (Cambridge).
Hinds, S. (1998), *Allusion and Intertext: Dynamics of Appropriation in Roman Poetry* (Cambridge).
Hirschberger, M. (2004), *Gynaikōn Katalogos und Megalai Ēhoiai: Ein Kommentar zu den Fragmenten zweier hesiodeischer Epen* (Munich).
Hölscher, U. (1967), "Die Atridensage in der *Odyssee*," in H. Singer and B. von Wiese (eds.), *Festschrift für Richard Alewyn* (Cologne): 1–16.
Holzberg, N. (1993), *Die antike Fabel: eine Einführung* (Darmstadt).

Hooker, J. T. (1975), "Review of T. Krischer, *Formale Konventionen der homerischen Epik* (Munich) 1971," *JHS* 95: 192.
Hooker, J. T. (1980), "The Apparition of Heracles in the *Odyssey*," *LCM* 5: 139-46.
Horsfall, N. M. (1979), "Stesichorus at Bovilllae," *JHS* 99: 26-48.
Horsfall, N. M. (2003), *Virgil's Aeneid 11: A Commentary* (Leiden).
Horsfall, N. M. (2008), *Virgil's Aeneid 2: A Commentary* (Leiden).
Howald, E. (1924), "Meleager und Achill," *RhM* 73: 402-25.
Howes, G. E. (1895), "Homeric Quotations in Plato and Aristotle," *HSCP* 6: 153-237.
Immisch, O. (1889), "Ad Cypria carmen," *RhM* n.s. 44: 301-94.
Jacobs, F. (1793), *Ioannis Tzetzae Antehomerica, Homerica et Posthomerica* (Leipzig).
Jacobstahl, P. (1934), "The Nekyia Krater in New York," *Metropolitan Museum Studies* 5: 117-45.
Janko, R. (1992), *The Iliad: A Commentary, Volume IV: Books 13-16* (Cambridge).
Janko, R. (1998), "The Homeric Poems as Oral Dictated Texts," *CQ* 48: 1-13.
Jedrkiewicz, S. (1989), *Sapere e paradosso nell'antichità: Esopo e la favola* (Rome).
Jens, W. (1955), "Die Dolonie und ihr Dichter," *StG* 8: 616-25.
Jensen, M. S. (1980), *The Homeric Question and the Oral-Formulaic Theory* (Copenhagen).
Jensen, M. S., et al. (1999), "Dividing Homer: When and How Were the *Iliad* and the *Odyssey* Divided into Songs?," *SO* 74: 5-91.
Johnson, W. J. (1998), *The Sauptikaparvan of the* Mahābhārata: *The Massacre at Night* (Oxford).
Jones, P. V. (1997), "Introduction," in G. M. Wright and P. V. Jones (eds.), *Homer: German Scholarship in Translation* (Oxford): 1-46.
Jouan, F. (2004), *Euripide: Tragédies, Tome VII, 2e partie. Rhésos. Texte établi et traduit* (Paris).
Kakridis, I.-Th. (1944), Ομηρικές έρευνες (Athens) [= 1949, *Homeric Researches.* (Lund)].
Kakridis, I.-Th. (1982), "Μετακένωσις," *WS* 16: 5-12.
Kakridis, P. (2001), "Κίκονες," in M. Païsi-Apostolopoulou (ed.), *Eranos. Proceedings of the 9th International Symposium on the* Odyssey (Ithaki): 481-7.
Karanika, A. (2011), "The End of the *Nekyia*: Odysseus, Heracles, and the Gorgon in the Underworld," *Arethusa* 44.1: 1-27.
Karanika, A. (2014), *Voices at Work: Women, Performance, and Labor in Ancient Greece* (Baltimore).
Katz, M. (1991), *Penelope's Renown: Meaning and Indeterminacy in the* Odyssey (Princeton, NJ).
Kelly, A. (2006), "Neoanalysis and the Nestorbedrängnis: A Test Case," *Hermes* 134: 1-25.
Kelly, A. (2007), *A Referential Commentary and Lexicon to Homer*, Iliad VIII (Oxford).
Kelly, A. (2008), "Performance and Rivalry: Homer, Odysseus, and Hesiod," in M. Revermann and P. Wilson (eds.), *Performance, Iconography, Reception: Studies in Honor of Oliver Taplin* (Oxford): 177-203.
Kelly, A. (2012a), "The Audience Expects: Penelope and Odysseus," in E. Minchin (ed.), *Orality, Literacy, and Performance in the Ancient World* (Leiden and Boston): 3-24.
Kelly, A. (2012b), "The Mourning of Thetis: 'Allusion' and the Future in the *Iliad*," in Montanari, Rengakos, and Tsagalis (2012): 221-65.
Kelly, A. (2015), "*Ilias parva*," in Fantuzzi and Tsagalis (2015b): 318-43.
Kelly, A. (2018), "Homer's Rivals? Internal Narrators in the *Iliad*," in Ready and Tsagalis: 351-77.
Kelly, A. (forthcoming), "Homer and Hipponax," in V. Cazzato and E. Prodi (eds.), *Framing Hipponax* (Cambridge).
Kilb, H. (1973), *Strukturen epischen Gestaltens im 7. und 23. Gesang der Odyssee* (Munich).
Kirk, G. S. (1962), *The Songs of Homer* (Cambridge).
Klingner, F. (1940), "Über die Dolonie," *Hermes* 75: 337-68 [= 1964. *Studien zur griechischen und römischen Literatur* (Zurich and Stuttgart): 7-39].
Knauer, G. (1964), *Die Aeneis und Homer. Studien zur poetischen Technik Vergils mit Listen der Homerzitate in der Aeneis* (Göttingen).
Köhnken, A. (1971), *Die Funktion des Mythos bei Pindar. Interpretationen zu sechs Pindargedichten* (Berlin).
Kopff, E. C. (1981), "Virgil and the Cyclical Epics," *ANRW* II.31.2: 919-47.

Korenjak, M. (1998), "Homerische Intertextualität ohne Formeln? Zwei phorminx-spielende Helden in Ilias und Odyssee," *MD* 40: 133–43.
Kovacs, D. (2002), *Euripides: Bacchae, Iphigenia at Aulis, Rhesus* (Cambridge, MA, and London).
Kraus, W. (1948), "Meleagros in der Ilias," *WS* 63: 8–21.
Krischer, T. (1971), *Formale Konventionen der homerischen Epik* (Munich).
Kullmann, W. (1955), "Die Probe des Achaierheeres in der Ilias," *MH* 12: 253–73 (= 1992: 38–63).
Kullmann, W. (1956), *Das Wirken der Götter in der Ilias. Untersuchungen zur Frage der Entstehung des homerischen "Götterapparats"* (Berlin).
Kullmann, W. (1960), *Die Quellen der Ilias: Troischer Sagenkreis* (Wiesbaden).
Kullmann, W. (1968), "Vergangenheit und Zukunft in der Ilias," *Poetica* 2: 15–37 (= 1992: 219–42).
Kullmann, W. (1977), "*Homer-Probleme* by Albrecht Dihle. Review," *Gnomon* 49: 529–43 (= 1992: 198–215).
Kullmann, W. (1981), "Zur Methode der Neoanalyse in der Homerforschung," *WS* n.s. 15: 5–42 (= 1992: 67–99).
Kullmann, W. (1984), "Oral Poetry Theory and Neoanalysis in Homeric Research," *GRBS* 25: 307–23 (= 1992: 140–55).
Kullmann, W. (1991), "Ergebnisse der motivgeschichtlichen Forschung zu Homer (Neoanalyse)," in J. Latacz (ed.), *200 Jahre Homerforschung—Rückblick und Ausblick* (Stuttgart): 425–55 (= 1992: 100–34).
Kullmann, W. (1992), *Homerische Motive. Beiträge zur Entstehung, Eigenart und Wirkung von Ilias und Odyssee*, ed. R. J. Müller (Stuttgart).
Kullmann, W. (1995), "The Two Nekyiai of the *Odyssey* and their Oral Sources," in M. Païsi-Apostolopoulou (ed.), *ΕΥΧΗΝ ΟΔΥΣΣΕΙ. Από τα Πρακτικά του Ζ΄ Συνεδρίου για την Οδύσσεια (3–8 Σεπτεμβρίου 1993)* (Ithaki): 41–52 (= 2002: 147–54).
Kullmann, W. (2002), "Nachlese zur Neoanalyse," in A. Rengakos (ed.), *Realität, Imagination und Theorie. Kleine Schriften zu Epos und Tragödie in der Antike* (Stuttgart): 162–76.
Kullmann, W. (2005), "Ilias und Aithiopis," *Hermes* 133.1: 9–28.
Kullmann, W. (2012a), "The Relative Chronology of the Homeric Catalogue of Ships and of the Lists of Heroes and Cities within the Catalogue," in Andersen and Haug (2012): 210–23.
Kullmann, W. (2012b), "Neoanalysis between Orality and Literacy: Some Remarks Concerning the Development of Greek Myths Including the Legend of the Capture of Troy," in Montanari, Rengakos, and Tsagalis (2012): 13–25.
Kullmann, W. (2015), "Motif and Source Research: Neoanalysis, Homer, and Cyclic Epic," in Fantuzzi and Tsagalis (2015b): 108–25.
Lamari, A. A. (2017), *Reperforming Greek Tragedy: Theater, Politics, and Cultural Mobility in the Fifth and Fourth Centuries BC* (Berlin).
Lamberton, R. (1988), *Hesiod* (New Haven and London).
Lambrou, I. (2015), *Homer and the Epic Cycle: Dialogue and Challenge* (Ph.D. diss., University College London).
Lambrou, I. (2018), "Homer and Achilles' Ambush of Troilus: Confronting the Elephant in the Room," *G&R* 65.1: 75–85.
Lämmert, E. (1991[8]) [1st ed. 1955], *Bauformen des Erzählens* (Stuttgart).
Lang, M. L. (1969), "Homer and Oral Techniques," *Hesperia* 38: 159–68.
Laser, S. (1949), *Studien zur Dolonie* (Diss., University of Kiel).
Laser, S. (1958), "Über das Verhältnis der Dolonie zur Odyssee," *Hermes* 86: 385–425.
Latacz, J. (1977), *Kampfparänese, Kampfdarstellung und Kampfwirklichkeit in der Ilias, bei Kallinos und Tyrtaios* (Munich).
Lattimore, R. (1951), *The Iliad of Homer* (Chicago).
Leaf, W. (1900–2), *Homer: The Iliad*, 2 vols. (London).
Leaf, W. (1915), "Rhesus of Thrace," *JHS* 35: 1–11.
Leaf, W., and M. A. Bayfield (1962), *The Iliad of Homer*, vol. I (London).
Leone, P. A. M. (1995), *Ioannis Tzetzae Carmina Iliaca* (Catania).

Leumann, M. (1950), *Homerische Wörter* (Basel).
Liapis, V. (2009), "*Rhesus*: Myth and Iconography," in J. R. S. Cousland and J. R. Hume (eds.), *The Play of Texts and Fragments: Essays in Honour of Martin Cropp* (Leiden and Boston): 273-91.
Liapis, V. (2011), "The Thracian Cult of Rhesus and the *Heros Equitans*," *Kernos* 24: 95-104.
Liapis, V. (2012), *A Commentary on the* Rhesus *Attributed to Euripides* (Oxford).
Lightfoot, J. L. (1999), *Parthenius of Nicaea: The Poetical Fragments and the Ἐρωτικὰ Παθήματα* (Oxford).
Lissarague, F. (1980), "Iconographie de Dolon le loup," *RA* (n.s.) 1: 3-30.
Lohan, W. (1890), *De librorum titulis apud classicos scriptores Graecos nobis occurrentibus* (Diss., University of Marburg).
Lohmann, D. (1970), *Die Komposition der Reden in der Ilias* (Berlin).
Lohmann, D. (1988), *Die Andromache-Szenen der Ilias. Ansätze und Methoden der Homer-Interpretation* (Zurich).
López-Ruiz C. (2014), *Gods, Heroes, and Monsters: A Sourcebook of Greek, Roman, and Near Eastern Myths in Translation* (Oxford).
Lord, A. B. (1953), "Homer's Originality: Oral Dictated Texts," *TAPA* 84: 124-34.
Lord, A. B. (1990), "Foreword," in J. S. Miletich (ed.), *The Bugarštica: A Bilingual Anthology of the Earliest Extant South Slavic Folk Narrative Song* (Urbana): vii-xviii.
Lord, A. B. (2018³) [= 1960], *The Singer of Tales* (Cambridge, MA).
Lucarini, C. M. (2019), *La genesi dei poemi omerici* (Berlin).
Lundon, J. (2002), "Aristotle, Aristarchus and Zielinski on the Narration of Simultaneous Events in Homeric Epos," *Proceedings of the 11th International Conference of Classical Studies (Kavala, 24-30 August 1999)*, vol. II (Athens): 581-91.
Lünstedt, P. (1961), *Untersuchungen zu den mythologischen Abschnitten der D-Scholien* (Diss., University of Hamburg).
Lyne, R. O. A. M. (1987), *Further Voices in Vergil's* Aeneid (Oxford).
Maas, P. (1933), "Zu griechischen Wörtern," *ZVS* 60: 285-6.
Maass, E. (1884), "Die Iliasscholien des Codex Leidensis," *Hermes* 19: 534-68.
Mackie, H. (1997), "Song and Storytelling: An Odyssean Perspective," *TAPA* 127: 77-95.
Macleod, C. W. (1982), *Homer*: Iliad, *Book XXIV* (Cambridge).
Manton, G. R. (1962), "Virgil and the Greek Epic: The Tragedy of Evander," *Journal of the Australian Universities Language & Literature Association* 17: 5-17.
March, J. R. (1987), *The Creative Poet: Studies on the Treatment of Myth in Greek Poetry* (London).
Marks, J. (2008), *Zeus in the* Odyssey (Washington, DC).
Maronitis, D. N. (1971), *Ἀναζήτηση καὶ νόστος τοῦ Ὀδυσσέα. Ἡ διαλεκτικὴ τῆς Ὀδύσσειας* (Athens).
Maronitis, D. N. (1983), "References latentes de l'Odyssée à l'Iliade," in *Melanges Edouard Delebecque* (Aix-en-Provence): 279-91 [= 2004: 133-46].
Maronitis, D. N. (1998), "*Ἀοιδός-Ἀφηγητής-Ποιητής: εσωτερική ποιητική της Οδύσσειας*," in *Ομηρικά (από τα Πρακτικά του Η´ Συνεδρίου για την Οδύσσεια, 1-5 Σεπτεμβρίου 1996)* (Ithaki): 57-75 [= 2004: 101-15].
Maronitis, D. N. (2004), *Homeric Megathemes: War-Homilia-Homecoming* (Lanham, MD).
Martin, R. P. (1989), *The Language of Heroes: Speech and Performance in the* Iliad (Ithaca, NY, and London).
Martin, R. P. (1992), "Hesiod's Metanastic Poetics," *Ramus* 21: 11-33.
Martin, R. P. (2001), "Rhapsodizing Orpheus," *Kernos* 14: 23-33 (= 2020a: 205-16).
Martin, R. P. (2020a), *Mythologizing Performance* (Ithaca, NY).
Martin, R. P. (2020b), "Homer in a World of Song," in Pache (2020): 36-48.
Matthews, M. (1976), *The Expression ΥΠΕΡ ΜΟΙΡΑΝ in Homer* (Ph.D. diss., Harvard University).
Mazon, P. (1943), *Introduction à l'Iliade* (Paris).
McClellan, A. M. (2017), "The Death and Mutilation of Imbrius in the *Iliad*," *Yage* 1: 159-74.

McLeod, W. (1988), "The Bow at Night: An Inappropriate Weapon?," *Phoenix* 42.2: 121–5.
Merkelbach, R. (1960), "Aiante," *Glotta* 38: 268–70.
Mervyn Jones, D., and N. Wilson (1969), *Scholia vetera et scholia Tricliniana in Aristophanis Equites* (Groningen and Amsterdam).
Meuli, K. (1954), "Herkunft und Wesen der Fabel. Ein Vortrag," *Schweizerisches Archiv für Volkskunde* 50: 65–88.
Minchin, E. (2001), *Homer and the Resources of Memory: Some Applications of Cognitive Theory to the* Iliad *and the* Odyssey (Oxford).
Minchin, E. (2018), "The *Odyssey* after the *Iliad*: Ties that Bind," in R. Simms (ed.), *Brill's Companion to Prequels, Sequels, and Retellings of Classical Epic* (Leiden): 9–30.
Minchin, E. (forthcoming), "Moving Towards Textualization: Evidence for Poetic Preparation in Homer," *YAGE* 8.
Monda, S. (2011), "The Coroebus Episode in Virgil's *Aeneid*," *HSCP* 106: 199–208.
Monro, D. B. (1884), "The Poems of the Epic Cycle," *JHS* 5: 1–41.
Monro, D. B. (1901), *Homer's* Odyssey, 2 vols. (Oxford).
Montana, F., and F. Montanari (2022), "The Ecdotic Problem of the Mythographus Homericus: Some Thoughts on the Scholiastic Side," in J. Pagès and N. Villagra (eds.), *Myths on the Margins of Homer: Prolegomena to the Mythographus Homericus* (Berlin): 31–56.
Montanari, F. (1995), "The Mythographus Homericus," in J. G. J. Abbenes, S. R. Slings, and I. Sluiter (eds.), *Greek Literary Theory after Aristotle: A Collection of Papers in Honour of D. M. Schenkeveld* (Amsterdam): 135–72.
Montanari, F. (2002), "Ancora sul Mythographus Homericus (e l'*Odissea*)," in A. Hurst and F. Létoublon (eds.), *La mythologie et l'Odyssée. Hommages à Gabriel Germain* (Geneva): 129–44.
Montanari, F. (2010), "The *Iliad* Plot in Ancient Scholarship. The Case of Book Ten (*Doloneia*)," *TC* 2: 1–17.
Montanari, F., and P. Ascheri (eds.) (2002), *Omero tremila anni dopo* (Rome).
Montanari, F., A. Rengakos, and C. Tsagalis (eds.) (2009), *Brill's Companion to Hesiod* (Leiden).
Montanari, F., A. Rengakos, and C. Tsagalis (eds.) (2012), *Homeric Contexts: Neoanalysis and the Interpretation of Oral Poetry* (Berlin).
Moran, W. S. (1975), "Μιμνήσκομαι and 'Remembering' Epic Stories in Homer and the Hymns," *QUCC* 20: 195–211.
Morard, A. (1963), "Notes sur le chant X de l'Iliade," *Bulletin de l'Association Guillaume Budé* 22: 385–403.
Morris, I., and B. Powell (eds.) (1997), *A New Companion to Homer* (Leiden).
Morrison, A. D. (2007), *The Narrator in Archaic and Hellenistic Poetry* (Cambridge).
Morrison, J. V. (1992), *Homeric Misdirection. False Predictions in the* Iliad (Ann Arbor).
Morrison, J. V. (1997), "*Kerostasia*, the Dictates of Fate, and the Will of Zeus in the *Iliad*," *Arethusa* 30: 273–96.
Most, G. W. (1992), "Il poeta nell'Ade: catabasis epica e teoria dell'epos tra Omero e Virgilio," *SIFC* 10.1-2: 1014–26.
Most, G. W. (1997), "Hesiod's Myth of the Five (or Three or Four) Races," *Proceedings of the Cambridge Philological Society* 43: 104–27.
Most, G. W. (2018), *Hesiod*. Loeb Classical Library, 2 vols., revised edition (Cambridge, MA).
Most, G. W. (2024), "Heracles in Hesiod," in Tsagalis: 131–45.
Motzkus, D. (1964), *Untersuchungen zum 9. Buch der Ilias unter besonderer Berücksichtigung der Phoinixgestalt* (Diss., University of Hamburg).
Moulton, C. (1977), *Similes in the Homeric Poems* (Göttingen).
Mueller, M. (2009²) [= 1984], *The Iliad* (London).
Muellner, L. (1976), *The Meaning of Homeric* εὔχομαι *through its Formulas* (Innsbruck).
Mühlestein, H. (1986), "Ein Halbvers und einige Epitheta aus vorhomerischer Dichtung," *MH* 43: 209–20 (= 1987: 174–85).
Mühlestein, H. (1987), *Homerische Namenstudien* (Frankfurt).

Nagy, G. (1979 = 1999²), *The Best of the Achaeans: Concepts of the Hero in Archaic Greek Poetry and Myth* (Baltimore).
Nagy, G. (1990), *Greek Mythology and Poetics* (Ithaca, NY).
Nagy, G. (1996a), *Homeric Questions* (Austin).
Nagy, G. (1996b), *Poetry as Performance: Homer and Beyond* (Cambridge).
Nelson, T. J. (2021), "Intertextual *Agones* in Archaic Greek Epic: Penelope vs. the *Catalogue of Women,*" *YAGE* 5: 25–57.
Nelson, T. J. (2022), "Iphigenia in the *Iliad* and the Architecture of Homeric Allusion," *TAPA* 152.1: 55–101.
Nelson, T. J. (2023), *Markers of Allusion in Archaic Greek Poetry* (Cambridge).
Nesselrath, H.-G. (2020), "Heracles in Homer," in A. Rengakos, P. Finglass, and B. Zimmermann (eds.), *More than Homer Knew—Studies on Homer and his Ancient Commentators* (Berlin): 27–36.
Newton, R. M. (1997), "Cloak and Shield in *Odyssey* 14," *CJ* 93: 143–56.
Nitzsch, G. W. (1862), *Beiträge zur Geschichte der epischen Poesie der Griechen* (Leipzig).
Nøjgaard, M. (1964), *La fable antique: la fable grecque avant Phèdre*, vol. I (Copenhagen).
Norden, E. (1926³), *P. Vergilius Maro: Aeneis Buch VI* (Leipzig and Berlin).
Notopoulos, J. A. (1964), "Studies in Early Greek Oral Poetry," *HSCP* 68: 1–77.
Noussia-Fantuzzi, M. (2015), "The Epic Cycle, Stesichorus, and Ibycus," in Fantuzzi and Tsagalis (2015b): 430–49.
Nünlist, R. (1998a), *Poetologische Bildersprache in der frühgriechischen Dichtung* (Stuttgart and Leipzig).
Nünlist, R. (1998b), "Der homerische Erzähler und das sogenannte Sukzessionsgesetz," *MH* 55: 2–8.
Nünlist, R. (2009), *The Ancient Critic at Work: Terms and Concepts of Literary Criticism in Greek Scholia* (Cambridge).
Olson, S. D. (1990), "The Stories of Agamemnon in Homer's *Odyssey*," *TAPA* 120: 57–71.
Olson, S. D. (1995), *Blood and Iron: Stories and Storytelling in Homer's* Odyssey (Leiden).
Olson, S. D. (2012), *The Homeric Hymn to Aphrodite and Related Texts: Text, Translation and Commentary* (Berlin).
Pache, C. (ed.) (2020), *The Cambridge Guide to Homer* (Cambridge).
Page, D. L. (1955), *The Homeric* Odyssey (Oxford).
Pagès, J. (2007), *Mythographus Homericus: estudi i edició comentada* (Diss., Autonomous University of Barcelona).
Pagès, J. (2017), "Apollodorus' *Bibliotheca* and the Mythographus Homericus: An Intertextual Approach," in J. Pàmias (ed.), *Apollodoriana: Ancient Myths, New Crossroads. Studies in Honour of Francesc J. Cuartero* (Berlin): 66–81.
Panzer, I. (1892), *De Mythographo Homerico restituendo* (Diss., University of Greifswald).
Parry, A. (1971), "Introduction," in M. Parry: ix–lxii.
Parry, A. (1972), "Language and Characterization in Homer," *HSCP* 76: 1–22.
Parry, M. (1971), *The Making of Homeric Verse. The Collected Papers of Milman Parry, edited by Adam Parry.* (Oxford).
Pedrizet, P. (1910), *Cultes et mythes du Pangée* (Paris and Nancy).
Pelliccia, H. (2003), "Two Points about Rhapsodes," in M. Finkelberg and G. G. Stroumsa (eds.), *Homer, the Bible, and Beyond: Literary and Religious Canons in the Ancient World* (Leiden): 97–116.
Penglase, R. (1994), *Greek Myths and Mesopotamia. Parallels and Influence in the Homeric Hymns and Hesiod* (London and New York).
Perry, B. E. (1970), *Aesopica: A Series of Texts Relating to Aesop or Ascribed to Him or Closely Connected with the Literary Tradition that Bears His Name* (Urbana, IL).
Pestalozzi, H. (1945), *Die Achilleis als Quelle der Ilias* (Zurich).
Petegorsky, D. (1982), *Context and Evocation: Studies in Early Greek and Sanskrit Poetry* (Ph.D. diss., University of California at Berkeley).
Petzl, G. (1969), *Antike Diskussionen über die beiden Nekyiai* (Meisenheim).

Phillips, E. D. (1957), "A Suggestion about Palamedes," *AJP* 78.3: 267-78.
Platte, R. (2017), *Equine Poetics* (Washington, DC).
Pontani, F. (2007-), *Scholia Graeca in Odysseam*, 5 vols. to date (I: *scholia ad libros α-β* [2007]; II: *scholia ad libros γ-δ* [2010]; III: *scholia ad libros ε-ζ* [2015]; IV: *scholia ad libros η-θ* [2020]; V: *scholia ad libros ι-κ* [2022]) (Rome).
Porter, A. (2014), "Reconstructing Laomedon's Reign in Homer: Olympiomachia, Poseidon's Wall, and the Earlier Trojan War," *GRBS* 54.4: 507-26.
Porter, A. (2022), *Homer and the Epic Cycle: Recovering the Oral Traditional Relationship* (Leiden).
Postlethwaite, N. (1988), "Thersites in the *Iliad*," *G&R* 35: 123-36.
Powell, B. B. (1991), *Homer and the Origin of the Greek Alphabet* (Cambridge).
Prince, G. (1973), "Introduction à l'étude du narrataire," *Poétique* 14: 178-96.
Probert, Ph. (2016), "Zeus on the Stud Farm? Against a Homeric Instance of *attractio relativi*," *Mnemosyne* 69.3: 365-81.
Pucci, P. (1987), *Odysseus Polutropos: Intertextual Readings in the* Odyssey *and the* Iliad (Ithaca, NY).
Pucci, P. (1998), *The Song of the Sirens: Essays on Homer* (Lanham, MD).
Quint, D. (2022), "Heroism and Loot in the *Iliad*," *YAGE* 6: 16-50.
Rabel, R. J. (1997), *Plot and Point of View in the* Iliad (Ann Arbor).
Ramersdorfer, H. (1981), *Singuläre Iterata der Ilias* [A-K] (Köningstein im Taunus).
Ranke, F. (1881), *Die Doloneia* (Leipzig).
Rankin, H. D. (1972), "Thersites the Malcontent: A Discussion," *SO* 47: 36-60.
Rawles, R. (2018), *Simonides the Poet: Intertextuality and Reception* (Cambridge).
Ready, J. L. (2011), *Character, Narrator, and Simile in the* Iliad (Cambridge).
Ready, J. L. (2018), "Performance, Oral Texts, and Entextualization in Homeric Epic," in Ready and Tsagalis: 320-50.
Ready J. L. (2019), *Orality, Textuality, and the Homeric Epics: An Interdisciplinary Study of Oral Texts, Dictated Texts, and Wild Texts* (Oxford).
Ready J. L., and C. C. Tsagalis (eds.) (2018), *Homer in Performance: Rhapsodes, Narrators, and Characters* (Austin).
Redfield, J. (1975), *Nature and Culture in the* Iliad: *The Tragedy of Hector* (Chicago).
Reece, S. (1994), "The Cretan *Odyssey*: A Lie Truer than Truth," *AJP* 115: 157-73.
Reece, S. (2009), *Homer's Winged Words: The Evolution of Early Greek Epic Diction in the Light of Oral Theory* (Leiden).
Reichel, M. (1994), *Fernbeziehungen in der Ilias* (Tübingen).
Reichel, M. (1998a), "Narratologische Methoden in der Homerforschung," in H. L. C. Tristram, *New Methods in the Research of Epic/Neue Methoden der Epenforschung* (Tübingen): 45-61.
Reichel, M. (1998b), "How Oral is Homer's Narrative?," *PLLS* 10: 1-22.
Reichel, M., and A. Rengakos (eds.) (2002), *Epea Pteroenta: Beiträge zur Homerforschung. Festschrift für Wolfgang Kullmann zum 75. Geburtstag* (Stuttgart).
Reinhardt, K. (1956), "Zum homerischen Aphroditehymnus," in *Festschrift Bruno Snell zum 60. Geburtstag am 18. Juni 1956 von Freunden und Schülern überreicht* (Munich): 1-14.
Reinhardt, K. (1961), *Die Ilias und ihr Dichter* (Göttingen).
Rempe, J. (1927), *De Rheso Thracum heroe*, (Diss., University of Münster).
Rengakos, A. (1995), "Zeit und Gleichzeitigkeit in den homerischen Epen," *Antike und Abendland* 41: 1-33 (= 2006: 85-134).
Rengakos, A. (2002), "Zur narrativen Funktion der Telemachie," in A. Hurst (ed.), *La mythologie de l'Odyssée. Hommage à Gabriel Germain* (Geneva): 87-98 (= 2006: 74-84).
Rengakos, A. (2006), *Το χαμόγελο του Αχιλλέα: θέματα αφήγησης και ποιητικής στα ομηρικά έπη* (Athens).
Rengakos, A. (2015), "*Aethiopis*," in Fantuzzi and Tsagalis (2015b): 306-17.
Richardson, N. J. (1993), *The* Iliad: *A Commentary, Volume VI: Books 21-24* (Cambridge).
Richardson, S. (1990), *The Homeric Narrator* (Nashville, TN).

Rieu, E. V. (1946; revised by D. C. H. Rieu 1991, with Introduction, Index, and Glossary by P. V. Jones), *Homer: The Odyssey* (London).
Rinon, Y. (2006), "*Mise en abyme* and Tragic Signification in the *Odyssey*: The Three Songs of Demodocus," *Mnemosyne* 59: 208-25.
Ritchie, W. (1964), *The Authenticity of the Rhesus of Euripides* (Cambridge).
Robert, C. (1901), *Studien zur Ilias* (Berlin).
Robert, F. (1950), *Homère* (Paris).
Rosen, R. (1990), "Poetry and Sailing in Hesiod's *Works and Days*," *CA* 9: 99-113.
Ross, D. O. (1975), *Backgrounds to Augustan Poetry: Gallus, Elegy, and Rome* (Cambridge).
Rousseau, P. (1990), "Le deuxième Atride: Le type épique de Ménélas dans l'*Iliade*," in M-M. Mactoux and E. Geny (eds.), *Mélanges Pierre Lévêque* 5: *Anthropologie et société* (Besançon): 325-54.
Rousseau, P. (1992), "Remarques complémentaires sur la royauté de Ménélas," in M. Woronoff (ed.), *L'univers épique: rencontres avec l'antiquité classique II* (Paris): 69-75.
Ruijgh, C. J (1974), "Review of T. Krischer, *Formale Konventionen der homerischen Epik* (München) 1971," *Mnemosyne* 27: 418-21.
Russo, J., M. Fernández-Galiano, and A. Heubeck (eds.) (1992), *A Commentary on Homer's Odyssey, vol. III: Books xvii-xxiv* (Oxford).
Rüter, K. (1969), *Odysseeinterpretationen: Untersuchungen zum ersten Buch und zur Phaiakis* (Göttingen).
Rutherford, I. (2009), "Hesiod and the Literary Traditions of the Near East," in Montanari, Rengakos, and Tsagalis: 9-35.
Rutherford, I. (2015), "Pindar's Cycle," in Fantuzzi and Tsagalis (2015b): 450-60.
Rutherford, R. B. (1985), "At Home and Abroad: Aspects of the *Odyssey*," *PCPS* 31: 133-50.
Rutherford, R. B. (2001), "From the *Iliad* to the *Odyssey*," in Cairns (2001b): 117-46.
Rutherford, R. B. (2013²), *Homer* (Cambridge).
Rzach, A. (1922), "Kyklos," *RE* 22: 2347-435.
Saïd, S. (2011), *Homer and the Odyssey* (Oxford); first published as *Homère et l'Odyssée* (Paris, 1998).
Sammons, B. (2009), "Brothers in the Night: Agamemnon and Menelaus in Book 10 of the *Iliad*," *Classical Bulletin* 85: 27-47.
Sammons, B. (2014), "A Tale of Tydeus: Exemplarity and Structure in two Homeric Insets," *TC* 6.2: 297-318.
Sammons, B. (2017), *Device and Composition in the Greek Epic Cycle* (New York).
Sbardella, L. (1994), "Tracce di un epos di Eracle nei poemi omerici," *SMEA* 33: 145-66.
Sbardella, L. (2012), *Cucitori di canti: Studi sulla tradizione epico-rapsodica greca e i suoi itinerari nel VI secolo a.C.* (Rome).
Scafoglio, G. (2004), "Proclo e il ciclo epico," *GFA* 7: 39-57.
Schadewaldt, W. (1938 = 1966³), *Iliasstudien* (Darmstadt).
Schadewaldt, W. (1965⁴), *Von Homers Welt und Werk: Aufsätze und Auslegungen zur homerischen Frage* (Stuttgart).
Scheer, E. (1908), *Lycophronis Alexandra*, 2 vols. (Berlin).
Schefold, K. (1993), *Götter und Heldensagen der Griechen in der früh- und hocharchaischen Kunst* (Munich).
Schein, S. L. (2002), "The Horses of Achilles in Book 17 of the *Iliad*," in Reichel and Rengakos: 193-205 (= 2016: 11-26).
Schein, S. L. (2016), *Homeric Epic and its Reception: Interpretive Essays* (Oxford).
Scheub, H. (2002), *The Poem in the Story: Music, Poetry, and Narrative* (Madison, WI).
Schironi, F. (2018), *The Best of the Grammarians: Aristarchus of Samothrace on the* Iliad (Ann Arbor).
Schischwani, S. (1994), *Mündliche Quellen der Odyssee* (Diss., University of Freiburg).
Schlunk, R. R. (1974), *The Homeric Scholia and the Aeneid: A Study of the Influence of Ancient Homeric Literary Criticism on Vergil* (Ann Arbor).

Schmit-Neuerburg, T. (1999), *Vergils Aeneis und die antike Homerexegese. Untersuchungen zum Einfluß ethischer und kritischer Homerrezeption auf* imitatio *und* aemulatio *Vergils* (Berlin).
Schmitt, R. (1967), *Dichtung und Dichtersprache in indogermanischer Zeit* (Wiesbaden).
Schmitz, T. A. (1994), "Ist die Odyssee 'spannend'? Anmerkungen zur Erzähltechnik des homerischen Epos," *Philologus* 138: 3–23.
Schoeck, G. (1961), *Ilias und Aithiopis. Kyklische Motive in homerischer Brechung* (Zurich).
Schütrumpf, E. (2008), *Heraclides of Pontus: Texts and Translations* (Piscataway, NJ).
Schwabl, H. (1982), "Traditionelle Gestaltung, Motivwiederholung und Mimesis im homerischen Epos," *WS* 99: 29–62.
Schwabl, H. (1986), "Zum Problem der traditionellen Kompositionsformen bei Homer, *WS* 99: 39–61.
Schwartz, E. (1887–91), *Scholia in Euripidem*, 2 vols. (Berlin).
Scodel R. (1998), "Bardic Performance and Oral Tradition in Homer," *AJP* 119: 171–94.
Scodel R. (1999), *Credible Impossibilities: Conventions and Strategies of Verisimilitude in Homer and Greek Tragedy* (Stuttgart and Leipzig).
Scodel, R. (2002), *Listening to Homer: Tradition, Narrative & Audience* (Ann Arbor).
Scodel, R. (2012), "Hesiod and the Epic Cycle," in Montanari, Rengakos, and Tsagalis: 501–15.
Scodel, R. (2024), "Heracles on Cos," in Tsagalis: 63–86.
Scott, W. C. (1974), *The Oral Nature of the Homeric Simile* (Leiden).
Seeck, G. A. (1998), "Homerisches Erzählen und das Problem der Gleichzeitigkeit," *Hermes* 126.2: 131–44.
Seitel, P. (2012), "Three Aspects of Oral Textuality," in R. F. Bendix and G. Hasan-Rokem (eds.), *A Companion to Folklore* (Malden, MA): 75–93.
Severyns, A. (1928), *Le Cycle épique dans l'école d'Aristarque* (Liège).
Shapiro, H. A. (1989), *Art and Cult under the Tyrants in Athens* (Mainz).
Sheppard, J. (1922), *The Pattern of the* Iliad (London).
Shewan, A. (1911), *The Lay of Dolon* (London).
Siikala, J. (2003), "'God Spoke Different Things': Oral Tradition and the Interpretive Community," in L. Tarkka (ed.), *Dynamics of Tradition: Perspectives on Oral Poetry and Folk Belief* (Helsinki) 21–34.
Singor, H. W. (1992), "The Achaean Wall and the Seven Gates of Thebes," *Hermes* 120: 401–11.
Slatkin, L. M. (2011), *The Power of Thetis and Selected Essays* (Washington, DC).
Snodgrass, A. M. (1998), *Homer and the Artists. Text and Picture in Early Greek Art* (Cambridge).
Spelman, H. (2018), "Pindar and the Epic Cycle," *JHS* 138: 182–201.
Stanford, W. B. (1959^2), *The* Odyssey *of Homer* (London).
Stanley, K. (1993), *The Shield of Homer* (Princeton, NJ).
Steinen, K. T. (1992), "Ambushes, Raids, and Palisades: Mississippian Warfare in the Interior Southeast," *Southeastern Archaeology* 11: 132–8.
Stelow, A. R. (2009), "The *Aristeia* of Menelaos," *CJ* 104: 193–205.
Stelow, A. R. (2020), *Menelaus in the Archaic Period: Not Quite the Best of the Achaeans* (Oxford).
Strasburger, G. (1954), *Die kleinen Kämpfer der Ilias* (Frankfurt).
Strolonga, P. (2018), "Variations of the Myth of the Abduction of Ganymede: Intertextuality and Narratology," *YAGE* 2: 190–217.
Taplin, O. (1990), "The Earliest Quotation of the *Iliad*," in E. M. Craik (ed.), *Owls to Athens* (Oxford): 109–12.
Taplin, O. (1992), *Homeric Soundings: The Shaping of the* Iliad (Oxford).
Taplin, O. (1999), "Spreading the Word through Performance," in S. Goldhill and R. Osborne (eds.), *Performance Culture and Athenian Democracy* (Cambridge): 33–57.
Thalmann, W. G. (1984), *Conventions of Form and Thought in Early Greek Epic Poetry* (Baltimore).
Thalmann, W. G. (1988), "Thersites: Comedy, Scapegoats, and Heroic Ideology in the *Iliad*," *TAPA* 118: 1–28.
Theiler, W. (1947), "Die Dichter der Ilias," in *FS f. Edouard Tièche* (Bern): 125–67 [= 1970: *Untersuchungen zur antiken Literatur* (Berlin): 11–47].

Thilo, G., and H. Hagen (1881-1902), *Servii Grammatici qui feruntur in Vergilii carmina commentarii*, 3 vols. (Leipzig).
Thomas, O. (2020), *The Homeric Hymn to Hermes* (Cambridge).
Thomas, R. (1992), *Literacy and Orality in Ancient Greece* (Cambridge).
Thomas, R. F. (1986), *Virgil:* Georgics i-ii (Cambridge).
Thompson, S. (1955-8), *Motif-Index of Folk-Literature: A Classification of Narrative Elements in Folktales, Ballads, Myths, Fables, Mediaeval Romances, Exempla, Fabliaux, Jest-Books, and Local Legends*, revised edition, 6 vols (Bloomington, IN, and London).
Thornton, A. (1970), *People and Themes in Homer's* Odyssey (London).
Thornton, A. (1984), *Homer's* Iliad: *Its Composition and the Motif of Supplication* (Göttingen).
Tomaschek, W. (1893-4), *Die alten Thraker*, 2 parts (I: 1893; II.1-2: 1894) (Vienna).
Torres-Guerra, J. B. (1995), *La* Tebaida *homérica como fuente de* Ilıada *y* Odisea (Madrid).
Torres-Guerra, J. B. (2015), "*Thebaid*," in Fantuzzi and Tsagalis (2015b): 226-43.
True, M. (1995), "The Murder of Rhesos on a Chalcidian Neck-Amphora by the Inscription Painter," in J. B. Carter and S. Morris (eds.), *The Ages of Homer. A Tribute to Emily Townsend Vermeule* (Austin): 415-29.
Trypanis, C. A. (1963), "Brothers Fighting Together in the *Iliad*," *RhM* n.s. 16: 289-97.
Tsagalis, C. (2003a), "*Odyssey* 24.191-202: A Reconsideration," *WS* 116: 43-56 (= 2008: 30-43).
Tsagalis, C. (2003b), "The Homeric Formula νυκτὸς ἀμολγῷ," *Classica et Mediaevalia* 54: 5-40 (= 2008: 153-87).
Tsagalis, C. (2004), *Epic Grief: Personal Laments in Homer's* Iliad (Berlin).
Tsagalis, C. (2006), "Poet and Audience: From Homer to Hesiod," in F. Montanari and A. Rengakos (eds.), *La poésie épique grecque: métamorphoses d'un genre littéraire* (Vandoeuvres-Geneva): 79-130.
Tsagalis, C. (2008), *The Oral Palimpsest: Exploring Intertextuality in the Homeric Epics* (Washington, DC).
Tsagalis, C. (2009), "Hesiodic Poetry and Poetics," in Montanari, Rengakos, and Tsagalis: 131-77 (= 2023: 209-55).
Tsagalis, C. (2011), "Towards an Oral, Intertextual Neoanalysis," *TC* 3.2: 209-44 (= 2023: 3-33).
Tsagalis, C. (2012a), "Deauthorizing the Epic Cycle: Odysseus' False Tale to Eumaeus (*Od.* 14.199-359)," in Montanari, Rengakos, and Tsagalis (2012): 309-45 (= 2023: 163-20).
Tsagalis, C. (2012b), *From Listeners to Viewers: Space in the* Iliad (Washington, DC).
Tsagalis, C. (2014a), "Preface," *TC* 6.2: 239-46.
Tsagalis, C. (2014b), "γυναίων εἵνεκα δώρων: Interformularity and Intertraditionality in Theban and Homeric Epic," *TC* 6.2: 357-98 (= 2023: 312-54).
Tsagalis, C. (2016), *Ομηρικές μελέτες: προφορικότητα, διακειμενικότητα, νεοανάλυση* (Thessaloniki).
Tsagalis, C. (2017), *Early Greek Epic Fragments I: Antiquarian and Genealogical Epic* (Berlin).
Tsagalis, C. (2018a), *Τέχνη ραψωδική: η απαγγελία της επικής ποίησης από την αρχαϊκή έως την αυτοκρατορική περίοδο* (Thessaloniki).
Tsagalis, C. (2018b), "Performance Contexts for Rhapsodic Recitals in the Archaic and Classical Periods," in Ready and Tsagalis (2018): 29-75 (= 2023: 463-510).
Tsagalis, C. (2020a), "The Meta-Narrative Moment: Rhesus' Horses Revisited," *TC* 12.1: 92-113.
Tsagalis, C. (2020b), "The Darkest Hour: Odysseus' Smile and the *Doloneia*," in A. Rengakos, P. Finglass, and B. Zimmermann (eds.), *"More than Homer Knew": Studies on Homer and his Ancient Commentators* (Berlin): 53-88.
Tsagalis, C. (2022), *Early Greek Epic Fragments II: Epics on Herakles (Kreophylos and Peisandros)* (Berlin).
Tsagalis, C. (2023), *Early Greek Epic: Language, Interpretation, Performance* (Berlin).
Tsagalis, C. (ed.) (2024), *Heracles in Early Greek Epic* (Leiden).
Tsagalis, C. (forthcoming), *Omero: Iliade, vol. III: Libri IX-XII (testo e commento)*, Fondazione Lorenzo Valla-Mondadori (Milan).
Tsagarakis, O. (1992), "The Flashback Technique in Homer," *SIFC* 85: 781-9.
Tsagarakis, O. (2001), "On Simultaneous Actions in Homer," in M. Païsi-Apostolopoulou (ed.), *Eranos: Proceedings of the 9th International Symposium on the* Odyssey, *2-7 September 2000* (Ithaki): 355-66.

Turkeltaub, D. (2020), "Immanence," in Pache: 165–6.
Urban, G. (1996), "Entextualization, Replication, and Power," in M. Silverstein and G. Urban (eds.), *Natural Histories of Discourse* (Chicago): 21–44.
Usener, K. (1990), *Beobachtungen zum Verhältnis der Odyssee zur Ilias* (Tübingen).
Ustinova, Y. (2002), "Either a Daimon, or a Hero, or Perhaps a God: Mythical Residents of Subterranean Chambers," *Kernos* 15: 267–88.
van der Valk, M. (1963–4), *Researches on the Text and Scholia of the* Iliad, 2 vols. (Leiden).
van Dijk, G. J. (1997), *Ainoi, Logoi, Mythoi. Fables in Archaic, Classical, and Hellenistic Greek* (Leiden).
van Rossum-Steenbeek, M. (1998), *Greek Readers' Digests? Studies on a Selection of Subliterary Papyri* (Leiden).
Vergados, A. (2013), *The Homeric Hymn to Hermes: Introduction, Text, and Commentary* (Berlin).
Vergados, A. (2014), "Form and Function of Some Theban Resonances in Homer's *Iliad* and *Odyssey*," *TC* 6.2: 437–51.
Vodoklys, E. J. (1992), *Blame-Expression in the Epic Tradition* (New York and London).
von der Mühll, P. (1940), "Der Dichter der Odyssee," *Jahrbuch des Vereins Schweizer Gymnasiallehrer* 68: 80–103.
von Kamptz, H. (1982), *Homerische Personennamen* (Göttingen).
Wackernagel, K. (1877), "Zum homerischen Dual," *Kuhns Zeitschrift* 23: 302–10 (= 1953: *Kleine Schriften* [Göttingen]: 538–46).
Walker, H. J. (2016), "Horse Riders and Chariot Drivers," in P. A. Johnston, A. Mastrocinque, and S. Papaioannou (eds.), *Animals in Greek and Roman Religion and Myth* (Newcastle upon Tyne): 309–33.
Walsh, T. (2005), *Fighting Words and Feuding Words: Studies in the Semantics of Anger in Homeric Poetry* (Lanham, MD).
Wathelet, P. (1989), "Rhésos ou la quête de l'immortalité," *Kernos* 2: 213–31.
Wehr, O. (2015), *Die Ilias und Argos. Ein Beitrag zur homerischen Frage* (Frankfurt).
Welcker, F. G. (1835–49, vol. 2: 1865²), *Der epische Cyclus, oder die homerischen Dichter*, 2 vols. (Bonn).
Wessner, P. (1931), *Scholia in Iuvenalem vetustiora* (Leipzig).
West, M. L. (1978), *Hesiod: Works and Days. Edited with Prolegomena and Commentary* (Oxford).
West, M. L. (1988), "The Rise of the Greek Epic," *JHS* 108: 151–72 (= 2011b: 35–73).
West, M. L. (1997), *The East Face of Helicon: West Asiatic Elements in Greek Poetry and Myth* (Oxford).
West, M. L. (2001), *Studies in the Text and Transmission of the* Iliad (Munich and Leipzig).
West, M. L. (2002), "'Eumelos': A Corinthian Epic Cycle?," *JHS* 122: 109–33 (= 2011b: 353–91).
West, M. L. (2003a), *Greek Epic Fragments: From the Seventh to the Fifth Centuries* BC (Cambridge, MA, and London).
West, M. L. (2003b), "*Iliad* and *Aethiopis*," *CQ* 53: 1–14 (= 2011b: 242–64).
West, M. L. (2005), "*Odyssey* and *Argonautica*," *CQ* 55: 39–64 (= 2011b: 277–312).
West, M. L. (2006), "Archilochus and Telephos," *ZPE* 156: 11–17 (= 2013b: 6–16).
West, M. L. (2007), *Indo-European Poetry and Myth* (Oxford).
West, M. L. (2011a), *The Making of the* Iliad*: Disquisition and Analytical Commentary* (Oxford).
West, M. L. (2011b), *Hellenica: Selected Papers on Greek Literature and Thought*, vol. I: *Epic* (Oxford).
West, M. L. (2012), "Towards a Chronology of Early Greek Epic," in Andersen and Haug: 224–41.
West, M. L. (2013a), *The Epic Cycle. A Commentary on the Lost Troy Epics* (Oxford).
West, M. L. (2013b), *Hellenica: Selected Papers on Greek Literature and Thought*, vol. II: *Lyric and Drama* (Oxford).
West, M. L. (2014), *The Making of the* Odyssey (Oxford).

West, M. L. (2015), "The Formation of the Epic Cycle," in Fantuzzi and Tsagalis (2015b): 96–107.
West, M. L. (2017), *Homerus: Odyssea* (Berlin).
West, S. R. (1967), *The Ptolemaic Papyri of Homer* (Cologne and Opladen).
West, S. R. (1981), "An Alternative Nostos for Odysseus," *LCM* 6: 169–75.
West, S. R. (1988), "The Transmission of the Text," "Books I–IV," in Heubeck, West, and Hainsworth: 33–48, 51–245.
West, S. R. (1989), "Laertes Revisited," *PCPS* 35: 113–43.
Whallon, W. (2000), "How the Shroud of Laertes Became the Robe of Odysseus," *CQ* 50.2: 331–7.
Whitman, C. H. (1958), *Homer and the Heroic Tradition* (Cambridge, MA).
Wilamowitz-Moellendorff, U. von (1884), *Homerische Untersuchungen* (Berlin).
Wilamowitz-Moellendorff, U. von (1916), *Die Ilias und Homer* (Berlin).
Wilamowitz-Moellendorff, U. von (1925), *Die griechische Heldensage* (Berlin).
Wilce, J. M. (2009), *Crying Shame: Metaculture, Modernity, and the Exaggerated Death* (Malden, MA).
Willcock, M. M. (1964), "Mythological Paradeigma in the *Iliad*," *CQ* 58: 141–54.
Willcock, M. M. (1977), "Ad Hoc Invention in the *Iliad*," *HSCP* 81: 41–53.
Willcock, M. M. (1978–84), *The* Iliad *of Homer*, 2 vols. (London).
Willcock, M. M. (1983), "Antilochos in the *Iliad*," in *Mélanges E. Delebecque* (Aix-en-Provence and Marseilles): 477–85.
Willcock, M. M. (1989), "The Poet of the *Doloneia*" (Review of G. Danek, *Studien zur Dolonie*, 1988), *CR* 39.2: 178–80.
Willcock, M. M. (1997), "Neoanalysis," in Morris and Powell: 174–89.
Willcock, M. M. (2002), "Menelaus in the *Iliad*," in Reichel and Rengakos: 221–9.
Wilson, D. F. (2002), *Ransom, Revenge, and Heroic Identity in the* Iliad (Cambridge).
Witte, W. (1908), *Studien zu Homer* (Frankfurt).
Wood, C. P. (2022), "Formular Mutation and the Oral Character of the Cyclic 'Thebaid'," *YAGE* 6: 51–68.
Zielinski, T. (1899–1901), "Die Behandlung gleichzeitiger Ereignisse im antiken Epos," *Philologus Suppl.* 8: 407–49.
Zirkle, C. (1936), "Animals Impregnated by the Wind," *Isis* 25.1: 95–130.

General Index

Achaean Wall 42–3, 70–2, 74, 79–80, 94, 98–9, 148, 154, 169, 188, 203 n. 64, 292 with n. 66
Achilles 1, 6 with n. 26, 14 n. 68, 20, 22 with n. 114, 23–4, 26–7, 29, 31, 34 with nn. 57–9, 36, 40–1, 45–54, 56–8, 60 n. 222, 62–5, 68–71, 74–6, 79–86, 88–94, 96–9, 101–2, 104–11, 113–15, 118–23, 129, 132–3, 136–7, 139–40, 144, 148–9, 156, 158 n. 155, 161–7, 169–76, 181–3, 185 with nn. 99–100, 188, 190, 193–6, 200–4, 211–12, 216 n. 7, 222–3, 225 with n. 66, 228–9, 232–4, 238–40, 242–3, 245–6, 255 n. 16, 259–61, 263 n. 64, 265–6, 270–3, 280–7, 290 n. 60, 294–6, 298–300
actorial motivation 5
adaptation 5–7, 14, 60, 63, 67 n. 6, 81 n. 70, 167 n. 30, 277, 293–5
adharma 260 n. 50
adjusted flexibility 259 n. 45
aemulatio 40
Aeneas 22, 25, 27, 31, 57 n. 205, 73 n. 32, 76 n. 51, 91 n. 108, 98, 103 n. 1, 106 n. 15, 108 with n. 25, 110 n. 33, 112–15, 117–18, 120, 122–5, 198 n. 40, 212, 242, 256 n. 19, 261, 264, 266–70
Agamemnon 3, 20, 23–5, 29, 34 n. 59, 36, 40, 42–4, 47–8, 56, 69, 74–9, 83 n. 84, 87, 89 n. 100, 92–3, 95–8, 100, 105, 111 with n. 35, 122 n. 80, 125, 131–2, 134–9, 141–2, 144 with n. 77, 147 n. 93, 151–7, 163 n. 8, 166, 168–71, 178 n. 68, 181, 184–5, 187–99, 201–4, 207–8, 213, 228, 237 n. 107, 244, 254–5, 271 n. 110, 273, 283–4, 290 n. 60, 292, 295 n. 87, 298
Ajax (Locrian/Oileus) 31, 49, 57 n. 205, 77–9, 89 n. 100, 92–3, 95, 154–5, 188, 209 n. 95, 239 n. 114, 281 n. 26
Ajax (Telamonian) 6 n. 26, 31, 49, 53, 57 n. 205, 75–9, 83–4, 89 n. 100, 92–3, 95, 97–9, 105–7, 109, 111, 115 n. 58, 118, 120–2, 153–4, 164 n. 17, 170 n. 42, 172 n. 48, 174, 178, 185 n. 100, 188, 192–3, 196–8, 200, 202, 205 n. 69, 209 n. 95, 212, 220 n. 34, 232, 270 n. 106, 272 n. 113, 283–6, 300

allusion
 and backward references
  "chain" pattern 77–8
  narrative sequence in pairs of episodes 75
  reversal in paired episodes 79
 and forward references
  Achilles' horses 80–1
  isolation before defeat 80
  solidarity brings victory 80–2
  λόχος and πόλεμος *see* theme of ambush/*lokhos* and theme of regular warfare/*polemos*
 compressed indexing of a source by means of phraseology 43
 direct quotation of the source 40
 explicit or implicit references to other epic traditions 41
 inversion or reversal of the source 40
 parody of the source 41
 self-reflexive tropes 43
 splitting of the source 41
alternative *Odyssey(s)* 65
Amyntor 146–7
analepsis 112
androktasiai 67
Antilochus 5–6, 31, 37, 48, 50–2, 74 n. 41, 106 n. 15, 111, 115, 122–3, 158 n. 155, 164 n. 15, 204 n. 64, 260 n. 55, 281 n. 21
Apollo 30, 35, 47–9, 52, 56 n. 199, 70 n. 14, 83, 88 n. 95, 90 with n. 102, 100–2, 105–6, 109, 113, 117–18, 120 n. 75, 125, 146 n. 85, 156, 168 n. 34, 172–3, 189, 221 n. 49, 233, 257, 263 n. 64, 292 n. 66
applied song 32
Aristarchus 7 n. 30, 12, 73 n. 34, 146, 150 n. 117, 167–8, 176–9, 266
aristeia 15, 22, 67, 78, 82–3, 92, 97, 149, 164 n. 15, 171, 186, 197 n. 39, 206–7, 216–18, 222–3, 226–7, 229, 231–2, 236–8, 240–1, 260, 269, 281 n. 23, 287, 289, 294–5
arming 16 n. 84, 25–6, 57, 126, 133–4, 144–6, 148–9, 152 n. 126, 159–61, 193–4, 204, 249, 255 with n. 13, 298
Asteropaeus 84, 164 n. 16, 226 n. 73, 233–4, 279

GENERAL INDEX

Athena 31, 36–7, 41–2, 46–8, 74–5, 83, 89–91, 98, 100–2, 113 n. 47, 117–18, 129, 132, 144 n. 76, 149, 152, 166 with n. 27, 172–3, 179 n. 76, 182–3, 189, 191 n. 8, 206–7, 211–3, 215–7, 227–9, 231–3, 237 with n. 107, 241–2, 255 with n. 16, 257, 268, 281 n. 26, 283, 290 n. 56, 298
authenticity 1–3, 7–8, 12, 14–16, 19–22, 24–5, 28, 36 n. 77, 68 with n. 7, 74 n. 40, 81 n. 70, 96, 126, 297–8
authorship 4 n. 22, 6–8, 13, 61, 67 n. 6, 69, 125, 128, 130, 151, 159
Autolycus 146–8, 160
autonomy 13, 280–2

Bellerophon 22–3
book division 2–3

Calchas 23, 55 n. 192, 93, 95, 125, 165 n. 24, 232–3, 268
Cassandra 93, 96, 265 with n. 80, 272 n. 113, 281 n. 26, 289–90, 292
Catalogue of Ships 55–6, 64–5, 105–6, 195 n. 26
Catalogue of the Best of the Achaeans 105, 107, 109, 114, 118–21, 123
Catalogue of Trojans and Allies 105
character-text
 discrepant from narrator-text 5–6
chariot-driving 103–4, 122 n. 78
Chimaera 22
Chromius, 106 n. 15, 108, 114, 124 n. 89
citation 13, 18, 37 n. 79, 40, 47–9, 55, 64, 66, 82 n. 81, 91, 95–6, 191, 235 n. 103, 275, 281 n. 26, 297
clothing 5, 16 with n. 84, 25–6, 57, 126, 133–7, 139 n. 41, 141 n. 55, 143–4, 146 n. 84, 149, 161, 298
cohesion 13, 54, 56–7, 75, 244 n. 1
competitive impulse 10 n. 49
complexity of conception 92 with n. 110
Coroebus 27, 164, 219–20, 260–1, 264–7, 275–7, 281–2, 286–93, 296, 300
crystallization 7 n. 30, 60, 280
Cyclic/cyclic 1 n. 1, 5, 9–10, 12, 15, 19, 27, 29, 36, 38–9, 42 n. 114, 63 with n. 241, 65–6, 165 n. 21, 175 with n. 55, 187, 197, 218 n. 19, 220, 225–6, 229–30, 232–3, 236, 238 with n. 108, 240–1, 243, 260–1, 270, 272 n. 115, 274–5, 278–80, 282, 287–9, 292–4, 296, 299
cyclic impulse 9 n. 42
cyclic tinge 9–10, 66, 243

Dares 114
Demodocus 12, 29–32, 294
dharma 260 with n. 50
diffusion 28, 34–5, 38, 60–1, 63, 297
Diomedes 2–4, 13 n. 67, 15, 17–27, 30–1, 36, 38, 41–3, 56, 58 nn. 205 and 208, 69, 71–87, 89–93, 96–104, 106–12, 114–18, 120–5, 132, 134, 138–41, 144–6, 148–9, 152, 155–6, 158–68, 170–2, 175, 177, 179–80, 182, 185–6, 188–90, 193 n. 16, 197–8, 200, 202–17, 220 with n. 34, 222, 227–9, 231 with n. 86, 233, 237–9, 241–3, 255–8, 261–7, 269–71, 274–5, 280–8, 290–3, 295–6, 298–300
Diores 101
direction of allusion/flow/influence/transference 36, 51–2, 63, 94 with n. 112, 147 n. 95, 244 n. 1, 289
divine will 28, 31
Dolon 2–3, 21 n. 107, 56–8, 71, 74 n. 37, 77, 80–1, 83–6, 88–91, 93, 95–6, 99, 102 with n. 132, 109, 115 n. 58, 121 n. 75, 129–32, 134, 139–40, 142–45, 148–50, 156 n. 145, 160 n. 161, 166–8, 170 n. 42, 175, 178–81, 183–5, 187, 189, 203, 205–6, 208–11, 213, 216 n. 7, 228 n. 80, 242–3, 245, 255–6, 260, 262 with n. 63, 264–5, 268–73, 295 with n. 86, 298–9
duel(s) 21 n. 107, 47, 67, 69 with n. 11, 76 n. 51, 91–2, 98–9, 136–7, 158, 163–4, 176, 182, 194, 197–8, 241 n. 131, 263 n. 64

Echemmon 106 n. 15, 108, 114, 124 n. 89
Einzellied 11, 13–4
embedded songs 28, 32
entextualization 25, 28, 54 with n. 186, 56, 297
Epic Cycle
 Cypria 14 n. 68, 35–6, 40–1, 58 n. 205, 64–5, 76 n. 50, 78–9, 81 n. 72, 99, 163 n. 8, 165 with nn. 21 and 24, 175–6, 190–2, 194–9, 202, 207 with nn. 84–5, 223 n. 61, 260 n. 55, 279, 281 n. 23, 285, 288 n. 49
 Aethiopis 12, 48–54, 58 n. 206, 62, 64, 121 with n. 77, 164 with n. 15, 218 n. 19, 222, 226–7, 229, 238 n. 108, 263 n. 64, 279, 281 with n. 21, 284–6, 289, 295–6, 300
 Ilias parva 12–13, 32 with n. 36, 62, 70 nn. 15–18, 81 n. 73, 99–100, 143, 164 with n. 15, 175 n. 52, 185 n. 100, 208, 219–21, 232, 238 n. 108, 241, 261, 263 n. 64, 265–6, 269–72, 274–6, 279, 281–9, 291–4, 296, 300
 Iliou persis 12, 62, 70 n. 18, 164, 175 n. 52, 261, 279, 281–2, 288–9, 292 with n. 67

GENERAL INDEX 323

Nosti 29, 32 with n. 36, 36, 40 with n. 103, 44–5, 100 n. 129, 279
Telegonia 279
epichoric 65
Epipolesis 78, 100, 199 n. 50
Eumelus 90, 104–9, 113–14, 117–18, 120–3, 221 n. 49, 239 n. 119, 278 n. 4
Euryalus 27, 145, 244 with n. 3, 260–1, 266–75, 278, 282
Eurypylus 27, 158, 164 with n. 15, 220, 222–3, 226–7, 229, 233, 235–6, 238–9, 263 n. 64, 279–82, 286–7, 289, 292–3, 296
evaluation 32, 46 n. 138, 56, 58, 66, 68, 96, 100, 106, 124, 196 n. 31, 214, 234, 239 n. 119, 282
event-list 4
evolution 3–10, 18–19, 24–5, 27–8, 66, 85, 161, 293, 298–9

fable 85–6
Faktenkanon 1 n. 4, 4, 9, 19 with n. 97, 60, 172, 211
fate 6, 28, 30–2, 41, 45, 58, 63–4, 80–1, 89, 91, 100, 102, 108 n. 24, 140, 212 n. 112, 242–3, 253, 262, 270, 273
Fenik's Law 21 n. 110
fixity 1 with nn. 3 and 5, 7 n. 29, 9, 19, 33, 66 n. 254
flashback 22, 24–5
foreshadowing 22, 24–5, 36, 48, 81, 161, 165 n. 21
funeral games
  for Achilles 49, 52, 64, 121 with n. 77
  for Patroclus 19, 22, 25, 50, 52, 64, 90, 103 with n. 1, 106–9, 117–25

Ganymedes 112–13, 115 n. 57, 122
generic/genre 28, 32–3, 38, 142 n. 62, 241, 297

Hector 6, 15, 24–7, 31–2, 38, 45–6, 48–53, 56–8, 64, 69 with nn. 11–12, 71–4, 76 nn. 51–2, 79–86, 88–99, 101–2, 108–11, 113 nn. 44 and 46, 121 n. 75, 125, 132–3, 136–7, 139–40, 143–4, 148 n. 104, 152, 154–6, 161–89, 192–214, 216 n. 7, 220, 225, 228–9, 233–4, 240–4, 246, 255, 258, 261–2, 264, 266–8, 271–3, 280–2, 286, 289–90, 294–300
Hector-phase/Hector-version 26, 162, 166, 171, 175, 184 n. 96, 186–7, 195, 197–9, 207, 209–11, 213–14, 242, 244, 290, 299
Nyktegersia
  Brothers deliberating 191–2
  Brothers devising a plan 192–3
  Doubting a hero 197–9
  Fear in front of grave danger 193–4
  Placing the council 203–4
  Plan finalized 200–2
  Praying before undertaking a difficult task 206–7
  Seeking advice about the implementation of the plan 195–7
  Selecting the protagonists 202–3
  Sleeplessness caused by a pressing need 190–1
  Summoning the leaders 194–5
  The arming scene 95, 134, 141 n. 53, 144–6, 148–51, 153, 158–61, 204–6, 274
The *Doloneia* proper
  Dedicating the spolia 213
  Dolon in the Hector-version 209–11
  Mission aborted 189, 211–13
  The disclosure of information 211, 267–8
  The two-mission motif 208–9
Hera 31, 40–1, 91 n. 108, 149, 166, 215–16, 227–9, 232–4, 237 with n. 107, 254, 268
Heracles 30, 32 with n. 36, 36–7, 39 with nn. 94–5, 62 with n. 237, 79 n. 63, 113–14, 169 n. 39, 194 n. 24, 223, 232, 238, 241, 265 n. 82, 278 with n. 4, 283
Hippocoon 101, 117, 185–6, 257–8, 274–5
hoplon krisis 283–4
horses
  of Achilles 53 with n. 182, 58 with n. 211, 80–1, 83, 85–6, 88 with nn. 95 and 99, 96, 102 with n. 135, 104–10, 114–15, 118–21, 140, 166, 181, 185, 211 n. 106, 216 n. 7, 239–40, 242–3, 272, 298
  of Aeneas 22, 25, 73 n. 32, 98, 103 n. 1, 108 with n. 25, 110 n. 33, 110 n. 33, 112–15, 118, 120, 122–5
  of Diomedes 83, 90, 104 n. 6, 106–7, 112, 114–15, 117–18, 120–1
  of Rhesus 14–5, 17–9, 22, 25, 57, 65, 69, 73 n. 32, 81 with n. 70, 83, 90, 94, 99–101, 103 with n. 1, 107, 109–11, 114–17, 124–5, 129, 145, 160, 171 with n. 43, 174 n. 51, 205, 213, 215, 217 n. 9, 231 with n. 86, 233–4, 237–41, 243, 245, 256 with n. 20, 261–3, 265 n. 82, 267–9, 273–5, 288, 290 with n. 59, 295 with n. 86, 298–9
Hypnos 5, 50 n. 157

Idaeus 45, 47
Ilus 45, 177
immortalization 5
inauthenticity 3, 11–12, 18–23, 28, 81 n. 70, 126
indexical potential of time 28, 35

324 GENERAL INDEX

indexing 43, 59, 64, 66
interpolation 19, 23, 25, 39, 67–8, 103, 288 n. 49, 293
intertextuality 18–19, 30, 39 n. 89, 59, 65 n. 253, 193, 196
intratextual, intratextuality
   backward 21, 24–5, 39, 70, 72, 75, 84, 96, 298
   explicit 23, 41, 185
   forward 21, 24–5, 39, 68, 70, 72, 80, 84, 86, 91 n. 108, 298
   implicit 25, 41, 70–1, 298
   verbal 24–5, 87–91

lament/lamentation 14 n. 68, 32, 49, 120, 175–6, 185–6, 195 n. 26, 198 n. 40, 253–4, 256–8
Laomedon 37 n. 83, 112–14, 233 n. 98, 265 n. 82, 292 n. 66
leopard 73 n. 34, 136 with nn. 26–7, 137–8
line of development *see* direction of allusion/flow/influence/transference
linos 32
lion 41, 84–6, 135, 137–41
Lycomedes 154, 203 n. 64, 220, 293

Mahābhārata
   and Aśvatthāman 245, 247, 252–8, 292
   and Dhṛṣṭadyumna 245, 252, 256
   and Duryodhana 245, 259, 261
   and Kṛpa and Kṛtavarman 245, 249, 253–6, 258, 292
   and the *Aeneid* 260–75
   and the *Doloneia* 245–60
   and the Kauravas 245–6, 260 with n. 49
   and the Pāṇḍavas 245, 252, 256, 260
   and Yudhiṣṭhira 253, 256–8
maidens' choral song 32
maiden's song 32–3
markedness 24 n. 127, 40, 48–9, 134 n. 22
meaningfulness 40, 48–50, 134 n. 22, 140
Meges 77–9, 155, 188, 220, 293
*Meleagris 32, 39, 61
Memnon 5–6, 14 n. 68, 37, 41 n. 106, 45, 48, 50–3, 111, 123 n. 87, 164 with nn. 15–16, 222, 226–7, 229, 235–6, 238 with nn. 108–9, 260 n. 55, 262 n. 64, 279–82, 286, 289, 295 n. 86
*Memnonis 5–6, 14 n. 68, 32 with n. 36, 36, 38, 41 n. 106, 48–54, 64, 99 n. 124, 121, 212 n. 112, 260 n. 55
Menelaus 20, 31, 35, 49, 55–6, 74 with n. 41, 76–9, 83, 87–8, 91–3, 95, 104, 106 n. 15, 123 n. 82, 131–2, 134, 136–40, 144 with n. 77, 151–6, 159–60, 163 n. 8, 165–6, 168, 171 n. 44, 178 n. 68, 182–3, 187–9, 191–9, 202–3, 207 n. 84, 209 n. 95, 213, 233, 237 n. 107, 239 n. 114, 254–5, 281 n. 26, 283, 293
Meriones 73–4, 78, 93, 95, 123 n. 82, 144, 146–9, 159–61, 203–5, 209 n. 95, 255, 274
metacyclic 10
meta-epic 6, 34
metapoetic 21, 28–31, 38, 40, 44, 59, 61 n. 234, 121–2, 297
mirror-text 107, 120, 123
misdirection 71–2
mnesterophonia 33, 288 n. 52
Monro's Law 123
moonlight 145 with n. 78, 270–2, 285
multiple correspondence 51
Muse/Muses 29–30, 33–4, 36–7, 49, 105, 214, 215, 218 with n. 15, 221–2, 238–9, 258 n. 42, 264 n. 69
Mythographus Homericus 26, 177 n. 65, 217 n. 8, 221–3, 225, 227, 230 with n. 83, 235–6
mythological reference 25, 28, 59 with n. 220, 61–2, 65, 297

narrative inconsistency 5, 48–9, 192, 200–1, 295 n. 86
narrator-text *see* character-text
nekyia/-ai 28, 32, 165 n. 21
Neoanalysis, neoanalysts 5–6, 9 n. 40, 14–15, 18–19, 24–5, 27–8, 38–40, 45, 48, 51–2, 60, 66, 192, 261, 275, 297–8
Neoptolemus 27, 164 with n. 15, 175 n. 52, 219–23, 229, 238 n. 109, 280–2, 286–7, 291–3, 296, 300
Nestor 14 n. 68, 21, 32, 35, 43–4, 47–8, 50, 55, 58 n. 209, 61–2, 73–5, 77–80, 87, 93, 97–8, 100, 108–9, 114–15, 123 n. 82, 132, 134, 137–8, 140 n. 51, 148, 151–5, 157, 160, 163 n. 6, 166–8, 171, 173–4, 177–80, 185 n. 100, 187–8, 192–204, 209 n. 96, 213, 216 n. 7, 245, 254–5, 268, 271 n. 110, 273, 284 n. 34, 295 n. 86
Nisus 27, 145, 244 with n. 3, 260–1, 266–75, 278, 282
notional cycle 9–10, 179 with n. 81, 261, 275, 278–9
Nyktegersia see Hector-phase/Hector version

Odysseus 1–2, 5–6, 12–15, 17–18, 20, 22, 24–7, 29–38, 40–1, 43–4, 46, 49, 51, 53, 55–6, 58 with nn. 205–6 and 208, 60 n. 222, 65–6, 69, 71 n. 22, 73–9, 81–5, 89–91, 93, 96, 98–102, 109–11, 115–18, 120–1, 125, 132, 134, 137–51, 155–6, 158–63, 165 with nn. 21 and 23, 167–72, 174–5, 177–86, 188–9, 193–4, 198–200, 202–13, 215–17, 220, 222, 227–9, 231, 233, 237–9, 242–3, 255–6, 258, 261–7, 269–71, 274–5, 280–8, 290–3, 295–6, 298–300

Oenotropi 165 with n. 24, 207 n. 85
opposition in imitation/contrast imitation 40, 48–50, 79 with n. 63, 268–9, 271, 275, 292
oral epic tradition
  innovation 6, 9–10, 15–16, 40, 53, 110–11, 212 n. 109, 291
  stability 6, 9
Othryoneus 93, 95–6, 289–90
overconfidence 85–7, 102, 216 n. 7, 243, 298

paean 32
Palamedes 81, 165 with nn. 19 and 21, 199 n. 50, 207 with n. 85, 285
Palladium 27, 38 n. 86, 44, 70, 82, 99–100, 164, 208 with 89, 232, 241, 263 n. 64, 265–6, 269–72, 275–7, 280–2, 285 with n. 38, 287–8, 290–2, 300
parallelism 16, 51, 56–7, 126, 129 n. 11
para-narratives 32
pardalis see leopard
Patrocleia 121
Patroclus 3, 5–7, 19, 22–5, 29, 31, 36, 48–53, 58, 62 n. 237, 64, 69, 74 with n. 41, 79 n. 63, 80–4, 88–91, 94, 102–3, 107–8, 111, 117, 119–25, 136 n. 27, 144, 148–9, 158 with n. 155, 161, 164, 169–70, 173–4, 183, 185, 195 n. 28, 201 with n. 55, 212 n. 109, 240, 243 with n. 134, 246 n. 10, 260 n. 55, 298
Pegasus 23
Peiroos 75, 90 n. 102, 100–1, 220 n. 34
Peleus 53, 58 with n. 210, 105, 107 n. 19, 111, 114 n. 47, 119–20, 240
Penelope 5–6, 8, 12, 91 n. 108, 146, 212 with n. 110
Penthesileia 12, 164 with n. 15, 176 n. 62, 218 n. 19, 222, 226, 229, 235–6, 238 with nn. 108–9, 262–3, 279–82, 286, 289
Phemius 29 with n. 9, 33, 43, 55
Phoenix 34, 55, 57 n. 205, 61 with n. 235, 99, 146–8, 174, 178–9, 200–2
phorminx 34 with n. 59
poetic memory 28, 37 with n. 80
Polydamas 80, 154–5, 166–7, 220–1
Poseidon 31, 53 n. 183, 58 with n. 210, 91–3, 95, 107 n. 19, 114 nn. 47 and 49, 119–20, 224, 239–40, 292 n. 66
post-post-traditional singer 15 with n. 80
Priam 45–7, 51, 69 with n. 12, 71 n. 22, 91 n. 108, 113 n. 46, 133, 166, 176 n. 62, 195 n. 28, 220, 223 with n. 61, 225, 233 n. 98, 265 n. 80, 281 n. 26, 289–90
priamel 77
prismatic reflection 52

progressive iteration 21
proprietorial rights 8 with n. 36
proto-*Iliad*/*Urilias* 39, 52
proto-*Odyssey*/*Urodyssee* 39, 68 n. 7
ptocheia 44, 70, 164, 263 n. 64, 265, 280 with n. 16, 282, 285 n. 38, 288 n. 52, 291

Quellenforschung 15
quotation *see* citation

refraction of the model 52
repetition
  of phraseology 24 n. 125, 60, 68 n. 7, 70, 87–8, 184
  of scene/situation 21, 47, 95, 134 n. 23
Rhamnes 274–5
Rhesus
  and Eioneus 110, 184 n. 93, 218–21, 234, 239, 293
  and Euterpe 214–15, 218, 221 with n. 49, 239 n. 113, 264 with n. 69
  and motif of "late-arriving ally" 27, 93, 164 with nn. 15–16, 218 n. 19, 222–3, 226, 229, 234–6, 279–80, 286–90, 295 n. 85
  and Strymon 13 n. 67, 214–15, 218–19, 233 n. 98, 238–9, 264 with n. 69
Rhesus-story
  oracle version 15, 22, 26, 110, 214–16, 227–8, 230–4, 236–41, 243, 246 n. 7, 259, 261–70, 272–6, 278–80, 288–91, 295 with n. 86, 299–300
  Pindaric version 171, 215–19, 227, 229, 231–2, 234, 236–9, 255–6, 261 n. 57, 280, 289, 291 n. 62, 294–5

Sarpedon 5, 14 n. 68, 30–1, 45, 49–51, 58 n. 205, 107 n. 19, 154, 182–3, 197 n. 38, 212 with nn. 109 and 112, 238, 242, 260 n. 55, 295 n. 86
Scamander 15, 22, 65, 108, 110, 125, 215, 217 n. 9, 219 with nn. 28–9, 228, 231 with n. 91, 233–4, 237–40, 262–4, 295 with n. 86
self-consciousness 28 n. 3, 35–7, 59 n. 218
shaping 3–10, 14, 18–19, 24–5, 27–8, 54, 66–7, 85, 148, 161–2, 164 n. 16, 172, 184 n. 96, 199 n. 50, 211 n. 106, 214, 242, 275, 289, 294, 297–8
shepherd's songs 32
silence 2, 22–3, 29 n. 8, 68, 123–5, 201
Simoeis 228, 233–4
solidarity 24, 80–1, 270
South Slavic epic/song culture 4 n. 17, 10 n. 45, 33, 66 n. 254, 151 n. 21

326 GENERAL INDEX

speech/speeches 16, 21 n. 107, 23 n. 122, 25–6, 33–4, 44, 46, 49, 55–6, 62, 71 with n. 22, 75–6, 79 with n. 61, 87, 92–3, 98, 126–33, 152 n. 126, 156, 161, 164 n. 17, 167, 171 n. 44, 177, 186 n. 105, 190 n. 1, 193, 197, 201, 203, 233, 254, 256 n. 20, 258–9, 264 n. 68, 298
Spiegelungseffekt 118–23
spies/spy/spying 2 with nn. 10 and 12, 15, 24, 26, 43, 56–8, 70–1, 73–4, 76–80, 82–3, 85, 87, 93, 97, 99, 101–2, 110–11, 129, 132, 134, 138–41, 143–6, 148–50, 156 n. 145, 160, 162–4, 166–8, 170–2, 174–5, 178–82, 184–5, 192–4, 196, 198, 200–1, 202–6, 208–13, 214–17, 228 n. 80, 237, 241–3, 245, 255–6, 262, 264–9, 271 with n. 109, 273–4, 295, 298–9
stable skeleton of narrative 1, 60, 242
structural grammar 9 n. 29

tampering with sources 5
teichomachia 3, 98–9
text
 portability of/portable 34, 55 n. 193
texte spéculaire 86
Thanatos *see* Hypnos
Theban epic/tradition 10 n. 44, 36, 42–3, 61 with n. 230, 203 n. 64, 207 with nn. 81 and 86, 268 n. 92, 278–9
theme (of)
 Achilles' horses *see* horses, of Achilles
 ambush/*lokhos* 18, 21–2, 26, 68 n. 7, 70, 82, 95
 companionship 74 n. 44
 cunning intelligence/*metis* 68–9, 142 n. 67, 200, 283
 Diomedes' preeminence 78
 disguise 265–6
 first to strike 89
 Hector tries to acquire enemy's weapons 102
 Hector's gradual victory 96
 impenetrability of the divine armor 54
 isolation before defeat *see* allusion, forward references
 joint deliberation 191
 lone wolf 143 n. 74, 148 n. 105
 moonlight betrays a hero during night mission 271
 night/nocturnal attack/raid 13–14, 16, 20, 27, 70, 94, 99, 101, 125, 141, 145 n. 78, 150 n. 113, 170 n. 42, 188, 198 n. 46, 209, 244–6, 255–6, 258–60, 266, 269–70, 276–7, 294–6, 298–300

 participation in the war 79
 potential death of Hector 170 n. 42
 pride brought low 85
 regular warfare/*polemos* 78, 101, 188, 199, 246, 273
 second Achilles 97, 102, 172, 185, 202, 225 n. 66
 seduction 149
 siege of a walled city 79 n. 63
 special mission 280, 282
 strife 41
 travel 69
 treachery 265
 wrath of Achilles/*menis* 1, 47, 62–3, 76, 108 with n. 24, 122–3, 193 n. 19, 196 n. 30
Thetis 14 n. 68, 23, 34 n. 57, 47–9, 58, 76 n. 50, 88, 107 n. 19, 111, 114 n. 47, 120, 156, 158, 240
Thrace 11, 13–14, 124, 186, 214, 218, 222, 256
Thrasymedes 50, 73–4, 140 n. 51, 144, 148–9, 159–61, 203–5, 209 n. 95, 255, 274
traditional referentiality 60 with n. 222, 169
transference
 of episode(s)/scene(s) 9, 13–14, 49, 52, 281–2, 290, 292–3, 296
 of features/themes 24, 28, 33, 45, 51, 143, 196, 265, 267–8, 270–1, 275, 297
 of motifs 9 with n. 40, 15, 28, 39, 42, 45, 51–2, 54, 63 with n. 243, 193, 199, 208 n. 91, 212 n. 112, 244 n. 1, 272, 275, 286, 297
 of narrative structure/sequence 45, 48, 68, 91–6
 of phraseology 16, 21, 24, 28, 39, 45, 48, 67–8, 70, 88 with n. 94, 91, 102, 144, 147, 167, 171–2, 177, 254, 266, 297–8
Trojan Horse *see* Wooden Horse
Tros 112–15, 122

unity of composition 21, 24, 72
utterance 38, 43, 55–8, 131, 297

wedding song 32–3
whip 83, 90, 116–18, 125, 145, 160, 205
wolf 85–6, 143 with nn. 70 and 74, 264 n. 72
wolfskin 143–4, 150 n. 116, 205, 264 with n. 72
women's work songs 32
Wooden Horse 12, 31, 70, 104 n. 5, 121 n. 75, 125, 286, 294, 298
writing 1–2, 7 n. 29, 9, 16, 63

Zielinski 25–6, 126, 150–61, 299
Zitat 66

Index of Passages

GREEK

AELIAN
Varia Historia
  13.14 2 with n. 11, 13 n. 67

AESOP
Fabulae
  219 85

ANTHOLOGIA PALATINA
  11.442 13 n. 67

ANTISTHENES
Ajax
  1 284 n. 34
Odysseus
  1 284 n. 34

APOLLODORUS
Bibliotheca
  1.3.4 221 nn. 40 and 43–4
  2.5.9 113 n. 47
  3.12.8 233 n. 98
Epitome
  3.6 194 n. 23, 202
  3.7 199 n. 50
  3.26 64 n. 248
  3.32 70 n. 14
  4.4 227, 238 n. 110
  5.1 218 n. 19, 227, 263 n. 64
  5.3 218 n. 19, 222, 226–7
  5.8 81 n. 73, 232 n. 95
  5.9 263 n. 64
  5.9–10 232 n. 96, 241 n. 127, 281 n. 22
  5.11 218 n. 19
  5.11–12 263 n. 64
  5.11–13 287
  5.12 226
  5.12–13 227
  20.1 49

APOLLODORUS OF ATHENS (*FGrHist*)
  244 F 146 221 n. 40

APOLLONIUS RHODIUS
  1.1015–52 265 n. 77

ARCHILOCHUS (*IEG*)
  frs. 172–81 86

ARISTOPHANES
Ecclesiazusae
  1029 285 n. 39

ARISTOTLE
Historia Animalium
  606b 136 n. 26
  612b10 150 n. 116
Poetics
  1454b30 3 n. 14
  1455a2 3 n. 14
  1459b4–7 288 n. 48
  1459b26–8 150 n. 117
  1462b 11
Rhetoric
  1417a13 3 n. 14

BACCHYLIDES
  3.97–8 8 n. 36
  13.114–20 79 n. 63, 163 n. 8

CLEMENT
Stromateis
  1.104.1 176 n. 57

CONON
  4 219 n. 22
  34 285 n. 39

DEMETRIUS OF SCEPSIS
  fr. 68 147 n. 89

DICTYS CRETENSIS
  2.45 219 n. 23
  3.15 176 n. 62

EPIC CYCLE
Thebais, Fragments (*GEF*)
  fr. 9 42 n. 114
  fr. 11 104 n. 11
Cypria, Summary
  ll. 110–12 191 n. 6
  ll. 110–17 194 n. 23
  ll. 111–13 196 n. 34
  ll. 111–21 78 n. 60
  ll. 118–19 194 with n. 23, 196 n. 32
  ll. 119–21 194 n. 23
  l. 145 64 n. 248
  ll. 152–3 35, 207 n. 84
  l. 154 79 n. 63, 163 n. 8

EPIC CYCLE (cont.)
  l. 166 207 n. 85
  ll. 125–6 176 n. 56
  ll. 125–8 281 n. 23
 Cypria, Fragments (GEF)
  frs. 16-17 (PEG) 199 n. 47
  fr. 20 (PEG) 176 n. 56
  fr. 25* 70 n. 14
  fr. 26 36, 165 n. 24
  fr. 27 81 n. 72, 165 n. 20, 207 n. 85
  fr. 30 81 n. 72
  fr. 31 175 n. 52
 Aethiopis, Summary
  ll. 175–6 218 n. 19, 226
  ll. 176–7 229
  l. 177 222, 226
  l. 185 218 n. 19
  ll. 185–6 53 n. 177, 226
  ll. 186–7 48, 281 n. 21
  l. 188 227
  ll. 188–9 48
  l. 189 48, 50, 229
  l. 191 50 n. 154
  ll. 191–2 48–9
  ll. 191–5 263 n. 64
  l. 193 49
  ll. 193–5 284 n. 34
  ll. 198–9 49 with n. 151
  l. 201 49
 Aethiopis, Fragments (GEF)
  fr. 3 49
 Ilias parva, Summary
  ll. 208–9 53 n. 184
  ll. 208–10 270 n. 106
  l. 211 70 n. 15
  ll. 211–12 241 n. 127, 281 n. 22
  ll. 211–13 81 n. 73
  ll. 211–15 241 n. 126
  l. 212 287
  ll. 212–14 164 n. 9
  ll. 213–14 263 n. 64
  ll. 213–16 183 n. 90
  ll. 217–18 164 n. 10, 281 n. 22
  ll. 217–21 287
  l. 219 218 n. 19, 226
  ll. 219–20 281 n. 23
  l. 220 222, 227, 229
  l. 221 263 n. 64
  ll. 224–5 143 n. 69
  ll. 224–7 70 n. 16, 164 n. 11, 208 n. 88
  ll. 224–9 81 n. 73, 287
  ll. 226–7 291
  ll. 228–9 38 n. 86, 70 n. 17, 82 n. 74,
    164 n. 12, 208 n. 89, 241 n. 127, 281 n. 22

  ll. 230–2 164 n. 13
  ll. 230–6 70 n. 18
 Ilias parva, Fragments (GEF)
  fr. 2 185 n. 100, 270 n. 106, 284 n. 34
  fr. 7 263 n. 64
  fr. 8 143 n. 69
  frs. 8–10 208 n. 88
  fr. 9 143 n. 69
  fr. 11 99 n. 126, 145 n. 78, 208 n. 89, 270–1,
    285 n. 37
  fr. 14 176 n. 57, 272 with n. 113
  fr. 15 293 n. 72
  fr. 16 293 n. 73
  fr. 17 293 n. 81
  fr. 21 220, 293 n. 75
  fr. 22 293 n. 74
  fr. 23 219–20, 293 n. 76
  fr. 24 220 n. 33, 265 n. 80,
    281 nn. 23 and 26, 286–8, 290–1,
    293 n. 77
  fr. 26 293 n. 78
  fr. 27 293 n. 79
  fr. 28 293 n. 80
  fr. 29.1–5 175 n. 52
  fr. dub. 32 (PEG) 284 n. 34
  P. Ryl. 22 218 n. 19, 226, 265 n. 78,
    281 n. 23, 287–8, 290–1
 Iliou persis, Summary
  ll. 241–5 70 n. 18
  l. 268 175 n. 52
 Nosti, Summary
  ll. 279–80 191 n. 8
  ll. 301–2 36

EPIC FRAGMENTS OF UNKNOWN
  AUTHORS
 Minyas
  fr. 7* 37 n. 78

EUDOCIA
 Violarium
  920 233 n. 98

EURIPIDES
 Fragments (TrGF)
 Philoctetes
  test. iv c [c] 81 n. 73

[EURIPIDES]
 Rhesus
  346–8 218 n. 16, 221 n. 47
  393 221
  399–403 225 nn. 70–1, 290 n. 60
  406–11 289
  407–11 225 n. 67
  408–11 289 n. 53
  418–19 267 n. 88

426–8 225 n. 66
426–33 225 n. 68
426–42 241 n. 131
444–6 216 n. 7
447–9 216 n. 7, 290 n. 57
461–2 284 n. 32
498–509 288 n. 52
501–2 288 n. 52
501–7 288 n. 52
501–9 288 n. 52
505–7 212 n. 112
538–9 288 n. 52
539 288 n. 52
539–41 288 n. 52, 290 nn. 55 and 57
580–1 211
585–641 231 n. 88
595–605 231 n. 88
595–607 212
595–641 231 n. 88
600 231 n. 88
600–4 231 n. 88
605–6 211
605–7 212 n. 112
607 212 with n. 112
622–3 256 n. 20
670–1 255 n. 17
710–19 288 n. 52
761 256 n. 27
761–9 256 n. 25
763–4 228 n. 80, 256 n. 23, 261 n. 58
769 256 n. 27
890–982 258 n. 42
931–3 225 n. 68

EUSTATHIUS
Commentarii ad Homeri Iliadem
6 13 n. 67
788.49–50 169 n. 38
813.54–6 181
817.27 221 n. 40
817.27–8 231 n. 86
822.19 285 n. 39

HELLANICUS (*EGM*)
fr. 26b 113 with n. 47
fr. 139 233 n. 98

HERACLES PONTICUS
fr. 111 221 n. 40

HERODOTUS
1.61.4–62.1 13 n. 67
1.62.4–63.1 13 n. 67
1.64.1 13 n. 67
2.116 3 n. 14, 82 n. 81
4.35.3 10 n. 46
7.114 233 n. 98
7.25 218 with n. 21

HESIOD
Opera
72–6 149
75 149
161–8 278–9
202–12 86
654 147 with n. 95
Theogony
209–10 169 n. 39
339–40 219 n. 26
573–84 149
576–7 149
984 45

[HESIOD] (M-W)
Catalogue
fr. 23a.27–30 36 n. 74
fr. 43a.61–4 39 n. 94
fr. 43a.64 113 n. 47
fr. 62 115 n. 57
fr. 148(b) 224
fr. 165.10 113 n. 47
fr. 280 37 n. 78

HESYCHIUS
δ 1881 285 n. 39

HIPPONAX (*IEG*)
fr. 72 263 n. 65

HOMER
Iliad
1.1 63
1.2 46
1.16 93
1.34–42 47 n. 141
1.35–52 35 n. 67
1.45 73 n. 34
1.106–8 125
1.149 135 n. 25
1.159 137 n. 30
1.165–6 46
1.194–5 227
1.227 82 n. 82
1.240–4 48
1.245 47–8
1.249 31
1.264–7 224
1.284 97 n. 119
1.348–56 47 n. 141
1.366–92 156
1.375 93
1.396–407 34 n. 57
1.417 45
1.430–87 69
1.453 35 n. 67
1.472–4 32
1.604 32

HOMER (*cont.*)
2.11–15 55 n. 192
2.28–32 55 n. 192
2.42–6 134–5
2.43 135
2.48–52 190 n. 3
2.50–2 156–7
2.53–4 157
2.56 143 n. 68
2.72–4 157
2.73–5 195 n. 29
2.79–83 195 n. 29
2.84–6 157
2.87–93 157
2.101–8 135, 147 n. 93
2.156–81 228
2.173–206 75 n. 47
2.182 228 n. 76
2.182–7 142 n. 67
2.183 143 n. 68
2.217–19 58 n. 206
2.220–1 58 n. 206
2.260 199 n. 50
2.279–393 75 n. 48
2.287 106 n. 15
2.308–19 255 n. 14
2.317–30 55 n. 192
2.408 137 n. 30
2.422–9 56 n. 196
2.455–83 56 n. 199
2.494–760 56 n. 199, 105
2.505 61 n. 230
2.563–6 61 n. 230
2.572 61 n. 230
2.586 137 n. 30
2.594–600 29
2.721–5 64
2.723 64 n. 248
2.761–79 105, 107
2.763 106, 114, 239 n. 119
2.763–6 90
2.763–7 120
2.764 104
2.766–7 90 n. 105, 113, 117 n. 60
2.767 113 n. 45
2.768 283–4
2.768–9 97, 99, 120
2.769–70 118
2.772 123 n. 83
2.773–5 119, 122 n. 78
2.775–7 119
2.775–9 122 n. 78
2.778 104
2.783 30
2.816–77 56 n. 199, 105
2.844–5 75, 220 n. 34
3.2–7 56 n. 199
3.15 56 n. 199
3.16–19 73 n. 34
3.16–20 73 n. 34
3.17 73 n. 34
3.17–20 134 n. 21, 136
3.19 73 n. 34
3.23–6 137 n. 31
3.27 137
3.28 137
3.39–57 137 n. 30
3.125–8 34, 43
3.184–9 289
3.186 290
3.186–9 290 n. 60
3.204–24 207 n. 84
3.205–6 35
3.208 33
3.209–10 155 n. 143
3.212 33
3.329 97 n. 119
3.330–8 159 n. 157
3.330–9 160
3.339 159
4.8 61 n. 230
4.97 102 n. 132
4.127–40 183 n. 89
4.148 203 n. 60
4.153 203 n. 60
4.155–82 198 n. 40
4.178–81 203 n. 60
4.354 199 n. 50
4.364–421 108 n. 21
4.368–400 197 n. 39
4.372–99 61 n. 230
4.374 198 nn. 45–6
4.374–5 30
4.375 30, 42 n. 114
4.384–400 207
4.389–90 61 n. 230
4.390 42 n. 113
4.392–3 82 n. 82
4.401 61 n. 230
4.406 42, 61 n. 230
4.408 61 n. 230
4.422 78
4.223–421 78
4.446-5.37 158
4.457 178 n. 71
4.471–2 143 n. 74

INDEX OF PASSAGES 331

4.507–13 100
4.507–16 90 n. 102
4.514–16 100
4.520–38 75
4.527–31 100, 220 n. 34
4.530 101
4.532 101
4.532–5 100
4.535 101
5.1 3 n. 14
5.4–7 255 n. 16
5.8–26 108
5.25–6 114
5.49–50 233, 239 n. 114
5.49–58 198 n. 40
5.62 33
5.76–8 233, 239 n. 114
5.84 198 n. 45
5.95–105 35 n. 67
5.115–20 42
5.116–17 36
5.125–7 61 n. 230
5.144 220
5.152–5 239 n. 114
5.159–65 108
5.165 114
5.180–216 114 n. 51
5.221–3 124
5.221–38 256 n. 19
5.222 114–15
5.222–3 125
5.229 143
5.261 112 n. 41
5.261–2 112 n. 39
5.263–4 112 n. 40
5.266–7 114
5.267 198 n. 45
5.272 112–13
5.273 114 n. 48
5.279 35 n. 67
5.295–6 112 n. 41
5.297–327 108
5.303 169
5.337 146 n. 85
5.366 240 n. 121
5.394–7 91 n. 108
5.472–92 197 n. 38
5.561–75 198 n. 40
5.576–89 106 n. 15
5.601–4 172
5.638 30
5.640–2 113 n. 47
5.651 113 n. 47

5.662 212
5.671–3 31
5.674–5 31 n. 32, 212
5.676 212
5.699 45
5.711–845 228
5.711–846 237 n. 107
5.767–93 92 n. 111
5.768 240 n. 121
5.773–7 233
5.787 228
5.788–90 79 n. 63, 163 n. 8
5.800–8 61 n. 230
5.800–24 207
5.844–5 146 n. 85
5.855–9 37 n. 81
6.5 97 n. 119
6.5–11 75, 220 n. 34
6.37–65 198 n. 40
6.97 113 n. 45
6.119–36 98
6.188–9 82 n. 82
6.199 45
6.222–3 61 n. 230
6.279–80 152
6.279–81 154–5
6.286–312 152 n. 128
6.289–92 3 n. 14, 82 n. 81
6.311 3 n. 14
6.357–8 43
6.402–3 233
6.407–39 71 n. 22
6.447–9 220
6.456 33
6.466–81 175 n. 52
6.480 90
6.487 31
6.506–12 108 n. 24
6.523 197 n. 38
7.9 224
7.11–12 220
7.93 163 n. 6
7.96–102 193 with n. 20, 198 n. 40
7.109–19 193 n. 21, 203 n. 60
7.113–14 163 n. 8
7.132–56 62
7.142 143
7.161–9 56 n. 196
7.163 98
7.164 135 n. 25
7.171 202
7.193–4 153
7.206–7 153

HOMER (cont.)
7.211 97 n. 119
7.234 129 n. 11
7.260–2 212
7.268–72 212
7.270–1 172 n. 48
7.270–2 172
7.324 33
7.375 33
7.399–402 98
7.403–4 98
7.442 198 n. 45
7.444 169
7.452–3 292 n. 66
7.476–7 157
8.1–56 157
8.42 104
8.45 240 n. 121
8.47–52 292 n. 66
8.79–91 14 n. 68
8.80 80 n. 66
8.90–117 100 n. 128
8.91–5 98
8.99–158 98
8.104 115
8.105–8 114–15
8.106 115 n. 53
8.106–7 112 n. 41
8.108 112–13
8.117–21 108
8.167–70 212 n. 111
8.167–71 108
8.170 98
8.189 168
8.190 110 n. 33
8.191–5 74
8.191–7 102
8.194–5 108
8.197 102 n. 131
8.228 228
8.253–7 56 n. 196
8.261–6 56 n. 196
8.266–72 205 n. 69
8.309–11 172 with n. 48, 212
8.350–96 228
8.350–484 237 n. 107
8.354–6 166
8.355–6 294 n. 82
8.362 37
8.362–9 37
8.402–8 55 n. 192
8.416–22 55 n. 192
8.490–1 72
8.508–9 209 n. 97

8.510–11 209 with n. 98
8.510–16 209
8.517–22 71 n. 23
8.522 71
8.529–34 71 n. 23
8.532 71 with n. 22
8.532–3 71 n. 22
8.532–4 98–9
8.534 90
8.543–4 72 n. 24
8.553–63 209 n. 97
8.562 209 n. 97
8.564–5 72 n. 24
8.565 23 n. 122
9.32–44 98
9.32–49 197
9.50–1 111 n. 35
9.53 87
9.66–7 203
9.69 87, 202 n. 60
9.74–6 87
9.75–6 204 n. 66
9.75–9 204
9.76 72 with n. 26
9.78 204 n. 66
9.80–8 203
9.81 74
9.81–6 203 n. 64
9.85–7 204 n. 65
9.104 200–2
9.158–61 202 n. 60
9.160 202 n. 60
9.160–1 203 n. 60
9.168–70 202
9.182 179 n. 73
9.182–3 200–1
9.186 34
9.189–91 29, 34 with n. 58
9.192–8 200–1
9.193–4 34
9.232 72
9.232–3 72 n. 26
9.236–9 170
9.237 163
9.237–8 163
9.239 86, 143 n. 73
9.304 163
9.304–6 163 n. 5
9.305 86, 143 n. 73, 163 n. 7
9.351–6 163
9.352–5 79 n. 63, 163 n. 8, 174
9.355 163 n. 8
9.372 135 n. 25
9.388–92 202 n. 60

INDEX OF PASSAGES 333

9.392 203 n. 60
9.421–6 200
9.423 196 n. 30, 200–2
9.447 147 n. 91
9.448 147
9.524 35 n. 61
9.524–5 34, 55
9.527–8 34 n. 60
9.624–42 164 n. 17
9.651 163
9.655 163
9.659 33
9.673 43 n. 126
9.673–5 111 n. 35
9.697–709 164 n. 17, 190 n. 1
9.698–700 98
9.707–9 295 n. 87
9.708 103
9.708–9 98, 111 n. 35
9.710–11 76 n. 52, 111 n. 35
9.712–13 152
10.1–4 247
10.1–202 14
10.1–253 258
10.3 247
10.3–4 246
10.5 228 n. 79
10.5–10 247
10.11 247
10.12–16 247
10.17–20 93, 192 n. 12, 196 n. 30
10.18–19 196 n. 35
10.19 33, 196 n. 30, 200–2
10.19–20 195 n. 30
10.21 152 n. 125
10.21–4 134–5
10.23–4 135, 142 n. 62
10.24 152
10.25–8 137 n. 28
10.26–8 198 n. 40
10.27–8 191 n. 9
10.29–30 142 n. 62
10.29–31 134, 136
10.32–3 191 n. 7
10.34 151 n. 122
10.34–5 152
10.37 152 n. 126, 171 n. 44, 193 with n. 14
10.37–8 178 n. 68
10.37–41 193
10.39 171 n. 44
10.39–41 193
10.41 171 n. 44
10.43–4 87, 178 n. 68, 248
10.43–5 87, 204 n. 66

10.44 171 n. 44
10.45 171
10.45–6 93
10.46–52 168–70, 193 with n. 15
10.47 171 with n. 44
10.47–8 171
10.47–9 166, 216 n. 7, 294 n. 83
10.47–50 171 n. 44
10.47–52 174, 192 n. 13
10.48 166 n. 27
10.48–9 143, 169
10.50 171 with n. 43
10.50–2 166 n. 28
10.51 110
10.52 166 n. 27
10.53 197 n. 37
10.53–6 153
10.53–9 93
10.54–6 248
10.55–6 153 n. 138
10.62–3 153 n. 136
10.70 198
10.80–1 141 n. 60
10.89 198 n. 45
10.91 196
10.92 193
10.93 93, 95
10.98–9 267 n. 87
10.104–7 163 n. 6, 193
10.105–7 93
10.114–18 137
10.116 198
10.117 198
10.117–18 197 n. 36
10.121 197–8
10.123 199
10.124 151
10.129–30 199
10.131–4 138
10.133–4 142 n. 62
10.149 138, 142 n. 62, 145, 205 n. 67
10.152–4 271 n. 110
10.155–6 275
10.160 152 n. 125
10.164–7 203 n. 62
10.177–8 85, 134, 138, 142 n. 62
10.178 145, 205 n. 67
10.180 155
10.196 74
10.199–200 72
10.200 72 n. 29
10.203–579 14
10.204–6 194
10.204–10 173–4, 248

HOMER (cont.)
10.204–53 93
10.206 177–8
10.206–7 268
10.206–10 194, 268 n. 97
10.207–10 166–8
10.208–10 167 with n. 32, 177
10.212 82 n. 77
10.214–17 168, 194, 273
10.215–16 58 n. 209
10.220–6 99
10.222–4 145
10.222–6 202
10.224–6 93, 145 n. 81
10.226 115 n. 55
10.227–31 79, 209 n. 95, 258
10.227–32 99
10.229 74
10.234–40 163 n. 8
10.234–53 203 n. 61
10.235–9 202 n. 60
10.237–8 202 n. 60
10.237–40 203 n. 60
10.239 202 n. 60
10.240 203 n. 60
10.242–7 82, 202, 249
10.243 38 n. 85
10.244–5 206 n. 77
10.245 198 n. 45
10.247 145 n. 81, 207 n. 85
10.250 38
10.251–3 141 n. 60, 145 n. 78, 248, 271–2
10.252 272 n. 114
10.254 200
10.254–71 93, 249
10.255 21, 74
10.255–7 73–4, 140 n. 51
10.255–61 158
10.255–62 274
10.255–71 148 n. 102
10.256–8 205 n. 67
10.259–61 205 n. 67
10.260 73 n. 34, 158–9
10.261–5 146
10.266 147 n. 91
10.266–7 143
10.266–71 146
10.267 33, 85 n. 90, 146 n. 85
10.272–3 93, 200
10.274–6 251, 255 n. 15
10.275–6 228 n. 80
10.278–82 206 n. 76, 250, 290 n. 56
10.279 198 n. 45, 206

10.282 110 with n. 31, 168–70, 179 with nn. 75 and 78, 266
10.284–5 36
10.284–94 206, 250
10.289 166 n. 27
10.292 169
10.292–4 168
10.294 169
10.295–8 93
10.297–8 139 with n. 40, 141 n. 61, 250
10.299 156
10.299–312 156 n. 144
10.299–511 14
10.303–31 211 n. 106
10.305–6 81, 85, 102, 216 n. 7, 272 with n. 118
10.308 203
10.309–12 167 n. 31, 174
10.316 58 n. 206
10.322 81 n. 68
10.322–3 81, 85, 272 with n. 118
10.325–6 203
10.325–7 184
10.329 228 n. 79
10.329–31 228 n. 79
10.330 24, 88
10.330–1 81, 102, 216 n. 7, 272 with n. 118
10.331 88 with n. 99
10.333 149 n. 111
10.333–5 134, 148 n. 103, 205 n. 67
10.334 85, 264 n. 71
10.335 149–50
10.336–7 264 n. 75
10.339–40 271 n. 110
10.339–464 93
10.345 178 n. 70, 268
10.349–50 200
10.354–6 210
10.364 200
10.365–77 205 n. 70
10.366–7 250
10.366–8 251
10.367–8 88, 270–1
10.371–4 145
10.378–81 80, 140 n. 46
10.387 210 n. 99
10.388–9 184 n. 97, 210 n. 100
10.391 86, 211 n. 104
10.391–3 58, 80
10.391–9 184 n. 97
10.391–411 211 n. 106
10.392 81 n. 68
10.392–3 81 n. 68
10.401 88 n. 99

INDEX OF PASSAGES

10.401–4 298
10.402–4 120 n. 75
10.406–7 110, 167, 184 with n. 98
10.406–8 211
10.408 167
10.409–11 167–8, 177, 185
10.411 167
10.413–22 209
10.414–15 168 n. 35
10.414–16 178 n. 67, 184 n. 97
10.419–20 228 n. 80
10.420–1 168 n. 35, 228 n. 80
10.424–5 184 with n. 92, 209 n. 93
10.427–41 209 n. 94
10.434 124 n. 90, 178 with n. 69, 261 n. 58, 268
10.434–5 93, 184 n. 93
10.435 220
10.436 125, 239 n. 116
10.436–7 109, 125
10.436–41 222
10.437 125, 233 n. 98, 239 n. 117
10.440–1 295 n. 86
10.447–53 256 n. 20
10.447–57 140 n. 48
10.455–6 145, 205 n. 71
10.455–7 89
10.457 140 with n. 49
10.458 150 n. 114
10.458–9 205 n. 67
10.458–68 211
10.460–3 115 n. 58
10.466–7 84
10.467 141 n. 60
10.468–9 200, 264 n. 73
10.471 228 n. 80, 252, 267
10.474 252
10.475 101
10.478 89
10.479–81 252, 256 n. 20
10.482 250
10.482–3 251
10.483 252, 256 n. 24
10.483–4 100, 205 n. 72
10.484 145
10.485–6 139 n. 39
10.485–7 138 n. 38
10.487–8 108, 205 n. 72, 252
10.488 84
10.489–93 101
10.490–1 73 n. 30
10.490–3 84
10.494–5 252
10.494–6 100, 108, 205 n. 72

10.494–7 93
10.495 145, 220 n. 34
10.496 84, 274 n. 131
10.496–7 253
10.498 83 n. 84, 104 n. 6
10.498–9 101
10.498–501 101, 116
10.499–506 145 n. 82
10.500 205 n. 74
10.500–1 90, 118 n. 73, 145 n. 80
10.504–6 90
10.506 257
10.507–8 83, 228 n. 80
10.507–11 100
10.509–10 212
10.509–11 118 n. 72, 213 n. 114, 250
10.511 228 n. 80
10.512 228 nn. 76 and 80
10.512–13 90
10.513–14 101, 104 n. 6
10.514 240 n. 121
10.515 90
10.515–17 90
10.515–19 83, 100
10.516 205 n. 74
10.516–17 117
10.522–3 253, 258 n. 38
10.526–31 211
10.528 90
10.530 118 n. 73, 240 n. 121
10.535 109
10.541 290
10.541–2 213 n. 113, 253, 258 n. 44
10.544 43 n. 126
10.545–51 295 n. 86
10.547 109, 239 n. 118
10.547–50 109
10.550 171
10.561–3 178 n. 70
10.565 254, 258 n. 44, 290
10.566–9 115
10.567–8 115 n. 58
10.567–9 109
10.570 74 n. 37, 90
10.570–1 115 n. 58
10.575–9 84
10.577–8 200
11.1 23 n. 122, 224, 246 n. 10
11.10–14 23 n. 122
11.15–16 23 n. 122
11.15–46 149 n. 110
11.56–60 149 n. 110
11.72–3 143 n. 74
11.94 83 n. 84

HOMER (*cont.*)
11.109 83 n. 84
11.143 83 n. 84
11.146–7 89 n. 100
11.159–61 112 n. 41
11.179 83 n. 84
11.225–61 89 n. 100
11.292–5 139 n. 41
11.312–19 74
11.314–15 171
11.349–67 212
11.363 172 with n. 45
11.365–6 172 n. 49
11.369 99
11.379 99 n. 123
11.411–20 147
11.420–1 147
11.430 44, 144 n. 76, 298
11.471 81 n. 71
11.472–97 285 n. 42
11.517 21
11.604 212 n. 109
11.717–21 224
11.734 169
11.767–70 194 n. 23
11.794–5 14 n. 68
12.20 219 n. 25, 239 n. 114
12.20–2 234 n. 101
12.39 113 n. 45
12.41–9 139 n. 41
12.299–306 41
12.366–9 154
12.416 169
13.1–382 92 n. 109
13.24 104
13.43–4 93
13.46 154
13.52 93, 95
13.52–8 93
13.101–16 163 n. 8
13.105–6 79 n. 63
13.112–14 93
13.125–8 30
13.126–35 93
13.159–62 73
13.165–8 73 n. 33
13.168 73
13.202–3 89 nn. 100–1
13.215–38 93
13.235–7 93
13.249 147 n. 93
13.249–73 93
13.274–310 82 n. 82
13.275–94 93

13.276–7 82 n. 82
13.288 198 n. 45
13.295–7 93
13.304–62 93
13.366 169
13.363–82 93
13.365–7 289
13.366–7 290 n. 57
13.400–1 106 n. 15
13.477–9 204 n. 64
13.518 204 n. 64
13.541 204 n. 64
13.576 204 n. 64
13.650 74 n. 38
13.751–3 154
13.772 95 n. 115
13.792–4 164 n. 16, 226 n. 73
14.9–10 73–4
14.9–11 74 nn. 40 and 42
14.9–12 21 n. 108, 74 n. 40
14.11 73 n. 36
14.91 34
14.109–32 98
14.113–14 224
14.114–25 61 n. 230
14.124–5 224
14.153–362 237 n. 107
14.165–86 149
14.313–28 55 n. 192
14.315–27 41
14.379–81 98
14.402–8 73
14.433–9 233
14.443–4 239 n. 114
14.465–8 89 n. 100
14.493–507 89 n. 100
15.221 45
15.263–9 108 n. 24
15.271–80 139 n. 41
15.314–17 112 n. 41
15.347 90
15.390–4 158
15.455 220
15.468 73 n. 34
15.678–86 104 n. 6
15.722–3 79 n. 63, 163 n. 8
16.1–2 158 n. 155
16.1–3 51
16.34–7 14 n. 68
16.36–100 48
16.41–2 53 n. 181
16.51 14 n. 68
16.76 171 n. 44
16.109 84 n. 87

INDEX OF PASSAGES 337

16.130–44 53 n. 179
16.131–44 161 n. 164
16.149–51 104, 240 n. 122
16.152–3 107 n. 19
16.152–4 107 n. 19
16.179–83 33
16.208 169
16.247 82 n. 77
16.306 178 n. 71
16.306–27 50
16.321–7 74
16.339–41 89 n. 100
16.380 110 n. 33
16.380–1 107 n. 19
16.381 107 n. 19, 114 n. 47, 240 n. 125
16.383 110 n. 33
16.431–61 212 n. 112
16.450 14 n. 68
16.457 5
16.467–9 107 n. 19
16.480–5 49–50
16.666–83 14 n. 68
16.675 5
16.788–857 49
16.818–57 48
16.823–8 139 n. 41
16.826 84
16.828 84
16.860–1 102
16.866–7 53 n. 183
16.867 88 n. 99, 107 n. 19, 114 n. 47, 240 n. 125
17.13 90–1
17.21–2 139 n. 41
17.71–81 102
17.75–8 88 nn. 95 and 99
17.75–81 83
17.76–8 102, 120 n. 75
17.125 53 n. 180
17.126 89 n. 101
17.130 83
17.194–7 53 n. 178, 111 n. 36
17.210 148 n. 104
17.213–14 111 n. 36
17.240 95
17.242 95
17.281–3 139 n. 41
17.377–83 74 n. 41
17.400 103
17.400–1 104
17.426–40 81 n. 69
17.443 53 n. 183
17.443–4 114 n. 47, 240 n. 125

17.448–9 24, 88
17.448–50 53 n. 182
17.449–50 102
17.450 111 n. 36
17.472–3 88 n. 97, 111 n. 36
17.503–5 102 n. 133
17.540 90–1
17.685–705 74 n. 41
17.690 81 n. 71
17.693 111 n. 36
17.695–6 51
17.715–61 49
17.716 31
18.1–2 51, 158 n. 155
18.21 111 n. 36
18.26–7 14 n. 68
18.27 195 n. 28
18.30–1 49
18.35–71 14 n. 68, 49
18.39–49 56 n. 196
18.74–7 23
18.79 23
18.82–3 111 n. 36
18.84–5 53 n. 178
18.95–6 52 n. 172
18.96 14 n. 68
18.130–2 111 n. 36
18.133 88
18.151–64 49
18.203–31 255 n. 16
18.254–66 166
18.275 33
18.287 79 n. 63, 163 n. 8
18.318–22 86
18.333–5 89 n. 101
18.334–5 89 n. 100
18.335 111 n. 36
18.442–56 158
18.493 32 with n. 43
18.526 32
18.567 32 n. 42
18.569–72 32
18.610 240 n. 124
19.10–18 111 n. 36
19.146–53 169
19.150 169
19.287–300 49
19.315–37 49
19.367–83 111 n. 36
19.369–91 148 n. 104
19.374 240 n. 124
19.381 240 n. 124
19.398 240 n. 124
19.400 104, 240 n. 122

338 INDEX OF PASSAGES

HOMER (*cont.*)
19.408–17 104
19.420 104
20.28 79 n. 63
20.33–40 56 n. 199
20.40 233
20.68–74 56 n. 199
20.73–4 233
20.75 56 n. 199
20.112–55 237 n. 107
20.145–8 37 n. 83, 113 n. 47
20.147 37 n. 83
20.164–75 86
20.204 35
20.221–9 115 n. 57
20.224 61 n. 230
20.226–9 115 n. 57
20.246–7 206 n. 78
20.248–9 30
20.286 169
20.306 220
20.336 31
20.359 198 n. 45
20.376–8 172
20.438–54 172
20.449–54 172 with n. 46
20.481–2 89 n. 100
20.499–500 84
21.16 103
21.17–18 84
21.131 233 n. 98
21.139–83 164 n. 16
21.144–7 233
21.153 129 n. 11
21.155–6 226 n. 73
21.182 84, 164 n. 16
21.214–32 233
21.281 165
21.305–23 234
21.328–41 234
21.394–9 37 n. 81
21.441–57 37 n. 83
22.7–24 56 n. 199
22.22–4 108 n. 24
22.25–130 56 n. 199
22.56–77 170 n. 42
22.58–68 220
22.77–8 195 n. 28
22.99–104 80
22.99–108 167
22.104 86
22.111–22 80
22.131 56 n. 199
22.164 29 n. 14

22.206–7 88, 271 n. 107
22.208–13 14 n. 68
22.213–14 173
22.214–47 237 n. 107
22.226–305 172
22.245 90–1
22.258–9 111 n. 36
22.261 139 n. 45
22.262 139
22.289–95 73 with n. 33
22.322–3 53, 111 n. 36
22.322–63 48
22.327 89
22.337–54 71 n. 22
22.339–42 140
22.346–7 86
22.368–9 111 n. 36
22.351 71 n. 22
22.351–2 71 n. 22
22.352 71 n. 22
22.359–60 48
22.360 49
22.378–84 14 n. 68
22.379–84 173–4
22.380 166 n. 28
22.391–4 32
22.393 89
22.393–4 170 n. 41
22.396 89
22.396–404 102 n. 134
22.398 89
22.402–3 89, 140 with n. 50
22.405 140 with n. 50
22.408–11 220
22.416–28 186 n. 103
22.431–6 186 n. 103
22.433–5 170 n. 42
22.477–514 186 n. 103
23.6–11 120
23.16 113 n. 45
23.22–3 84
23.40–2 84
23.58–61 190 n. 2
23.78–81 36
23.80–1 36
23.110–897 49
23.178 258
23.233–8 91 n. 108
23.242 104
23.264 29 n. 14
23.272–86 119
23.276–8 120
23.277–8 53 n. 183, 114 n. 47, 240 n. 125
23.283 123 n. 83

INDEX OF PASSAGES   339

23.283–4 81 n. 69
23.287–538 98, 107 n. 18
23.288 120
23.289 106 n. 14, 120
23.291 115 n. 53
23.291–2 115
23.295 104
23.309–10 115
23.345–8 114 n. 49
23.346 61 n. 230
23.362–4 118 n. 71
23.378 115 n. 53
23.382 117 n. 63
23.382–400 116
23.383 90, 117 n. 61
23.385 117 nn. 64–5
23.387 118 n. 66
23.388 90, 118 n. 67
23.388–9 118 n. 68
23.389–90 118 n. 69
23.391 90 n. 104
23.391–2 118 n. 70
23.651–897 107 n. 18
23.679 61 n. 230
23.700–39 120
23.702 29 n. 14
23.798–825 120
23.811–25 98
23.826–9 64
24.39–45 86
24.234–7 289
24.265–8 45
24.281–508 45–7, 91 n. 108
24.322–7 45
24.347–8 45
24.349–51 45
24.437 45
24.461 45
24.465–7 45
24.468–9 45
24.475–6 45
24.477–9 46
24.486–506 46
24.507–12 46
24.550–1 220
24.591 258
24.605 73 n. 34
24.614–17 168
24.720–2 32
24.720–81 185, 258 n. 40
24.723–6 32 n. 46
24.725–45 186 n. 103
24.728–30 295 n. 84
24.728–31 170 n. 42

24.734–9 175 n. 52
24.736–8 175 with n. 53
24.748–59 186 n. 103
24.762–75 186 n. 103
24.778–81 69, 298
24.779–80 176 n. 62
24.804–5* 235
Odyssey
1.1 63
1.2 196 n. 31
1.4 46
1.29 36 n. 74
1.93 176
1.169–77 56 n. 196
1.179–89 56 n. 196
1.184 34
1.194–5 56 n. 196
1.285 176
1.298–300 57 n. 202
1.299 36 n. 74
1.301 36
1.325 29 n. 13
1.325–7 29
1.326–7 29 n. 16
1.338 29 n. 17
1.340–1 29
1.336 29 n. 13
1.346 29 n. 13
1.351–2 35, 55
1.421–7 190 n. 2
2.80 47–8
3.94–5 35, 55
3.95 196 n. 31
3.106 196 n. 31
3.110 22 n. 114, 123 n. 86
3.162–83 100 n. 129
3.186–7 35
3.193 57 n. 202
3.197 36 with n. 74
3.203–4 35, 57 n. 202
3.204 8, 55
3.261 169 n. 39
3.267–71 29 nn. 7 and 13
3.307 36 n. 74
3.313 36
3.337 171 with n. 44
4.17 29 n. 13, 32
4.17–18 29 n. 7
4.187–9 37
4.242–58 288 n. 52
4.244–6 143 n. 69
4.257 291
4.324–5 35
4.325 196 n. 31

HOMER (cont.)
  4.368–9 165 n. 22
  4.505 171 n. 44
  4.590 107 n. 19
  4.601–8 115 n. 58
  4.614 55 n. 192
  4.614–19 55 n. 192
  4.615 55 n. 192
  4.615–16 55 n. 192
  4.616 55 n. 192
  4.617 55 n. 192
  4.617–19 55 n. 192
  4.678 33
  4.777 33
  5.1 224
  5.61 32
  5.105 44
  5.309–12 38 n. 84
  5.312 165
  5.370–1 104 n. 6
  5.483 147
  5.487 147
  6.101 32
  6.130–6 41
  6.162 35
  6.252–3 46
  6.255–7.154 46–7, 91 n. 108
  6.260–1 46
  6.291–6 46
  6.317–20 46
  6.321–2 46
  7.20 46
  7.30 46
  7.49–50 46
  7.50–77 46
  7.78 46
  7.80 177
  7.137–8 46
  7.142–3 46
  7.145 46
  7.146–52 46
  7.154–5 46
  8.43 29 n. 13
  8.62 29 n. 13
  8.63–4 31
  8.73–4 30, 35
  8.73–82 29 n. 10
  8.74 8
  8.83 29 n. 13
  8.110–14 56 n. 196
  8.115–17 274 n. 129
  8.266–366 29 n. 11
  8.367 29 n. 13

  8.403–5 274
  8.471 29 n. 13
  8.475 29 n. 14
  8.479–81 29 n. 13
  8.483 29 n. 13
  8.487 29 n. 13
  8.489–91 31, 35
  8.492 57 n. 202
  8.492–3 31
  8.494 30
  8.496 30–1
  8.498 30
  8.500–20 29 n. 12
  8.521 29 n. 13
  8.539 29 n. 13
  8.580 8
  9.3–4 29 n. 13
  9.19–20 40 n. 104, 46
  9.263–6 57 n. 202
  10.221 32
  11.225–32 32 n. 36
  11.271–4 169 n. 37
  11.367 33
  11.441 36
  11.482–91 32 n. 36
  11.508–37 32 n. 36
  11.519–20 223
  11.522 32 n. 36, 235
  11.543–60 38 n. 84
  11.543–64 284 n. 36
  11.601–26 32 n. 36
  11.601–27 36–7
  11.617–26 36
  11.628–9 36
  11.630 36
  11.630–1 32 n. 36
  11.632–3 36
  12.70 40 with n. 104, 57 n. 202
  12.119–20 37 n. 81
  12.184 44 n. 127
  12.184–91 44 n. 128
  12.189–91 34
  12.219 147
  12.226–7 37 n. 81
  12.330–2 165 n. 22
  13.204 196 n. 31
  13.293 144 n. 76
  13.429–38 35 n. 67
  14.72–7 147
  14.131 33
  14.196–201 57 n. 202
  14.414–39 147
  14.457–8 141 n. 54

14.474 141 n. 60
14.475–7 141 n. 57
14.481 141 n. 52
14.483 141 n. 60
14.484–503 141 n. 58
14.485 141 n. 60
14.489 141 n. 56
14.494 141 n. 60
14.529 141 n. 53
14.530 141 n. 53
14.468–503 140, 142 with n. 67
14.482 142 n. 62
14.495 143 n. 68
14.500–1 143 n. 68
15.15 225
15.312 196 n. 31
16.64 196 n. 31
16.118–19 159
16.151 196 n. 31
16.456 35 n. 67
17.26–9 147
17.46–51 56 n. 196
17.385 29 n. 13
17.518–21 30
19.221–48 142
19.225–8 142 n. 65
19.246–7 142 n. 64
19.357 45 n. 135
19.393–466 148 n. 100
13.394–466 147 with n. 93
19.395–6 148
19.443 147
19.452 147
19.491 45 n. 135
19.518–22 30
19.547 32
19.577 73 n. 34
20.120–1 137 n. 32
20.134 45 n. 135
20.287–302 35 n. 67
21.75 73 n. 34
21.233 159 n. 159
21.381 45 n. 135
21.406–9 30
22.2 73 n. 34, 159 n. 159
22.41 45 n. 135
22.290–1 35 n. 67
22.345–9 43
22.347 33
22.348–9 29
23.124–5 30
23.133–6 32–3
23.143–52 32

23.296 12 with n. 57
24.36–92 38 n. 84
24.37–92 32 n. 36
24.47–62 49 with n. 151
24.60–1 32
24.71–9 22 n. 114, 123 n. 86
24.76–9 51
24.85–92 49
24.115–17 199 n. 47
24.115–20 194 n. 25
24.121–90 6
24.196–8 43
24.196–202 32 n. 36
24.197 29
24.197–8 8, 43
24.200 8, 29, 40

HOMERIC HYMNS
Hermes
   178 146 n. 85
   283–5 146 n. 85
Aphrodite
   58–65 149
   202–40 41
   217 104 n. 8
Ares
   2 45 n. 134

MARSYAS II (*FGRHIST*)
   136 F 7 221–2, 238 n. 112

NICANDER
Theriaca
   196–7 150 n. 115

PANYASSIS
Heracleia
   fr. 17 37 n. 78

PARTHENIUS
Narrationes Amatoriae
   36 241 n. 131
   36.1 225 nn. 66 and 69
   36.4 225 n. 70

PAUSANIAS
   8.25.5–6 114 n. 49
   10.27.1 219–20, 287–8

PAUSANIAS ATTICUS
   δ 14 285 n. 39

PHOTIUS
Lexicon
   δ 637 285 n. 39

PINDAR
Olympians
   9.48–9 10 n. 46

342 INDEX OF PASSAGES

PINDAR (*cont.*)
   Pythians
      1.53 81 n. 73
   Nemeans
      4.26–30 39 n. 94
      8.26 284 n. 34
      10.64 169 n. 39
   Isthmians
      6.31–3 39 n. 94
      8.26–48 114 n. 47
Fragments (S-M)
   262 214–15, 221, 294 n. 83
PISANDER (*EGEF*)
   test. 2 278 n. 4
PLATO
   Cratylus
      428c 3 n. 14
   Ion
      539b 3 n. 14
   Leges
      802a 10 n. 46
   Republic
      493d 285 n. 39
      614b 3 n. 14
PLUTARCH
   Lycurgus
      4.4 13 n. 67
QUINTUS SMYRNAEUS
   13.21–2 267 n. 86
   13.171 267 n. 86
   13.174 265 n. 80
   13.174–5 265 n. 79, 290 n. 57
   13.176–7 265 n. 80
SCHOLIA
   in *Aristophanis Equites*
      1056a 284 n. 34
   in *Dionysii Thracis Artem Grammaticam*
      180.1–2 12 n. 56
   in *Euripidis Hecubam*
      910 176 n. 57
   in *[Euripidis] Rhesum*
      Hyp. (a) 221 n. 43, 229 n. 81
      Hyp. (c) 221 n. 42
      346 221–2
      393 221 with nn. 40–1
   in *Homeri Iliadem*
      1.59 223 n. 61
      1.264 224
      1.399 177
      1.399–400 176 n. 58
      1.400a–b 176 n. 58
      2.455–6 186 n. 105

3.18a 73 n. 34
3.19–20 73 n. 34
3.126–7 34 n. 54
3.374b 182–3
5.25 106 n. 15
5.662 182–3
7.9 224
8.53a 157 n. 153
8.284 177
9.182 178–9
9.192a 179 n. 77
9.197a 179 n. 77
10.1 11–12, 13 n. 67
10.1a 2 n. 11
10.3–4 20–1 n. 107
10.11 152 n. 125
10.23b 138 n. 34
10.23d 138 nn. 34–5
10.134a 138 n. 37
10.206 178 n. 69
10.258 271 n. 109
10.260 145
10.282 266 n. 85
10.282a 177, 179
10.299a 156 n. 145
10.299b 21 n. 107, 156 n. 145
10.335a–c² 150 n. 114
10.391b 211 n. 104
10.406 180–1
10.407b 180–1
10.409a 167
10.414–15 182–3
10.433–4 183, 185 n. 101
10.435 15 nn. 75–6, 110 with nn. 29–30, 214–15, 217, 221–2, 225–7, 229–30, 235–6, 238 n. 110, 242 n. 133, 255 n. 18, 261, 263–4, 276, 288, 291 nn. 62–3, 294 nn. 82–3
10.496–7 228 n. 80, 267
10.499c 145 n. 82
10.519 185, 258 n. 40
10.561 178 n. 70
10.568a¹ 115 n. 58
11.1 224
11.672 224
11.741 177
13.408b¹⁻² 186 n. 105
14.119 224
16.140c 185
18.486 224
19.119 177
19.398a¹⁻² 240 n. 124
20.237 233 n. 98
21.76b 186 n. 105

22.188 69, 99 n. 124, 176
23.660 225
24.257b 70 n. 14
24.605b 168 n. 34
in Homeri Odysseam
　1.93 176 with n. 59
　1.285 176
　3.307a 176
　3.313 176 n. 59
　4.425 288 n. 52
　11.519–21 223 n. 60, 235 with n. 102
　15.16–17 225
　23.296 12 with n. 57
in Lycophronis Alexandram
　18 233 n. 98
　344 176 n. 57
　831 221 n. 42
in Pindarum
　Nem. 2.1c 13 n. 67
in Tzetzis Carmina Iliaca
　2.190 221 n. 42
SOPHOCLES
　Ajax
　　445–9 284 n. 34
　　1135–6 284 n. 34
　　1243 284 n. 34
　Philoctetes
　　592 81 n. 73
　　606–8 282 n. 27
Fragments (*TrGF*)
　Philoctetes in Troy
　　frs. 697–703 13 n. 65
SUDA
　δ 1164 285 n. 39
THEOCRITUS
　Epigrams
　　22 278 n. 4
THUCYDIDES
　1.9.4 3 n. 14
　1.10.4 3 n. 14
　2.39 222 n. 56
TIMOTHEUS (*PMG*)
　fr. 791.211–12, 216–17 10 n. 46
　fr. 796 10 n. 46
TZETZES
　Anecdota Graeca
　　1.6 13 n. 67
　Posthomerica
　　719–21 176 n. 57
　　773 176 n. 57
　Prolegomena Allegoriae Iliadis
　　172–3 233 n. 98

LATIN

CICERO
　De officiis
　　3.116 103
　De oratore
　　3.137 13 n. 67
ENNIUS
　Annales
　　288 267
HYGINUS
　Fabulae
　　102 81 n. 73
LIVY
　3.70.6 103
PLAUTUS
　Bacchides
　　954–5 265 n. 82
SERVIUS
　Commentarii in Vergilii Aeneidem
　　1.469 221 n. 40, 232 n. 97,
　　　262 nn. 60–1, 264
　　1.469–73 241
　　2.13 232 n. 97, 240–1, 265 n. 82,
　　　295 n. 84
　　2.81 14 n. 68
　　2.166 269 n. 100
　　3.16 14 n. 68
　　9.307 271 n. 109
SCHOLIA
　in Iuvenalem
　　6.655 223 n. 61
TACITUS
　Annales
　　4.48.1 267
VIRGIL
　Aeneid
　　1.456–7 241
　　1.466 264 n. 68
　　1.469 231, 264 n. 68
　　1.469–73 230 n. 85, 241, 261
　　1.470 261 n. 58
　　1.470–3 232
　　1.472–3 241, 261, 267 n. 91
　　2.13 240 n. 120, 241 with n. 130, 295 n. 84
　　2.13–14 265 n. 82
　　2.341–2 265 n. 78
　　2.342–3 265 n. 79
　　2.343–4 265 n. 80
　　2.345–6 265 n. 80
　　2.355–6 264 n. 72
　　2.358 264 n. 74

VIRGIL (cont.)
  2.359 264 n. 76
  2.389–90 265 n. 81
  2.410–12 265 n. 77
  5.286–361 122 n. 80
  5.295 274 n. 129
  8.83 262 n. 59
  9.179–80 274 n. 129
  9.186 266
  9.189–90 267
  9.192–3 266–7
  9.195–6 269
  9.236–7 267 n. 86
  9.240–3 268
  9.243–5 269
  9.263–74 272
  9.275–80 272
  9.303–7 274 with n. 128
  9.314–66 268 n. 95
  9.324–8 274
  9.325–6 275 nn. 133–4
  9.326 274 n. 131
  9.327–8 275 n. 132
  9.373–4 271
  9.404–9 271 n. 112
  9.420–45 275

SANSKRIT

Mahābhārata
  8.69 253
  10.1–25 253
  10.1.3–4 247
  10.1.30 247
  10.1.32 247
  10.1.32–3 246–7
  10.1.32–42 251
  10.1.33 247
  10.1.34–5 247
  10.1.34–42 251
  10.1.44 248
  10.1.53 248, 252
  10.1.59 248
  10.1.64 250
  10.2–5 258
  10.2.31 248
  10.3.24–5 248
  10.3.26 248, 252
  10.3.27 252
  10.3.28 252
  10.3.28–9 248
  10.3.29 248
  10.3.30 248
  10.3.33–5 252
  10.4.8 249
  10.5.35–6 249
  10.5.37 250
  10.7.2–66 250
  10.8.8 252
  10.8.11 252
  10.8.26–7 253
  10.8.37 253
  10.8.140–1 253
  10.8.148–9 254
  10.10.9–25 253, 256 n. 26
  10.11.4–25 253
  10.64–7 253

Rāmāyana
  6.22.18 256 n. 22
  6.23.7–31 258 n. 43

Rigveda
  1.60.5 104 n. 10